Non dilexerunt animam suam usque ad mortem.
The Latin, *Non dilexerunt animam suam usque ad mortem*, translates, "... they loved not their lives unto the death." Revelation 12:11

On The Cover: *Massacres at Salzburg* took place in 1528 when Prince-Archbishop Cardinal Matthaus Lang of Salzburg issued mandates sending police in search of Anabaptists. Many were captured and killed. This engraving illustrates the sufferings and sacrifices these Dissenters endured when their government, in conjunction with established religion, attempted to coerce and impose uniformity of religious belief. Hence, this picture is a reminder of the cost of religious liberty and the ever-present need to maintain the separation of church and state. We use this art to represent our Dissent and Nonconformity Series.

The

ISRAEL OF THE ALPS

Drawn by S. Bough, from a sketch by Dr. Muston.　　　Engraved by S. Bradshaw

CHÂTEAU-QUEYRAS.
IN THE VALLEY OF THE GUILL, DAUPHINY

BLACKIE & SON, GLASGOW. EDINBURGH & LONDON.

The Israel of the Alps,
A HISTORY OF
The Waldenses.
VOL. I.

PRA DU TOUR.
WHERE THE VAUDOIS BARBAS PREPARED FOR THE MINISTRY.

Blackie and Son;
GLASGOW, EDINBURGH AND LONDON

THE ISRAEL OF THE ALPS.

A COMPLETE

HISTORY OF THE WALDENSES

AND THEIR COLONIES;

PREPARED IN GREAT PART FROM UNPUBLISHED DOCUMENTS.

BY ALEXIS MUSTON, D.D.,

PASTOR OF THE PROTESTANT CHURCH AT BOURDEAUX, DRÔME, FRANCE.

TRANSLATED

BY THE REV. JOHN MONTGOMERY, A.M.

WITH A DOCUMENTARY APPENDIX ON THE ORIGIN OF THE WALDENSES,

BY THE TRANSLATOR.

VOL. I.

LONDON:
BLACKIE & SON, PATERNOSTER BUILDINGS, E.C.;
GLASGOW AND EDINBURGH.
1875

NUMBER ONE IRON OAKS DRIVE • PARIS, ARKANSAS 72855

Thou hast given a *standard* to them that fear thee;
that it may be displayed because of the truth.
-- Psalm 60:4

*Reprinted
by*

THE BAPTIST STANDARD BEARER, INC.
No. 1 Iron Oaks Drive
Paris, Arkansas 72855
(501) 963-3831

THE WALDENSIAN EMBLEM
lux lucet in tenebris
"The Light Shineth in the Darkness"

ISBN #1-57978-538-7

AUTHOR'S PREFACE.

"No people of modern times," says Boyer, "exhibits so much analogy to the ancient Jewish people, as the Vaudois of the Alps of Piedmont; no history has more abounded in marvels than theirs, no church in martyrs."

These words sufficiently explain the title of the present Work, *The Israel of the Alps*.[1] Let me state its origin and its object.

For more than fifteen years, I have been occupied with assiduous researches into the history of the Vaudois. My intention was to have taken up again the volume published in 1834, and to have carried out the work on such a scale as would have made it amount to eight or ten volumes octavo.

But a work of such a size could not have served to supply the actual wants of the public. I proposed, therefore, to publish separately the *Sources of the History of the Vaudois*, with the principal historic documents, and a rapid but complete sketch of the history itself. On the one hand, however, circumstances have compelled me to renounce the idea of publishing the *Sources;* on the other, I have found that a complete summary of the history of the Vaudois could not be comprehended in a single volume, because the unpublished part of that history is as considerable as that already known, or perhaps even more so.

The question of the origin of the Vaudois and of the organiza-

---

[1] The choice of this title has been influenced by another consideration. The author of this work had commenced, in 1834, the publication of a *History of the Vaudois*, of which only the first volume has ever appeared. If he had given to the present work the title of a *History of the Vaudois*, it might have been confounded with the previous work, from which it is in reality quite distinct. The volume published in 1834, by Levrault, at Strasburg (where it is still to be found, as well as at Reinwald's, in Paris), contains a description of the Vaudois valleys, with dissertations, and a great number of quotations relative to the origin and doctrine of the Vaudois. This large amount of matter has not been again embodied in the *Israel of the Alps*. The previous volume also contains a map of the valleys, and fac-similes of the principal authors who have treated of Vaudois history. Far from being a sort of former edition of the present work, the previous volume would rather serve as an introduction to it, rendering it more complete.

tion of their church, prior to the Reformation, required to be re-examined. The primitive character of their doctrines had not been completely determined, for want of documents. The particular histories of the Vaudois of Le Queyras, of Barcelonette, of Vallouise, and of Freyssinières, had never been written in a connected manner; the histories of Merindol and of Cabrières had been often written, but never elucidated; it was likewise necessary that the documents connected with the judicial proceedings which preceded and followed the decree pronounced by the court of Aix, on the 18th of November, 1540, should be subjected to a fresh scrutiny, which, to the best of my knowledge, had been attempted by no one.

Details relative to the Vaudois martyrs, will be found in this work collected for the first time. The very interesting history of the churches of Saluces was almost unknown, and here forms half a volume.*

There was a gap betwixt the close of the very full chronicle of Gilles, and the period at which Léger commences his documentary history. A second gap occurred betwixt Léger and Arnaud; and from that writer to our own days, no considerable collection of new documents was to be met with.

Very many histories of the Vaudois had, indeed, been written, general or particular, extensive or brief. Each of them contains interesting facts, or presents interesting historic views; but nowhere is there to be found a collection of documents, arranged with just regard to the proportionate value of historic facts. There have been few events in our history of so great importance as those which led to and those which followed the official re-establishment of the Vaudois in their own country; yet the most complete historians have hitherto scarcely taken the least notice of them. A whole volume of the present work is devoted to these remarkable facts, which occupy only a few pages in the works of my predecessors. The expulsion of the inhabitants of the valleys, in 1686 and 1687, was not narrated in detail, except in contemporary pamphlets, which have now become very rare; the expulsions of 1698 and 1730, have not been so narrated at all. The first part only of the history of the Vaudois colonies in Germany had been written, but not in the French language. The whole of this history will be found in *The Israel of the Alps*. That of the Vaudois of Pragela, who, at one time, were themselves alone more numerous than the inhabitants of all the other Vaudois valleys put together, had never been written in any language; eight chapters are devoted to it in this work. Finally, from 1730 to our own days, new historic

* [The original is in four volumes.]

phases have brought the Vaudois under the indirect influence of the philosophy of the eighteenth century, under that of the French Revolution, that of the Austro-Russian invasions, and that of the empire of Napoleon. Nothing of all this had been related as its historic importance deserved; and it is only since the Restoration, that documents have been printed which begin to throw a sufficient light upon the destinies of the Vaudois church.

In the present work, all these gaps have been filled up; and if it be thought that these volumes surpass the limits of an abridgment, I would say, Gather together the works which have been written on the Vaudois—run over their tables of contents—compare it with that of the present work, and see if these volumes do not comprehend more variety of matters than all the other books which have been written on this subject, which, however, would of themselves, form a large library, as any one may satisfy himself, by casting a glance over the *Bibliography* with which *The Israel of the Alps* concludes. PERRIN (an 8vo volume of 248 pages) has only furnished me with matter for two half chapters; GILLES (a 4to volume of more than 600 pages), has furnished me with three complete chapters and seven half chapters; I have derived a whole chapter and four half chapters from LÉGER (a folio volume of 212 and 385 pages); from ARNAUD (an octavo of 407 pages), I have derived two chapters and a half; and the whole of the German authors who have written on the Vaudois colonies, have supplied me only with what amounts to about three half chapters. All the rest has been drawn from works exclusively relating to particular parts of the subject, or from unpublished documents.

Whatever judgment may therefore be formed of the present work, I venture to think, that it must be admitted to have really given a new aspect to the history of the Vaudois; and that *The Israel of the Alps* not merely contains the most complete history of the Vaudois which has hitherto been published, but that, were all which has hitherto been published collected together, it would be equivalent only to a very limited portion of what is here presented. As far as the nature of the work permitted me, I have always allowed the authors from whom I had occasion to quote, to speak in their own words—not merely in order to afford the reader a gratification which otherwise he could have found only by searching into rare books or manuscripts, but more especially in order to give greater variety to the narrative, and to restore as far as possible the impress of contemporary emotions.

It has often happened that I have discovered errors in the works which I have consulted, even in those of greatest reputation and learning; I have corrected them, according to the best of my information, but without taking any particular notice of them; for this would have produced no change in the page which contained the error, and I would have thought it somewhat at variance with that gratitude which we owe to writers who have devoted their labours to subjects in which we are most warmly interested.

The number of these inaccuracies forbids me to presume that my own work can be exempt from them. I would be very thankful if any one would put it in my power to remove them. If it had not been printed as fast as it could be prepared, I would already have corrected some slips,[1] and would likewise, I doubt not, have changed some strong expressions here and there, which the horrible character of the facts narrated has drawn involuntarily from my indignant pen. These reflections of a writer's own feelings may render his style more animated, but are scarcely compatible with the calm dignity of history. Besides such errors of style, and errors of the press, there must unquestionably be many other imperfections discoverable in this work. But as it is the first which presents the history of the Vaudois in a complete form, and is certainly the most accurate of all yet in existence upon that subject, I hope for some indulgence as due to the long and laborious researches which it has cost me.

These researches have been prosecuted most of all in the *State Paper Office of the Court of Turin*. The papers there preserved having been put into my hands only in bundles unarranged, I have taken notes from them and quoted them with few exceptions according to a running number which marks the order in which I received them. The *Diplomatic Archives* of France supplied me with many precious documents, for which I am indebted to the kindness of M. Guizot, then minister of foreign affairs. The *Records of the Council of State* of Geneva, have been made available for *The Israel of the Alps,* by the obliging attentions of the minister, M. le Fort. I obtained access to the *State Paper Office* of the Grand Duchy of Hesse-Darmstadt, through M. Du Thill, then minister of the interior. The archives of Baden, of Stuttgart, of Frankfort, of Berlin, and of the principal cantons of Switzerland, have also been consulted, either by myself in person or by correspondents. The records of the old *Court of Accounts* at Grenoble, those of the *Senate* and of the *Court of Accounts* at Turin, have likewise augmented my store of materials. I have been indebted for numerous documents to the municipal archives of Pignerol, of

---

[1] The present translation enjoys the character of a new edition, in virtue of corrections and additions by the Author.

Lucerne, of Fenestrelles, of Briançon, of Gap, and of some other towns both of Piedmont and of France. And here I ought to express my deep-felt gratitude to my relative and friend, M. Aillaud, professor at Pignerol, who searched for me the archives of the *Intendance* of that city. Access to those of the bishopric was obtained for me by the author of *Historical Researches concerning the Origin of the Vaudois* (see the *Bibliography*, section II., § iv., No. 9). Without referring in this place to anything else than the researches which he facilitated, I value too highly the privilege of having been enabled to complete them in such a manner, not to testify a just sense of gratitude to him on that account.

I have derived much assistance from the admirable collection of rare pamphlets, comprising also a number of valuable manuscripts, contained in the *Royal Library* at Turin. I owe an expression of my thanks to MM. De Promis, Des Ambroix, De Coccillo, De Saluces, Duboin (son of the celebrated civilian, whose great collection he still continues to increase), Bonnino, deputy-keeper of the records of the Court of Accounts, and Sclopis, author of *The History of the Laws of Piedmont*, who have facilitated my researches by their communications, their kind offices, or their advice. The learned M. Cibrario, member of the historical commission for the *Monumenta Patriae*, and of the Academy of Sciences at Turin, has with similar kindness taken an interest in my labours. He has, moreover, been at the trouble of making some researches himself, and sending me several documents of very great interest, which otherwise I could not have procured.

At Paris, I have found no less disposition to assist me. M. De Salvandy, then minister of public instruction, caused a very important manuscript to be placed at my service, which, without his authority, I could not have consulted. M. Michelet was kind enough to point out to me in the national archives of France, some documents hitherto unknown.[1]

---

[1] A voluminous record of an investigation concerning the hardships inflicted by *John de Roma* upon the Vaudois of Provence. The following is the title marked upon a detached slip—"[Cayer de procédures, &c.]:—Record of proceedings in 1533, in virtue of a commission from Francis I., King of France, of date 12th February, 1532, against John de Rome, of the order of the Jacobins, who, after having been expelled from Avignon by the Cardinal de Clermont, withdrew into Provence, where, without being legally recognised or authorized, he performed the functions of an inquisitor, and conducted himself towards the lieges of that province in an outrageous and vexatious manner, contrary to all public order."

This manuscript, which, according to another note, used to be contained in a bag, and was not included in the *Inventory* under the head of *the Government of Provence*, consists of eight quires of paper, of small folio size. On the back is affixed the rescript of Francis I., which authorizes the prosecutions. The deposi-

M. Sordet, keeper of the records of the *Hôtel de Ville* at Geneva, and Professor Diodati, curator of the library there, as well as the pastors Lavit, Claparède, Vaucher-Mouchon, &c., have, in the most obliging manner, facilitated my researches. I have been permitted to consult the *Archives of the Venerable Company*, known under the name of the *Archives of St. Peter*. The distinguished historian, Professor Merle D'Aubigné, has assisted me, both by giving me the benefit of his information and by communicating documents in his possession. And, finally, I am indebted to M. Lombard-Odier, banker, for a copy of an interesting manuscript, the work of a proscribed Vaudois in 1729. I am not less bound, however, to express my thanks to my young fellow-countrymen, MM. Tron, Geymonet, Parise, Bert, Rivoire, and Janavel, then students at Geneva, who were kind enough to employ themselves in transcribing for me everything that I required. M. Monastier, an author, who, like them, is a native of the valleys of Piedmont, and has produced a recent and much-valued history of the Vaudois, communicated to me notes and extracts which he collected when engaged in his own labours. Another native of the valleys, M. Appia, in whom the French church at Frankfort recently lost an eminent and venerated pastor, most freely made me welcome to the whole resources of his rich collection of documents connected with the history of the country of his birth, and gave me the benefit of all his information, his advice, and his reminiscences. I regret that this just tribute of my gratitude can only be paid to his memory. A venerable Vaudois pastor, the late M. Mondon, the successor of Scipio Arnaud in one of the Vaudois colonies in Germany, but whose removal from this world preceded by a long time that of M. Appia, expressed the same interest in my undertaking. To him I owe the use of the first sheets of the original manuscript of the *Return*, now deposited at Berlin.

In the Vaudois valleys, the gentlemen holding offices connected with the Table have, in more instances than one, placed at my disposal official documents and notes most valuable for their accuracy; and the pastor M. Joshua Meille, and his son-in-law, M. Volle,

tions of the witnesses commence on the first page of fol. 84.—*National Archives of France*, compartment J, No. 851.

An unpublished letter of Margaret of France, Duchess of Savoy, dated from Turin, 1 June, 1566 ["*Thurin ce premier jour de juing* 1566"], and relative to the Vaudois, has also been communicated to me by Professor Ch. Bonnet; but too late to be of much service. It will be published, along with other valuable documents, the fruits of the researches of that learned professor, in a *Life of Renée of France, Duchess of Ferrara*, which will shortly gratify the impatient expectations of all who are acquainted with his patient and admirable labours.

have in other ways contributed to the increase of my collection of unpublished papers. I am bound to make the same acknowledgment in regard to M. Gay, of Le Villar, and M. Antoine Blanc, of La Tour, as well as to my friend M. Amédée Bert, whose *Historic Scenes*, recently published, have excited in Italy so great an interest in favour of the Vaudois.

Amongst foreigners, the reverend Dr. Todd, of Dublin, and above all others, the reverend Dr. Gilly, of Durham, have laid me under particular obligations by transmitting to me information which they alone were able to furnish.

Finally, I owe the warmest expressions of gratitude to Professor Schmidt, author of the *History of the Cathari*, who has been kind enough to look over the proof-sheets of the *Bibliography* of *The Israel of the Alps;* as also to MM. Mailhet, Arnaud, and Olivier, who have gone over the manuscript and the proof-sheets of the whole work.

I cannot mention all the public libraries to which I have been more or less indebted in the preparation of this work. Those of Lyons and Grenoble contain ancient Vaudois manuscripts in the Romance language; as do also those of Geneva, Zürich, and Dublin. Those of Avignon and of Carpentras possess other manuscripts, which, although more modern, are not less interesting.

M. Frossard, author of a *History of the Vaudois of Provence*, and M. Barjavel, author of the *Historical Dictionary of Vaucluse*, have augmented, by the fruits of their studies, the notes which I had already collected on the subject treated of by the first of these writers.

I have attempted, in various ways, to have researches made at Prague, in order to discover, if possible, some documentary traces of the relations anciently subsisting betwixt the Vaudois and the evangelical churches of that country; but these attempts have been fruitless.

The charter-chests of a number of families have been opened to my investigations—amongst others, those of the Counts of Lucerna—but at a time when I could not go in person to examine them. I have not the less pleasure in recording here the respectful expression of my gratitude.

It would have been equally desirable to have seen, if possible, the episcopal records of Suza and of Saluces—those of the Archbishopric of Turin, and of the Inquisition formerly existing there—those of Aceil, of Carail, of Dronier, and of other towns, in which the Vaudois had numerous adherents in days of yore—as well as those even of the Holy Office at Rome. And I have no doubt that there are still many sources of information altogether unknown to me. However, I have succeeded in forming, I believe, the most numerous collection of historical documents, relative to the Vaudois, which any historian has as yet possessed. I am especially happy in having been enabled to fill up the lamentable blanks which have hitherto existed in that memorable history.

But the operation of accumulating a great mass of historical materials is no more the distinguishing function of the historian, than the operation of bringing together the materials of a building is the distinguishing function of the architect. With the same materials may be erected either a monument of striking beauty, or one of the most commonplace description. What gives its proper character to a work of art, is its leaving in the mind a precise idea corresponding with the purpose for which it was intended. France possesses two such works, the smallest and the greatest of their kind, I believe, in Europe—the *Maison carrée* of Nismes, and the Cathedral of Strasburg, of which both the one and the other leave a distinct idea, an abiding impression, in the mind —an impression which will remain in the memory of the traveller more vivid and perfect than that of the street in which, perhaps, he has long had his abode. Unity, harmony, and proportion distinguish those things of which our minds thus readily take hold. Without these qualities in the completed work, a great collection of materials is nothing else, in history or in architecture, than a mere heap: these alone give the work a higher character, whether it be great or small. I do not deny that I have been ambitious that my little work should exhibit these characteristics.

Hitherto, the chronological method has been almost exclusively followed in all the histories of the Vaudois. This method consists in relating, year by year, all which occurs in the different countries, or different series of facts with which we have to do. It appears, at first sight, the most natural, and would be in reality the best, if each fact had neither cause nor effects. On the contrary, it is only the linking together of these causes and effects that renders our view of any fact complete; but as the origin of events is often to be traced far back, and the consequences stretch far into the future, the chronological method breaks up the connection, cutting asunder the exhibition of a fact and its consequences, by the account of a contemporaneous fact which has no relation to it. It follows that blanks are concealed from observation amidst these incomplete exhibitions of historic facts; and these blanks are often involuntarily produced by the very pen of the writer, who is compelled, by the chronological succession, to pass from one fact to another, instead of proceeding in a continuous manner with the development of the same fact. This development, then, becomes like a broken picture, whose fragments are scattered at great distances. It is what might be expected, that the reading of histories written after this method ordinarily leaves in the mind none but very confused historic ideas, or rather leaves it without precise and dominant ideas.

The analytic method, on the contrary, after having classified the events, exhibits them in all their amplitude. Their aspect is presented entire and distinct, and consequently the mind of the reader more readily lays hold of the unity of the whole group. But this method is necessarily very tedious and difficult. After the documents have been collected, a selection and critical examination must be made: those which may serve as sources of historic information must be placed by themselves, and valid authorities must be distinguished from doubtful testimonies. It is then expedient to arrange them all in chronological order, with the view of having a general representation of the whole subject which is to be investigated. After this, the whole must be divided into distinct epochs, in order to detach from the historical picture the different outlines which are afterwards to be filled up with details. It is then necessary to fix upon the series of documents in each epoch, relating to facts of the same nature, and to withdraw from the group those which relate to things of a different kind. Finally, it remains to arrange these different series of documents, with a view to the historic exhibition of the facts which they tend to establish, so that these facts shall elucidate each other. All these things have been done for the *History of the Vaudois* which I now give to the public, of which, perhaps, I may say that the plan has cost me more time and trouble than anything else in the work. I venture to hope that its simplicity would prevent this from being perceived. Whatever may be the scale upon which it may yet happen that the *History of the Vaudois* shall be again taken up—whether it shall be extended to ten volumes or reduced to one—this plan, I believe, will always be found suitable.

The two chapters which treat of the Vaudois martyrs, are the only ones in this work which I have borrowed, without modification, from my original publication. Numerous notes have been appended to those which I have had to compose entirely from unpublished documents—such, in particular, as the two first chapters of the fourth volume—[Part II., Chapters xviii. and xix.]—the matter for which, although presenting little variety, was very considerable in amount; and, in general, all those which treat of the history of the Vaudois from 1690 to 1814.

If circumstances should permit me, hereafter, to publish entire the documents which I have used as authorities, the suppression of which has, more than all other things, contributed to restrict this book to moderate dimensions, I will have accomplished almost all that I would desire or think it in my power to do with regard to the history of the Vaudois.

An examination of the various arguments by which it has recently been attempted to disprove the existence of the Vaudois previous to Valdo, will be found in the Bibliography at the end of this Work.[1] In some instances, I did not possess the means of verifying, for this Bibliography, the titles of certain works with which I was unacquainted. I have not, however, on that account, thought it necessary to refrain from noticing them, according to the indications of them which I had obtained.

Something would, no doubt, have been gained, with regard to a number of important questions concerning the original sources of the history of the Vaudois, had they been here subjected again to the fiery trial of a better sustained and more profound analysis. Many things may yet remain to be said concerning the origin of the Vaudois, and their relations with the other sects of the middle ages. But the present work was meant to contain statements of fact rather than dissertations, and to have dwelt in this way upon particular points would not have consisted with its plan. A desire to present as condensed a historic narrative as possible, and an ambition to fill up the immense blanks which still subsisted in the modern history of the Vaudois, have been paramount in directing the preparation of those volumes. I have been obliged to carry on my labours in a little village, destitute of any learned library, and at a great distance from the printing-office. This will account for *errata*, a mere allusion to which will certainly be enough to obtain for them the indulgence of intelligent readers, who will easily rectify slight imperfections.

I have thought it my duty to indicate, at the head of each chapter, the authorities and sources of information particularly connected with each, and I conclude *The Israel of the Alps* with a list of the works which form general sources of information, relating throughout to the whole history of the Vaudois. Notwithstanding the large number of authors contained in this list, there are but few of them who can be regarded as authorities, the greater part having

---

[1] Concerning the opinion which would make the Vaudois derive their origin from Valdo, see *Bibliogr.*, part I. sect. II. § iii. article 24. Concerning the antiquity of the Vaudois MSS. in the Romance language, see part II. sect. I. § i. Concerning the *Nobla Leyczon*, see the same section, § iii., MS. 207, art. 5, &c.

done nothing but copy from one another. Besides, with the exception of the earlier ones, who have derived their information from original documents, and of a few subsequent writers, who have brought the aids of an exact criticism to the elucidation of obscure points, the rest are only of inferior interest. Yet there is none of them to be despised, for they may be found to present valuable details of fact, and new views of passages of history.

If I had written, as was my original intention, a critical and documentary history of the Vaudois, I would have quoted almost all these works, and made parts of them the subject of discussion. Having attempted nothing here but to narrate events as completely and as briefly as possible, I have confined myself to the authorities upon which I depend for them—all discussion has been avoided, and all means of abridgment have been studiously employed.

The mere substance of official documents has almost always been given—speeches have not been given at full length—narratives of judicial examinations have been transformed into simple dialogues, by which means the diluting phrases, "Being then asked," "He replied," &c., have been avoided. Occasionally in place of mentioning in succession the written communications of a negotiation, I have suppressed them altogether, saying merely, "It was then proposed," "It was replied," &c. And when the documents which I had before me proved respecting any historic personage, and upon the authority of sure witnesses, that such a personage had spoken to such or such an effect, had made such or such an answer, or had brought forward such or such considerations, I have thought it right to substitute for the narrative form that of direct address, making the person himself speak instead of relating what he said. This method was common with the historians of antiquity; and whilst I have been very reserved as to the use of it, I have always attended with the greatest care to the exact accuracy of the words, as expressing the thought which they were meant to convey. I shall perhaps be told that it is the duty of the historian neither to abstract nor to add. But in what sense? What sort of text is it of which not a single word may be changed? When he has before his eyes a number of different accounts of the same event or series of events, a number of documents, of which each by itself is insufficient, but which taken together present the subject in a clear enough light—when he has to pursue his search for the truth through a heap of judicial records, police reports, diplomatic notes and private correspondence, contemporary publications bearing the stamp of party spirit, narratives intentionally falsified or involuntarily left incomplete, journals varying in the accuracy of their information, &c.—is it not from the comparison, the combination, and the persevering and critical examination of all these confused elements, that history must be framed? It is as important, in such a case, that the materials should be rightly estimated and classified, as that they should be of large amount.

I shall not say more on this subject. There are, of course, in this book, imperfections which I am aware of, and others of which I am ignorant. I can only offer, by anticipation, the expression of my gratitude to those who may be pleased to point out to me any improvements of which it may be susceptible. But if I am accused of being inaccurate, upon the sole ground of my having departed from the ideas hitherto prevalent, I must reply—Look to the sources from which my information is derived, and inform yourselves, before you pronounce an opinion.

I am far from concealing that my sympathies are with the oppressed and against their oppressors; but I have never been consciously inaccurate; and in every instance in which the facts of history have called me to say anything to the credit of the adversaries of the Vaudois, I believe that I have done it as fully and as frankly as possible.

There exist already a large number of histories of the Vaudois. They are all incomplete. Another recapitulation would have served no purpose. I assigned myself the task of writing their history, so as to make it complete. That undertaking presented difficulties which it may well be believed were not small, as no one had yet surmounted them. In default of other good qualities, the long and fatiguing labours which I have been obliged to undergo, in order to attain my object of presenting the truth without blanks, may perhaps obtain for me the approbation of my readers and of the Vaudois who love their native land.

I have prayed God to support me in my labours; and I pray him now to render them serviceable to my native country and to the truth.

ALEXIS MUSTON.

BOURDEAUX (DRÔME), 18 *September*, 1850.

TRANSLATOR'S PREFACE.

THE translation of this work was undertaken in the belief, which remains unshaken in the translator's mind, of its being the most complete and interesting history of the Vaudois yet given to the world. The lively and graphic style, of which the English reader may perhaps find here but an imperfect representation, although it adds much to the value of the work, is far from being its chief merit. The author has evidently devoted no small amount of labour to its preparation, both in the acquisition and in the arrangement of his materials. He has added to the stores of historic information previously accumulated, and has elucidated points that were formerly obscure, by his researches amongst documents inaccessible to previous historians. He has also, more fully than any previous author, brought the whole history of the Vaudois into one view—not only that of the Church in the Piedmontese valleys from the earliest period to the present day, but also that of the Vaudois inhabiting the French territory, of the Vaudois settlement in Calabria, and of the colonies which Vaudois exiles founded, who sought a refuge from persecution in different parts of Germany.

Few subjects have greater claims to the regard of all Christians than that of which this work treats. Even if the opinion were admitted, against which Dr. Muston contends, that the Vaudois derived their name and their origin as a distinct Christian community from Peter Waldo, the merchant of Lyons, who became a preacher of righteousness, and a witness against the corruptions of the Church of Rome, in the end of the twelfth century, it would be impossible to regard without deep interest that light shining in the midst of darkness throughout so many centuries, and the testimony so long maintained, amidst so many conflicts, by these Reformers before the Reformation. But the interest with which we contemplate the Vaudois (or *Waldenses*), is greatly increased when we acknowledge them as possessing a still higher antiquity—

as giving his name and, in part at least, his knowledge of the truth to Waldo, instead of deriving theirs from him—as forming a connecting link between the primitive church and the churches of the Reformation.

The reader of Vaudois history cannot read with unmingled pleasure. History records no deeds of cruelty more atrocious, no persecutions more terrible. But scenes which the benevolent mind would fain shut out from its contemplation, are yet invested with the highest and most enduring interest by the triumphs of faith, or possess a very great historic value as manifestations of the spirit of Popery, and as proofs of the identity of the Church of Rome with that Babylon of the Apocalypse, in which, when the Lord makes inquisition for blood and proceeds to the judgment long deferred, shall be found "the blood of prophets, and of saints, and of all that were slain upon the earth."

The high testimonies of approbation which Dr. Muston's work has received from the historians Thierry and Michelet, the late lamented Dr. Gilly, and others most competent to judge, have already in part been made known by the publishers in their prospectus of this translation. The translator may be permitted to add, that the manner in which Dr. Muston's work has been treated, even by those continental writers who, in magazines and in works recently published, have argued in support of opinions contrary to his, on the important question of the origin of the Vaudois, has been such as to exhibit their high sense of its importance. Dr. Herzog, in his recent work on this subject (*Die romanischen Waldenser, ihre vorreformatorischen Zustände und Lehren, u. s. w.*), describes Dr. Muston's history as containing a rich store of precious materials. Constant reference has been made to it in the whole of the recent discussions concerning the Vaudois.

To the question of the origin of the Vaudois, the translator has ventured to devote an Appendix. He would have been glad to have entered more largely into this subject than he has been able to do—the necessary limits of the work preventing him. His desire, however, was not so much to adduce any argument of his own, which he could scarcely pretend to do, as to exhibit the state of the controversy on the Continent concerning the historic apostolicity of the Vaudois—a question of great interest and importance, although certainly not of so great importance as some have ascribed to it. This he has in some measure endeavoured to do; and imperfect as it is, he is not without hope that the appendix devoted to this subject, may be of use in directing attention to facts and arguments with which, if he may judge from all he has seen in print, very few persons in this country seem to have much acquaintance.

It may be proper, and yet, perhaps, it is not quite necessary, for the translator here to say that he does not hold himself responsible for every sentiment contained in the work which he has translated, nor wish to be understood as assenting to it. He differs from the author in some instances in which he has not thought it requisite to append any note; but in no case did he think it warrantable to change what the author had written. Dr. Muston has been allowed to speak for himself, and to say to the British public what he originally thought fit to say to that of France and Switzerland. On various points, religious, political, and historical, the translator would have expressed himself otherwise; but he remembered that the work was Dr. Muston's and not his, and he is confident that it will find general approbation among the religious public of Britain, for the evangelical, liberal, and generous sentiments with which it is pervaded.

The work, as now issued, is not, however, a mere translation of the *Israel of the Alps*, as published six years since in France, but possesses, at the same time, the character of a second edition. Some corrections and additions have been made by the author, and maps and plates now accompany the work for the first time. The plates are chiefly, as will be seen, from sketches by Dr. Muston himself.

The translator has only to add, that concerning the form and spelling of proper names, he felt considerable difficulty. The French form, generally used in the original, is sometimes the least familiar to British readers. It has been thought best to prefer the most familiar form—French or Italian, as it might be. And if a perfect uniformity has not in all cases been preserved, it is hoped that no difficulty will thence arise to the reader.

J. M.

INNERLEITHEN, *November*, 1857.

CONTENTS.

VOL. I.

	Page
AUTHOR'S PREFACE,	v
TRANSLATOR'S PREFACE,	xvii

INTRODUCTION.

PRELIMINARY REMARKS ON THE ORIGIN OF THE VAUDOIS... 1

PART FIRST.

HISTORY OF THE VAUDOIS FROM THEIR ORIGIN, TO THE TIME WHEN THEY WERE CIRCUMSCRIBED WITHIN THE VALLEYS OF PIEDMONT ALONE.

CHAPTER I.—Origin, Manners, Doctrine, and Organization of the Vaudois Church in Ancient Times............17

CHAPTER II.—FIRST PERSECUTION—YOLANDE AND CATTANÉE. (From A.D. 1300 to A.D. 1500.)—Persecution and Conflicts about the year 1308—Persecution by Yolande, Duchess of Savoy, in 1476; and by her son, Charles I., Duke of Savoy, in 1485—Bull of Extermination against the Vaudois by Pope Innocent VIII. in 1487—Crusade against them—Albert Cattanée, the Pope's Legate—Defeat of the invading force in the Italian valleys—Negotiations with the Duke of Savoy—Strange fancies then prevalent among Papists with regard to the Vaudois............30

CHAPTER III.—HISTORY OF THE VAUDOIS OF THE VAL LOUISE, FROM THEIR ORIGIN TO THEIR EXTINCTION. (A.D. 1300 to A.D. 1500.)—Some account of the Val Louise—Early persecutions there—The Inquisitor Borelli—Martyrdoms at Embrun in the end of the 14th century, and desolation of the Vaudois valleys in France—Cattanée—Massacre of the whole population of the Val Louise in 1488............37

CHAPTER IV.—HISTORY OF THE VAUDOIS OF BARCELONNETTE, LE QUEYRAS, AND FREYSSINIÈRES. (A.D. 1300 to A.D. 1650.)—Some account of the Valley of Barcelonnette—Persecution in 1560—Return of the fugitive population—Persecution in 1623—The Vaudois finally expelled—The Valley of Freyssinières—Early persecutions—The Inquisitor Ployéri—Martyrdoms in the end of the 15th century—Relaxation of persecution by Louis XII.—Brief of Pope Alexander VI.—Struggles of the 16th century—The Protestants seize Embrun—Lesdiguières—The Valley of Queyras in the end of the 16th century—Struggles and Successes of the Protestants—

Page

The Revocation of the Edict of Nantes—Present Protestantism of the French valleys—Neff. 44

CHAPTER V.—HISTORY OF THE VAUDOIS OF PROVENCE.—MÉRINDOL AND CABRIÈRES. (A.D. 1350 to A.D. 1550.)—Settlement of the Vaudois in Provence—Persecutions of the 16th century—Cruelties of Menier D'Oppède—Proceedings against the inhabitants of Mérindol—Singular Deliverance of many from death—The Vaudois of Cabrières—Cardinal Sadolet—Cardinal De Tournon—The Bishop of Cavaillon at Mérindol—Edict of Francis I. suspending prosecutions—Revocation of that Edict surreptitiously obtained—Menier D'Oppède destroys Mérindol, Cabrières, La Coste, and other places, and butchers their inhabitants—Protestantism in modern times on the slopes of the Leberon..53

CHAPTER VI.—THE VAUDOIS IN CALABRIA. (A.D. 1400 to A.D. 1560.)—Settlement of the Vaudois in Calabria—Montalto, St. Xist, and other places founded by them—La Guardia—Correspondence maintained between the Vaudois of Calabria and those of the Alps—John Louis Paschal appointed pastor—Commencement of persecution in 1559—Sufferings of Paschal and of Mark Uscégli—Paschal conveyed to Rome—Attempts to induce him to recant—His martyrdom—Cardinal Alexandrini in Calabria—Falsehood and cruelty—Slaughter of the Vaudois of St. Xist and La Guardia—Fearful massacres and atrocities—Escape of a small remnant of the Calabrian Vaudois to Piedmont—Protestantism extinguished in Calabria..................72

CHAPTER VII.—INFLUENCE OF THE REFORMATION IN THE VAUDOIS VALLEYS.—THE SYNOD AND THE BIBLE. (A.D. 1520 to A.D. 1535.)—Deputation of the Vaudois to the Reformers—The deputies arrested as they return—Martyrdom of Peter Masson at Dijon—Synod at Angrogna in 1532—Dissensions—Letter from the Churches in Bohemia—Synod at Pral, 1533—Olivétan's Bible—Mission of Martin Gonin to Geneva—He is arrested on his way home, and put to death at Grenoble....................................93

CHAPTER VIII.—HISTORY OF A NUMBER OF MARTYRS.—Brief notices of many martyrs—Martyrdom of Stephen Brun at Embrun, in 1538—Of Bartholomew Hector at Turin, in 1556—Of John Vernoux, Anthony Laboric Quercy, and three others, at Chambery, in 1555—Letter of the martyr Quercy to his wife—Narrow escape of the Barba Gilles in the neighbourhood of Chambery—Geoffroy Varaille burned alive at Turin in 1558—Nicholas Sartoire at Aosta, in 1557—Extraordinary escape of a Vaudois minister—Martyrdoms of Mathurin and his wife, and of John De Cartignon, at Carignan, in 1560—Brief notices of other martyrs—Horrible cruelties inflicted on Odoul Geymet..105

CHAPTER IX.—HISTORY OF THE EVANGELICAL CHURCHES OF PAESANE, PRAVIGLELM, AND SALUCES. (A.D. 1550 to A.D. 1580.)—The marquisate of Saluces—Inquisitors sent to extirpate heresy in 1308—Persecutions of 1499-1510—Margaret De Foix, Marchioness of Saluces—Expulsion of the Vaudois from Saluces—They take refuge in the other valleys—Their return to Saluces in 1512—Influence of the Reformation—Increase and extension of the church..128

CHAPTER X.—HISTORY OF THE PROGRESS AND EXTINCTION OF THE REFORMATION AT CONI, AND IN THE PLAIN OF PIEDMONT. (A.D. 1550 to A.D. 1580.)—The Reformation in towns near the Vaudois valleys—Timidity—Perse-

Page

cution—Many of the Protestants take refuge among the Vaudois—Martyrdom of the Pastor Jacob—Protestantism in Turin—Persecutions in various parts of Piedmont—The churches of Coni and Carail—Persecutions—Suppression of the Reformation in Coni..136

CHAPTER XI.—HISTORY OF THE REFORMED CHURCHES OF CARAIL, CHIÉRI, AND DRONIER. (A.D. 1560 to A.D. 1605.)—Commencement of persecution against the Reformed Church of Carail—The noble family of Villanova-Sollaro—Activity of the Popish clergy—Suppression of the Reformation at Carail—Condition of the church in the marquisate of Saluces—St. Bartholomew's Day—Vacca, Archdeacon of Saluces, resists the massacre of the Protestants—French civil wars—The marquisate of Saluces becomes part of the dominions of the Duke of Savoy—The Protestant Church of Dronier —Its suppression—Persecuting measures adopted against the Vaudois of Praviglelm, and of the whole upper valley of the Po..............................143

CHAPTER XII.—A SKETCH OF THE VICISSITUDES ENDURED BY THE CHRISTIANS OF THE VALLEYS SITUATED AROUND THE VAUDOIS VALLEYS, PARTICULARLY THOSE OF BUBIANO, LUCERNA, CAMPILLON, AND FENIL. (A.D. 1560 to A.D. 1630.)—Protestants in the neighbourhood of the Vaudois valleys forbidden to attend religious meetings there—Fines and confiscations—Count William of Lucerna—Treaty of Cavour—Castrocaro, governor of the Vaudois valleys—Unsuccessful attempts to proselytize at Lucerna and Bubiano—Certain of the Vaudois summoned to Turin—Interview of Valentine Boulles with the Duke of Savoy—Theological discussion between a Vaudois pastor and a Jesuit—Captain Cappell—Systematic persecution of the Protestants of Lucerna—Confirmation of Vaudois privileges—Extortion and injustice—Peter Queyras and Bartholomew Boulles—Arrests—Sufferings of the Protestants of Bubiano and other places—Final prohibition of Protestantism beyond the limits of the Vaudois valleys...........................155

CHAPTER XIII.—REVIVAL OF THE EVANGELICAL CHURCHES OF SALUCES, AND NEW VICISSITUDES TO WHICH THEY WERE SUBJECTED. (A.D. 1602 to A.D. 1616.)—Valleys of the Stura, the Vrayta and Valgrane—Edict of 12th June, 1602—The Protestants driven into exile—Persecution conducted by the Capuchin Ribotti—Effects of long-continued oppression—The *Digiunati*—Irritation and disorder—Negotiations—The Duke of Savoy grants favourable terms to the Vaudois—Protestant churches spring up anew—Popish missionaries—Expatriation of Protestants—Their manifesto—A breathing time 174

CHAPTER XIV.—CONCLUSION OF THE HISTORY OF THE CHURCHES OF SALUCES; PARTICULARLY OF THOSE OF ACEIL, VERZOL, ST. MICHAEL, AND PRAVIGLELM. (A.D. 1616 to A.D. 1633.)—Lesdiguières intercedes for the Vaudois of Saluces—Increase of Protestantism in the valleys of the Stura and of Mayra—The Bishop of Saluces at Dronier—Protestant worship interrupted—Proscriptions—Vexations—Renewed intercessions of Lesdiguières—Disorders—Plot for a general massacre of the Reformed in the province of Saluces—Outrages and cruelties—Martyrdom of Peter Marquisy and Maurice Mongie—The pope grants to the Duke of Savoy a tithe of ecclesiastical revenues for six years—Further persecutions—Sentence of banishment against the inhabitants of Praviglelm and Paësane—Intercession of Lesdiguières—The churches of Saluces gradually weakened by continued persecutions—Victor Amadeus—Extinction of the churches of Saluces...184

xxiv   CONTENTS.

Page

CHAPTER XV.—MORE MARTYRS. (A.D. 1535 to A.D. 1635.)—Inquisitorial proceedings instituted both by the Court of Aix and the Senate of Turin—Martyrdom of Catalan Girardet—The pastor of Pral treacherously murdered—Intercessions of the Elector Palatine on behalf of the Vaudois—The Secretary of the Palatine Legation arrested on account of his being a Protestant minister—Conspiracy against the state, a deceitful pretext for severities against the Vaudois—Sufferings of the French Vaudois—Martyrdom of Romeyer, a merchant of Villar d'Arènes, at Draguignan—Many persons put to death on account of religion—Gaspar Orsel delivered from the inquisitors—Capture and escape of the pastor of Praviglelm—Brief notices of sufferers—M. Jean of Marseilles—Secret murders in prison—Martyrdom of Peter Marquisy and Maurice Monge of Aceil—Sufferings and release of Paul Roëri de Lanfranco—The case of Sebastian Bazan—Imprisonment and trials of Bartholomew Coupin—His attempted escape—His death—The brothers Malherbe—Daniel Peillon........................200

PART SECOND.

FROM THE TIME WHEN THE VAUDOIS WERE RESTRICTED WITHIN THE LIMITS OF THEIR VALLEYS, TO THE DATE OF THEIR TOTAL BANISHMENT.

CHAPTER I.—MATTERS PRELIMINARY TO THE SECOND GENERAL PERSECUTION OF THE VAUDOIS OF THE VALLEYS OF PIEDMONT. (A.D. 1520 to A.D. 1560.)—Increasing number of attendants at the public worship of the Vaudois—Building of places of worship—Friendly disposition of the Dukes of Savoy in the earlier part of the 16th century—Pope Paul IV.—Commissioners of the Parliament of Turin sent to the valleys in 1556—Fanaticism—Firmness of the Vaudois—Profession of faith—Threatenings of persecution—Charles and Boniface Truchet, seigneurs of Le Perrier—Their attempt to seize the minister of Rioclaret—Flight of the people of Rioclaret—An aged pastor and another prisoner burned alive at Pignerol—The people of Rioclaret saved by the other Vaudois, who take up arms for their assistance—Remarkable fate of the seigneurs of Le Perrier—Philip of Savoy, Count of Racconis, at Angrogna—Many instances of violence—Poussevin, commandant of Fossano—His argument in favour of the mass—The syndics of the valleys refuse to send away the pastors—An army collected against the Vaudois in 1560—Vain attempts to bring them even to apparent concessions—Friendly interposition of Count Charles of Lucerna....................233

CHAPTER II.—HISTORY OF THE SECOND GENERAL PERSECUTION WHICH TOOK PLACE IN THE VAUDOIS VALLEYS. (A.D. 1560 to A.D. 1561.)—The army under the command of the Count De La Trinité marches against the Vaudois—Its excesses even against adherents of the Church of Rome—Remarkable proof of the estimation in which the morality of the Vaudois was held—First skirmishes—Successive defeats of the Count De La Trinité—Attempted negotiations—The Count De La Trinité visits the Pra-du-Tour

Page

—His perfidy—Combats—Cruelties—A large sum extorted from the Vaudois to secure the withdrawal of the invading army—Further treachery—The Vaudois send their pastors to Pragela—Outrages and horrible atrocities—Unsuccessful deputation to the Duke of Savoy—The Vaudois swear a covenant in the Val Cluson—They adopt measures for more effective resistance—Partial contests, in which the Vaudois are successful—They take Le Villar—Their *Flying Company*—Further defeats of the assailants—Treacherous attempt to engage the Vaudois in negotiations, and to attack them by surprise—Final defeat of the Count De La Trinité, and terms of peace granted to the Vaudois 250

CHAPTER III.—CASTROCARO, GOVERNOR OF THE VALLEYS. (A.D. 1561 to A.D. 1581.)—Distress prevailing in the valleys—Refugees from Calabria—Castrocaro appointed Governor of the Valleys—His scheme for the gradual destruction of the Vaudois Church—He proceeds to impose new restrictions—His arbitrary proceedings—His duplicity—He misrepresents the Vaudois at Court—Kind intentions of the Duchess of Savoy—Gilles Des Gilles, pastor of La Tour, seized and committed to prison—Castrocaro frustrated in some of his attempts—New dangers—A solemn fast—Deliverance from fear—Further arbitrary measures of the Governor—A new covenant sworn by the Vaudois—Charles IX. of France writes to the Duke of Savoy in favour of the persecuted Protestants of the plains of Piedmont—Massacre of St. Bartholomew—Threats of Castrocaro—Consternation of the Vaudois —They are re-assured by the Duke of Savoy—Francis Guérin, pastor of St. Germain, boldly challenges a popish priest to public controversy—Death of the Duchess of Savoy—Controversial discussions—A son of the pastor of La Tour carried off by night—Castrocaro's tyranny and misgovernment become known to the Duke of Savoy—He refuses to appear at Turin, and is carried thither a prisoner—The reward of a traitor and persecutor 277

CHAPTER IV.—STATE OF THE VAUDOIS DURING THE REIGN OF CHARLES EMMANUEL. (A.D. 1580 to A.D. 1630.) GLI BANDITTI.—Troubles in the valley of Pérouse—The Jesuits in the valley of Lucerna—A solemn fast of four days—Deaths of two aged Vaudois pastors—War between France and Savoy—Sufferings of the Vaudois—Proceedings of the Romish clergy—Apostasy of a Vaudois minister, Andrew Laurent—His consequent miseries—The Jesuits in the Valleys—Discussions between them and Vaudois pastors—Ubertin Braida, priest of La Tour—The *Banditti*—The *Digiunati*—Irritation and excesses—A fast—Governor Ponte—Count Charles of Lucerna—Captain Galline attacks Bobi, but is defeated and spared by the Vaudois—Count Charles of Lucerna obtains favourable terms for the Vaudois, and tranquillity is in some measure restored—Death of Vaudois pastors—New alarms—A fast—Earthquake—The regiment of the Baron De La Roche in the Valley of Lucerna—The Vaudois compelled to pay a large sum of money—Disunion among them—Further injustice and exactions—Destruction of a number of places of worship—Continued vexations—Rorengo, Prior of Lucerna—Resistance to the establishment of monks in the valleys 289

CHAPTER V.—THE PLAGUE AND THE MONKS. (A.D. 1627 to A.D. 1643.)—Famine—The Vaudois prevented from obtaining employment—Extraordinary storms—Convent erected at La Tour—War between France and Savoy—Sufferings of the Vaudois—The plague—Meeting of the pastors at Pramol—Deaths of pastors—Terrible ravages of the disease—Three pastors alone left in the valleys—New pastors obtained from Geneva—Victor Amadeus I.—Rorengo and the pastor Gilles—Government commissioners in the valleys—Polemical works—Public discussions—Anthony Léger...310

CHAPTER VI.—THE PROPAGANDA. (A.D. 1637 to A.D. 1655.)—Charles Emmanuel II. of Savoy—The Duchess Christina of France—Disputes as to the regency—The Propaganda instituted—Rorengo—Placido Corso—Public discussions—Crimes and cruelties—Terrible conflagrations—Civil war—The Vaudois support the Duchess Christina—Protestant worship prohibited at St. John—Other severe edicts—Women in the Propaganda—The Marchioness of Pianesse—Her dying charge to her husband—The residences of the monks burned at various places in the valleys—False charge brought against a Vaudois pastor, of having instigated the assassination of a priest...321

CHAPTER VII.—THE PIEDMONTESE EASTER, OR THE MASSACRES OF 1655. (Saturday, the 24th of April, being Easter Eve.)—Proceedings of the Society *de propagandâ fide*—Gastaldo, the duke's lieutenant in the valleys—Severe measures—Prolonged and fruitless negotiations—The Marquis of Pianesse—His deceitfulness—He puts himself at the head of troops for the extermination of the Vaudois—Indecision of the Vaudois, who are in part deceived by false pretences—Janavel—The Vaudois resist the Marquis of Pianesse at La Tour, but are defeated—Further combats —Further treachery of Pianesse—Massacre on the day before Easter—Fearful atrocities—M. Du Petitbourg refuses to conduct his troops upon occasion of this massacre—His subsequent exposure of its enormities......337

CHAPTER VIII.—JANAVEL AND JAHIER. (April to June, 1655.)—The fugitive Vaudois find an asylum in the French dominions—Janavel, with a small band, obtains wonderful victories over the troops of Pianesse—Pianesse has recourse again to the arts of treachery—He ravages Rora, but is attacked and defeated by Janavel as he retires with his booty—Pianesse marches against Rora with almost ten thousand men—Janavel's wife and daughters made prisoners—His constant resolution—The Duchess of Savoy and the French court—Mazarin refuses to take part against the Vaudois as she desires—Cromwell offers them a refuge in Ireland—Intercessions of foreign powers—Collections made for the Vaudois in Protestant countries—The Vaudois continue in arms—Another Vaudois troop takes the field under Jahier—Janavel makes an attempt to seize Lucernette, but fails—Jahier and he effect a junction—They seize St. Segont—Further successes—Janavel is severely wounded—Jahier is killed..........355

CHAPTER IX.—END OF THE CONFLICT, NEGOTIATIONS, AND PATENTS OF GRACE. (June to September, 1655.)—Foreigners come to the assistance of the Vaudois—Further successes of their arms—They fail in an attempt, conducted by the French General Descombies, to take the Fort of La Tour —Intervention of Cromwell—His ambassador, Morland, at Turin—Treaty of Pignerol..373

CHAPTER X.—INFRACTIONS OF THE TREATY OF PIGNEROL—LÉGER'S VICISSITUDES. (A.D. 1655 to A.D. 1660.)—Grievances not redressed by the Treaty of Pignerol—The Fort of La Tour—Continued operations of the

Propaganda—Gastolda, governor of the valleys—New vexations—Violations of the treaty—Question of the right to meet for public worship at St. John—Léger, pastor of St. John, the object of the particular hostility of the Romish party—He is condemned to death, and flees from the country—His labours and trials in his exile—Odious conduct of Charles II. of England, with regard to money collected in that country during the time of Cromwell, for the Vaudois..381

CHAPTER XI.—THE WAR OF THE OUTLAWS. (A.D. 1660 to A.D. 1664.)—De Bagnol, commandant of the fort of La Tour—*Gli Banditti*—This troop of proscribed and desperate men makes reprisals on the persecutors of the Vaudois—Edict of 25th June, 1663—Treachery and violence—The Vaudois assailed by troops under the Marquis De Fleury—Defeat of the assailants—Edict of 10th August, 1663—The Vaudois, under Janavel, continue the defensive war—An attempt to divide the Vaudois by getting a few of their number to consent to the conditions of the edict of 10th August—Intervention of foreign Protestant powers............................390

CHAPTER XII.—MEDIATION OF SWITZERLAND; TREACHERY OF ST. DAMIAN; CONFERENCES AT THE TOWN'S-HOUSE OF TURIN; ARBITRATION OF LOUIS XIV. (A.D. 1664 to A.D. 1680.)—Conferences between the ambassadors of the Protestant cantons of Switzerland and delegates of the Duke of Savoy—Complaints against the Count De Bagnol—His defence—Charges brought against the Vaudois—The question of public worship at St. John—Treacherous invasion of the valleys during the conferences—Further negotiations—Terms agreed upon—Difficulties still renewed—Death of Charles Emmanuel II...402

CHAPTER XIII.—EXILE OF JANAVEL, REVOCATION OF THE EDICT OF NANTES, PRELIMINARIES OF A FOURTH PERSECUTION. (A.D. 1680 to A.D. 1685.)—Janavel retires to Geneva—Louis XIV.—Revocation of the Edict of Nantes—Janavel becomes apprehensive of danger impending over the Vaudois—The Duke of Savoy in a condition almost of vassalage to France—Demands of the French monarch with regard to the Vaudois—He urges the duke to extreme measures—The Propaganda and the Papal nuncio second his efforts—Janavel's letter to his brethren in the valleys, and directions for their conduct in the approaching struggle...................414

CHAPTER XIV.—COMMENCEMENT OF THE FOURTH GENERAL PERSECUTION IN THE VALLEYS. (January to the end of April, 1686.)—Edict of 31st January, 1686—Consternation in the valleys—Delegates meet at Angrogna—Petition to the Duke—Attempted intervention of the Protestant cantons of Switzerland—the valleys invaded by French troops—Organized resistance—Endeavours of the Swiss ambassadors—Proposal that the Vaudois should leave their native country—Division of opinion among them—They finally resolve to abide by and defend their valleys—Celebration of the Lord's Supper at Easter, 1686...426

CHAPTER XV.—WAR AND MASSACRE IN THE VALLEYS. (April to May, 1686.)—The Swiss ambassadors endeavour to secure a place of refuge for the Vaudois in Brandenburg—The valleys invaded by the combined troops of France and Piedmont—Catinat, the French commander-in-chief—His treachery—Successes of the invaders—Cruelties and outrages—Gabriel of Savoy—His treachery towards the Vaudois—Fearful cruelties—Conflicts—Massacres—Prolonged sufferings and martyrdom of Leydet, pastor of Pral..437

CHAPTER XVI.—TERMINATION OF THE CONTEST; MEMOIRS OF A PRISONER; CAPTIVITY AND DISPERSION OF THE VAUDOIS IN VARIOUS TOWNS. (A.D. 1686—May to September.)—The last body of defenders of the valleys—Further treachery practised against them—The valleys, after great massacres and devastations, seem entirely reduced—The invaders depart—New bands of Vaudois appear in arms in the valleys of Lucerna and St. Martin—It is at last stipulated that all the surviving Vaudois shall be permitted to go into exile—Journal of a prisoner—Sufferings of the prisoners..452

CHAPTER XVII.—TOTAL EXPULSION OF THE VAUDOIS, WHO ARE CARRIED AWAY TO VERCEIL, OR CONDUCTED INTO EXILE. (September, 1686, to September, 1687.)—Sympathy manifested by Swiss and other Protestants—Vaudois refugees begin to arrive at Geneva—Vaudois children detained as proselytes—Sufferings of Vaudois who, to escape persecution, had apostatized—Sufferings of those who went into exile—Arrival of successive bands of exiles at Geneva—Their kind reception there—Continued detention of most of the Vaudois pastors by the Duke of Savoy............464

LIST OF ENGRAVINGS.

VOL. I.

                     PAGE

CHATEAU QUEYRAS, IN THE VALLEY OF THE GUIL, DAUPHINY,
Frontispiece.

 On the right are the Mountains of Arvieux, on the left the gorge of the River Guil, where it struggles through a continued gulf, flanked by walls of tremendous rocks fringed with pines. For several miles the river occupies the whole breadth of the defile, with the exception of a narrow path hewn out of the rock, which in some places will scarcely allow two persons to pass.

PRA DU TOUR, IN THE MOUNTAINS OF ANGROGNA,   *Engraved Title.*

 Here the ancient Vaudois had the school of their Barbas or Pastors, the secret source of those vivifying missions which they sent to both extremities of Italy. Not a vestige, however, can now be traced of the buildings of the ancient college which formerly existed in this mountain retreat. The Vaudois regard the Pra du Tour almost as a sacred spot. A Roman Catholic chapel was erected here, with the view of drawing over the Waldenses to the Church of Rome, but the project, as might have been expected, signally failed.

PANORAMIC VIEW OF THE VAUDOIS VALLEYS, . . . 17

 This view is taken from the Mountain of Lucernette, and affords a very comprehensive and interesting prospect of the Vaudois country.

THE CONFLUENCE OF THE GUIL AND THE DURANCE, . 40

 On the left are the Mountains of Freyssinière; towards the centre is the town and fort of Mont Dauphin, situated on a lofty rock at the junction of the two rivers. The defences of this fortress, which commands four valleys, and is considered one of the keys to France, were designed by Vauban, in 1694. A little further to the right is the small town of Guilestre; behind is the gorge of Queyras; and on the right are the mountains which separate this valley from that of Barcellonette.

LIST OF ENGRAVINGS.

PAGE

THE TOWN OF SALUCES, IN THE VALLEY OF THE PO, . . . 128

    The principal objects are the ancient castle of the Marquises of Saluces, now converted into a house of correction; and the cathedral, with its lofty and elegant tower, erected in the fifteenth century. In the distance is seen Mount Viso, one of the highest of the Alps, from the flank of which the Po takes its rise.

THE TOWN OF LE VILLAR, IN THE VALLEY OF LUCERNA, . . 268

    Looking west. In the centre of the town, to the right, is the Protestant church, with a tower surmounted by a spire. The building with the square tower, a little to the left, is the Roman Catholic church. In the distance are seen the mountains forming the extremity of the Valley of Lucerna.

THE TOWN OF BOBI, AND MOUNT BARIOUND, IN THE VALLEY OF LUCERNA, ... 448

    The view is taken from the wood of Balsille. Mount Bariound, the cleft summit of which presents an appearance so remarkable, formed one of the strongholds of the Waldenses in their celebrated "Return" in 1689. It commands a magnificent view, extending to the banks of the Po.

THE

ISRAEL OF THE ALPS.

INTRODUCTION.

PRELIMINARY REMARKS ON THE ORIGIN OF THE VAUDOIS.

The origin of the Vaudois forms one of the most interesting questions of ecclesiastical history. I regret that the narrow limits of this work, and the want of sufficient resources of learning within my reach, do not permit me to treat it so thoroughly as I would have desired. It merits a lengthened and profound discussion; it is a subject much richer than it at first sight appears. A man of learning, and possessed of the necessary means for the investigation of this question, would doubtless find his labour abundantly rewarded.

All that I can do at present, is to lay before the reader a few considerations, such as have occurred to me in my studies, and which have sufficed to determine my own opinion on this point. There are, however, persons of high standing, who do not agree with me concerning the existence of the Vaudois anterior to Valdo. The passages which I proceed to quote are extracts from private correspondence; I hope their publication will not be thought an indiscretion, but rather a tribute of respect to the learning of the writers, and an evidence of my own impartiality.

"I believe," says M. Schmidt, "that the Vaudois Church has no need of any attempt to exalt her reputation, by placing before her historic period a sort of fabulous period, remounting to the days of the apostles; that church appears to me to have sufficient claims to respect, when she is regarded as tracing her origin to a simple layman of Lyons, whose piety, moderation, and courage may always be an example to us. To have clearly asserted the doctrine of the gospel three centuries before the Reformation, and to have maintained it thenceforward with heroic fidelity, in the midst of persecutions and of martyrdoms, is, in my estimation, so honourable, that I have not even a wish to embellish this indisputable fact, by the addition of a long period which is not certain at all. . . . . Having, then, the positive fact of Valdo, why should I not be satisfied with it, at least so long as it cannot be *proved* that there were Vaudois before him?"[1] "On the point now under consideration, the most eminent ecclesiastical historians of Germany, MM. Gieseler and Neander, have long ago renounced the opinion which refers the origin of the Vaudois to the days of the apostles. They trace them back only to Valdo. . . . You bring forward the edict issued by Otho IV. in 1209, and thence conclude that the Vaudois must have been numerous and ancient in the valleys of the Alps. Numerous let it be granted that they were, although in strictness it might be disputed. . . . But as to their being ancient, that is, more ancient than Valdo, I do not think that it follows. Valdo began his career at Lyons about 1170; nine years afterwards he solicited from Pope Alexander III. authority to preach. After the lapse of other five years, in 1184, Lucius III. pronounced an anathema against his disciples. From 1184 to 1209 is a period of twenty-five years, or rather from 1170 to 1209 are thirty-nine years; during this interval of nearly forty years, the Vaudois may have spread far enough, and in fact they did; only consider the facility with which the adversaries of Rome then propagated their doctrines; consider, in particular, the state of mind then prevailing throughout Upper Italy. . . . I shall say nothing of the arguments which you deduce from the Milanese ritual, and from the Epistle to the Laodiceans. . . . How I think on these points you may see from my last letter."—He reckons these arguments insufficient.—"All the certain facts, established by historic documents, are without exception subsequent to 1170, that is to say, to the appearance of Valdo. Prior to this epoch, there is not so much as one. Produce me the least possible fact anterior to this epoch, and I lay down my arms."[2] "You quote to me a bull of Urban II., mentioning the *Vallis Gyrontana* as a focus of heresy in 1096. In the first place, allow me to say, I have never maintained that there were no manifestations of an anti-catholic spirit before the days of Valdo. But in order to establish a true historic connection, a perfect identity of doctrines, it would be necessary to know that heresy of which the focus was in the aforesaid valley. . . . Even admitting that the heresy in question was analogous to the Vaudois doctrines, this would only prove that before Valdo there were

[1] Letter from M. Schmidt, author of the *History of the Cathari*, Strasburg, April 28, 1850.   [2] From the same, May 26, 1850.

already persons who believed something similar to what he afterwards believed; but to conclude, therefore, that he derived either his birth or his doctrine from these men, is to make a great *saltus in probando*."[1]

The reader will here observe that M. Schmidt grants almost all that I desire, for it is by no means necessary to prove that Valdo was descended from the Vaudois; it is enough if the Vaudois be acknowledged to have existed before his time.

I think it my duty also to quote the words of M. Gieseler on this subject, from a letter which he was kind enough to address to me:—
"In the first place, you remind me that, according to the testimony of authors comparatively recent, Peter de Bruys was sprung from a certain valley, which Urban II., in the year 1096, describes as infested with heresy; and thence you think yourself entitled to infer, that the doctrine which Bruys held in common with Valdo, flourished in that valley before Valdo's time. Indeed, it cannot be doubted that before the days of Valdo, Peter de Bruys and Henry condemned the errors of the Catholic Church, as well as the monstrous opinions of the Cathari, and sought to return to the pure doctrine of the Holy Scriptures. Nor is it improbable that Peter sowed the seeds of his doctrine in his native valley, and left followers there; and thus we can explain how Urban might call that valley full of heretics. And it is also likely enough, that of the remaining disciples of Peter and Henry, many joined the Valdenses (Vaudois), in whom they found the same zeal for the doctrine of the Bible; and thus it probably came to pass, that no trace of the Petrobrusians and Henricians appears at any subsequent period. But that the Vaudois themselves existed before the days of Peter de Bruys, and that Peter himself was one of them, I can by no means admit. For, in the first place, he taught many things very contrary to the doctrine of the Vaudois. He denied that infants ought to be baptized, and that the sacrament of the body and blood of Christ was celebrated after its celebration by Christ himself. He required monks to marry. On the other hand, it is well known that the Vaudois did not at first oppose the doctrine and institutions of the Catholic Church, and that they sought only the free preaching of the simple doctrine of the gospel. Moreover, they held celibacy in high estimation; and their leaders themselves lived in celibacy."[2] Such is the principal argument of M. Gieseler in this letter, of which a part only is here given. The opinions of Neander, Herzog, and Schmidt on this point are substantially

[1] Letter from M. Schmidt, author of the *History of the Cathari*, Strasburg, July, 10, 1850.   [2] Letter dated Gottingen, June 20, 1850.

the same. I cannot discuss it here; but I must observe, 1st, that the doctrines of Bruys are more extreme than those of the Vaudois; 2d, that doctrines held in protestation against the Romish Church existed before the birth of Bruys, in the very valley in which he is said to have been born;[1] 3d, that Bruys may have derived from the valley of his birth, and which was one of the Vaudois valleys of Dauphiny, the germs of that opposition to the Romish Church which became the leading characteristic of his own opinions, after these had become independent of the influences predominant around him in his earliest years; 4th, that the extremeness in the opinions of Bruys, discordant with the moderate character of the Vaudois, may itself have led him to withdraw to a distance from them, in order to make proselytes elsewhere; 5th, that this spirit of moderation, which it is generally acknowledged that the Vaudois have displayed, is the usual fruit of time and experience; and that if it was already manifested among them in the days of Bruys, it would be an evidence of the long previous existence of those whom it characterized; and, 6th, that whilst the antiquity of the Vaudois would explain the calm maturity of their doctrines, the excitable character of Bruys would account for the violent extremeness of his. All analogies appear to me to be in favour of my opinion.

In these various letters the difficulty has also been represented to me of deriving the name *Vaudois* from *Vaux*, or *Valdenses* from *Vallis*, as well as the vagueness of the expressions of Otho IV. in his edict of 1209, and the want of documents anterior to the 12th century. I have examined most of these objections in other parts of this work. My readers will estimate for themselves the value of these objections, and of the answers made to them. But I think it right still to add here a few of the reasons which lead me to regard the Vaudois of the Alps as of greater antiquity than the days of Valdo of Lyons.

In the first centuries of the Christian era, each church founded by the disciples of Christ had a unity and an independence of its own. They were united by the same faith, but that faith was not imposed by authority upon any one. Each of these churches thus had its independent organization, as each individual may have his particular constitution and mode of life, whilst the general characters of human life are common to all men. That desire for a visible unity, which characterizes all human governments, impelled the Emperor Constantine to seek the union of all the Christian churches of the empire under a uniform legislation. The spirit of domination soon extended from the civil government to the ecclesiastical;

---

[1] See Chap. i., and notes.

the institution of patriarchs[1] preceded that of the papacy;[2] the latter was slowly matured,[3] and the exclusive character which its organization finally assumed, caused the separation which then took place between the Eastern and Western churches.[4]

Scarcely had this rupture taken place when Popery stirred up the Crusades,[5] and soon afterwards those internal persecutions by which it effected the destruction of the Albigenses.[6] But down to this time the Bible had been read in the vulgar tongue in France;[7] and in Piedmont[8] the diocese of Milan maintained its independence, the Ambrosian ritual preserved there the recollections of the 4th century, and the Vaudois could still find shelter and peace behind this venerated shield.[9]

St. Ambrose did not acknowledge any authority on earth as superior to that of the Bible;[10] and he wished that for the study of it, men would recur to the original text.[11] If any passage appeared obscure, he did not admit that the word of man should interfere with the word of God in order to determine its sense, but he recommended the Christian to endeavour to decide for himself the doctrinal import of obscure passages, by comparing them with other passages of Scripture relating to the same subject.[12] The Bible was to be elucidated only by its own light. Moreover, he declared that nobody could pretend to call himself the successor of St. Peter, unless he had the faith of St. Peter; and he said with regard to a certain

---

[1] It was the second Council of Constantinople, in 381, which gave the title of *patriarchs* to the bishops of Rome, Constantinople, Alexandria, and Antioch.

[2] It was Boniface III. who received for the first time, in 1607, the title of *Œcumenical Bishop*, or Universal Pontiff.

[3] The principal institutions of Catholicism, the celibacy of the priests, ecclesiastical investiture, &c., are to be referred to the days of Gregory VII., who was elected pope in 1073, although the establishment of some of them had been attempted before.

[4] This schism, long foreseen upon account of a number of increasing differences which the autonomy of the Christian churches at that period still permitted to subsist, may be regarded as completed in 1054, by the excommunication which Leo IX. pronounced against the Patriarch of Constantinople.

[5] The first Crusade was preached by Urban II. to the Councils of Placentia and of Clermont, in 1095 and 1096.   [6] In 1209.

[7] The Council of Toulouse, held in 1129, prohibited the reading of the Bible in the vulgar tongue.

[8] See in the Bibliography at the end of this work (Part II. sect. i. § 11), what relates to the translations of the Bible made by the Vaudois into the vulgar tongue.

[9] The diocese of Milan originally comprehended Liguria, Emelia, Flaminia, Venetia, the Cottian Alps (where the Vaudois valleys are), the Grajan Alps, and Rhetia, now the country of the Grisons.

[10] St Ambros. *De fide, ad Gratianum*, lib. i. c. 4. This and the following citations are extracted from a series of articles entitled "Origini et dottrine della Valdese," published in the journal *La Buona Novella*.

[11] *De Spiritu Sancto*, lib. ii. c. 6, and *De Incarnatione*, c. 3.

[12] St. Ambrose, Sermon XIII. on Psa. cxviii.

pope, Pope Liberius, that he was a decided Arian.[1] The sinner, according to him, is justified only by the merits of Christ;[2] we can derive no merit from our own works,[3] the sacraments confer no grace of themselves, they are only the visible sign of that which we receive from the Saviour.[4] St. Augustine, who was the disciple of St. Ambrose, admitted only two sacraments, Baptism and the Lord's Supper, and there is no reason to believe that his master ever acknowledged a greater number. Nor was the worthy Bishop of Milan any more a believer in the bodily presence of Christ in the Eucharist,[5] or in the renewal of his sacrifice at each celebration of the sacrament of the Supper.[6] It may readily be believed that he must have rejected as idolatrous all worship rendered to other objects than the Divine Being;[7] and as to the worship of images, he called it Paganism.[8]

St. Ambrose occupied the see of Milan for twenty-three years, he died in the year 397, and the influence of his evangelical doctrines long continued to be felt in his diocese. Nor did he stand alone in the maintenance of these doctrines. One of his contemporaries, Philastrius, Bishop of Brescia, condemned also, like him, the worship of images,[9] maintained the authority of the Bible, rejected that of Rome,[10] rejected also all pretension to meritorious works,[11] and added to the influence of St. Ambrose by that which he himself exerted. His successor, Gaudentius, and Rufinus of Aquileia, maintained the same doctrines.[12] The latter, a simple priest, having been condemned by Pope Anastasius, as a partizan of the followers of Origen; the Bishop of Aquileia, to whose authority he was immediately subject, maintained him notwithstanding in the post which he occupied, thus affording us a proof of the ecclesiastical independence which the north of Italy enjoyed at that period. This bishop, who is called by St. Jerome one of the best instructed and most pious prelates of his time, did not, any more than his predecessors, recognize any authority superior to that of the Bible,[13] and it ought to be observed that in explaining the passages on

---

[1] *De Pœnitentia*, lib. i. c. 6.
[2] *De Jacobo et Vita Beata*, lib. i. c. 5, 6, &c.   [3] *De bono mortis*, c. 2.
[4] *De Spiritu Sancto*, lib. iii. c. 2. *Epist.* lxxxiv., lxxi., &c.
[5] *Comment. in Luc.*, lib. x. c. 14.   [6] *De officiis*, lib. i. c. 14.
[7] *De fide, ad Gratian.*, lib. i. c. 7.
[8] *De officiis*, lib. i. c. 26. *De fuga sœculi*, c. 5.
[9] *Hæreses*, c. 49.   [10] Ibid. c. 40, 41.   [11] Ibid. c. 47.
[12] As to Philastrius, see his letter to Benevolus, and his sermons; the second of which is certainly intended to combat the notion of the real presence of the body of Christ in the Eucharist. As to Rufinus; on the authority of the Bible, see *Apud Cypr.* pp. 552 and 553; on the objects of faith, see his treatise on the Creed, &c.
[13] *Sti. Cromatii Sermones*, serm. II. pp. 162, 175, &c.

which it has since been attempted to found the doctrine of purgatory, he makes no mention of that popish dogma.[1] His successor, Niceas, who lived about the year 420, also formally rejects the whole theory of personal satisfaction and expiation, acknowledging the right to pardon sins as belonging to God alone, and the merits of Christ as obtaining pardon for us.[2]

The end of this century was disturbed by the invasions of the barbarians. Aquileia and Milan were ravaged by Attila; the Huns, the Heruli, and the Goths successively burst into Upper Italy; and we need no written testimonies to convince us that Rome, with difficulty able to defend herself, could not then extend over these countries an authority to which they had not been subjected before, and from which we afterwards find them free.

In the commencement of the following century, St. Laurence, who was translated from the see of Novara to that of Milan, about the year 507, declares, contrary to the opinions at present received among Papists, that repentance is the only means by which we can obtain the pardon of our offences, and that pardon cannot come to us by the intercession of any creature whatever, nor by any human absolution, but only by grace and the love of Christ. Finally, says he, we must trust in God rather than in men.[3] Ennodius, in his *Life of St. Epiphanius, Bishop of Pavia*, in relating the circumstances which attended the death of that prelate, makes no mention of confessor, or absolution, or indulgence, or cross, or banners, or images, or holy water, or litanies, or any of the other things which are so prominent at the present day in the popish ceremonial on such an occasion.

About the middle of the 6th century, a part of the bishops of Upper Italy[4] refused to adhere to the decisions of the Council of Chalcedon, held in 553; and in 590, nine of them separated themselves from the Roman Church, or rather they solemnly renewed the protestation of their independence of it. The bishops being then elected by the people of their diocese, we may presume, without doing any violence to history, that the latter were imbued with the same doctrines and with the same spirit.

The permanence of this state of things in Upper Italy, is attested in the 7th century by a new Bishop of Milan, Mansuetus, A.D. 677. To combat the opinion that the pope is the head of the church, he directs attention to the fact that the Councils of Nice, Constan-

---

[1] *Sti. Cromatii Sermones*, serm. II. p. 166.
[2] *Ad virginem lapsam*, inserted in the works of St. Ambrose.
[3] See, in Mabillon, *Vetera Analecta*, the three discourses of this bishop, which are still extant. Pp. 20–40.   [4] Those of Venetia, Istria, and Liguria.

tinople, Chalcedon, and many others, had been convoked by the emperors, and not by the pope. This bishop himself was not afraid to condemn Pope Honorius as a Monothelite;[1] and thus gives us a new proof of the independence then enjoyed by the diocese of Milan, across which the Vaudois would have been obliged to pass, in order to reach Rome.

The kingdom of Lombardy itself was solicitous for the preservation of this independence. Thus everything contributed to its maintenance; and it may be supposed that, satisfied with the first successes obtained in the towns, Rome thereafter paid less regard to the relics of independence which might still subsist in the mountains. We know, moreover, that ancient manners and ancient liberties have at all times been less easily eradicated from such situations.

However, we are not reduced to the necessity of supporting this idea by mere inferences; and the 8th century still presents us with examples of resistance to the pretensions of the papal see in Upper Italy. As these pretensions are more strongly urged, we find the resistance also becoming more vigorous in the following centuries, and we can follow its traces quite on to the 12th century, when the existence of the Vaudois is no longer doubted by anybody.

The Council of Narbonne, at which a number of bishops of Upper Italy were present, recommended to the faithful no other prayers than the *Pater* and the *Credo*. The Council of Frankfort, at which also Italian prelates were present, formally condemned the worship of images. St. Paulinus, Bishop of Aquileia, maintained, like his predecessors, the symbolical character of the Eucharist,[2] the nullity of satisfactory works,[3] the sovereign authority of the Bible in matters of faith,[4] and the efficacious mediation of one only mediator between God and man, even Jesus Christ.[5]

But the grasping ambition of the Church of Rome, overcoming by degrees the resistance made in quarters nearest to its centre of action, forced back towards the chain of the Alps, the limits, still becoming narrower, of that independence inherited from past ages, which had at first opposed it over the whole of Upper Italy. This independence was defended, in the 9th century, by Claude of Turin; in whom, at the same time, we behold the most distinguished advocate of evangelical doctrines whom that age produced. Whilst the Bishop of Milan[6] contented himself with deploring the corruption of the Roman Church,[7] by which he had been

---

[1] See the investigation of this fact in the *Buona Novella*, i. 298.
[2] In his book *against Felix D'Urgel*, written by order of Charlemagne, p. 1766.
[3] Ibid. p. 1792. [4] Ibid. p. 1795. [5] Ibid. p. 1790. [6] Angilbert.
[7] See an extract from these complaints in the *Buona Novella*, i. 326.

reduced to subjection, but in whose iniquities he did not take part, the Bishop of Turin boldly declared against the innovations which she had so long sought to introduce into the sphere of his influence and power. The numerous works of this prelate on different books of the Bible,[1] had prepared him for defending it against the attacks of Popery; and strong in the might of truth, Claude of Turin owned Jesus Christ as the sole Head of the church,[2] attached no value to pretended meritorious works, rejected human traditions, acknowledged faith alone as securing salvation, ascribed no power to prayers made for the dead, maintained the symbolical character of the Eucharist, and, above all, opposed with great energy the worship of images, which he, like his predecessors, regarded as absolute idolatry.[3]

Thus the doctrines which characterized the primitive church, and which still characterize the Vaudois Church at the present day, have never remained without a witness in the countries inhabited by the Vaudois; and if men had been silent, the Bible would have spoken. In the 10th century, Atto, Bishop of Verceil, still appears as their defender; he maintains the authority of the word of God, and does not admit that of the fathers of the church, except in so far as they agree with it; insisting that the church is founded only upon the Christian faith, and not upon the pre-eminence of any apostle or pontiff—that the pope has no administrative authority beyond the see of Rome, and that all the faithful ought to partake of the Eucharist.[4]

But the oppressive tendencies of the Church of Rome manifested themselves in the cruel measures of which the Jews were then the victims. Ignorance and superstition made rapid progress. The light of human learning passed for a time to the midst of Mahometanism. The conflicts in Spain and in Italy against the Mahometan power, were for a little while an obstacle in the way of the pontifical despotism.

In the 11th century, although there were already numerous monasteries in Lombardy, the vows of those who entered them

[1] In 815 he wrote three books on Genesis and a commentary on St. Matthew. Next year he published a commentary on the Epistle to the Galatians, and, soon after, another commentary on the Epistle to the Ephesians. In 821 he wrote four books on Exodus; in 823, a commentary on Leviticus. There is also ascribed to him a commentary on the book of Ruth, but none of his works have been printed except his commentary on the Epistle to the Galatians.

[2] *Comment. in Galat.*, Bibl. PP. i. 810.

[3] On these various points see the same work of Claude on the Galatians, pp. 789–844; the extract which Mabillon gives from his commentary on Leviticus, and also a citation by Meyer, lib. iii. c. 14, as referred to in the *Buona Novella*, i. 528. [4] In D'Achery, *Spiceleg. vet. auct.*

were not yet rendered irrevocable by any other authority than that of their own consciences; and in the 12th century all the priests of Upper Italy were still free from the yoke of the celibate. This independence, so long disputed by Rome and maintained by the Lombard clergy, was a protecting shield for the Vaudois valleys.

Thus we see that the Apostolic Church of Italy, disowned and proscribed by papal pride, gradually retired from Rome, withdrew into Upper Italy, and sought a retreat in the wilderness to preserve her purity. We see her first sheltered in the diocese of Milan, where Popery still pursues her. She then retires into the diocese of Verceil, and thither also the hostile pretensions of Popery are extended. She takes refuge in the diocese of Turin, but Popery still gains upon her, and at last she seeks an asylum in the mountains. We find her in the Vaudois valleys!

The inhabitants of these valleys, previously unregarded, became an object of attention from the 12th century, not because they were new opponents of Rome's domination, but because they remained alone in their opposition. Rendered distinct by her isolation, their church found her own pale a separate one for this reason only, that she herself had never changed. But as they did not form a new church, they could not receive a new name; and because they inhabited the *valleys*, they were called *Vaudois*.

Let us now see how these events are reflected in their own writings.

St. Peter and St. James, in addressing their epistles to *the Catholic Church*, show us that it was something very different from *Catholicism*. They meant by the Catholic Church the whole body of Christians of that time—Christians who were apostolic. Now the Vaudois, in their most ancient works, written in the Romance tongue, at a date when there existed schismatical sects which have now disappeared, speak of themselves always as being in union with the Catholic Church,[1] and condemn those who separate from

---

[1] Aquesta nostra fe katholica se conten en li articles de la fe e en le sagrament de la sancta gleysa.—[This is our catholic faith, which is contained in the articles of faith, and in the sacraments of the holy church.]—Vaudois MSS. of Geneva, No. 208, fol. 3.

Non te conselha daquilli que son devis de la sancta gleysa.—[Take heed not to follow the counsel of those who are separated from the holy church.]—MS. 209, Treatise on Repentance.

Nos creen qu'el meseyme Dio eslegis a si gloriosa gleysa . . . . ma quilla sia sancta e non sozca.—[We believe that God himself has chosen unto himself the glorious church . . . that it may be holy and undefiled.]—MS. 208, de li Articles de la fe, § 5.

Sobre totas cosas nos desiren lonor de Dio e lo perfeit de la sancta gleysa, e que nos sian fedels membres de Yeshu Xrist.—[Above all things, we desire the

it,[1] but, at the same time, the doctrines which they set forth in their works are only those of the primitive Catholic Church, and not at all those of later Catholicism. The successive corruptions which gradually constituted it, were everywhere introduced by small degrees, and did not for a long time reach the threshold of their secluded valleys.

When they did become known there, the Vaudois boldly stood up *against that variety of invented things*,[2] which they called *a horrible heresy*,[3] and unhesitatingly pointed them out as the cause why the Church of Rome had departed from the primitive faith.[4] They no longer give to Popery the name of *the Catholic Church*, but speak of it as *the Roman Church;* and then also they openly separated from it,[5] because it was no longer the primitive church,

honour of God and the profit of the holy church, and that we may be faithful members of Jesus Christ.]—MS. 208, fol. 14.

Crezen la sancta gleysa esse funda tant fermament sobre la ferma peyra, que las portas d'enfern, non poissan per alcuna maniera prevaler encontra ley.—[We believe that the holy church is so firmly founded upon the rock that the gates of hell cannot, in any manner, prevail against it.]—Geneva MS. 208, fol. 15.

[1] Pren conselh de le bon preyre, daquello lical son conjoint a la gleysa antica e apostolica, ressemilhant dobras de sanctita e de fe. Ma non te consellur daquilh que son devis de la sancta gleysa.—[Take counsel from good priests, from those who are united to the ancient and apostolical church, in the similarity of works of holiness and of faith. But take not counsel from those who separate from the holy church.]—Geneva MS. 207, Treatise on Repentance.

Cum le sant doctor dion
Alcuna cosa, o affermant
Sobre oppinion tant
Coma fe, hereticant.

—[When the holy doctors say anything, or affirm upon [*human*] opinion as a matter of faith, they fall into heresy.]—Geneva MS. 208, fol. 15.

[2] Circa la varieta de las cosas emergent.—Vaudois MSS. in library of Trinity College, Dublin, C. V. 22, fol. 180, and Geneva MS. 208, fol. 14.

[3] La horrenda heretication.—Ibid.

[4] Ayczo es la causa del department de la Gleysa Romana.—(Dublin MSS. C. V. 25.) *Here is the cause of the deviations of the Roman Church*. In recent copies, and in works printed since the Reformation, this title is to be found in the following form, *Ayczo es la causa* DEL NOSTRO *departiment de la Gleysa Romana, i.e.*, Here is the cause of our separation from the Roman Church; and the work, in fact, has for its object to cut off all connection with that church, so that, without violence to its contents, either of these different forms may be adopted.

[5] The following are the first lines of the last-quoted work, according to the MS. of Dublin, class C. V. 25.—(I am indebted for this communication to the obliging kindness of the learned Dr. Gilly, author of so many remarkable works on the Vaudois, and who has just published, from the original MSS., their ancient translation of the gospel according to St. John):—

Al nom del nostre Segnor Yeshu Xrist! Amen.—[In the name of our Lord Jesus Christ! Amen.]

La causa del nostre departiment de lunita de la costuma de la Romana Gleysa, e de totas cosas semblant en part o en tot en aquellas cosas, lasquals contradiçon a la verita: es de doas manieras. Luna causa es la verita saludivos: lautra la falsita

such as theirs had been left to them by their fathers, but a corrupt church, delighting in vain superstitions.

Here, let me remark, we have one of the strongest intrinsic proofs of the apostolic descent of the Vaudois, for the Church of Rome was also, in its origin, the Apostolic Church, being under the guidance of St. Paul, and if the Vaudois had been separate from it from the beginning, they could not have been apostolic themselves; if they had separated from it at a later period, without previously having had any independent existence, their existence would only have dated from that separation. But, on the contrary, they had existed from the commencement of the common life; that life had been preserved amongst their mountains; they might probably believe that it was also preserved elsewhere, and when its corruptions became so striking, that the primitive apostolical character of the Church of Rome was completely effaced, they refused to give it the name of Catholic, and showed in what it had departed from true catholicity.

It may, perhaps, be said, that there were no Christians in the Alps in the time of the apostles. But the Apostolical Church did not die with the apostles; in the era of the martyrs the seeds of it were sown all over Italy. The Ambrosian office, which the Vaudois were reproached for having retained after it had been abolished elsewhere,[1] was not set up except in the 4th century; and the Epistle to the Laodiceans, which they preserved in some of their manuscripts,[2] also leads us back to the same date.

Thus the name Vaudois, in its original use, did not designate a particular sect, but merely the Christians of the valleys. When this name had become a term of reproach among the Papists, the ignorance of the middle ages made it synonymous with *magician*

---

contraria a la salu.—[The cause of our separation from the ritual unity [*unity of the customs*] of the Roman Church, and from all things, in whole or part, having resemblance thereto and contrary to the truth, may be viewed in two ways. The one is [*a regard to*] the truth which saves: the other, to the falsehood which is contrary to salvation.]

La verita pertenent a la salu es de doas manieras: luna essential, o substancial, l'autra ministerial; josta loqual cosa e la falseta, es departia parellhament en falseta substancial, e en falseta ministerial.—[The truth pertaining unto salvation may be viewed in two ways, in its substantial essence and in rites; and wherever falsehood is found, it will be found equally as falsehood in substance and falsehood in rites.]

Farther on they distinctly use the word *Reformation* in respect of all the abuses which have been introduced into the church, pronouncing it to be necessary, if that church wishes still to be called Christian. Still farther on they plainly point it out as the *Antichrist*.—See Perrin, pp. 253-295.

[1] Fournier, *Hist. des Alpes*, &c.—MS. of Gap, p. 263.
[2] *Bible Vaudoise*, public library of Lyons, No. 60.

or *infidel;*[1] but the Vaudois themselves called themselves only by the name of Christians, and above all, endeavoured to merit it.

That the Vaudois, notwithstanding their small number, remained the representatives of the universal church, and were the precursors and not the disciples of the Reformation, is entirely owing to the word of God, the gospel of Christ. It may be that they did not understand it always so well as the Reformers; that they shared in some of the religious forms of the Romish Church; that they even admitted doctrinal articles which we do not admit at the present day (the distinction, for example, betwixt mortal and venial sins); it is not their infallibility for which we would contend, but that which gave them their strength, their unity, their perseverance in the gospel, in one word, their individuality as a church, at once Catholic when viewed in reference to the Bible, and Protestant when viewed in reference to Catholicism; their maintenance of the absolute authority of the word of God, and of the doctrine of salvation by Jesus Christ. The Vaudois, therefore, are not schismatics, but the continued inheritors of the church founded by the apostles. This church then bore the name of Catholic, and was persecuted by the Pagans. Afterwards, becoming powerful and persecuting in its turn, it underwent a vitiation of its very nature in Catholicism, whilst it was preserved in the Vaudois valleys simple, free, and pure, as in the time of persecution.

We find, accordingly, that the writers nearest to the time of Valdo do not speak of the Vaudois as if they were the disciples of that reformer, but present them to our notice as if they derived their origin from their valleys.[2] Moreover, it was in these valleys that, according to writers of the same country, opponents of the Vaudois, Peter de Bruys, the precursor of Valdo, was born;[3] from

---

[1] See Jacques Duclerc, *Memoires sur la Vaudoiserie d'Arras.*—MS. of the ancient library of the abbey of Saint Waast, at Arras, fol. G. Even *Joan of Arc* was condemned as a *Vaudoise.*—See Mézeray, Michelet, &c.

[2] *Dicti sunt . . . a valle densa.*—(Bernard, *Contra Valdenses et Arianos* in Gretzeri Opera, t. xii., prefatory part of the work.) *Valdenses . . . . eo quod in valle.*—(Eberhard, *Liber Anti-hæresis,* c. xxv.) This writer elsewhere calls the Vaudois by the simple name of *Mountaineers,* which still further confirms the idea that he regarded them as originally belonging to their mountains.—See *Max. Bibl. Patrum,* vol. xx. col. 1039.)

[3] Father Albert, (in his *History of the Diocese of Embrun,* i. 56), and the Jesuit Fournier, (in his *History of the Maritime or Cottian Alps,* and particularly of their metropolitan city, Embrun, a MS. in fol., of which the original, in Latin, is at Lyons, and the translation, which I quote, in the library of the Little Seminary at Gap), also Raymond Juvenis (author of unpublished *Historical Memoirs* and *Procureur du Roi,* at Gap, about the end of the 17th century), say that *Peter de Bruys derived his descent from the Val-Louise,* one of the Vaudois valleys of Dauphiny.

which it would follow that the doctrines common to these two reformers must have been known in these valleys before the appearance of Valdo. These doctrines, in fact, are already alluded to before that period, and even in official documents.[1]

The name of Valdo seems to have been neither a baptismal[2] nor a family name.[3] If it was only a designation, we may suppose that it was given in consequence of his connection with the Vaudois of the Alps,[4] and his propagation of their doctrines. But even if a Christian at Lyons named Valdo,[5] had participated in these doctrines, and had left his disciples the name of *Vaudois*, it would not follow that the Vaudois of the Alps were the disciples of Valdo. We even find this name and these doctrines in a poem in the Romance tongue anterior by half-a-century to Valdo. But the date of the poem has been disputed; it shall be examined in a subsequent part of this work.[6]

The edict of Otho IV., of date A.D. 1209, ascribes to the Vaudois of Piedmont a notoriety and an influence so great, that it may

---

[1] The Val-Louise is mentioned as *infested with heresy* so early as the year 1096, in a bull of Urban II., cited by Brunet, Seigneur de l'Argentière.—(*Collection of Acts, Papers, and Proceedings relative to the perpetual* emphyteosis *of the Tithes of the Briançonnais*, p. 55.) In this bull the Val-Louise is called *Vallis Gyrontana*, from the name of the *Gyron*, or *Gyr*, a torrent which flows through it. Concerning the different names of this valley, see at the commencement of chap. iii. of part I. of this work.

[2] Because he was called *Peter*.—"*Predicto* Petro, quidam se adjunxit *qui dictus erat* Johannes, *et erat de Lugduno*."—Philichdorfius, *De Hæresi Valdensium*, c. i. *Bibliotheca Max*. PP. t. xxv. 278.

[3] Family names were not in use at that period. Individuals received some designation derived from their profession, their personal appearance, or their character, as, *James the Weaver*, *Thomas the Red*, *Richard Cœur-de-Lion*, &c.

[4] In his character of a *foreign merchant*. To this notion is objected the difficulty of deriving the words *Valdo* and *Valdenses* from *vallis*, a valley. But how many words have we which have not followed, in their formation, the rules of an exact etymology? These arbitrary derivations were especially numerous in the middle ages. The objection would be of force only if that disputed derivation were the fact supposed in a hypothesis of our framing, but it existed already in the days of Valdo. *Valdenses . . . . dicti sunt . . . . a valle densa.*—(See note at bottom of p. 13.) Moreover, Eberhard de Bethune calls the Vaudois *Vallenses*, giving the same etymology of the word.—(See note above referred to.) De Thou calls them indifferently Vallenses, Valdenses, or Convallenses.—*Histor.* lib. xxvii., &c.

[5] The name of Valdo was not rare in the middle ages. In 739 we have *Valdo*, Abbot of St. **Maximin**, at Trèves; in 769, and in 830, the same name occurs again amongst the *freemen*, subscribers for donations to the abbey of Wissembourg; in 786 lived *Valdo*, Abbot of Richenau, near St. Denys; in 881 *Valdo*, Bishop of Freissingen; in 907 *Valdo*, member of the Synod of Vienne; in 960 *Valdo*, Bishop of Como, &c.—Letter of M. Schmidt, May 26, 1850.

[6] *La Nobla Leyczon*, bearing the date A.D. 1100. For discussion of the subject of this date, see in the Bibliography of the *Israel of the Alps*, part I. sec. ii. § 3, art. xxiv., and part II. sec. i. § 3; MS. 207, art. v.

be presumed they were already of long standing in the country.¹ Supposing that the disciples of Valdo had taken refuge in the Alps about the end of the 12th century, it would be very difficult to admit that they could have so filled both the Vaudois valleys of Dauphiny and those of Piedmont in less than one generation, as to have acquired that influence which is ascribed to them, alike by this edict on the one hand, and by that of Alphonso of Arragon, Marquis of Provence, on the other.² It would be impossible to account for such an increase, save on the supposition that the new refugees had already in that country brethren of their own religion;³ whilst their settling in that country can hardly be explained but by supposing the previous existence of their brethren in religion there.⁴ On either of these suppositions, the Vaudois of the Alps must have been prior to the disciples of Valdo.

The idiom of the *Nobla Leyczon* being the language of the Alps, and not that of the Lyonnais,⁵ this poem must have been written by inhabitants of the mountains, and not by strangers. But since it cannot have been composed, except between the years 1100 and 1190⁶—since in 1100 the disciples of Valdo of Lyons were not yet in existence—since in 1190 scarcely six years had elapsed from the time of their banishment from Lyons,⁷ and it is not probable that in so short a time they could have acquired a new language, so as all at once to endow it with the most perfect works which it had yet produced—since, moreover, in the precarious position in which they were placed, they must have had something else to do than to write poems—and, finally, since in the *Nobla Leyczon* there is no mention of Valdo nor of his disciples, not even an allusion to their existence, I am compelled to believe that it is

---

¹ See *Monumenta Patriæ*, III. col. 488. The fault found with the Vaudois in this decree is in these words, *Zizaniam seminant*, which, according to the notion of some, would seem to indicate that their presence in that country was recent, but, in my opinion, would rather imply that their activity had increased.

² In 1192, according to D'Argentré (*Collectio judic. de novis errorib*. t. i. fol. 83),— in 1194, according to Eymeric (*Directorium Inquisit*. p. 282), Alphonso II. was *Marquis of Provence*. The *Vaudois* are named in that edict. We may therefore consider them as existing *in Provence* at that date.

³ Without this it can scarcely be explained how they could have known that they would find an asylum there.

⁴ That is, if the disciples of Valdo did indeed take refuge in the Alps.

⁵ See the Bibliography of the *Israel of the Alps*, part II. sec. i. § 1, art. vii. and § 2, MS. 7. ⁶ The same Bibliography, part I. sec. ii. § 3, art. xxiv.

⁷ In 1179 Valdo presented to Pope Alexander III. a translation of the Bible into the vulgar tongue, and was present at the Council of Lateran, where divers heretics were condemned. But it does not appear that Valdo was of the number, as Mapes, Archdeacon of Oxford, who was present at that council, reports that the Pope embraced Valdo and granted him part of the things which he demanded. This is

not among the disciples of Valdo that we are to look for the author of that poem.

In fact, if the Vaudois of Lyons had found it necessary to write such a work, it is evident that they would have written it in the language which was familiar to them, that is to say, in the idiom of the Lyonnais, and not in that of the Alps. And, even supposing that they could have known the latter idiom, I confidently say that they would not have employed it, at least, not unless there had been already in the Alps natives who held the same doctrines with themselves, for otherwise, these natives would have been their adversaries, and the disciples of Valdo, whose object it was to conceal themselves, would have avoided the language of their adversaries, rather than made choice of it. Whence I conclude, that these poems were not their productions;—that they are to be ascribed to natives of the Alps who spoke that language;—and that these natives were Vaudois anterior to Valdo.

Their history is only a portion of the great history of the martyrs; they acquired new importance, from century to century, by the very calamities which they endured. Their importance, always religious, does not secure their title to a place in the political records of the nations; yet the place of this people, so small in numbers, is one of such prominence in the records of human opinion, that the course of their history through calm and storm up to the present day, is to be traced with the greatest interest.

Their existence, by exceptional provision, under an oppressive and violent government, has now terminated. The era of the martyr people has lately been brought to a close by the hand of modern liberty. Let us trust that we may look upon the past as a history concluded, and that a new career opens up to the Vaudois of glorious progress in the future. May they always carry along with them the true spirit of Christianity!

confirmed by the *Chronicle of Laon*, according to which it even appears that Valdo had obtained authorization for preaching, but under certain reservations. Moneta also gives us to understand the same thing.—(Authors cited by Gilly, *Romaunt Version*, Introd. p. lxxxix.-xciv.) But these reservations were probably not attended to; and Valdo was condemned in the Council of Verona (by Lucius III., in 1184), when the emperor engaged to exert himself for the extirpation of heretics. It was in consequence of this condemnation, between 1185 and 1188, that Valdo was expelled from Lyons with his disciples.

Drawn from Nature by Alexis Muston

GENERAL VIEW OF THE
TAKEN FROM THE VALLEYS

1 Lucernette.   2 Lucerna.

VALLEY
5 Valley of Salabial or Lucernette.   6 Valley of Rora.   7 Valley of Lucerna or Pelis.

MOUNTAIN
10 Mount Viso, overlooking the Valley of the Po.
11 Mount Friouland overlooking the Valley of Rora.
12 Mount Brouard.
13 Mount Palavas, overlooking the Valley of Lucerna and particularly the Basins of Bobi and Le Villar.
14 Le Cournaout, the central highest peak overlooking the Valleys of Lucerna Augrogna and La Tour.

BLACKIE & SON; GLASGOW.

Engraved by T. A. Prior

VAUDOIS VALLEYS.
OF LUCERNETTE

3 La Tour. 4 Saint John.

8 Valley of Augrogna,(the lower part, opening into the Valley of Lucerna). 9. Basin of St. John.

15 Mount Vaudalin, over--looking the Basins of LaTour and Augrogna.
16 Peak of Cella Veilla.
17 Côte Roussine,over--looking the Pra del Tour.
18 Mountains of laVachere overlooking the Valley of Augrogna.
19 Les Sonnaillettes, the highest point of the Costiere of S!John.
20 Costiere of Saint John.

EDINBURGH & LONDON.

PART FIRST.

HISTORY OF THE VAUDOIS, FROM THEIR ORIGIN TO THE TIME WHEN THEY WERE CIRCUMSCRIBED WITHIN THE VALLEYS OF PIEDMONT ALONE.

CHAPTER I.

ORIGIN, MANNERS, DOCTRINE, AND ORGANIZATION OF THE VAUDOIS IN ANCIENT TIMES.[1]

The Vaudois in the Early Ages—their Ecclesiastical Independence—their *Barbas*, or Ministers and Missionaries—their Adherents in different parts of Italy—their Church Government, and Mode of Worship—their Doctrine—Sacraments, Confession, &c.—Persecutions—Persecution by the Emperor Otho IV. in 1209.

THE Vaudois of the Alps are, in my opinion, primitive Christians, or descendants and representatives of the primitive church, preserved in these valleys from the corruptions successively introduced by the Church of Rome into the religion of the gospel. It is not they who have separated from Catholicism, but Catholicism which has separated from them by changing the primitive religion.

Hence arises the impossibility of assigning any precise date for the commencement of their history. The Church of Rome, which at first also was a part of the primitive church, did not change all at once; but as it became powerful, it adopted, along with the sceptre, the pomp, the pride, and the spirit of domination which usually accompany the possession of power; whilst, in the retirement of the Vaudois valleys, that primitive church was reduced to an obscure existence, retaining its freedom in its isolation, and thenceforth little tempted to abandon the pure simplicity of its first days. The independence of the diocese of Milan, to which the Christians of the Alps then belonged, and that of which the episcopal see of Turin

[1] AUTHORITIES.—Ancient Vaudois MSS. in the Romance language, deposited in libraries—of Lyons, No. 60; of Grenoble, No. 488 (ancient shelves, 8595); of Geneva, Nos. 43, 206, 207, 208, 209; and of Trinity College, Dublin, class A. IV. 13, class C. V. 18, 21, 22, class C. IV. 17 and 18.

gave evidence, by opposing the worship of images in the 9th century,[1] must have contributed to their security in that situation.

The Vaudois have been represented as deriving their origin from Valdo of Lyons, and it is indisputable that that reformer had disciples to whom he left the name of Vaudois; but this is not sufficient to prove that the Vaudois of the Alps derive their origin from him. Many circumstances, on the contrary, seem to establish their existence anterior to his time,[2] and perhaps it was from them that he derived the name by which he is now known.[3]

The Vaudois valleys could not always preserve that unnoticed independence in which their security consisted. Catholicism having gradually attired itself in new forms of worship unknown to the apostles, made the contrast daily more striking between its pompous innovations, and the ancient simplicity of the Vaudois. In order, therefore, to reduce them to the despotic unity of Rome, there were sent against them the agents of a ministry equally unknown to apostolic times. These were the inquisitors.[4] In consequence of the resistance which they encountered in these retired mountainous regions, the valley of Lucerna was placed under ban.[5] But this measure served only to make more manifest the line of demarcation betwixt the two churches; for whilst the Vaudois had not schismatically separated themselves from the Catholic Church, whose external forms they still retained, they had their own clergy, their own religious service, and their own parishes.

Their pastors were designated Barbas.[6] It was in the almost inaccessible solitude of a deep mountain-pass that they had their school, where the whole influences of external nature were opposed to anything soft and yielding in the soul.[7] They were required

---

[1] See, in particular, the *Life of Claude of Turin*, who occupied the episcopal see for more than twenty years after having declared against these innovations.—Basnage, *Church History*, ii. 1308.

[2] BERNARD DE FONTCAUD (de fonte calido), who died in 1193 (Herzog, *De orig. et pristino statu Wald.*, &c., p. 2), wrote *Contra Valdenses et Arianos*. He makes no mention of Valdo in this work. The Vaudois are classed with the Arians, but not confounded with them. EBERHARD, or EVRARD DE BETHUNE (*Biblioth. Max.* PP. t. xxiv.), the time of whose death is unknown, but cannot be far from that of the preceding author, speaks of the Vaudois without speaking of Valdo, from which it may be inferred that he knew nothing of the latter, who was probably his junior, and that the Vaudois of whom he speaks are anterior to Valdo.—See the Bibliography at the end of this work, part I. sec. ii. § 3, art. xxiv.

[3] In consequence of his probable connection with the Vaudois valleys, for he was a foreign merchant, and his name was Peter.

[4] Driven from the Valley of Angrogna in 1308, they reappeared in that of Lucerna in 1332.—Brief of John XXII., July 20, 1332.

[5] In 1453, by Nicolas V.—See the concluding chapter of the Bibliography.

[6] A title of respect; in the Vaudois idiom literally signifying an *uncle*.

[7] This pass, situated in the valley of Angrogna, is called *Pra du Tour*.

to commit to memory the Gospels of St. Matthew and St. John, the general epistles, and a part of those of St. Paul. They were instructed, moreover, during two or three successive winters, and trained to speak in Latin, in the Romance language, and in Italian. After this they spent some years in retirement, and then were set apart to the holy ministry by the administration of the Lord's Supper, and by imposition of hands. They were supported by the voluntary contributions of the people. These were divided annually in a general synod: one part was given to the ministers, one to the poor, and the third was reserved for the missionaries of the church.

These missionaries always went forth two and two, to wit, a young man and an old one. The latter was called the *Regidor*, and his companion the *Coadjutor*. They traversed Italy, where they had stations organized in many places, and secret adherents in almost all the towns. At Venice they reckoned 6000;[1] at Genoa they were not less numerous. Vignaux speaks of a pastor of the valley of Lucerna, who was away from it for a period of seven years.[2] The Barba Jacob was returning from a missionary tour in 1492, when he was arrested by the troops of Cattanée on the Col de Coste-Plane, as he passed from the valley of Pragela to that of Freyssinières;[3] and the records[4] of judicial investigations directed against the Vaudois from 1350 to 1500, and so often quoted by Bossuet,[5] make mention also of the characteristic circumstance of these habitual journeys.

What a delightful and truly festival time it must have been to these scattered Christians, when the missionary pastor came amongst them, expected all the year with the certainty of the regularly returning seasons!—a time soon past, but fraught with blessings, and in which the fruits of the soul and the harvest of the Lord made progress towards maturity.

Each pastor was required to become missionary in his turn. The younger ones were thus initiated into the delicate duties of evangelization — each of them being under the experienced guidance of a man of years, who, according to the discipline of his church, was his superior, and whom he was bound to obey in everything, as matter of duty, and not merely out of deference. The old man, on his part, thus made his preparation for repose, by training for

[1] Gilles, p. 20.   [2] Quoted by Perrin, p. 241.
[3] Perrin, p. 241, marginal note 4.
[4] These records formerly belonged to the private library of Colbert, from which they passed to that of the Marquis of Seignelay. Bonnet and Lelong quote them in their dictionaries. I know not what has become of them. A manuscript in folio, in the library of the Little Seminary of Gap, contains a number of fragments of them, which I have consulted.   [5] *History of Variations*, b. xi. § ci. *et seq*.

the church successors worthy of it and of himself. His task being accomplished, he could die in peace, with the consolatory assurance of having transmitted the sacred trust of the gospel into prudent and zealous hands.

Besides this, the Barbas received instructions in some trade or profession, by which they might be enabled to provide for their own wants. Some were hawkers, others artisans, the greater part physicians or surgeons, and all were acquainted with the cultivation of the soil and the keeping of flocks, to the care of which they had been accustomed in their early years. Very few of them were married; and their perpetual missions, their poverty, their missionary tours, their life always spent amidst warfare and dangers, make it easy to understand the reason of their celibacy.

In the annual synod, which was held in the valleys, inquiry was made concerning the conduct of the pastors, and changes of residence were made amongst them. The Barbas actually employed in the ministry, were changed from place to place every three years—two of them always exchanging places with one another, except the aged men, who were no longer removed. A general director of the church was named at each synod, with the title of president or moderator. The latter title became more prevalent, and continues to this day.

The Vaudois Barbas were bound to visit the sick, whether sent for or not. They nominated arbiters in disputes; they admonished those who behaved ill, and if remonstrances produced no effect, they went the length of excommunication; but it was very rare. Their preaching, catechizing, and other exercises of instruction and devotion, were generally similar to those of the Reformed churches, except that the worshippers pronounced, with a low voice, the prayer which preceded and that which followed the sermon. The Vaudois had likewise hymns, which they only sung in private; which, moreover, agrees with what we know of the customs of the primitive church.

Their doctrines were equally analogous, or rather were remarkably identical with those of the apostolic times, and of the earliest fathers of the church. They may be briefly summed up in these few words:—*The absolute authority and inspiration of the Bible* [1]—

---

[1] Nos creen .... tot czo qu'es contenu al velh e al novel Testament esser segella e auctentica d'l sagel d'l sant Sperit ... e tota la ley d'Xt. istar tan ferma en verita que una lettra o un poinct d'ley meseyma, non poissa mancar ni deffalhir.— [We believe that all which is contained in the Old and New Testaments is sealed and authenticated by the seal of the Holy Spirit, ... and that the whole law of Christ is so firmly established in truth, that not one letter nor one point of it can be lacking or fail.]—Vaudois MS. of Trinity College Library, Dublin, C, V, 22,

EARLY VAUDOIS CHURCH.

the Trinity in the Godhead[1]—*the sinful state of man*[2]—*and free salvation by Jesus Christ*[3]—but above all, *faith working by love.*[4]

It may, perhaps, surprise many to be told that, before the Reformation, the Vaudois never disputed with the Romish Church the number of the sacraments which it received.[5] They, in fact, contented themselves with remarking that Jesus Christ instituted only two of them; and as the gospel, upon which they always founded, had not formally indicated that number, nor even made use of the word *sacrament*, it was very natural for them to acquiesce concerning this point in the decision of the church, as they afterwards did in that of the Reformers.[6]

under the title *Tresor e lume de fe*, fol. 176, *et seq.*, and in No. 208 (unpaged) of the Vaudois MSS. of Geneva.

[1] Lo premier article de la nostra fe es que nos creyen en un dio payre tot poissant, . . . local dio es un en trenita.—[The first article of our faith is, that we believe in one God, the Almighty Father, . . . which God is one in Trinity.]—Authorities as above. Dublin, fol. 180.—Geneva, *de li articles d'la fe*. See also the catechism, *Interrogations menors*, published by Perrin, &c.

[2] Nos sen conceopu en pecca e en miseria. Larma tray soczura de pecca. Pecca, soczura, enequita sovent, pensen, parlen, eobren fellonosament.—[We are conceived in sin and in misery. The soul carries along with it a defilement of sin. Sin, defilement, and iniquity attend us; we think, speak, and act wickedly.]—*La Barca*. MS. of Geneva, No. 207, and of Dublin, No. 21.

[3] This point of doctrine is the special subject of the fourth article of faith set forth in the Dublin MS. No 22, and Geneva MS. No. 208.

L' hereta celestial, el meseyme, Xrist, filh de dio, promes donar a li veray cootivador de la fe.—[Jesus Christ, himself the Son of God, promises to give the heavenly inheritance to those who truly continue in the faith.]—Geneva MS. 609.

Nostra salu . . . e premierament en la eslecion e donacion de gra delle sua gracia, fayent agradivols, . . . secondament en la participacion del merit de notre Segnor Salvador Yeshu Xrist.—[Our salvation is primarily in the election and free gift of his grace, making us agreeable to him. Secondly, in the participation of the merits of our Lord and Saviour Jesus Christ.]—MS. of Dublin, C, V, 25, first piece: *Ayczo es la causa del despartiment de la Gleysa Romana*.

[4] Non possibla cosa es ali vivent, complir li comandament de dio silh non han la fe: e non puon amar luy perfectament ni cun carita silh non gardan li seo comandament.—[It is impossible for any in this life to fulfil the commandments of God if they have not faith; and they cannot love him perfectly, nor with a proper love, if they keep not his commandments.]—Vaudois MSS. of Geneva, No. 208, fol. 2.

[5] The Vaudois MS. of Dublin, C, V, 22 (left-hand side of fol. 181), contains a tract *de li set sacrament*. This is partly found in the MS. 208 of Geneva, fol. 17-26, and in MS. 209, fol. 9, where marriage is called *lo cart sagrament* de la gleysa*, with this observation:—

Enayma el fo aiosta non despartivolment al cal el es desser garda sant e non socza.—[Although it has been added, not according to an exact classification, yet it ought to be kept holy and not polluted.]

[6] The passages of the Vaudois writings in the Romance language, which have been

* The diversity of orthography, which may be remarked in the same words of different quotations, is owing to the difference of copies, or of the era at which they were made; sometimes, but rarely, to the negligence of the copyists; and often to the uncertainty of the orthography itself, before the language was properly formed.

They admitted *Confession*;[1] but let us observe in what circumstances. Confession, say they, is of two kinds; the first must be made to God from the inmost heart; without which, no one can be saved.[2] The second kind is that which is made with audible voice to the priest, in order to receive counsel from him; and this confession is good, when that of the heart has preceded it. But, alas! many confide only in the latter, and fall into perdition.[3]

They admitted the sacrament of *Repentance*, but again let us note how. "Acts of repentance are excellent, and becoming on the part of every sinner; but they must proceed from abhorrence of sin, and sorrow for having committed it. Otherwise it is a false repentance, and a false repentance alienates a man from God as much as a true repentance brings him near to him."[4] Such a false repentance is that which reposes upon vain satisfactions; for what good thing

already published, and which have tended to give currency to a different opinion, either on this question or on the following, must have been modified in the copies which have served as the basis of these publications, for they do not correspond with the primitive text of the most ancient MSS. Many proofs of this might be adduced, but the plan of the present work forbids. It is sufficient for me to guarantee the correctness of my own quotations, which have all been taken from the original MSS.

[1] See Dublin MS. 22, fol. 243, *et seq.*; Geneva MS. 209, fol. 17,—and 207, concluding treatise *de la Penitencia*, fol. antepenult.; and concerning *absolution*, which they did not admit, see Dublin MS. 22, fol. 383.

[2] Al repentent se conven la confession, lacal es en dui modo. La promiera es interior, czo es de cor al Segnor dio. . . . E sencza aquella confession, alcun non se po salvar.—Geneva MS. 207, final treatise, article *Quartament*.

[3] La seconda confession es vocal, czo es al preyre, per pilhar conselh de luy, e aquesta confession es bona, cun aquella premiera . . . sere devant anna. Ma oylas! moti home despreczan aqucsta interior . . . e solament se confidan a la vocal, e aquella creon que lor sia abastant a salu . . . e cagic en despercion.—Subsequent part of the same paragraph. See also Geneva MS. 209, treatise *de la Penitencia*, with some modifications in the terms. The same treatise is to be found in the sixth shelf of MSS. at Dublin, art. 37.

[4] Such is the general import of the treatise on *Repentance*, Dublin MS. 22; Geneva MS. 207, at the end, and MS. 209, at the beginning.

En ayma lome sapropria a dio e al regne de li cel per la vera penitencia; enayma el se delogna de dio e del regne de li cel per la falsa penitencia.—[As much as man draws near to God and to the kingdom of heaven by true repentance, so much does he alienate himself from God and from the kingdom of heaven by a false repentance.]

La vera es habandonnar lipecca comes et plorar lor, e degitar totas las caysons de li pecca, e doler se sencza fin, e annar a dio de tot lo cor. . .—[True repentance is to forsake sins which we have committed, and to mourn over them, and to avoid all occasions of sin, lamenting [*the commission of sin*] without ceasing, and going to God with the whole heart.]

Donca lo repentent deo irar lo pecca . . . e aquilh que non han en odi li pecca de li autre, e non desvian lor segont lo lor poer . . . aitals non son veray penitent, &c. (the beginning and end of the treatise.)—[He who repents must therefore hate sin . . . and he who does not abhor it even in others, turning them from it to the utmost of his power . . . such a man knows nothing of true repentance.]

can you do that you were not bound in duty to have done? and if you do not those things which you ought, what shall you substitute for them? The whole world could not deliver us from our sins; but he alone has made satisfaction for them, who is both Creator and creature at once, namely Christ.[1]

Therefore, with good reason, they add that idolatry has no other cause than these false opinions by which Antichrist takes away grace, truth, authority, invocation, and intercession from God, in order to ascribe them to the ministry and to the works of his own hands, namely, the saints and purgatory.[2]

The Vaudois, however, do not cease to recommend *almsgiving*,[3] as a means of fighting against sin, by the giving up of those riches which might have served as its instrument, and by the help of the prayers of the poor thus solicited.[4] It is with the same object that they recommend *fasting*, by which a man is humbled;[5] but fasting without charity is like a lamp without oil, it smokes and does not

---

Encara al pentent conven la satisfacion, e aquesta es de greu condicion . . per laqual alcun punis la cosa non raczonivol laqual el fey; e aquesta satisfacion perman en tre cosas czo es en oracion, en dejunis e en almosinas, &c.—[There is still one thing of great importance pertaining to him who truly repents, to wit, satisfaction . . . . by which there are some who punish the unreasonable thing which they have done; and this satisfaction consists in three things, namely, prayer, fasting, and alms.]—Same treatise *de la Penitencia*.

[1] En tant sistent punicion o véniancza quant es aquel contra loqual l'a pecca. Donca la pena o loffencza es non mesurivol, e non mesurivol es dio contra loqual ha pecca. Donca oylas, non deoria peccar per alcuna cosa, ni encar per tot lo mont. Car tot le mont non poeria deslivrar del pecca. Donca lo es manifest que alcun de si non po satisfar per lo pecca; ma aquel sol satisfare, local es creator e creatura czo es Xrist, local a satisfait per li nostra pecca.—[The pardon or punishment ought in reason to be according to the greatness of him against whom we have sinned. Wherefore there is no more proportion betwixt the punishment and the offence, than there is betwixt God and the sinner. [The offence is infinite against an infinite God.] Wherefore, alas! a man ought not to commit sin for the sake of anything, not even of the whole world, for the whole world could not deliver us from sin. It is, therefore, manifest that no one, of himself, could offer satisfaction for sin; but that he alone could satisfy who is both creator and creature at once, to wit, Christ, who has satisfied for our sins.]—Extract from Geneva MS. 209, obtained through the obliging attention of M. Tron, minister, native of the Vaudois valleys. It is to be found, also, at the end of MS. 207, and in the Dublin MS. 22, fol. 358.

[2] Non es alcuna altra causa didolatria sinon falsa opinion de gratia, de verita, de authorita, d'envocation, d'entrepellacion [*intercession*], laqual el meseyme Antechrist departic de dio e en Li menestier e en las authoritas e en las obros de las soas mans, e a li sanct e al purgatori; e aquesta enequita de Antechrist es dreitament contra de la fe, e contra lo premier comandament de la ley.—Vaudois book of *Antichrist*, quoted by Perrin, p. 287, Leger, p. 81, and Monastier, p. 355.

[3] *De l'almosina*, Geneva MS. 209, p. 21, and in the *Vergier de consolacion* which concludes the volume. See also the *Liber Virtutum* of MS. 206, and this last-named treatise in the Dublin MS. 22.

[4] Geneva MS. 209, p. 40.   [5] Id. art. *Remedi contra li pecca*.

give light.¹ *Prayer* is, according to them, essentially implied in love;² and they add that patience, and constancy, and gentleness, and resignation, and charity, are the seal of the Christian.³ As for those who would devolve upon others the care of their salvation, seeking the prayers of priests and of monks, masses, indulgences, *neuvaines*, &c., they forget the word of God, which declares that every one shall bear his own burden.⁴ They recommend, indeed, that men should go to the priests, who have *the power of binding and of loosing;*⁵ but let us take notice how they understand this, "that is to say, who know how to give good advice for a man's deliverance from the bondage of sin."⁶ Not that they expect any

¹ Lo dejuni sencza lalmosina non es alcun ben; czo es sencza lalmosina de carita et es pardonar a li seo enemis e prager per lor; lo dejuni sencza l'almosina es enayma la lucerna sencza holi, laquel fma e non luczis.—[Fasting without almsgiving does no good: to wit, without the almsgiving of charity, which consists in pardoning our enemies, and praying for them. Fasting without almsgiving is like a lamp without oil, which smokes and does not give light.]—Geneva MS. 209, fol. 20.

² Aquel non laissa de aurar loqual non laissa damar; e aquel laissa de amar local laissa de aurar.—[He ceases not to pray who never ceases to love; and he ceases to love who ceases to pray.]—Vaudois MS. of Geneva, 209, fol. 8. This admirable sentiment is much more just than that of M. Courier, so often quoted, *He who works, prays,* and it is more evangelical! In this quotation may be seen an example of the variableness which then prevailed in orthography; *local* and *loqual; damar* and *de amar.*

³ Donca, non basta a lome de junar et orar et far autras cosas; car aquestas cosas son petitas; ma sufrir patientament czo que dio permet, play plus a dio que aquellas cosas que lome eilegis de si, cun czo sia que aquellas cosas aiudon.—[Wherefore it is not enough for a man to fast, to pray, and to do other [*such like*] things; for these things are small. But to suffer patiently what God permits, pleases him more than these things which are of the choice of man himself; however these things contribute to it.]—Geneva MS., end of the volume, and Dublin MSS., vol. vi. § 11.

⁴ La penitencia es vana lacal es derecezo feria e socza plus greoment. Car li geyment non profeitan alcuna cosa se li pecca son replica. Moti scampan lacrimas non deffalhivolment e non deffalhon de peccar. Cum lome retorne al pecca la cayson es aquesta: car el non es converti a dio de tot lo cor. Es decebivol aquesta penitencia permanent en comprament de messas preypals, en communion annuals e en hinficar capellas . . . &c.—[The repentance is vain, which [*admitting of relapse*] is again more seriously broken and defiled; for lamentations are good for nothing, if the man falls back into sin. Many cease not to shed tears, and cease not to sin. When a man falls again into sin, the reason is that he has not been converted to God with his whole heart. That repentance is deceitful which is limited to the purchase of presbyterial masses, to annual communions, and the decoration of chapels.]—Passages extracted from the first four paragraphs of the treatise *de la Penitencia,* Geneva MS. 207, at the end.

⁵ Aquel que se vol verament pentir quera lo prever local sapia ligar e desligar.—[He who would truly repent should go to the priest, who knows how to bind and to loose.]—*De la Penitencia,* art. iv. § 2.

⁶ Ligar e desligar, czo es ben conoisse lo pecca, e ben conselhar.—[To bind and to loose, signifies, to discern sins well and to give good counsel [*to the sinner*].—Geneva MS. 209, art. *de la Penitencia.*

absolution from them, for this they designate a delusive thing;[1] but because, they say, as a sick man seeks the best physician who can assist nature in him, and free him from his malady, even so the sinner ought to seek the best counsellor in order to get quit of sin;[2] and that feeling of guiltiness, the strength of which attests the sensibility of the soul in which it is experienced, presses so sore amongst these rustic and ancient Vaudois, that they never cease to bring forward the expression of it again and again in their different works. "We have turned aside from the path of truth. The light of righteousness shines not in us." "The sun of understanding is covered with clouds; iniquity holds us fast in its trammels."[3] "I am weak for that which is good, and strong for that which is evil."[4] "In the name of God, my brethren, renounce the world, that you may follow the Lord."[5] "The works of man are of little avail for salvation."[6] Such is their mode of speaking. They like-

[1] . . . Se cre satisfar par li seo pecca per czo que li es encharja del preire. . . . Aquesta penitencia decebivol perman en assolucion preipals. . . .—[. . . He supposes he has made satisfaction for [*the guilt of*] his sins, because he has intrusted the priest with them. . . . Such is the delusive repentance which priestly absolution engenders.]—Same treatise, *De la Penitencia*, No. 207, art. ii. and iii.

[2] Coma fay lo malate per recobrar la sanita corporal, cerca lo melhor mege . . . &c.—[As the sick man does in order to recover his bodily health, seeking the best physician . . . &c.]

Enayma spiritualment per lo bon conseil de li bon preire . . . &c.—[So spiritually, by the counsels of good priests* . . . &c.]

Car silh refudan desser ressemilhadors de li apostol, ilh faren a vos come iuda.— [For if they refuse to be like the apostles, they will serve you like Judas.]—Same treatise; but in MS. 209, for the last leaves of MS. 207 have been torn off, and are awanting.

[3] Nos haven erra de la via de verita, e lo lume de justicia non luczis a nos, e lo solelh dentendament non nasque a nos. Nos sen lacza en las vias denequita e sen anna en las vias greos, e haven mesconoysu la via del Segnor.—MS. 207, last treatise, § vi. The following is a literal translation of these last phrases:—"The sun of understanding has not risen [been born] for us; we are entered into the ways of iniquity, and have walked in evil ways, and have not known the ways of the Lord."

[4] Temeros soy a far ben e forment pereczos,
E ardi a far lo mal e mot evananczos.

—[I am timorous, and very slow to do good; but courageous and very forward to do evil.]—Vaudois Poems. *Confession of Sins.* Dublin MSS. C, V, 21.

[5] Prego vos carament per l'amor del Segnor,
Abandonna lo segle serve a dio cum temor.

—[I pray you affectionately, by the love of the Lord, to abandon the world, and to serve God without fear.]—*Lo Novel Comfort.* Geneva MS. 207, and Dublin, 21, first part.

[6] Cant lome ha sapiencia e non ha lo poer
Dio li o reconta perfait cant el ha bon voler;
Ma cant elha poiscencza e grant entendamcnt
Li profeita mot poc cant al seo salvament.

* It is not to be taken for granted that this word *priest* was exclusively applied to the Catholic priests; it was probably also a general designation which the Vaudois gave to their pastors; for, in respect to the consecration of these pastors, it is said that they were received into the office of the priesthood, *en l'offici del preverage.*—*Book of George Morel.* Dublin MSS. C. V. 18.

wise add that it is impossible for man to perform his duties without faith. "Yes, I know that thou canst do nothing by thyself; but call upon the Lord for help, and he will hear thee."[1]

Finally, let us take notice that the Vaudois acknowledged, like the Catholics, the distinction rejected by Protestants, betwixt *mortal sins and venial sins*;[2] but that they were very far from meaning by these terms to extenuate the heinousness of any sin, because they said of sin in general, "Sin annihilates man, and brings him down from the position which he ought to occupy."[3] These terms, moreover, which may be traced to a very high antiquity in the annals of the church, might be thought to derive countenance from that passage of St. John, "All unrighteousness is sin; and there is a sin not unto death."[4]

The Vaudois had also their own *houses of retirement from the world*.[5] In the number of the thirty-two propositions which were

—[When a man has understanding and has not power, God accounts him perfect, if so be that his will is right; but when a man has [*mere*] power and [*barren*] knowledge, this avails him very little for his salvation.]—*La Novel Sermon*, another Vaudois poem, contained in the same MSS., published entire by Hahn, and fragments of it by Raynouard and Monastier.

[1] Non possibla cosa es a li vivent complir li comandament silh non han la fe. (Geneva MS. 508, fol. 2.) Yo say que tu non poyres far ayczo de tu meseyme; ma apella dio, lu teo ajudador, e el esauczire tu, si tu seres fidel e istares curios [*desirous*] de la toa salu.—Geneva MS. 209, fol. 20.

[2] For this see the same MS. 209, fol. 20 and 21; MS. 208, *exposicio de li X comandament*, at the exposition of the fourth commandment; MS. 207, *sensec de la penitencia*, art. vi. § 2. This word *sensec*, which has sometimes been translated *sentiment* or *sensation*, signifies merely *followeth*. It is a form of expression frequently employed in passing from one subject to another; thus, after having treated of spiritual almsgiving (prayers, counsels), the author writes, *ara sensec della lmosina corporal*, "Here followeth of corporal almsgiving."

[3] Lo pecca non es alcuna cosa natural, ma es corrucion del ben, e defet de gracia, car lo pecca aniquilla lome e lo fay defalhir del bon esser.—[Sin is not anything natural [*having its existence in the proper nature of things*], but is the corruption of good, and want of grace; for sin annihilates man, and deprives him of all good existence [*well-being*].—*Qual cosa sia pecca*. Geneva MS. 209, fol. 21.

[4] 1 John v. 17.

[5] Alcun d'nos ministres d'levangeli, ni alcunas de las nostras fennas non se maridan.—Exhibition of the practices and doctrines of the Vaudois Church before the Reformation, presented by the Vaudois deputies to the Reformers.—*Book of George Morel*. MSS. of the Bible in Trinity College, Dublin, C, V, 18. (Dr. Todd, the librarian, has given, at considerable length, a monograph of this MS. in No. 113 of the British Magazine, p. 397, *et seq*.) Another passage may still be given from this MS. relative to the ordination of the Barbas,* and to the subject of this note:—Tuit aquilh liqual se recebon entre de nos en l'offici del ministier evangelic

* The Barbas, or Vaudois pastors, do not appear to have had a particular dress. An eye-witness describes them as clothed in a long white woollen robe (which probably means nothing more than an ample garment, with long skirts).—National Library of Paris, MSS. of Brienne, vol. 204.—*Informations of 25th October*, 1544; deposition of the third witness.—Others have seen some of them wearing a gray dress.—*Judicial Investigations concerning the Vaudois*; MSS. of Trin. Coll. Lib., Dublin, C. V. 19, vol. ix § 18; and in Allix, "*Some Remarks*," &c., p. 318.

ascribed to them, and which were affixed upon the gates of the cathedral of Embrun, in 1489, the following occurs, "They deny that a Christian should ever take an oath." I cannot say, however, that they have anywhere made so absolute a declaration on this subject; but it is certain that they considered it as a fruit of perfection, that truth should never need from the lips of man the guarantee of any kind of oath. The perfect man, said they, ought not to swear;[1] and these words imply, on the other hand, the lawfulness of oaths, from the very absence of perfection, for no one is perfect here below.

Their opposition to the Church of Rome was always founded upon the Bible;[2] the character of a Christian, according to them, was to be found in the Christian life, and the Christian life was a gift of the grace of God.

The Barbas went once a year to each of the scattered hamlets of their parishes,[3] in order to listen to each person apart in a *private confession*. But this confession had no other object than to obtain the salutary counsels of Christian experience, and not a delusive absolution.

venent la plus part del gardament de las bestias e del coltivament della terra, e de heta de 25 o alcuna vecz de 30 ancz, e al pos tot sencza letras. E prove li predit requerent entre de nos, trecz o quatre mecz dyvern, per trecz o quatre ancz, si illi son de manieras convenivols e agradivols . . . . Apres aquestas cosas, li predit requerent son amena en alcun luoc, alcal alcunas nostras fennas, lasquals son nostras, serons* en Jeshu Xrist vita en vergeneta; e en aquest luoc li predit demoron un an el alcuna vecz ducs; e poi en apres aquest temp consuma, son receopu cum lo sagrament de la eucharistia, e cum limposicion de las mans en loffici del preverage e della predication; e en apres aiczo li trameten predicar duy a duy.

These ideas, so precisely expressed, serve to corroborate what we have said before. Part of these details may be found in Schultetus, *Annales Evangelii Renovati*, and in Ruchat's *History of the Reformation in Switzerland*, t. iii.

[1] Neun perfect non deoria husar de jurament.—Chap. xvi. of the *Vergier de Consolacion*, Geneva MS. 209; and Dublin MS. C, IV, 27.

[2] In no polemical writing of the time will we find so large a number of quotations from the Bible as in those of the Vaudois. Many of the passages which they quote are at the present day differently understood, but nowhere was the authority of the Bible ever more respected.

[3] Plebeculam nostram semel singulis annis quia per diversos vicos habitant, adimus, ipsamque personam in confessione clandestine audimus.—Exhibition of the customs of the Vaudois Church, made by its deputies (George Morel and Peter Masson) to the Reformers.—Quoted by Schultetus, *Annales Evangelii Renovati*, p. 299. We may suppose that the *district examinations* prevailing at the present day in the Vaudois Church are a relic of this custom. Each pastor is bound to go annually to each of the principal hamlets or *quarters* of his parish, to conduct there a separate religious service, to receive communications, and to give the most confidential advices, according to circumstances.—A. M.

* To follow on, to *continue*; hence the word *series*. This, therefore, is not an error of the transcriber, as has been supposed, and a proposal made to read *servon* (*serve*); moreover, it is impossible to say, *servon en Jeshu Xrist*. The translation of the passage is, *spend their life in virginity in Jesus Christ*.

Such was, in its principal features, the state of the Vaudois Church of the middle ages. In a poem in the Romance language, entitled *La Nobla Leyczon*, and which is of the date of the end of the 11th century, or the commencement of the 12th, the Vaudois are said to have been already persecuted upon account of their customs and their doctrines. We may form a ready notion of that war of a corrupt world against a people, the severe purity of whose manners condemned at once its disorders and its superstitions. "If there be any one of whom it is said, that he will not slander, nor swear, nor lie, nor be guilty of dishonesty, or theft, nor give himself up to dissoluteness, nor revenge himself upon his enemies, they call him a *Vaudois*, and exclaim 'Death to him!'"[1] But these were, unquestionably, nothing more than the results in particular and isolated instances of that hostility which the spirit of evil always excites in the hearts of worldly persons and impenitent sinners, against the visible fruits of evangelical sanctification.

The first measures of a more general character, adopted by the secular authorities for the destruction of the Vaudois, do not appear to have been earlier than the year 1209. At that epoch Otho IV. was elected Emperor of the West, at Cologne, by a part of the empire, and crowned at Aix-la-Chapelle. This ceremony took place in 1198; but, in 1206, he was defeated by Philip of Swabia, his rival, and retired to England, to the court of King John, his uncle. He returned two years afterwards, having heard of the death of his rival. He was then recognized by the diet of

---

[1] I give the text of the passage according to the different versions:—

. . . . e nos o poen ver
Que si n'i a alcun bon que ame a teme Jeshu Xrist
Que non volha maudire, ni jurar, ni mentir
Ni avoutrar, ni aucir, ni penre de l'autruy,
Ni venjar se de li seo enemis
Ilh dion qu'es Vaudes e degne de punir.

—(Raynouard, *Selections from the Original Poetry of the Troubadours*, ii. 73-103, v. 367-372 of the poem.) This version agrees with that of the Geneva MS. 207; that of the Cambridge MS. published by Morland, pp. 99-120, presents the following text, with which I have contrasted, in italics, the different readings of the version published by Léger, pp. 26-30:—

. . . . e nos o poen voyr
Morland: Que sel ama alcun bon quel vollia amar Dio e temer Jeshu Xrist
Leger: *Que sel se troba alcun bon que vollia amar Dio e temer Jeshu Xrist*
Que non vollia maudire ne jurar [*ni jura*] ni mentir
Ni avoutrar, ni aucir [*aucire*] ni penre de l'autruy
Ni veniar se de li sio enemic
Illi diczon [*dison*] quel es vaudès [*Vaudès*] e degne de punir [*murir*].

The text of the *Nobla Leyczon*, published by M. Hahn (*Geschichte der Waldenser und verwandter Sekten*, Stutgard, 1848), agrees with that of Raynouard.

Frankfort; and in the following year he repaired to Rome, in order to be crowned emperor by Pope Innocent III., who had always favoured him in opposition to Philip. On this journey he passed through Piedmont; but Thomas, the then reigning Count of Savoy, had taken part against him in his disputes with Philip, who, in recompense for his support, had given him the towns of Quiers, Testona, and Modon. Otho IV., irritated against the old partizan of his rival, thought good to avenge himself of him by weakening his power within his own states, and for this purpose he gave to the Archbishop of Turin, who was a prince of the empire,[1] authority to destroy the Vaudois by force of arms. So that the long course of successive persecutions through which they were to pass, was not commenced by the Duke of Savoy, but by his enemies; and when, at a later period, the house of Savoy itself adopted the same methods of cruelty and depopulation, it was never of its own spontaneous movement, but from foreign influences, of which the most pressing were those of the court of Rome.

The branch of the Counts of Piedmont reigned for 176 years, and the last four of them bore the title of Princes of Achaia. Their residence was at Pignerol, and you will not find, says the Marquis of Beauregard, in his *Historical Memoirs*,[2] that these princes, who dwelt so close to the Vaudois, or the first Marquises of Saluces, ever persecuted them. It has even been supposed that some of the Counts of Lucerna,[3] immediate vassals of the empire, and principal lords of these valleys, at a very ancient period, were partakers of their religious opinions.

Thus was the primitive church preserved in the Alps to the very period of the Reformation. The Vaudois are the chain which unites the reformed churches with the first disciples of our Saviour. It is in vain that Popery, renegade from evangelical verities, has a thousand times sought to break this chain; it resists all her efforts. Empires have crumbled—dynasties have fallen—but this chain of scriptural testimony has not been broken, because its strength is not from men, but from God.

---

[1] The title of Prince of the Empire had been given in 1160 to the bishops of Turin, Maurienne, and Tarantaise, by Frederic I., with the object also of weakening the house of Savoy, which had abandoned his party to espouse the cause of the pope, Adrian IV., in the politics of the time. The papacy has brought ruin even on its supporters. [2] II. 5.

[3] Some writers have alleged that the arms of the Counts of Lucerna bore, like the seal of the Vaudois churches, a torch (*lucerna*), surrounded by seven stars. But this is an error; the escutcheon of that family bears *argent, three bands gules*. This coat of arms is, moreover, exhibited above the title of the *Memoire istoriche* of Rorengo, in virtue of his title of *Conti di Luzerna*.

CHAPTER II.

FIRST PERSECUTION.—YOLANDE AND CATTANÉE.[1]

(FROM A.D. 1300 TO A.D. 1500.)

Persecution and Conflicts about the year 1308—Persecution by Yolande, Duchess of Savoy, in 1476; and by her son, Charles I., Duke of Savoy, in 1485—Bull of Extermination against the Vaudois by Pope Innocent VIII. in 1487—Crusade against them—Albert Cattanée, the Pope's legate—Defeat of the invading force in the Italian valleys—Negotiations with the Duke of Savoy—Strange fancies then prevalent among Papists with regard to the Vaudois.

IN the beginning of the 14th century (somewhere about the year 1308), the inquisitors having entered the valley of Angrogna, where already synods of 500 delegates were sometimes held,[2] the Vaudois repelled them by force of arms.[3] It is even alleged that the Catholic prior of the place lost his life in this collision.[4] Few details of these events have been preserved, and they do not seem to have been productive of any very important consequences.

It was a foreigner, a female, the sister of Louis XI., who first signalized herself by exciting bloody persecutions against the Vaudois; from which glory and martyrdom equally resulted to them. Her name was Yolande, and she had become the wife of Amadeus IX., one of the mildest and most charitable of those dukes of Savoy whose names are an honour to their dynasty. She was left a widow in 1472, and named regent of his dominions. After this we find her called *Violante*, perhaps in consequence of an alteration of orthography occurring in the public documents of the time, or perhaps in allusion to her cruel and vindictive character.

On the 23d of January, 1476, without having previously found any fault with the Vaudois, without having expressed any displeasure against any of their proceedings, without alleging for her severities any reason but their religious belief, she commanded the Seigneurs of Pignerol and Cavour to bring them back, by whatever means, to the pale of the Romish Church. The Vaudois demanded that that church itself should be brought back to the gospel. The

---

[1] AUTHORITIES.—*Léger, Gilles, Perrin.*—"*Memoirs of Albert Cattanée*," contained in the *proofs* of the "*Hist. de Charles VIII.*," by *Godefroy.* Paris, 1634, fol. pp. 277-300.—"*De Vita Emmanuelis Philiberti*," fol. *Aug. Taur.* 1596.—"*Memoires pour servir a l'Hist. du Dauphiné*," fol. Paris, 1711. By *Valbonays.*—*Chorier,* &c.
[2] "Frequentes congregationes, per modum capituli . . . . in quibus aliquando quingenti Valdenses fuerunt congregati."—Brief of John XXII., 23d July, 1332.
[3] "Manu insurrexerunt armata."—Id.   [4] Loco cit.

duchess convoked her great vassals to consult with them as to the means of reducing to silence these hardy Protestants, if we may employ the term a century before the Reformation. But she had not time to give effect to her designs, for very soon after she was forcibly carried off, by order of the Duke of Burgundy, who was at war with Louis XI., and who feared that she would give some assistance to the French king.

The Vaudois, however, had refused to abjure their evangelical heresy, and Charles I., the second son of Yolande, having mounted the throne, gave orders that an investigation should be made concerning this resistance (A.D. 1485). The result of this investigation was laid before the Holy See in 1486, and exposed, for the first time, in an official manner, the wide difference which the lapse of ages had produced betwixt the Vaudois, always faithful to the primitive religion, and the Romish Church, which had gradually become more and more degenerate.

In the following year Innocent VIII. fulminated against them a bull of extermination, by which he enjoined all temporal powers to take arms for their destruction. He summoned all Catholics to a crusade against them, "absolving beforehand all who should take part in this crusade from all ecclesiastical penalties, general or special, setting them free from the obligation of vows which they might have made, legitimating their possession of goods which they might have wrongfully acquired, and concluding with a promise of the remission of all sins to every one who should slay a heretic. Moreover, he annulled all contracts subscribed in favour of the Vaudois, commanded their domestics to abandon them, forbade any one to give them any assistance, and authorized all and sundry to seize upon their goods."[1]

Forthwith some thousands of volunteers, persons ambitious of distinction, vagabonds, fanatics, men without lawful employment, needy adventurers, plunderers of every description, and pitiless robbers and assassins, assembled from all parts of Italy to execute the behests of the pretended successor of St. Peter. This horde of depredators and brigands, an army worthy of a pontiff whose own life was scandalous,[2] marched upon the valleys, in company with 18,000 regular troops, jointly furnished by the king of France and the sovereign of Piedmont.

[1] This bull may be seen in Léger, II. c. 1, pp. 8-20.
[2] Innocent VIII. was the father of eight children; whence the distich of that period:—

"*Octo nocens genuit totidemque puellas;
Hunc merito poterit dicere Roma patrem.*"

And of what extraordinary crimes, then, could this pontiff have regarded the unhappy Vaudois as guilty? He lays no crime to their charge; he acknowledges, on the contrary, in his bull of extermination, that their principal means of seduction was their great appearance of sanctity. To massacre Christians because their good conduct attracted the esteem and sympathy of their neighbours! it could only have been thought of by that haughty and merciless power which they themselves already ventured to call Antichrist. But how could a people so few and so feeble resist such formidable forces as now came to assail them? At the very commencement of their history, the Vaudois seem on the point of being crushed and annihilated for ever. And so they would have been, if the hand of God had not undertaken their defence. It was He whose breath filled the ranks of their enemies with infatuation, and the hearts of his children with courage.

The papal legate commissioned to watch over the execution of these sanguinary orders, was an archdeacon of Cremona, named Albert Cattanée, generally called De Capitaneis. He fixed his head-quarters at Pignerol, in the convent of Saint Lawrence, and sent preaching monks to attempt the conversion of the Vaudois before attacking them with arms. These missionaries were utterly unsuccessful. He then proceeded in person to the valleys. The inhabitants sent two deputies[1] to him, who addressed him in these terms: "Do not condemn us unheard, for we are Christians and loyal subjects; and our Barbas are ready to prove, either in public or in private, that our doctrines are agreeable to the word of God, for which reason they ought rather to be held worthy of praise than of blame. It is true that we have not thought fit to follow the transgressors of the evangelical law, who have long ago departed from the tradition of the apostles; we have not thought fit to conform ourselves to their corrupt precepts, nor to recognize any other authority than that of the Bible; but we find our happiness in a life of simplicity and purity, by which alone the Christian faith strikes its roots deep, and spreads out its branches. We contemn the love of wealth and the thirst of power with which we see our persecutors consumed; and our hope in God is stronger than our desire to please men. Take heed that you draw not his wrath upon yourselves by persecuting us, and be assured that, if God wills it. all the forces which you have assembled against us will avail you nothing." This holy confidence did not deceive them. God

---

[1] The names of these deputies were John Campo and John Desiderio. The details following are from the *Memoirs of Albert Cattanée*, preserved amongst the *proofs* of the *History of Charles VIII*.

willed it, and that army of invaders vanished from around the Vaudois mountains like the rain that has fallen on the sands of the desert.

The inhabitants concentrated themselves on the most inaccessible points; the enemy, on the contrary, were spread out over the plain, and whether from incapacity for strategy, or from his pride moving him to make a grand display of his military force, Cattanée thought proper to commence an attack upon all points at once; so that from the village of Biolets, situated in the marquisate of Saluces, to that of Sezanne, which belonged to Dauphiny, his lines, without any depth, occupied all the country. He proposed to destroy by a single effort the hydra of heresy. By a single effort his own forces were shattered; for his lines, weakened by the way in which they were extended, were everywhere broken, his battalions driven back in precipitate flight, and assailed in rear by those whom they had come to assail.

The weapons employed in this combat were only pikes, swords, and bows. The Vaudois had hastily made for themselves great bucklers, and even cuirasses, of the skins of beasts, covered again with the thick bark of chestnut-trees, in which the arrows of the enemy stuck without doing them any harm. These arrows, coming with reduced force by reason of the distance, and because they were shot from a lower towards a higher ground, penetrated into the bark without having power to pass through it; the Vaudois, on the contrary, skilful, energetic, and, above all, full of confidence in God, and better posted for defence, shot down from above with an advantage which gave them the victory.

There was, however, one post where, notwithstanding the vigour of their defences, the enemy seemed on the point of forcing a passage. It was the central point of this great line of operations on the heights of St. John, where they abut upon the mountains of Angrogna, at a place called Rochemanant. The crusaders had invaded this quarter from beneath, mounting step by step, and closing their ranks around that natural bulwark behind which the Vaudois had sheltered their families. Seeing their defenders yield, these families threw themselves upon their knees with many tears; women, and children, and old men united together in fervently crying, "*O Dio aijutaci!* O Lord, help us! O my God, save us!" This cry of prayer was the only cry which broke from their hearts in their distress, and arose to heaven. But their enemies laughed at it, and seeing this company upon their knees, hastened their advance. "My fellows are coming—they are coming to give you your answer," exclaimed one of their chiefs, surnamed *the Black of*

Mondovi, because of his swarthy complexion; and immediately, joining bravado to insult, he raised the visor of his helmet, to show that he was not afraid to encounter the poor people whom he insulted. But at that moment a steel-pointed arrow, let fly by a young man of Angrogna, named Peter Revel, struck this new Goliath with such violence, that it penetrated into his skull, between his eyes, and laid him dead. His troop, struck with terror, fell back in disorder; a panic seized them; the Vaudois took advantage of the moment, and impetuously rushed forward, hurling their adversaries before them, and, eagerly continuing the pursuit, swept them into the very plain, where they left them vanquished and dispersed. Then, re-ascending to their families so miraculously delivered, they likewise flung themselves upon their knees, and all together gave thanks to the God of armies for the victory which they had just gained.

"O Dieu de mon salut, Dieu de ma delivrance!"

[O God of my salvation, God of my deliverance] might they have sung, if that beautiful hymn had then been composed. But they had all its sentiments in their hearts. It is trust in God which is the real strength of man; the humble Israel of the Alps was then invincible, like the people of Moses under the command of Joshua.

A new attempt was made next day to seize on that formidable post, where the strength of victory from on high seemed seated with these heroic mountaineers. The enemy took a different route; ascending by the bottom of the valley of Angrogna, in order to penetrate to the Pra du Tour, whence, mounting by La Vachera, they would have been masters of the whole region. But a dense and dangerous mist, such as sometimes unexpectedly appears in the Alps, settled down upon them just at the very moment when they were entangled in the paths most full of difficulty and of peril. Ignorant of the locality, marching apprehensively, uncertain of the route which they ought to take, and not able to advance except singly, over rocks, upon the brink of precipices, they gave way before the first assault of the Vaudois, and not being able to range themselves in order of battle, they were easily defeated. The first who were repulsed fell back precipitately, overthrowing those who were next to them; the confusion spread further and further; disorder reigned everywhere; the retreat became a flight, the flight a catastrophe, for those who attempted to retrace their course slid over the humid rocks, of which the edge was concealed by the mists. Others, again, thinking to find in these sinuosities a way of escape, precipitated themselves into the chasms in which the former had already perished. Very few succeeded in making their escape; the greater part losing their way in the depths of the ravines, or on the crests of the rocks.

This decisive defeat, which is to be ascribed to the will of God rather than to the arms of the Vaudois, accomplished the deliverance of that valley, in which the troops of Cattanée never appeared again. The detachment which was destroyed in so complete and unexpected a manner, was the last which showed itself upon the banks of the Angrogna before the period of the Reformation. The captain who commanded it was called Saguet de Planghère, and the chasm into which he fell is called to this day, after the lapse of four centuries, the *Toumpi de Saguet*—Saguet's hole.

On the mountain of Roderi, in the valley of Pragela, the Vaudois, says Cattanée, favoured by the nature of the grounds, put the crusaders to flight, by rolling down upon them avalanches of rock; after which they descended, attacked them in close combat, and prolonged the battle until evening. A few, however, were made prisoners, and conducted to Mentoules, to be subjected to the ceremonies of a vain abjuration.

The legate charged with the commission of extermination next proceeded to Dauphiny, to the valley called the Val Louise, of which we shall presently speak; but, before concluding this chapter, it remains to be told that one battalion of the enemy, seven hundred strong, having come from that valley to the valley of St. Martin, by the Col d'Abriès, was observed above Pral, directing its course towards the village of Pommiers. Thither the Vaudois repaired to wait for it. The soldiers, inflamed with pride by the massacre which they had just perpetrated in Dauphiny, entered the hamlet in disorder, dreaming only of pillage, and supposing themselves already victors. But, being suddenly attacked on all sides, they were unable to make any defence, and were all slain or put to flight. Those who escaped in the first instance, perished, ere long, amongst these unknown mountains, everywhere occupied by courageous defenders. The bearer of the colours concealed himself alone in a ravine, where he remained two days; after which, cold and hunger compelled him to come out, and to seek an asylum from the Vaudois, who supplied him with all that he required, showing that generous forgetfulness of offences, with which Christ inspires his faithful servants. Having recovered strength, he rejoined the army to which he belonged, and was able to inform them of the total defeat of his companions. Thus was this army dissipated, which, to a people so few in number, was really formidable. But it was to them that it was said, "Fear not, little flock, for it is your Father's good pleasure to give you the kingdom,"[1] and, as they themselves said, "If God be for us, who can be against us?"

After these expeditions, productive neither of advantage nor of glory, the Duke of Savoy withdrew his troops — dismissed the legate, upon the pretext that his mission was terminated — and sent a bishop amongst the Vaudois in order to bring them to take the first steps with the view of obtaining a peace, of which the assurance was held out to them. The interview of this envoy with the evangelical Christians of the Alps, took place at the hamlet of Prasuyt, situated on the confines of the communes of Angrogna and St. John. It was resolved that the Vaudois should send a representative of each of their churches to their prince, who was to come to Pignerol to receive them. It was during the conferences there held, that this prince asked to see some of their children, that he might satisfy himself, by personal observation, whether they were really born with black throats, rough teeth, and goats' feet, as the Catholics pretended. "Is it possible," said he, when he saw a number of them with his own eyes, "that these are the children of heretics? What charming creatures they are! they are by far the prettiest children I ever saw." Thus was overthrown a ridiculous prejudice, but which could not fail to be powerful in an age so little enlightened as to admit of its finding its way even to the mind of a prince.

Superstition, obscuring the moral and religious perceptions, casts its shadows equally over all the regions of human intelligence; as, on the other hand, also, the light of the gospel enlightening the soul which is opened to receive it, elevates, augments, and purifies all the powers of the mind. Of this, the Vaudois themselves are a proof, for they had taken their place, three centuries before these events, at the head of modern literature, having been the first to write in the vulgar tongue. That which they then used was the Romance language, for all the early remains of which we are indebted to the Vaudois. It was from this language that the French and Italian were formed. The religious poems of the Vaudois still continue to be the most perfect compositions belonging to that period; and they are also those in which the rays of the gospel shine with the greatest brightness.

Thus—whilst the colossal shadow of the Roman empire, when its sun was sinking, and the no less dreadful shadow of the pontificate, whose ambition succeeded to that of the empire, still covered Italy— the summits of the Alps were already brightened with a new

---
[1] Luke xii. 32.

dawn, which the Reformation was afterwards to extend over the whole world. It is not because the Vaudois were the precursors of the Reformation that we connect them with the primitive church, but because they were primitive Christians, and pioneered the way for the Reformation. Their past history illustrates what the gospel teaches all to expect; but none will have sorer trials to endure than those of the martyr people, whose glory, like that of Christ, is derived from sufferings, wrongs, and abasement.

CHAPTER III.

HISTORY OF THE VAUDOIS OF THE VAL LOUISE, FROM THEIR ORIGIN TO THEIR EXTINCTION.[1]

(A.D. 1300 TO A.D. 1500.)

Some account of the Val Louise—Early persecutions there—The Inquisitor Borelli—Martyrdoms at Embrun in the end of the 14th century, and desolation of the Vaudois valleys in France—Cattanée—Massacre of the whole population of the Val Louise in 1488.

THOSE primitive Christians, who have received the name of Vaudois, did not inhabit some of the valleys of Piedmont only, but also of France. Of what consequence were the boundaries of the two states to them? Their only desire was to live in tranquillity and in proximity to each other. We find them, from time immemorial, in the profound retreats of the Briançonnais as well as amongst the Alps of Italy.

The valleys which they appear to have most anciently inhabited

---

[1] AUTHORITIES.—*Gilles, Perrin.*—"*Lettres sur la Vallouise,*" by *Father Roussignol.* 8vo, Turin, 1804. — "*Mémoires de Cattanée,*" in Godefroy, "*Hist. de Charles VIII.*"—"*Recueil des Actes, pièces et procédures concernant l'emphitéose perpétuelle des dîmes du Briançonnais,*" &c., 24mo, 1754.—" *Les Transactions d'Imbert, dauphin du Viennois, Prince du Briançonnais, et Marquis de Sezane,*" &c., fol. 1645.—*Chorier*, "*Hist. Gén. du Dauphiné,*" fol.—*Thuanus*, "*Histor. sui Temporis,*" lib. xxvii. — "*Mémoires pour servir a l'Hist. du Dauph.,*" (Paris, 1711), fol. (*Valbonays.*)—MS. "*Hist. Gén. des Alpes . . . et partic. d'Embrun leur Métropolitaine,*" fol. translated by *Juvenis.* Gap; Library of the Little Seminary. (The original is at Paris, and a copy at Lyons).—"*Inventaire des Archives de la Cour des Comptes, à Grenoble,*" 34 vols. fol. (Reg. du Briançonnais et de l'Embrunois.)—*Aymari Rivallii*, "*De Allobrogibus,*" 4to, National Library, Paris, No. 6014. — "*De Episcopis Ebredunensibus.*" Library of Lyons, carton 119. "*Collectanea Hist.*," fol. 900.—See also the MS. 735 in the same library, as well as "*Gallia Christiana,*" t. iii. pp. 1052-1100, and proofs, 177.—"*Pièces concernant l'Archevêché d'Embrun.*" Paris Library, vol. 517, 518 of the "*Fonds Fontanieu*" and "*Fonds Gaignières,*" portfolios A, 134, 154.—"*Mémoires sur l'Egl. Métrop. d'Embrun.*" Library of Grenoble, No. 439, MS. in 4to.—"*Mémoires sur le Dauphiné.*" Library of Valence, MSS. Nos. 162 and 2125, fol.

are, on the side of France, those of Freyssinières, Val Louise, and Barcelonnette; on the side of Piedmont, those of the Po, of Lucerna, and of Angrogna, as also those of Pragela and St. Martin.

Val Louise is a deep and bleak ravine, which descends from Mount Pelvoux to the basin of the Durance. It was formerly called *Val Gyron*,[1] from the name of the Gyr, a torrent which flows in it. At a later period it was named *Val Pute*, in Latin *Vallis Putœa*, because of the great number of hills or *puyts* which it contains, as the names of its villages attest: Puy St. Vincent, Puy St. Eusebe and Puy St. Martin—*puya*, in the patois of the country, still signifying an eminence. As to the name Val Louise, it is generally said to have been derived from Louis XII., the father of his people, in commemoration of benefits which he had thought its inhabitants worthy to receive.[2]

They began to be persecuted between 1238 and 1243;[3] and again, a century after, in 1335, we find amongst the current accounts of the Bailiff of Embrun this singular article, *Item, for persecuting the Vaudois, eight sols and thirty deniers of gold* ;[4] as if the persecution of these Christians of the Alps had then become a regular part of the public service, a constant duty and always attended to. Alas! it was but the expression of that continual and increasing hatred with which Popery, based upon tyranny, has always regarded the gospel, the source of all kinds of liberty.

One of the Vaudois brethren of the valley of Lucerna[5] had purchased from the dauphin, John II., more than five hundred years ago, a good house in the Val Louise, which he had presented to the brethren of that neighbourhood, in order that they might be able to hold their religious meetings in a more becoming manner; but the Archbishop of Embrun caused it to be destroyed in 1348, excommunicating by anticipation any one who should attempt to rebuild it; and twelve unfortunate Vaudois, who were seized upon that occasion, were subjected to all the tortures which superstition and cruelty could inflict. Conducted to Embrun, in front of the cathedral, in the midst of a great concourse of people, surrounded by fanatical monks, and clothed in yellow robes, upon which were painted red flames, symbolical of those of hell, to which they were deemed devoted; they had an anathema pronounced against them,

---

[1] It is thus designated, *Vallis Gyrontana*, in a bull of Urban II., of date A.D. 1096.

[2] This name may, however, be found in use under Louis XI., as appears by his letters, dated from Arras, 18th May, 1478.

[3] Chorier, lib. xii. c. 5.   [4] *Raynaldi Annales*, n. 69.

[5] His name was Chabert. See *Inventories of the Records of the Court of Accounts at Grenoble*, the volume concerning the Briançonnais.

their heads were shaved, their feet made bare, and ropes passed round their necks; after which, at the sound of the bells which tolled their funeral knell, the Catholic clergy raised a chant of execration and of death. The poor captives were dragged, one after another, to a pile, surrounded with executioners. O saintly souls! not captives but free indeed, filled by the Spirit of the Lord with a courage so strong and so meek, those pictured flames with which your tunics were covered, were the symbol only of those flames in which you were to be consumed! From the midst of death you passed not into the torments prepared for the slaves of the wicked one, but into the blissful serenity of that heaven which is promised to the faithful servants of the Lord, on the wings of your faith and of the prayers of your friends!

The fire was applied to the pile; and the martyrs, who had lived like the primitive Christians, were found able also to die like them. The executioners quickly strangled them; their bodies returned to the dust, of which they were made, and their souls ascended to God who gave them.

When a church is persecuted, we have a sure sign that it is a living church; that its progress in sanctification grates upon the wicked, disquieting and irritating them, and arming against it their selfish passions. The inquisitors even caused the bodies to be disinterred from their graves, of those who were named to them as having died without receiving the aids of the church, because they thought the Redeemer sufficient for them; and these exhumed bodies, after their memory had been cursed, were cast into the flames. Their ashes were dispersed to the four winds; and as fanaticism is always united, in the Church of Rome, with the most sordid interests and passions, all the property which they had left to their heirs was confiscated, insomuch that even the alienations which had taken place since their decease, to the prejudice of the archiepiscopal exchequer, were declared null. It may be imagined what trouble, what disorder, what desolation such animosities must have produced in families: but their most valued possessions were not those which were thus taken from them; and if the love of money leads to crime, the love of the treasures of heaven leads to holiness. All that could be done, however, to daunt simple and courageous hearts was tried upon this occasion. To these sacrilegious ceremonies of violating graves, breaking open coffins and publicly burning their contents, all the people had been convoked, in name of that fearful church which thus pursued its victims even in death; and still more powerfully to strike men's minds by this apparatus of terror, all persons present were adjured with imprecations to regard with abhorrence the doctrines on account of which these corpses had been deprived of the rest of the tomb; but they remained steadfast in their faith even when they beheld the bones of their fathers scattered. This steadfastness was afterwards to be put to sorer trials.

A young inquisitor, named Francis Borelli, obtained from Pope Gregory XI. urgent letters addressed to the King of France, to the Count of Savoy, and to the governor of Dauphiny, calling upon them to unite their forces for the purpose of extirpating this *inveterate heresy* from the Alps. But it was stronger even than kings, for it was the word of God, the gospel of the earliest times, the counsel of eternity. The inquisitor as to religion undertook the charge of the carnal weapons which were intrusted to him; and the persecutions directed by Borelli did not leave the most secluded village out of their net. Like the fabulous robe of the centaur, which consumed the body upon which it was flung, it laid hold of entire families, of the populations of whole districts, of those who were not perfectly submissive everywhere, and very soon the prisons of these vast provinces were not sufficiently spacious to contain the multitude of prisoners. New dungeons were constructed for them, but with such haste that they wanted everything but what was necessary to cause suffering to the captives.

The valley of the Durance, with its side valleys of Le Queyras, Freyssinières, and Val Louise, was more shockingly decimated than any other district. It might have been thought that the plague had passed over it: but it was only the inquisitors!

Borelli commenced by causing all the inhabitants of these valleys to be summoned before him. They did not appear, and he condemned them for not appearing. Thenceforth, always liable to be surprised by his assassin bands, they suffered doubly from their own dangers and from the distress of their families. One was seized on the road, another in the field, another in his house. No one knew, when he embraced his father at worship in the morning, if he would see him again at evening prayer; and the father who sent away his sons to the harvest field could have no confidence that they would eat of that which they went to reap.

We may imagine what painful anxieties must then have succeeded, under the domestic roof, to the peace of former times! For fifteen whole years this work of depopulation, misery, and bloodshed, was carried on in these mountains in name of the Catholic religion. The deadly breath which laid so many low, which ruined so many families, and made so many hearts desolate, was breathed from the Vatican—that dreadful mount, which resembles

Drawn by S. Bough, from a sketch by Dr. Muston.   Engraved by J. H. Kernot

CONFLUENCE OF THE GUIL AND THE DURANCE.
THE TOWNS OF MOUNT DAUPHIN AND GUILESTRE AND THE MOUNTAINS OF DAUPHINY.

BLACKIE & SON, GLASGOW. EDINBURGH & LONDON.

Olympus only in its false gods, Sinai only in its thunders, and Calvary in bloodshed.

At last, on the 22d of May, 1393, all the churches of Embrun were decked out as for a great solemnity; the Church of Rome had a festival, for blood was to flow. The pagan images, which load her altars with their gilded insensibility, remind us of those idols at whose feet human victims were wont to be immolated. All the clergy, covered with their theatrical ornaments, were congregated in the choir. Double ranks of soldiers kept the people within the nave and surrounded a troop of prisoners. And who were they? Soldiers of Christ who came to contend for the faith. What was their crime? That faith itself. How many are there? Listen! their names are just to be read, and their sentence pronounced. What is that sentence? The same for all; condemned to be burned alive. The list is read, and eighty persons from the valleys of Freyssinières and Argentière are already devoted to the pile. But no inhabitant of the Val Louise has yet been mentioned— that quiet retreat, opening amongst the rocks like a dove's nest— will it be spared? No. Popery does not forget it; her watchword is Death: she can admit of no alternative but to be burned alive upon the earth for resisting her, or to serve her and go to hell. The Vaudois had thought it better to resist, and a new catalogue of one hundred and fifty names, all belonging to the Val Louise is read over in that church, now no longer the house of God, but rather a den of infamy, a cave of hangmen: and after each name there sound, like a funeral knell, those fatal words which crown them all—" condemned to be burned alive!" It was the half of the population of that unhappy valley; and in these lists— which appear to us so execrable, but to the Church of Rome so natural—might sometimes be found, one after another, the names of all the members of the same family. In this horrible solemnity, no fewer than two hundred and thirty victims were devoted at once to the stake, in the name of the God of the gospel. And for what reason? For having been faithful to the gospel.

But the secret of these numerous condemnations is still more shameful than even their cruelty; the property of the condemned was confiscated for behoof of the bishop and the inquisitors. The spoils of these poor people went to provide for the junketings of the clergy.

Beyond all question, unity of faith must at that time have made great progress in that afflicted country; but it was the solitude of the desert that long prevailed in these depopulated mountains, which the inquisitors professed to have reduced to the peace of the church; they should have said to the silence of the tomb. But everything comes to an end upon earth—even fanaticism; as the wolves abandon a charnel-house which they have emptied of its contents, so the inquisition retired from these impoverished valleys.

France was then groaning under the pressure of her wars with the English, Dauphiny being one of the last provinces which remained faithful to the feeble king, Charles VII. A young girl, Joan of Arc, soon reopened to her the gates of Rheims and the path of victory. During this time the Vaudois churches slowly recovered a little. Like the flowers of their own rocks, made hardy by the storms, their energy increased in the midst of dangers; and as the winds bear the fragrance of flowers to a distance, so the gale of persecution propagated their evangelical faith. Thus the influence of these churches increased by reason of their very sufferings. The violent and ferocious animosity of the Popish paganism equally increased. Such was the state of things when the close of the 15th century approached, that epoch at which, as we have seen in the preceding chapter, Innocent VIII. opened against the Vaudois a crusade of extermination.

It was in the month of June, 1488, that the papal legate, Albert Cattanée, having attempted in vain to subjugate the valleys of Piedmont, passed into France by Mount Genèvre, where he hanged eighteen of the poor people whom he had made prisoners. He descended to Briançon, a town which had been described to him as being then particularly infested with heresy; thence he marched upon Freyssinières, whose inhabitants, few in number and ill-provided with arms, retired to the rock which rises above the church, but the troops surrounded it and made them prisoners.

Success inspiring these fanatical soldiers with courage, or rather with ferocity, they invaded, with great shouts, the deep ravine of Val Louise. The Vaudois, terrified and perceiving that they could make no resistance to forces twenty times their number, abandoned their poor dwellings, set the old people and the children as hastily as possible upon their rustic beasts, drove their flocks before them, and carrying with them what they could of provisions and domestic utensils, bade a last adieu to the homes in which they were born, and retired, praying to God and singing hymns, to the steep slopes of Mount Pelvoux. This giant of the Alps, which has been called the Visol of the Briançonnais, rises to the height of more than 6000 feet above their valley. At about a third part of this elevation there opens in the mountain an immense cavern, called *Aigue Fraide*, or *Ailfrède*, because of copious springs of water, fed by the snows, which continually flow from it. A kind of platform, to which there is no possibility of mounting but by fearful precipices, extends to the opening of the cavern, whose majestic vault very soon contracts into a narrow passage, and expands again into an immense irregular hall. Such was the asylum which the Vaudois had chosen. In the farthest part of the grotto they placed their women, children, and old men; the flocks were disposed of in the lateral apartments of the rock; the strong men placed themselves at the entrance, after they had built up the approach to it, filled the path with rocks, and committed themselves to the care of God. Cattanée says that they had carried with them victuals enough to maintain themselves and their families for more than two years. All their precautions were taken, their intrenchments could not be forced; what had they to fear?

Their danger was in the very confidence which these human precautions had inspired. Reposing securely in the means of defence which they had provided for themselves, they forgot too much that it is faith alone which will remove mountains and deliver from the greatest perils.

Cattanée had with him a bold and experienced commander, named La Palud. This captain, seeing that it was impossible to force the entrance of the grotto on the side by which the Vaudois had approached it, because of the intrenchments by which they had sheltered themselves, redescended into the valley, gathered together all the ropes which could be procured, and once more climbed the Pelvoux, promising to his soldiers a complete victory. Wheeling round the rocks, they clambered up the steep slope, and fixing cords above the opening of the cavern, slid down in full equipment right in front of the Vaudois. If the latter had put more confidence in the protection of God than in that of their intrenchments, they would not have been seized with fear when they saw these prove insufficient. Nothing could have been more easy or natural than to cut the ropes by which they saw their enemies descend, or to kill them in succession as they arrived within reach of their weapons, or to hurl them into the abyss which the platform overhung, before they had time to act upon the offensive. But a panic seized the unfortunate Vaudois, and in their distraction they precipitated themselves amongst the rocks. La Palud made a frightful slaughter of those who attempted any resistance; and not daring to enter into in the depths of the cave from which he saw these terror-stricken people issue, he heaped up at the entrance all the wood which he could find; the crusaders set it on fire, and all who attempted to come out were consumed by the flames or died by the edge of the sword. When the fire was extinguished there were found, says Chorier, under the vaults of that cavern, 400 little children smothered in their cradles, or in the arms of their mothers. There perished upon this occasion, he adds, more than 3000 Vaudois. It was the whole population of Val Louise. Cattanée distributed the property of these unfortunates amongst the vagabonds who accompanied him; and never since that time has the Vaudois Church arisen again from her ashes in these blood-stained valleys.

Thus the very men whom prayer made victorious in the most critical moments, were utterly destroyed in circumstances the most favourable for defence, in consequence of putting too much confidence in themselves. And how many may we every day see fall in consequence of distrusting themselves too little, which is, in fact, not trusting in God as they ought!

This terrible example shown to the other Vaudois churches, plunged them into grief, but led them also to prayer; and thereby their spiritual strength was renewed, so that, if some still died beneath the palms of martyrdom, the mother church made a successful resistance, holding up the standard of the cross.

CHAPTER IV.

HISTORY OF THE VAUDOIS OF BARCELONNETTE, LE QUEYRAS, AND FREYSSINIÈRES.[1]

(A.D. 1300 TO A.D. 1650.)

Some account of the Valley of Barcelonnette—Persecution in 1560—Return of the fugitive population—Persecution in 1623—The Vaudois finally expelled—The Valley of Freyssinières—Early persecutions—The Inquisitor Ployeri—Martyrdoms in the end of the 15th century—Relaxation of persecution by Louis XII.—Brief of Pope Alexander VI.—Struggles of the 16th century—The Protestants seize Embrun—Lesdiguières—The Valley of Queyras in the end of the 16th century—Struggles and Successes of the Protestants—The Revocation of the Edict of Nantes—Present Protestantism of the French valleys—Neff.

BEING in Dauphiny, we may as well pursue the story of the vicissitudes which the ancient Vaudois experienced all around the present Vaudois valleys, before resuming the series of events which have befallen them in the latter down to our own days.

[1] AUTHORITIES.—The same as in the preceding chapter, and, in addition, "*Hist. Géogr. Ecclés. et Civile du Diocèse d'Embrun, par M***.*" 1783, 2 vols. 8vo. (The author of this work was Father Albert. It was to it that a reply was made in the "*Cinq Lettres par un Vaudois des Gaules Cisalpines.*" The author of the latter work was Paul Appia. It is also worthy of being consulted.)—*Ladoncette,* "*Statistique des Hautes-Alpes,* 8vo.—*Félix Neff, Memoirs, Biographies.*—Also, various papers in the archives of Gap, Embrun, Briançon, Pignerol, and Turin, too numerous to be particularly mentioned.

The Vaudois were, in process of time, rooted out, not only of the Val Louise, but also of Barcelonnette, Saluces, Provence, and Calabria, where they were anciently established. They have likewise more recently been exterminated in the valley of Pragela.

The valley of Barcelonnette is a deep ravine, shut in upon all sides by almost inaccessible mountains. It belonged in former times to Piedmont, but it was in the possession of France from 1538 to 1559, after which it reverted to Piedmont till 1713, when it was finally ceded to France in exchange for the two little valleys of Sexare and Bardonèche, situated towards Briançon.

This vale of Barcelonnette, with the little lateral valleys which open into it, anciently bore the name of Terres-Neuves (the *New Lands*), probably because they had been recently discovered. It is not known at what date the Vaudois began to occupy them. Farel preached there in 1519. The place of worship was at Les Josiers. The inhabitants, much interested and delighted to hear the voice of the reformer, gloried that the doctrines of their fathers, in all their evangelical completeness, were thus publicly proclaimed. But this publicity attracted to those who professed them the dreaded attention of the Church of Rome. The ferocious inquisitors ascended even to that peaceful retreat of poverty and prayer. This took place in 1560, the same year in which the valleys of Méana, of Suza, and of Pragela, were laid waste.

"The persecution," says Gilles, "raged so fiercely then against the faithful of these countries, that they were all made prisoners or compelled to flee, so that they were for a long time wanderers amongst these wild mountains, and in great want of food and shelter. Those who were seized, and who refused to abjure, were sent to the galleys. As for apostates, their condition was not much better, for besides the remorse of conscience which continually tormented them, they were distrusted and despised, so that some of them also returned to the right way." These last, who, having become Catholics, returned again to the gospel, received the name of *Relapsed*. The severest penalties were denounced against them, but the Catholics themselves had little esteem for men who were converted with the knife at their throat. How could they even respect doctrines for whose advancement the use of such means was found necessary?

However, a few years after (in 1566), a rigorous edict enjoined all the Vaudois of Barcelonnette to embrace Catholicism, or to leave the dominions of Savoy within the space of one month, under pain of death and confiscation of goods. The greater part of them resolved to retire into the valley of Freyssinières, which belonged to

France; but it was then the time of Christmas, the most inclement season of the year; the women and children became faint by the way; the snow which covered the mountains augmented the fatigue and dangers of the route; night had come on before they could reach the ridge, so that the proscribed race were obliged to lie down upon a bed of frozen snow, and the cold so seized upon them in their sleep as to change the sleep of many into that of death. Those who died were soonest at the end of their sufferings, but how keen must have been the anguish of the survivors who next morning had to behold sixteen of their children corpses, stiffened by the frost in the arms of their wretched mothers! The survivors, with great difficulty, reached the fraternal asylum which was opened to them.

The governor of Barcelonnette would then have distributed amongst the Catholics the possessions abandoned by these unhappy fugitives, but, to the credit of the inhabitants of these mountains, it must be told that no one would consent to accept them. These Catholics were far behind in the path in which their Church had advanced.

The Vaudois, therefore, were at liberty to return to their abodes, and take possession again of their property. The authorities winked at their return, without which these districts must have remained waste, and these mountains unpeopled; but in order to the exercise of public worship, they were under the necessity of traversing the glaciers again, and repairing to Vars in the dominions of France. And these humble Christians, already so severely tried, did not hesitate to travel that long and arduous journey, several times a year, to enjoy the privilege of mutual edification, and to receive the benediction of a pastor. What a lesson for the Christians of our day!

But, half a century after, in 1623, severities were recommenced. A Dominican monk, named Bouvetti, obtained authority from the Duke of Savoy to institute proceedings against the Vaudois of Barcelonnette, to whom he brought a new edict of abjuration or exile. This edict was mercilessly carried into execution by the governor of the valley, Francis Dreux, so that, after many fruitless petitions and efforts to obtain some mitigation of their lot, the Vaudois, unshaken in the faith of their fathers, were compelled again to forsake their native country, to which they were now never to return, going into hopeless exile, and seeking an asylum in countries less afflicted than their own. Some retired into Le Queyras and the Gapençois, others to Orange or Lyons; some went to Geneva, and many to the Vaudois valleys of Piedmont, which they regarded as their mother country. Thus was this retired valley left to silence and depopulation, which had been happy when it was forgotten, and in which, whilst it was forgotten, the gospel had been proclaimed and enjoyed in peace.

The persecuting Church gloried in this destruction as a triumph. Thus human passions, to glorify themselves, take for their pedestal the very vices which serve them, and, encouraged by the errors of his age, the man of power makes a merit of his excesses and misdeeds.

The inhabitants of Freyssinières, whose laborious habits and blameless manners the illustrious and unfortunate De Thou has so well described, made resistance to their persecutors. Louis XII. indeed had said, after a judicial investigation concerning them, "These brave people are better Christians than we." But they were so in virtue of the gospel, and Rome could not endure this. From the commencement of the 13th century to the end of the 18th, she never ceased to persecute them; and between the year 1056 and the year 1290, five bulls of different popes demanded their extermination. The inquisitors preyed upon these unhappy valleys from the year 1238; and in order to discover if an accused person were really guilty, we are told that these official defenders of the Catholic faith applied to him a red-hot iron; if it burned him it was a sign of heresy, and he was condemned. What times and what manners! Would to God that the uncertainty of the documents would permit us not to believe such things!

In 1344, says an old MS., the greater part of the people of Freyssinières being persecuted, fled into the valleys of Piedmont; but they returned with the Barbas, resisted the inquisitors, and were soon stronger than before.[1] It remained for the inconceivable cruelties of Borelli and of Veyletti to enfeeble them anew. Louis XI. put an end to the proceedings of these agents of the holy office in 1478. They were succeeded by Francis Ployéri, whom Cattanée left there after his extermination of the whole Vaudois of Val Louise.

This inquisitor commanded the inhabitants of Freyssinières to appear before him at Embrun. They knew that it was in order to obtain from them an abjuration of their faith; it could therefore be of no use for them to go, and no one went. Thereupon they were condemned to death for contumacy, as rebels, heretics, and *relapsed;* and, as usual, all the goods of these poor people were confiscated for the profit of the Church. This was the thing which interested and attracted her most, and which constituted her motive

---

[1] MS. Memoirs of Raymond Juvenis, in the Libraries of Grenoble and Carpentras.

for these condemnations. What cared her monks for the sorrows, the inexpressible distress, and misery of our families, if they could provide well for themselves, and give themselves up to all the grossness of their clerical sensuality! All of the unfortunate Vaudois who could be apprehended were therefore committed to the flames without more formality; for the surest means of seizing upon confiscated lands was to slaughter their owners; and whosoever ventured to intercede for the condemned, were it a son for his mother or a father for his child, was immediately thrown into prison, brought to trial, and often condemned as an abettor of heresy.

The Vaudois had no repose till after the death of the feeble Charles VIII., which took place in 1498. Deputies from almost all the provinces of the kingdom then repaired to Paris, to be present at the coronation of Louis XII. The inhabitants of Freyssinières were there also represented by a procurator, who was commissioned to lay their complaints before the new sovereign. Louis XII. remitted this business to his council; the pope was written to upon the subject, and commissioners, both apostolical and royal, that is to say, representing the pontifical power and the royal authority, were named to proceed to the spot and there make exact inquiry into the facts of the case.

Having arrived at Embrun, they caused all the papers connected with the proceedings instituted against the Vaudois by the inquisitors to be laid before them, found fault with the bishop, and annulled all the condemnations pronounced for contumacy against the inhabitants of Freyssinières. But the bishop would not assent to an arrangement which entailed upon his clergy the loss of the property acquired by these odious confiscations. He grounded his resistance upon what one of the commissioners had said publicly in the hostelry of the Angel, where they had been lodged, "Would to God that I were as good a Christian as the worst of these people!" from which the prelate concluded that this judge must have favoured the heretics at the expense of justice. However, Louis XII. ratified the decisions of the commissioners by letters dated at Lyons, 12th October, 1501, and the commissioners obtained from the pope a brief which rendered the king's decision binding upon the clergy. This pope was Alexander VI., and the brief was obtained through the intermediation of his son, Cæsar Borgia, who had come to France, bringing to Louis XII. a bull of divorce, in exchange for which he received, along with the title of Duke of Valentinois, the very part of Dauphiny in which the valley of Freyssinières is situated.

Borgia and Alexander VI. had something else to do than to trouble themselves about the doctrines which were professed there! The inhabitants had treated an ecclesiastical tribunal with contumacy, and an absolution was necessary for this in order to render inoperative those proceedings which the king desired to have annulled; nothing could be refused to the king, and Alexander VI. was generous in the matter of absolutions. But the cause for which one was sought appeared to him too insignificant for such long writings. Nothing but contumacy; a pretty peccadillo! And so, to make it something worth the trouble, he granted to the Vaudois a comprehensive absolution, not only from that of which they were charged, but also from all sorts of fraud, usury, larceny, simony, adultery, murder, and poisoning; for no doubt these things being so common at Rome, it was quite natural to suppose them equally common everywhere. The simple and austere life of the Vaudois stood in no need of these sin-breeding indulgences, and the evil which resulted from their employment remained entirely with the church which had recourse to them.

Half a century after, during the heat of the wars which filled up the 16th century, an attack was directed against the Vaudois of Freyssinières and Le Queyras, by the military commandant of Embrun, who marched against them at the head of 1200 men belonging to Embrun and the Briançonnais. But Lesdiguières, then scarcely twenty-four years of age, hastened by the Champsaur to the defence of his brethren in the faith. He encountered their enemies at St. Crispin and cut them in pieces.

The Protestants, in their turn, thought to seize upon Embrun. A stratagem was devised for this purpose. The day of the feast of the Conception, in December, 1573, was fixed for the execution of it; but it was mismanaged, and its author, Captain La Bréoule, having fallen into the hands of the Catholics, was strangled, dragged through the mud, quartered, and the parts suspended upon four gibbets at the four gates of the city. Twelve years after, Lesdiguières seized the place. He first attacked the town of Charges, which was fortified. The inhabitants and soldiers, trusting in the fortifications, did nothing but chat and divert themselves. Lesdiguières, advancing by paths which were concealed from observation, planted his ladders against the walls and entered the town. "We are come to dance with you," said he, making his appearance. The garrison were declared prisoners; they attempted to defend themselves and perished by the sword. A regiment of 500 arquebusiers came from Embrun to retake this place, but they fell into an ambuscade which Lesdiguières had planted for them at the hill of La Coulche, where they were cut in pieces. The victorious chief then caused the approaches to Embrun to be reconnoitred, and took possession of it on the 17th of November, 1586. A part of the soldiers who defended it retired into a sort of central fortress, of which there still remains a portion called the *Tour Brune*, contiguous to the ancient bishop's palace. Fire was applied to it, and during this fire the papers of the episcopal archives were thrown out of the windows in order to save them. Among them were the records of investigations against the Vaudois; a soldier laid hold of them and sold them, and from hand to hand they have passed into the hands of our historians. The cathedral of Embrun then became a Protestant church, for the bishop had fled at the commencement of the siege, with all his clergy.

Two days after this exploit Lesdiguières proceeded to besiege Guillestre, which was taken, and of which he levelled the walls, never since rebuilt. He then ascended the rugged valley of the Guill and took Château Queyras. The resistance which he met with at this place increased the irritation of his troops and the effervescence already prevailing in the valley. The victorious Protestants incurred the guilt of bloody reprisals against the Catholics, by whom they had been so long oppressed. For some years previous in particular, troops of fanatics had frequently assailed their habitations and passed through their villages, scattering everywhere desolation and death, instigated to these outrages generally by Captains De Mures and De La Cazette.

In 1583, the Reformed of Queyras being threatened with a speedy attack, called to their aid their brethren in faith from Piedmont, for considerable forces were preparing to attack them. The Vaudois of the valley of Lucerna were the first to arrive for their defence. They seized on Abriès; the enemy were masters of Ville Vieille, situated two hours' march lower down. A traitor, named Captain Vallon, left the Catholic troops, came to Abriès, and said to the Protestants, "I am one of your brethren; I have been made prisoner, and they have made me swear not to take up arms again, but I have obtained permission to leave the camp, and I am come to tell you that if you do not retire you will all be cut in pieces." "You spy!" exclaimed the Vaudois, "if you would not be cut in pieces yourself in the first place, begone immediately." The traitor disappeared, and the enemy's forces advanced. The cavalry came by the bottom of the valley, and two bodies of troops by the lateral slopes of the mountains. The Vaudois were intimidated at the sight of forces so superior to their own. "What! are you afraid?" cried Captain Pellenc of Le Villar. Let a hundred men follow me, and God will be with us! All followed him. Captain Fraiche, who had already delivered the Vaudois of Exiles from the soldiers of

La Cazette, was the first to rush upon the enemy. He caused their centre to give way, but their two wings closing together, the little Vaudois troop was on the point of being surrounded. They retreated over the heights of Val Préveyre; there they met their brethren of the valley of St. Martin, who had also come on the same summons; then they resumed the offensive with impetuosity · they had the advantage of the ground, and the avalanches of stones which they rolled down before them broke the first ranks of the Catholics. They dashed into the opening, struck down, dispersed, overwhelmed, and swept away the aggressors, and pursued them as far as Château Queyras. The skirmishes which afterwards took place were terminated by the victory of Lesdiguières, who made himself master of the whole valley, where cruelties and spoliations, unworthy of their name, were then perpetrated by the Protestants. Lesdiguières maintained his protectorate there until the Edict of Nantes. The Vaudois then had it in their power to enjoy the free exercise of their worship. During the 17th century they had pastors at Ristolas, Abriès, Château Queyras, Arvieux, Moline, and St. Véran. These pastors were sent by the synod of the valleys of Piedmont, as the Barbas had been in former times, who cherished with so much care the sacred fire of the primitive faith in churches much more distant.

The revocation of the Edict of Nantes was attended with the destruction of their places of worship, and their renewed proscription. It is well known what numbers of French Protestants were then driven into exile. Those of Le Queyras re-entered the valleys of Piedmont with the Vaudois who had been expelled from thence.

Under the reign of Louis XV., the reformed religion being still interdicted, the Protestant churches of Dauphiny had their meetings for worship "in the wilderness," like those of Gard and the Cévennes. When a meeting was to be held anywhere, the villagers might be seen descending separately and by different paths, their spades over their shoulders as if they were going to the field, and then they met in some solitary retreat, where the psalm-books were drawn forth from their labourers' dresses. Entire families travelled great distances to be present. They left home in the evening and travelled all night. At the outskirts of villages the men took off their shoes and walked barefooted along the silent street, lest the clatter of their iron-shod soles should betray their passing. The feet of the beast which bore the wife and children were wrapped in cloths, which prevented noise; and the caravan, fatigued but rejoicing, arrived with much emotion at the furtive rendezvous of prayer and edification. Sometimes, it is true, the soldiers of the gendarmerie, then called the maréchaussée, suddenly made their appearance, when all were engaged in the exercises of piety, and in the king's name arrested the pastor. Bloody collisions took place. The bullets of Popery oftener than once mangled the gospel of Christ; but the "assemblies of the wilderness" dissolved in one quarter, were resumed in another. Where, by the incessant confiscations of which they were the object, copies of the Bible had become too rare to suffice for the wants of all, societies of young people were formed, with the view of committing it to memory, and in this way saving themselves from that privation of it with which they were threatened. Each member of these pious associations was intrusted with the duty of carefully preserving in his recollection a certain number of chapters, and when the assembly of the wilderness met again, these new Levites, standing around the minister, with their faces towards the people, instead of the reading of the interdicted pages, recited in succession, and each in his turn, all the chapters of the book named by the pastor for common edification.

It was thus that the Protestant churches of France passed through these stormy times. In the valleys of Dauphiny, which were anciently Vaudois valleys, the descendants of these glorious martyrs have survived their misfortunes, and still subsist at Freyssinières, Vars, Dormilhouse, Arvieux, Molines, and St. Veran. A recent apostolate, displaying, like those of the ancient Vaudois, the fervour which animated the primitive church, has connected with these countries the name of Felix Neff, which history has already placed alongside of that of Oberlin, the famous benefactor of the Vosges. The young missionary and the aged patriarch had the same ardour; for souls do not become aged, and what are our years in comparison with eternity? Even centuries are nothing. Happy are these churches which have combated during centuries for a cause that cannot be destroyed, and whose contests and triumphs shall be celebrated in the world of immortality!

The chapters following will show us the heroic and patient defenders of this cause in other places also, but everywhere the same.

CHAPTER V.

HISTORY OF THE VAUDOIS OF PROVENCE.—MÉRINDOL AND CABRIÈRES.[1]

(A.D. 1350 TO A.D. 1550.)

Settlement of the Vaudois in Provence—Persecutions of the 16th century—Cruelties of Menier D'Oppède—Proceedings against the inhabitants of Mérindol—Singular deliverance of many from death—The Vaudois of Cabrières—Cardinal Sadolet—Cardinal De Tournon—The Bishop of Cavaillon at Mérindol—Edict of Francis I. suspending prosecutions—Revocation of that Edict surreptitiously obtained—Menier D'Oppède destroys Mérindol, Cabrières, La Coste, and other places, and butchers their inhabitants—Protestantism in modern times on the slopes of the Leberon.

THE Vaudois established themselves in Provence during the reign of Charles II., who possessed vast lordships at once upon both sides of the Alps, and who therefore assumed the title of Count of Piedmont and of Provence. This was about the end of the 13th cen-

---

[1] AUTHORITIES.—"*Histoire de l'exécution de Cabrières, de Mérindol, et d'autres lieux de Provence; ensemble une relation partie. de ce qui passa aux cinquante audiences de la cause de Mérindol,*" par Louis Aubery de Mauriez. 4to, Paris, 1645.—Camerarius, "*De excidio reliq. Valdensium . . . lugubris narratio.*" Heidelberg, 1606. (Edited thirty years after the death of the author, by his nephew, Louis Camerarius.)—"*Hist. mémor. de la persèc. et saccagement du peuple de Mérindol, Cabrières, et autres circonvoisins.*" 32mo, 1556. (Ascribed to Du Bellay, Seigneur of Langez, who was commissioned by Francis I., in 1541, to make an investigation concerning the Vaudois of Provence.)—"*La persèc. de ceux de Mér. et Cabr., peuples fidèles en Provence.*" Crespin, *Hist. des Martyrs*, edit. 1619, fol., from fol. 133 to fol. 159, and fol. 182 to 186.—"*Les Vaudois de Provence, par Louis Frossard.*" 8vo, 1848, pp. 287.—"*Essai histor. sur les Vaudois de Provence . . . par Paulin Roman.*" 4to, Strasbury, 1839.—"*Observ. sur les preliminaires de l'exécution de Cabrières et de Mér.,*" by *Nicolay*, in the *Hist. de l'Acad. des Inscript. et Belles Lettres*, t. xviii. p. 377 (a superficial work).—Dreux de Radier, *Articles critiques sur l'exéc. de Cabr. et de Mér.*, in the *Journal de Verdun*, Sept. 1753, p. 189.—"*Revue de Comtat,*" Nos. for February and March, 1839. "*Sur les debats judiciaires qui eurent lieu devant la chambre du roi en 1450; Jacobi Auberii, Parisiensis Advocati, pro Merindolis et Caprariensibus actio,*" . . . fol., Lyons, 1619. Some of the pleadings on the other side have also been published. See, amongst others, that of the defender of Menier (the advocate Robert), &c. Many small pamphlets were published after Aubery's pleadings. De Thou speaks of these events in his history, book v. The lives of the Baron of Oppède and of the Baron of La Garde, who took part in these proceedings, have been published separately.

MSS.—"*Plaidoyers et autres actes intervenus en la cause de ceux de Mérindol et Cabrières, depuis 1540 jusques en 1554,*" a folio of more than 1000 pages, National Library, Paris, No. 204. (It is by this MS. that I have been chiefly guided in this work.)—"*Pièces concernant l'affaire de Mérindol,*" en 1540, Library of Aix, No. 798.—"*Enquête contre Jean de Roma, en 1520.*" Paris (Archives de la République, section Hist.).—"*Discours des guerres de la conté de Venayssin et de la Provence,*" . . . by *Loys de Perussiis*, 4to (Library of Avignon).—"*Hist. de la ville*

tury. At the commencement of the next century, the persecutions directed against the Vaudois of Dauphiny caused some of them to take refuge with their brethren in the faith upon the banks of the Durance.

At the close of the ten years' war between Louis II., Count of Provence, and Raymond of Toulouse,[1] this district remained depopulated; and as Louis II. was obliged to sell part of it in order to provide for the expenses of that war, the Seigneurs of Boulier Cental, and of Rocca Sparviera, bought from him at that time the valley of Aigues, which stretches from north to south along the soft slopes of the Leberon. But these seigneurs already possessed, in the marquisate of Saluces, great estates cultivated by Vaudois. They engaged some of that people, therefore, to come and cultivate their new possessions likewise, and these lands were conveyed to them by *emphyteosis*, that is to say, upon perpetual lease.

From the most distant parts of Calabria, where other Vaudois were also settled, numbers of them returned to the valleys from which they originally sprung, and passed from thence into Provence, as there were also some from Provence who went to settle in Calabria; so great was then the fraternity subsisting among all these communities, or rather these dispersed parishes of an united church.

"In place of priests and of curés," says a Catholic author of that country,[2] "they had ministers who, under the name of Barbas, presided in their secret religious conventicles. However, as they were seen to be quiet and reserved, and as they faithfully paid their taxes, tithes, and seigneural dues, and were moreover very industrious, they were not disturbed upon the subject of their practices and doctrines."

But the Reformers of Germany, to whom they sent a deputation along with their brethren of Piedmont, warmly urged them to abandon this reserve, reproaching them as guilty of dissimulation, because their exercises of religion were only conducted in secret. Scarcely had they made a more open display of their separation from the Church of Rome, when inquisitors were sent against them.

d'Apt," by Remerville. Library of Carpentras.—"*Hist. de la ville de Pernes* . . . *avec ce qui s'est passé de plus intéressant* . . . &c." (The author of this MS. was Dr. Giberti.) In the same library, Nos. 606 and 607.—De Cambis Velleron, "*Annales d'Avignon*," first volume. Library of Avignon.—MSS. of Peyresk. Reg. xxxi. vol. ii., at fol. 361, &c. Library of Carpentras.

[1] From A.D. 1389 to A.D. 1400.

[2] *Histoire des guerres excitées dans le comtat Venaissin, par les Calvinistes du XVIe siecle*, t. i. p. 39. This work, published anonymously, was written by Father Justin, a Capuchin monk, of Monteux, near Carpentras.

One of these, called John de Roma, perpetrated many outrages during a period of ten years which he spent in that region.[1]

At last the king caused him to be imprisoned, and an investigation, whose voluminous records are preserved to this day,[2] was made concerning his exactions and cruelties. Nevertheless, the proceedings which he had instituted were continued. In 1534, says Gilles, the Bishops of Sisteron, Apt, Cavaillon, and others, each in his own diocese, caused inquisition to be made for the Vaudois, and filled the prisons with them. Learning that these heretics derived their origin from Piedmont, they wrote about them to the Archbishop of Turin, and he named a commissioner, who wrote to Provence that these proceedings should be suspended until he had made more perfect inquiry on his side. But the Bishop of Cavaillon replied, on the 29th of March, 1535, that thirteen of the prisoners had already been condemned to be burned alive. Of this number was Anthony Pasquet, of St. Ségont. The spirit of the martyr who gave his name to that village was not yet extinct there. Others had died in prison; the bishop mentioned in particular Peter Chalvet, of Rocheplate. Thus the intervention of the commissioner, who was himself a native of Rocheplate, was ineffectual to counteract the zeal of these prelates, and especially of the Parliament of Provence, more eager apparently for condemnations than for justice.

Clement VIII., a year before his death, promised plenary indulgences to all Vaudois who should return to the bosom of the Popish Church. None availed themselves of the offer. The pope complained to the King of France, who wrote on the subject to the Parliament of Aix; and the Parliament ordered the seigneurs of the lands occupied by the Vaudois, to compel their vassals to abjure or to quit the country. As they refused, an attempt was made to overcome them by intimidation. Some of them were cited to appear before the court of Aix, to explain the causes of their refusal; they did not attend, and the court condemned them by default to be burned alive. Thereupon their brethren took up arms; one named Eustace Maron put himself at their head, and they proceeded to rescue the prisoners. The authorities became alarmed, the effervescence extended, and a civil war was just on the point of breaking out in the district. The king, Francis I., was informed of it, and thinking to pacify all, he caused a general amnesty to be proclaimed in July, 1535, on condition that the heretics should abjure within six months.

Tranquillity was restored, and the six months passed away;

[1] From A.D. 1521 to 1532.
[2] National Archives, Paris (Michelet, Letter of April 20, 1839).

no one had abjured, and each of the seigneurs or magistrates in these regions arrogated the right of arbitrarily exacting the required abjuration, or punishing the Vaudois at his own pleasure by confiscation and imprisonment. This latter mode of proceeding may be said to have become truly fashionable. It was known that the Christian would rather give up his fortune than his creed, and he was deprived of his fortune in order to punish him for retaining his faith. It was a new way of acquiring wealth. Many availed themselves of it to a large extent; Ménier D'Oppède went beyond all bounds. He was poor, of Jewish descent, a man of doubtful integrity, of unquestionable selfishness, infatuated with self-conceit, like all men of little minds, and disdaining people of low rank with a pride all the more contemptuous because he himself was but a miserable upstart. The apostasy of his grandfather seemed to irritate him all the more against the religious steadfastness of the Vaudois; the sternness of his character prevented his shrinking from the use of any kind of means, and his ambition made all kinds lawful. Marching with a troop of armed men, he would seize the Vaudois in their fields. "Call upon the saints for deliverance," he would say to them. "There is no other mediator between God and man," the Vaudois would reply, "but he who is both God and man, that is Christ." "Thou art a heretic; abjure thy errors." Upon the refusal of the Vaudois, he flung them into the cellars of the castle of Oppède, which served him for a prison, and did not release them without the payment of a large ransom, or if they died, he confiscated their goods.

These shocking depredations were particularly numerous in 1536. Next year the *procureur-general* of the Parliament of Provence, solicited at once by the fanatical clergy and by the interested spoliators, made a report, in which he represented that the Vaudois were daily increasing. On this report the king required the court to repress the rebels; and the year following (June, 1539) he authorized it to take cognizance of the crime of heresy. After the month of October in that same year, the court issued warrants for the arrestment of 154 persons, whom two apostates had denounced as heretics.

It may be imagined what an excessive fermentation such measures must have produced in the country; and though we can here give only a brief sketch, we may say that no historian has yet combined together those details, an acquaintance with which, however, is necessary, that the course of events may be understood. In circumstances such as these, a spark may cause a conflagration. This actually happened in the manner which we now proceed to show.

The mill of the Plan d'Apt was an object of desire to the magistrate of that town. He denounced Pellenc, the miller, as a heretic. Pellenc was burned alive, and his mill confiscated for behoof of the man who had denounced him. Some young men of Mérindol, in whose Provençal veins the Italian blood still boiled, were unable to contain their indignation at such iniquities, and in their ignorance of legal forms, to which, however, no recourse would have remained for them, they executed justice after the manner of the populace and according to the notions which children form of it; they destroyed, during the night, the mill of which the man who had destroyed their brother had so unrighteously obtained possession as the price of his blood. The magistrate of Apt made his complaint to the court of Aix, and named the persons whom he suspected of having had a hand in this business. The court, although it was vacation time (it was in July, 1540), held an extraordinary meeting, and ordered the apprehension of eighteen suspected persons. The officer commissioned to intimate to them the decree of the court, proceeded to Mérindol, where he found all the houses deserted. "Where are the inhabitants of this village?" said he to a poor man whom he met upon the road. "They have taken refuge in the woods," said the other, "because they were told that the troops of the Count de Tende[1] were coming to kill them." "Go and seek them," said the officer, "and tell them that no harm will be done to them." Some Vaudois came, and the officer summoned them to appear before the court within the space of two months from that date.

On the 2d of September they all met, and addressed a petition to the court, in which they protested their submission to its authority and their loyalty to the king, entreating the court not to lend an ear to their enemies, who would mislead it in the execution of justice, "for," say they, "in the summons which has been served upon us we find persons indicted to appear before you who are dead, and others who never existed, and children of so tender an age that they cannot even walk alone." The court, annoyed that simple countrymen should point out such mistakes in its decrees, replied that they must appear, without concerning themselves about the dead. The Vaudois consulted an advocate to know what they ought to do. "If you wish to be burned alive," said he, "you have nothing to do but to come." The poor people did not attend; and the day for which they were summoned being past, the court of Aix, on the 18th of November, 1540, pronounced against them an inconceivable sentence, condemning to the pile twenty-three persons, of whom only seventeen were designated by name. "The court," such are also the

[1] Then Governor of Provence, August, 1540.

further terms of that sentence, "delivers over their wives and their children to any one who can lay hold of them, prohibits all and sundry from giving them any assistance, and as the village of Mérindol is notoriously known to be a retreat of heretics, appoints all the houses and buildings of that place to be demolished and burned."

This decree caused a general indignation amongst all persons of enlightenment, especially amongst all the generous spirits belonging to the noblesse and the bar, as may be inferred from the following anecdote, borrowed from the writers of the time:—The President of the court of Aix was dining with the bishop of that city. "Well, Monsieur de Chassanée," said a woman, who lived in a shameless manner with the prelate, "when are you to execute the decree of Mérindol?" The president made no answer. "What decree do you mean?" asked a young man. The lady informed him. "It must certainly be a decree of the parliament of women," ironically exclaimed the youthful D'Allenc, one of the most eminent of the Arlesian noblesse. A councillor named De Sénas gravely affirmed its sad reality. "No; it is impossible to believe anything so barbarous," exclaimed the Seigneur of Beaujeu. A member of the parliament, who was also one of the company, thought to put an end to the conversation by a joke. "Ah! Seigneur de Beaujeu," said he, pointing to the young lady, as she sat between the bishop and the president, "if you are going to attack the gowns you will have no easy work of it!" The witticism caused a laugh, but the person to whom it was addressed replied with indignation, "It is atrocious! I have had to do with the inhabitants of Mérindol, and nowhere have I met with more decent people." "I would have been astonished," said the mistress of the episcopal palace, "if nobody had been found to defend these misbelievers!" "I would have been still more surprised," rejoined the young man, "if a new Herodias had not loved to see the shedding of innocent blood." "Come! come!" said the aged De Sénas, "we are here to enjoy ourselves, and not to dispute." Hereupon the discussion terminated; but, a few days, after the Count D'Allenc waited upon the President Chassanée, appealed to his sentiments of justice and humanity, and obtained a suspension of the decree. The court itself was alarmed at the decree which it had passed, and wrote to the king to remit the matter to his judgment.

Francis I. commissioned Dubellay, Seigneur of Langez, to repair to Provence, and make investigation as to the conduct of the Vaudois. "They are quiet and peaceable people," says he, in his report, "reserved in their manners, chaste and sober, very industrious, but very little in the habit of attending mass." Upon this report, the monarch proclaimed a general amnesty (by letters, dated 18th February, 1541), whereby, leaving all that was past to be forgotten, he granted pardon to all the accused, upon condition that within three months they should abjure their errors of doctrine. These letters of grace, which came to the court in the beginning of March, were not published by it till the month of May. There remained only a fortnight for the Vaudois to avail themselves of them; but, if it had been only one moment, they would not have sought to prolong their lives by abjuring the truth and giving up their souls to death. On the contrary, they proclaimed their persecuted doctrines more distinctly than ever, by a confession of faith, drawn up on the 6th of April, 1541. This was sent to Francis I., and the Sire de Castelnau read it to him; each point of doctrine being supported by passages of the Bible. "Well! and what have they got to say in answer to this?" exclaimed the king. But his unsettled and shallow mind could not remain faithful to the impressions which it had received; he very soon forgot these words of approbation which a scriptural production had drawn from him—a production of which, indeed, enlightened Catholics themselves could not but approve.

The illustrious and learned Sadolet, whose features Raffaele has preserved to us in a celebrated painting, and who was then Bishop of Carpentras, caused a copy to be sent to him; and it is here that, for the first time, the Vaudois of Cabrières appear upon the stage, for they belonged to the diocese of Carpentras, whilst Mérindol formed part of that of Cavaillon. They made haste themselves to convey to Cardinal Sadolet a copy of their common confession. "We are ready," said they, on presenting it, "not only to abjure, but to be subjected to the severest penalties, if it can be shown to us, from the Holy Scriptures, that our doctrines are erroneous." The cardinal answered them kindly, acknowledged that they had been the objects of black calumnies,[1] invited them to come and hold conference with him, and endeavoured to convince them that without changing in any respect the purport of their confession, they might mitigate its terms. He did not seek to hide from them that he himself was desirous of a reform in Catholicism. If the Vaudois had always been examined before men such as he, blood would not have been shed.

Sadolet wrote to the pope that he was astonished to see proceedings adopted against the Vaudois, whilst the Jews were spared; but his protection was soon withdrawn from them by his removal from the country; for, being called to Rome, he lost sight of them,

[1] *Meras calumnias et falsas criminationes* . . . .

and the Vaudois had now none to deal with but their persecutors.

The term of amnesty, announced by the letters of grace, being expired, the court of Aix commanded the Vaudois to send six mandatories, to declare whether they intended to take advantage of it and to conform to its conditions. One man alone presented himself, named Eslène: "We are ready to abjure," he once more said, "upon condition that our errors be proved to us." Others claimed the benefit of the amnesty without reservation; and of this number were those persons in particular who had been condemned by the decree of the 18th of November, 1540; so that the decree ceased, by this very circumstance, to have any object, yet afterwards it served as a pretext for their total extermination. This fact, which has not been noticed by any writer, exposes the disorder and iniquity then existing where the Vaudois were concerned, in respect of what was called the administration of justice.

A whole year now elapsed without any very notable incident, except the martyrdom of an humble hawker [colporteur] of books, who was surprised at Avignon in the very act of selling a Bible. His trial was soon finished: in the eyes of the Church of Rome his crime was unpardonable. All means were tried in order to make him abjure, but he had been too long familiar with the word of God to bow to the word of men. His steadfastness (which the evangelical colporteurs of our days seem to have inherited, and which they display in the midst of humiliating treatment sometimes experienced by them, where their predecessors would have incurred the penalty of death) did not forsake him in his last moments. Condemned to be burned alive at the place of public execution, he was chained to a post, to which the volume of the Holy Scriptures was also attached. "Ah!" cried he, "how can I complain of my being put to death, when the word of God is burned along with me?" The Bible and the Christian were consumed together in the flames; but the Vaudois were only the more confirmed in their faith and constancy.

The Cardinal De Tournon, stirred up against them by the Legate of the Holy See, transmitted to the king information that the clergy had condemned the Confession of Faith which they had presented. The king demanded to be apprised of the results which had been produced by the letters of grace which he had granted, and at the same time wrote to the governor of the province[1] requiring him to cleanse that region of heresy.

The Bishop of Cavaillon was one of those who most strongly

---

[1] Then the Sire de Grignan.

maintained that they should *make an end at once* with the heretics. The court of Aix delegated him, along with one of his councillors, to make inquiry at Mérindol how the Vaudois stood affected with regard to religion. Having arrived in the village, he sent for the *bailli*, whose name was Maynard, and for the principal persons of the place, and without touching upon any question of doctrine, said to them, "Abjure your errors, whatsoever they may be, and I will hold you as dear as I now hold you guilty: if not, then tremble for the penalty of your obstinacy." "Would your grace," said the bailli, "be pleased to tell us what points we are required to abjure?" "It is needless," said the bishop; "a general abjuration will satisfy us." "But according to the decree of the court," said they, "it is upon our Confession of Faith that we ought to be examined." "And what is that?" said the bishop's councillor, who was a doctor of divinity. The bishop presented it to him, saying, "See! the whole thing is full of heresy." "In what place?" said Maynard. "The doctor will tell you," replied the prelate. "I would need two or three days to examine it," remarked the theologian. "Very well! we will come back next week."

Eight days after, the doctor of divinity went to his bishop. "My lord," said he, "I have not only found this paper conformable to the Holy Scriptures, but, moreover, I have learned to understand them better during these two or three days, than during all the rest of my life." "You are under the influence of the devil," said the prelate. The councillor withdrew; and as we shall not meet with him again in the course of this history, it may here be added that this circumstance led him to search the Scriptures still more than he had yet done, and that, a year after, he went to Geneva, where he embraced Protestantism. Had the Confession of Faith of the Vaudois churches produced only that result, there is enough of good in the conversion and salvation of one immortal soul, to make us regard it with feelings of satisfaction, whatever temporal misfortunes may have ensued from it.

However, a few days after the bishop had dismissed this conscientious theologian, he filled up his place at Cavaillon with a doctor of the Sorbonne, recently come from Paris.

With him the prelate returned to Mérindol. They met some children on the way, and the bishop gave them a few pieces of money, recommending them to learn the *Pater* and the *Credo*. "We know them," said the children. "In Latin?" "Yes; but we cannot give the meaning of them except in French." "What need is there of so much knowledge?" said the bishop; "I know many doctors who would be at a loss to give the meaning of them." "And what purpose would it serve to know them, if one did not know what the words meant?" replied Andrew Maynard, who now made his appearance before them. "Well, do you know it yourself?" said the prelate. "I would think myself very unhappy if I were ignorant of it," replied the bailli. And he explained the meaning of a portion. "I could not have believed," exclaimed the churchman, with a peculiar clerical oath, "that there had been so many doctors at Mérindol." "The least among us could tell you as much as I," replied the bailli; "only ask one of these children, and you shall see." But, as the bishop kept silence, he went on: "If you will permit, one of them shall himself ask questions at the rest." And they did it so readily and beautifully, that everybody marvelled.

The bishop then, sending away all the strangers, said to the Vaudois, "I know very well that there is not so much ill amongst you as people think; nevertheless, to satisfy men's minds, it is necessary that you should submit to some appearance of abjuration." "What would you have us to abjure," said they, "if we are in the truth?" "It is nothing but a mere formality that I require of you," said the bishop; "I demand neither notary nor signature. Let the bailli and the syndic only make an abjuration here, in secret, and in your name, as vague as they please, and I will put an end to all these prosecutions." The Vaudois kept silence, and made no reply. "What is it that restrains you?" said the bishop, to remove all difficulty; "if you do not think fit to keep by that abjuration, nobody will be able to convict you, neither by your act nor your signature." But the upright and honest minds of these simple mountaineers could not enter into such sinuosities of popish consciences. "We are frank and sincere, my lord," said they, "and we are not disposed to do anything that we cannot keep by." Oh! do not the reservations and prudent dissimulations of worldly wisdom seem wretched indeed, when contrasted with that generous blindness of honesty and truth! For if the Vaudois had but thought fit to say, "We abjure our errors," making application of that expression to some other thing altogether than their doctrines, perhaps they might have been saved. But Jesuitism is not of Vaudois origin. The bishop withdrew.

On the 4th of April, 1542, he returned with a recorder of the tribunal, and a commissioner of the parliament. The inhabitants of Mérindol were summoned together again: the papers in their case were read; some remarks were exchanged betwixt the bailli and the recorder; but the commissioner becoming impatient, commanded them to be silent, and required the Vaudois to give their conclusive reply. "Our reply," said they, "is, that our errors ought to be pointed out to us." The commissioner asked the bishop to do it. The bishop replied that public report was a sufficient inculpation of the heretics. "And was it not to ascertain if these reports were well founded that the investigation was appointed?" said Maynard, in name of the Vaudois. The bishop, sufficiently embarrassed, then called upon a preaching monk, who was with him, to preach a sermon to them. The monk pronounced a long discourse in Latin, and every one withdrew. But the commission not having followed up this investigation, another year passed, during which the Vaudois enjoyed some measure of tranquillity. Nay, the inhabitants of Cabrières du Cantal (for there is also a Cabrières d'Aigues), having been attacked by a band of marauders, amongst whom were some soldiers of Avignon, addressed their complaints to Francis I.; and the monarch, comprehending at last the intrigues of their enemies, signed, of his own accord, on the 14th of June, 1544, an edict, by which he suspended all proceedings commenced against the Vaudois, ordaining that they should be re-established in all their privileges, and that those of them who were prisoners should be set at liberty, and which concluded with these words, "And seeing that the Procureur-General of Provence is a relative of the Archbishop of Aix, *their sworn enemy*, a councillor of the court shall be appointed in his place to inform me if they are innocent." It looked as if all was on the point of being thus brought to an end; and seeming just to approach a peaceful conclusion of this agitated drama, we are farther than ever from anticipating the terrible catastrophe with which it was really to close.

The court of Aix, before publishing the letter of Francis I., sent one of its officers, named Courtin, to Paris, in order if possible to obtain the revocation of it. A sum of sixty livres was allowed him for this journey. He had letters of recommendation to the Cardinal De Tournon, and to the *Procureur du Roi* of the privy council. In a meeting of this council, on the 1st of January, 1545, the letters of revocation were presented to the king for signature. Francis I. signed them without reading them; afterwards he repented of it, and inquiry was made by whom these letters had been prepared, and by whose hands they had been brought to him. The name of the *Procureur du Roi* in the privy council was John Leclerc. "Was it you," he was asked, "who signed this paper?" "I have no recollection of it." The seal was broken; there was no signature. The persons commissioned to inquire into the matter sent for Leclerc's substitute, whose name was William Potel. He was asked, "Was it you who prepared the paper?" "Yes, but I did not sign it." "Who got you to write it?" "It was M. Courtin, an officer of the Parliament of Provence." "Why did you not sign it?" "Because it wanted the packet of documents connected with it." "By whom were these letters of revocation, which have been surreptitiously obtained and illegally drawn up, introduced into the privy council?" "By Monsieur the Cardinal De Tournon." The cardinal was called. "Who gave these documents to your eminence?" "The officer of the court of Aix, sent by the president, D'Oppède" (for D'Oppède had succeeded Chassanée in 1543). "Whose business was it to present them for his majesty's signature?" "The grand chancellor's." This dignitary was sent for, and the letters of revocation were exhibited to him. He was asked if he had ever had them in his hands. He said, "Yes; but as they did not appear to be regular, I did not think it proper to present them for signature to the king." "Then who presented them?" "He who countersigned them." They looked and found that this was the minister De L'Aubespine. He was summoned before the commission, and acknowledged his signature, but he said that the paper had not been written in his office. None of his clerks had any better recollection of it. The hand of the clergy, working in secret, had left no trace of the tortuous course by which these letters had passed. Moreover, says the advocate-general of 1550, the seal was of white wax, and the counter-seal green, a thing quite unusual.

It is therefore beyond doubt that these letters had been dishonestly fabricated, and presented at unawares for the signature of the king. Let us now see what they contained.

"Considering," it is there said, "that the heretics of Lucerna have established themselves in Provence, and preach there; that the Vaudois publicly manifest their heresy, that they trouble the country . . . . &c., the court of Provence shall proceed to execute the decree of the 18th of November, 1540, all letters of grace of later date notwithstanding, and we ordain the governor of the province to apply himself with all vigour to the execution of justice in this matter."

What justice, O God! what iniquity! And this business becomes blacker still, if we consider that the privy council, even if the papers had come to it in the regular way, had no power to decree anything contrary to the letters of grace and evocation, which had been granted by the monarch himself. It was an equally flagrant, and still more deplorable contravention of law, that whilst the decree of the 18th of November, 1540, only bore the condemnation of a small number of the inhabitants of Mérindol, yet under the pretext of the execution of that decree was included the destruction by fire and sword of a whole population, occupying seventeen villages, all of which were ravaged and destroyed.

Scarcely had this sanguinary order been obtained, when Courtin sent it to D'Oppède, by an express courier. This courier arrived at Aix on the 13th of February, 1545. The court of Aix immediately wrote to Courtin, signifying its great satisfaction; to M. De Grignan, Governor of Provence, requiring him to have troops ready for their service; and to the Cardinal De Tournon, congratulating him on the triumph which he had obtained.

Here, again, a new infraction of judicial forms took place. The Vaudois, who were trusting to the suspension of proceedings, in terms of the royal letters of 14th June, 1544, ought to have received immediate notification of these new papers, which gave effect to the original decree. They received no notification of the kind; all was carefully concealed from them; the troops were collected in silence; and advantage was taken of the feeling of security amongst the poor people to make preparations for their death. The enemies of the Vaudois did not wish that they should have time to address to their sovereign a reclaiming petition, which might have led to a detection of the villainy of which he had been the dupe, and of which they were to be the victims. They only waited until a certain Captain Poulain, Baron of La Garde, who was then in Piedmont, and who was soon to conduct a body of veteran troops to Roussillon, should pass through Provence, in order to employ these troops in that service. He arrived on the 6th of April. From the 7th to the 11th all the necessary preparations were made for the execution of that retroactive sentence, which had never even been notified to those whom it concerned. The next day, the 12th of April, was the Sabbath; nevertheless, the court met on the summons of Menier D'Oppède. The king's advocate, whose name was Guérin, formally demanded the execution of the decree, to which these letters of revocation were supposed to have restored all its force. The court accorded his demand, named commissioners, and required D'Oppède, as the king's lieutenant, in absence of the governor, to take vigorous measures for the execution of justice— an odious mockery! Immediately after, D'Oppède wrote to the Warden of Apt to take arms and seize upon all the heretics of the neighbourhood; he then caused his commissioners to set out, who that same evening arrived at Pertuis.

At the same time orders were sent to the inhabitants of Lourmarin to prepare billets for 1000 infantry, and 300 cavalry. The inhabitants replied by taking up arms. The summons was repeated; they demanded a delay of twelve hours to consider of it. "What!" it was answered, "shall subjects make terms with their prince?" The Châtelaine of Lourmarin, Blanche de Lévis, came in person to intercede for them. She was not listened to. Thereupon she went to the public square of the village, into the midst of the inhabitants, and with many tears adjured them to lay down their arms, and not to expose themselves to certain destruction. "Our destruction will only be the more speedy if we do so," was their reply. "But at least send a petition," said she. "Well," said they, "let them only allow us to leave the country, and we will abandon our property to those who wish to get possession of it by our death." But the poor châtelaine could give them no assistance in this matter. The Lady of Cental also wrote to D'Oppède to entreat him to spare her vassals. But Captain Vaujuine had already arrived at Cadenet. The troops spread over the country commenced to pillage and to burn. The first column, led by D'Oppède, marched upon Lourmarin. The second, conducted by the Baron of La Garde, marched upon La Motte and Cabrières d'Aigues. The third, under the orders of Vaujuine and De Redortier, proceeded towards Mérindol and Cabrières du Comtat.[1]

D'Oppède commenced, upon the way, by setting fire to the houses of La Roque, Ville Laure, and Trezemines, which had been deserted by the Vaudois; he did the same at Lourmarin, where 114 houses were destroyed by the flames. He then ordered the officers and the consuls of Apt to collect all the forces possible at Roussillon, and to proceed thither and await his orders.

On the 18th of April, the united troops of D'Oppède, Vaujuine, Redortier, and Poulain, appeared before Mérindol. The inhabitants had fled from it, but a young man, whom some circumstance had detained in the fields, was seized by the spoilers. His name was Maurice Blanc. He was tied to an olive tree, and the soldiers making a target of his body, seemed to delight in insulting his agony by discharging their pieces at him from a distance. He expired, pierced by five arquebuse balls. Just so many were the wounds which his Saviour had received upon the cross. The young martyr of Mérindol committed his soul to him, with the exclamation, "O Lord, receive my spirit into thy hands!"

They then set fire to the village, which was entirely destroyed. Some women, says a person who was present, having been surprised in the church, were stripped of their garments, and the barbarians, making them join hands as for a dance, compelled them, by severely pricking them with their daggers and pikes, to march round the castle, amidst shouts of laughter and outrages, of which they were

---

[1] According to the report of this expedition, drawn up by Brissons, criminal recorder to the court of Aix, who was associated with the commissioners in order to draw it up.

the objects. After this they took them, already covered with blood, and flung them, one after another, from the top of the rock upon which the castle was built. Many others were taken elsewhere and sold. A father had to go as far as Marseilles to redeem his daughter. A young mother, who was fleeing across the corn-fields with her infant in her arms, was seized and violated by these soldiers, or rather brutes, whilst she still continued to hold her babe pressed to her breast. An old woman, whose age secured her from similar outrage, was treated by them in a way which insulted both humanity and their own religion. They shaved her in the form of a cross, and having decked her with some worthless ornaments, dragged her through the streets, chanting in derision, after the manner of priests. This took place at Lauris, on the way between Cabrières and Avignon. The procession arrived where there was an oven ready for baking bread, and the soldiers, pushing their victim forward with their weapons, said to her, "Go in there, you old damned wretch!" The poor woman was going in without resistance, so much had she been tormented, when those who had heated the oven objected, and prevented her from being thrown into it.

Amidst such brutalities, a thousand times repeated, under different and more revolting forms, the army came to Cabrières. It was a fortified town in the territories of the pope. The king's troops had no power to touch it without the consent of the pontiff. But the vice-legate, Mormoiron, hastened to put into the hands of D'Oppède the most unlimited powers for this expedition.

They arrived at Cabrières on the 19th of April, which was also a Sabbath. The walls were battered from morning to night, in order to make a breach in them—a becoming sanctification of the day of the Lord! The Vaudois, who were shut up in that place, prayed and offered an unyielding resistance. The attack was continued all night without effect. On Monday morning D'Oppède put a stop to the firing. He wrote, with his own hand, to the Vaudois, that if they would open the gates of their town he would do them no harm. He probably knew that, according to the decision of the Council of Constance, there is no necessity for keeping faith with heretics. The Vaudois, less familiar with the canonical science, which teaches perjury, than with the Bible, which enjoins sincerity, judged by its maxims of the king's word, or that of the President of the court of Aix, and opened to him the gates of Cabrières. The first troops which entered were the veteran bands of the Baron of La Garde, newly arrived from Piedmont, men inured to all the dangers of war. It was by them that the carnage was to be commenced, but knowing the terms of capitulation which had been agreed upon, the soldiers asserted that it concerned their honour to oppose the infraction of them. The commissioners of the court of Aix and of the vice-legate entered into a discussion with them upon this point. Meanwhile Menier D'Oppède caused the principal persons of the town to be called, who came with unhesitating confidence. They were eighteen in number. Their hands were tied, and they were ordered to the midst of the troops. They supposed that they were only made hostages, to secure the tranquillity of the rest of the population. But as they moved along the ranks of the Provençal troops commanded by D'Oppède, his son-in-law, named De Pourrières, struck with his cutlass the bald head of an old man, whose tottering step had caused him to touch him in passing. "Kill them all!" cried D'Oppède, seeing him fall, and in a moment these dastardly and fanatical troops fell upon them and butchered them. After they were dead, the same De Pourrières, and the Sire de Faulcon, went about amongst them and mutilated their corpses.

The heads of these unfortunate men were carried about on pikes. The passions of the soldiery were roused; the signal for massacre had been given. Some women, shut up in a barn, which was set on fire, sought to save themselves by leaping from its walls. They were received upon the points of partizans and swords. Others had retired into the castle. "Their death! their blood!" cried D'Oppède, and pointed out to his soldiers the way to their place of refuge.

But how shall I describe the scene which took place in the church? It was the most horrible and sacrilegious scene of all; for it was there that a great number of the women and young girls of the place had taken refuge. The soldiers rushed upon them, stripped them, committed the most shocking outrages upon them, and then some were thrown down from the steeple; others were taken away to be still further abused. Pregnant women might be seen with their bellies ripped up, and the bloody fruit of their womb fallen from them. Mutilated bodies, still breathing, lay scattered before the porch. The advocate Guèrin, who was present there, said in his deposition, "I think I saw four or five hundred poor souls of women and children killed in that church."

The prisoners who were not put to death by order of the president, were sold by the soldiers to those who recruited for the royal galleys. However, the vice-legate would not suffer any quarter to be given. Such was the spirit of Popery in its most exalted representatives. This legate also, having learned that twenty-five persons, the greater part of whom were mothers of families, were concealed in a cave towards Mys, although it was not within the boundary of the papal territories, marched thither with soldiers to destroy them. Arriving at the entrance of the cave, he gave orders for discharges of musketry, but no one came out. Thereupon he caused a great fire to be kindled in the mouth of the cave, and every living creature in it was stifled to death. Five years after their dried bones were still to be seen, as was ascertained in those judicial investigations of which we are presently to speak. The general results of these investigations, which may here be stated, were, that in this extermination 763 inhabited houses, eighty-nine stables, and thirty-one barns were burned. As to the number of the slain, it could not be ascertained with precision, but it was estimated at more than 3000.

Whilst he was still at Cabrières, D'Oppède received a message from the Seigneur of La Coste, praying him to spare his vassals. This was on Monday evening. "Let them make four breaches in their walls," replied D'Oppède, "and then we shall see." On Tuesday morning the breaches were commenced. Two officers, with a few soldiers, arrived. The Seigneur of La Coste offered them a refreshment before the gate of the castle. Two domestics served it. The soldiers sat down to eat, and whilst they eat there arrived, with a great sound of drums and trumpets, the bulk of the forces of Menier D'Oppède, marching as to an assault. The inhabitants of the little town were alarmed, closed the gates, and interrupted the making of the breaches, which had been commenced. The soldiers scattered themselves through the gardens of the castle, which were on the outside of the walls of the town, tore up the plants, cut down the fruit-trees, burned the arbours, and dragged about over the parterres, which they had covered with ruin and confusion, their prisoners, whom they cruelly maltreated. Within the walls the soldiers who had got admission killed the two domestics who served them.

Next day, being Wednesday, the 22d of April, D'Oppède wrote to the syndics of La Coste to persuade them to open the gates of the town, promising justice and protection. The gates were opened, and that instant the furious soldiery rushed into the streets, destroying, plundering, ravishing, massacring, and burning in all directions. A little warren lay behind the castle. Thither the soldiers dragged the captives whom they seized, to deprive them of their honour before depriving them of their life. Mothers attempted to defend their daughters, and to save them from the perpetrators of these brutalities. One, seeing the fruitlessness of her efforts, pierced her bosom with a knife, and held it out bleeding to her daughter, that she might stab herself with it also. "Oh! I am overcome with all these horrors," exclaims the king's advocate, who pleaded in the *evocation* of this affair before the court of Peers. " Spare me from speaking of the wretches who flung themselves from the top of the walls, or hanged themselves upon the trees, or stabbed themselves, the victims trodden under foot, or wandering about and dying of famine, or torn by the ravens, or seized and killed, or sold and sent to the galleys."[1] The very cattle of these poor people perished for want of shelter, for it was forbidden to harbour a Vaudois, or anything that had appertained to them. A poor woman, ready to die of hunger, asked a morsel of bread at the door of a farm-house. "It is forbidden," they said. "If men forbid you, God commands you," cried she. But that cry did not save her, and the Church of Rome was able to reckon one triumph more.

What, then, became of such of these unfortunate Vaudois as succeeded in making their escape from present death? Assembled upon the wild brows of Leberon, they prayed God to enlighten their enemies, and entreated from him the strength which they needed, that they might not be tempted, in consequence of their misery and their calamities, to abandon their faith or to adopt any evil course. Their calamities were not yet, however, at an end, for after the regular troops came the marauders. The inhabitants of the village of Les Jourdains scoured the country with flags flying, and returned to their homes with mules laden with booty. Those of Puypin rifled their own churches, hoping that this spoliation might be laid to the charge of the Vaudois. Those of Mount Furon killed or sold some wandering children, whom they contrived to seize. Those of Garambois murdered an old man in a cistern. In short, there was nothing but violence, spoliation, and death everywhere. The country-house of Cantal, which was then the most beautiful in Provence, was burned.

The lady of that place, as guardian of her son, whose lands had been ravaged, addressed a complaint to the king. This complaint was brought before the second tribunal of the kingdom, called the Queen's Chamber. The parties concerned in these ravages were cited to appear before this court, but they refused, sheltering themselves behind the authority of the decrees, in virtue of which they pretended to have acted. It became necessary to revert to the decrees themselves, and to examine them; but for this the Queen's

---

[1] . . . . *Viros et morte peremptos,*
Indigna : raptasque, soluto crine, puellas ;
Et late miseris subjecta incendia vicis.

The Chancellor Michel De L'Hôpital. *Epist. ad Franc. Olivarium* . . . *de causa Merindolii* . . . &c.

Chamber was not competent, and the case was carried before the supreme tribunal of the kingdom, called the King's Chamber, afterwards called the Court of Peers. Thus it came to pass that all these acts of iniquity and barbarity were inquired into by judicial investigations, the records of which place them all in a clear light, though to those who have not consulted them the connection of events is sufficiently obscure.

This case was tried in September, 1551, during the reign of Henry II., who sought to cleanse away this stain of blood from the memory of his father. Nevertheless, the most guilty were not punished; the advocate Guérin alone was condemned to death, and D'Oppède returned in triumph to Provence. But we may form some notion of all the intrigues which the clergy must have put in operation to save him, from the fact that on the news of his acquittal hymns of thanksgiving were sung in the churches.

Public prayers were made in Provence to ask of God the preservation and speedy return of this illustrious defender of the faith! "Truth prevails over all." This maxim of history condemns him now. Its tribunal, superior even to that of the Court of Peers, is not accessible, like the tribunals of men, to the corrupting influences of the mighty, whom it judges even in their graves.

Those of the Vaudois who survived retired into the valleys of Piedmont, and afterwards returned to Provence when the storm was past. The revocation of the Edict of Nantes overthrew once more the places of worship which they had rebuilt upon the banks of the Durance. Under the deplorable reign of Louis XV. the vexatious treatment of the Protestants was continued in a more hypocritical and more undignified manner. At the present day Protestantism flourishes again on the desolated slopes of the Leberon, but religious indifference has wrought greater ravages amongst souls than the persecutions of former times. The inhabitants of these regions scarcely know their history. May the remembrance of their ancestors, recalled in these pages, lead them to an imitation of them! That Bible which made them so great, even in adversity, can alone restore the Vaudois character to these churches, which have forgotten their very origin, and lost even the dignity of misfortune.

CHAPTER VI.

THE VAUDOIS IN CALABRIA.[1]

(A.D. 1400 TO A.D. 1560.)

Settlement of the Vaudois in Calabria—Montalto, St. Xist, and other places founded by them—La Guardia—Correspondence maintained between the Vaudois of Calabria and those of the Alps—John Louis Paschal appointed pastor—Commencement of persecution in 1559—Sufferings of Paschal and of Mark Uscégli—Paschal conveyed to Rome—Attempts to induce him to recant—His martyrdom—Cardinal Alexandrini in Calabria—Falsehood and cruelty—Slaughter of the Vaudois of St. Xist and La Guardia—Fearful massacres and atrocities—Escape of a small remnant of the Calabrian Vaudois to Piedmont—Protestantism extinguished in Calabria.

It has been already mentioned that the Vaudois had also churches in Calabria. The following is the account which Rorengo gives of their emigration thither.

Two young men of the Vaudois valleys happened one day to be in Turin, in a hostelry, to which also a Calabrian nobleman came to lodge. The young men talked about their affairs, and the desire which they felt of going and settling somewhere out of their own country, where the cultivation of the soil began to be insufficient for the wants of the population. The stranger said to them, "My friends, if you choose to come with me, I will give you delightful plains instead of your rocks." The young Vaudois accepted his offer, on condition of their obtaining the consent of their families, which they went to ask, and in the hope that they might not be the only ones to accept this offer, but that others of their fellow-countrymen would accompany them.

The people of the valleys did not think it proper to come to any determination before acquainting themselves with the places in which it was proposed to establish them. For this purpose they sent commissioners into Calabria, accompanied by the two young men to whom the lord of the place had offered land.

"In that country," says Gilles, "there were beautiful streams

---

[1] AUTHORITIES.—*Perrin, Gilles, Léger.*—*M'Crie, "History of the Progress and Suppression of the Reformation in Italy, in the 16th century"* (translated). Paris, 1831, 8vo, p. 290.—*Meille, "Les Vaudois en Calabre au XIVe S."* In the *Revue Suisse*, ii. p. 647-658, and 687-709.—*Thomaso Costa, "Seconda parte del compendio del l'istoria di Napoli,"* p. 257.—*A Porta, "Historia Reformationis Ecclesiæ Rheticæ,"* ii. 210, 310.—*Partaleon, "Rerum in ecclesia gestarum historia,"* p. 337. —*Giannone, " Hist. gén. du roy. de Naples."*—*Hondorff, " Theatrum histor.,"* &c. *Rorengo, Crespin,* &c.

(Still unconsulted.—Archives of Cosenza, of Naples, and of the Inquisition at Rome.)

and little hills, clothed with all sorts of fruit-trees growing promiscuously, according to the soil which they affected, such as olive and orange trees. In the plains were vines and chestnuts; along the lower hills, walnuts, oaks, beeches, and other hardwood trees; on the slopes and crests of the mountains, larches and firs. Everywhere were to be seen in abundance lands fit for cultivation, with few to cultivate them."

In the Vaudois valleys of Piedmont, on the contrary, there were more labourers than there were fields for them to cultivate; they were like a bee-hive which has become too small through the prosperity and increase of its population. Emigration was therefore soon resolved upon, and a new swarm of these heaven-blessed and flourishing families prepared to transport to a distance their industrious habits and pure manners, indicative throughout of the spirit of the first times of the gospel.

The young people who were to go made haste to marry; those who had properties sold all; and every one put his affairs in order. It must have been in the year 1340 that this took place;[1] and never before had these peaceful valleys known so general a movement, an agitation so great and so profound, extending everywhere amongst their families. The festivities which celebrated their domestic alliances were mingled with the grief of separations. More than one nuptial procession was changed into the caravan of exile. They could say, indeed, like the Hebrews, setting out for the promised land, "The tabernacle of the Lord shall go before us," for they bore with them their hereditary Bible, the gospel of consolation and of courage, that holy ark of the new covenant and of peace of heart. Yet the old men, and still more the poor mothers, must have wept many tears on beholding the departure, for an unknown region, of those youth in whom were centred all the earthly hopes of their declining days. Accordingly, the whole Vaudois family accompanied the first steps of this young colony on its departure. At the base of their mountains they embraced and wept, praying together to the God of their fathers to bless them always, both the one portion and the other, at the two extremities of Italy.

Thereafter the emigrants moved away in silence from their native country, and most of them never to return to it again. They took twenty-five days to reach Calabria, not accomplishing their journey without many privations, and perhaps regretful longings after their native land, becoming dearer to them the farther that they removed from it. But they bore a part of their country along with them, as they were entirely surrounded with fellow-countrymen and with

---

[1] Compare, as to this date, Perrin, p. 196, and Gilles, p. 19, lines 10 and 24.

familiar objects; above all, they bore with them in their hearts that confidence in the Almighty which is better than country or home.

Having arrived at the places which they were to inhabit, they agreed upon the conditions of their settlement. The lords of the soil granted them very favourable conditions. According to the terms agreed upon, the Vaudois were bound only to pay a certain quit-rent to the owners, and upon this were left at liberty to manage their agricultural labours according to their own pleasure. The right was granted to them of combining themselves in one or more independent communities, of naming their own rulers, both civil or ecclesiastical, and, finally, of imposing rates and collecting them without being bound to demand any authorization, or to render any account of what they did. These conditions, thus arranged, became a sort of charter to the Vaudois in this new country.

Thus was there secured to them an amount of liberty very great for that period; and their sense of its value is proved by the fact, that they caused these conditions to be drawn out in an authentic instrument, which at a later period was confirmed by the King of Naples, Ferdinand of Arragon.

The first little town founded by these new colonists was situated near the town of Montalto; and as the inhabitants had passed, in order to settle in it, over the mountains which separate that region from Upper Italy, the place of their residence was called Borgo d'Oltramontani, the town of Outremont, or town of the Ultramontanes. Half-a-century later, they built St. Xist, which became afterwards the capital of that colony. During the interval, and after the foundations of these towns were laid, the hamlets of Vacarrisso, L'Argentine, St. Vincent, Les Rousses, and Montolieu sprung up, the names being in general merely those of the places where they were built. These numerous villages attest the increasing prosperity of a country previously almost without inhabitants.

It is, indeed, remarkable what a civilizing influence the gospel possesses, diffusing blessings amongst the people everywhere, in proportion to the purity in which it is received. The Vaudois churches, so flourishing in the midst of a land filled with superstition and wretchedness, presented then the same contrast which is still remarked in our own days between Protestant and Catholic countries. Let men draw what inference they may, it is indisputable that Brazil, where the Church of Rome is absolute, is very inferior in enlightenment, in morality, and in prosperity, to the United States of North America, where Protestantism has diffused so much of liberty and life. In Europe, what a difference betwixt Spain, the country of inquisitors, and Germany, the country of the Reformation; betwixt Catholic Ireland and Protestant Scotland! France itself has only improved in its condition as Catholicism has lost power. And under the sky of Italy, in these fertile regions of Calabria, at the period to which our history relates, the industrious and united Vaudois made the striking contrast to appear for the first time.

Peacefully enjoying the privileges which they had obtained, faithful in the payment of their taxes and their tithes, and satisfied to abide within the restricted circle of their own beliefs and affections, they might have been supposed to be reserved for the happiest destinies. Yes! God gave them, indeed, all the means of quiet happiness, but Rome took them away. The Marquis of Spinello, struck with the improvements which they had introduced in the lands intrusted to them, invited them to his estates likewise. He authorized them to surround with walls the town which they built. This town was, for this reason, called La Guardia, as being appointed to perform the principal part in *guarding* their country.

Towards the end of the 14th century, their brethren of Provence being persecuted, many of them returned to the valleys from which their fathers had emigrated; but finding them too densely peopled to be able to accommodate new inhabitants, and some even of their own inhabitants desiring also to leave their native land, they formed together a new emigration, descending again into Italy, and settling on the frontiers of Apulia, not far from their Calabrian brethren. The villages which owed their origin to these new colonists, were all surrounded with walls, and were called by the same names with those which their inhabitants had left. There was a *La Cellaie*, after a place in the valley of Angrogna; a *Faët*, after a place in the valley of St. Martin; a *La Motte*, after a place at the base of the Leberon, near Cabrières d'Aigues, in Provence.

Even in A.D. 1500, some Vaudois left Freyssinières and Pragela, to settle in Calabria. They fixed their residence upon the banks of a little river, called the Volturate, which flows from the Apennines into the sea of Tarentum. Latterly, says Gilles, they extended themselves into divers other parts of the kingdom of Naples, and even into Sicily.

It is evident that the blessing of God rested upon these Vaudois colonies in their prosperity; and not only agriculture, but the sciences flourished among them; for Barlaam of Calabria, of whom Petrarch was the disciple, was himself, according to some writers, a disciple of the Vaudois. Sprung from all parts of the Alps where their brethren dwelt, they formed amongst themselves a representation of the whole Vaudois nation. We may therefore imagine what satisfaction they must have felt in that country, in which they found, as it were, all their native countries brought together. Moreover, they frequently received visits from pastors of the valleys. The Vaudois Synod renewed the appointments for this purpose every two years. Each of these pastors was accompanied by a fellow-labourer younger than himself, and after two years' sojourn amongst their brethren of these churches, they returned to the mother church; for the Vaudois Church did not act upon the principle of assigning the same field of labour to its pastors for the whole period of their ministry.

But they did not take the same road, in their return to the valleys, which they had followed in going to Calabria. If they had gone by the right of the Apennines, by Genoa and Naples, they returned by the left, along the coasts of the Adriatic. This change of route was not without design;[1] for in almost all the cities of Italy, as in Genoa, Venice, Florence, and even Rome itself, they had brethren, and a private house in which they met. It was not until they had accomplished this evangelistic pilgrimage, of which the last station was Milan, that the missionary pastors returned to their own country. It must have been an occasion of great Christian joy for these poor isolated souls, whose secret sympathies made them look so eagerly for the coming of their pastors, when a preconcerted signal by the stranger who knocked at their door, made him known as the missionary from the Alps, whom the Vaudois Church sent to them once every two years.

Conducted with every demonstration of kindness into the hospitable abode, where the recollection of the Barbas who had preceded him was preserved as a family treasure, from generation to generation, he found that abode his own, and that family his flock; a small flock no doubt, but under the care of the Good Shepherd. The faithful minister carried with him his commission in the gospel, which he was always ready to exhibit. How eagerly they must have pressed around him, and questioned him regarding the churches which he had visited in his journey, the brethren with whom he had met, and the Barba who had been with them two years before![2] Frequently the replies communicated melancholy news, and then they prayed together, and meditated on the Sacred Books. The man of God, a stranger and a pilgrim on the earth, received, according to the custom of the ancient Vaudois and of

---

[1] Gilles, p. 20.   [2] Meille, *Rev. Suisse*, ii. 653.

the primitive church, the evangelical confession of these humble believers, and then parted from them to go on his way, and to seek other hidden ones whom he was to comfort and confirm. Gilles relates that his grandfather, upon a visit which he made to the faithful in Venice, was assured by themselves that they were about 6000 in number.[1]

But all improvement, however slight, which purifies the heart, elevates also the mind, and developes the understanding. This we have already seen illustrated in the way in which the Vaudois distinguished themselves, as the first to make use of their common language for the composition of verse—that beautiful Romance language, which was extinguished in the blood of the Albigenses, and with which a literature full of promise, and a civilization that might have proved important for the world, irrecoverably perished. In Calabria, likewise, attention was drawn to the Vaudois by the enlightenment which distinguished them in an age of darkness; and when the Reformation had broken out, the Church of Rome, becoming more observant of religious movements—whilst these, on the other hand, acquired a greater strength—could not but fix her eyes upon those Protestant churches which had preceded Protestantism, those primitive churches which had survived the apostolic times. Their existence was their condemnation: they must needs be utterly destroyed.

Already, at different times, says Perrin,[2] "the clerical race had made complaint that these ultramontanes did not live religiously, like other people; but the seigneurs restrained the curés, saying that these cultivators of the soil came from distant and unknown regions, where, perchance, the people were not so much addicted to the ceremonies of the church; but that in the main they were remarkable for honesty, charitable towards the poor, punctual in paying their rents, and full of the fear of God; that therefore there was no reason why their consciences should be troubled about a few processions, images, or lights, which they had less than the other people of the country." This restrained those who looked upon them with ill-will, and prevented for a time the murmurs of their neighbours, who, not having been able to draw them into alliances by intermarriage, became jealous when they saw their lands, their cattle, and their labours, more blessed of Heaven than their own. Thus they remained in liberty, prospering as the people of God, even in the land of bondage. The priests themselves, says Meille, had never levied such large tithes as since the Vaudois had come to make the country more productive. To drive

---

[1] Gilles, p. 20.   [2] P. 197.

them away would have been to render themselves poor, and they held their peace.

However, the Calabrian brethren came to know that their fellow-Vaudois of the Piedmontese valleys, yielding to the counsels of the Reformers, had erected places of worship, instead of the private houses in which they had previously been accustomed to assemble; and they thought it their duty also to make an outward manifestation of their existence as an evanglical church. "But the Barba who was then with them, an aged and prudent man," says the historian Gilles, whose great-grandfather he was, "represented to them that zeal must be contented without always pushing things to the uttermost; for it was necessary for them to consider if, in their circumstances, they were able to act as freely as their brethren of the Val Lucerna, and to make themselves as conspicuous, without endangering the destruction of their churches. In short, he counselled them to bend to the times, and even secretly to put their affairs in order, so that they might retire to a place of safety in the moment of peril." "Some," adds the chronicler, "followed his counsel, and were saved; others, who thought it judicious, proceeded, but slowly, to act upon it, and in this way many lost their lives; but the majority did nothing, either because they were too much attached to that country to be able to make up their minds to quit it, or because they had too much confidence in God to entertain any fear." In the meantime, the Barba Stephen Négrin, of Bobi, in the valley of Lucerna, succeeded the aged Barba Gilles, who returned to his native country.

But the Calabrians wished to have a settled pastor, who should not quit them. For this purpose they sent to Geneva one of their number, named Mark Uscegli, and familiarly know by the name of Marquet, one of those endearing names of childhood, which are sometimes retained in later life. He was commissioned to solicit from the Italian Church which then existed there, the means of having a minister in Calabria, who should reside amongst his brethren of that country, and devote himself entirely to them. His request was granted; and to this honourable but perilous post a minister, still very young, was nominated, himself also a Piedmontese, who had quitted the profession of arms to become a soldier of Christ, and who had prepared for the ministry of the gospel by a course of study recently terminated at Lausanne.

The name of this young man was John Louis Paschal; he was born at Coni, and two days before his being selected to be sent into Calabria, he had been betrothed to a young woman of his own nation, Camilla Guarina, born like himself in Piedmont, and who like himself had fled to Geneva, in order to live according to the gospel. When he made known to her the call which he had received, and asked her consent to leave her and go into Calabria, the poor girl could only answer him with tears. "Alas!" she exclaimed, "so near to Rome, and so far from me!" But she was a Christian, and she submitted.

Paschal set forth, accompanied by Uscegli, by another pastor, and by two schoolmasters also destined for the Vaudois. The name of this second pastor was Jacob Bovet; he also was from Piedmont, and he suffered martyrdom at Messina, in 1560. These two friends, natives of the same country, brethren in faith, in devotedness, and in courage, were not to be separated, even in death.

Scarcely had Paschal arrived in Calabria, when he began to preach the gospel in public, as was done at Geneva, the Vaudois desiring it, and his own zeal urging him so to do. "Thereupon," says Crespin, "there arose a great noise in these countries, that a Lutheran had come and was destroying everything by his doctrines. The ignorant murmured, the fanatical exclaimed that he must be put to death with all his adherents. The Vaudois alone pressed around him with the joyous affection of brethren, and always hungering the more for the word of life, the more that he multiplied it to them, like the bread broken by the Lord. Thereupon the Marquis Salvator Spinello, principal feudal lord of the Vaudois, who at that time happened to be at Foscalda, a little town near La Guardia and St. Xist, sent to ask the attendance of some of the inhabitants of these towns, that they might explain matters to him. The Vaudois thus summoned, entreated their minister, Paschal, to accompany them, and to state their reasons for the course which they had pursued." This was in the month of July, 1559.

Mark Uscegli went along with them, and when they had arrived at Foscalda they went into a hostelry before going to appear before the marquis. There a secret friend of their doctrines, who was one of that nobleman's own household, came to request a conversation with them. "Listen to me," said he; "you have powerful enemies; the best defence of the feeble is to keep out of their way; I advise you therefore to go back without presenting yourselves." "What!" exclaimed Paschal, "shall I skulk away without defending myself, without contending for the truth, without pleading for my beloved church!" "The only object of pleading is to gain a cause," replied the prudent adviser; "in this instance it can only be gained by keeping silence." "That would not only be feeble, but shameful," rejoined the young minister, breaking out in holy ardour; "the Christian is not to measure his strength, but to do his duty.

Moreover," added he, "the help of God cannot fail us in this conflict; where is there more strength than in his word?" "Its strength goes for nothing with those who do not listen to it. Take heed! you will not be judged according to the word of God, but according to that of men." "What then!" replied the courageous pastor, "the honour of defending the word of God is better than that of triumphing over men." "You will defend it better by preaching it to your churches, which desire it, than by exposing it to the contempt of those who wish to suppress it." "But it is my churches themselves which are called to account, and their pastor ought to be there." Besides all this, Paschal felt so profoundly convinced, so assured, so strong in the excellence of his cause, that he did not despair of being able to make it good, even before the most prejudiced minds. One soul brought captive to the foot of the Saviour's cross was of more value, in the estimation of the pastor, than all earthly good. The secret emissary, who came to give this warning of human wisdom, retired discomfited before this holy foolishness of the cross. The Vaudois presented themselves accordingly before the Marquis of Spinello, accompanied by their young and ardent defender.

But he had not to contend, as he expected, in an honest contest, by reasons and gospel statements, against errors sincerely held. His enemies desired not truth but silence; they wished not to destroy error, but the protests which were made against it. Poor Paschal, therefore, had the grief of being at once deprived of the friends whom he already had, and of the adversaries whom he expected to find. The marquis, after having heard him for some moments, during which the Vaudois kept silence, sent them away, whom alone he had cited, and retained Louis Paschal and Mark Uscegli as prisoners, who came to defend them. They remained for eight months in the prisons of Foscalda; to youth and mental activity an anticipation of the tomb! But the tomb is the gate of heaven to redeemed souls, and celestial consolations cheered the two young Christians in their dungeon.

After this long period of trial they were removed to the prisons of Cosenza, where it would seem that Mark Uscegli was subjected to torture, for we read these words in a letter of Paschal, written on the 10th of March, 1560, "God has preserved me alone from the torture." Alas! it was only to reserve him for martyrdom.

"My companion, Marquet," says he, in another place, "was solicited by the Count D'Acillo to recant, and as he particularly put forward the authority of the pope to pardon all sin, Marquet said, 'If the pope had had the power of pardoning sins, it would have been needless for Jesus Christ to have come and died for sinners.'"

A Spaniard, who was present, exclaimed, "What! a clown, that can neither read nor write, will meddle and dispute!" "We have nothing to do with disputations," said an auditor of the Holy Office, who was also there, "but to know if thou wilt abjure, ay or no." "No," replied Uscegli. "Ah, well then, it goes the devil's way!" replied the auditor, and signed himself four times with the sign of the cross. From this moment we hear nothing more of poor Marquet; and it makes one's eyes fill with tears to find that infantile diminutive applied, at the close of his torture, to the young man whom his mother had so called amidst the caresses which she lavished upon his childhood.

In the month of April, Paschal was conducted from Cosenza to Naples, along with twenty-two prisoners condemned to the galleys, and three companions, whom he does not name. "The person who was appointed to conduct us," says he, in a letter addressed to his afflicted bride, "put on me manacles so tight that I could not repose either by day or by night. I was obliged to bribe him to open them a little, and he did not take them off till he had succeeded in getting from me all the money which I possessed. The galley slaves were fastened by the neck to a long chain; they got nothing but coarse herbs for their food, with a slice of bread, and when one of them fell down from inanition and fatigue, they forced him to rise again by beating him unmercifully." Is it possible that sinful men can so treat their brethren? But the despotic and merciless spirit of Rome would transform brethren into executioners. "During the night," continues the prisoner, "the beasts were better treated than we, for at least they gave them litter, whilst, as for us, we were left on the bare ground."[1] Nine days were spent in this way ere they arrived at Naples, and in the bark which conveyed them thither he ceased not to preach and exhort, proclaiming the fulness and the necessity of the salvation which is by Jesus Christ. It is evident that he was one whom menaces and maltreatment could not intimidate.

Paschal was brought to Cosenza on the 7th of February; he left it on the 14th of April. He entered the prisons of Naples on the 23d of that month, and was transferred to those of Rome on the 16th of May, 1560. There this fervent and zealous disciple of Christ arrived with irons on his feet and hands! But consider how Christ endured such contradiction of sinners against himself, and remember that thus they persecuted the prophets which were before

[1] Letter of Paschal, in Crespin, fol. 514.

you. Blessed, without doubt, must this new apostle of the Gentiles be deemed, imprisoned, like St. Paul and St. Peter, in that great city of Rome, which has always aimed at reigning over the earth. "Blessed are they that are persecuted for righteousness' sake, for theirs is the kingdom of heaven."[1]

He entered the city by the Gate of Ostium, the same by which also the apostles and primitive martyrs were conducted into it. Fourteen centuries had passed, and the same scenes were to be renewed again in the name of the idols of Popery, more bloody than those of the Gentiles. Paschal was imprisoned in the Tower of *Nona*, where very few, says Crespin, were permitted to see him. Already dead as to his connection with the world, nothing can be known of the proceedings with regard to him, save only that he was frequently interrogated and urged to recant, but without effect.

His brother, Bartholemew Paschal, who had neither abjured Roman Catholicism nor the brotherly affection of the carnal heart, resolved to make an attempt to save him, or at least to see him again. Determining to undertake a journey to Rome for this purpose, he set out from Coni, with a recommendation from the governor of that city, and a letter from the Count de la Trinité, whose name has so melancholy a celebrity in the annals of the Vaudois valleys, where we shall presently see that he conducted an atrocious persecution. In consequence of these introductions from persons so powerful, and so high in credit at the papal court, and perhaps, also, because it was hoped that his influence might lead his brother to abjure, Bartholemew Paschal succeeded in making his way to the gloomy and fetid dungeon where John Louis was confined.

"I went last evening," he wrote to his family, "to pay my respects to the Grand Inquisitor of the faith, the Cardinal Alexandrini, but when I spoke to him of my brother, he replied sharply, that that fellow had been a great pest in the country, and that even in the bark he had done nothing but preach his nonsense." Is not this the very way in which the pagan inquisitors of former times must have spoken of St. Paul? "I then went," he says, "to speak to the judges who examined him. They told me that he became always more and more obstinate, and that his was a bad business. I entreated them in his favour, and they replied that for any other crime, however enormous, pardon might have been possible, but that for having attacked the Church, at least unless he recanted, there could be no pardon." Was this indeed the church of Him who pardoned his executioners? "Then," continues Bartholemew Paschal, "I returned to seek the cardinal, and at last I obtained

[1] Matt. v. 10.

leave to visit my brother. Great God!" he exclaims, "it was frightful to see him amidst the gloom of these damp walls, meagre, pale, enfeebled, bareheaded, his arms tied with small ropes, which went into the flesh, ill of fever, and not even having straw to lie upon."

"Do good even to your enemies," said Jesus and the apostles.

"But," continues the letter of Bartholemew, "desiring to embrace him, I cast myself down upon the ground, and he said to me, 'My brother, why do you distress yourself so much? Know you not that a leaf cannot fall from a tree without the will of God?' The judge who accompanied me imposed silence upon him, saying, 'Hold your peace, you heretic!' And I added, 'Is it possible, my brother, that you are obstinate in disowning the Catholic faith, which everybody else holds?' 'I hold that of the gospel,' he replied. 'Think you, then,' said the judge, 'that God will condemn all those who do not follow the doctrine of Luther and Calvin?' 'It is not for me to determine,' replied he, 'but I know that he will condemn those who, knowing the truth, do not profess it.' 'You speak of truth—you disseminate errors.' 'Prove me that by the gospel.' But the judge, instead of answering his question, said to him, 'You would have done far better to have remained still in your own house, enjoying your inheritance, and dwelling among your brethren, instead of rushing into heresy and losing all that you had.' 'I have nothing to lose upon the earth,' he replied, 'that I must not lose sooner or later, and I acquire an inheritance in heaven, which all the powers of the earth shall not be able to take from me.'"

Is not this still the language of the primitive Christians, and of their idolatrous persecutors, who only lived for the good things of this world?

During three whole days, successive members of the Holy Office dealt with Paschal, for more than four hours at each time, in the hope of inducing him to recant, and perhaps, also, of being able then to give him up to his brother; but they could get no concession. "Then," resumes Bartholemew, "I entreated him to yield a little, and not to bring upon his family the disgrace of a condemnation. 'Must I honour my Saviour less than them, that I am to become perjured to him?' 'You will honour him in your heart, although you remain in the Church.' 'If I am ashamed of him on the earth, he will deny me in heaven.' 'Ah! my dear brother, return to the bosom of your family, we would all be so happy to have you there.' 'Would to God that we were all met again, united in the Saviour's love! for my native skies would be pleasanter to me than the vaults of this prison. But if I remain here, it is because Jesus abides with me, and my Saviour is better to me than my family.' 'Would it be to lose him, to come with us?' 'Yes; for the gate of my dungeon will not open except by means of an abjuration, and that would be the loss of my soul.' 'Your friends, then, are nothing to you?' 'Jesus says, he that is not ready to give up his father or his mother for my sake, is not worthy of me.' Then," says Bartholemew, "I went the length of promising him the half of all that I had, if he would come back with me to Coni; but he, with tears, answered me that to hear me utter such words afflicted him much more grievously than the fetters with which he was bound: 'for' said he, 'the world passeth away, with the lusts thereof, but the word of God endureth for ever.' And when I wept also, he added, 'God grant me such strength that I may never forsake him!' Then the monk said to him, 'If you will die, die then!'"

We see, in these three personages, the regenerate man, whose soul speaks according to the Spirit of God; the natural man, full of regard for the things of this world, of which he knows the value, and yet also full of kindly affection; and, finally, the man besotted by superstition, such as Rome has made him, ignoble and cruel, interrupting the intercourse of soul and heart, the conversation between the martyr and his brother, by such gross invectives as have now been related.

"Three days after," the brother of John Louis Paschal continues, "I found means to speak with him again, and when the monk was proceeding to exhort him anew, he said to him, 'All your arguments are founded upon human prudence, but do not shut your eyes to the grace of God, for you will be inexcusable before him.' 'The monk was very much astonished, and said 'God have mercy on us!' 'O, that he may!' added the prisoner. But the day following, without uttering a word, he made a sign to me that I should begone, having perceived that the inquisitors had begun to suspect me; and so I left him without speaking, and returned to Piedmont."

Here we have still the natural man, timid, because he has no strength but his own, in contrast with the Christian, invincible, because he confides in the strength of Christ.

Now thou art alone, then, poor Paschal! buried alive in the bowels of the earth, waiting to be consumed alive by the fire! But the best of fathers, of brothers, and of friends is still ever with thee!

"The affection which I bear to you," he writes to his bride, "increases with the increase of my love to God; and the more that I have made progress in the Christian religion, the more also have I loved you." Then, giving her to understand that his death might soon be expected, he says, "Console yourself in Jesus Christ; and let your life be an exhibition of his doctrine." Such were the exhortations which Paschal addressed to Camilla Guarina, who was to mourn him as his widow, without having become his wife.

On Sabbath, the 8th of September, 1560, he was conducted from the tower *Di Nona* to the convent *Della Minerva*, there to hear his condemnation. "He confirmed, with a steadfast and joyful heart," says Crespin, "all the answers which he had already given, rendering thanks to God for having called him to the glory of martyrdom; and next day, being Monday, the 9th of September, he was conducted to the square of the castle of St. Angelo, near the bridge over the Tiber, where the pile had been prepared." Pope Pius IV. was present at this execution; "but," observes Perrin, "he would have been glad to have been elsewhere, or that Paschal had been dumb, or the people deaf; for that worthy man spake many things which moved the spectators and displeased him much." Upon this account the inquisitors caused him to be presently strangled, fearing, perhaps, that his voice might still be raised in midst of the flames to proclaim the truth. The flames, therefore, only consumed his corpse, and his ashes were cast into the Tiber.

Thus died this courageous martyr, removed from his consort before having married her, and from his congregation before having resided among them, but not removed from the profession of the Christian faith without having done it service; for his example itself was of more value than all the sermons which he could have preached throughout the course of his life.

During his captivity, the Marquis of Spinello, who had ever previously shown himself the zealous protector of the Vaudois, in consequence no doubt of the solid advantage which he derived from their rents, being apprised of the severity of the court of Rome, and fearing, not without cause, that it might be extended to the lands which owned him as their feudal superior, thought proper at least to prevent the consequences of the accusation which was already brought against him, of having introduced and favoured heretics. Perhaps he might also hope, by coming forward against them, to keep in his own hands the means of affording them more efficacious protection. Be this as it might, he himself accused them of heresy, and demanded from the Holy Office the means of bringing them to submission. "However, it was well known," says Gilles, "that in secret he desired their preservation. Upon this," continues he, "the Bishop of Cosenza applied himself to that business; and the marquis, under the guise of assisting him, always contrived to effect some mitigation of his measures."[1]

But the proceedings of Paschal and his companions having made known at Rome the importance of the evangelical churches of Calabria, the Holy Office deemed it not too much to send thither the Grand Inquisitor himself. Cardinal Alexandrini, fresh from the execution of the young and courageous pastor of these ancient churches, which he also had witnessed, prepared therefore to visit them. He arrived at St. Xist, accompanied by two Dominican monks, who put on an aspect of the greatest affability, like the wolves in sheeps' clothing of whom the gospel speaks. They caused the inhabitants to be assembled, and said that their intention was to do no harm to anybody (by and by they slaughtered every one); that they were come only to bring them in an amicable way to cease listening any longer to any ministers but those sent by the bishop; and that if they would dismiss the Lutheran schoolmasters and preachers by whom the neighbourhood was still infested, they would have nothing to fear. And then, no doubt, in order to obtain evidence for themselves as to the number who had a regard for the rites of the Church of Rome, they caused the bell to ring for mass, and summoned the people to attend it. No one came. All the inhabitants with one consent left the town, and retired into a wood, leaving in their houses only a small number of children and of aged persons. The monks, without appearing to feel at all irritated, went through the mass by themselves; then, leaving that deserted town, they proceeded to La Guardia, of which they took the precaution to close the gates behind them.

The bells were rung; the people assembled. "Most dear and beloved Christian brethren," said the monks, "your brethren of St. Xist have abjured their errors, and unanimously attended at the most holy mass; we invite you to follow so wise an example; otherwise we shall be obliged, with great sorrow, to condemn you to death." This treacherous language left no room for hesitation between the two alternatives; the people, filled with alarm, thought it best to follow the example of their brethren, who, of course, had acted without constraint, and submitted to hear mass. After this ceremony the gates of the town were opened. Some of the people of St. Xist arrived, and the truth was discovered. Immediately the whole population of La Guardia, indignant at such treachery, and ashamed of their own weakness, assembled again in the public square, crying from all sides that Rome lived only by errors and

[1] Gilles, p. 178.

superstitions. The monks endeavoured to calm the irritated people, who, in order to avoid hearing them any longer, resolved to go and join in the woods their neighbours of St. Xist. But the Marquis of Spinello arrived, and endeavoured to restrain them; and with difficulty, says M'Crie, by his representations and promises, succeeded in preventing them from carrying their design into execution. Thus already were the Vaudois divided, part in the town, and part in the woods.

The Grand Inquisitor, in virtue of the powers with which he was invested, now required the aid of the military to execute his commission. Two companies of soldiers were placed at his disposal. He sent them into the woods of St. Xist to bring back the fugitives; but scarcely had they discovered their retreat, when they fell upon them, crying, "Kill! kill!" The unfortunate Vaudois tried to make their escape; the soldiers pursued them in all directions, as if they were engaged in the destruction of wild beasts. At last some of the fugitives gathered upon a mountain, and demanded a parley. The captain of the soldiers advanced. "Spare us!" they exclaimed, "spare us! what harm have we done you? Have pity on our wives and children! Have we not been here for centuries, without having given any cause of complaint? Are we not loyal subjects, industrious labourers, and peaceable well-doing people?" "You are devils, transformed into angels of light, to seduce the simple," was the reply, "but the Holy Office has unmasked your errors." "Well, then," said they, "if we may not be permitted to profess the faith of our forefathers in peace, in these countries which we have rendered fertile, we offer to leave them, and to retire into another country." "You will go to sow there the poison of your heresy. No mercy for the rebels!" cried he. And giving the order for his troop to attack them, he advanced with his men amongst the rocks where the Vaudois had sheltered themselves. But seeing the fruitlessness of their endeavours, the necessity of fighting, and that the only hope of safety for their families was in victory, which depends upon God alone, the fugitives laid hold of such weapons as they had been able to make or provide themselves with, loosened masses of rock, which they hurled upon their assailants, crushing many to death, and then rushed out and dispersed them, killing half of their number, and finally intrenched themselves anew upon the heights which they had so valiantly defended.

But what avails courage against numbers, without miraculous assistance, like that which was granted to the Israelites against Sennacherib? Cardinal Alexandrini addressed himself to the

Viceroy of Naples, representing the legitimate self-defence of the Vaudois as an open rebellion against authority. The viceroy set out in person, at the head of his troops, and arriving at St. Xist, made proclamation that all should be destroyed by fire and sword if the Ultramontanes did not abjure their heresy.

This was not the means to subdue them; for, determined not to abjure, they resolved also to defend themselves. Their party immediately acquired a strength and an unity which till then they had wanted. The Vaudois with enthusiasm fortified themselves on the mountains; and their position very soon became so formidable, that the viceroy did not venture to attack them with the troops which he had brought. Thereupon he issued a new proclamation, by which he offered to all the fugitives from justice, and banished and condemned persons who lived as vagabonds in the kingdom of Naples, pardon of their offences, on condition that they should come and range themselves under his banners for the extermination of the heretics. This was just what Cattanée had done; and such are the supporters of the cause of Rome, whence blood and infamy everywhere flow, as a sponge soaked in mud empties itself when it is grasped in the hand.

A multitude of outlaws of the worst character, and wretches of all ages, marauders and robbers, who knew all the paths of the Apennines, offered themselves for his service. The Vaudois were surrounded, pursued, waylaid on the approach to their place of retreat, and slaughtered by men in ambush; the forests, in which they could not be got at, were set on fire; the greater part of them perished, and many of those who made their escape, died of famine in the caverns to which they retired.

But what did the monks and inquisitors now do? "We cannot endure the sight of bloodshed!" they exclaimed, "these exterminations are revolting to us; O! come, come with us into the fold of the Church; with us you will find nothing of that display of warlike weapons which is so disagreeable to men of peace." And the better to testify their aversion to it, they removed to a distance from the town, inviting the inhabitants of La Guardia who still survived to join them there without arms. Alas! poor people, always deceived by the great deceiver of the nations, the woman who speaks with a sweet voice, and afterwards precipitates both bodies and souls into hell! they still listened to this perfidious invitation; they assembled, but the soldiers were concealed close by, and seventy Vaudois, the number of the first disciples of our Lord, were seized and loaded with chains. These new confessors of the gospel, in presence of a new Paganism, more cruel and more treacherous than the ancient, were carried prisoners to Montalto. There they were subjected to torture; the inquisitor, Panza, made them all endure the rack, the cords, the wheel, the iron wedges, or the boiling water, to compel them not only to abjure their religion, but also to denounce their brethren and their pastors!

O Rome, hypocrite that thou art! shedding crocodile tears because thou canst not now, in thy decrepitude, glut thyself with human flesh as in time past; what need have we in contending against thee, to enter into the lists of controversy? Thine own acts condemn thee better than our words, and thy history shall be thy burial-dress. The truth is every day preparing it for thy reception; and when the gospel shall have overcome thy principles of hatred and of pride by its maxims of humility and love, it will triumphantly inscribe upon thy tomb, Hate only evil, but love the evil-doers.

One of the things which the torturers were especially anxious to obtain from those who were submitted to their hands, was the confession of the pretended abominations of which the Vaudois were accused, and with which it was desired to reproach their morals, on the testimony of their own brethren. Is this Holy Office of the Catholic faith, then, to be accounted a court of justice, or a den of villains, which seeks not only to slaughter its victims, but to load them with infamy?

Stephano Carlino, from whom they thought to extort this confession, was tortured in so horrible a manner, says M'Crie, that his bowels were forced out of his belly. Another prisoner, named Verminello, had promised, in the extremity of his suffering, to attend mass. This yielding made the inquisitor hope that by augmenting the violence of the tortures he would at last extort a confession of the crimes which he was so desirous to fasten upon the Vaudois, and of which no testimony had yet been obtained. With this view, the unhappy captive was kept for eight whole hours on an instrument of pain, called the *hell*, but Verminello constantly denied the truth of these atrocious calumnies. Bernardino Conto was covered with pitch at Cosenza, and burned alive before all the people. Another martyr, named Mazzone, was stripped of his garments and scourged with small iron chains, and when his flesh had been thus torn in pieces, he was dragged through the streets, and killed at last by blows with burning billets of wood. Of his two sons, the one was flayed alive, as a sheep is flayed by the butcher, and the other was flung down from the summit of a tower.

To this same tower a young man was conducted, of prodigious

strength, and who upon that account had been surnamed Samson. But the strength of the Christian's soul was still more remarkable than the physical strength of the Israelite. As he had resisted all attempts which had been made to get him to abjure, he was urged at least to confess. "I only confess to God," replied he. "Come to mass, or you are a dead man." "Jesus says, if ye believe in me, though ye were dead ye shall live." "Well! kiss this crucifix." "My Jesus is not upon that piece of wood, but in heaven, from which he shall come again to judge the living and the dead." "You will not kiss it?" "I do not choose to be an idolater." And the soldiers flung him down upon the pavement. Much injured, but still alive, he implored the mercy of God. The viceroy happened to pass by. "What piece of carrion is that?" said he, looking at him. "A heretic, who could not die." The ruler gave him a kick upon the head, saying, "Make him food for the pigs." Yet the poor young man continued to live for twenty-two hours before he breathed his last. Which was most contemptible in all this?—king or priest? But before these powers the nations of the earth still prostrate themselves. O when shall Christ make them free!

Sixty females of St. Xist, as Gilles relates, were tortured in such a way, that the cords having entered into their flesh, and no relief being given them, devouring vermin were engendered in their wounds, which could only be killed by quicklime. Some of them consequently died in the dungeons into which they were cast; others were burned alive, and the best-looking were sold, as in Turkey, to the highest bidders, who, of course, were also the basest of men.

But all these atrocities were yet surpassed by the barbarous scenes enacted at Montalto, under the government of the Marquis Buccianici. "Poor wretches!" exclaims an eye-witness,[1] "eighty-eight prisoners were shut up in a low chamber. The executioner came; he entered and laid hold of one, and after having wrapped a linen cloth round his head, he led him out to the ground adjacent to the building, caused him to fall down upon his knees, and cut his throat with a knife. The blood spouted upon his arms and clothes; but removing the bloody cloth from the head of the man whom he had killed, he entered again, took another prisoner, and slaughtered him in the same manner. My whole frame still shudders when I figure to myself the executioner with his bloody knife between his teeth, and the dripping cloth in his hand, his arms red with the blood of his victims, going in and coming out again almost

---

[1] Ascanio Caraccioli, M'Crie, p. 295.

a hundred times in that work of death. It is impossible to imagine the gentleness and patience of these poor people, who were thus taken like lambs from the fold. All the old men met their death with imperturbable calmness. I could scarcely restrain my tears at the time. And about eight o'clock a decree was issued, which condemned to the torture a hundred women who were afterwards to be put to death. The number of the heretics who were arrested in Calabria is said to have amounted to 1600, and they were all condemned to die. It is said that they originally came from the valleys of Piedmont."

"Some of them," adds a Neapolitan historian,[1] "had their throats cut; others were sawn through the middle of the body, or flung headlong from the tops of rocks. The father saw his son die, and the son his father, without showing the least sign of grief, but, on the contrary, glorying in their being delivered from their woes, and going to rejoin one another in the bosom of that Jesus who died for them." And the historian from whom I quote mocks at this heavenly resignation, and says that it was an evil spirit of which these resigned victims were possessed. The same thing was said of Jesus Christ. Blessed are they who tread with such faith the path of sorrow which He trod!

Another eye-witness, who was one of the suite of Cardinal Alexandrini, thus completes this mournful story: "Before my lord's arrival, eighty-six relapsed heretics had been flayed alive, and then cut into two parts, and the pieces placed upon stakes all along the road for a space of thirty-six miles. This mightily strengthened Catholicism, and considerably shook the cause of heresy. There are already 1400 of these Ultramontanes in the prisons; some still wander amongst the mountains, but ten crowns are promised for every head that is brought in. Soldiers have been sent in pursuit of them, and every day some prisoners are secured. Their number has at last become so considerable, that my lord, along with the Commissary and the Grand Vicar of Cosenza, have resolved to subject the greater part of them only to penance, excepting the most obstinate, who will be put to death. As for the preaching ministers and leaders of this sect, they will be burned alive. Five of them have already been sent to Cosenza, in order to undergo that punishment, anointed with rosin and sulphur, so that, being gradually consumed, they may suffer the more for correction of their impiety. Many women remain prisoners, all of whom will be burned alive. Five of them are to be

---

[1] Thomaso Costo, *seconda parte del Compendio dell' Istoria di Napoli*, p. 257.

burned to-morrow." This letter is dated 27th June, 1561,[1] and terminates with a gross joke about the state of pregnancy of some of these ill-fated females.

When our indignation is roused against the authors of such atrocities, we are ready to declare that the Church of Rome should be called the church of devils. Pagans, barbarians, savages could not act so cruelly; it was left for Popery to degrade man beneath the level of the brutes. A man is burned alive! it is a terribly laconic expression! How much pain and suffering does it describe! What, then, when a whole people is given over to such a death! Can we fail to recognize in persecuting Rome the great whore of the Apocalypse, drunk with the blood of saints and of martyrs? the abominable city, in which is found the blood of all those who have been slain on the earth?[2]

The pastor, John Guérin, who came to Calabria from Bobi to succeed the Barba Gilles, already mentioned, died of hunger in the prisons of Cosenza, because he would not renounce the gospel—the immortal food of his soul amidst all his cruel torments. The four principal persons of the town of La Guardia were hanged upon trees, on a little hill called Moran. The town of St. Agatha, near Naples, paid also its tribute of victims to Rome's thirst for blood. And how many more places besides these, of which the very names have not reached us! For two years the rage of the monster, whom the Vaudois called Antichrist, devoured that unhappy country. For two whole years the piles were always kindled, the prisons choked, the executioners bathed in blood.

A few of the unfortunate Vaudois succeeded in making their way back to the valleys of Piedmont. But through what a series of difficulties and perils! Orders were given to the keepers of all bridges, and to those who had the charge of vessels, or of any kind of conveyances, that they should suffer no traveller to pass without a note from the priest of his parish. Innkeepers were threatened with severe penalties who should receive strangers without this safe-conduct; so that these poor persecuted people were constrained to travel by night, passing rivers by fording, hiding themselves in the woods, living upon roots, upon what they could timidly glean in the fields, and the fruits which they found on some kinds of trees; yet thus did a number of families, the females habited in male attire, succeed, after multiplied dangers and unparalleled fatigues, in regaining the retreat of their forefathers. O, how blissful to them after hardships so great and protracted, must have

---

[1] It was written by Luiggi d'Appiano, and is preserved by Gilles, pp. 182-4. I have only given extracts. [2] Rev. xvii. 5, 6; xviii. 24.

been the peaceful security of the Vaudois valleys, which, however, were also to be subjected to much suffering!

But it appears that all the Vaudois of unhappy Calabria were not yet destroyed; for Pius IV. afterwards sent the Marquis of Butiana to accomplish the extirpation of heresy in that country, and in order to encourage him in the work, promised to reward his success by granting a cardinal's hat to Joseph Butiana, his son. He had no difficulty in succeeding. The Inquisition, that great prop of Popery, which has declined ever since it was abolished —that power of hell, which, however, has not prevailed against the church of God—had long enough wrought its work of ruin now in these evangelical districts.

The people of Rome themselves, irritated at the bloody atrocities which it had perpetrated, burned its palace on the death of Paul III. This, no doubt, was because they were not so good Catholics as they ought to have been. Accordingly, Pius IV., whose pontificate was signalized by the events which we have just narrated, transported the seat of the Holy Office to the opposite bank of the Tiber, to the same place which is said to have been occupied by the ancient circus of Nero, in which so many of the primitive Christians were delivered over to the teeth of wild beasts. And these were primitive Christians, too, who perished at Cosenza, at La Guardia, and at St. Xist; only for wild beasts were substituted the priests, the monks, and the inquisitors of the Church of Rome.

CHAPTER VII.

INFLUENCE OF THE REFORMATION IN THE VAUDOIS VALLEYS.— THE SYNOD AND THE BIBLE.[1]

(A.D. 1520 TO A.D. 1535.)

Deputation of the Vaudois to the Reformers—The deputies arrested as they return —Martyrdom of Peter Masson at Dijon—Synod at Angrogna in 1532—Dissensions—Letter from the Churches in Bohemia—Synod at Pral, 1533—Olivétan's Bible—Mission of Martin Gonin to Geneva—He is arrested on his way home, and put to death at Grenoble.

THE great events of the Reformation, the report of which was fraught with such dismal consequences in Calabria and in Provence, could not remain without influence on the Vaudois valleys,

[1] AUTHORITIES.—*Gilles, Léger.—Claude Baduel,* "*Acta Martyrum* . . ." (A translation of Crespin.)—"*Bible of Olivétan*" (printed at Serrières, near Neuchâtel, in 1535); the preface.—*Id.* for the *Brief Discours des persécutions sur-*

from which the evangelical churches of these countries had originated in former times. Let us contemplate the condition of Catholicism, of the Reformation, and of the Vaudois at that period.

The first Christian churches founded by the apostles were religious societies, united to one another by the bonds of faith and charity, but independent in their organization. Hence, the particular churches could remain long united to the universal church, without renouncing that liberty of conscience which belonged to them in their individual capacity. The Vaudois Church is an instance in point; and the long strife which the Papal Church had to maintain, in order to reduce the greater part of other churches under its authority, affords a more general, but a certain proof that they were not from the first subject to it. The word church then signified no more than a simple assembly; and the distinctive characteristic of the Christian assemblies was that they were churches of brethren.

Catholicism, in its first establishment, changed the meaning of all these words; it desired to have dominion over the world, and availed itself for this purpose of the elements of that Paganism which had recently been supreme. Setting up again the fragments of its broken altars—restoring, for the sake of their imposing character, its old abandoned pomps—it connected the recollection of idolatrous festivals with altered names and new legends; in a word, it adopted the forms of Paganism in order to attract the Pagans to itself; and this it called converting them! The grandeur of Catholicism arose, therefore, entirely from the grandeur of the religions which preceded it; but, at the same time, it stifled the Christian spirit beneath the magnificence of these borrowed externals; spiritual worship gave place to a worship consisting in spectacles, and whilst there was no intention of renouncing the gospel, the gospel was supplanted. The invasions of the barbarians had just overthrown the Roman empire, and Catholicism was nothing else than the result of a hideous combination of corrupt Paganism with the savage barbarism which destroyed the ancient civilization. Then was this church seen to

---

venues . . . &c. Geneva, 1620.—"*Le Manuel du vray chrétien* . . ." par Daniel Pastor, ministre en Pragela. 8vo, 1652.—"*Risposta al libro del Sr. Gillio titolato Torre evangelica*. . . ." 1628. Ruchat, "Hist. de la Réform. de la Suisse . . ." 1728. 6 vols., vol. iii. The continuation of this work, which was still unpublished in 1836, has since been published.—*Scultetus*, "*Annales Evangelii renovati.*"—MSS. in Trin. Coll. Libr. Dublin, C, V, No. 18, containing a *Collection de lettres et d'autres pièces relatives à la mission de George Morel, et de Pierre Masson, auprès des Réformateurs, en* 1530. (A particular account of this MS. may be seen in the *British Magazine*, No. cxiii., p. 397, *et seq.*)—Documents sent to me by M. Merle D'Aubigné; viz., Letter from the churches of Bohemia to the Vaudois, in 1533; Letter, Adamus to Farel, &c.

grow up to all the height of that edifice of past times which had been cast down; and, like a building spared in a great inundation, stood alone for centuries within a level but darkened horizon, amidst the ruins of the ancient world gradually disappearing or undergoing change.

Its pride increasing with its strength, Popery now aimed at subjecting the temporal powers to the spiritual power, of which it arrogated the name to itself; and thus did it unconsciously proclaim the superiority of mind over matter, even whilst it had, so to speak, wedded itself to matter in its wholly material worship. The human mind awoke, and protested against a worship so unworthy of itself; the dawn of restored letters cast its first rays upon the Bible, which also gave forth its protest; all generous hearts gathered around it, with the ardour of life, to destroy in its name the carnal forms of a monument of death; and, as two chords in unison vibrate in response to one another, notwithstanding the distance which separates them, the sensation at once produced in the Vaudois Church by the Reformation, gives evidence of the secret harmony which existed between them, and which alone could account for the feeling of mutual affection with which the hearts both of the Vaudois and the Reformers were suddenly moved. The Vaudois hastened to send to the Reformers some of their Barbas, George Morel, of Freyssinières, and Peter Masson, to whom in Latin documents is given the name of Latomus.

"It is not without surprise," said they to Œcolampadius, "that we have learned the opinion of Luther with respect to freewill. All creatures, even the very plants, have properties peculiarly their own; and we would suppose that such is the case with men also, to whom God has given strength to do good, to some more, and to some less, as the parable of the talents appears to teach. And as to predestination, we are much troubled about it, having always believed that God created all men for eternal life, and that the reprobate only become so by their own fault; but if all things take place of necessity, so that he who is predestinated to life cannot become reprobate, nor those who are destined to condemnation attain salvation, of what use are sermons and exhortations?" They came afterwards to understand that the Divine foreknowledge has nothing to do with man's prudential arrangements, and that the will itself is a gift of the grace of God, from whom all things derive their life, motion, and being, and the heart of man its willing and its doing according to his good pleasure. On this point, as on many others, the Reformers of Switzerland and of Strasburg gave the Vaudois evangelical replies, which filled them with joy.

As they returned with their treasure, and passed through Dijon, on their way home to Dauphiny, their pious conversation revealed them to be Lutherans. This was crime enough in that inhospitable city.

France, however, had preceded Germany and Switzerland in a reforming movement, which was evidently destined either to revive or to destroy the Catholic Church. Nowhere had the imperious ambition of Popery been more energetically repressed than by the French nation. The sister of the reigning monarch, Margaret of Valois, Duchess of Alençon, had become a convert to the gospel under the learned and unpretending instructions of a professor of the Sorbonne, and a bishop of Meaux.[1] But in France, also, a reaction displayed itself so much the more strongly, as the avowal of Bible doctrines had been made with greater reserve.

The Vaudois delegates, returning from Strasburg to the valleys, were arrested, as we have seen, at Dijon. The particulars of this event are not known, but the issue was that George Morel succeeded in making his escape, with the precious packet of letters and religious instructions which he bore to his compatriots; but, as if no other price than that of a martyrdom would have been proportionate to their worth, Peter Masson sealed them with his blood, dying on the 10th of September, 1530, with the calmness of a Christian who feels that he is redeemed.

The glorious news had already resounded amongst these mountains that Popery was falling to ruins, and that the everlasting gospel was rising again as a sun of life to shine upon a renovated world. In 1526, a pastor of Angrogna, named Gonin, had been in Germany, and had brought back the publications of Luther.

Several conferences were held, to discuss the explanations given by the Reformers. It was necessary that their minds should be brought to harmony, even as their hearts were harmonious already. Finally a synod was held in the commune of Angrogna, to which representatives of all the Vaudois parishes repaired, not only from the valleys, but also from Calabria, Saluces, Provence, and Dauphiny. This solemn assembly was held in the open air, at the hamlet of Chanforans, in presence of all the people.[2] It met on one of those shady pieces of level ground situated half-way up the mountains, in a verdant amphitheatre, shut in like an arena for giants by the distant slopes of the Pra du Tour, then crowned with sparkling snows.

---

[1] Lefèbvre and Brissonnet.
[2] *En presencia de tuti li ministri et eciam Dio del populo.* (MS. of George Morel, Dublin, C, V, No. 18.)

SYNOD AT ANGROGNA.

Already a rapid change of opinions and relations had taken place all around the Vaudois valleys; many persons who until then had remained indifferent to the gospel, had begun to seek after it. The seigneurs of Miradol, Rivenoble, and Solaro, appeared at the council of faith and liberty. Some of the Reformers of Switzerland also came thither. Farel came mounted on a white horse, with that noble demeanour which belongs to persons of high birth. Saulnier accompanied him, and all thronged around the steps of these illustrious but unassuming men, who came to seal the compact of brotherhood between the successors of the primitive church and the promoters of a new era of evangelization. The Synodal Assembly met at Angrogna, on the 12th of September, 1532, and lasted for six days.

"The Reformers," says one who was present at that meeting, "were greatly rejoiced to see that people, who had ever proved faithful—that Israel of the Alps, to whose charge God had committed for so many centuries the ark of the new covenant—thus eager in his service. And examining with interest," says he, "the manuscript copies of the Old and New Testaments in the vulgar tongue which were amongst us"—it will be perceived that it is a Vaudois who speaks—"correctly copied with the hand at a date beyond all memory, they marvelled at that favour of Heaven which a people so small in numbers had enjoyed, and rendered thanks to the Lord that the Bible had never been taken from them. Then, also, in their great desire that the reading of it might be made profitable to a greater number of persons, they adjured all the other brethren, for the glory of God and the good of Christians, to take measures for circulating it, showing how necessary it was that a general translation should be made of it into French, carefully compared with the original texts, and of which large numbers should be printed." All the Vaudois applauded the design, and, according to the author just quoted, joyfully agreed to the work proposed;[1] so that it is to the existence of these ancient Vaudois manuscripts, the first in which the Bible was ever presented in the vulgar tongue (being what was then called the Romance tongue), that the Christian world was afterwards indebted for the first complete translation of the Bible printed in French.[2]

This preliminary decision of the Vaudois Synod was not, it is evident, one of the least important. They proceeded then to the

---

[1] These details are derived from the prefatory notes in Olivétan's Bible, fol. 3 (right hand): *Apologie du translateur*.
[2] The translation of Guiart des Moulins was prior to this, but it was not made from the original languages.

discussion of the articles upon which there existed some diversity of opinion between the Vaudois and the Reformers.

The first question which was examined related to the subject of oaths. Jesus Christ says, "Let your yea be yea, and your nay, nay."[1] The Christian must never lie. When an oath is tendered to him, is it lawful for him to swear? The assembly decided in the affirmative.

The second question received the following answer:—"No works are to be called good but those which God has commanded, and none are to be called evil but those which he has forbidden." This doctrine, which seems to imply the possibility of things indifferent in the life of man, is a slight modification of the ancient opinions of the Vaudois, according to which everything in us, without exception, is either good or evil.

In the third place, auricular confession was rejected, as contrary to Scripture; but mutual confession and secret reproof were maintained.

The next question is delete in the contemporary manuscript from which these particulars are derived, but these are the words of it: "Does the Bible forbid us to work on Sabbath?—Conclusion: Men may not engage on that day in any works but those of charity or of edification."

Afterwards we read: "Articulate words are not indispensable to prayer; genuflections, beating of the forehead, trembling and agitation, are things superfluous. It was decided that Divine service ought to be carried on in spirit and in truth."

"Is the imposition of hands necessary?" Both this question and the answer to it are delete in the manuscript, but the words can still be read, as follows:—"The Apostles made use of imposition of hands, as also did the Fathers of the church; but it is an external thing, in which every one is left at liberty."

The thirteenth question bears that marriage is prohibited to no one. The fifteenth, that to attempt to impose vows of celibacy is an antichristian thing and work.

The last eight articles are these:—

"XVIII. Every kind of usury is forbidden in the word of God." (By usury was then understood the receipt of any kind of interest for money lent.) This sentence is also effaced; but there remains after it a statement that loans ought to be made and granted in mere and entire charity.

"XIX. All the elect have been specially chosen before the foundation of the world.

---

[1] Matt. v. 37.

"XX. It is impossible that those who are appointed unto salvation should not be saved.

"XXI. Whosoever asserts freewill denies completely the predestination of God.

"XXII. The ministers of the word of God ought not to wander about, nor to change their residence, unless it shall be for the good of the church.

"XXIII. They are warranted to have, for the maintenance of their families, other revenues besides the fruits of apostolical communion."

There is then, also, something said of the sacraments, which according to the Holy Scriptures are reduced to two, Baptism and the Lord's Supper.

Hence it appears that questions the most diverse, relating to worship, discipline, and doctrine, were discussed in this interesting meeting. It was terminated by words full of brotherly kindness and prayer:—"Since it has been according to the good-will of the Most High," we read in the account already quoted, "to permit us to assemble in this place so large a number of brethren, we have with one consent agreed to the present declaration. The spirit which animates us being not of men, but of God, we implore Him that, according to the directions of his love, nothing may henceforth divide us; and that when we are far separated from one another, we may always remain united in the same mind, whether for the teaching of these doctrines, or for expounding to others the Holy Scriptures." Such was the declaration signed by the greater part of those who were present. However, this agreement was not unanimous; for there were, says Gilles, a number who dissented, and two pastors having refused to sign, withdrew from the Synod. Thus, although based upon the gospel, these first articles of faith, framed by the breath of men, became the cause of the first schism which ever broke out in the Vaudois Church. It must be observed, however, that the two dissenting pastors did not belong to the valleys, but to Dauphiny.

They proceeded to Bohemia, to the brethren of that country, who maintained, though by rare intercourse, a constant connection with the Vaudois churches, amongst which their spiritual guides came to receive instruction in the word of God. The Barbas whom they found officiating there, had therefore also passed some time in the valleys in their youth. But the report of the crusade which had been raised against them in 1487, had caused the Bohemians to take for granted the entire destruction of these beloved and primitive churches of the Alps. The two ministers who then arrived amongst them from these churches, re-assured them therefore on this point; but they complained bitterly that foreign doctors had brought amongst them new doctrines, which the Synod of Angrogna had too readily adopted. Thereupon the churches of Bohemia wrote a fraternal letter to those of Piedmont, entreating them not to lay aside their ancient customs, and, above all, to be very circumspect in the matter of doctrine.

The Dauphinese ministers brought back this letter to the valleys, eight months after they had left them. A new synod was held at Pral, on the 14th of August, 1533. The communication from the brethren of Bohemia was there considered, to which it was replied that no doctrine had been nor would be received in the Vaudois Church on the authority of human doctors, but only on that of the Bible. This synodal assembly approved also of the resolutions of the preceding year. The foreign pastors, persisting in their dissent, retired from the valleys; but a fact less excusable than their dissent, was the abstraction of several ancient manuscripts and papers concerning the history of the Vaudois, of which they took possession before they went away.

Whilst the dissenters were signalizing themselves in a manner so little to their credit, the strict and devoted body of the Vaudois clergy steadfastly pursued the paths of that faith which worketh by love, preparing with the utmost diligence the translation of the Bible, which the Synod of Angrogna had resolved to print.

Ten years before, the four gospels had already been published in French, by Lefebvre D'Etaples.[1] The remainder of the New Testament, and thereafter some fragments of the Old, appeared at Antwerp, from 1525 to 1534. Olivétan, who was appointed to superintend the Vaudois version, doubtless profited by these labours; but it must be believed that other Vaudois likewise assisted him, for the preface to the Bible which bears his name is dated *from the Alps, this seventh of February*, 1535. It is a large folio volume, of somewhere about 2000 pages (for the sheets are not numbered). It is printed in Gothic characters, in two columns, with remarkable neatness, and bears the following title: *La Bible qui est toute la saincte escripture, en laquelle sont contenus le Vieil Testament et le Nouveau, translatés en françoys, le Vieil de Lebrieu et le Nouveau du Grec.*[2] Then follows this motto, from the prophet Isaiah: *Ecoutez cieulx, et toi terre preste laureille, car Leternel*

---

[1] Printed at Paris in 1523.

[2] The Bible; that is, the whole of the Holy Scriptures, in which are contained the Old Testament and the New, translated into French, the Old from the Hebrew, and the New from the Greek.

parle.[1] The name of the prophet quoted is written *Isaiah*, which recalls, better than the modern French orthography [*Esaïe*], the Hebrew pronunciation. The date of this publication is noted at the end of the volume, in these terms: *achevé d'imprimer en la ville et comté de Neufchastel, par Pierre de Wingle, dict Pirot, l'an M.D.XXXV., le iiijsme jour de Juing*.[2] This Bible cost the Vaudois 1500 golden crowns; and it would be surprising that a people so few in number should be able to make such very considerable sacrifices, if we did not know that faith makes the greatest works possible, and that the feeblest can do all things when Christ strengthens them.

This undertaking, originated through the influence of Farel, himself a Frenchman, was also prosecuted with a special regard to the Reformed Church of France. The Vaudois, who address that church as a sister, say to her in the preface—calling to remembrance the refuge which the disciples of Valdo had sought amongst them—"The poor people who make you this present were driven forth and banished from your company more than three centuries ago; they are the true people of patience, who, in faith, and hope, and charity, have silently vanquished all the assaults and efforts which their enemies have been able to make against them." "They are the people of joyous affection and of constant courage," replied the churches of France by one of their synods; "their name is the little flock; their kingdom is not of this world; their motto is *piety and contentment;* they are a church which has endured conflicts, and is embrowned and sun-scorched without, but fair and of goodly appearance within; whose footsteps the greater part amongst us have failed to follow; for religious zeal exists only in the monuments of history, and in the ashes of our fathers, which are still warm with their ardour for the propagation of the gospel." These admirable sentences, so true at that period, but much more true in our days, are extracted from a little work composed by order of the Synod of Briançon, held from the 25th to the 30th of June, 1620. It is entitled, *A Brief Account of the Persecutions which have in these days befallen the churches of the Marquisate of Saluces*.[3]

These churches likewise belonged to the great Vaudois family; and of them we shall presently come to treat. But before bringing this chapter to a close, I must still speak of the Vaudois minister of the parish within which was held the Synod of 1532, the Barba

---

[1] Attend, O heavens, and give ear, O earth, for the Lord hath spoken.

[2] The printing was completed in the city and county of Neufchâtel, by Peter de Wingle, called Pirot, in the year 1535, on the 4th day of June.

[3] *Brief discours des persecutions advenues en ce temps aux Eglises du marquisat de Saluces.*

Martin Gonin, pastor of Angrogna, who, in order to complete the work of instruction and of renovation set on foot by that synod, undertook to go in person to Geneva, to procure the religious publications necessary for his countrymen. He had formerly visited the churches of Provence, and he was now to visit those of Switzerland. This Christian mission, which the enemies of the gospel rendered very perilous, was undertaken in 1536. The Bible of the Vaudois had been published in 1535; so that, a year after having diffused through the world the book of books, this people, as eager to be instructed as to teach, demanded in return from the world, the tribute of that enlightenment for which it was indebted to the Bible.

Gonin had already, in 1526, made an excursion amongst the Reformers, and had brought back a great number of books. The worthy Barba left the valleys again, ten years after, at the conclusion of winter, because the roads being then more difficult and less frequented, were also less closely watched. Another Vaudois, by name John Girard, accompanied him to Geneva, where he intended to found a printing establishment, specially with the view of providing for the wants of his own countrymen. He did actually found it, and it fell to his lot afterwards to print the narrative of the first persecutions undertaken against the Vaudois in the 16th century. As for Barba Martin Gonin, after having made choice of the books which he was commissioned to procure, he set out again for the Vaudois valleys, in the month of March, 1536.

The Duke of Savoy was then at war with the King of France, who had just seized upon Bresse, Savoy, and great part of Piedmont. The Bernese took advantage of these circumstances to re-assert their claim to the right bank of the Leman, which the Duke of Savoy still possessed. It was at this time that they seized upon the Pays de Vaud, and that they embraced the Reformation. They had carried their invasions as far as Chablais and the Pays de Gex.

To shun these scenes of conflict, Martin Gonin was obliged to take a different road from that by which he had formerly travelled; he went through France, and as he traversed the Champsaur in order to reach the Gapençois, and thence to gain the Vaudois valleys of Dauphiny, he incurred the suspicion of being a spy of the Duke of Savoy, and was arrested. He was conducted to Grenoble, where he was examined by some members of the Parliament, and obliged to reply to their interrogatories; but they, being persuaded of his innocence, commanded him to be set at liberty. The jailer, before giving effect to this decision, and with the intention unquestionably of robbing his prisoner of any valuables which he might find about him, took upon himself to search him, under pretext of making him free of all possible suspicion. Having set about this odious proceeding, he thought that he discovered papers concealed under the lining of his dress. These were no other than the brotherly letters of Farel, Saulnier, and other ministers of Geneva, which these worthy servants of Christ had sent to their Christian brethren in the valleys, by the hands of their pastor. The jailer took possession of these writings, and to justify himself to the judges, perhaps to gain credit for his bad action, he delivered them to the provost, who commanded him to convey Gonin back to prison.

Two days after, the captive was summoned to a new examination, as a person accused of Lutheranism. Being called upon to reply, he said, "I am not a Lutheran, for Luther did not die for me, but Jesus Christ only, whose name I bear." "What is your doctrine?" "That of the gospel." "Do you go to mass?" "No." "Do you acknowledge the authority of the pope?" "No." "Do you acknowledge that of the king?" "Yes; for the powers that be are ordained of God." "But the pope is also one of the powers that be." "Only by the support of the devil." At these last words the judges, in a fury, instead of proceeding further with the examination of the accused, who demanded to be allowed to prove all his beliefs from the Bible, commanded him to be silent, declared him a heretic, and condemned him to death.

But Grenoble was a city of more enlightenment than Dijon. The new light had penetrated to it. The seigneurs of Bonne, Villars, Mailhet, and Bardonanche, with other families of high descent, had already in some measure imbibed those doctrines which made them, in the contests that soon followed, strenuous defenders of the Reformation. It was dreaded that the evangelical language of the Vaudois Barba might excite too much sympathy; it was thought proper, therefore, that his execution should not be public, "for fear," as the narratives say, "that his engaging manners and fair speech should create some commotion amongst those that should be present." Accordingly, it was resolved that he should be strangled by night, and that his corpse should then be cast into the Isère.

Meanwhile, the humble martyr prayed for the advancement of the kingdom of God, for his afflicted family, for his church, and his fellow-countrymen. "O Lord!" he cried, from the depths of his dungeon, "be pleased to hasten that happy time when there shall be only one flock and one Shepherd!" He sought consolation in the present from the hope of the future, and the Lord answered his prayer, by hastening his own entrance into the felicity of heaven. On the 26th of April, 1536, about three o'clock in the morning, unaccustomed feet were heard on the damp stair of his prison. The light of a dark lantern fell upon its dismal steps. The door was opened, and the executioner and his assistants appeared on the threshold. "I see plainly what you come for," said the pastor, prepared to die; "but do you think to deceive God?" "In what?" inquired they. "You intend to throw me into the river, when there is nobody to see; but will not God see you?" "Get your ropes ready," said the executioner to his men, without replying to the Christian martyr. "And you, poor sinners," said Gonin to the other prisoners, "remember that there is pardon in one only, that is in Jesus Christ; and were your souls red even as crimson, he could make them white as snow." "What is the meaning of this talk?" said his companions in misfortune. "The stains most indelible, even according to human laws," he replied, "can be washed out by Him. Repent, and be converted, for the kingdom of God is at hand."

"Are the ropes ready?" said the executioner, interrupting him. The assistants stepped forward, and proceeded to carry into effect what was called human justice. They bound the hands of the martyr. They then conducted him to the banks of the Isère. There the executioner, having tied a rope to one of his feet, allowed him to kneel and to pray to God; afterwards he put a small rope round his neck, and passing a stick through it, twisted it in such a way as to tighten it more and more. No longer able to breathe, Gonin fell upon the ground. Here the strangulation was finished, and when they saw that he was motionless, they cast him into the river. But the coolness of the water restored the doomed man to life: his body quivered, his limbs moved—would he then survive that execution? No; the executioner, with foresight of such a possibility, retained hold of the rope which he had attached to the foot of the victim. He kept the convulsed and dying body floating until its agonies were ended. The movements communicated through the cord became more and more feeble, and when the last quiverings had ceased in that double suffocation by rope and by water, the line was cut, and the river bore away the body of the Vaudois martyr, whilst his soul winged its flight to heaven.

CHAPTER VIII.

HISTORY OF A NUMBER OF MARTYRS.[1]

Brief notices of many martyrs—Martyrdom of Stephen Brun at Embrun, in 1538—Of Bartholomew Hector at Turin, in 1556—Of John Vernoux, Anthony Laborie Quercy, and three others, at Chambery, in 1555—Letter of the martyr Quercy to his wife—Narrow escape of the Barba Gilles in the neighbourhood of Chambery—Geoffrey Varaille burned alive at Turin in 1558—Nicholas Sartoire at Aosta, in 1557—Extraordinary escape of a Vaudois minister—Martyrdoms of Mathurin and his wife, and of John De Cartignon, at Carignan, in 1560—Brief notices of other martyrs—Horrible cruelties inflicted on Odoul Geymet.

"THERE is not a town in Piedmont," said a Vaudois Barba, in his memoirs,[2] "in which some of our brethren have not been put to death."

Jordan Tertian was burned alive at Suza; Hyppolyte Roussier was burned at Turin; Villermin Ambroise was hanged on the Col de Méane; Ugon Chiamps, of Fenestrelle, was taken at Suza, and conducted to Turin, where his bowels were torn out and flung into a basin, without his sufferings being terminated even by this frightful torture. Peter Geymonat, of Bobi, died at Lucerna, with a living cat in the interior of his body. Mary Romaine was buried alive at Roche-Plate. Madeleine Fontane suffered the same fate at St. John; Michel Gonet, a man almost a hundred years of age, was burned alive at Sarcena. Susanna Michelin, at the same place, was left in a dying state upon the snow. Bartholomew Frache, having been hacked with sabres, had his wounds filled with quicklime, and expired in this manner at Fenil. Daniel Michelin had his tongue torn out at Bobi, for having praised God. James Baridon died, covered with brimstone matches, which they had fastened between his fingers, and about his lips, his nostrils, and all parts of his body. Daniel Rével had his mouth filled with gunpowder, which

---

[1] AUTHORITIES.—*Perrin*, pp. 151-160.—*Gilles*, pp. 53, 67, 74, 134, 180, 208, 290, 318, 426, 454, 553, &c.—*Léger*, part ii., pp. 115-138.—*Crespin*, fol. edition of 1619, fol. 3, 117, 320-334, 418-422.—*Rorengo*, "*Memorie historiche* . . ." pp. 64, 66.—*Fournier*, "*Historie des Alpes maritimes et Cottiennes, et particulièrement d'Embrun leur métropolitaine* . . . ." &c. MS. in fol. Translation of Juvénis; Library of the Little Seminary at Gap, fol. 260-320. (The original is in Latin, and is in the Library of Lyons. There is a copy at Paris.)—"*Cartulaire de l'Abbaye d'Oulx*," MS. fol.; Archives of the Bishopric of Pignerol.—*Memoirs of the Capuchin Missionaries* (in Italian), in the same archives.—Archives of Grenoble (of the Court of Accounts, the Parliament, and the former Bishopric).

Still unconsulted.—Documents to be found in the archives of the Holy Office, and of the archbishopric of Turin; the bishoprics or municipalities of Asti, Carignan, Pancalier, Carail, Saluces, and Suza; and the archives of the Inquisition at Rome. Vignaux, quoted by Perrin, p. 151.

was set on fire, and the explosion of which tore his head in pieces. Mary Mounin was taken in the *Combe* of Liousa; the flesh of her cheeks and of her chin was removed, so that the jaws were exposed, and in this way she was left to die. Paul Garnier was slowly mangled at Rora, Thomas Marguet mutilated in an indescribable manner at the Fort of Mirabouc, and Susanna Jaquin cut in pieces at La Tour. A number of young women of Taillaret, in order to escape outrages still more dreadful to them than death, flung themselves from a precipice, and perished among the rocks. Sarah Rostagnol was cleft up through the middle of her body, and was left in a dying state on the road from Eyrals to Lucerna. Anne Charbonnier was impaled alive, and borne in this state like a banner, from St. Jean to La Tour. At Paësane, Daniel Rambaud had his nails torn out, then his fingers were cut off, then his feet and hands were severed by blows of hatchets, and then his arms and legs were separated from his body, upon each refusal that he made to abjure the gospel.

There is not a rock in the Vaudois valleys which may not be looked on as a monument of death, not a meadow but has been the scene of some execution, not a village but has had its martyrs. No history, however complete, can contain a record of them all. I shall relate a few of the most striking facts, in connection with the circumstances which led to them. In the present chapter I shall only seek to collect together those which occurred in an isolated manner, before the era of great persecutions. The first memorial in this martyrology belongs to the valleys of Dauphiny.

Two years after the martyrdom of Martin Gonin at Grenoble, a young man, named Stephen Brun, born at Reortier, in the valley of the Durance, was imprisoned at Embrun as a heretic. He was a simple farmer; but God is glorified in the humblest of his creatures, and often chooses the weakest to confound the strong.

Stephen had a wife and five children; they therefore attempted to persuade him to abjure for the sake of his family. "Those who do the will of God are my family!" said he. "Do you really wish to leave your wife a widow, and your children orphans?" "Christ says to them, 'I will not leave you orphans.' He is the heavenly husband of faithful souls. An immortal Redeemer is better than a husband who must die." "But can you not postpone your death by coming to mass." "Say, rather, that I would hasten it, for that would be the death of my soul." "Are you not afraid of the punishment which is in preparation for you?" "Christ says, 'Fear not those who can only kill the body, but rather fear him who is able to cast both soul and body into hell?'" "Prepare, then, for death." "I prepare for immortality." And when they came to announce to him his condemnation, he exclaimed that it was his liberation.

The day of his execution having arrived, the executioner came to tell him that his death was now to take place. "It is life," said he, "of which you assure me!"

It was on the 16th of September, 1538, a tempestuous day. Stephen was fastened in the centre of a pile, which had been raised on the esplanade of the episcopal palace of Embrun. Scarcely had the fire been set to it, when it blazed with prodigious violence beneath the feet of the martyr. But the flames, being carried away by the wind, scarcely ascended to his chest, and did not choke him, as happens when they rise over the head. The fire consumed in succession his limbs and the lower parts of his body, but Stephen continued to breathe, and was still alive after an hour of this cruel torment. An hour passed in the flames: what an age of distress! The first martyr mentioned in the Bible, that other Stephen who was stoned, did not confess his Saviour with more courageous resolution. When the wood of the pile had been renewed, the fire seemed as if it would go out without taking away the life of the sufferer. Stephen remained always standing, like Shadrach in the furnace. Hereupon the executioner, who held in his hand a long iron hook, used for stirring the fire, gave him a blow on the head with it, to kill him, and stabbed him in the bowels, which gushed out into the fire when he drew back the hook. At last the body of Stephen fell, and they covered it with burning brands, which very soon reduced it to ashes.

"They that will live godly," says St. Paul, "shall suffer persecution." Jeremiah and Daniel were cast into the pit and to the lions; Isaiah was sawn asunder with a wooden saw; Zechariah was slain between the temple and the altar; St. John was beheaded. "Which of the prophets have not your fathers persecuted?" said the first Stephen to the Pharisees. That martyr, whilst they stoned him, saw the heavens opened, and the Son of man, who, seated at the right hand of the Father, called him to himself. The poor martyr of Reortier expired without any wonders appearing around him, but in him God did make wonders to appear.

"Wherein, then, consists the power of the martyr?" exclaims a Catholic orator. "It consists in his being right, and altogether right, and in being able to say, Kill me! but ye shall not make me speak anything but what I now speak. I know no power in the world more formidable than that of a man strong in his convictions, and allowing himself to be put to death for his doctrines. It was thus that the salvation of the world began." It was thus, we may add, that the Christian church kept its ground in the Vaudois valleys, and that it sprung to new life in the world at the voice of the Reformers.

But the antichristian power, which St. Paul calls the son of perdition, and which exalts itself above all that is called God, setting itself in opposition to God, makes it its great object to destroy the Bible in order to maintain its supremacy. A hawker of Bibles became at this time its victim, and although he was not a native of the Vaudois valleys, a memorial of him is entitled to a place in their history, because he was doing them a service, and his blood was mingled with that of their martyrs.

Bartholomew Hector was born at Poictiers. Having become acquainted with the gospel, he retired to Geneva with his wife and children. Being settled there, in order to earn a living for his family, he went from place to place, selling copies of the Holy Scriptures. He had come to Piedmont in the month of July, 1555, and had already disposed of a large number of Bibles in the hamlets of the Vaudois valleys. One day, having ascended to the very highest summer huts [*chalets*] upon the mountains of Angrogna, he stopped at the Alp of La Vachère. (The name of Alp or Alpage is given to the places to which the Vaudois shepherds conduct their flocks in summer. During the brief period that they are free from snows, these lofty peaks seem as if they hastened to clothe themselves with flowers, and pour forth in a few days all the riches of their annual vegetation). Next day he proceeded to a place still higher up, the Alp of Infernet, whose rapid slopes look down upon the immense rocks of the Pra du Tour. The vender of Bibles was not to be arrested by the obstacles of the path, and the weight which he carried seemed light when he thought of the good which he was to do; for it must not be forgotten that at these great elevations, so remote from the ordinary abodes of the Vaudois people, the herdsmen and *alpagers* who attend their flocks, are necessarily in part deprived of that spiritual nourishment which would be presented to them in the centre of their parish.

Bartholemew Hector, satisfied, it would appear, with his excursion, resolved to proceed from the Alp of Infernet to that of Laouzoun, and thence to the valley of St. Martin. But on his way down he was arrested at Rioclaret, by the seigneurs of the place, named Truchet, who had him conveyed to Pignerol, from which a catalogue of his books was forwarded to the senate of Turin.

After having left him to suffer and to pray for seven months, forgotten in the prisons of Pignerol, they thought fit at last to take steps in his case. His first examination took place on the 8th of March, 1556.

"You have been caught selling heretical books," they said to him. "If the Bible contains heresies in your estimation, in mine it contains the truth." "But they make use of the Bible to keep people from going to mass." "If the Bible keeps them from it, it is because God does not approve of it; for the mass is a piece of idolatry." This last reply made his position a great deal worse in the eyes of the defenders of the state worship, which owned no salvation apart from itself. "Out of Christ," said the colporteur, "I grant that there is no salvation, and by His grace I will not forsake Him."

His examination was resumed next day. He endeavoured to set forth the doctrines of the gospel. "We will hold no discussions with error," said the court. "But judges are appointed to discern between error and truth; permit me then to prove that I am in the truth." "If you are not in the Church, you are not in the truth." "I am in the Church of Christ, and I prove it by the gospel." "Return to the Church of Rome, if you would save your life." "Jesus says, 'He who would save his life shall lose it, and he who shall lose his life for my sake, shall live for ever.'" "Think of the abjuration which is required of you; it is the only means left you of saving yourself." "What about the saving of my body, if I lose my soul?" The urgency and threats employed to get him to abjure, thus remaining without effect, he was sent to Turin.

It was not the Duke of Savoy who was then sovereign of that country, but Francis I., the nephew of Charles III., whom he had driven from the throne.

Bartholomew Hector appeared before new judges, who were much inclined to lenity. But the strength of his convictions could bend to no compromise. "If you are resolved not to abjure your faith," they said to him, "at least you may retract your former declarations." "Prove to me," said he, "that they are erroneous." "It is not *proving* that is in question, but *living*," said they. My life is in my faith," he replied; "it is it which has made me speak." The judges, not venturing to take upon themselves the condemnation of a man so simple and so firm, and to whose charge no crime was laid, came to a decision, on the 28th of March, 1556, to remit the case to the inquisitors. It was just what Pilate did when he delivered Jesus into the hands of lawless men, and sent him away from the judgment hall.

On the 27th of April, the humble vender of Bibles appeared

before the Holy Office. It would seem that his evangelical and penetrating discourse, the sincere faith of his soul, and his modest and resigned air, had troubled the conscience even of that tribunal; for the inquisitors adjourned the case, and adjoined with themselves for trial of it the Vicars-General of the archbishopric of Turin and of the abbey of Pignerol. In their presence Hector remained always the same; there was a change of his judges, but no change of his cause.

He was again assured that for a simple retractation his life would be spared. Greater men than he have not looked so narrowly into such a question. But those who are first upon the earth are often the last in heaven. He who was one of the last here below, manifested a celestial resolution and mildness in the midst of these temptations. "I have said the truth," he exclaimed; "how can I change my words and make a retractation? Can a man change the truth as he would change his garment?" Truly, the poor seller of Bibles was well worthy of his noble employment; his pious hands did not profane the book which he distributed to men; why should men have pronounced against him a sentence of death?

Further delay was, however, granted him to reflect and abjure; but the more he reflected, the more he was convinced. Eternity would have passed without his abjuring. The period allowed him expired on the 28th of May; but it was prolonged to the 5th, and then to the 10th of June, with fresh exhortations to him each time to recant. It is perhaps more difficult to resist the urgency which is accompanied with indulgence than violence and severity. But Hector, without abating his humility, swerved not a hair's-breadth, saying, that whoever should take away one tittle from the Holy Word, should lose his part in the kingdom of heaven. He preferred to lose his part, already so full of trouble, in terrestrial existence.

The ecclesiastical tribunal, faithful to the traditions of Rome, by which the commandments of God have been so often annulled, could only declare him guilty of heresy. But it did this as if with regret; for, in delivering him to the secular arm, it recommended him to the indulgence of the judges who were to pronounce the penalty incurred by this crime. The law was express; the penalty was death. The secular judges, therefore, sentenced the man to be burned alive, in the square of the castle at Turin, on a market day. This sentence was passed on the 19th of June, 1556; but from regard to the recommendation of the ecclesiastical judges, the court authorized the executioner to strangle the condemned man during the kindling of the pile. When the sentence was read to him in the prison, he exclaimed, "Glory be to God, for that he has thought me worthy to die for his name!"

Other persons still came to persuade him to abjure, promising to obtain for him in that case the revocation of the sentence. Hector urged them to be converted, and to embrace the gospel. His discourses were so touching, and so full of unction, that he was threatened with having his tongue cut out, if he took upon him to speak to the people on his way to the place of execution. Perhaps a dread of the effect which he might produce, may serve to explain the long indulgence of his judges. Be this as it might, Hector paid no attention to the threat, and during his whole course from his prison to the pile, he ceased not to utter words of Christian truth.

Certainly there was in this man a power by which his affrighted judges were unconsciously overborne; for, at the moment of his ascending the pile, a new emissary arrived from the court to promise him life and liberty even then, if he would only retract his heretical opinions. He had only to say, I disavow all heresy; it would have pledged him to nothing; he might have retained his beliefs, he might have returned to his family; how many strong reasons might have been urged to excuse such reservations! But no such artifice of expression even occurred to the candid mind of the persecuted Christian; to him it would have appeared a disavowing of his faith—an absolute recantation. Accordingly, standing by the pile which was about to reduce him to ashes, and beside the executioner who was presently to strangle him, the humble colporteur of the Alps, upon this unexpected intelligence of a pardon which it would have been so easy for him to have secured, instead of replying to the messenger, fell on his knees, and said, "O Lord! give me grace to persevere unto the end; pardon those whose sentence is now to separate my soul from my body; they are not unjust but blind. O Lord! enlighten by thy Spirit this people who are around me, and bring them very soon to the knowledge of the truth." The people wept, astonished that such a man should be put to death, who spake only of God. But the executioners, having received orders to perform their work, caused Hector to ascend the pile; the wood was kindled, powder and sulphur were thrown upon the fire to conceal the last agony of the martyr, and at the same moment he fell down strangled; so that his death was very quick, and might even be called very pleasant, as he fell asleep with such security in the bosom of his God.

Somewhere about the same time, a pastor of Geneva, named

John Vernoux, had been sent into the Vaudois valleys to exercise the ministry of the gospel. He was one of the first fellow-labourers of Calvin, along with whom he had taken part in the Synod of Poictiers, which accomplished the organization of the Reformed Church of France. When he came to the valleys he was accompanied by Anthony Laborie Quercy, formerly a *royal judge* at Caiart, who had abandoned the magistracy to devote himself the more actively to the cause of the gospel. Having sojourned for some months in Piedmont, they returned together to Geneva, in order to make the arrangements necessary for their permanent settlement amongst the Vaudois.

These arrangements having been made, and their preparations terminated, they again left Geneva for the valleys, accompanied by two friends, named Batailles and Tauran, and by a third named Tringalet, who had no intention to follow them any farther than the frontiers of the Genevese territory, but who, being a most intimate friend of Anthony Laborie, could not bring himself to leave him at the appointed time of separation. "I will not leave you," said he; "I will go with you to these Vaudois valleys, which have preceded our blessed Reformation in the way of salvation." "The Vaudois have never been reformed," said another, "they are still primitive Christians, witnesses of the Apostolic Church." "You increase my impatience to see them," said he; "it is of the Lord; I am resolved not to leave you." His mind was made up, and they did not part. The whole five proceeded together towards the valleys of Piedmont.

Having passed through a part of Savoy, they arrived at Faucigny, where they received a mysterious warning that they would need to be upon their guard. They turned aside from the great roads, and took the mountain paths. But it became evident that whoever gave them warning had been possessed of good information, for in the gorges of the Col Tamis they were descried by soldiers of the maréchaussée,[1] who laid hold of them. Being carried prisoners to Chambéry, they made no attempt to conceal their faith, and received many solicitations to renounce it. But Christian faith, when it has been felt in the heart, is not a consort that can be so readily parted with.

On the 10th of July, 1555, after a long conference, in which he vainly attempted to convince them of heresy, the judge who conducted the examination exclaimed, "Of what use is all this? do you not know that you will be put to death as heretics, if you do not relinquish your errors?" "Yes," replied the pastor Vernoux,

[1] An armed police.

"the first thing which we learned from our Master was, that whosoever will follow him must expect persecution." "But Jesus does not command you to die?" "He tells us that as many as will walk in his steps must take up his cross; and he bore his own cross to Calvary." "You are very young men: think upon the life that is before you." "The life which is before us is in the heavens, and, far from extinguishing our hope, you give us more impregnable assurance of it." "Is it possible that men can speak in this way of a condemnation to death?" "It is by death that our souls attain to the fulness of their life." And in spite of all which the judges could do to obtain some concession on their part, nothing could triumph over the heroic firmness of these courageous disciples of Christ. They were, indeed, worthy to preach his word who could thus die for him! Blessed are the pastors whose lives correspond to such deaths!

Being declared guilty of heresy, the two pastors, Vernoux and Laborie, who were already numbered amongst the clergy of the Vaudois churches, and their three travelling companions, were delivered over to the secular tribunals. By a first sentence, of date the 21st of August, 1555, they were only condemned to the galleys, but the king's procurator appealed from this judgment, and the case had to be tried anew. The respect felt for them appears to have increased as their case proceeded. So, when Laborie refused to take oath upon a crucifix, they brought him a Bible, which was contrary to all ordinary practice, for Popery had proscribed it everywhere. Again, after his examination, the president kindly laboured to show him that he might live in peace and serve God as freely in his own proper place of abode as at Geneva. Laborie, who preferred to live in exile along with fellow-believers, rather than in his native country, where the gospel did not yet prevail, mildly replied, "The primitive Christians called one another brethren, and awakened Christians must still have brethren." "But," said the president, "it is not serving God to withdraw in a scandalous manner from the Church." "The scandal is owing to those who have abandoned the purity of his worship, and not to those who return to it," said Laborie. Thereupon the president, assailing him on the subject of his doctrines, endeavoured to prove to him by the Holy Scriptures, that man was not predestinated from all eternity, either to evil or to good; that a great many of the Catholic ceremonies, although superfluous, were nevertheless tolerable, as the gospel did not condemn them, and as St. Paul himself had circumcised Timothy, although he made so great an opposition to circumcision.

It was a thing so rare at that time for a Catholic judge to condescend to enter the arena of discussion with the Bible in his hand, that I have thought it necessary to mention it. This dealing with Scripture, moreover, making him familiar with evangelical doctrine, could not fail also ere long to create in his own mind some misgivings on the subject of heresy.

The accused frankly declared their opinions. Circumcision, they said, was founded upon a commandment of God, whilst the popish superstitions had no other origin than the errors of man. Not being able to convince their prisoners, the judges entreated them, with almost paternal earnestness, to return of their own accord to the Church, and not to compel them unwillingly to pronounce an inevitable condemnation. They even added, that they themselves desired a true reform in the Church, but not out of the Church. "Would to God, gentlemen," said Laborie, upon hearing this, "that all the ecclesiastics of France thought as you do, for we would very soon be of one mind; and if I am a heretic, my lord president is not far from being like myself." The councillors smiled; and one of them replied, "Nay, you must become like him, and not he like you."

But this irresolute, undecided position, intermediate between truth and error, between the church and the world, between Christ and Belial, will not do for men of candid and devoted hearts. It is the broad way in which many walk; but the newly-appointed pastors of the valleys and their Christian friends walked in a more narrow and a less agreeable path; less agreeable, I mean, for the worldly, but more productive of happiness for the children of Christ.

After this sitting they separated Laborie from his companions, and finding himself alone, he prayed earnestly to God that he would not suffer him to fall. "Thus I continued," he says, in one of his letters, "praying and meditating till two o'clock in the morning."

Next day he adjured his judges, by the regard they had for their immortal souls, not to put away from them the knowledge of salvation which was offered them. He represented to them the duties of their office, and told them that being appointed defenders of the truth, they ought not to condemn the truth. "If we are not in the truth," said he, "prove it; if we are, acquit us; for you have to judge the cause of Jesus in our persons, and you cannot be amongst those who judge in ignorance, for God has given you much light." "They listened to me," he says, "for about an hour without interruption, and I saw that some of the younger ones wept." "Did not God enjoin Moses to punish heretics?" said one of the most skilful. "I granted him that," says Laborie, in his own account of the examination, "and even cited the case of Servetus, who had endured the penalty of his crime at Geneva; but only take heed, said I, that you do not treat the true children of God as heretics!" "Ah, well! my friend," said one of the judges, "give us a simple retractation of your heresies, without specifying any of them." "It would be as base in me to make a half-abjuration of the truth, as to recant it altogether." "This will commit you to nothing in respect of the future; and your life may still be useful, even to your own cause." "I should serve it ill, if I were to begin by betraying it." "You will do it still less service when you are dead." "The death of the faithful is a seed of life, which remains behind them longer than their works would have done." This was indeed to renounce life for the sake of immortality.

On the 28th of August, all the five were condemned to be burned alive. They were left at liberty to see one another, to write to their friends, their relatives, and their colleagues at Geneva. "We give thanks to God," say they, "and await the hour, commending ourselves to your prayers." The most admired stoicism of antiquity is not worthy to be compared with this serene and impressive resolution of the Christian's soul. Courage shines forth only upon occasions; but resignation is courage become habitual and abiding. It originates not with man, but with God.

Anthony Laborie was united in marriage to a young woman who had been born a Catholic, but converted to the gospel. The following are passages of the letters which he wrote to her in order to prepare her for her approaching widowhood:—

"Anne, my beloved sister and most faithful spouse, you know how well we have loved one another, so long as it has pleased the Lord to leave us together; his peace has continually remained with us, and you have completely obeyed me in everything. I pray you, therefore, that you be always found such as you have been, and better, if it be possible, when I am no more. If your youth is alarmed at the world and poverty, I advise you to marry again, with another brother who equally fears God; and thenceforth think no more of me as having been your husband, but as a handful of ashes; for from this moment we are no longer united, except by the bond of that fraternal charity, in which I hope for your prayers so long as I am alive. When your father shall be apprised of my death, I doubt not but he will seek after you to win you back to Popery; but I entreat you, in the name of the Lord, to remain firm in your adherence to the truth. Trust in God; pray to him, love him, and serve him, and he will not forsake you. Our little girl, as well as yourself, will be dear to him;

for he is the protector of the widow and the father of orphans. The example of Moses should suffice to assure you of this."[1] What affecting thoughts are contained in these grave and calm sentences!

Calvin also addressed to the prisoners at Chambéry exhortations which may be reckoned austere. "Since it has pleased God to employ you in this service [martyrdom], continue to do as ye have begun. If the door is closed against you, that you may not edify by doctrine those to whom you had dedicated your labours [the Vaudois], the testimony which you bear will not fail to console them even from afar; for God will give it power to resound where human voices never could have reached."[2] What men and what times were these! And is this only the chief of a sect; is it not rather another Moses, the legislator of a people newly won to the Lord, who dares to speak of martyrdom as of an ordinary service? And what disciples are these men devoted to a cruel death, who bid farewell to their families as if only for a brief separation! O Lord! increase our faith; it seems as if faith itself had died upon the piles of the martyrs!

The prisoners at Chambéry still remained ignorant of the day when their execution was to take place. One morning they were brought forth from the prison; they supposed that they were to be led to some new examination; but a friend found means to acquaint them on the way of the fate which awaited them. "Let us give thanks to God," said Laborie, "that he has thought us worthy to be martyrs for himself!" But the pastor Vernoux, more sensitive, and liable to be moved by unexpected impressions, could not help being seized with an involuntary agitation. A cold sweat covered his temples; he fell into a nervous trembling; his resolution seemed about to fail. But all at once he found himself inwardly strengthened, the soul reinvigorated the body, the hand of God sustained him. "My brethren," said he, with humble firmness, "I pray you be not scandalized at my weakness, for I have experienced within myself the most terrible conflict which could possibly be endured. But glory be to God, who by his spirit has overcome the flesh! Let us go forward! I can do all things through Christ which strengtheneth me."

And his Saviour did not abandon him. For the executioner having laid hold of him to fasten him first to the pile, he demanded a moment for prayer, and it being granted him, these words proceeded from his dying lips, breathing the assurance of his heart: "O Lord God, Eternal and Almighty Father, I confess before thy Holy Majesty that I am nothing but a poor sinner, incapable of

---

[1] Crespin, fol. 329. [2] Crespin, fol. 332, 333.

myself of doing any good. Be pleased, then, to have compassion upon me, O God of all goodness, the Father of mercy, and to pardon my sins for the love of Jesus Christ thy Son, my only Redeemer!" He knelt upon the pile, and pronounced that admirable confession of sins, which proceeded for the first time from the lips of Theodore Beza, in midst of the great Synod of La Rochelle. This affecting and powerful prayer is well known, as still in use in the reformed churches. But how much more impressive must it have been when uttered by that pastor, on the top of the pile on which he was to die, than as pronounced from pulpits, by so many careless voices, without danger and too frequently without life!

Laborie stepped upon the pile with firmness of manner and a joyful countenance, as if he had been going to a festival. And that triumph of these regenerate souls was indeed a festival. Isaac may have groaned upon Mount Moriah; but behold! the Christian pastor offers himself for a holocaust with joy in his heart and a smile upon his lips. How mighty the power of that faith which works such wonders!

Tringalet prayed for his enemies. The two other martyrs also spoke some pious sentences, and all five having been strangled, were left to the flames, which only devoured their corpses.

A short time after, the Barba Gilles, already mentioned in the history of the churches of Calabria, returning from these countries by Venice and the Tyrol, passed into Germany, and making his way back through Switzerland, stopped at Lausanne. There he made the accquaintance of a young pastor of great talent, but of a very delicate constitution, named Stephen Noel. Having obtained his consent to devote his services to the Vaudois churches, they set out for together for Piedmont; but in passing through Savoy, they were accosted one evening in an hostelry near Chambéry, by an officer of justice, who began to address them "with a profusion of compliments," says Gilles, "which were by no means desired." They passed themselves off as relatives of some soldiers whom they were going to see in the camp. (It was during the time of the wars of Francis I. in Italy). But the officer of justice, not seeming more than half satisfied, expressed his desire of having further conversation with them in the morning. They had no wish to wait for him; and through the protection of their host, who favoured them (but above all through that of God, who kept them in safety), they were enabled to make their escape during the night, turned aside into by-paths, and arrived safe and well in Piedmont.

But there, also, other martyrs were to shed their blood. The reader will recollect the crusade commenced by Innocent VIII.

against the Vaudois. Amongst the chiefs who signalized themselves at the head of these sanguinary troops, was a Captain Varagle (pronounced Varaille), whose son, a youth of remarkable intelligence, entered into orders in 1522. He resided at a short distance from the Vaudois valleys, in Busque, a little town more isolated from the rest of the world than almost any other in Piedmont. His rapid progress in learning, his knowledge of theology, and his eloquence in the pulpit, attracted the attention of his superiors.

It was at this period that the influence of the Reformation was everywhere felt. The Church of Rome perceived the necessity of strengthening its tottering power. The Synod of Angrogna, at which Farel and Saulnier had been present, had just given a more lively impulse to that movement of disquietude, of inquiry, and of awakening, which then agitated all the better class of minds. Young Varagle was chosen for the work of repressing it. (His name was Geoffrey, and I shall write his surname Varaille, in order to conform the orthography to the pronunciation.)

To him was intrusted the difficult task of visiting the principal cities of Italy, in order to restore the credit of the Romish Church by his eloquent discourses. An Observantine monk of the convent of Monte Fiascone, in the county of Urbino, was commissioned to accompany him. His name was Matteo Baschi, and it was he who, reforming the order of the Cordeliers in 1525, originated that of the Capuchins, which very soon reckoned nearly 500 convents in Europe, and more than 25,000 monks. With these two missionaries ten other members of the secular clergy were joined for this important enterprise.

Being compelled, in order to accomplish it, to examine for themselves the arguments employed by the reformed against Catholicism, they soon perceived their force, and presently became themselves suspected of an inclination in favour of the doctrines which they were appointed to combat. These suspicions grew into certainty, and they were all imprisoned at Rome upon this serious charge. Their captivity lasted for five years.[1] It may be supposed that this long detention was not long enough to efface from their minds the impressions which were regarded with so much alarm; if their minds were upright and sincere, this seclusion, as it kept them from attending to anything else, was only calculated to confirm them the more. Such was its effect on Varaille.

Renouncing from the first all active opposition to the Reforma-

[1] Minutes of the sittings of the Parliament of Turin, of 27th and 28th September, 1557.

tion, he attached himself to the Legate of the Holy See at the court of France, and accompanied him to Paris, where he abode for some time. But the distant rays of the Reformation, that dayspring from on high, which opened up the era of modern liberty by the outbreaking light of the gospel, reached him with still greater power in the French capital. The massacre of the Vaudois of Mérindol and of Cabrières, the case relative to which was about this time pleaded before the Court of Peers, excited his indignation and disgust against a church drenched with the blood of the righteous. Compelled unquestionably by his conscience, he spontaneously quitted the high position which he occupied at Paris, and proceeded to Geneva, in order to study the new doctrines at their fountain.

What an epoch was that in which the great interests of religion had so powerful a reality, that a regard to them alone was sufficient to change, in this way, the whole course of a life!

Varaille was at this time nearly fifty years of age; but his faith made him young again, and, filled with an ardour which his youth had not known, he cast off without hesitation all his previous connections, ready to begin life anew with a moral strength which he had never possessed before. This man, laden with half a century of Popery, had felt the truth of the words spoken by our Lord to Nicodemus, and humbly received the imposition of hands, that he might be numbered amongst the evangelical pastors destined to defend that cause with which all that he had previously had to do had been in the character of an adversary. The Vaudois churches now applied for a pastor who could preach in Italian. Geoffrey Varaille was sent to them, and was settled in the parish of St. John. Here, then, was he in these same valleys in which his father had conducted a persecuting crusade. O, how unlike are God's ways to our ways! The son was called to take charge, as a pastor, of that same flock which his father had sought to exterminate.

After having spent some months in the valleys, he desired to see the little town of Busque, where he was born; his family was not yet quite extinct there, and a few evangelical Christians who began to appear in that place, were to him a family whom his heart did not less dearly love. This journey, however, was not without perils; he received notice that spies were employed by his enemies to watch his movements. But his courage seemed to have increased with his years, as if under his white hairs the ardour of youth had returned along with evangelical fervour. In truth, the life of the soul is in old men a youth without decay, the dawn of immortality.

Nevertheless, he enjoyed the satisfaction of visiting his family, and edifying the brethren at Busque, without anything happening to him. But on his return, passing by Barges, at the base of the Mount Viso, he was denounced by the Prior of the abbey of Staffarde (to which a part of the Vaudois valleys had been granted in the 9th century),[1] and arrested by a criminal officer, a nephew of the Archdeacon of Saluces.

He was treated with respect; a richly furnished house was assigned him for his prison, and he was even allowed to be at large upon parole. How many ordinary prisoners would have taken advantage of it to have fled! But the true Christian is not like one of those Papists who declared in their council[2] that a man may break his word without breaking the law of God. Having even learned that some of the reformed of Bubiano, who formed part of his parish, had an intention of coming to deliver him by force, he sent them word to refrain, and to leave the matter in the hands of God. And yet the edicts of Francis I., who had conquered Piedmont, and of Henry II., who then reigned there, authorized the greatest severities against him.

After several examinations he was conducted to Turin, firmly bound. The responses which he made to his judges, and the written arguments which he presented to them in support of his religion, are a monument of his talents, his knowledge, and his piety.

During his imprisonment, Calvin wrote to him from Geneva a letter in Latin, of which the following is a translation:—

"Most dear and beloved brother!—Whilst the news of your imprisonment has extremely grieved us, the Lord, who can bring light out of darkness, has united therewith a cause of joy and consolation, in the spectacle of the fruits which your affliction has already produced, and the glory which sustained St. Paul ought also to impart courage to you; for if you are bound, the Word of God is not bound, and you have it in your power to testify regarding it to many, who will spread farther abroad the seed of life which they have received from your mouth. Jesus Christ requires this testimony from every one; but he has laid the obligation in a more especial manner upon you, by the seal of the ministry which you have received, to preach the doctrine of salvation which is now assailed in your person. Remember, then, to seal, if need be, with your blood, that doctrine which you have taught with your mouth. He has promised that the death of his own shall be precious to him; let this recompense suffice you. I shall dwell no longer on this point, persuaded that you repose confidently on him, in whom, whether we live or die, our eternal happiness is to be found. My

---

[1] Amongst others, the *Combe of Giausarand*, or *Val Guichard*. See *Monumenta patriæ*, T. I., No. DXIII, anno 821. [2] Oecum. Const. 1415.

companions and brethren salute you.—Geneva, 17th of September, 1557."

It would have been pleasant to have met with more tender outpourings of the heart, in the great man whose name a portion of the Christian church still bears. But perhaps this inflexibility was necessary to that commanding influence over the minds of others by which he consolidated the Reformation.

The humble Vaudois pastor encouraged no one to face death, but he went forward to it himself with a heroic firmness. When the sentence of death was announced to him, he said with a solemn voice, " Be assured, gentlemen, that you will sooner want wood for piles, than ministers of the gospel to seal their faith upon them; for they multiply daily, and the word of God endures for ever." The court, Crespin says, pronounced sentence of death against him, rather for fear of reproach, than from conviction that he deserved it. O Pilate, Pilate! how numerous are thy race in the world!

Geoffrey Varaille was burned alive in the square of the castle at Turin, on the 29th of March, 1558. When he had ascended the pile the executioner approached; it was thought that he meant to apply the fire. Not at all; he knelt at the feet of the martyr, entreating him to pardon him the death which he was about to inflict upon him. " Not only thee," replied Varaille, "but all those who have caused it." Then, whilst the assistant executioners applied the fire in front, the principal executioner strangled him from behind; "and many people," says Crespin, " relate, as a notable fact, that a dove flew around the fire and rose into the air, which was esteemed a sign of the innocence of the martyr. But for the circumstances of this death, we have confined ourselves to the principal matter, without curiously staying upon mere externals." The true miracles of the gospel are the miracles of faith, for the gospel of Christ is the power of God unto salvation, unto all those that believe.

Along with Varaille, says Gilles, there was conducted to the place of execution, a good old man, who had already suffered much for the cause of truth, and after he had been compelled to witness the death of that worthy martyr of the Lord, and had been whipped, red hot irons were taken from that same pile, and he was marked with them, with the king's mark.

In the same year, a young man, who was born at Quiers, a short distance from the Vaudois valleys, happening to be at Aosta, on Good Friday, heard a preacher who said that the sacrifice of Jesus Christ was renewed daily in the sacrifice of the mass. "Christ has only died once," murmured the young man, "and he is now in heaven, from which he will not come again until the last day." "You do not, then, believe in his corporal presence in the host?" demanded a clerk, named Ripet. "Truly, God forbid! Do you know the creed?" "Yes; but what of that?" "Is it not there said that Jesus is now seated at the right hand of the Father?" "Yes." "Well, then, he is not in the host." Not being able to reply to this argument, they imprisoned him who used it.

He was twenty-six years of age; his name was Nicolas Sartoire. His friends contrived to secure his escape by night; he then left the town of Aosta, the ancient Augusta Prætoria, a place full of ruins and superstitions, and as he had already dwelt at Lausanne, he took the way by the St. Bernard, to take refuge in Switzerland. But at the village of St. Remy, the last which he would have had to pass through before crossing the frontier, he was arrested anew, and brought back to prison. His friends of Aosta then wrote to those whom he had at Lausanne, that they should apply to the authorities of Berne, who might demand him, as an inhabitant of that country. These attempts were made, but without effect. Nicolas Sartoire was tortured. "Retract your errors!" said the ecclesiastical judge. "Prove to me that I have errors." "The Church condemns you." "But the Bible acquits me." "You incur the punishment of death by your obstinacy." "He who shall persevere unto the end shall be saved." "You wish, then, to die?" "I wish to have eternal life." And torments, as well as solicitations, were without effect.

After the rack, he was made to endure the strapado, but his courage did not forsake him. "And for his obstinacy," says the sentence, "he was condemned to be burned alive." His friends implored him to retract; assured, they said, of being able still to obtain his pardon. "The pardon which I desire," he replied, "I have already obtained from my God." This courageous child of the Lord died on the pile, at Aosta, on the 4th of May, 1557, refusing to the last to purchase life by abjuring his religion.

About the same time, says Gilles, one of the ministers of the valley of Lucerna, returning from Geneva, was taken prisoner at Suza, and conducted thence to Turin. He displayed the same steadfastness, and his judges displayed the same barbarity. He was condemned to be burned alive. But it appears that his dignity, his gentleness, and the imposing and modest seriousness of his speech, had produced a profound impression upon those around him, for the day of the execution being come, one of the executioners feigned himself ill, and concealed himself; the other, after having put to death some malefactors, afraid of being compelled to execute the minister, fled; so that the execution being prevented from taking place, the minister found means to make his escape, and returned to his church.[1] Gilles has not preserved the name of this pastor; he relates in the briefest way this extraordinary history, in which we see the executioners fleeing before the victim—the executioners more conscientious than the judges, and refusing to have anything to do with the execution—the executioners giving the Church of Rome a lesson of humanity! Many others Christians of the Vaudois valleys, or of the places adjacent, were also condemned to death in the 16th century; but very rare were the instances in which they succeeded in escaping the execution of the sentence, and the example is perhaps unparalleled of a pastor returning to his church after having been spared by four or five executioners.

In 1560, many of the reformed or Vaudois of Piedmont were made prisoners, having been surprised in the very fact of social prayer and religious assemblies beyond the limits of the actual territory of the Vaudois valleys; and by a procedure more worthy of Mahometans than of Christians, they were condemned to be burned three days after their incarceration, without pleadings, without examination, without the formalities of trial, and simply on the strength of the accusation alone.

However, if they made profession of Popery, they were set at liberty; but if they refused to go to mass their heresy was demonstrated; in that case they had these three days allowed them to abjure, and if they did not yield, an end was put to their life. Abjuration or death: such was the language of the jurisprudence matured beneath the shade of Catholicism.

It was in the town of Carignan that the executions commenced. A French fugitive, named Mathurin, was the first seized. The commissioners enjoined him to abjure his religion if he would escape death. He preferred to die. "We give you three days to reflect," said they, "but after that time you will be burned alive if you refuse to come to mass." The family of Mathurin were more distressed than himself. He had married a Vaudois woman. His wife applied to the commissioners for leave to see him. "Provided that you do not harden him in his errors," said they. "I promise you," she replied, "that I will not speak to him except for his good." The commissioners never thought of any greater good than life, and conducted the young woman to the prisoner, in the hope that she would persuade him to prolong his days by a recantation.

But the courageous daughter of the martyrs dreaded, on the contrary, that her husband might be induced to follow that course out

[1] Gilles, chap. x. p. 67.

of affection for her, or through human weakness, and the good which she wished to do him was to confirm him in his resolution. "Accordingly," says our old chronicler, "she exhorted him, in presence of the commissioners, as earnestly as possible, steadfastly to persevere in his religion, without putting the death of the body, which is of brief duration, in the balance against the eternal salvation of his soul." The commissioners, transported with rage, on hearing language so different from what they expected upon her part, loaded her with reproaches; but she, unmoved and earnest, continued to address her husband, saying to him, with a firm and gentle voice, "Let not the assaults of the wicked one make you abandon the profession of your hope in Jesus Christ." "Exhort him to obey us, or you shall both be hanged," cried the magistrates. "And let not the love of this world's possessions make you lose the inheritance of heaven!" said the Christian woman, without pausing in her calm exhortations. "Heretical she-devil!" they exclaimed, "if you do not change your tone, you shall be burned to-morrow." "Would I have come to persuade him to die rather than to abjure," she replied, "if I could myself seek to escape death by apostasy?" "You should fear, at any rate, the torments of the pile." "I fear him who is able to cast both body and soul into a more terrible fire than that of your billets." "Hell is for heretics; save yourselves by renouncing your errors." "Where can the truth be if not in the words of God?" "This will be the destruction of you both," said the magistrates, if that name can be given to such cruel fanatics. "Blessed be God!" said the woman to her husband, "because having united us in life, he will not separate us in death!" "Instead of one, we shall have two of them to burn," sneeringly muttered the executioner's satellites." "I will be thy companion to the end," the heroic woman simply added. "Will you come to mass and have your pardon?" said the magistrates again. "I would much rather go to the pile and have eternal life." "If you do not abjure, Mathurin shall be burned to-morrow, and you three days after." "We shall meet again in heaven," replied she, mildly. "Think of the delay that is still granted you." "The length of it is of no consequence, for my resolution is for life." "Say, rather, it is for death." "The death of the body, but the life of the soul." "Have you nothing else to say to us, you damned obstinate wretch?" "Nothing; except that I beseech you not to put off my execution for three days, but to let me die with my husband." Her request was granted. She had entered the prison a free woman, but she remained a captive, and only came out again to mount the pile.

The name of this woman was Joan, and this name, pronounced in such circumstances, involuntarily recals that of Joan of Arc. Why should not the heroism of the Christian woman be admired as much as that of the young female warrior of Orleans? Ought the victims of faith to be less thought of than those of battle? Alas! one may more readily become illustrious in this world by taking the lives of his enemies, than by giving his own for the love of the brethren. But those who do so give their lives, do it not with an eye to worldly glory.

The two martyr spouses had a last evening of prayer and meditation to spend together on this earth. It is pleasing to think that it cannot have been the least sweet of their evenings, for Jesus says, "Wherever even two shall be met in my name, I will be with them, in the midst of them." And when were the conditions of that promise ever more completely realized than at that hour?

Next day, being the 2d of March, 1560, a pile was formed in the public square of Carignan, and there these worthy confessors of the gospel died, holding one another by the hand, and with souls united in the love of the Saviour.

A new pile was formed twelve days after, in the same place, for the execution of a young man who had been arrested three days before, on the way from Lucerna to Pignerol. His name was John De Cartignon, and as he was a jeweller, he was called Johanni delle Spinelle. He had already been a prisoner upon account of religion; it was upon this account that he had retired to the valley of Lucerna, for he was not a native of it. Finding himself once more a captive, he concluded that this would be the last time. "My deliverance," he said, "will not come from men, but from God." And, indeed, God sustained him, for he endured the torment of his execution with rare courage.

The inquisition called these atrocious barbarities acts of faith—*autos da fe*. Such were, therefore, the acts of the Catholic faith; those of the Protestant faith were glorious martyrdoms. Which are most worthy of the name?

"In 1535," says Gilles, "Bersour having been commissioned to proceed against the Vaudois, laid hold of so great a number of them that he filled with them his castle of Miradol, and the prisons and convent of Pignerol, as well as the dungeons of the inquisition at Turin." Many of the prisoners were condemned to be burned alive. One of them, Catalan Girardet, of St. John, on his way to the place of execution, lifted two stones, and rubbing them one against another in his hands, said to the inquisitors, "See these impenetrable pebbles; all that you can do to annihilate our churches, will no more destroy them than I can wear away and destroy these stones." He endured his death with admirable firmness. These words of his have caused his name to be preserved; but how many others died like him, and with the same courage?

Many prisoners also perished without its being ever known what became of them! Such was the case at this period with Mark Chanavas of Pinache, Julian Colombat of Villar Pérouse, and George Stalè of Fenil.

Let us bestow a thought upon these unknown victims, whose sufferings and courage perhaps increased together during whole years of unmeasured distress, occasioned at once by their being forgotten, and by disease and hunger. Some one striking circumstance is enough to give distinction to a name, but this perseverance throughout ages (for in dungeons a year is an age), this termless resignation, does it not require even more strength of soul, and ought it not to excite in us even more profound sympathies than the enthusiasm of a moment?

A few years later, the pastor of St. Germain was brought by a traitor within the grasp of a troop of malefactors in the pay of the abbey of Pignerol. Some of his parishioners, who attempted to defend him, were arrested along with him. But the torments and death of the victims of Rome, and the victories of their faith, were things then so common, that Gilles, without even mentioning the name of this pastor, merely tells us that, after having overcome all the temptations which were employed in order to make him abjure, he was condemned to be burned alive by a slow fire; and adds that some women of St. Germain, who were prisoners along with him, were constrained to carry faggots to the pile where their pastor was patiently enduring martyrdom. What a picture, however, is here presented to us of holy resolution maintained in the midst of horrors!

Still later, in 1560, the hamlet of Les Bonnets, situated between La Tour and Le Villar, was assailed by soldiers, who came at once from both of these last-named places, where at that time were fortifications, which are now demolished. After having destroyed and pillaged everything, they bore off fourteen prisoners. Two men alone had escaped them. These men hastened to post themselves above a steep slope by which the aggressors must pass. No sooner had the troop of spoliators got upon this declivity with their prisoners, than the two Vaudois, who lay concealed, set in motion a great number of stones, which rolled down upon them, and threw them into confusion, so that twelve of the prisoners found opportunity of taking to flight. The two captives who remained in the hands of the assailants both belonged to a family named Geymet; the name of the one was John, that of the other Udolph. They were conveyed to the castle of La Tour. There, after both cruelties and promises had been employed in order to make them abjure, the captain of the garrison, named Joseph Banster, strangled John Geymet with his own hands. Udolph was fastened to a table, stripped of his garments, and put to death by an unparalleled torture. The following is the simple and laconic account which Gilles gives of it:—" The soldiers having collected a great number of those creatures which live in the dung and carrion of animals, filled therewith a bowl, which they placed upon his belly, and fastened it to his body, so that these vermin went into his entrails and devoured him, he being yet alive. These cruelties have been related by the very soldiers of the garrison. Thus died this poor martyr, in the sixtieth year of his age."

Here let us pause. The mind recoils, horror-stricken, from the thought of so many victims, and of such atrocious refinements of cruelty. Was this a race of savages, who could ruthlessly shed so much blood? And if they did it in name of their religion, ought not that religion to be execrated of mankind? Can altars which have been served by the inquisition, by Jesuitism, and by simony, pretend a right to the servile homage of civilized men! Cain killed his brother through envy, in a moment of passion, without having known the light of the gospel; he killed him alone; but Rome, which assumes the name of Christian, beneath whose very tiara the tradition of assassination has been transmitted—Rome has destroyed thousands of victims, has murdered them in cold blood, has premeditated their death, has prolonged their agonies, has invented refinements of torture, and whensoever the interests of her own empire were concerned, her work has been to betray, to corrupt, and to kill.

But these poor oppressed ones, the victims of her tyranny—these Christians who enjoyed no rest, and martyrs who exhibited no weakness—knew also well that it is said in the gospel, " Blessed are they who are persecuted for righteousness' sake, for theirs is the kingdom of heaven." But it is not necessary to suffer martyrdom in order to die unto the Lord; and every Christian, however mean his condition, says, in the words recorded in ancient Bible history, "Let me die the death of the righteous, and let my last end be like his."

CHAPTER IX.

HISTORY OF THE EVANGELICAL CHURCHES OF PAËSANE, PRAVIGLELM, AND SALUCES.[1]

(A.D. 1550 TO A.D. 1580.)

The Marquisate of Saluces—Inquisitors sent to extirpate heresy in 1308—Persecutions of 1499-1510—Margaret De Foix, Marchioness of Saluces—Expulsion of the Vaudois from Saluces—They take refuge in the other valleys—Their return to Saluces in 1512—Influence of the Reformation—Increase and extension of the church.

IN the bottom of the basin and on the elevated level grounds of Paësane, and in the deep valleys of Cruzzol and Onzino, where the head-waters of the Po descend from Mount Visol, the Vaudois appear to have had their most ancient settlements in the province of Saluces. It has been alleged that their origin amongst these mountains was contemporaneous with that of the other Vaudois who inhabit the left bank of the Po. But Gilles informs us that the inhabitants of Praviglelm, Biolet, and Biétonnet, came from the valley of Lucerna. This emigration must be referred to a very remote date, since those who descended from it had peopled the

---

[1] AUTHORITIES.—*Perrin, Gilles, Léger, Rorengo.*—"*Brief discours des persécutions advenues aux eglises du marquisat de Saluces.*" Genève, chez Paul Marceau, 1620. (This work was composed by order, and printed at the expense of the Synod held at Briançon in June, 1620.)—"*Memorabilis historia persec. bellorumque in pop. vulgo* Valdensem *appellatum*, &c." Genevæ. Excudebat Eustathius Vignon M.D.LXXXI. (Small 8vo, of 150 pages in italics.)—"*Relatione all'eminentissima congregatione de propaganda fide, dei luoghi di alcune valle di Piemonte, all'A.R. di Savoja sogetti* . . ." Torino. No date, small 18mo, pp. 523.—Massi, "*Storia de Pinerolo* . . ." 3 vols.—Semeria, "*Storia della chiesa metropolitana di Torino.*" 8vo. 1840.—"*Le banissement des gens de la religion prétendue réformée, hors des estats de Savoye, le tout, selon l'ordonnance et arrest de l'Inquisition et Sénat de Piedmont.*" Paris, M.D.C.XIX. (Relates exclusively to the Vaudois of Saluces.)— "*Lettres des fidèles du marquisat de Saluces, souveraineté du duc de Savoye, envoyées à MM. les Pasteurs de l'Eglise de Genève, contenantes l'histoire de leurs persécutions,* . . . . &c."—"*Jouxte la copie ecrite à Genève.*" 1619.—Soleri, "*Diario dei fatti successi in Torino,* . . . &c."—Muletti, "*Mém. hist. sur le marquisat de Saluces,*" (t. vi.)—Costa de Beauregard, "*Mém. hist. sur la maison roy. de Savoie.*" Turin, 1816. 3 vols. 8vo.—"*Litteræ quædam nondum editæ . . . ex authographis . . . edidit Bretsneider.*" Leipsiæ, 1835. 8vo.—(Contains a letter of the pastor of Praviglelm, dated 23d July, 1563.)—General and particular histories of Piedmont, and of the Marquisate of Saluces.—"*L'Art de vérifier les dates.*"—Histories of France (for the period during which Piedmont was included in the French dominions).—Various documents found in the archives of Saluces, Lucerna, Pignerol, and Turin.—A MS. of the Royal Library at Turin, the "*Chronicle of the family of the Sollaros*" (in Italian).—Private letters of MM. Cibrario, Duboin, César of Saluces, &c.—Some of the authorities here noted belong to the subsequent chapters.

Drawn by S. Bough from a sketch by Dr. Muston. Engraved by J. H. Kernot

THE TOWN OF SALUCES.
MOUNT VISO IN THE DISTANCE.

BLACKIE & SON, GLASGOW, EDINBURGH & LONDON.

MARQUISATE OF SALUCES.

marquisate of Saluces, and we find that the Vaudois were already there in the 13th century. We know, indeed, that the Vaudois of Provence issued from it; and in the confession of faith which they presented to Francis I., on the 6th of April, 1541, they refer their settlement in Provence to more than 200 years before that date.

The Vaudois of Saluces themselves, including those of the valleys of the Po, gave out that they and their fathers had existed in that country from time immemorial.[1] Perhaps it was this which gave rise to the opinion, which has recently been expressed, that the Vaudois of all other parts of Piedmont issued from these districts;[2] but Gilles positively affirms that those of Saluces themselves derived their origin from the valley of Lucerna.[3]

The marquisate of Saluces dates its existence from the 12th century. This tract of country was given as a dowry to Beatrix, grand-daughter of Adelaide of Suza, who enlarged the abbey of Pignerol, and in whose behalf the emperor, Henry the Aged, her son-in-law, erected the fiefs of the territory of Saluces into a marquisate. They remained, therefore, dependent, as secondary fiefs, upon the *marche* of Suza, and when the territory of Seuzie passed into the hands of the Counts of Savoy, these counts found themselves also the *suzerains* of the Marquises of Saluces.

In 1308 inquisitors were sent into this region to destroy heresy; but after having been repulsed and defeated in discussion, they sustained a new defeat in their attempt to triumph by means of violence. Surrounded in a castle, and retained as prisoners by the inhabitants of the district which they came to convert, and who seemed to be unanimous in repelling them, they were compelled to submit to conditions instead of imposing them, and retired from these countries without having even commenced the work for which they had come thither.[4] Pope John XXII., in his brief to John de Badis, intimated to the Marquises of Saluces, to the Counts of Lucerna, and to the Duke of Savoy, his desire that they would assist the inquisition with all their power against these disorganizers of the Church of Rome. But the power most formidable to that church, and effectual in disorganizing it, is the word of God, and not the rebellion of men. Let the Bible reign in any place,

[1] Perrin, p. 185. Léger, p. cxi.
[2] *De Rougemont, "Précis d'ethnographie, de statist. et de géographie hist."* t. i. p. 210. [3] Gilles, p. 18.
[4] *Prænominati hæretici ipsum Inquisitorem in quodam castello patenter et publice obsederunt, sic eum oportuit quod inde recedere, inquisitionis hujusmodi officio relicto, totaliter imperfecto.*—Brief of John XXII. to John de Badis, 23d July, 1332.

and there Popery must be overcome. This appeal of the pontiff had no other result than the apprehension of a Barba of the valley of Lucerna, named Martin Pastre. He was on his way to the churches of Saluces, and he justified, by a courageous martyrdom, the choice which had been made of him for that evangelical mission.

The edict of the Duchess Iolande, in 1476, enjoining the châtelains of Pignerol, Cavour, and Lucerna, to cause all the Vaudois of the Italian Alps to return within the pale of the Catholic Church, could not but affect in some measure those on the right bank of the Po; but it was in 1499 that they began to be assailed with the most direct violence.

Margaret de Foix, the widow of the Marquis of Saluces, finding herself free from his control, and being a slave to her confessor, became in the hands of fanaticism a ready instrument of persecution. She was connected by family ties with Pope Julius II., and obtained from him the creation of a bishopric in the marquisate. In return for this favour, she erected, at her own expense, the episcopal palace in which Anthony de la Rovera, the first bishop of Saluces, and nephew of Julius II., was received more as a prince than as a pastor. It was she, also, who built the church of St. Clara, in which her tomb may be seen unto this day; but whilst she built churches of stone, she sought to destroy the living church, which preserved within it the gospel of the earliest times; and at the instigation of the clergy by whom she was surrounded, she issued a decree, by which the Vaudois were enjoined, under pain of death, to embrace Catholicism or to quit the country.[1]

The unfortunate people retired to the banks of the Po. The marchioness would have pursued them, but the seigneurs of Paësane, with whom the fugitives had found shelter, represented that to themselves alone, in concert with the bishop and the inquisitors, belonged the right of proceeding in that way against any persons on their lands; their own vassals, moreover, were almost all of the Vaudois faith. The marchioness then purchased from the bishop and inquisitors the right of prosecution which belonged to them; and being thus possessed of two-thirds of that barbarous jurisdiction, she sent out *missionaries*, whose first act was to ordain all the inhabitants of St. Frons, Praviglelm, Paësane, Biolet, Biétonet, Serre di Momian, and Borga d'Oncino, to come and perform an act of penitence at Paësane, before Brother Angiolo Ricciardino de Saviglian.

No one came, and the prosecutions commenced. Two men were

[1] Muletti, vi. 29, 331.

arrested at St. Frons. "To what place do you belong?" "To these mountains." "Are you Vaudois?" "We all are." "Abjure the heresy." "When it has been proved to us." It was not proved, but the two Christians were thrown into prison. Two others were arrested in another place, and likewise declared themselves Vaudois. The one belonged to Praviglelm, and the other to Oncino. "None of our people will abjure," said they to the inquisitors. The Marchioness of Saluces then armed 200 men, and caused them to march towards the mountains. The greater part of the inhabitants fled to Barges with their cattle, but some were taken and cast into prisons. Their trial having been finished, *and tortures not spared*,[1] five of them were condemned to death on the 24th of March, 1510. Their execution was reserved for Palm Sunday. Human victims! the offerings of the Church of Rome to its false gods!

The Vaudois prisoners were to be burned alive, in a meadow situated opposite to the paternal home of one of them, named Maynard. This name, which occurs also amongst the persecuted in Provence, attests the affiliation of the Vaudois churches of the two sides of the Alps. The pile was prepared, but when the day came, there fell such a quantity of rain and snow, that the wood could not be got to burn. The execution was put off to the next day. During the night, a secret friend managed to convey a file to the unhappy captives, and they freed themselves from their fetters, and glorifying God for this deliverance, took refuge at Barges with their brethren in the faith.

The executioners revenged themselves upon other prisoners for the flight of these victims. Mary and Julia Gienet, with one of their brethren, named Lanfré Balangier, were burned alive on the bank of the Po, on the 2d day of May following. But the prisons were not yet emptied. Many were subjected to the ignoble and cruel punishment of the bastinado, and many died under these atrocious inflictions. Some of their companions in captivity perished by slow degrees in the subterranean dungeons of the castle of Paësane. Some made profession of repentance, a small number were pardoned, and all who could make their escape retired to Barges, and from thence into the valley of Lucerna.

The property of these poor people was confiscated, two-thirds of it going to the Marchioness of Saluces. It was a profitable business, for she made more by it than the right of prosecution had cost her. Accordingly, she gave a share of the spoils of the heretics to the monks of Riffredo. The traffickers in human blood are

[1] *Uditi testimonii, non risparmiati itormenti.*—Muletti, vi. 385.

a step in advance of brutes, which give up no part of their prey. The last third of these confiscations was divided betwixt the seigneurs of Oncino and Paësane, on whose lands they had taken place. They had opposed the murder, but they shared the spoil.

At length, on the 18th of July, 1510, which the reader will observe was before the Reformation, the Inquisition caused the Vaudois place of worship to be demolished; which a contemporary manuscript calls the *synagogue of the heretics*, saying that it was white and of good appearance on the outside, but full of windings within, and constructed almost like a labyrinth!

Next year, also, five Vaudois were burned alive at St. Frons. Unfortunate race, but worthy of admiration! Confiscation deprived them of their property, their families were decimated by the sword, the piles of their martyrs became more and more numerous, but their faith did not perish.

All those who had escaped the weapons of the soldiers and the flames of the Holy Office, and who were hidden in the mountains, or had fled to Barges and Bagnols, retired to the valley of Lucerna, where seigneurs more powerful and more just protected their vassals against such aggressions. And what shows better than any other consideration the primitive brotherliness which really prevailed amongst the Vaudois, and the profound practical charity which governed their lives, is the fact that all this large number of refugees lived for five whole years with the poor mountaineers of those Vaudois valleys, which had been the cradle of their race.[1] Sharing at once in their bread and their worship, praying and labouring with them, the proscribed refugees continued always expectant of some termination of that precarious state of things. They were mostly divided amongst the communes of Angrogna, Rora, and Bobi, and had named a syndicate, commissioned to watch over their common interests.

Numerous applications were made as soon as possible to the Marchioness of Saluces that they might be permitted to return to their ancient possessions. All these petitions remained unanswered. However, the prolonged sojourn of so many new families with a people themselves so few as the inhabitants of the valley of Lucerna, was a thing that must some time have an end. To recover possession of their native country was a duty recommended to them by a regard for others, enforced by justice, and which it belonged to their courage to perform. An intrepid man stood up in the midst

---

[1] They did not all arrive at the same time, but successively from A.D. 1505 to 1510, and their removal took place in 1512. Some of them, therefore, must have remained only two years, and some of them seven.

of them. "My friends!" he exclaimed, "let us return to our own inheritances! it will be the best way of gaining possession of them." "But will not those who occupy them prevent us?" "We will take again, in spite of them, what they took in spite of us. Let us put our trust in God! his blessing is upon justice and not upon iniquity. If we have been persecuted for our faith, we shall also be protected by it, for it is of God, and God is mightier than our enemies." They assembled in arms in the valley of Rora, set out by night, traversed the mountains of Crussol, descended into the valley of the Po, reached their ancient abodes, fell like thunder upon their plunderers when unarmed, fought with them, overthrew them, pursued those who made any resistance, cleared the country of them, got the upper hand in it through the terror which audacity and success inspire, re-established themselves in their hereditary possessions, and brought back to their old abodes the faith of their forefathers. Only five Vaudois lost their lives in this expedition. Why did they not more frequently listen to the voice of that courage which restored to them their native land! Valour has a more imposing effect than weakness; and the moderation of the Vaudois has many a time doubled the arrogance of their enemies.

After this the churches of the valley of the Po enjoyed tranquillity for some years. The news of the Reformation began to agitate men's minds. We have seen what effect was thereby produced in the other Vaudois valleys. New light was diffused everywhere. The evangelical doctrines spread all around these mountains, which, for so long a time before, had been brightened by the dawn of that bright day.

As in France the upper classes of society were the first to produce defenders of the Reformation, so the noblest families of Piedmont soon partook of the honour of being connected with it. In the province of Saluces the seigneurs of Montroux opened their castle for the religious meetings of the new reformed. Several members of the family of Villanova Sollaro embraced their religion. The Duke of Savoy himself wrote to them several times to persuade them to relinquish it. These urgencies, from so high a quarter, added still more importance, in public estimation, to the profession of evangelical religion which they were intended to overthrow. The number of the reformed increased instead of diminishing; they demanded pastors, and, until these should come, betook themselves with eagerness to the regular preaching which went on in the valley of Lucerna.

This influx of hearers from other parts, who thus crowded to the living springs of grace as to another Siloah, very soon became so considerable that the Duke of Savoy prohibited his subjects, who did not belong to the Vaudois valleys, from being present at these preachings.[1] At the same time, he himself sent Catholic missionaries to oppose the progress of these doctrines. But the doctrine was the doctrine of the gospel, and they were to oppose God! therefore they failed. Yet Duke Philibert displayed all possible personal activity to promote the success of his preachers. He wrote no fewer than four letters, in the month of May, 1565, to the Châtelain, to the Podestat, to the Official, and to the inhabitants of Carail, in order to recommend the missionary whom he sent to them.

But as the whole marquisate of Saluces was then under the dominion of France, these endeavours produced little effect there. On the contrary, the number of the reformed increased daily, and in consequence of the *Edict of Pacification*, newly obtained by the King of Navarre in favour of his co-religionists, the church of Dronèro, one of the most flourishing in the marquisate, obtained from the Royal Council letters-patent,[2] which authorized the opening of a Protestant place of worship without the gates of the town. Louis de Birague, who at this time succeeded the Count de Nevers as the king's lieutenant in the province of Savoy, wrote to the court to have this authorization withdrawn. Charles IX. himself[3] replied, in these terms:—"*By the advice of our much honoured lady and mother,[4] we declare by these presents, that in the edict of pacification we never intended to comprehend the exercise of religion in the towns of Piedmont.*"[5] Thus did Catharine de Médicis exercise her fatal power even over these churches of brethren! But their courage was not daunted; and next year they spontaneously organized themselves as reformed churches. They had pastors, deacons, and consistories, and established a regular religious service, which only could not always be conducted in public.

France was then desolated by wars of religion; the Huguenots had been massacred at Vassy and in Champagne; the Guises excited the Catholic party; the Protestant party was supported by the Bourbons. These intestine commotions distracted the attention of the government from the external provinces. The churches of Saluces, protected by their isolation, were permitted peacefully to increase beyond the reach of these distant storms. Accordingly, in a few years they became numerous and flourishing. The times of quiet are those which offer the least materials for history. Happy

---

[1] Edict of 15th February, 1560. [2] Dated 6th June, 1563.
[3] From Dieppe, 7th August, 1563. [4] Catharine de Médicis.
[5] This letter is preserved in the Archives of Pignerol, class xxv. file I. No. 3.

is the people all whose vicissitudes can be comprehended in a page! But spiritual history advances with all the conversions which take place when that of human actions stands still. This epoch was one of the most fruitful for the gospel in the province of Saluces. Ten pastors, serving twenty-one churches, independent of those of Coni, Carail, and Ozasc, already exercised the gospel ministry there in 1567.[1] By this we may see with what life they were filled, and what splendid promise they gave for the future, if liberty of conscience might have been allowed to prevail. But the great conquests of humanity are not attained in a day. In yielding liberty Rome would have fallen into destruction; but it is by her own tyranny that she is doomed to perish.

Let us leave the churches of Saluces to the enjoyment of their short-lived prosperity, and consider what was then taking place around them in other parts of Piedmont.

[1] The following are the names of these pastors, and of the parishes which were assigned them by the Synods of 2d June and 14th October, 1567, held, the one at Praviglelm, the other at Dronèro, or Dronier:—

The pastor Galatée (who was sent to plead the cause of these churches before Charles IX.) had for his field of labour *Saluces*, *Savillan*, Carmagnole, *Lavodis* (Lévadiggi), and *Villefalet*. (The names in italics are those of places where there was a place of worship.)

The minister Segont de Masseran (Mattervo) had in his district *Verzol*, Alpease, and Costilloles.

Francis Trucchi served the church of *Dronier*; Andrew Lacianois those of *St. Damian*, *Paillers*, and *Cartignano*; Peter Gelido that of *Aceil* (Asceglio); James Isoard those of St. Michael, *Pras*, and *Chianois*.

Francis Soulf was pastor of Praviglelm; and Bertrand Jordan of Biolet, and of *Biétonct*.

Besides these, two other pastors, who were not present at the Synod, served the churches of *Demont* and *Testeone*. Lastly, there was also a pastor at *Carail* (Caraglo), whose name is not preserved.

CHAPTER X.

HISTORY OF THE PROGRESS AND EXTINCTION OF THE REFORMATION AT CONI, AND IN THE PLAIN OF PIEDMONT.[1]

(A.D. 1550 TO A.D. 1580.)

The Reformation in towns near the Vaudois valleys—Timidity—Persecution—Many of the Protestants take refuge among the Vaudois—Martyrdom of the Pastor Jacob—Protestantism in Turin—Persecutions in various parts of Piedmont—The churches of Coni and Carail—Persecutions—Suppression of the Reformation in Coni.

IN the space between Turin and the Vaudois valleys, there is perhaps not a single town in which the religious reformation of the 16th century did not find adherents, and obtain the sympathy of many.

Catholicism had fallen into a state of degradation of which we can scarcely form an idea at the present day. An inquisitor of Racconis,[2] writing to the Holy Office of Rome in 1567, says, " I cannot describe to you the utter decay of everything connected with religion in this country; the churches in ruin, the altars despoiled, the sacerdotal vestments tattered, the priests ignorant, and all things held in contempt." Like the quickening dawn of morning, the evangelical revival, therefore, spreading over that bare and arid soil, restored life and vigour, and a thousand unexpected views of heaven and of earth opened at once before the spiritual vision of men. Life increased along with truth; the dew came with the light. The people, who had hitherto partaken of the immovable petrifaction of Popery, now illustrated and verified that saying of the Saviour's forerunner, " Even of these stones God is able to raise up children to Abraham." But, like children, also, they were weak and timid. That dawning light was not then able to give them either the courage of conviction or the martyr's faith. Moreover, the most artful partisans of Rome restrained the natural development of the new opinions, by appearing to participate in them. " A reform is necessary," said they; "every one feels it; the Church will make it; this is not the time for separating from her."

Such was the language of Dominic Baronius,[3] who was at that time in Piedmont, and who was oftener than once in communication

---

[1] AUTHORITIES.—The same as in the preceding chapter.

[2] His name was Cornelio D'Adro; his letter is dated the 22d of October, 1567. (Archives of Turin.)

[3] He was a native of Florence; his namesake, Cæsar Baronius, who was a cardinal, and librarian of the Vatican, was a Neapolitan.

with the doctors of the Vaudois churches. Perhaps his conviction was sincere, seeing that he wrote, in his book on *Human Institutions*, with reference to the serious corruptions which Popery had introduced into the celebration of the Lord's Supper, "Weep ye, and lament, for the sacrilegious profanation of this divine mystery! I would restrain my pen, but, O God! the zeal of thy house consumes me. Impiety, idolatry, ambition, venality surround thine altars!" And yet he did not dare openly to abandon that idolatry and impiety. Rome pardoned his offence upon account of his submission. "He affected to wonder," says Gilles, "that he found no danger in launching out against the abuses of the papacy, but in the time of persecution he made use of a hypocritical dissimulation, and persuaded others to do the same." Maximilian of Saluces, one of his adherents, wrote thus to the Vaudois pastors: "We condemn, as well as you, the errors of the Papal Church, we desire that they may be reformed; but, in the first place, it is necessary that we reform ourselves inwardly, and that we know how to accommodate ourselves to circumstances, and not to expose ourselves to needless perils in too sharply attacking received usages." Such was also the language of Erasmus, and even to a certain extent that of Melancthon.

The Vaudois pastors expressed themselves with less eloquence, but they acted with more courage. "Our rule of conduct," said they, "ought to be that declaration of Jesus, 'Whosoever shall confess me upon earth, him will I confess in heaven; and whosoever shall deny me upon earth, him will I deny in heaven.' We choose rather to be rejected by the Papal Church than by our Saviour."

The pastors of Geneva likewise sent to the different towns of Piedmont in which the gospel had begun to be introduced, letters strongly encouraging to perseverance. Celsus of Martiningue, who was pastor of the Italian church in that town, wrote to Baronius, with the view of inducing him to follow a course more open and evangelical. But the greatest effort to which the convictions of the latter, who was an abbé, ever proved equal, was that of introducing certain modifications in the manner of celebrating mass. He would have wished to reunite the two parties, and that by measures deemed sufficient upon both sides; but his example caused many persons to stop half-way in a course which would otherwise have resulted in a complete change. This hesitation on the one side, augmented the decision upon the other. The duke was solicited to issue an express prohibition of Protestant religious services beyond the bounds of the Vaudois valleys, and to restrain those from repairing to the valleys who did not inhabit them. This prohibition was published on the 15th of February, 1560.

Proceedings were immediately commenced against the Protestants in Piedmont. The uncle of the reigning duke had been stirred up to undertake the charge of these proceedings himself. "The officers of justice," says Gilles, "were incessantly running up and down, apprehending upon the highways, in the fields, and even in their houses, persons obnoxious upon account of their religion, whom they afterwards delivered into the hands of the commissaries." These commissaries were inquisitors, and the stake was their ultimate argument. Two martyrs were burned alive at Carignan, in the beginning of the year.

The Protestants, affrighted, like a flock of sheep surprised in a novel and dangerous situation, dispersed in disorder. Those of Carignan and of Vigon retired to Quiers or Chiéri; those of Bubiano and of Briquèras to La Tour. As at that time a part of Piedmont belonged to France, the fugitives were able to get out of reach of the inquisitorial prosecutions both in the French villages and in the Vaudois valleys, where the religious liberty which was at that time assailed but energetically defended, was in the following year officially guaranteed.

The officers of justice then turned in the direction of Suza, entered the valley of Méane, and made a great number of prisoners. Their pastor, named Jacob, was condemned to be burned alive. "The will of God be done on earth as it is in heaven," said the old man. And amidst the torments which the earth had in store for him, he served the Lord with as lively a faith as the elect can amidst the celestial beatitudes. Pardon was offered him upon condition of his abjuring, but he refused; and that he might not be able to make a public profession of his faith, he was conducted to the pile with his mouth gagged, and his arms tied. There he was burned in a slow fire. But his countenance, full of resignation and of resolution during this cruel torture, so shook the minds of the judges, that the Senator De Corbis resolved to have nothing more to do with such prosecutions; and the Count of Racconis, says Gilles, "was so softened towards the reformed, that thereafter, instead of persecuting them, he did all that was in his power to procure their deliverance from their troubles." Thus the silent death of the martyr was productive of more advantage to his brethren than a victory won in the field of battle. He had conquered on the pile, where courage is more difficult than in the excitement of combat.

The city of Turin at that time belonged to France. In it there were pastors who preached publicly to an audience which always became more and more numerous. The Catholic clergy obtained the appointment of deputies, who were commissioned to present themselves before Charles IX., in name of the inhabitants of that city, to induce him to take measures for repressing this Protestantism. The young monarch replied, on the 17th of February, 1561, by a letter to the governor of Turin, and a proclamation to his "good and loyal subjects," in both of which he announced his resolution not to suffer the practice of the reformed religion either in the city or in the vicinity. Scarcely had these documents arrived at Turin, when the Protestant pastors were ordered to remove from it. It would appear that they had very soon after contrived to return, for it was found necessary to renew this order of banishment next year. This was only the prelude to a more general measure. Catharine de Médicis had written, at the same time with her son, to the Duke of Savoy, to inform him that the king's intention was to put an end to the reformed worship throughout the whole extent of Piedmont. She therefore entreated Emmanuel Philibert to take steps for the same purpose in his own dominions.

It might have been hoped that the duke would not have entered into these violent measures, as his wife, Catharine of France, sister of Henry II., was favourable to the Reformation, having acquired a knowledge of it in the company of the Queen of Navarre, and of René of France, the daughter of Louis XII., who participated in the new opinions. But Philip of Savoy, uncle of the duke, had been gained to the Catholic party by the Archbishop of Turin, and prepared to aid it by force of arms. It was he who, under the name of the Count of Racconis, distinguished himself in a manner so little to his honour, in the persecutions instituted at this time against the inhabitants of the Vaudois valleys, as we shall shortly see. The influence which he then exercised over his august nephew, united with that which the brief of Pope Pius IV. must have had—a brief dated 15th November, 1561, by which that pontiff adjured all the inhabitants of Piedmont to be upon their guard against heresy, and to put it away from them—decided Emmanuel Philibert to adopt severe measures against the Protestants. The courtier prelates by whom he was surrounded, incessantly endeavoured to interest his thirst for glory in their annihilation; they would have liked to have destroyed by a single blow all those evangelical churches, of which the germs began to appear so full of life in all parts of Piedmont. The first step taken was to enjoin all magistrates to watch over assemblies *for religion;* that was the expression employed; the next was to forbid these assemblies. Those who were taken in the fact of joining in social prayer and meditation on the Scriptures, were treated as criminals. The towns of Chiéri, Ozasc, Busque, and Frossac, became the theatres of cruel and often bloody proceedings against the reformed. Of this we have seen proofs in the preceding chapter, in perusing the details which have been preserved concerning some of their inhabitants who suffered martyrdom at that time.

The Countess of Moretta, who protected the reformed, was herself obliged to retire before their persecutors. The Countess of Carde, who also protected them, having died, they were constrained either to go to mass or to leave their native land. The same injunction was intimated to those of Ozasc and of Frossac. These simple and sincere men, although newly born to the gospel life, were already nourished with the pure spiritual milk which strengthens the soul of the Christian. They had tasted that the Lord is gracious, and rather than abandon his ways, they renounced their country, their goods, the homes in which they were born, and their hereditary fields, in order to preserve their religion. These unfortunate persons, or rather these happy faithful ones of Christ, almost all repaired to the valley of Lucerna, where they were kindly received, as the fugitives of Paësane and St. Frons had been half-a-century before.

Meanwhile, in the churches of Coni and Carail there had been an increase of the number of awakened souls, who from a little flock grew up more and more into a holy nation, a peculiar and willing people; and as the dawning light first touches the summits of the mountains in the horizon over which it is to spread, so it was chiefly amongst the upper classes that the doctrines of the Reformation were received.

After a war of twenty-three years, peace had been concluded betwixt France and Spain.[1] The Duke of Savoy had been the ally of the latter power, and had lost all his possessions, which, however, were now restored to him, with the exception of Turin, Pignerol, and Saluces. Many of the seigneurs who fought by his side had embraced Protestantism. So long as their aid seemed necessary to him, he had allowed these valiant adherents of the Reformation to enjoy liberty of conscience and religious quiet, which the recollection of their services secured to them. But scarcely had the more eminent of the secular clergy resumed the place of these men of arms around their sovereign, than the voice of honour was succeeded by that of the church. The duke was

[1] By the treaty of Chateau Cambresis, April, 1559.

told that having returned to possession of his hereditary states, his glory required the re-establishment also, in its integrity, of the religion of his ancestors. It was by these artful methods that a prince was induced to become the executioner of his most faithful subjects, to weaken his states, and to destroy his people; and this they called glory! "Woe unto them!" says the prophet, "that call evil good, and good evil."

The duke began by interdicting the Protestants from all kinds of public worship beyond the limits of the Vaudois valleys; then he issued an edict at Coni,[1] by which all the inhabitants were required to give up to the magistrates all books *of religion* which they might possess. As the Bible is simply called *the book*, so the profession of its doctrines revived by the Reformation was simply called *religion*. These terms, by general use, came to be acknowledged as part of the language, the popular good sense, which instinctively created this form of speech, thus unconsciously attesting the truth that religion was indeed there and there alone.

The Duke of Savoy at the same time enjoined his subjects to attend the preaching of the missionaries whom he was about to send them. But what did the missionary thus recommended preach at Carail? *Che Dio faceva far l'invernata bona, accioche d'il mese seguente avanzas* (sic) *a fare di legna per poter bruschiar gli luterani;* that is, "that God was giving them so mild a winter that year, in order that they might be able to save wood for burning the heretics in the succeeding months." It may be imagined that this eloquence was not very persuasive in the way of inducing souls to prefer the religion of the stake and pile to that of the gospel. Accordingly, the preacher was very soon forsaken; but, in the month following, on the 28th of December, 1561, a fresh edict renewed the order to deliver up all bibles to the magistrates, and enjoined all the inhabitants of the country to go to mass without more ado. But the number of those who refused was so great, that no step durst be taken to obtain the execution of this edict. Nay, about this time Emmanuel Philibert conceded the free exercise of their worship to the inhabitants of the Vaudois valleys;[2] the seigneurs who had followed him in the war still enjoyed in their independence the benefit of the remembrance of their recent exploits; and it was impossible to proceed with severe measures so quickly as the Church of Rome would have desired.

But a few years after, in 1565, the same prince having commanded the Vaudois to abjure within the space of two months,

[1] 28th September, 1561.
[2] At Verceil, on 10th January, and at Cavour, on 3d July, 1561.

effect was given in the Church of Coni to the edict of 1561. Each family was required to appear before the magistrates, and to make a declaration of Romish orthodoxy, under peril of the severest penalties.

It may be conceived that these obstacles must have had the effect of retaining in the Church of Rome men who perceived its errors, but were timid—men of enlightened minds, but feeble, who had embraced the cause of the Reformation. However, there were still found fifty-five families who, in presence of the magistrates, had the courage openly to renounce all connection with Popery, and to declare themselves Protestants. It was an act of proscription; and accordingly the greater part of them, knowing the full consequence of that avowal, made haste of their own accord to set their affairs in order, to sell what they possessed, and to retire elsewhere.

A few only of the most influential and respected obtained, under special security from a Catholic proprietor, the favour of retaining both their properties and their beliefs, but solely on condition that they should abstain from any religious exercise, whether in their houses or elsewhere, under pain of total confiscation of all that they possessed. The poorer class, less encumbered with this world's goods, had rejected all shackles; the rich suffered them to be imposed upon them. The Protestant party was divided; it would have been better for them if they had resisted together, for the Bible assures us that there is great strength in the unity of brethren. It was at this same period that the young martyr of Coni, whose life has been given in the history of the Vaudois of Calabria, died at Rome. That humble Bethany from which he derived his birth, was less cruelly treated than the adopted church to which he devoted himself; but the flock that was beginning to be formed at Coni disappeared, as well as the ancient Church of Calabria.

The bundle being loosed, each separate stick is easily broken. The humbler of the people had removed from the place; the noble families retired to their estates, hoping to live there in greater freedom and tranquillity. It seemed, in fact, as if they were forgotten for some time, and they allowed themselves to be lulled into a false security; but very soon, by a gradual process, noiselessly and secretly, they were decimated; their most eminent members were taken away, the persons of greatest zeal being arrested in their dwellings, on the pretext, always plausible, that they had been guilty of family prayer and of the secret worship of their God.

Of these new prisoners there were some who made their escape; part of them by their courage, and part by means of bribes. Some perished in dungeons, a number were put to death, and some at last abjured, under the constraint of violence, the faith which they had embraced from conviction.

Thus that church ceased to exist upon the banks of the Stura, where, thenceforth, the truth shed only rare and trembling gleams. It was brought into being beneath the radiance of Divine grace; its enemies sought to drown it in blood; and it may be said of it, that its beauty departed from it as soon as it ceased to be free. The light placed under a bushel is in a fair way for going out.

CHAPTER XI.

HISTORY OF THE REFORMED CHURCHES OF CARAIL, CHIÉRI, AND DRONIER.[1]

(A.D. 1560 TO A.D. 1605.)

Commencement of persecution against the Reformed Church of Carail—The noble family of Villanova-Sollaro—Activity of the popish clergy—Suppression of the Reformation at Carail—Condition of the church in the marquisate of Saluces—St. Bartholomew's Day—Vacca, Archdeacon of Saluces, resists the massacre of the Protestants—French civil wars—The marquisate of Saluces becomes part of the dominions of the Duke of Savoy—The Protestant Church of Dronier—Its suppression—Persecuting measures adopted against the Vaudois of Praviglelm and of the whole upper valley of the Po.

THE church of Carail was destined to endure nearly the same vicissitudes as that of Coni. In the first place, a list of the reformed was demanded from the magistrates.[2] In this list were immediately included nearly 900 persons, although many were absent, and their names did not appear there.[3] An ancient house at Carail, that of Villanova-Sollaro, was distinguished by attachment to the doctrines of the gospel; and it was under its protection that the church against which proceedings were now commenced had risen and been sheltered. The Duke of Savoy caused letters to be written about the commencement of the year[4] to the heads of this noble family, that if they wished to retain the favour of their prince, they must cease to extend their support to a heresy already too widely spread. But the seigneurs of Sollaro, whilst they protested their

---

[1] AUTHORITIES.—The same as in Chapter IX.
[2] In the month of March, 1565.
[3] Letter of Gioanetto Arnaudo, one of the commissioners appointed to prepare this list. Chronicle of the family of Villanova-Sollaro. (MS. of the Royal Library at Turin.) [4] 27th February, 1565.

devotedness to their sovereign, demanded the privilege of proving also their devotedness to their religion.

After the list was prepared, Emmanuel Philibert himself wrote to them,[1] and summoned the Count of Sollaro to his presence. He urged him, in the strongest manner, to return within the pale of the Church of Rome, sternly declaring his resolution not to suffer two religions in his dominions. But the count respectfully replied, that he would render to Cæsar the things which were Cæsar's, but to God the things which were God's.

A few days after the duke sent a missionary to Carail,[2] commanding all the inhabitants of the town to attend his preaching. The greater part of the reformed refused to go. Thereupon an officer of the Council of State apprised the syndics that they must get ready a special list of these latter within the space of four days;[3] and at the same time there arrived a proclamation by the duke, in which he exhorted all the reformed of the town to change their doctrines, threatening them with his wrath if they persisted in their heresy. The greater part of these Christians now took to flight, which left a great blank, and spread desolation over the country. The duke perceived that he had gone too far, or rather too fast, and he sought to bring them back, by causing a letter to be written to them on the 20th of May, in which he urged them to return to their homes, promising that no new step should be taken without new notice. But this new notice was not long of making its appearance. On the 10th of June an edict was published, by which all the Protestants of Carail who would not abjure were ordered to leave the country within the space of six months. A year was allowed them to effect the sale of their properties, by agents appointed for that purpose.

A number of efforts were made to obtain the revocation of this edict, at once so unjust, so impolitic, and so barbarous. The Duchess of Savoy besought her husband to recal it. The seigneurs of Sollaro, who enjoyed a credit merited alike by their enlightenment, their illustrious rank, and their virtues, repaired to the presence of their sovereign, who seemed at first to yield to their remonstrances; but scarcely were they gone when the influence of the Catholic clergy enveloped him again; and on the 30th of November, 1565, the Podestat of Carail received orders to have the edict of the 10th of June put in execution. In this state of things the reformed had only to choose between the two alternatives, abjuration or exile. They did not hesitate, but made their preparations for departure.

[1] On the 14th of April.
[2] He arrived at Carail on the 28th of April.   [3] On the 8th of May, 1565.

Popish charity, however, thought fit not even to leave them the solace which remains for the proscribed; the inhabitants of the neighbouring districts were prohibited from receiving the fugitives.

We may form some notion of the character and the activity which Rome must have displayed in these proceedings against so great a number of people, by her bloodthirsty eagerness, in the case of a single person, neither of title nor rank. In that same year the Cardinal Bobba wrote from Rome to the Duke of Savoy, by order of his Holiness (what a title of mockery!), to inform him that he would recal the nuncio accredited to his court, if he refused to put to death a relapsed heretic of Vercelli. The letter is dated from Rome, 22d of October, 1566. The name of the prisoner was George Olivet. He was a proselyte whom Catholicism had not been able to retain. His *Holiness*, the *Holy* Church, the *Holy* Office demanded that he should die; it was made an occasion of diplomatic rupture; and these pretensions to holiness which Popery is continually putting forth in the midst of the most odious iniquities, involuntarily recal what has been said of bravery—those who boast of it most have least of it in reality. From this document we learn that the Duke of Savoy, notwithstanding his severities, was still accused of resistance to the plans of Rome. No master can be more difficult to serve than tyranny, and none is more ungrateful.

Orders were therefore transmitted to the governors of the surrounding towns, that the fugitive reformed should not be received in them. Emmanuel Philibert even wrote to this effect to the governors of Saluces, Nice, and Provence, as well as to Charles IX., to whom by this means he hoped to make himself agreeable. The instructions did not bear that shelter must be absolutely refused to the reformed, but that they must not be received without their promising to abjure. This measure, however, was equivalent to an absolute proscription, for if they had chosen to have abjured, they would have had no need to have sought shelter so far from home.

The good Duchess of Savoy, fully perceiving how inhuman and senseless these arbitrary orders were, besought her husband at least to postpone the execution of them till he had gone in person to Carail, to judge with his own eyes of their propriety. Emmanuel Philibert arrived at Carail about the end of the month of August, 1566. Two days before his arrival he had commanded all Protestants not belonging to it to leave it. On his approach, the reformed of the place fell into the error of betaking themselves also to flight. That flight was regarded as a mark of alienation from their soverign, and of sympathy for the strangers whom he had just expelled. It may be imagined that good reasons might perhaps be assigned for these movements, but in reality the people only yielded to a feeling of alarm and apprehension, which did not stay to reason.

The duke was irritated, and immediately caused a proclamation to be issued in Carail, expressly forbidding any kind of provisions being carried out of the town, in order to punish in this way the reformed who had unfortunately left it upon his arrival.

Such a reception was certainly little calculated to induce a long stay, and he very soon departed again, leaving a garrison in the town, the soldiers of which were to be maintained and lodged in the very houses of the Protestants, whether fugitive or remaining at home, until the latter should return to Catholicism. But as those who had fled did not come back to the town, they were summoned to appear before the Podestat of Coni, who was then advocate-fiscal, and a noted opponent of biblical doctrines. These wandering and dispossessed families not daring to appear before him, he pronounced against them sentence of confiscation of property, and of banishment.

The Archbishop of Turin then repaired to Carail,[1] in the hope of bringing back the people the more readily to the Church of Rome. He made his appearance there escorted by a numerous suite, and manifested at first only paternal and benevolent feelings, calling the fugitive Christians poor wandering sheep. He sent them safe-conducts, and invited them to conference with himself. Some came, but the greater part stayed away, and of those who came a small number were drawn back to Popery. The sentence of banishment and confiscation was confirmed against those who did not appear, or who resisted the solicitations of the prelate.

However, indications of war having appeared between Savoy and France, Emmanuel Philibert gave orders to the Podestat of Coni to restore the dispersed Protestants to their residences, on condition that they should abstain from all exercise of their religion, under pain of death. The rich returned; the poor preferred exile. But those who returned were not long till they found reason to repent of it. They were arrested one after another, under pretext of religion, as had already been done in the town of Coni. Once arrested, if they refused to abjure, they were allowed to perish in the prisons, unless, indeed, they were sent to the galleys.

[1] On the 20th of September, 1566.

The family of Villanova-Sollaro displayed the greatness of true nobility amidst these adversities. They had supported the Protestant Church in the days of its growth, and they did not abandon it in its downfall. Conviction imposes a necessity as well as nobility,[1] said these ancient seigneurs of a region once so flourishing and now rendered so desolate. There were six brothers of this family. The chancellor, Count of Stropiano, their relative, assembled them in name of his royal highness, to entreat them to abjure, but they were immovable. "Let our sovereign," said they, "demand any other sacrifice, and we shall have pleasure in making it." "He repeats to you, by my mouth," said the chancellor, "that it is his resolution not to suffer two religions in the country." These noble Protestants understood the threat conveyed in these words, returned to Carail, sold a part of their lands, and retired to the marquisate of Saluces, then in the possession of France. During five years of trouble and domestic agitation, they were sometimes in France, sometimes in Piedmont, wanderers and always kept in alarm. The narrative of these events has been preserved in the chronicle which still exists of that illustrious and ill-fated house.

In 1570, the seigneurs of Sollaro were summoned to appear before the Senate of Turin, with other persons of rank, guilty, like them, of having returned to the gospel, an offence which the Church of Rome could by no means pardon. Through the influential intercessions made for them, amongst which the first place must be assigned to those of the Duchess of Savoy and of the Elector Palatine,[2] the prosecutions against them were suspended for a short time. But they were subsequently renewed; and the Sollaros were condemned and banished, their property confiscated, and the members of their family dispersed and forgotten.

The third of these six brothers retired to the valley of Lucerna, where his descendants continued to exist for more than a century. Of this branch of the family was that pious and beautiful Octavia Sollaro, whose sad story Gilles has preserved in one of the pages of his simple and unadorned chronicles.

One of the descendants of this third brother, called Vallerio Sollaro, appeared before the Synod of Villar, held in 1607, in order that he might obtain the hand of a young girl of the valley of St. Martin, who refused to marry him because he was of noble

[1] An allusion to the French proverb, *Noblesse oblige.*—TRANSLATOR.
[2] He had sent to Turin, in February, 1566, a special ambassador, named Junius, The advocate-fiscal, Barberi, having learned that his secretary, Chaillet, was a Protestant minister, caused him to be arrested in the very hotel of the ambassador. To this secretary we are indebted for a narration of all the operations of the embassy, in a long letter, preserved by Gilles, chap. xxxiii.

birth, and she was a simple peasant. The representations which the Synod itself addressed to the young noble on the unsuitableness of so unequal an alliance, did not shake his resolution, and the marriage took place. The ancient escutcheon was not, however, dishonoured by this alliance; for the antiquity of the Vaudois family was higher still, and its patents of nobility, inscribed in the word of God, are more imperishable than the heraldic distinctions of men.

Whilst in the territories of the Duke of Savoy the Church of Carail thus disappeared before tyrannic persecution, the churches of Saluces enjoyed, under the dominion of France, a toleration equal to the other Protestants of that country; but their pastors were mostly foreigners, some natives of Switzerland, some of the Vaudois valleys, and some of other parts of Piedmont.

In these latter regions all foreigners had already been commanded to leave the country within the space of twenty-four hours.[1] Next year, the Vicar of Chiéri, a town not far from Saluces, received orders to cause all Protestants to depart from that territory, who had fixed their residence in it without his authorization, or whose permitted time of sojourn had expired.[2] The Duke of Savoy at the same time demanded of the lieutenant of the king of France in the province of Saluces,[3] that he should cause all who were not born within the kingdom to remove out of his government, and that he should not receive any fugitive natives of Piedmont who might retire to it. The governor of Saluces gave orders accordingly. Persons not natives of the province were commanded to quit it with their families within the space of three days, and prohibited from returning to it without special permission, under penalty of death and confiscation of goods.[4]

This blow was principally directed against the pastors who were not natives of the marquisate; but not being able to determine upon forsaking their flocks, they remained in the country. Truchi, a native of Cental in Provence, and Soulf, a native of Coni in Piedmont, were imprisoned at Saluces. Their colleague, Galatée, although a very aged man, repaired to La Rochelle to address the King of Navarre in their favour, and was happily successful. The Duke of Nevers, governor of Saluces, even received orders to set all the prisoners at liberty.[5] These poor churches, after a brief alarm, raised their heads again with more than their former courage, like a vigorous plant, which the storm, that does not

---

[1] Edict of 20th April, 1566.　　[2] Edict of 1st April, 1567.
[3] Then the Duke of Nevers.　　[4] Decree of 19th October, 1567.
[5] By letter, dated 14th October, 1571.

altogether break it down, causes to strike root more deeply in the soil.

Upon hearing of the marriage of the King of Navarre (Henry IV.) with Margaret of France, the sister of Charles IX., they thought themselves secure of a long period of peace. But they left Catharine de Médicis out of their calculations. All at once burst the sanguinary thunders of St. Bartholomew; sixty thousand victims butchered in a few days. The news of this event were welcomed in Catholic countries with transports of inexpressible joy. Pius V. had just died, after having launched a bull of excommunication against all princes who tolerated heretics in their dominions. He did not live to enjoy the slowly ripened fruit of his labours; but his successor, Gregory XIII., although less cruel than he, did not repudiate the heritage. He caused a medal to be struck, public rejoicings to be made, and *Te Deum* to be sung in honour of this prodigious extermination.

An order to cause all the Protestants of the province of Saluces to be massacred in one night, had been sent to Birague, who was then governor. Ignorant that this measure related to the whole of France, he was troubled at the order, and submitted it to the Chapter of the place. Some gave their opinion in favour of a complete and immediate execution of it; but sentiments more humane were also expressed, and here I cannot but proclaim the Christian joy which I feel in being able to ascribe them to a Catholic priest, the Archdeacon of Saluces, Samuel Vacca by name, who strenuously opposed the massacre of the Protestants. "It is only a few months," said he, "since we received letters-patent from the king, that the pastors who were in confinement should be set at large, and their flocks left at liberty. But nothing has since happened which can be regarded as a reason for such a change; it must be supposed that this cruel order has been occasioned by false reports. Let us inform his majesty that these are honest and peaceable people, and that nobody has anything to lay to their charge, except in regard to their religious opinions, and if the king persists in his design, it will always be but too soon to carry it into execution."

Thus the Protestants of Saluces were saved, for the reprobation which immediately arose against these base butcheries prevented the renewal of them. Rorengo censures this moderation, saying that it served only to strengthen the cause of heresy; let us hope, on the contrary, that it will serve to cover many inquisitorial sins and cruelties, veiling them with the grateful and blessed recollections which are connected with the name of one worthy old man. Why are there not more to emulate his fame! "The time is coming," says a writer on political economy, "when Rome would give all the St. Bartholomews, all the proscriptions, all the *autos-da-fe* in the world for a single act of faith, of hope, and of charity."

Amidst the anxiety which the news of these massacres occasioned almost everywhere, the Duke of Savoy hastened to re-assure the Vaudois valleys, by strongly declaring that he reprobated such crimes; and at Saluces also, a number of Protestant families, dreading the execution of the orders which had been received, took refuge with Catholic families, on whose kindness they could reckon, and who sheltered them as brethren till the storm was past. Thus did humanity triumph on the Italian side of the Alps, and it is a pleasant page of our history, in which we can twice pay so just a tribute to our adversaries and our sovereigns.

In 1574, the Marshal de Bellegarde was appointed governor of the province of Saluces. He was a man superior to the prejudices of his time. This appointment followed upon the return of Henry III., who quitted the throne of Poland, from which he fled as from a prison, to mount the throne of France, left vacant by the untimely, mysterious, and terrible death of Charles IX.

The new governor, by his impartiality to all under his jurisdiction, was not long of exciting the complaints of the Catholic party, then all powerful at the court. But the king himself became a partisan; he consented to be chief of the League, setting an example of coalition to those of the opposite side. Lesdiguières stood forward as leader of the reformed in the rich valleys of the Isère and the Durance. When things were in this state the Marshal was requested to resign his government. The reformed entreated him not to leave them, and De Bellegarde remained at Saluces. The governor of Provence was ordered to march against him; but Lesdiguières, at the head of the Protestants of Dauphiny, hastened to his support. The Vaudois of Lucerna and of Pragela joined him, and the governor of Saluces was maintained in his position. Complaints were made to the Duke of Savoy, relative to the aid which his subjects had lent to a stranger; remonstrances were addressed by the duke to the magistrates of the valleys, and prosecutions commenced against the Vaudois who had taken arms; but the almost simultaneous death of the Marshal and the prince put an end to this affair.[1]

During this time, however, the churches of Saluces increased in strength. The pastor of St. Germain,[2] who had already brought the Catholics of Pramol to embrace Protestantism, had, with ardour

---

[1] The Duke of Savoy died on the 30th of August, 1580, and the Marshal De Bellegarde on the 4th of December of the same year.
[2] Francis Guérin.

and activity worthy of a soldier of the cross, followed the Vaudois troops as they passed into the marquisate, and remained in that territory in order to give greater consistency and strength to the Protestant communities which were already there, by organizing them in a manner similar to that of the churches of the valleys. A general synod was held for that purpose at Château Dauphin, in which all these churches were represented.

In the valley of Maira, the Catholic and Protestant chiefs even formed a common alliance, promising one another, says Gilles, "good friendship and union, without injury or reproach on account of religion; but, on the contrary, mutual aid in case of necessity, against any assailant whomsoever." The people have always understood more of brotherhood than kings and pontiffs. A religious system pervaded by the spirit of formalism and the feelings of a body corporate, unites men not in a brotherhood, but in an association.

At this time, therefore, the churches of Saluces had peace, and flourished. The numerous conversions which we have related, sufficiently prove that this fine country was not hostile to the Reformation, and that it would nowhere have spread more rapidly, if human thought had been respected in that liberty which inalienably belongs to it. But the sword, chains, and fire, were employed to combat thought,—the arms of the Romish Church, but not of the gospel. Neither kings nor pontiffs have ever respected liberty any more than brotherhood.

It is probable that the reformed churches of Saluces would have subsisted unto this day, like those of Dauphiny and the Cevennes, if that province had remained under the dominion of France. Henry IV. soon ascended the throne, and during a number of years these churches continued to increase and to gain strength. The Edict of Nantes, issued in 1598, appeared to give them a lasting stability. But war was then raging between France and Piedmont, and the marquisate of Saluces was successively taken and retaken by the two powers, until it remained at last in the possession of the Duke of Savoy, in terms of the treaty of 17th January, 1601, concluded at Lyons, betwixt Henry IV. and Charles Emmanuel. By this treaty, the King of France ceded to the duke his possessions in Piedmont, to wit, the provinces of Saluces and Pignerol, in exchange for La Bresse and Le Bugey. It was said in reference to this exchange, that the King of France had made a ducal peace, and the duke a royal one.

But it must be observed that, twelve years before this event, in 1588, Charles Emmanuel had already seized upon the marquisate, taking advantage of the civil wars by which France was then paralyzed. Scarcely had he made himself master of this province, than, faithful to the engagements into which he had entered with his allies, he began to require the reformed churches of Saluces to conform to the Catholic worship. The letter which he wrote them to this purpose is dated 27th March, 1597. The evangelical party respectfully replied that they were grateful for the interest which his royal highness testified in their spiritual welfare, but that they entreated him to do them the favour to respect their conscientious convictions, and to maintain things as they were when they became his subjects:—"Our religion is founded on the Holy Scriptures," said they in conclusion, "as are also our loyalty and our behaviour, and we hope that your royal highness will always find in us faithful subjects, upright citizens, and serious Christians." The duke pushed his efforts no farther at that time, the province of Saluces being then a very insecure possession. But after the treaty of Lyons, when he found himself its undisputed master, he issued a decree by which all Protestants were required to quit his dominions within two months, unless they abjured within fifteen days.[1] Disregard of this decree was to be punished with loss of life and confiscation of goods.

The most considerable of the Protestant churches which had arisen was at that time the church of Dronier (Dronèro), situated at the entry of the valley of Mayra (Valle di Magra), in one of the richest basins of that fertile country. "Scarcely," says Rorengo, "were there any traces of Catholicism there to be seen."[2] In the first instance, missionaries were sent thither, who made few proselytes; and thereupon Charles Emmanuel was solicited to employ means more expeditious. The Church of Rome has never triumphed except by aids which have nothing to do with conviction and the power of truth. In this we have one evidence that it cannot defend itself nor triumph by the word and faith; it needs the help of violence and servility. Why, then, should it be called a church?

When the edict of proscription, apostasy, or death, was issued by the Duke of Savoy, the Church of Dronier showed its respect for the covenant of its God. An earnest and respectful supplication, enforced by strong arguments, was addressed to the sovereign on the part of the Vaudois and the reformed. Meanwhile they were fervent in prayer, and as they were encouraged to hope for the revocation, or at least the mitigation of that barbarous edict, they soothed themselves with the idea that it might be only a passing gust, after which they would again enjoy the calm. The threatening aspect

---

[1] July, 1601.   *Memorie istorichi*, p. 145.

of the clouds which began to arise in the horizon of their happiness, betokening calamity, they regarded as a warning to serve God better, and not to forsake him.

With such thoughts they allowed the time pointed out in the edict to slip over, without having sold their properties or made their preparations for departing,—I do not say without abjuring, for of that none of them thought. At the end of two months they received inexorable orders to conform without delay to the clerico-ducal edict. Then, full of affright and anxiety, taken by surprise, losing their self-possession, beset upon all hands by the most pressing solicitations from monks and magistrates, trembling for their families, and scarce knowing what they did, a great number of that disorganized church were hurriedly gained over to the ranks of the Church of Rome. It was against their consciences; but that was of no consequence to Popery. It gloried in these external conversions, as it still glories in its mere external and material unity, which hypocrisy always suffices.

Those who had strength enough of faith to forsake their country and all that they possessed, withdrew to France, or to Geneva, or to the Vaudois valleys, where they found an asylum, notwithstanding the edict which banished them from the ducal dominions.

They had nothing left! the world would say. But are the treasures of a good conscience and the peace of God nothing?

It seems surprising, however, that all the reformed and Vaudois of the province did not act with more energy and concert, opposing a courageous resistance to these iniquities. Their adversaries themselves were afraid of it; and therefore they had spread the report on all hands, and did not cease to repeat that, although the edict was so general, it was not meant against any but the Protestants of the plain, and that those of the mountains would not be disturbed, provided always they kept themselves quiet during the proceedings against the former. "Bear ye one another's burdens," says the Bible, "and so fulfil ye the law of Christ." The inhabitants of the mountains left their Christian brethren of the plain to bear their trials alone, and in their turn they had none to help them in those which awaited themselves. Scarcely had the Protestants been got out of the way who occupied the districts nearest to the great towns, when the injunction to conform to the edict was formally addressed also to those of the most retired villages. The influence under which this edict was concocted, was effectual to extend still further its range of depopulation and death.

Hitherto, however, no threat had been addressed to the Vaudois of Praviglelm and of the whole upper valley of the Po, where they had exercised their evangelical worship from time immemorial. They regarded the maintenance of it as a right acquired by antiquity, and did not think it possible that it could be disputed. But the crying injustice of which their brethren were the victims ought to have opened their eyes; for if justice and humanity were not respected in the plain, what reason was there they should be respected amongst their rocks? And if they could bear to see the acts of injustice which touched not themselves, why should they not be exposed to similar sufferings?

But they did not reason so far, and as they were told that the edict did not concern them, they lived as tranquil as if it had never existed. At last, when all their brethren were banished or dispersed, they were given to understand in their turn that they must submit to the edict as well as the others.

Then these apathetic mountaineers, seeing the question assume the form of one of life and death for themselves, transported with an indignation which perhaps they had long restrained, flew to arms without premeditation or concert, made vows of courage and mutual aid, and by their union, their energy, and their valour, saved, for some time, at least, their imperilled cause. Abandoning their flocks, their houses, and their families, they assembled in arms, and threatened the Catholics amongst whom they dwelt that they would destroy all with fire and sword, if any ill befell their wives or their children. They then descended to the plain, marched against their oppressors, seized upon the fortress of Château Dauphin, and threatened to lay everything waste if the measures which had already caused so much distress were not revoked in so far as they were concerned.

The Catholics, who had never suffered from the neighbourhood of the Protestants, and who must have well understood the reason of their irritation, were the first to intercede for them, less from desire of justice than from fear of their resentment. Numerous petitions were addressed to Charles Emmanuel; the magistrates of the country themselves gave advice that a troop so determined should not be driven to despair; a former pastor of Praviglelm, Domenic Vignaux, who was then pastor at Villar in the valley of Lucerna, and who had preserved friendly relations with the governor of Saluces, joined his entreaties to those of the inhabitants of the country in favour of his former parishioners; and at last the inhabitants of those deep valleys where the Po takes its rise, were permitted to return to their abodes, and to preserve their religion.

This success was obtained without effusion of blood, so true it is that energy spares it more than feebleness. How many martyrs have perished, one after another, by the most cruel sufferings, who, if they had acted in concert, would have been saved by the mere display of courageous resistance! But notwithstanding their present triumph, the Vaudois of Praviglelm, in consequence of having held their peace when their brethren were proscribed, fell afterwards into that state of isolation which is fatal; and their churches, like the other churches of Saluces, are now destroyed. In the following chapters we shall see some of the events which led to their extinction.

CHAPTER XII.

A SKETCH OF THE VICISSITUDES ENDURED BY THE CHRISTIANS OF THE VALLEYS SITUATED AROUND THE VAUDOIS VALLEYS; PARTICULARLY THOSE OF BUBIANO, LUCERNA, CAMPILLON, AND FENIL.[1]

(A.D. 1560 TO A.D. 1630.)

Protestants in the neighbourhood of the Vaudois valleys forbidden to attend religious meetings there—Fines and confiscations—Count William of Lucerna—Treaty of Cavour—Castrocaro, governor of the Vaudois valleys—Unsuccessful attempts to proselytize at Lucerna and Bubiano—Certain of the Vaudois summoned to Turin—Interview of Valentine Boulles with the Duke of Savoy—Theological discussion between a Vaudois pastor and a Jesuit—Captain Cappel—Systematic persecution of the Protestants of Lucerna—Confirmation of Vaudois privileges—Extortion and injustice—Peter Queyras and Bartholomew Boulles—Arrests—Sufferings of the Protestants of Bubiano and other places—Final prohibition of Protestantism beyond the limits of the Vaudois valleys.

WE have already seen that, in the beginning of the year 1560, the Duke Emmanuel Philibert had prohibited all the inhabitants of his dominions from going to hear the Protestant ministers in the Vaudois valleys, and from celebrating the reformed worship without the limits of these valleys.[2] But this edict did not specify how far their limits were to extend. Commissioners were appointed, who were to determine this at their discretion, according to the cases which arose, and to prosecute those who were guilty of what they should deem contraventions of the edict.

But as the contravention of the edict was punishable with a fine of 100 crowns,[3] and as the half of this sum was to go to the

[1] AUTHORITIES.—The same as in Chapter IX.
[2] Edict of Nice, 15th February, 1560.   [3] In terms of the above edict.

informers, there were sure to be found, in the vicinity of the Vaudois valleys, some ardent lovers of Catholic worship and of the money of the reformed, who would lie in wait as spies of the humble pilgrimage of the Christians of the plain going to the mountain assemblies. The monks of the abbey of Pignerol even took into their pay a troop of miscreants, who scoured the country and made prisoners of these poor people. Whilst this troop chiefly devoted its labours to the valley of Pérouse, it carried its efforts and its ravages as far as Briquéras, Fenil, and Campillon. There, moreover, their place was more than supplied by Count William of Lucerna. A vain silly man, who delighted in showing himself off like a peacock on a richly caparisoned horse, making a display of his glittering ornaments, he had dissipated his fortune in the pursuit of pomp and pleasures, and he thought to recover it again by the wages of espionage. It was he who advised the Duke of Savoy to build the fort of Mirabouc.[1]

"At that time," says Gilles, "the most influential and wealthiest of the inhabitants of Garsiliano, Fenil, Bubiano, and other little towns situated in the vicinity of the Vaudois churches, were of the same religion with us, and very diligent in their attendance on our worship. Nay, the greater part of the population of Campillon and Fenil was Protestant."

The Count of Lucerna gathered about him a few persons of birth and brutality like his own, and of these, along with his domestics well armed, he formed a little troop of brigands, or rather of sbirri, whose exploits consisted in surprising and arresting the Protestants as they went to the valleys to attend the religious assemblies. These noble adventurers hoped to enrich themselves by the spoils of their victims, and they even settled by anticipation the division of the property of most of them. Captain Scaramuzza had the property of Claude Cot, of Vigon, who took refuge in the valley of Lucerna in 1560. Count William obtained an assignation of 1000 crowns, of which 800 were to be taken from the commune of Rora, and 200 from those of the plain; but the general persecution which then arose against all the inhabitants of the valleys, and which was terminated by the treaty of Cavour (concluded on the 5th of June, 1561), made that right of spoliation worthless, and destroyed all the future prospects of these banditti.

By this treaty, all the Protestants of Bubiano, Fenil, Briquéras, and other towns contiguous to the territory of the valleys, were

---

[1] By letter, dated Bubiano, 24th October, 1560. It is in the State Archives, amongst the *Correspondence of Emmanuel Philibert with his Ministers;* but the Duke of Savoy at that time was Charles III.

authorized to repair thither freely, and to attend public worship. The Vaudois won their liberty of conscience by the most generous efforts and the most heroic exploits. The inhabitants of the towns just named, whose goods had been confiscated, and who had been obliged to flee, were allowed to return freely to their possessions. Of this number were three lawyers of Campillon, the Podestat of Angrogna, who belonged to Bubiano; Clarenton, a physician, and Reinier, a lawyer, also of that town; Anthony Falc, who afterwards devoted himself to the ministry; Daniel and Baptist Florius, as well as a great number of merchants, farmers, and artisans of every description.

The above-mentioned towns thereafter enjoyed some years of real tranquillity, for which they were indebted to the energy of the Vaudois people, who had secured it for them.

Without having the right to open places of worship, the inhabitants of these towns had the right of repairing to those of the Vaudois, and of celebrating family worship in their own houses. They even had it in their power to send for the pastors in case of sickness, or in order to the funeral service of those of their own religion. In 1564, however, the Dominican Garossia attempted to apply to them the provisions of an edict of the year preceding, relative only to other towns of Piedmont, by which the Catholics were interdicted from having anything to do with the Protestants. He attempted also to take from them the Bibles and religious books which they used; but, resting upon the terms of the treaty of Cavour, they sheltered themselves from his designs: and by the confirmation of all their privileges, which was granted to the Vaudois in 1574, for the payment of 4000 crowns, they still obtained a further abatement of the restrictions under which they were placed.

But the clergy, by their unprincipled proceedings, gradually obtained the upper hand again. In 1565, Castrocaro, then governor of the valleys, caused the place of worship at St. John to be closed; and the Countess of Cardes, the Baroness of Termes, and other persons of high rank, who were accustomed to come from their castles, to attend at the celebration of the Lord's Supper in the valleys, according to the reformed worship, received orders to abstain from so doing in future. The Vaudois pastors met and resolved to resist the iniquitous attempts of the governor. They wrote to the Duchess of Savoy, and by her good offices they obtained from Emmanuel Philibert a new confirmation of their liberties. However, intrigues and vexations of every kind continued to press upon the scattered Protestants of Piedmont. The goods of Claude

Cot, a rich burgess of Vigon, had been confiscated. The ambassador of the Elector Palatin was then at Turin. The Duke of Savoy wanted to make him a present: "Would your royal highness," said he, "give me the house which has been confiscated at Vigon." It was bestowed on him in absolute possession, by a ducal patent of the 12th of April, 1566. The worthy ambassador, Junius, immediately restored it to the persecuted family. But Junius had no sooner departed, than Castrocaro, who was then governor of the Vaudois valleys, prohibited all the reformed of Lucerna, Bubiano, and Campillon, from attending the Protestant worship of the valleys, under pain of death.[1] He caused those who did not give heed to this order to be apprehended. They appealed to the duke: the Vaudois also sent two deputies to represent to him that the Edict of Cavour authorized their fellow-Protestants of the plain in attending their worship. A new authorization confirmed the privilege, and all who had been made prisoners upon this occasion were released, through the intercession of the good duchess.

But by degrees the limits were narrowed within which burned the radiant fires of evangelical truth and of independence; and at last, by an edict of the 25th of February, 1602, the towns of Lucerna, Bubiano, Campillon, Briquéras, Fenil, Montbrun, Garsiliano, and St. Segont, the only towns in which religious liberty was maintained, were completely detached from the territory of the valleys. This was done in the hope that the bond being thus broken which attached the Protestants of the plain to those of the mountains, their unity of faith would be equally broken, and their mutual relations and brotherhood.

Forthwith the governor of the province and the Archbishop of Turin repaired to these regions, accompanied by a grand train of preaching monks, polemical clergy, Capuchins, Jesuits, and missionaries, in hope of accomplishing at once the conversion of all the Protestants. When a few trembling green leaves still remain upon the uppermost boughs of a tree which the winds have swept bare, a light breeze will be enough to bring them down. But the sap by which these churches were nourished still retained all its vitality.

The prelate having arrived in the beginning of the month of February, had taken up his abode in the palace of the counts of Lucerna. After having held some private conferences with the count and the governor, he began by causing all the heads of Protestant families residing in Lucerna to be summoned into his pre-

---

[1] This order was dated 21st April, 1566.

ATTEMPTS TO PROSELYTIZE.

sence. "There were a good number of them," says Gilles, "and these among the principal families of the country, who had always dwelt in it from time immemorial." His royal highness, they were told, was resolved not to suffer two religions in that town, "and he has sent us to you," said the prelate and governor, "for your own good, that you may make up your minds to live as good and faithful Catholics, which if you do not, you will be obliged to sell your goods and leave the country." Of course these insinuating speeches did not remain unanswered; but more energetic language was next employed. "You cannot resist the orders of your sovereign without being accused of rebellion, and then you will be treated as rebels; whilst if you return to your duty," that is to say, to the Church of Rome, "not only will you save all your property, but you will be largely rewarded." "If it is a duty," replied the more resolute ones firmly, "why speak of reward? and if not, why try to make us deviate from our duty?" "Those will be rewarded who do what is agreeable to their sovereign." "Our fidelity ought to be agreeable to him, and he would have reason to doubt it if we were unfaithful to our God." The greater part of the Protestants of Lucerna, therefore, remained unmoved by the offers and the threats with which they were plied; but the resolution of some gave way. Presently proclamation was made that exemption from taxes was granted to those who had newly become Catholics, and to those who should intimate an intention of following their example.[1]

The archbishop, the governor, and the count then proceeded to Bubiano, where all to a man were inflexible.

Attributing this unanimous resistance to the heads of two or three eminent families, as zealous for their religion as influential and honourable in virtue of their station, they caused them to be cited to Turin, before the Duke of Savoy. There were Peter Morèse, Samuel Falc, and the brothers Matthew and Valentine Boulles. The last-named had married a young woman, by birth a Catholic, but converted to Protestantism, a god-daughter of the Count of Lucerna. On their arrival in Turin they were surrounded by devoted courtiers, who said to them, "Take care what you do! for our prince is very angry at you four, for having prevented the conversion of the Protestants of Bubiano. He proposes to speak to you in a friendly way; but if you think proper to oppose him, you may expect something rough and disagreeable." They paid little

---

[1] These exemptions were dated on the 22d of February. They were renewed on the 10th of May, and are to be found in the Archives of the Court of Accounts at Turin. Reg. *Patenti e concessioni*, No. xxvi. fol. 198 and 268.

heed, however, to these artful suggestions, and presented themselves at the palace, where his highness caused them to be informed that he would receive them in private, one by one.

Valentine Boulles was the first introduced. The duke spoke kindly to him. "I desire," said he, "that my subjects should all be united in the same religion; and knowing how useful you have it in your power to be in promoting these views in the part of the country in which you dwell, I have thought fit to see you, that I may myself exhort you to follow the religion of your prince, and to gain your neighbours to it. Be persuaded," added he, "that in acting thus, besides the spiritual advantage which will thence result to yourself, you will reap other benefits, by which you will learn how great satisfaction you have given to your sovereign." "After the service of God," replied the Christian, "there is none to which I deem it so much an honour to devote myself as that of your highness; and I am ready heartily to spend in it my life and my property. But my religion is more precious still to me than my life. I believe it to be the true religion, the only religion founded upon the word of God, and I cannot abandon it without losing all peace, all consolation. Your highness may rest assured of my devotedness to your service, but be pleased to leave me my religion, without which I could not live." "And think you, then," rejoined the duke, "that I have not taken care for the salvation of my soul? If I were not persuaded that my religion is the true one, I would not follow it, and I would not try to get any other person to follow it. However, I am disposed to make those who embrace it understand how agreeable their so doing is to me; but I do not wish to do violence to anybody's conscience. You may retire."

Valentine Boulles was conducted out by another gate from that by which he had entered, and his companions were told that he had yielded to the solicitations of his prince, and had become a Catholic. They having then been successively introduced, replied to the duke, that having lived hitherto in the Protestant religion, they would have deemed it a precious favour to have been permitted to die in it, but that if his highness demanded the contrary, they were ready to do all that was agreeable to him. "That is really agreeable to me," said the duke, "and I will know how, in fitting time and place, to make you know it."

Notwithstanding these words of favour, they went out little comforted by their weakness; but what was their grief when they learned the firmness of their brother, and the more satisfactory words which the duke had addressed to him, leaving him his freedom of conscience! The poor men were so humbled for their fall, that far from waiting to receive the favours of their prince, they had scarcely returned to the valleys when they made public profession of repentance, to expiate that fault and re-enter the fellowship of their church. The promise to the contrary had doubtless been wrung from them by a sort of surprise, but advantage was taken of it to represent to the duke that the conversion of the Vaudois was not so difficult a thing to secure, their adversaries not being ashamed to say that, like the sheep of their fields, they would all follow where the first went. "These persons," they said, "were made to believe that the first had become a Catholic, and the rest agreed to abjure; afterwards they learned that he had remained in his errors, and they immediately returned to them. Let your highness, then, display a little energy in the work which has been undertaken, and when two or three families have been converted, all the rest will follow like a flock." Such were the irreparable consequences of that momentary weakness. The rising again, it is true, was as prompt as the fall had been sudden, the repentance as deep as its occasion had been serious; but nothing could destroy the impression which that moment had produced.

The honourable firmness of Valentine Boulles had been respected by the prince, and the Vaudois, respected like him, might have found in their sovereign's justice reason to entertain better prospects for the future; for men will treat those more considerately whom they respect, than those whom they despise, and whose constancy they hope to shake; and from that time forth the inhabitants of the valleys were treated with a sort of disdain and rigour, very unlike the habitual moderation of Charles Emmanuel. If each of the persons summoned from Bubiano had only studied his conscience, and not considered his situation or what another might have done before him; if each of them had replied to the prince with the noble and respectful firmness of the first who appeared in his presence, perhaps their church would have been saved. But its enemies saw their opportunity for making a first assault upon it, and they did not suffer the opportunity to escape them.

Immediately afterwards, in fact, an order was published, requiring all the Protestants of Lucerna, of Bubiano, of Campillon, and of Fenil, to become Catholics, or to leave the country within five days, under pain of death and confiscation of goods.

The churches of the valley lost no time in addressing a petition to the sovereign, setting forth arguments to persuade him to revoke this edict. They reminded the duke that, in returning from the Fort of Mirabouc, taken from the French in 1595, he had said to the Protestants who came to congratulate him at Villar, "I will make no change in regard to your religion; and if any one molest you, I will redress it as soon as I am informed of it." To this the duke caused it to be replied that he had not changed his intentions concerning them, but that what was being done related solely to the heretics dwelling beyond the limits of their valley. The governor of Pignerol, renewing his previous orders, then enjoined the Protestants who were in these latter circumstances to quit their abodes within two days, unless they obtained special permission from the archbishop to remain. Some individuals went to the prelate to obtain this; but, as may well be supposed, he insisted, in the first place, upon having an abjuration from them. "We would not like to abjure without knowing wherein our religion is wrong," replied the people with simple good sense. Forthwith appeared clergy, and monks, and Jesuits, who entangled them amidst a confused mass of theological arguments, for which the reading of the Bible had not prepared them. "We cannot dispute with you," replied they, "but if you would be pleased to confer with our pastor, and to prove to him that the mass and other ceremonies of your worship are not contrary to the word of God, we promise you that we will attend them without so much scruple."

The archbishop, thinking himself sure of victory, made haste to send a safe-conduct to the pastor, Augustus Gros, who had been named to him, and who was himself a former Augustine monk of Villefranche, converted to Protestantism. But he, remembering the decision of the Council of Constance, which sanctions breach of faith on the part of a Catholic towards persons of another communion, refused to go to Bubiano, and proposed St. John or Angrogna for this meeting, "not refusing," said he, "to confer with the prelate, or with those of his theologians whom he may think proper to send, with the weapons of the word of God, and according to the conditions essential to a sober and well-conducted debate."

The archbishop accepted this proposal, and nominated to enter the lists a Turin professor, by name Anthony Marchesi, a doctor of theology, and rector of the Jesuits in that capital. The commencement of the conferences was fixed for the 12th of March. They were opened, on the part of the Catholics, by the exposition of this thesis—*The mass was instituted by Jesus Christ, and is to be found in the Holy Scripture.* The Jesuit displayed great talent in his argument in support of it. But the pastor, coming after, and exposing in detail, one after another, all the parts of the mass, demanded that the whole ceremonial should be shown him in the Bible. Marchesi was then obliged to grant that the greater part of the rites had been instituted by the Church of Rome at divers times and in diverse circumstances. "Then," said the pastor, "I promise to go myself to the mass, and to exhort my hearers to go, provided that it be stripped of all these human additions, and restored as it was instituted by Christ." The Jesuit looked down to the ground; silence prevailed throughout the meeting, and the president of the conference declared that, this first question being exhausted, the consideration of that of auricular confession would be put off till next day.

Each went his own way, but the Papists returned no more. Some time afterwards Augustus Gros was informed that the Jesuit boasted of having had the advantage in this conference. "I would have been very much surprised if he had spoken otherwise," replied the pastor; "he had not the courage to confess the truth contained in the word of God; what could be more confidently expected, then, than that he would deny a truth uttered by the lips of men?"

The archbishop, with all his suite, retreated after this unsuccessful conference; and instead of the great triumph of conversion, with the expectation of which they had flattered themselves, the enemies of the Protestants were obliged to be contented with subjecting them to partial and vexatious treatment in a multitude of ways.

Valentine Boulles, in particular, the first of the persons summoned from Bubiano who had appeared before the Duke of Savoy, and whom they accused of having destroyed, by his perseverance, all the good effects of that experiment, was exposed to incessant recriminations. His wife, a Catholic by birth, was daily subjected to urgent solicitations that she should return to the church in which she had been baptized. Wearied out at last by this life of perpetual oppression, they resolved to flee from it, and to seek a more tranquil existence, with the peaceful exercise of their religion and conjugal happiness, in the seclusion of a retreat at a distance from all these wicked annoyances. They therefore quitted Bubiano, and settled at the lower part of the valley of Lucerna, in the little village of Bobi.

In 1619, a Protestant joiner having died at Campillon, the seigneur of that place objected to his being buried in the ordinary cemetery of the Protestants, which was contiguous to that of the Catholics, pretending that the proximity of the mortal remains of a heretic would pollute the holy earth set apart for the reception of the coffins of faithful Papists. Alas! they place holiness in the earth rather than in the heart; a cemetery is the fit emblem of their church, which is motionless as death. Why should human pride and fanaticism carry division even into the tomb?

It must be observed that, a few days before, an edict prohibiting the Vaudois from assembling at a funeral in greater number than six persons, had been secretly published. I say *secretly published*, because it concerned the Protestants alone, and had been read only at the close of the Catholic service. The greater part of those interested in it were therefore completely ignorant of it. The seigneur of Campillon, to carry out his opposition to this funeral, collected his armed retainers. The Protestants, on their side, took arms, under the direction of Captain Cappel. The obsequies took place without a conflict, in consequence of the firm front presented by the Vaudois, but all who were present were denounced as having infringed the edict. The trial of this case belonged to the podestat of Lucerna; but, by an infraction of the juridical laws then in force, the provost-general of justice took it up, and sent out his officers in pursuit of the Vaudois, who were very soon entangled amidst the meshes of inextricable assignations, protocols, compearances, examinations, confrontings, and proceedings, to such a degree that no criminal case ever assumed such formidable dimensions as this. An unjust judge is the scourge of a people!

The greater part of the accused were condemned for contumacy, but it was thought proper that they should be made prisoners. The most difficult to lay hold of was Captain Cappel, "a terrible man," says Gilles, "and who made himself to be much dreaded."

Treachery came to the aid of injustice. The colonel of a regiment offered a company to this redoubtable captain, and invited him to meet him on that business at Pignerol. "Remember your Virgil," said one of his friends, to whom he made known this proposal—

"Timeo Danaos et dona ferentes."[1]

But his own boldness prevailed over this prudent advice. He repaired to Pignerol, was conducted into the castle, and retained a prisoner. From thence he was transferred to Turin, thrown into a dungeon, and condemned to death. Two Vaudois, Samuel Truchi and the minister Guérin, brothers-in-law of Lesdiguières, besought that illustrious general to intercede for the unfortunate captain; and in September, 1620, Lesdiguières, having come to Turin, obtained a pardon for Cappel. However, he was destined to die in prison; for in 1630 he was arrested anew, and died of pestilence in the prisons of Pignerol.

After he was first arrested, the provost-criminal caused all the other Protestants who had been present at the funeral of the poor artisan of Campillon, to be summoned to appear before him within three months. At the end of that time, not having appeared, they

---

[1] I dread the Greeks, even when they come with gifts.

were all condemned for contumacy, and declared to be banished from the dominions of his royal highness. Thereupon their fellow-Christians of all the valleys made common cause with them, offered them an asylum, and interceded with the sovereign. For fear that the duke might find fault with the unjust severities of which they had been made the victims, and that at the close of the reckoning the seigneur of Campillon, the eager mover in the whole affair, might find himself in a dangerous predicament, that seigneur thought proper to interpose in their favour. We shall by and by see whether or not he was sincere in so doing.

His interposition was offered to the Vaudois by a Papist, who called himself a Protestant. This commencement did not promise much sincerity. The seigneur signified his confidence of obtaining remission of the sentence, provided the co-religionists of the parties would address a petition to the sovereign in which they should offer him money. This might have seemed a gross insult to his royal highness, but he knew nothing about it, for his seigneural excellence of Campillon took charge both of the petition and the money. Meanwhile the provost-criminal continued to carry his sentence into execution against the Protestants residing at Lucerna, on the right bank of the Pélis.

At length the Vaudois themselves sent deputies to Turin. The duke was not there; his ministers demanded from them 5000 ducatoons (nearly 30,000 francs[1]), that an end might be put to the vexations of which they complained. It may well be said that they were all alike, seigneurs, provosts, and ministers. The deputies could not venture to engage for the payment of such a sum; the 3000 livres which the seigneur of Campillon had already taken charge of had made them timid; they returned to the valleys, and the provost continued more actively his prosecutions, processes, intimations, and sentences, which always issued in heavy expenses.

At last, they learned that Charles Emmanuel was on his return to Turin. New deputies immediately repaired thither; a new petition was presented, new difficulties were every day thrown in their way, and finally they retired, leaving the charge of their business to two delegates remaining on the spot—Anthony Bastie, a notary of St. John, and James Fontaine, the gonfalonier or standard-bearer of Le Villar. At the end of some months they obtained a draft of a decree, of which the following were the principal provisions:—The ancient privileges of the Vaudois to be confirmed, and all the proceedings commenced against them, upon account of religion, to be abolished, upon payment of the sum of 6000 duca-

---

[1] Or about £1200 sterling.

toons (34,800 francs[1]). It contained an injunction, moreover, that the Protestants should not labour in public on the days of the Catholic festivals; that they should *show reverence* to processions, or retire out of their way; and finally, that they should close the new place of worship which they had opened at St. John (at Les Stalliats).

"May it please your royal highness," said the deputies to Charles Emmanuel, "for many years the humble confidence which your faithful Protestant subjects[2] have reposed in your goodness, has been entertained with fair words and good hopes, without any amelioration of their condition. At the present time it is still proposed to restrain the exercise of our religion, and on this account a considerable tribute is exacted from us." They might have added, in reference to the proceedings which it was proposed to abolish, "Ought the cessation of an injustice to be purchased? and would its long continuance not rather give a right to compensation?"

Be these things as they might, the duke replied with his accustomed amiability and suavity, saying that *there was nothing he desired more than to see them contented.* But those who surrounded him were less noble, less just, and, above all, less disinterested. When the Vaudois deputies were about to depart, to carry this reply to the valleys, the procurator-fiscal caused them to be arrested and detained until the complete payment of the 6000 ducatoons, which the advisers of his royal highness had decided to impose upon the Vaudois.

This was on the 12th of March, 1620; they were kept prisoners for five months in the castle, which still stands beside the museum of painting in Turin; and on the same day the governor of Pignerol, Ponte by name, upon the suggestion of the Archbishop of Turin, caused twelve Vaudois to be likewise incarcerated, who had come to the market of Pignerol. There was no help for it but to resolve upon payment of the tribute demanded. Long negotiations still took place, and at last, on the 20th of June, 1620, an edict was issued conformable to the projected arrangement, save only that it contained nothing relative to the Catholic festivals and ceremonies.

Next year, in the month of April, new annoyances were commenced against the Vaudois, in regard to a valuation of property, which required them to present themselves individually at Pignerol, which some of them had failed to do. The great means employed

---

[1] Or about £1400 sterling.

[2] *Sujets de la religion.* The Protestants are frequently designated *gens de la religion*, or *religionnaires.*—TR.

against the Vaudois, which consisted in raising criminal prosecutions, on pretext of rebellion against the orders of the sovereign, was again resorted to; and in order to escape, these unfortunate adherents of a persecuted religion consented to augment their tribute by another 1000 ducatoons.

This sum was apportioned amongst all the inhabitants of the valleys, although those of Campillon alone had been originally the cause of the tribute. The distress was great; many families were obliged to pinch themselves in the very necessaries of life, and murmured at such hardships. Then it was that the monks and Jesuits set their emissaries to work amongst the poorer and more isolated. This influence was brought to bear, especially along the disputed boundary line where Protestantism was in contact with Romanism, in the towns of Bubiano, Campillon, Fenil, Garsiliano, and Briquéras.

The agents of the clergy, both regular and secular, under pretence of compassion for the hardships endured by these poor families, offered, with all appearance of generous interest, not only to pay their quota of the debt for which the Vaudois were subscribing, but also to obtain for them a long exemption from taxes, and even immediate rewards, on condition that they would only consent not to reject boons still more precious, namely, the abandonment of Protestantism, and the adoption of the Church of Rome. A number were prevailed upon, and thus sold themselves, yielding to the fallacious and gilded seductions of the tempter.

Thus, under these perpetual assaults, these scattered churches, consisting of no great numbers of persons, were weakened, being constantly exposed to the danger either of violence or of temptation. And when in our own days we see so much religious indifference prevailing amongst religious communities not only enjoying freedom, but loaded with gifts, addressed with invitations rather than with threats, surrounded with encouragements instead of obstacles, honoured instead of being despised for the discharge of their duties—when we see scriptural faith and life extinguished before the breath of selfishness and corruption, by the mere power of the infirmities of our nature—we may well be astonished that the scattered Christians of the plain of Piedmont should have been able to survive at all, during a whole century, the numerous falls which made gaps in their ranks, or the strokes of persecution which were meant for their destruction.

I cannot recount in detail all their distresses, all the troubles with which they were beset, or the injuries to which they were for a long time subjected. Charles Emmanuel might, perhaps, have been inclined to be favourable rather than hostile to them, but when the animosity of the government against them was abated, they had to endure that of private enemies. After the judicial proceedings followed the doings of the fanatics.

In 1624, for example, two Protestants being in the public square of Bubiano, some new converts reproached them with remaining faithful to a religion which had never made men anything but martyrs. "If I were in the prince's place," said one of them, "I would very soon make you abjure." "In what way?" "By force." "We thank God that he has given us a prince more moderate than you." This saying was reported to the magistrates in the following amended form: "The Protestants said that the prince is less zealous for religion than the new converts."

"The prince is insulted!" exclaimed the Catholics. The magistrates, urged on by their clamours, caused the two unfortunate Protestants to be prosecuted for the crime of lese-majesty. They were not only heretics, but rebels. The name of the one was Peter Queyras, and that of the other, Bartholemew Boulles. They succeeded at first in withdrawing from the pursuit of which they were the objects, and which, to say the truth, does not seem to have been urged with much rigour. The whole affair seemed to be forgotten, when Queyras was one day invited to dine with a seigneur of the valley. His conduct will show whether or not the seigneur was truly noble. He caused his servants to arrest the Protestant, and deliver him to the sbirri of Lucerna. He was cast into prison, and Boulles, his innocent accomplice in the language laid to his charge, thereupon fled to the mountains of Rora.

Queyras was conveyed to the dungeons of Turin. His liberation was demanded in vain. The inquisition supposed that a new victim had come into its hands. But the wife of the prisoner took her infant in her arms, went and cast herself at the feet of the prince, and informed him that the words spoken by her husband were a tribute to the wisdom of the sovereign, and not an insult to him; and supplicating in favour of the father of the child which she carried with her, she had the good fortune to obtain the pardon which she asked. "A faithful wife," says the Bible, "is a treasure from the Lord." The princes of the house of Savoy almost never showed themselves unjust or cruel, unless under the influence of the Church of Rome.

Next year (in 1625) a senator came to Bubiano, and, in virtue of secret informations of which he was possessed, caused many persons to be apprehended in that district. A petition was addressed to Charles Emmanuel, to obtain the enlargement of the captives. The duke replied that that business belonged to the judge Barbéri, who had been commissioned to inquire into it; but his benevolence did not forget it, and after a time they were set at liberty.

Thus the Protestants of Bubiano and of the neighbouring towns still retained, at that date, some measure of liberty of conscience, which they owed to the sovereign's toleration; for, according to the edict of 28th September, 1617, their religion was not to have been tolerated for more than three years beyond the bounds appointed by the edict of 1602. Not residing within these boundaries, they must have abjured, or sold their goods, to withdraw to some other quarter, or have incurred the penalties pronounced by the edict. Some authors even say that only three months were allowed them for this purpose; and eight years had now already passed without their having either abjured or sold their lands. They might, therefore, hope for the permanent continuance of this favour, the prolongation of which had been tacitly conceded to them by the kindness of the sovereign. The monks and the inquisitors were only the more eager to proceed against them; they wished to make victims of them, and not to see them indulged.

One day ten young persons were apprehended on their way to Pignerol; the monks of the abbey turned it to their own account. Subsequently a man and woman, both advanced in life, were seized at Briquéras, and conducted to Cavour. The inquisition made them its prey. Every now and then, indeed, travellers or foreign merchants were surprised on their journeys, and cast into dungeons, where they often remained without being heard of more.

In 1627 a number of persons were arrested simultaneously at Bubiano, Campillon, and Fenil. The prisoners were in the first place conveyed to Cavour, then to the castle of Villefranche, after which nothing more was to be heard of them. Their relatives, their friends, and all their compatriots were deeply afflicted. Urgent solicitations were addressed to Count Philip of Lucerna, who appears to have been no stranger to these acts of violence, and from whom none but evasive answers could be obtained. The Vaudois then addressed a petition to their prince, and sent deputies to present it to him. A person of noble birth offered his intervention with the sovereign; it was accepted; they set out and came to Turin. "I have a friend in great favour at court," said their new protector; "intrust me with your petition to show it to him, and I promise you his support." The petition was given up, but not returned. The Vaudois demanded it. "I have presented it to the duke," replied their noble friend, "but his highness was excessively angry, because of a report which accused you of having taken arms to rescue the prisoners by force. I have assured him of the falsehood of that report, and I hope to calm him completely; but you will be obliged to make some outlay, and you will not forget, in particular, to pay me the great expenses which I have incurred on this occasion."

The people of the valleys were much discontented with the turn which this affair took, and found great fault with their deputies for having let the petition pass out of their hands, which they ought themselves to have presented to the sovereign. At last a reply was obtained, and they were informed that this business was remitted to the judgment of the Archbishop of Turin and the grand chancellor. To the latter they therefore addressed themselves; but he replied that his highness, and the heir presumptive of the crown, were about to take it into their own consideration. The unhappy captives were therefore transferred to Turin, after a preventive detention of several months, ignorant even what crime was laid to their charge. The brother of Sebastian Bazan, whose name we shall meet with again in the next chapter of martyrs, was amongst the number of these prisoners. Some more weeks passed, during which the archbishop died; and after this, upon the renewed petition of the Vaudois, the duke ordered the chancellor to bring the affair to a close.

On the 21st of July, Barbéri, abusing his high position, repaired to Lucerna, escorted by a troop of constables and officers of justice, or rather brigands; for, violently entering the houses of the reformed, they pillaged at discretion, and drew up an inventory of what they left. They went on to Bubiano, where they repeated the same proceedings, and thence, in like manner, to Campillon and Fenil. After this he published an order, requiring all the notaries and syndics of these communes to render him an exact account of all the possessions of the Protestants, who, he said, were all guilty, in one way or other, and merited, without exception, to be condemned to death, and to have their goods confiscated; but that, of his clemency, he would permit them to live, on condition that they should pay a large ransom. What justice! What a senator!

The Vaudois, indignant, refused to pay this monstrous tribute. Thereupon the report was spread that an army was coming to exterminate them. The inhabitants of Bubiano, and of the other towns of the plain, hastened to convey their families to the mountains, and to carry off whatever they had most valuable. The mountaineers, on the other hand, descended in arms, and posted themselves before Lucerna, to be ready to receive the army that was spoken of. But another senator, named Syllan, being then at Lucerna on his own private business, sent emissaries to re-assure the

Vaudois as to this subject. He afterwards caused them to be informed, that if they would pay the expense of Barbéri's troop it would be withdrawn, and the movables which had been taken away would be restored.

It seemed a little hard to pay the expense of the injustice to which they had been subjected; but the Catholics of Bubiano and the other towns above-named, offered to the Vaudois to pay for them the half of the sum, in order to be delivered from that horde whose presence was disastrous for all. This act of brotherliness upon the part of the people was more Christian than all the acts of persecution on the part of the church. The offer was accepted, and Barbéri accordingly went away with the tribute which he had sought. But it soon came to be known that he had received no orders from the prince to act against the Vaudois; and they therefore drew up a detailed account of all the hardships to which they had been subjected, and it began to be spoken of that they should be made to pay something again, in order to get a stop put to them, when unexpected circumstances occurred, which completely changed the aspect of this affair.

Many persons had been apprehended at Lucerna, Garsiliano, and Briquéras, but it often happened that when the case of one of these prisoners was to be proceeded with, he was not to be found. On the other hand, the informations against persons alleged to frequent the Protestant worship in the valleys, multiplied so much, that the higher authorities could not conceive that the Vaudois had so great a number of adherents in Piedmont. What rendered the whole thing still more incomprehensible was, that some of the captives who had disappeared from the prisons were again seen at liberty amongst the mountains. Let us tell the whole story of this mystery at once. The informers received a reward from the magistrates, and the inferior magistrates received a ransom from the accused, who were too happy to escape in this way from these unjust and cruel prosecutions. The prospect of these ransoms and recompenses had made the whole neighbourhood of the valleys a mere prey to a set of informers. But the work of the wicked deceives him. These informations began to include persons higher in station and influence, who, instead of compounding, proved the falsehood of the accusation, and brought the accuser to punishment.

Thereupon the superior authorities, whose uprightness is one of the glories of Piedmont, suspended all the prosecutions which had been begun. A severe investigation was instituted concerning the previous course of these proceedings, and many false witnesses were discovered, who had caused the innocent to be condemned, and who were in their turn condemned to the galleys. But the Church of Rome, which attacks evangelical truth, must needs defend calumny; and, by the intervention of the Jesuits, many of these false witnesses succeeded in escaping the punishment to which they had become liable.

The Vaudois made no complaints; they were too happy to have their brethren restored to them. The prisoners of Villefranche were set at liberty. Those of Campillon and Bubiano, of Fenil and Briquéras, were not long of returning to the bosom of their families. The attempts directed against them had resulted in mischief to their enemies. The feet of the plotters of evil were taken in the snares which they themselves had hid. The eternal wisdom of Heaven never fails to be justified in these things by the perpetual folly of men.

In consequence of this restoration to legal rights, the Christians of Bubiano, Campillon, and Fenil—where the reformed, Gilles says, were more numerous than the Catholics [1]—obtained the privilege of continuing, *secondo il solito* (according to use and wont), the free exercise of their family worship, as well as the power of repairing to the valleys for public worship, and even of sending for the Vaudois pastors in case of sickness or death. Their right to have a Protestant schoolmaster was also recognized.

This was nothing more than what was allowed by the edicts of the 10th of January and 5th of July, 1561; but it was a great victory to have maintained them. The Catholic clergy were not long of disputing their enjoyment of the fruits of it, and, under the most futile pretexts, raised prosecutions against the Vaudois, which always concluded with the alternative of apostasy or a ransom, "insomuch," says the author above quoted, "that there was no fault so petty but it was very difficult to settle for it without this condition, nor crime so enormous that it was not readily to be pardoned to those who would abjure their religion."

The monks, in particular, ceased not to complain of the pretended vexations which they endured from the Vaudois. At La Tour, for example, where an ancient Protestant cemetery was just beside the walls of their convent, and the use of the cemetery had upon that account been interdicted [2] to those of our religion, it so happened that the inmates of the cloisters exposed some of the bones in digging the foundation for a wall. A Vaudois woman gathered up the bones and buried them. Forthwith the monks wrote to Turin that the Vaudois impeded them in their labours, carried away their materials, were guilty of thefts from them, &c. And

[1] Gilles, p. 402.   [2] By decrees of 2d July, 1618, and 25th June, 1620.

in this manner, upon false reports, severe prosecutions sometimes lodged the innocent in prison.

La Fontaine was not yet born: but it seems that the fable of the wolf and the lamb was already known; for the learned and simple historian who relates these facts, boldly compares these monks to the wolves, "incessantly crying," says he, "that the lambs were troubling the water."

But the monks were kept in countenance by others; and sometimes the secular authorities, and sometimes the seigneurs, played the part of the *wolves*. We have seen proof of this in the ambuscades of William of Lucerna, and the ransoms of those who were condemned. In 1629, for example, a Protestant of Campillon, named Perron, was assailed in his own house by a band of constables, whom his four sons and he valiantly repelled for half-a-day. One of his sons was killed, and another dangerously wounded. But particulars of this kind are so numerous, that they cannot all be mentioned.

Under the reign of Victor Amadeus I., orders were given to the authorities of Lucerna, Bubiano, Briquéras, Campillon, and Fenil, and often reiterated, to proceed with the extirpation *of the heretics* who could not be got to relinquish their heresy. These orders were dated on the 9th and 11th of November, 1634, the 6th and 27th of May, 1635, the 10th of April, 1636, and the 3d of November, 1637. But whether the sentiments of the sovereign were milder than his words, or whether the indulgence of the judges mitigated the severity of his decrees, the Vaudois continued to exist in these towns, where they had existed so long.

An edict of 28th January, 1641, definitively pronounced their goods confiscated everywhere without the limits of the valleys. On the 17th of February, 1644, they were forbidden to come without the territory of these valleys, except for the purpose of trafficking at the fairs; but it appears, nevertheless, that there were always some shoots of the old evangelical churches remaining at Lucerna, Bubiano, Campillon, Fenil, and Briquéras; for the prohibition against the Vaudois residing in these towns was frequently renewed at later dates. It is repeated in the edicts, amongst others, of the 31st of May and of the 15th of September, 1661, of the 31st of January, 1725, and of the 20th of June, 1730.

It was reserved for our days to see these unjust and puerile barriers at last disappear, which had been raised betwixt one set of people and another, in order to circumscribe thought. The doctrines of the gospel, like the enlightenment of civilization, will not be confined within manorial boundaries. What have the marches of a territory to do with the limits of error and of truth? May these fair regions soon recover, in their liberty, the gifts which once they exhibited so admirably in the days of their bondage!

CHAPTER XIII.

REVIVAL OF THE EVANGELICAL CHURCHES OF SALUCES, AND NEW VICISSITUDES TO WHICH THEY WERE SUBJECTED.[1]

(A.D. 1602 TO A.D. 1616.)

Valleys of the Stura, the Vrayta and Valgrane—Edict of 12th June, 1602—The Protestants driven into exile—Persecution conducted by the Capuchin Ribotti—Effects of long-continued oppression—The *Digiunati*—Irritation and disorder—Negotiations—The Duke of Savoy grants favourable terms to the Vaudois—Protestant churches spring up anew—Popish missionaries—Expatriation of Protestants—Their manifesto—A breathing time.

THE number of Protestants in the province of Saluces was not confined to the members of the churches which we have named, but in the valley of the Stura, in the valley of the Vrayta, and in Valgrane, there were fugitives from the great towns, who had retired to the most secluded villages. Thither each of them brought with him a portion of the evangelical light of their dispersed church, a spark of the common faith, which was thus extended in their exile.

Light has the property of communication without diminution; it enlarges its sphere by multiplying the centres from which it shines. Accordingly, the number of enlightened souls increased around the proscribed refugees, and these forgotten villages gradually became new churches. Moreover, many of the families which had embraced the external forms of Catholicism when it was imposed upon them by violence, hastened to return to the natural expression of their faith when the oppression had ceased.

Then, also, the persecuting attention of Popery was again drawn to them. The edict of the 25th of February, 1602, which interdicted Protestant worship without the limits of the Vaudois valleys, had no other object than to put an end to it in the towns of the province of Pignerol, situated on the outskirts of these valleys; but it was made a terrible weapon in the province of Saluces.

In the first place, missionaries were sent thither under the direction of Father Ribotti, in order that those who did not yield to their arguments might be treated as hardened and obstinate rebels.

[1] AUTHORITIES.—As in Chapter IX.

The governor of Dronéro and the vice-seneschal of Saluces were invited to assist in this enterprise.

The reformed then addressed a petition to Charles Emmanuel,[1] in the hope of obtaining some mitigation of the provisions of that edict, the force of which they felt, without being named in it. They entreated, amongst other favours, that they might not be subjected to any ecclesiastical jurisdiction, but only to the civil magistrates; and nothing could be more just, because the ecclesiastical tribunals belonged to the Church of Rome, and could not be expected to judge, but only to condemn the adherents of another communion. They asked, also, that those of their religious persuasion who had been for more than seven years settled in that part of the country, should not be driven into exile; and, finally, that mixed marriages, solemnized by Protestant ministers whilst the province belonged to France, should not be annulled. This was, however, the thing which the Catholic clergy demanded most of all, without any regard to the confusion of every kind which this measure could not fail to produce in families.

These three points were conceded to the Vaudois of Saluces. But before this was done, a priest of the neighbourhood had taken upon him to issue, upon his own private authority, an order of expulsion against all the reformed of his parish. This abuse of power was complained of to the Duke of Savoy, who replied that he would write upon the subject to the governor.

The reformed and the Vaudois originally belonging to this province, had therefore reason to hope that for them days of tranquillity were at last come; but through the solicitations of the Capuchins and Jesuits, the justice promised and the concessions obtained, very soon gave place to new severities. On the 12th of June, 1602, appeared the following edict:—

"Having laboured, by all means possible, for the extirpation of heresy, in order to the glory of God and the salvation of souls, we are grieved to learn that in the marquisate of Saluces, the people whom we have prohibited from the exercise of their worship live without ostensible religion, and thereby run the risk of falling into atheism. To prevent this horrible evil, we ordain all the adherents of the pretended reformed religion, whether born in the country or only settled in it, to embrace the Catholic faith within fifteen days, or to leave our dominions and to sell their properties within the space of six months, under pain of confiscation and death."

The Protestants of these regions, preferring the pains of exile to a base desertion of the faith of their fathers, left the province of

[1] On the 15th of May, 1602.

Saluces in a body, and retired once more to that Ephraim of the Vaudois valleys, where the exiled always found a refuge, where Christians always found brethren, and where sacred consolations were always ministered to the afflicted.

But many of them settled upon the left bank of the Cluson, in the valley of Perouse, at Les Portes, Pinache, Doublon, and Perouse itself, where, according to an edict recently promulgated,[1] the reformed worship was equally to be abolished; and the Capuchin Ribotti, always breathing out fury against the Vaudois, pursued thither also these unfortunate and fugitive victims.

Aided by the urgency of the nuncio, and solicitations directly addressed by Paul V. himself to the Duke of Savoy, Ribotti obtained an edict,[2] by which that prince renewed in a more general manner the prohibition to celebrate Protestant worship in his dominions, without the arbitrary limits to which the territory of the Vaudois valleys had been restricted. The Protestants did not make any haste to abjure, and the duke did not make any haste to punish; but by multiplying his prohibitions, he multiplied the claims which Popery could urge for the employment of measures so severe as to be effective. The prince, notwithstanding his natural mildness, could not refuse to cause the orders which he had already issued to be put in execution; but it may be easily enough seen, from the instructions which he addressed in these circumstances to the governors of provinces, that the real author of these cruelties was the pope, and not himself. "Desiring," said he, "that the holy enterprise of the extirpation of heresy should be accomplished in our dominions, and his Holiness having for this purpose sent missionaries, at the head of whom is Father Ribotti, we enjoin all our officers to render him all assistance."[3] Then, denying himself the credit of his own clemency, he recommended them to treat the Vaudois with some tenderness, and to make them suppose that they owed it to the personal kindness of Father Ribotti; for assuming, with good enough reason, that that monk would be pitiless, the duke wrote a private letter to the governor of Saluces, in which he said, "In order that his severities may not make him too odious to these poor people, you will take care to show them indulgence in some things, and to grant them some mitigations, as if they were owing to his intercession."[4] But the missionaries understood nothing of the employment of any such means; and at this juncture the above circular was issued, which was by no means calculated to calm men's tempers. The unhappy peasants, so often annoyed, proscribed, dispossessed, and now again

[1] 28th May, 1602. [2] Issued on the 3d of July, 1602.
[3] Circular of 5th September, 1602. [4] This letter is dated 8th July, 1602.

chased from their abodes, already also exasperated and excited by a troop of discontented and banished men like themselves, but who certainly had not the same Christianity, assembled in an armed band among the mountains. They proclaimed themselves the defenders of the oppressed, not concealing their intention of resisting the troops of the sovereign himself, if he should employ his troops against them or their adherents.

But there were no stores of provisions in the mountains; and for subsistence this body made frequent forays into the plain, supplying themselves with victuals by pillage, in which the Catholics, and those who had recently become Catholics, were the principal sufferers. Hence arose many reprehensible disorders.

This famished band received the name of the band of the *Digiunati*, and by the intimidation which they exercised, they compelled a number of Protestants who had recently become Catholics, to return to the Reformed Church, which violence had driven them to leave. Wretched and deplorable conversions on both sides! But what was only an exception with Protestantism, was habitual with the Church of Rome.

The Duke of Savoy, having been informed of these troubles, commanded the magistrates to cause the syndics of the communes which were frequented by the *Digiunati* to be summoned before them, and to make each of these syndics responsible for the disorders committed in his commune. At the same time, he enjoined the Protestants of the towns situated in the plain of Piedmont, on the border of the Vaudois valleys, to quit their abodes, or else to become Catholics within the space of fifteen days.[1]

The irritation of the parties had reached its height, when, in addition of all other calamities, a general famine aggravated the distress of the numerous families of Protestants, who, without having left the territories of Savoy, lived in wandering and banishment. The *Digiunati* became the agents of depredation and vengeance; and in spite of the severe but ineffective proceedings adopted against them—in spite of the express prohibition to give them any harbour, assistance, or supply of food—their number continued to increase. All the fugitive victims of persecution or of famine joined them. Exerting themselves in this vagabond and savage life to do as much injury as possible to their enemies, they became every day more dreaded. Their presence in the mountains afforded a kind of refuge for all who were persecuted, and the exasperation continually increased, from the combination of so many miseries and animosities.

[1] Orders of 2d March and 28th May, 1602.

Four young men of Bubiano having met with one of the agents of the Inquisition, killed him as they would a mischievous beast, and went to join the *Digiunati*. Another assassination was committed upon the person of a Catholic of Bagnols, who had come and joined himself to the refugees in order to betray them; "and besides these," says Gilles, "they performed many other acts of vengeance, which displeased well-disposed people, notwithstanding all the pretexts and all the reasons which they brought forward in opposition to their censures."

But disorder is like a conflagration; it increases by its own violence. And ought we to be astonished that these unfortunate people, with a price set upon their heads, should have endeavoured both to defend and to avenge themselves? In times of war the nations eagerly rush to that systematized murder, which decimates them without dishonour; and in times of persecution, is it not conceivable that proscribed persons, whose lives are more cruelly threatened than in a battle, may have been drawn into crimes of which, in other circumstances, they would have been incapable? What is said of offences may be applied also to these excesses—woe be to those by whom they come!

The inhabitants of the surrounding districts, moreover, including the Catholics themselves, although suffering from this state of things, regarded the resistance made by these unfortunate people, driven as they were to despair, as most natural; and all their wishes were, not for their death, but for an arrangement which would permit the proscribed to return to their ordinary life. "Scarcely were we arrived at Lucerna," says a traveller of that period, "when we were surrounded by men and women, entreating us with clasped hands that an accommodation might be come to. In this we remarked the judgment of God; for the banished people had been driven from Lucerna upon account of their religion, and now these were the Papists, who could not venture out of the town because of the banished." This traveller was the Count of Lucerna, who interposed on their behalf, and particularly on behalf of those of Saluces, who had been so long time dispersed. He demanded that a petition should be intrusted to him. All the Vaudois and Reformed churches, from Suza to Coni, constituting, as they said, one body in Christ, made haste to sign it.[1]

Meanwhile, the *Digiunati* continued their raids. Six of them having come down to Lucerna to buy victuals,[2] the Chevalier of

---

[1] In March, 1603. The reply of Charles Emmanuel was on the 9th of April.
[2] This was on the 6th of March, 1603.

Lucerna[1] and Captain Crespin of Bubiano, aided by 100 armed men, resolved to apprehend them. They cut off their passage at both ends of a narrow street, in which they were transacting business; and they, finding themselves hunted like deer, knowing that a price was set upon their heads, perceiving that they were surrounded, yet with no safety but in flight, rushed upon their enemies with the courage of despair, drove back the soldiers, killed the captain, and passed through the midst of the fifty men whom he commanded, without leaving a single prisoner in their hands. The soldiers pursued them, and the *Digiunati* took different routes, and all escaped, with the exception of one, who, having leaped from the top of a wall, broke his thigh in falling, and could not save himself. He was taken, fastened to four horses, and torn in pieces alive. This was not the way to calm men's minds.

At length the petition of the Vaudois was presented to Charles Emmanuel. The duke perceived how dangerous it was for the Catholics, as well as for the Protestants, that the causes of these fatal divisions should be perpetuated, and he decided[2] that all the banished should be permitted to return to their habitations, that the confiscations which had taken place of their goods should be annulled, and even that Protestants who had become Catholics should have the right to return to the church which they had left, if their consciences demanded it.

However, a certain number of the *Digiunati* were excepted from these provisions, and orders were renewed to deliver them up dead or alive. But this was only a desperate fraction of that numerous people who everywhere arose to hail with delight the restored religion of their fathers, insomuch that in that region, where, on the day before, all was Catholic, at least in appearance, a multitude of Protestant families suddenly flung off the veil of the established superstitions, and openly proclaimed their respect for the Bible. Thus the churches of Saviglano, Levadiggi, Demont, Dronéro, and St. Michael speedily re-appeared. Their elements were not to be formed, they were only to be united together again. Some of them were found to be stronger after this revival than they had been previously; as, for example, those of St. Damian, Verzol, and Aceil. But like those swarms of devouring locusts which return to a plain that sprouts again and becomes green, the Jesuits and Capuchins re-appeared in these countries when they began once more to flourish. This would have been of little consequence if they had kept

---

[1] The brother of the count, who offered to become intercessor for the Vaudois with the sovereign. The chevalier's name was Emmanuel, that of the count was Charles. [2] At Coni, 9th April, 1603.

themselves to preaching and discussions. The doctrines of the Bible would only have gained thereby; it is by conflicts that they are confirmed. Yes! by conflicts, but not by bloodshed.

These new missionaries[1] had, in the first place, frequent conferences with the pastors. The governor of the province took a fancy to bring them together at dinner, in order to be present at their discussions. A number of monks and Catholic priests were led, by these discussions with the Protestants, to embrace the gospel, which strengthened the Protestant cause. Thus the Reformed Church recruited itself, and added to its forces from the very ranks of those who came to combat against it. It was in the valley of the Vrayta, which at that time belonged to France, that that church most rapidly extended itself. "The Protestants," says Rorengo, "held their meetings there both by day and by night; their worship was public, and the poor Catholics themselves durst not set out their faces to go to mass, for fear of hearing the cry of *idolaters* raised against them !"

One of the ministers of this valley was a converted priest, and his example had been followed by numbers of his parishioners.[2] Short as the time had been during which the field had been left open to the Reformation, it had established itself everywhere, solely by the influence of the Bible, mightier than the secular arm.

It was in 1603 that the Capuchin missionaries came to the valley of the Vrayta, in order to prepare the way for the employment of new measures of severity. They first made their appearance at Château Dauphin, a place surrounded by wild and rugged mountains of vast height. Particular mention is made of their superior, Joseph de Tenda, and of Brother Zachary, author of four polemical volumes against the Reformation. From Château Dauphin they proceeded to the Val de Grano, and established missions at Carail, Aceil, and Verzol, at the entry to Saluces. They re-opened the deserted churches, restored the pageants of the Catholic worship, and renewed the annoyances against the Protestants. As for the Jesuits, they had one residence at Aceil, another at Dronier, another at St. Damian, and a fourth in the manor-house of Château Dauphin. What must have been the activity in mischief of all these men planted in different localities, and associated for the same cause,

---

[1] The Jesuits had, however, been introduced into the diocese of Saluces in 1596.
[2] Rorengo attributes his conversion to a motive adduced in so many cases, that it must certainly be deemed a very powerful one by those who so often allege it. It was, he says, from the desire to break the celibate, to which he had bound himself when he entered into orders; and as if it were not enough to have made it a crime in him to have taken a wife, the worthy Rorengo goes on to accuse him of bigamy. All this without proofs, as usual.—*Memorie Istorichi*, p. 178.

emulating each other in their exertions in their common work, stimulating each other to the destruction of heresy, convinced, perhaps, that theirs was the true religion, but animated with a bitter zeal, very remote from the spirit of the gospel! Was there not in this a real plague to the Protestants, analogous to that of the swarm of insects which brought upon Egypt desolation and death?

"It is impossible to relate all the efforts which these missionaries at that time made."[1] These words of Rorengo suggest much. We know not what the efforts were of which he speaks; but we may judge of a tree by its fruits; and at this time, says Perrin,[2] "not only was the free exercise of religion interdicted at Saluces, in the valley of the Mayra, which contained Verzol, St. Damian, Aceil, and Dronéro, but also, by a new edict, all the Protestants were required to become Catholics. Inquisitors were sent from house to house, and more than 500 families were compelled to go into exile. They retired into the dominions of France, part of them to Provence, where they aided in restoring the ancient Vaudois churches of the Leberon, part of them to Dauphiny, where they added to the churches of Pragela, which was then included in that province."

Thus, like the waters, which always follow a natural inclination in flowing towards the central basins among the hills, these people, truly attached to the gospel, kept by their spiritual native land when they removed beyond the horizon of the districts in which they were born.

But before thus dispersing and separating from one another—before thus going into exile—they drew up a declaration, which all the other churches of the Vaudois valleys subscribed along with them, in order to make known the causes of this proscription.

"Let all men know," say they, "that it is not for any crime or rebellion that we are this day deprived of our properties and our abodes. This happens by reason of an edict of abjuration or exile, which his royal highness, deceived, no doubt, by false reports, has issued against us. But our forefathers and our families having been brought up in the doctrine professed at this day by the Reformed Church, we are resolved to live and die in it. And, therefore, we declare and affirm, that this doctrine which they would prohibit to us, is held by us to be the only true doctrine—the only doctrine approved of God, and the only doctrine able to conduct us in the way of salvation. And if any one pretend that we are in error, far from being obstinate in defending it, we profess ourselves ready immediately to abjure it, upon our being convinced by the

---

[1] *Le diligenze de Padri missionarij, tanto gesuiti che capuccini, furono indicibili.* Rorengo, p. 179.   [2] P. 184.

word of God. But if it is attempted, by mere force and constraint, to make us change our beliefs, we prefer rather to renounce all that we have, yea, even our lives, rather than the salvation of our souls."[1] These noble and courageous words ought to have gained for the proscribed all the sympathy of generous minds. But they exasperated still more the Catholic clergy, and led them to adopt violent measures, by revealing to them their utter inability to convince. When, therefore, a number of these expatriated families showed an inclination to return to Piedmont, entering it again by the Vaudois valleys, an edict was obtained from Charles Emmanuel, by which all strangers were prohibited from settling in the valleys, and all Vaudois were prohibited from going beyond their limits.[2] But it would seem that these enactments, over the execution of which it was so difficult to watch, did not arrest the movement against which they were directed; for a little while after, new orders—obtained as before, by the solicitation of the Capuchins, the Jesuits, and the nuncio—recalled the attention of the governors of the province, not only to this particular edict, but to all the previous regulations adopted in a spirit of hostility to Protestantism.[3]

The year following (in 1610) the Duke of Savoy entered into an alliance with Henry IV. against the Spaniards, and in 1612 the wars of Montferrat began, which endured for four years; so that the attention of the monarch, and the influences which impelled him to action, were for a brief period abstracted from religious questions. This time of general agitation was therefore a season of tranquillity for the churches of Saluces. No doubt it was tranquillity only in a relative sense—not peace, but respite; not a regular and enduring state of rest, but temporary exemption from persecution. Yet, as in a stormy day, if the clouds but clear up a little, the darkest sky will immediately re-assume the colours of life, so an aspect of sudden prosperity, like a precarious sunbeam, re-appeared for a few years in these tormented churches.

Among the *Papers connected with the country of Provence*, under date 17th April, 1612, occurs a petition to the king, in the following terms:—"May it please your majesty to provide that persons belonging to the marquisate of Saluces, refugees in this country, may have power freely to pass and traffic in the territories of the Duke of Savoy, without being pursued after upon account of religion;"[4] and among the papers of Dauphiny of the same period

[1] This declaration is published entire by Perrin, pp. 185-189; and by Léger, P. I. ch. xvii. pp. 111-113.
[2] Edict of 2d July, 1609.   [3] Orders of 21st November, 1609.
[4] MS. of Peyresk, Library of Carpentras, Register XXXI. vol. I. fol. 361, art. xvii.

is a similar request, that "his majesty (the King of France) would exert his influence with the Duke of Savoy to obtain liberty of trading in his dominions in favour of the refugees of Saluces."[1] Both these points were conceded.

At the same time, the still existing churches of Saluces caused earnest solicitations to be addressed to the duke, through the mediation of Switzerland, that liberty of conscience might be granted to them. And in 1613, the Vaudois valleys having been required to furnish a contingent of troops for the war of Montferrat, it so happened that these troops were sent as a garrison into the province of Saluces. They had the privilege of meeting for the exercise of their worship, and their brethren in religion sometimes joined them in these little meetings, so as to increase their number, thus taking steps, as it were, to reclaim for themselves the enjoyment of religious liberty.

But meanwhile the Jesuits and the Capuchins, on the other hand, only became more active in watching and in prosecutions. To give some satisfaction to these worthy coadjutors, who found so little in the results of their preaching, the magistrates from time to time made new prisoners.

Those against whom the clergy were most active in directing severe proceedings were the *relapsed*, or those who had become Catholics *invitâ conscientiâ*, to whom the superstitions of the Catholic paganism rendered dearer still the simplicity of evangelical Christianity, and who made haste to return to it upon the first favourable opportunity, with firmer attachment than ever. But when they were discovered, they were denounced to the Holy Office, and often disappeared, noiselessly, in the mysterious chambers of the Inquisition.[2] However, the war continued, and the Vaudois came to be more and more needed; the secular power, less cruel than the church, gradually relaxed its severity; the Protestants of Saluces began to look around them and breathe freely. But for them to breathe at all was to worship God and serve him according to the gospel. "Those of Dronier," says a work of that period,[3] were the first to set the good example, and from the year 1616, they began to hold their meetings." These meetings were held in secret; but every day the number of faithful attendants was increased by new admissions. "The news soon travelled to Rome,

---

[1] MS. of Peyresk, Library of Carpentras, Register XXXI. vol. I. fol. 371, art. xxvii.

[2] *Si denunciava al Santo-Offizio, e cosi le cose passavano con molto quiete, con occultissima vigilanza.* Rorengo, p. 183.

[3] *Brief discours des persécutions advenues en ce temps aux fidèles des Eglises de Saluces.* Geneva, 1620.

the pope was very angry about it; his highness was apprised of it, and the clergy omitted no means of opposition."[1]

The Protestants would not have been able to have avoided some new catastrophe, but for a providential circumstance, which, on the contrary, gave them unexpected support. The events which led to it, and those which followed from it, will form the subject of next chapter.

CHAPTER XIV.

CONCLUSION OF THE HISTORY OF THE CHURCHES OF SALUCES; PARTICULARLY OF THOSE OF ACEIL, VERZOL, ST. MICHAEL, AND PRAVIGLELM.[2]

(A.D. 1616 TO A.D. 1633.)

Lesdiguières intercedes for the Vaudois of Saluces—Increase of Protestantism in the valleys of the Stura and of Mayra—The Bishop of Saluces at Dronier—Protestant worship interrupted—Proscriptions—Vexations—Renewed intercessions of Lesdiguières—Disorders—Plot for a general massacre of the reformed in the province of Saluces—Outrages and cruelties—Martyrdom of Peter Marquisy and Maurice Mongie—The pope grants to the Duke of Savoy a tithe of ecclesiastical revenues for six years—Further persecutions—Sentence of banishment against the inhabitants of Praviglelm and Paësane—Intercession of Lesdiguières—The churches of Saluces gradually weakened by continued persecutions—Victor Amadeus—Extinction of the churches of Saluces.

It has been already stated that at this time Charles Emmanuel was at war with Spain about the matter of Montferrat. He asked aid from France, and Lesdiguières was sent to him. This illustrious general, who was then regarded as the head of the Protestant party in France, entered the province of Saluces in 1617.

Indignant at the manifold annoyances to which those of his own church were subjected, he interceded for them with their sovereign. The court of Savoy readily understood that the leader of the reformed could not fight its battles with very much zeal if it persecuted his party. On the ground of prudence, therefore, some repose was granted to the Vaudois of Saluces; and on the 28th of September, 1617, the duke, being at Asti, issued a decree to this effect. He said—" Out of particular regard for a great personage, we grant permission to the Protestant refugees, and persons ban-

---

[1] *Brief discours des persécutions advenues en ce temps aux fidèles des Eglises de Saluces.* Geneva, 1620.

[2] AUTHORITIES.—The same as in Chapter IX.

ished from the marquisate of Saluces, to return and enter into free possession of their properties and their abodes, for a period of three full years;[1] to make arrangements about them, and sell them at their own pleasure during that time, they being prohibited, however, from spreading their heretical opinions or asserting their doctrines, upon pain of death. The prisoners detained upon account of religion shall be set at liberty, and enjoy the same privileges; and as to properties confiscated or sold, they shall be returned to their former owners upon a just indemnity, which we will grant to those who have acquired them."

These provisions would have been of great value if they had been permanent; but to assign them beforehand a limit so confined, was to grant nothing; it was only to sow the seed for fresh troubles and more ruin at a future time. The Protestants, nevertheless, showed themselves very grateful. Their conscientious sensitiveness was awakened only upon one point, and they wrote to the pastors of Geneva to know if they ought to accept this decree, seeing that it treated them as heretics.[2] Why did they not insist that these advantages should repose upon a less precarious foundation? The intercession of Lesdiguières obtained for them the omission of the reference to *heresy*, and in their honest simplicity these unsophisticated mountaineers, confiding in the justice of their prince, never imagined that he could make any revocation of this edict. With them what was just and true over night must needs be still just and true in the morning. The variations of the Catholic Church, in point of honesty, would be found still more numerous than those of the Protestant Church in point of doctrine. Sad changes were already in preparation for the Vaudois, notwithstanding these things at present favourable to them, to which the Papal Church was obliged, in the meantime, to submit, but to which it hoped soon to put an end.

Nevertheless, the happy effect which they in the first instance produced surpassed all expectation. In a few days the aspect of the country was altered. "The night before," say the Capuchins, "we would have thought it almost purged of heretics, and next day they make their appearance from all quarters, like the soldiers of Cadmus, who rose in full armour from the sand of the earth." In the valley of the Stura, which is deeper and more extensive than the others, Protestantism, which had never been eradicated, flourished again with more vigour than ever. It was in the town of Aceil (distinguished in our days as the birthplace of the famous

---

[1] Borelli says three months.
[2] Archives of the pastors of Geneva, vol. F, p. 174.

Cibrario, author of the history of European law during the middle ages), that the Reformation had the greatest number of adherents. The village of Pagliéro joined in this open profession of the gospel. The town of Verzol boldly declared for the same cause, but afterwards drew back. That of St. Michael, which appeared at first more cautious in its proceedings than the others, very soon acquired resolution, and followed Aceil with steadfastness.

The Protestants were, indeed, prohibited from having public assemblies, but the number of private meetings supplied the place of public worship; and, moreover, it was not long till they began to hold general congregations during the night, that climate being as mild as the climate of Nice. The secret of these congregations was not unfrequently betrayed by the joy which the people could not contain, either before they went to them or after they returned.

In the valley of Mayra, at Dronier, and other places,[1] so many made profession of Protestantism that the Catholics seemed to disappear. Many, instead of selling their lands, bought more; industrial activity, commerce, and agriculture, speedily made unusual advancement. It seemed as if they thought they had nothing to fear for the future; and this prosperity itself ought to have induced the Duke of Savoy to maintain the causes which had produced it, instead of destroying it, by allowing them to be removed.

It is well worthy of attention, that in all countries of the world in which Protestant doctrines have taken firm root, the people have prospered, as if an unseen benediction had been pronounced over them; and wherever Catholicism has maintained itself in greatest power, life has been extinguished, prosperity and morality have disappeared, as if under the influence of some mysterious curse.

The churches of Saluces recovered in one year all the lustre which belonged to them half a century before. "'These heretics," says Rorengo (whom we cite in preference to other authorities, not as the source of our information, but in confirmation of it), "commenced to play the lords amongst the poor and disconsolate Papists, who with terror found themselves on the point of being annihilated in that country."[2] They no longer ventured to make processions, but cried out against the tyranny of the reformed.

The festival of Easter, in 1618, had been celebrated at Dronier by so great a concourse of Protestants, that the Bishop of Saluces repaired thither the same week, to restore in some degree the honours of his deserted church. Notwithstanding his presence at Dronier, on the Sabbath after Easter, there was still so numerous

[1] *Memorie Istorichi*, pp. 184, 185.   [2] Ibid. p. 185.

an assemblage of the reformed, that all the apartments of the private house in which they met were occupied. The hall, the landing-place before the door, the steps, and even upon the street— every place was overflowing, eye-witnesses say, with members of the church who could not find admission.[1] The pastor had commenced his opening prayer; all the people were on their knees around him, even to the outer steps of the domestic sanctuary. At that moment the bishop arrived in great pomp, escorted by soldiers and officers of justice. "In the name of his royal highness," said he, "dissolve your congregation." But the voice which prayed to God, ceased not at the bidding of that which spoke to men. The pastor continued his prayer and thanksgiving; the officers of law drew up their minute of proceedings; the bishop waited until the end of the prayer, and then renewed his summons. "In the name of our apostolical authority," said he, "we forbid you all from assembling again henceforth, contrary to the edicts of his royal highness." "In the name of Jesus," the pastor then replied, "we do not recognize any apostolical authority except in the gospel which he has given to us by the apostles, and which we faithfully preach. As for the edicts, we do not violate them, since we are assembled in a private house." This reply was taken down in the minute of proceedings, and the bishop retired. But he consulted lawyers to ascertain the legal import of the edict, and learned with victorious satisfaction that the setting forth of doctrines was forbidden. In consequence, he came back three days after, with the grand referendary, Milliot, to summon the Protestants to appear before the authorities as having been guilty of proclaiming their doctrines, contrary to the terms of the edict under which they sheltered themselves.

The Christians perceived that there was in this a plausible pretext for condemning them; and for people who had so often been condemned without reason, there was ground enough of alarm in the presence of a specious reason. However, the prohibition of asserting their doctrines could only, in fairness, be considered as a prohibition of Protestants endeavouring to convert Catholics, because, surely, they could not be prevented from speaking amongst themselves of their own beliefs; and as the number of persons authorized to meet in a private house was not limited, it could not well be made a crime in them to hold meetings more or less numerous. But these simple and honest people did not dream of having recourse to such arguments of defence; their convictions were too strong to admit of their not seeking their propagation. This was to have declared their doctrines. And after justice had already

[1] *Brief discours*, ch. iii.

been denied them in so many instances more flagrant than this, a favourable interpretation of the law was what they would certainly not have obtained. They deemed it, therefore, more prudent to escape out of the way, and took refuge in the woods situated above Dronier. There they remained for forty days, like Jesus in the wilderness, fasting and praying to God, animated by an increasing ardour, an inextinguishable and delightful thirst for prayers, hymns, and pious meditations, for which their souls longed more eagerly, and in which they found increased satisfaction, in presence of danger and in the calm of these solitudes.

It was not, however, for want of courage that they took to flight; for the referendary Milliot having proceeded against them by individual citations, a number of Protestants, who had been omitted, spontaneously went and declared themselves partakers in the same transgressions, that is to say, in the same faith, and complained to the judges that they had not been included among the proscribed. Was not this devotedness of a sincere faith as noble and as courageous as a heroic resistance would have been?

The Catholics, seeing the town of Dronier almost deserted, and the fugitives self-condemned by their own apprehensions, fancied that they already saw their goods confiscated, and might divide them in anticipation of the event as already sure. But so great a number of Protestants had caused their names to be inscribed in the lists drawn up, that the magistrates shrunk from the necessity of adopting severe measures against such a multitude, and wrote to the Duke of Savoy, to remit the matter to his decision. On their side the Vaudois entreated Lesdiguières again to intercede for them, and Charles Emmanuel put an end to these uncertainties by covering all that was past with a general amnesty, after which he simply re-established the provisions of the edict of 28th September, 1617.

The fugitives thereupon returned to their abodes, more united and more fervent than ever; the Catholic clergy redoubled their efforts to give to their worship the sovereign pomp to which it was legally entitled, and for which it lacked only the attendance of a sufficient number of people. Processions, novenæ, and pilgrimages were multiplied. The parochial clergy received orders to preach sermons in their churches; proof sufficient of the negligence which had prevailed in this respect. The missionaries laboured to unite the force of argument with the magnificence of ceremonies; but power in reasoning depends upon truth, and truth is not to be determined by decrees, like the arrangements of a festival. These foreign merchants of crosses and amulets saw the public indifference increasing around them; they accused the Protestants of being the cause of that impious desertion, and accordingly their most earnest wishes were for the removal of Protestantism from the country. The reformed, upon their part, redoubled their zeal and ardour; and in consequence of this emulation between the two rival religions, many elements, by no means akin to piety, were mingled with their proceedings.

One day when the Bishop of Saluces,[1] accompanied by a missionary[2] and the superior of Coni,[3] was about to enter the parish church of Dronier, a voice amongst the crowd pronounced these words, " Ere long there will be no priests, nor monks, nor prelates!" The words certainly ought not to have been uttered; but perhaps it was nothing more than a remark made in a conversation betwixt two persons. Nay, it is possible that these words, even if uttered in an offensive manner, did not proceed from the mouth of a Vaudois, but from the perfidious lips of an enemy seeking their destruction. Be this as it might, this occurrence, which in our times it would be deemed puerile to notice, greatly excited the wrath of the bishop and the indignation of the clergy. It was reported to the sovereign; and as wounded pride exaggerates everything with which it comes in contact, these words were represented as manifesting intentions, and possessing a signification, perilous to the safety of the state, and it was necessary, at the very least, that the reprobation for which they called should extend to all the Protestants.

Count Milliot, to whom the histories now give the title of vice-chancellor, now made another visit to Dronier, and commenced by requiring[4] that all who desired to enjoy the benefit of the late edict[5] should come and have their names inscribed in a register to be kept for that purpose. The number of names inscribed accordingly was very considerable, for the number of the Protestants was increasing, and not diminishing. Many even of the Catholics ranked themselves along with them. Rorengo mentions a doctor of laws, a captain, and a physician.[6] This register of names was afterwards transmitted to the Senate of Turin.

Meanwhile the Catholics constantly sought to surprise the Protestants in the criminal act of public worship; and the Protestants, mistrusting the Catholics, kept upon their guard, went about armed, and were not sparing of disdain and recrimination against their adversaries. Thus the parties became more imbittered by their

---

[1] Ottavio Viale.
[2] Fra Marcello di Torino (Capuchin).
[3] Padre Giovani di Moncalieri.
[4] On 2d June, 1618.
[5] That of 28th Sept., 1617.
[6] P. 186.

very hostility. In such circumstances it is very difficult to avoid excesses, and the smallest spark will suffice to kindle a flame.

The Protestants were apprised that a noble personage, belonging to the family of Cardinal Almandi, had taken some steps against them. Indignation, fanaticism, and the savage excitement awakened by the wild solitudes to which they had so often been driven, armed the hand of an assassin.

The crime of the individual became a cause of offence against all. It was immediately reported to the sovereign, who, without delay, renewed the severe enactments of the ancient edicts; amongst others, those of the 25th of February, 1602, according to which the Protestant worship, mixed marriages, and the acquirement of property, were absolutely prohibited beyond the narrow limits of the Vaudois valleys. The leases and contracts by which they had taken or purchased lands from the Catholics were therefore annulled. At Aceil they had taken possession of the edifices of the Brotherhood of the Holy Spirit, and there they celebrated their worship. They were expelled from them, and prohibited from returning, under pain of death. Finally, an edict of Charles Emmanuel, of date the 2d of July, 1618, ordained all Protestant heads of families to bring, every man, a list of the names of his household to the magistrates of his canton, under penalty of a fine of 300 golden crowns, and of divers corporal punishments, even to imprisonment and the gibbet; whilst the Bishop of Saluces and the Capuchin missionaries watched, with an inexorable solicitude, to see that no one should enjoy his property beyond the expiry of the three years allowed by the edict of 28th September, 1617.

The fatal term drew near; conflicts became more numerous, especially upon occasion of funerals, at which the edict of 1618 had prohibited the Protestants from assembling in greater number than six persons, as well as from burying their dead in the Catholic cemeteries, or in ground inclosed with walls.

But in most of the communes at that time there was only one common cemetery; and in the towns where the Protestants had made one for themselves they had surrounded it with walls. It was now required that they should deposit the corpses of their brethren on the sides of the great roads, or in unclosed grounds, open to every comer, and exposed to all profanations.

Besides, their dead were taken from them, to be transported to the cemetery of the Catholics, if it were known that the deceased had received baptism in the Church of Rome. At St. Michael even this was exceeded. A Vaudois woman had been buried for three months in the Protestant burying-place, which was inclosed with walls. The priest of the parish ordered the body to be exhumed, and caused the half-broken coffin to be carried and deposited before the abode of her friends; one of whom, meeting the sacrilegious priest one evening on a lonely road, gave him some blows with a stick, to revenge this outrage.

Immediately fifty Protestants of St. Michael were cited to Saluces, and many of them were detained prisoners. They were set at liberty by the intercession of Lesdiguières.

At Demont, in the valley of the Stura, a few fanatical Papists, after a supper party, excited by wine, swore death to heretics, and resolved to pursue the first who made his appearance. Having recognized a young man who walked before them as a Vaudois, they drew their swords and attacked him. The young man carried a little axe; and not being able to escape from their attack by flight, he wheeled round and killed the foremost of his assailants. The rest then took to flight; but, some days after, they returned, better armed and in greater numbers, furiously took possession of the village, violated the women, injured or killed the men, flung the children upon the street, and plundered the houses like brigands; then, loaded with booty, they derisively summoned the whole population to appear at Turin.

Here a fact falls to be mentioned, equally honourable to the Protestants and to the Catholics of Demont, that the latter offered to bear a share of the expenses and losses occasioned by these disorders, and by those of the criminal process which followed. This shows how readily the two parties would have lived on good terms with one another, if the breath of Rome had not constantly excited the hatred of her adherents, whom she accused of allowing themselves to be corrupted whenever they displayed any charity. At Dronier, likewise, it was to a Catholic gentleman that the Protestants of the district owed their deliverance from a snare which was laid for them, and from the prosecutions which would have been the consequence of their having been left unwarned. Thus, wherever they were known, the Vaudois found protectors, even amongst their adversaries; the latter also became more Christian by their intercourse with them; for wherever Protestantism has prevailed, manners have always been softened. The missionary monks, who had not come under this influence, sometimes exhibited themselves in the pulpit, bearing a naked sword in one hand and a torch in the other, to exhort the people to destroy the heretics, declaring that it was of no use to make any attempt upon them but by fire and sword.[1] This was a surer method for Popery than to make attempts

[1] *Brief discours*, ch. iii.

by argument. But behold those who call themselves the ministers of God! men who pretend to grant absolution for the greatest crimes, but who have no pardon for the reading of the Bible, or for prayer!

To form a notion of these outrages, we must recollect that the episcopal palace of Saluces was the centre from which proceeded perpetual vexations to the Vaudois. But by and by their enemies went farther, and regretted that they had been spared at St. Bartholomew's-day; it was an error, they said, and must be remedied. Accordingly it was deemed a duty to arrange a scheme for a general massacre of all the reformed in the province of Saluces. Here, also, the members of the Catholic Church showed themselves to be less cruel than their spiritual guides, for the greater part of the inhabitants of the country refused to enter into that conspiracy. However, the design was not given up; but God permitted it to be discovered, and we shall now see how the Protestants came by the knowledge of it.

One of those who had the management of it, Fabricius De Pétris, picked a quarrel with a young Protestant, and attacked him, but was killed himself; and amongst his papers were found written evidences of this conspiracy.

The report of this discovery spread with the rapidity of lightning. The ferment which existed betwixt the two parties still increased. On both sides new excesses were committed every day, of which, however, the Protestants were more frequently the victims. Those of St. Pierre, for example, in the valley of the Vrayta, were expelled from their abodes by the parish priest and the provost of the town. A few days before, five inhabitants of Dronier had also been banished, and had retired to the valley of Lucerna.

It was now the year 1619, and the fermentation increased continually. The vexations to which the adherents of the Reformed Church were subjected, were multiplied upon all sorts of pretexts.

At Demont two Protestant families were cruelly afflicted. And what was laid to their charge? That they had contracted marriage within the degrees of relationship prohibited by the canons of some old council. The spouses were separated; the husbands sent to the galleys, and the wives condemned to be scourged in the public square.

But these judges, so cruelly exact in maintaining the arbitrary prohibitions as to the degrees of consanguinity, to which, moreover, the Catholics alone ought to have been subjected—these very Papists, who so promptly dissolved the family ties sanctioned by a union upon which the blessing of Heaven had been invoked—what respect had they for virtue? It may be learned from what follows. An apothecary at Dronier, named Marin, had two daughters of rare beauty. Towards the end of July one of the Capuchins of the town sent for this man; the other monks entered his house during his absence, and seized his daughters with violence. A coach waited at the door—it was that of the Bishop of Saluces—the victims of this odious abduction were flung into it and conveyed to Turin, without regard to their tears and supplications, without pity for the distress of their family.[1]

A month after[2] the same bishop caused a poor woman to be apprehended, against whom were brought most singular accusations. "She received at Geneva," her accusers said, "a great black robe; and, clothed in this hearse curtain, she mounted the pulpit amongst the reformed, took a cow's horn, and blew the Holy Spirit through that horn upon those who were present." The book from which we derive these particulars adds, with an air of simplicity, "It must be confessed that this was an invention sufficiently ridiculous!"[3] Yet for this was this unhappy woman subjected five times to the rack, and tortured in presence of clerical dignitaries and the administrators of justice in the district. The prefect, the bishop, and the inquisitor, were there; and this in the 17th century! Yes, in the 17th century, but under the dominion of Catholicism. And in the 19th century itself, in 1845, where Popery still reigns, have we not seen a woman condemned to death for the crime of heresy?[4]

Thus passed these dark and troublous days, the storm ever threatening to break. Towards the end of the year 1619, an extraordinary meeting of priests, monks, and popish bigots of every confraternity, was convoked at Saluces, to consult as to the means of dealing effectively and conclusively with the heretics. After a repast, at which all these worthy guests were assembled, they had the leading Protestants burned in effigy, as they could not just yet do the same thing for their persons. These pastimes of the Catholic clergy sufficiently show by what spirit they were animated. They were men of no seriousness and no humanity. Cruelty and buffoonery, baseness and barbarism, were the characteristics of these pre-

---

[1] All these particulars are taken from the *Brief discours sur les persécutions advenues en ce temps aux Eglises du Marquisat de Saluces*, ch. iv.

[2] On 22d August, 1619.

[3] The point is lost in the translation, depending upon the verbal expression, which cannot be preserved. *Bien cornue*, well-horned, is the phrase for *ridiculous*.—Tr.

[4] This condemnation took place in the Isle of Madeira, in August, 1845. See the journals for the month of September of that year; amongst others the *Débats*, *Siècle*, *Espérance*, &c.

tended ministers of the God of perfection and of love. On the side of the Reformers the discontent went on increasing. A conflict was inevitable, in which the weaker party must perish.

The inhabitants of Aceil, who were nearly all of the same communion, and who had never ceased to hold their evangelical assemblies, still took advantage of their numbers to continue them. The governor of Dronier, Andrea della Negra, was sent against them; he apprehended and lodged in the prisons of Saluces the two distinguished members of the church who habitually conducted these meetings for prayer. The name of the one was Peter Marquisy, of the other, Maurice Monge. The apprehension of the former took place in June, that of the latter in September, 1619. Both of them were shortly condemned to death by the Inquisition.

From this judgment they appealed to the Senate of Turin. It was hoped that some influence might be used with the Duke of Savoy to save them; but that prince was then absent; he had gone to Savoy to receive Christina of France, who was on her way to Piedmont. The senate was thus left to itself, or rather to the suggestions of the dignified clergy, all powerful at court. Most unfortunately for the interests of the prisoners of Aceil, a new tumult had taken place in that town. The governor of the province, the Count of Sommariva, was killed by a shot of an arquebuse, on the hills of Mongardino, to which he had pursued the insurgents. And in unconscious prosecution of those pagan notions so familiar to the Catholics, it was thought necessary to offer up Maurice and Marquisy as expiatory victims to the manes of the governor. These courageous leaders of the church of Aceil were forthwith executed at Saluces[1] about four o'clock in the morning. But notwithstanding the hour, the bishop of the diocese was present at their execution, being conveyed to the spot in his coach. All the particulars of their courageous and edifying death have been preserved in a letter written from Saluces on the morning after their execution, and published at Geneva some days after. Part of them shall be given in the chapter devoted to the history of the martyrs.

In return for so many concessions to the demands of Rome, the new pope, Gregory XV., granted to the Duke of Savoy, by his brief of 27th May, 1621, the privilege of retaining the tithe of ecclesiastical revenues for six years, upon condition of his devoting the money to the extirpation of heresy. The duke grasped the money, and the clergy pressed him to act. In February, 1622, he began to employ these resources, or at least to show that he was husbanding them for the stipulated work, by resuming the prose-

---

[1] This execution took place on the 21st of October, 1619.

cutions so often instituted against the Vaudois and the reformed of Piedmont, who did not abide within the narrow limits to which the territory of the Vaudois valleys had been circumscribed.

In the month of March following, the members of the church in Praviglelm and the surrounding communes were summoned to appear before the prefect of Saluces, under pain of death and confiscation. They might have repaired thither in so great numbers that the very display of firmness on their part would have awed their enemies. No penalty was yet denounced against those who might have obeyed. What made them hesitate? Perhaps the example of those who had been imprisoned when they made their appearance upon such a summons, with that kind of *vis inertiæ* which keeps the peasant from moving from his cottage, and a vague unreflecting fear of the tribunal of Saluces, which had proved so fatal to Protestants. Be this as it may, they did not attend. In place of acting vigorously, of showing themselves united and resolved, and firmly maintaining their rights, they exhibited in their conduct weakness and indecision—a severe censor might even say cowardice, for it is cowardly to abandon the defence of a right, as it is to shrink from the defence of one's native country. Not having appeared within the time prescribed, the inhabitants of Praviglelm and Paësane were all condemned to be banished from the dominions of his royal highness, and to be hanged if they fell into the hands of the authorities. As for their goods, it needs not to be said that they were confiscated. For the exchequer and for Rome, this was the clearest part of the business.

This sentence was passed at Saluces on the 15th of March, 1622, confirmed by the Senate of Turin on the 7th of June, and published at Paësane on the 29th of the same month.

The poor people had recourse to the intervention of Lesdiguières. But what had occurred? Being one day in company with the Cardinal Ludovisio of Bologna, Lesdiguières said to him, "When your eminence shall wear the tiara, I will renounce Protestantism." But eighteen months had now elapsed since Ludovisio had been elected pope, and Lesdiguières had changed his religion at the time he named. As one demits an office—as one delivers over goods upon an appointed day—the great general had laid down his religious beliefs when the almanac informed him that the time was come. However, he had not yet imbibed the inhuman spirit of his new church, and he wrote to Charles Emmanuel in favour of his former brethren in religion in the higher valleys.[1] "They have lived," said he, "without having given offence to any;

[1] This letter is preserved by Gilles, p. 421.

and they have always been countenanced in the exercise of their religion. Whatsoever decree your highness may have issued with regard to others, may it please your highness to permit them to enjoy in peace the benefit of your kindness, which will thus augment, in the persons of these poor people, the obligations which make me, Monseigneur, your very humble," &c. The letter is dated from Grenoble, 29th July, 1622. Lesdiguières wrote with the same object to the French ambassador at the court of Turin; and, in consequence, the Vaudois, without obtaining a formal revocation of the atrocious sentence, received nevertheless a promise that no steps would be taken upon it, and that they might live in peace on the little heritages that had been transmitted to them from their fathers. Some of them, however, who had already left the country, were apprehended on their return.

The same pope, who had received the abjuration of the French general, founded at that time (in 1622) the sanguinary congregation *de propagandâ fide et extirpandis hæreticis*, and canonized Ignatius de Loyola. This congregation was, for nearly a century, the most formidable engine which fanaticism and error ever employed to prevent the triumph of the doctrines of the Bible. But it was in Piedmont especially that the *Propaganda*, that disgraceful offspring of Jesuitism and the Inquisition, perpetrated its terrible ravages. We shall shortly see it at work in the Vaudois valleys. Meanwhile let us attend to its operations in the marquisate of Saluces, where it lost no time in establishing itself, and where it thenceforth became a permanent source of trouble and persecution.

In 1627, the valley of Stura was cruelly tormented by proselytizers. The last vestiges of Protestantism which remained at Carail, were rooted out, according to the heart's wish of the monks by fire and sword. It was now no longer necessary to have been present at the meetings of the reformed in order to be thrown into prison; it was enough not to go to mass. At St. Michael, at Pagliero, and at Demont, the incessant prosecutions to which the Vaudois were subjected, deprived these once flourishing little towns of the peaceful citizens to whom they owed their prosperity, to fill the prisons with victims, and to people the mountains with outlawed men. The greater part retired to France, but, ere long, France also became utterly inhospitable to them. The history of a family has been discovered at Berlin, which left Demont at this period, settled in Provence, and was afterwards expelled from the latter country at the time of the revocation of the Edict of Nantes. What miseries religious wars and antipathies have occasioned!

And how far must the general feeling have become alienated from the doctrine of Christ, ere that impious combination of words, *Religious wars and antipathies*, could be introduced into language!

Some of the many prisoners made by the Propaganda at this period, bought their lives by the payment of a heavy ransom. The fortune gathered by the father for his children, went to enrich convents, jailers, and executioners.

Thus impoverished, decimated, proscribed, and persecuted everywhere, these unfortunate churches of Saluces became weaker daily. For many years, every manifestation of evangelical life, except patience and resignation, was forbidden to them; and if the sacred fire survived in their paralyzed members, it was like the last pulsations of a heart slowly dying in the breast of a motionless sufferer, against whom the tortures of the Inquisition are still ferociously employed. O! why should religious congregations have acted like wild beasts, destroying human beings in this way?

In the higher valleys of the Po, at Oncino, Praviglelm, and Bietonet, the proscribed worship still survived for a time in the retirements of poor cottages and Alpine shepherds' huts. But it was not long that these first and last branches of the great Vaudois family, in the province of Saluces, were exempted from persecution. When the fire has devoured the outer parts, it spares not the heart of the tree.

In 1629, the Count De La Mente, who was lieutenant-general of the duke's armies in the marquisate, imposed a fine of 400 ducats on the Protestants of Praviglelm. They did not make haste to pay it. This, probably, was what had been expected; it was the triumph of the persecuting skill of the *Propaganda* and the clergy. Without loss of time, the Count De La Mente sent four hundred soldiers to Praviglelm to lay waste the fields, carry off the cattle, and plunder the dwellings of the unfortunate Vaudois. The booty was transported to Paësane, and 1000 ducats had to be paid before it was restored.

Another seigneur, envious of the success of this expedition, came some days after at the head of twenty-five men, in order to seize the pastor of Praviglelm, and to carry off some hostages, whom he would not have released afterwards without a heavy ransom. These poor mountaineers were abandoned to all incursions, as a country without a master is abandoned to the first who chooses to take possession. This time, however, they repelled the aggressor, with his twenty-five men; but he came back very soon, accompanied no longer by soldiers, but by monks. A few words will explain the meaning of this new expedition.

The captain of this cowled legion began by ordering all the inhabitants of the district to attend the preaching of the missionaries, under pain of a fine of a crown of gold for each instance of disobedience. The instances were numerous, and, under pretence of making the Vaudois pay the fines incurred, their crops and their goods were again seized. Hereupon the inhabitants of the valley of Lucerna decided upon taking arms, to go to the assistance of their brethren in the valley of the Po. At the same time, their first plunderer, the Count De La Mente, afraid that things might be carried too far, and that he himself might be brought to a reckoning, put an end to these scandalous extortions.

The plague which ravaged Piedmont in 1630, did not spare the inhabitants of these mountains; but this scourge, at all events, did not produce irritation and division amongst men. A new outbreaking of popish zeal soon succeeded it, attended by all these sad effects.

Victor Amadeus had ascended the throne; the nuncio, the prelates, the monkish congregations, and all the representatives of Popery thronged in haste around him. "What a glory it would be for your highness to carry into full effect at last the designs transmitted from generation to generation of your predecessors, and completely to extirpate heresy from your dominions! Not only would it be a glory; it is a duty. It would be the consecration of your accession!—the best security for the blessings of God upon your crown." Such was the language addressed on every side to the new sovereign. He was then forty-three years of age. Notwithstanding the natural firmness of his character, his prudence, and the capacity which he displayed of thinking and scheming for himself, by which he had already obtained the treaty of Ratisbon,[1] and that of Quiérasque,[2] restoring to him the possession of a great part of his dominions, he yielded at last to these suggestions.

Happily the Vaudois valleys of Lucerna, Perouse, St. Martin, and Pragela, belonged at that time to France; but, next to that great centre of Protestantism in Piedmont, the marquisate of Saluces contained the greatest number of its professors.

The duke issued, therefore, on the 23d of September, 1623, an edict, in the following terms:—

"The princes of the earth being appointed by God, ought to have nothing more at heart than the defence of his religion. Therefore, in order to restore peace to the church, and to give proof of our indulgence to the heretics of Saluces, who have rendered themselves liable to the penalty of death by their continued obsti-

---

[1] 13th October, 1630.   [2] 6th April, 1631.

nacy, we ordain that they abjure their errors within the space of two months after the publication of the present edict, and that according to the forms which shall be prescribed to them by the Bishop of Saluces. In this case we will remit to them all the penalties to which they have become liable; but if they allow that term to pass without abjuring, they will be required to quit our dominions, under pain of death."

This was the way in which a sovereign gave proof of his kindness towards his subjects; this was the way in which he pretended to do service to the Christian religion! In this edict, here much abridged, the churches of Biolet, Biétonet, Croésio, and Praviglelm are mentioned by name. It was the death-stroke for these unfortunate communities, and our chapter must now be closed with their last sigh.

Upon the publication of this edict, many Vaudois families, perceiving that the final agony of the evangelical churches of their dear valleys was nigh at hand, silently withdrew into exile, to Dauphiny. At the same time the Bishop of Saluces, exulting in his now approaching triumph, and inflated with the importance which the edict had given him, arrived in these poor villages, escorted by monks and soldiers. The *ultima ratio regum* is also the *ultima ratio Romæ*. Shall I relate how the prelate could make his boast of having *converted* numbers of those indigent families, who would not have had even a trifle to support them on their journey, if they had left their native land? No; but I will relate how others, abandoning their possessions, retired to the mountains, where, in the persons of these wandering outlaws, amidst the misery and distresses of exile, were extinguished the last relics of that Vaudois Church which flourished so long about the sources of the Po. Their houses were burned and demolished, their goods confiscated, their flocks seized and sold for behoof of the bishop, the monks, and the exchequer.

Let any one compare at the present day the moral and the general condition of the Vaudois valleys in which the gospel has been maintained, with the obscurity and decay into which those of the Stura and of the Po have fallen, from which it was banished at the expense of so much time and so many efforts, and he will see if Catholicism be favourable to the prosperity of nations. If the sphere within which this comparison is made be regarded as too limited, in being confined to these humble valleys, let him pursue in all quarters of the world the same parallel betwixt Catholic and Protestant countries, and he will arrive at the same result.

Thus were these interesting Vaudois communities extinguished, whose history no one has hitherto written. But the spirit which animated them has not disappeared. May it ever continue to animate what remains of the Israel of the Alps amongst the mountains so long moistened with the blood of martyrs!

CHAPTER XV.

MORE MARTYRS.[1]

(A.D. 1535 TO A.D. 1635.)

Inquisitorial proceedings instituted both by the Court of Aix and the Senate of Turin—Martyrdom of Catalan Girardet—The pastor of Pral treacherously murdered—Intercessions of the Elector Palatine on behalf of the Vaudois—The Secretary of the Palatine Legation arrested on account of his being a Protestant minister—Conspiracy against the state, a deceitful pretext for severities against the Vaudois—Sufferings of the French Vaudois—Martyrdom of Romeyer, a merchant of Villar d'Arènes, at Draguignan—Many persons put to death on account of religion—Gaspar Orsel delivered from the inquisitors—Capture and escape of the pastor of Praviglelm—Brief notices of sufferers—M. Jean of Marseilles—Secret murders in prison—Martyrdom of Peter Marquisy and Maurice Monge of Aceil—Sufferings and release of Paul Roëri de Lanfranco—The case of Sebastian Bazan—Imprisonment and trials of Bartholomew Coupin—His attempted escape—His death—The brothers Malherbe—Daniel Peillon.

As from each sheaf of a great harvest a grain used to be taken to make up the heap which was intended for the altar, so from each epoch we select a memorial, from each persecution a precious gem of courage and piety, destined to a place in the group of Vaudois martyrs, the offering of their churches on the altars of the true God.

That there may be no blank in this sketch, which is intended to refer to all the events of the history in connection with all the martyrdoms, let us first direct our thoughts to the circumstances which occasioned them.

At the period of the Reformation, the Christians of Provence and of the valleys made common cause with the Reformers. The attention of the Church of Rome was fatally drawn to them in the first instance in Provence, at the gates of Avignon. This Rome of the West could not be expected to do otherwise than contend against the religious awakening which menaced its predominance. The inquisitor, John de Roma, raised the first piles upon the slopes of Léberon. The proceedings against these victims led to the discovery, amongst the heretics of Provence, of many persons from the valleys of Piedmont. The court of Aix wrote concerning this

[1] AUTHORITIES.—The same as in Chapter VIII.

to the senate of Turin, and the senate named a commissioner (Pantaléon Bersour) to go to the places mentioned and take information.

Bersour returned from Provence with numerous particulars of precise information concerning the principal families of the Vaudois of Piedmont, and concerning the high antiquity and the extent of the ministry of the Barbas, which they carried on in silence, that it might bear the more fruit, and of which the distant ramifications were not suspected, even in the very places where they existed.

Like those marine plants which make their appearance on the surface of the waters only by a few green and almost unnoticed summits, but which pass through all the depths of the ocean to fix their roots in the primitive soil, the Vaudois, maintaining always their relation to the primitive church, had passed through centuries, and surmounted the increasing tide of superstition. Possessing no worldly eminence or personal distinction, they were not inapt to be confounded, by an indifferent observer, with the immense mass which surrounded them, and to this lowliness they owed their greatness. Their extension was carried on more successfully in the shade than it could have been in the blaze of day; they avoided the storm which might have broken on their heads; but so soon as attention and inquiry were directed to them, a discovery was made of the whole extent which their association, seemingly of so little importance, had secretly attained.

Bersour, furnished with the informations which he had received in Provence, repaired to the valleys, and continued the inquisitorial proceedings commenced by the court of Aix. Many witnesses were then brought to give evidence concerning this evangelical religion. One of them, Bernardin Féa of St. Segont, being interrogated by the judge who presided in the investigation concerning the intercourse which he had had with the heretics, replied in this manner:—

"Being at Briquéras in 1529, I met Louis Turin of St. John, who took me into his house on business. Our business being ended, another inhabitant of St. John, named Catalan Girardet, came to see us, and invited us to accompany him as far as La Tour, where he said we would hear things that were good; Louis Turin himself pressed me to accept the invitation, and we set out. When we had arrived at La Tour, Catalan conducted us behind the house of Chabert Ughet." (This was probably a descendant of the person who, in 1310, purchased from one of the last dauphins of the Viennois a house in Val Louise, that it might be used for the religious meetings of the Vaudois.) "We entered into a great apartment, where many persons were assembled. There a Barba, named Philip, preached, and after his duties were over, he asked me some questions, and instructed me in certain points of their religion."

"What did he say to you?"

"That there is no salvation but in Jesus Christ, and that we ought to do good works, not in order to be saved, but because we are saved."

However, as this witness had not ceased to attend mass, he was not disturbed, but a prosecution was commenced against Catalan Girardet, who had drawn him to that meeting.

Compelled to quit the valleys, Catalan was arrested at Revel, about the end of the year 1535, in course of which the evidence of Bernardin Féa had been given against him. He did not for an instant attempt to disguise his opinions; and being strongly urged to abjure them, he replied to the monks who came into his dungeon to tempt him to apostasy, "You will sooner persuade these walls to go on pilgrimage, than a Christian to deny the truth."

The fear of death had no greater effect in shaking his constancy. He was condemned to be burned alive. On the way to the stake, the monks who attended him still tried to persuade him to abjure. "Why should you be obstinate in your heresy?" said they; "your rude and barbarous sect will soon be, like your own flesh, consumed in a moment." Taking up two stones from the road, and rubbing them one against another, Catalan Girardet exclaimed in reply, "It would be easier for me to rub these stones to powder, than for you to destroy our churches!"

This assurance of the martyr was not mistaken. He died firm and serene, his countenance radiant, even as seen through the flames which devoured him, with the blessed certainty of that salvation which he had received, and of that eternal happiness which he was going to receive.

But is death endured for a profession of religion the only martyrdom? And has the Christian, visited with it for Christian works, no right to be also held in pious remembrance? A short time after the Count of La Trinité had laid waste the Vaudois valleys by fire and sword,[1] the pastor of Pral, named Martin, received a visit from two men who had been in the service of the seigneurs of Le Perrier, the cruel and perfidious Truchets, those relentless enemies of the Vaudois, who had already dragged to martyrdom Bartholomew Hector, the seller of Bibles. The pastor of Pral was a native of France; the two strangers called themselves Frenchmen; Martin received them as fellow-countrymen. They then expressed a desire to enter the Reformed Church, and the good

[1] See PART SECOND, ch. ii., of this History.

pastor continued to entertain them as his guests, whilst he sought to instruct them in the way of salvation.

His parishioners, however, warned him to be upon his guard; for there is in the common people an instinctive sagacity, which sometimes gives a presentiment of danger with an accuracy of judgment, independent of evidence; moreover, as these intruders had recently carried arms against the Vaudois, it was natural enough that they should regard them with distrust. Nevertheless, the simple good pastor believed in the sincerity of their conversion, and appealed on their behalf to the charity of his flock against the insinuations which were made respecting them. His benevolent representations did not re-assure the people of Pral, who saw, with so much the more displeasure, these ill-reputed strangers dwelling under the roof of their pastor, that the latter had no family and lived by himself; but the worthy man, considering them almost as his adopted children, continued to treat them with the most generous hospitality.

One morning, however, he did not appear at church at the ordinary hour of public worship. The people gathered anxiously around his dwelling. The door was bolted; they knocked; no one answered. Some neighbours then mounted upon the roof, and penetrated into the interior by a skylight, and presently their cries of grief announced to those without some bloody catastrophe. In fact, the pastor Martin was lying lifeless, and bathed in his blood. The monsters, whom he had received with kindness, had cut his throat and taken flight, after having plundered the house of their benefactor. The Vaudois pursued after the culprits, but in vain; no trace of them could be discovered; but some time after they boldly re-appeared in the valley, being again in the service of the seigneurs of Le Perrier, who thus made themselves their accomplices, and who, perhaps, had been the instigators of this odious assassination. No doubt there was imprudence on the part of the pastor, in the too generous reception which he gave to these cutthroats; but ought not he also to be reckoned a martyr, who died confessing the gospel by the works of a charity carried the length of self-sacrifice, as much as if that self-sacrifice had been made by a profession of religion?

In consequence of the persecutions of which this execrable crime was one of the last fruits, the Elector Palatine sent an embassy to the Duke of Savoy, to intercede with him on behalf of the Vaudois. They were at that time ill used, in a multitude of ways, by the councillor Barberi, whom Emmanuel Philibert had appointed his commissioner to treat with them. The secretary of the palatine's legation was a Protestant pastor. Barberi, thinking he might do what he pleased, caused him to be arrested by his minions at the very hotel of the ambassador; and without any other cause or pretext than simply that of his religion, he had the audacity to put him in prison. This fact, of itself, may give an idea of the fierceness which then characterized the proceedings against the Protestants; and by this we may understand how much the Vaudois must have displayed of prudence, of irreprehensible probity, of patient endurance, and of active virtues, to avoid giving any occasion to their adversaries, whereby these proceedings might appear anything else than barbarous cruelties, and flagrant acts of injustice. This secretary of legation, who himself was very soon released, wrote them an affecting letter on this subject, of which the commencement is as follows:—

"Dear brethren in the work of the Lord! All things work together for good to them that love God, and the violence to which I have been subjected will give occasion of reflection to his highness, who will from this time, I trust, show himself less prejudiced against you. If it should prove, however, that instead of becoming more mild, and moderating the severity at present exercised, the duke becomes more imbittered, be assured that it will be a plain token that God is about to interpose. But I trust that God will have pity on his highness, and hear the prayers, cries, and tears of those who groan under the burden of this horrible persecution, to turn the heart of their prince, and to inspire him with compassion for his people. As to the answers which the Chancellor Stropiano has made to our intercession for you, he accuses you of being disturbers of the public peace." (Such is the exact expression; so that it will be seen not to be of recent invention.) "He pretends that the Vaudois conspire against the state, and in support of that accusation, he quotes the case of nine religionaries who recently assembled in a frontier town" (at Bourg in Bresse, for that province was then a part of Savoy), "and whom he has caused to be imprisoned as conspirators."

We shall now examine into some particulars of these pretended conspiracies. A few Christians had met in a private house to meditate together on the word of God; after this exercise they prayed for the triumph of the gospel, when the officers of justice, guided by a pious, that is, a Catholic information, arrived upon the spot, surrounded the place of meeting, and seized all who were present. As the captives protested against this violation of a private abode, and as no cause of complaint could be found against them, they were accused of an imaginary conspiracy. Now, the men could not prove that they had not conspired, and so they were condemned to the galleys, as persons suspected of having conspired. "There is nothing new under the sun," says Solomon, and the same parodies on a court and on justice were repeated in 1793, against other doctrines, and in name of another fanaticism.

The Vaudois of Dauphiny and of Provence also paid, at this time, their tribute of martyrs to maintain the constant testimony of the Christian Church against the constant assaults of Antichrist.

The valley of the Grave, which descends from Le Pelvoux in a direction opposite to that of the Val Louise, had, in former times, been enlightened by some straggling rays of that evangelical light, whose centre of radiance was in the midst of the Vaudois valleys. A mercer of Villar d'Arènes, one of the most secluded villages of this valley, after having conducted his family to Geneva, that they might there be educated, and taught to walk in the ways of the Lord, was himself brought back to France by the necessity of attending to his business. Being particularly skilful as a worker of coral, Romeyer repaired to Marseilles in order to buy corals; and on the way he endeavoured to dispose of the goods which he carried with him. Passing by Draguignan, he showed them to a goldsmith of that town, named Lanteaume, who thought them very beautiful, and would have bought them, but the artist and he not being able to agree about the price, they parted without concluding a bargain. The Baron de Lauris was then at Draguignan, the son-in-law of Menier D'Oppède, whose name is written in letters of blood in the history of the Vaudois. Lanteaume, unwilling to allow the treasures which he had seen on the previous evening to pass out of his hands, advised Romeyer to exhibit them to a wealthy seigneur, who would probably purchase them, and named to him the Baron of Lauris. When the covetousness of the baron had been awakened by the sight of so good a prey, Lanteaume went and informed him that Romeyer was a Lutheran. Confiscation of goods followed, of course, upon a sentence of death. The two participators in this meditated spoliation understood one another precisely.

Romeyer was apprehended, at command of Lauris, by the *viguier* of Draguignan, in April, 1558. After he had undergone several examinations, in which he made a frank confession of his faith, the court of Draguignan met for his trial. An Observantine monk, who preached in that town during Lent, said, "I shall sing a mass to the Holy Spirit, that he may suggest to the judges to condemn that cursed Lutheran to death." But his mass did not produce all the effect which he expected from it; for a young advocate having risen at the bar of the court, pointed out that Romeyer had not been guilty of any offence, that he had neither preached nor taught his doctrine in France, that he was a foreigner, and did nothing in Provence but attend to his trade, and that therefore justice ought to protect him and not to condemn him.

All the bar supported this doctrine. The votes of the court were divided, one half for acquittal, and one half for condemnation. And of what sort of magistrates was this court composed? The following fact will show. One of them, named Barbesi, having heard the firmness spoken of, which Romeyer had shown in his examinations, came to see him in his prison. He was, as Crespin tells us, an illiterate, fat, ill-formed man, with a flat large nose, a hideous aspect, a sluggish disposition, and addicted to gluttony and lasciviousness. On his entrance, he coarsely addressed the prisoner: "What place do you belong to? What are you? What do you believe in?" "I am a native of Dauphiny," was the reply; "I dwell in Geneva; I trade in coral; I believe in God and in Christ my Saviour." "Do the people of Geneva believe in God? Do they pray to him? Do they serve him?" said the judge. "Better than you!" was the quick reply of the poor captive, whose feelings were wounded by such suspicions and language. Accordingly Judge Barbesi voted for his condemnation; but in consequence of the equal division of votes, the condemnation could not be pronounced.

The Observantine monk, who made this, so to speak, his personal affair, and who already saw the credit of his prayers and his masses singularly compromised in public opinion by the uncertainty of the court, caused the bells to be violently rung, got the populace to run together, and exclaimed that good Catholics ought not to suffer an infamous heretic, a Lutheran, a man already damned, to come and defile with impunity by his presence the devout town of Draguignan. He then went with his passionate advices to the official and the consuls of the town, representing to them that it concerned their honour to maintain intact the excellent reputation of their beloved city; and all together, supported by the ragged populace and a raging rabble of priests, proceeded to the doors of the magistrates, exclaiming that if they did not condemn the heretic to be burned, they would themselves be denounced to the parliament, the king, the pope, and all the powers of the world and of hell, in order that they might be punished.

This is what Popery calls religious fervour. This worthy monk had perhaps a little too much zeal! it might be hesitatingly admitted by the hypocrites of our days, whom Rome still makes much of as her most faithful adherents, but who give small evidence of Christianity.

The king's lieutenant, who at that period represented the government, reminded them of the respect due to judicial forms, which must not be violated, even in the case of this heretic. "Let him be put to death! Let him be put to death!" replied the people. "To the fire with him! To the fire with him! Let him be burned!" exclaimed the clergy. The magistrate abovenamed, not being able to appease the tumult, promised to go to Aix to refer the matter to the parliament, analogous to the *Cour Royale* of the present time. The populace would have dispersed, but the monk prevented them; and the consuls of the city sanctioned this sort of municipal comitiæ with their presence. It was resolved that four persons should go to Aix at the expense of the commune, to accompany the *Procureur du Roi*, and urge the condemnation of Romeyer. These four deputies were the first consul, by name Cavalien, Judge Barbesi, the advocate-general, and a registrar. But on the way they met one of the presidents of the court of Aix, named Ambrois, who said to them—"You surely need not make so much ceremony about the burning of a heretic." The deputation made haste to return, that they might hurry on the sentence of death, and the king's lieutenant pursued his way alone. Having arrived at Aix, he laid the whole matter before the court, which called up the case before itself, and interdicted the court of Draguignan from pronouncing sentence.

But fanaticism does not so readily let go its hold. Barbesi set out again for Aix, and obtained a decree that sentence should be pronounced in the court of first resort. This was, in fact, to obtain the condemnation, or rather the judicial assassination and legal tortures of poor Romeyer. He was accordingly condemned to undergo, first the rack, then the wheel, then to be burned alive, and that by a slow fire.—O justice! O charity! But did Popery ever know you?

Romeyer might still have escaped the infliction of this atrocious sentence at the expense of an abjuration; but the monk who was sent to make this proposal to him declared, as he came out from the prison, that he found him *pertinax*, and that he was a man already damned. The language of these men was as barbarous as their manners, as cruel as their doctrines.

The priests were immediately requested to announce, in all the surrounding parishes, that on the 16th of the month of May would take place, in public, the execution of a frightful Lutheran; and in the town of Draguignan proclamation was made, by sound of trumpet, that every good Catholic should bring wood for the pile.

The king's lieutenant, who had endeavoured to save Romeyer from this unjust execution, withdrew from the town, that he might not be a witness of it. But his substitute, accompanied by a number of judges, both civil and ecclesiastical, as well as by the consuls of the town, repaired in the morning to the prison of the condemned man, in order to apply the torture. They displayed before him the rack, the cords, the wedges, the bars of iron, and, in one word, all the instruments of torture invented by the successors of the martyred apostle. They said, "Denounce your accomplices and abjure your errors, instead of exposing yourself to these torments." "I have no accomplices," replied Romeyer; "I have nothing to abjure, for I profess nothing but the law of Christ. You now call it perverse and erroneous; but at the day of judgment God will proclaim it just and holy, to the confusion of its transgressors."

"Whereupon," says Crespin, "being placed upon the *gehenna*, and fearfully pulled by the cords, he cried without ceasing to God, that he would have pity upon him for the love of Jesus." "Implore the Virgin now!" said these idolaters. "We have only one Mediator," he replied. "O Jesus! O my God!—grace! grace!" and he fainted. "For upon his refusal the torture had been recommenced," says the chronicler, "and that in so violent a manner, that he was left for dead." Then the monks and the priests unloosed him from the wheel, fearing lest he should expire without being burned. The bones of his arms and legs were broken, and the points of the displaced parts of bone stuck out through the flesh. They gave him some cordials to recal him to life. He was then removed to the place of execution, and fastened by an iron chain to the stake, which rose from the centre of the pile. Even now a monk addressed him, saying, "Call upon the Virgin and the saints!" The poor mercer of Villar d'Arènes made a sign with his head in the negative. Thereupon the executioners set fire to the pile. As it was composed, in great part, of branches and bushes, the flame at first rose with rapidity, then the half-burned fuel sank together, so that the martyr remained suspended to the stake above the devouring fire. His inferior members were shrivelled, his entrails running out, and his poor body already half burned below, when his lips were still seen to move, without any sound proceeding from them, but attesting the martyr's last invocation of the Divine Being—his last appeal to that Christ who died for him.

And doubtless that appeal was heard. And doubtless that vengeful prophecy shall be fulfilled, which for eighteen centuries has been suspended over the head of the Apocalyptic monster, whose sins have reached up unto heaven, and whose mouth has drunk, unto intoxication, the blood of saints and of martyrs. Yet we are told that we ought to employ, with regard to the papacy, that reserve in expression which is proper enough in the case of a wicked man for whose conversion we may hope, but not as to the inveterate wickedness of ages! The tree is to be judged by its fruits; and if the old trunk, which has served as a gibbet for so many victims, bears fruits less fatal in our day, it is because of its decrepitude: but restore its strength or trace it to the source of its bloody sap, and you will find it the same as ever. Let it be known, and it must be condemned!

There were also three unfortunate persons who, in 1563, were left to die of hunger at Cabrières, in a deep pit; and forty persons put to death by the sword, the rope, or the fire in the valley of Apt; forty-six at Lourmarin, seventeen at Merindol, and twenty-two in the valley of Aigues. All these crimes were perpetrated fifteen years after the fearful massacres of which notice has been already taken.

But, to give an example of the arrogant opposition which the Inquisition sometimes made to the will of the sovereign, and even to the edicts which he had signed, disputing with him for its victims. After the articles agreed upon at Cavour in 1561, between Emmanuel Philibert and the Vaudois, they ought not to have been proceeded against in any way, for anything that had taken place during the war of 1560. However, a man belonging to St. John, Gaspar Orsel by name, had been made prisoner at that time, and to save his life he promised to become a Catholic; but after the peace had been concluded, he returned to the sincere profession of his faith and religion. The inquisitors caused him to be watched by spies, and in 1570 he was seized, tied with cords, and conveyed to the prisons of the Holy Office at Turin. Against this the Vaudois reclaimed, on the ground of the amnesty which had been granted. The duke ordained the inquisitors to release their prisoner, but they refused to obey. The Edict of Cavour was laid before them, which this detention contravened. "Our order is not subject to the secular power," replied the worthy Dominicans. They were very willing to take advantage of that power, but not to bow to it. Upon this, Philibert, irritated, informed them in reply, that all the frocked legions upon earth would not make him break his word, and that they must forthwith set the captive free, if they did not wish cannon to be sent to bury them under the ruins of their den.

On this unexpected language, the Holy Office found it necessary to yield. Orsel was set free, and the Duke of Savoy wrote to the Vaudois on the 20th of November, 1570, through the governor of the province, to re-assure them that they need no longer entertain any fear regarding further proceedings based upon similar promises of abjuration. The firmness which he showed in this instance in compelling respect for the edict which he had issued, is honourable to the character of the prince; but that edict itself had been obtained by the firmness which the Vaudois displayed in legitimate self-defence. The obstinacy of the Holy Office alone cannot be praised, for it was obstinacy in evil.

Although it thus appears that the attempts of the papal party were not always successful, but that those escaped against whom they were directed, I think it right to quote some other examples of their evil-doings, to give an idea of the dangers with which the Vaudois were perpetually surrounded.

The reader will remember that when they were menaced in one valley by the princes and seigneurs who ruled in it, they often retired to another beyond the bounds of their authority, or more powerful to resist them.

The pastor of Praviglelm, himself a native of Bobi, had already found such a refuge in the valley of Lucerna in 1592. It was at the time when the Duke of Savoy had just seized upon the marquisate of Saluces, and found his possession of it disputed by France. Some time after, beginning to think that he might be able to keep hold of his conquest, he began also to manifest a disposition to repress the reformed. The people of Praviglelm now received information that a project was on foot for seizing their pastor. They resolved to save him, and assembled for the purpose of opening a path for him through the snows towards St. Frour. But they were surprised by a company of soldiers belonging to the garrison of Revel, which seized the minister, and bore him off a prisoner. This took place during the night of the 27th of February, 1597.

The Vaudois immediately made the utmost exertions to have him restored to liberty. The governor of Revel gave them to understand that they might attain their object by the offer of a considerable ransom. The sum was speedily procured, for misfortune had given the Vaudois a spirit of devotedness; and the incessant perils which menaced them all, had created amongst them a feeling of unity and mutual sympathy, which realized that saying of St. Paul, "If one member suffer, all the members suffer with it."

But the Inquisition had no desire to hear of ransom and enlargement; it preferred blood to money; and the garrison of Revel having been obliged to remove to a distance for some military operations, the report went that the inquisitors were coming to carry off the prisoner. His name was Anthony Bonjour. His brother-in-law obtained leave to pay him a visit, under pretext of shaving him. Whilst performing this operation, he contrived to whisper into his ear with what danger he was menaced, and to slip a parcel of ropes under the apron which he had put upon him, saying in a low voice, "Put this in your pocket, and as soon as I am out of the way, lose no time, but let yourself down over the walls, at the rocks behind the castle, into the wood." And when he had taken leave, and before the minister had apparently recovered from his perplexity, he turned back, and said, "Save yourself, Master Anthony, save yourself; flee quickly, or you are lost!" The minister thereupon ventured to attempt his escape in this way, and reached without accident the base of the rocks upon which the castle was built. Meeting no one, he set out in the direction of the mountain; but he had not gone far when he met face to face a male and a female servant of the governor, who were returning to the castle. "Ah! you are making your escape," said they to the minister. "In God's name, let me flee," said he, "for they want to take my life." The persons to whom he spoke were of the common people; the sentiments of humanity had access to their simple souls; and so these servants held their peace, and the fugitive succeeded in reaching the steep and wooded slopes which overhang the town.

Scarcely had he fled, when there were heard in the castle and neighbourhood much noise of arms and of horses, military cries, barking of dogs, and, in short, all the agitation which ensues upon the discovery of an important escape.

As for the poor pastor, after having waited till evening in the impenetrable thickets in which he had hid himself, seeing the tumult succeeded by a calm, he bent his steps for Praviglelm, and arrived there in the middle of the night. His family were at prayer, his friends in distress, his congregation in dejection; but on the unexpected news of his deliverance (for he had been more than six months a prisoner), on the arrival of the father of the family, there were, says a contemporary, "around the good pastor restored to his flock, tears and rejoicings more than can be described."

In connection with this occurrence a strange coincidence must be noticed. It was to the absence of the governor and garrison of Revel that Bonjour owed his success in making his escape. The troops of that place had been sent against the Vaudois of the valley of Pragela; but the Vaudois were victorious, and made the governor of the castle of Revel himself a prisoner. "Ah, Sir!" said the leader of the Vaudois, "it is you who keep the minister of Praviglelm a prisoner." "I received orders to do so," he replied, "but that prisoner has always been well treated in my castle." "We will treat you in the same way here," said the Vaudois; "but you shall remain in our hands, as an hostage, till he be set free."

The men of Praviglelm, however, having assembled in arms, to the number of more than a hundred, conducted Anthony Bonjour to the place of his birth, in the village of Bobi, situated at the bottom of the valley of Lucerna. "He is now in safety," said his former jailer, on learning this news; "you asked me for his liberty; now he has it—grant me mine." Messengers were sent to Bobi to make sure of the fact. The aged pastor acknowledged the humanity which the governor of Revel had shown him, and the Vaudois of Pragela set the governor at liberty. This was being more generous than he had been, for they spared him the perilous chances of an escape, in which, perhaps, he would not have succeeded so well as his former captive.

Thus God in his goodness so ordered it, that this noble personage received the recompense of his humanity, and the humble minister of the valleys would have had, in this unexpected hostage, the means of deliverance secured to him, if his attempt at escape had not been successful. Anthony Bonjour continued to perform his pastoral functions in the valley of Lucerna for more than thirty years after this time, and died at Bobi, on the last day of October, 1631, after having escaped the ravages of the pestilence in the preceding year, and exercised the ministry of the gospel for more than half a century.

But the prisoners in general, and especially those of the Inquisition, by no means obtained so favourable an issue of their captivity.

That same year (1597) an attempt was made to carry off the pastor of Pinache, Felix Huguet; his house was plundered, and his papers carried to Pignerol, but he escaped the ravagers. Instead of this prey, which they had missed, the inquisitors caused his father and his brother to be seized, and they were thrown into the prisons of the Holy Office. The latter came out of prison at the end of three years, but after a promise of abjuration, which altered and saddened him, as if he had lost his soul. As for the aged father, nothing could shake his constancy. Threats and tortures assailed him in vain; disease weakened him without overcoming him; the desire of seeing his family again, and of being warmed in his last days by the sun of his native spot, had no greater effect in bending him to submission. He died slowly, put to death by being thus buried alive; and in the depth and darkness of his dungeon, resigned his soul into the hands of Him who is the light and the life, not only for a few days of sorrow here below, but also to all eternity.

Nevertheless, amidst his sufferings, without earthly consolation, in these deep and gloomy subterranean cells, where his groans died away without an echo, he must have spent many hours of great distress. He had also hours of delight. One night, at the time when the universal silence of the sleeping earth rendered more perceptible the distant noises which communicated their vibrations to the sides of their dungeon, the two captives of Pragela (for his son was still with him) heard, through the walls of the prison, Christian hymns and psalms sung by unknown voices in the neighbouring cell.

After some days of labour, the wall was pierced; and the Huguets, father and son, entered into communication with their brethren in captivity. "For these nine years," said one of them, "I have lain buried before my time in this tomb; but I rejoice that God gives me strength to suffer so long for his gospel. The truth is so glorious! Salvation is so precious! My blessedness daily increases, and I confidently hope to continue thus, singing psalms and confessing the truth, to the very end of my life." The name of this martyr is not known.

There were in that prison Vaudois, Piedmontese, and foreigners. One class were destined to die in public, another to have life slowly extinguished in the bowels of the earth. There were dungeons above dungeons; in the deepest the captives were left to die of hunger. There were others in which they were crushed under a stone table, which was moved by chains; sometimes also they were poisoned, or died of sickness. The most privileged died by the hand of the executioner.

The brother of another Vaudois pastor was amongst the number of the prisoners. His name was John Baptist Gros. The inquisitors, oftener than once, offered him his liberty, on condition that his brother Augustine should come and take his place. What a justice is that of Popery! The son of this unfortunate prisoner was also apprehended some years after. He endured a long captivity, with the same courage which his father had displayed. Firmly resisting all solicitations to apostasy, he at last obtained his deliverance; but he wasted away and died some time after, having contracted his mortal disease in the dungeons, whether it was properly disease or the effect of poison. Another minister of the valleys, named Grandbois, died also, it was never known in what manner.

That same year (still 1597), travellers returning from Turin said in the valleys, "We saw brought out of the dungeons of the Inquisition a venerable old man; tall, emaciated, sickly, but resigned, with white hair and a gray beard, whom they conducted to the square before the castle, to burn him alive. Enfeebled as he was, his look was full of spirit; and his courageous bearing and pious behaviour sufficiently told the cause of his death, for he could not speak; they had put a gag on his mouth; but he retained his firmness to the last. Although we inquired amongst the crowd, we were not able to find out his name, nor whence he was." "Alas!" said a young surgeon of Coni, who heard this, being then at La Tour, where the story was told, "these marks lead me to believe that this martyr was M. Jean, of Marseilles, with whom I became acquainted at Coni, in the following way. One evening I was in the Place de Notre Dame, where the governor of the town then was with some monks, when I saw a man pass by, such as you have just described. The governor interrogated him:—'Whence come you, Sir?' 'From Marseilles, Sir.' 'Whither are you going?' 'To Geneva.' 'What to do?' 'To live according to the law of God.' 'Can you not do that at Marseilles?' 'No, for they want to compel me to join in the mass, and in idolatry.' 'And are we, then, idolaters here at Coni?' 'Yes, Sir.' Thereupon the governor, much enraged, caused him to be imprisoned. I was often employed to convey to him alms and offerings on the part of the members of the church in our own town. He was incessantly singing psalms in his prison. The governor threatened him with the gallows if he continued it. 'As long as I live,' said he, 'I will sing the praises of my God, and as for death, I fear it not.' We were very urgent with the governor to have him restored to liberty. At last we obtained his liberation. He went to Turin, where I have learned that he had some discussions with the monks, and since that time I have heard nothing more of him; but, after your story, I must believe that his soul now reposes in peace in the bosom of his God."

The means employed against the evangelical Christians of the valleys were sometimes much more expeditious. During that same year (1597), Sebastian Gaudin, of Rocheplate, was taken and hanged at St. Segont. At a later date (in 1603), Frache, of Angrogna, who had been one of the Vaudois deputies assembled on the 19th of November, 1602, in the palace of the counts of Lucerna, to confer with these seigneurs concerning the sufferings to which the valleys had been subjected, was allured into a lonely house near

Lucerna, and never came out of it. The particulars of his death are not known, but it is probable that he was secretly assassinated. Two men of Le Villar perished in the same manner, in a house apart from all others in La Tour, where the troops of the Baron of La Roche had been placed in garrison. This was in 1611. These men disappeared without any one knowing what had become of them; but after the departure of the troops, their bodies were discovered under a dunghill. They still bore traces of the torments to which they had been subjected before they were slaughtered.

Mention has already been made, in the history of the Vaudois churches of the former marquisate of Saluces, of two faithful servants of God, who sealed with their blood the living faith of their souls.

Peter Marquisy was one of the elders of the evangelical church of Aceil; he held also a situation as a notary, and, according to the terms of the contemporary narrative from which we derive these particulars, "he acquitted himself very worthily, both in the one office and the other, always employing himself with great zeal in the advancement of the truth."[1] But the zeal on which God looked with approbation was to work him injury among men. Compelled to flee from his native country in order to escape the hands of his persecutors, he retired to Grenoble, where he suffered both from sickness and poverty. "The Reformed church of this place," adds our narrator, "can testify that he lived free of reproach, enduring, with all patience, the trial of his affliction." But he was unwilling that his family should suffer by his absence, and, with a view to put his affairs in order, he returned to Aceil in July, 1619. His intention was not to remain there long; but so soon as the murderous slaves of Popery were apprised of his arrival, they commenced to watch his movements, and by and by he fell into their hands. He was first cast into the prisons of the castle of Dronier; but ere long he was transferred to the dungeons of the Inquisition at Saluces.

A companion in affliction was given to him. With the lawyer was joined the soldier; but although their occupations had been so different, their lives were really the same; they were brethren in the faith, and they were brethren in martyrdom. The name of the new prisoner was Maurice Monge, or Mongie. He, as well as Marquisy, was a native of Aceil. Belonging thus to one place, they had, no doubt, oftener than once, partaken of the same communion, and could support one another in their common misfortune. Having shared together in the delights of Christ's table, they could encourage one another to bear testimony for him by their death. "We

[1] *Brief discours des persec. advenues du Marq. de Saluces*, chap. iii.

have had fellowship in his grace," said these Christians to one another, "let us go on to the fellowship of his sacrifice!"

Maurice Monge, it would appear, was a distinguished soldier; he had won honourable rank by his valour. He came to Saluces to ask pardon for his countryman, on the ground of an edict of toleration, recently obtained from the Duke of Savoy by the solicitations of Lesdiguières. But far from obtaining his request, he himself was deprived of liberty; the Inquisition claimed him as a prey of which it had got hold, and he was compelled to share the chains of him whom he had hoped to deliver.

The charges against Marquisy did not, however, seem to be so serious as to involve his death. He was accused of having failed to show proper respect to a Capuchin; of having read in public a Protestant book; prevented a Protestant woman from becoming a Catholic, and led a Catholic woman to embrace Protestantism. The two latter charges rested on no positive evidence. As for Maurice Monge, he was accused of being a *relapsed* person; and he frankly avowed that, having been at mass by constraint, he had hastened to return, as soon as he could, to the evangelical worship. "Do you believe," he was asked, "that our Lord Jesus Christ is corporally present in the host?" "O! as for that," said he, "I never believed it." "To the fire! to the fire!" exclaimed the judges. And from that time it was thought that this saying would cost him his life. Nor was the anticipation erroneous.

The two Vaudois were condemned to death, by a sentence pronounced on the 1st of October, 1619. They appealed to Turin. "But," says the narrative already quoted, "they could find no advocate nor procurator who would defend them; every one, indeed, saying that the cause was just and the sentence iniquitous, but no one daring to take up the case, for fear of being ruined." The papal nuncio, the Archbishop of Turin, and other ecclesiastics, actively exerted themselves to obtain a confirmation of the sentence of death, and easily succeeded, where, in fact, there was no opposition. Nothing now remained but to carry it into effect by a double murder.

On a dark autumn morning, before even the sun was up, on Monday, the 21st of October, 1619, the Bishop of Saluces left his palace in his carriage. Does he go to administer consolation in some case of great distress? What a zeal prompts him to go out so early in the morning! Let us follow the episcopal chariot. It stops before a scaffold. At the same moment a troop of soldiers and of monks approach the same spot. They come from the palace of the Inquisition, and bring with them the two captives of Aceil, who perceive that the hour of their death is come, and ask time to pray, but it is refused them, and the executioner immediately seizes upon Marquisy, in order to terminate his life. Some field-labourers, who have risen early for their work, and some of the humbler class of inhabitants of the town, who have got notice of the execution, hasten to the scene of death. Marquisy attempts to address them, but the executioner seizes him by the throat, and the soldiers strike him with their weapons. These words, however, escape from the lips of the martyr: "I see the heavens opened, and the angels wait for me!" "They are devils that wait for thee! damned wretch!" exclaims a monk. The bishop looks on from the window of his coach. The victim is dead, and the bishop still looks on. Another is brought; it is Maurice Monge. "Behold the corpse of your acolyte in heresy, misbeliever that you are!" says the fanatical monk. But Maurice, at that solemn moment, was above the reach of insults; they could not discompose his serenity. He deigned no reply to the unfeeling coarseness of the monk, but turning his eyes upon his friend, he said, with a mild voice, "Courage! we have gained the victory!" And thus he died, without ostentation and without weakness. He had braved death in the service of his prince, and how could he fear it in the service of his God!

Other prosecutions and other executions followed these. But nothing equalled in horrors the massacres of 1655, the terrible scenes of which would, of themselves, furnish a complete martyrology. Let us dwell, in preference, upon those rarer instances, more pleasant to contemplate, in which we find the persecuted obtaining their deliverance.

A skilful physician, Paul Roëri of Lanfranco, had come and settled in La Tour, in order to live there, without restraint, according to the gospel. Originally belonging to the neighbourhood, he was followed to his new residence by the reputation which he had acquired in Piedmont, and the Papists saw, with a jealous eye, the consideration and scientific enlightenment of the valleys thus augmented.

This physician, occupying himself in preparation of the medicines which he used, and in compounding which he almost exclusively employed vegetable substances (which, in these mountains, possess a remarkable energy), was accused, upon account of his crucibles and alembics, of spending his time in the fabrication of base money. One Sabbath, in the month of October, 1620, Roëri, having gone to the place of worship in St. John, was surrounded as he came out after service, by a troop of constables and officers of justice, under the directions of one of the principal seigneurs of the valley. The congregation, irritated at this procedure, surrounded the officers of justice in their turn, and might have made an end of them, by closing in upon them in anger, as easily as a sportsman chokes a bird in his hand; but the gentleman *sbire*, perceiving the danger, went into the church, and protested with an oath that religion had nothing to do with the cause of this arrest, and that if the innocence of Roëri were established, he would immediately be set at liberty. "No! no!" cried some of the Vaudois, "he is not guilty, we will answer for him." "If he is not, I swear by my honour," replied the gentleman, "that I will bring him back among you safe and sound."

After some further protestations, he was allowed to go away with his prisoner. The latter wrote from his dungeon, a few days after: "Dear brethren of the Val Lucerna, remember me in your prayers. The Lord grants me the means of writing to you, though I am bound to the strictest secrecy regarding it; I bless him for it, and acknowledge that this affliction is a rod in his hand, for the just correction of my faults. However, dear brethren, as to the crime of which I am accused, I swear before God that I am innocent of it. Were my soul naked before you, as it is before him, you would not see in it one thought which had the least connection with anything of the sort. Be so good, then, as to bestir yourselves without fear, to get me out of this place, with the help of God; whose will, however, and not mine, must be done."

A deputation was sent to the seigneur who kept him prisoner, to obtain his deliverance; but he refused to release him before his case had been tried. Roëri was then transferred to the prisons of the senate of Turin. A great number of letters were exchanged betwixt him and his brethren in the faith. The accusation fell to the ground of itself; but fanaticism stood firm. The prisoner was told that he would be delivered over to the Inquisition if he did not abjure without loss of time. The question was then no longer one relative to the fabrication of base coin.

The gentleman who committed him to prison had given his promise as a guarantee for his enlargement; but of what worth are the promises of oppressors? The curiosity of worldly people was of more advantage to the poor captive. His skill in distilling had been spoken about; the proceedings with regard to him had attracted much attention to his laboratory; the seigneurs of the court represented to Charles Emmanuel that science was interested in the preservation of such a practitioner, and that his highness himself might find a pleasure in seeing his experiments. And, in fact, the duke caused Roëri to be brought to his palace, placed a laboratory at his disposal, was present at the preparation of some medicines and essences, tried them, approved them, retained the skilful preparer of them in his service, and finally authorized him to return to the valleys. But he made him revisit Turin from time to time, to resume his operations in the laboratory of the palace, and renew the pharmaceutical stores of the royal household. "Roëri," says Gilles, "was carried off by the plague of 1630, after having rendered great assistance to those who were sick of the plague in St. Germain and the Val Pérouse, whither he had retired, as well as to all those of the neighbourhood."

Whilst the French possessed Piedmont (from 1536 to 1559), we have seen that a great number of towns, as Turin, Chivas, and Carignan, had pastors and places of worship belonging to the reformed religion. The town of Pancalier was also of this number. "Its inhabitants," says an old author, "used mostly to belong *to the religion*, and had the public exercise of it." Amongst the principal families of this city, figured that of Bazana or Bazan, of which we have now to speak, and that of Rives, which was allied to it. When liberty of conscience was extinguished in Piedmont, these noble families retired into the valley of Lucerna, where the evangelical worship was still permitted. But whilst his family still dwelt in Pancalier, Sebastian Bazan had already spent some years at La Tour, there to receive religious instruction; and at that time had formed a very intimate friendship with a young man of that country, Gilles, who was the companion of his studies, and who became afterwards the narrator of his martyrdom. In consequence, no doubt, of the recollection of this former friendship, and of the wants of the religious life, of which his sojourn in the valleys had made him sensible, Sebastian Bazan afterwards formed the desire, and adopted the resolution, of transferring his abode thither. After the death of his father, he and his two brothers and their families, accompanied by their aged mother, came and fixed their residence at La Tour. "He was," says Gilles, "a very zealous defender of the Protestant religion, a man of sincerity, and an enemy of all vice, so that the enemies of virtue and of truth could not easily endure him; but for the rest, he was a man held in great and universal esteem, and of good reputation."

He went to Carmagnole on the 26th of April, 1622, and the Papists sought to seize him. He was known for his courage as well as for his probity, and his adversaries therefore took precautions against the resistance which they thought he might attempt, and in which his valour might have made him successful, and surrounded him on all sides, leaving him no means of defence. He remained a prisoner for four months in the dungeons of that town, after which he was conveyed, on the 22d of August, 1622, to those of the senate of Turin.

The courageous captive did not want intercessors for his liberation, and Christian friends to console him. But the latter alone were successful. "What favours God has granted me in your letters and your prayers!" he wrote to Gilles on the 14th of July; "for every good thing comes to us from God, even the blessing of friendship, and it is he who endows his own with strength and hopefulness in their trials, such as our adversaries cannot credit, who accordingly seek to make us yield by long imprisonments, and by perpetually urging us to abjure; but I am assured that the Lord will never forsake me, and will sustain me to the end." In fact, as the Bible tells us, it is not a vain thing to trust in him; and Sebastian Bazan proved for himself the truth of the declaration. "My case," he continues, "has been remitted into the hands of his highness, from which I presume that if any great man who was in favour with him could be employed in it, my deliverance could easily be obtained." It was, indeed, already in itself a boon to be removed out of the hands of the inferior magistracy, always goaded on by the clergy; above all, it was a great matter to escape from those of the Inquisition. "Be so good," continues Bazan, "as to visit my family, and exhort my wife to remain constant in the fear of God. She has need to be affectionately admonished, and gently remonstrated with, which you know better how to do than I to write about it." Finally, commending himself to the prayers of his friend, he concludes with this most touching prayer, expressing the sentiments of a Christian in the language of a soldier: "May God work with his own hand to bring us to perfection, that, resting on his holy promises, we may triumph gloriously with our captain, Jesus Christ, in his glorious heavenly kingdom! From the prisons of Turin, this 14th of July, 1622."

His hopes, certainly, were not disappointed as to the life to come; but as to his terrestrial deliverance, they were. Instead of his case being remitted to the humanity of the sovereign, he passed from the prisons of the senate to those of the Inquisition.

Lasciate ogni speranza, voi ch'intrate! says Dante, speaking of the gates of hell. Yes! princes have been harsh, cruel, pitiless; but with them there was at least room for hope; in the horrors of Popery heaven and earth disappear, and nothing remains but hell! Yet never was reception more signalized by a slimy affectation of kindness and tenderness, than that which Bazan met at the Holy Office. Mild and flattering words, expressions of interest and even of affection, fervent and pious solicitations were in the first instance employed to get him to abjure. But the adopted son of the Vaudois valleys knew well enough that the most sanguinary monsters can give to their voices the gentlest tones, as the savage lynx attracts the sheep by imitating the bleating of lambs; and the calmness with which he remained steadfast in his convictions, in place of augmenting the esteem of his adversaries for him, had only the effect of drawing out their wrath. The most terrible threatenings succeeded the tenderest appeals. After threatenings came tortures; the lynx showed his teeth. But the victim did not yield; and the monster that held him captive did not grow weary of sporting with his torments.

Then, indeed, was the time to make intercession for the unfortunate prisoner; but the Inquisition, when it has got the scent of blood, does not let its victims escape. Yet powerful intercessions in favour of poor Bazan continued to be made in great number. Lesdiguières himself wrote to the Duke of Savoy. "I have been accustomed," he said, "to address my supplications to your highness, certain beforehand of not being refused." Alas! Catholic although he had become, he was still unacquainted with Popery. "I request of your highness the life and liberty of one called Sebastian Bazan, detained in the prisons of your city of Turin. He is a man with whom no fault can be found, except as to his religious opinions; and if those who profess the same religion with him ought to be punished with death, then great Christian princes, and even your highness yourself, will have difficulty in re-peopling your dominions. The King of France has granted peace throughout all his kingdom to those of that religion, and I boldly counsel your highness, as your very humble servant, to take the same way. It is the surest means of firmly establishing tranquillity in your dominions."[1]

Lesdiguières did not confine himself to this single letter; he wrote also two others, still with the same object. The Duke of Savoy insisted upon the Inquisition's acceding to these requests of humanity. But the inquisitors replied, with much mildness, humility, and apparent regret, that this case was no longer in their hands, but had been submitted to the decision of Rome. After this, some months more passed. For a year and a half, by a resignation which indicated both strength of conviction and energy of character, Sebastian Bazan protested against the violence which was done in his person to the Christian religion. And this constant firmness of a noble spirit, always serene and resolute, notwithstanding the de-

[1] Dated from Paris, 15th February, 1623.

pressing effect of the treatment received in the dungeons, encircles the head of the martyr with a halo of glory not less pure than that of the courage, more briefly tried, which braves the punishment of death.

But for Sebastian Bazan this glory also was reserved. On the 22d of November, 1623, sentence of death was notified to him. He was condemned to be burned alive. " I am contented to die," he mildly and courageously replied, " since it is the will of God, and will be, I trust, for his glory. But as for men, they have pronounced an unjust sentence, and they will soon have to give an account of it." Was it a mere fortuitous coincidence, or was it in truth an actual judgment of God? I know not; but he who had pronounced this unjust sentence, received the stroke of death that very evening in his own house. He died, therefore, even before the condemned man. Next day, however, (the 23d of November, 1623,) was the day fixed for the execution.

Before leading Sebastian Bazan out of his prison, they put a gag in his mouth, to prevent him from uttering gospel truth at the stake. But whilst the executioner was fastening him to it, the gag fell out, and the martyr proclaimed with a loud voice the cause of his death. "People," said he, "it is not for a crime that I am brought hither to die; it is for having chosen to conform myself to the word of God, and for maintaining his truth in opposition to error." The inquisitors made haste to put an end to this sort of language by causing the pile to be kindled. Then Sebastian Bazan began to sing the hymn of Simeon, in the metrical version of Theodore Beza, that touching hymn of the churches of his native country, which the faithful sing after having refreshed their souls in the communion of their Saviour:—

> " Laisse-moi désormais
> Seigneur, aller en paix,
> Car selon ta promesse,
> Tu fais voir à mes yeux
> Le salut glorieux
> Que j'attendais sans cesse!"

But his voice was very soon stifled by the flames, and according to eye-witnesses, many persons, even of high rank, wept on seeing him die.

Several other arrests, followed by cruel treatment, took place at this period; amongst others, that of Captain Garnier, of Dronier, who was apprehended for having conversed on religious subjects

---

[1] A simple and beautiful versification of the words of the aged Simeon, Luke ii. 29, 30.—Tr.

with one of his relatives. He was tied upon a horse, his hands being bound behind his back, and his feet under the belly of the animal. When those who had him in charge stopped at any hostelry, they left him in this condition before the house, after having attached the chain to the iron bar of some window, or to a ring in the wall. Being conducted in this manner to Turin, he was put in a prison of the castle, which was named the *purgatory*, and afterwards removed to another, called the *hell*. But after long time spent in investigation and prosecution of the case, he was released on a bail of 200 crowns of gold, and his promise not again to converse on religious subjects. He then retired to the valley of Lucerna, where he married; but having occasion to make a journey into Dauphiny, and desiring to revisit the place of his birth, he attempted to return by the valley of Dronier, and was assassinated on the Col de Tende, at the age of fifty-five years.

More particulars have been preserved to us of the last moments of Bartholomew Coupin, who was also settled in the valley of Lucerna, but who was born at Asti, about the year 1545. Having married a young woman of Bubiano, he settled at La Tour, where he carried on the trade of a woollen draper, and exercised the office of an elder in the consistory of that church. The affairs of his business, as well as the associations of his youth, having led him in 1601 to Asti, his birthplace, at the time of a fair, held in the month of April, he found himself in the evening at a hostelry, supping with strangers. Conversation having commenced among them, the person next him inquired where he resided. Coupin named La Tour. "I have been in your quarter," replied the questioner, "and lodged with a townsman, whose wife is from Montcallier." "No doubt it was Monsieur Bastie," said Coupin. "Yes, Sir," said the other; "he is *of the religion*, I have been told." "And so am I, at your service," said the woollen draper. "Do you not believe that Christ is in the host?" inquired the other. "No," replied Coupin. "What a false religion yours is!" exclaimed a person who till then had been silent. "False, Sir," replied the old man—for Coupin was then some sixty years of age—"it is as true that our religion is true, as it is true that God is God, and that I must die." He did not then think how soon these last words were to be realized! Nobody spoke again to answer him; but next day, the 8th of April, 1601, Bartholemew Coupin was apprehended by order of the bishop of that place. The officers of customs in the town had respected his religious opinions; the prelate had less charity, and caused him to be cast into the prisons of his palace.

Does any one imagine that St. John or St. Peter ever had prisons in their houses? But, indeed, their pretended successors are not bound in anything to resemble them!

Bartholomew remained two days in irons, far from his family, afflicted, but calling upon his God, in the unwholesome garrets of that palace, in which one of the dignitaries of the Papal Church complacently enjoyed the light of the sun in his gilded halls, and the sensual delights of the earth at his richly-served table. This was still very unlike the lives of the apostles, nor was it of such a mode of existence that Paul spoke to Timothy, as proper for a Christian bishop. But on the part of Popery, nothing in the way of interpretation or unfaithfulness ought to excite any surprise.

On the day after his apprehension, they brought Coupin a book, intended to overthrow the *Institutions* of Calvin. It had been composed by the previous bishop of Asti, whose name was De Punigarole. "Not knowing how to pass my time," says he in a letter, "I have read the whole of this horrid book, and even from it I have derived some benefit, having learned from it a number of sentences of Calvin, which are quoted in it." Thus the very means which were thought best for shaking his faith, served to confirm him. It was not for want of arguments of every sort, employed to overcome him; for poor Bartholomew was subjected to sixteen examinations of five hours each, before the grand vicar, the advocate fiscal, and a secretary named Annibal. The following are his own words to his family, in a letter which Gilles has preserved: "They asked me, besides what is in the Holy Scripture, about things of heaven, of earth, and of hell, and other things of which I never heard before; and I marvel at the grace which God gave me to enable me to answer, it seems to me, seven times more than I knew. O immortal God! thy word is indeed true, which tells thine own that they need not concern themselves about what they should say when they are brought before men for thy sake; because it shall be given them what they shall answer!" We may form some notion of the extent of these examinations, from the circumstance that frequently a quire of paper was not sufficient to hold all the questions and answers of a single sitting.

"On the 16th of April," says the prisoner, "when I was very much indisposed (for his advanced age, his detention, and his feeble health, had made him quite valetudinarian), they came to seek me in my prison, to conduct me to the tribunal. I passed through three grand apartments, and in the last I saw six prelates and lords gravely seated in arm-chairs.[1] 'Ah! my God!' thought I,

---

[1] "*Sur les chaises*," Coupin's letter says.

'this is my death!'" But the bishop saluted him, and, after having named to him the persons present, mildly said to him, "Bartholomew, we have prayed to God for you, that you may acknowledge your errors, and return to the bosom of the church. What say you?" "I say that I am in the true church, and that, by the grace of God, I hope to live and die in it." "If you would renounce that heresy," replied the bishop, "your valley would be all festivity and rejoicing upon your account." "It would rather deplore the news of my apostasy." "Have they no regard, then, for your life?" "Jesus says, 'He who will save his life shall lose it;' and it is eternal life which those who love me desire for me." "Have you nothing, then, which binds you to the earth?" "I have a wife and children; I have also some property; but God has taken away all this from my heart, to put there love for his service, to which, through his holy will, I shall remain faithful until death."

"There were upon the table," adds the martyr, "two Bibles, and a large paper book, on which were written, beforehand, the questions of the examination; and this with so many diabolical inventions, that the most learned man in the world could not have extricated himself from amongst them; and as for me, poor worm that I am, I answered as much as it pleased God; and if in anything I had difficulty as to reasons, I said to them—'I believe what the Holy Scripture teaches, and that is sufficient to prove the truth of my doctrine.'"

On the 29th of April they returned to the charge, to make him abjure. But he said to them—"You lose your time in seeking to overcome me, for I will never esteem myself overcome, knowing that you could not do it if there were a thousand of you against me." They said, "Do you then think yourself so learned?" "No, my lords," he replied, "I am a poor merchant, and very unlettered; but I wish to learn nothing from you in the matter of religion, and, therefore, I pray you to leave me in peace." "O what a peace!" cried the inquisitor who presided at these examinations. "Cursed heretic! obstinate Lutheran! thou wilt go to the abode of all the devils of hell; and thou likest this better than to be reconciled to the holy mother church!" "It is long," replied the prisoner, "since I was reconciled to the holy church, and that is the reason why I am so unwilling to leave it."

In the following month (from the 1st to the 15th of May) he was again frequently examined respecting the worship of images, the invocation of saints, the merit of works, justification, &c.; but in the end he said to them—"My lords, if an unarmed man were attacked by four or five men well armed, how could he protect himself? You are here opposed to me—so many learned folks, with books and writings prepared; how am I, a poor ignorant man, and without books, able to defend myself?" "You know too well how to do that, you wretch!" replied the inquisitor; "it would be better for you that your skull were not so well furnished." God, who puts the truth into the mouths of his children, puts wisdom and knowledge also into simple and upright hearts. It is not from the head, but from the heart, that the living convictions come by which men are enabled to brave death.

The bishop endeavoured to shake Coupin's determination by the means so well known to the Church of Rome, and which so often succeed with weak minds—the charm which is in prodigies, the power of the marvellous, and all this aided by cruel threatenings, and a long perspective of the torments from which a miraculous conversion seemed the only way of escape. "See you that building that stands there by itself?" said the bishop's secretary one day to the poor prisoner, whom he had brought down to a terrace. "Yes." "It is a prison." "Well!" "It is thirty-two years since I came to this palace." "What has that to do with yonder prison?" "Listen: one day there fell into our hands a singular heretic; nobody knew what he was. He was neither a Jew, nor a Lutheran, nor a Mahometan; nobody could tell his religious creed." "And, therefore, not being able to convict him of error, as they did not know his opinions, they must have released him!" "No: he was walled up over there, and a little nourishment was passed to him through a hole guarded with iron bars." "What became of him?" "He remained there for five years; many priests and monks came to instruct him and exhort him. All at once he was converted; and ever since that time he has done marvellous things." "As for me," replied Coupin, with the simplicity of a Christian, and the affecting good-nature of an old man, "I have but two or three steps to take in order to arrive at the good place of rest, and, by God's help, I will not turn back."

"However," says he himself, "many priests and preachers came also to console me and to disconsole me. The sieur John Paul Laro, a person of great rank, having come to see me, began to assail me about change of religion. 'A nephew of Calvin,' said he to me, 'being on a long journey, passed through Rome, where he fell sick. Being without money, he went to the hospital. Next day they wanted to confess him and to bring him the host, but he refused the sacraments. Having questioned him as to whence he came, they knew what he was, and the pope had him brought into his own presence. There he became a convert, and since that time he has done marvellous things.'" It was always the same conclusion. "Other persons also," says Coupin, "came to tell me similar fables."

Meanwhile, his fellow-countrymen, his friends, and his family, made very urgent efforts to obtain his liberty. All the notables of the valley of Lucerna, including even some Catholic seigneurs, who knew Coupin as an honourable and respected man, addressed a petition in his favour to the Duke of Savoy, from whom there was some hope of obtaining his liberation. The edicts in force authorized the Vaudois to profess their religion; the duke seemed disposed to apply them to the prisoner at Asti, but the Romish Church and the Inquisition always prevented it. "They blew to kindle the pile," says an author of that time.

However, they did not cease to employ, in order to overcome the firmness of the martyr, all the solicitations and all the means which could operate upon the heart of man. He had espoused, as his second wife, the daughter of a worthy notary of Bubiano, John Reinier by name, who had been, in 1560, one of three delegates of the valley of Lucerna, appointed to repair for conference, in name of the Vaudois, to the castle of Cavour.[1] Coupin obtained leave to receive a visit from his wife and his eldest son. They supped together: it was on the 15th of September, 1601. At the close of the repast, the bishop and the inquisitor arrived. "Well, Coupin, have you come to repentance? You see your wife and child: abjure your errors, and we shall immediately set you at liberty." But they made nothing of it, says Gilles; and his pious wife herself durst not ask him to renounce his religion for the love of this world. She could not but weep as she looked with admiration on this invincible firmness of a soul victorious over life. "My dearest," he said to her, "take heed to give good instruction to our children. Be a mother to them all!" (for he had two by his former marriage; their names were Martha and Samuel. The names of the others were Matthew, David, Bartholomew, and Mary). Then, when he had commended them all to the grace of the Lord, they took their last farewell with many tears. Now, after the lapse of three centuries, it is pleasant to think that they are re-united in heaven.

After their departure, Coupin found himself again alone in a lofty prison, for his cell was situated in the uppermost story of the episcopal palace. The friends whom he had at Asti, seeing the hour of his condemnation to approach, excited by the example of his courage, and vexed at the fruitlessness of all the efforts which they made in his favour, resolved, in despair of his case, to de-

[1] See Part II., ch. i.

liver him themselves, and to come and carry him off during the night.

All their precautions were taken with success. They made their way, without any one suspecting it, to the top of the palace, pierced the roof, descended into the garrets, removed a plank of the ceiling, and reached Coupin's prison. The poor man knew not, on hearing this noise, whether he ought to fear or to rejoice. Putting his trust in God, he remained calm. He waited till the ceiling of his cell was pierced, and a dark lantern made its appearance over the opening, when well-known figures presented themselves in the light of that liberty-bringing lamp, amidst the profound darkness of the night. "Silence!" said they to him, "we are friends. Fasten this rope around your body." "And why so much ado? If God think proper to deliver me from this place, he will deliver me without any need of my going out like a robber." "But what if it please God to make use of us for your deliverance? You see to how much danger we have exposed ourselves to come here! God protects us: would you disappoint his goodness and our labour?"

The aged captive suffered himself to be persuaded. Liberty had become more precious to him since he had been deprived of it. They drew him out of his chamber, and then from the roof of the palace they let him down to the street. His liberators followed with all haste, but the jailer and domestics had heard the noise; they rose and gave chase; the gates were opened amidst great din; the friends of Coupin became confused, and took to flight; he alone preserving his composure, but too feeble and too aged to follow them, waited tranquilly in the street till the jailer came to seek for him. He was seized, carried back to the bishop's palace, and shut up in a place of confinement still closer than before. His soul alone was free; his soul was happy, and felt no solitude, for Jesus Christ says to his people—"I am with you alway, even unto the end of the world."

This occurrence, however, had the effect of quickening the procedure against Coupin, and hastening on the termination of his bodily sufferings. The papers in his case having been sent to Rome, he was condemned to be burned alive. But on the day of execution he was brought forth dead from the prison in which he had been detained. Had he died by a natural or by a violent death? This question has not yet been resolved. Be that as it might, his corpse was cast upon the pile; and whilst Rome raised her chant of victory around the execution fire, the church of the apostles and martyrs, the Vaudois Church, and the living gospel, reckoned one triumph more.

Of these poor victims of persecution, it will be seen that a number had, by their birth, no connection with the Vaudois Church; but they belonged to it by their faith, and, in many instances, had fixed their residence in the valleys. Of this number was also Louis Malherbe, born at Busque, near Saluces, in 1558. After having passed through all the vicissitudes attendant upon the numerous persecutions which the Protestants of his native district were compelled to endure—by turns a prisoner and a fugitive—now enjoying his possessions, and now seeing them subjected to confiscation—wandering hither and thither, but always steadfast in the midst of his eventful life—in misery and in poverty, he only became ever the more attached to the doctrines for which he had so much to suffer. And if we love those things most which have cost us the greatest sacrifices, what must be God's love to those believing souls whose salvation has cost the sacrifice of the Saviour!

Louis Malherbe had taken a wife at Verzol; and, after many changes of residence, he settled at last at La Tour, like Roëri, Bazan, and Coupin.

His family had already paid its tribute of martyrdom. When Castrocaro was governor of the valleys, Captain Malherbe, the brother of Louis, paid with his life for the spirit of independence which animated him. This captain had been noticed by the Duke of Savoy for his valour; and being a person of great consideration in the valleys, he conducted himself as one who should rather be the associate of the counts of Lucerna, than of the governor of La Tour. The governor, upon this account, conceived an envious animosity against him; and on the evening of the 1st of November, 1575, he gratified it by an assassination. Malherbe had gone to sup with a relative; Castrocaro placed one of his officers, named Bastian, with a company of the garrison, in ambush on the way by which he must pass. The darkness of the night favoured their designs: the streets of La Tour were silent and solitary. Scarcely had Malherbe made his appearance when these assassins attacked him at unawares: he drew his sword against them, put himself in a posture of defence, repulsed them at first, and although thereafter more closely pressed, continued to fight, successfully defending himself, and always keeping his face towards his assailants, till he arrived at the door of his own house. It was situated opposite to where the present town's-house stands. The assassins, fearing lest he might escape, augmented their fury. Malherbe struck redoubled blows, with the hilt of his sword, upon the door, against which he had set his back; at the same time, he repulsed upon all sides the attacks of his adversaries. At the noise of the combat his relatives and friends ran hastily and opened the door, but it was too late. The mortal blow had been given; an instant had sufficed; his wearied arm had left his breast undefended, and he had just fallen, breathing his last. The murderers immediately took flight, and when the door of the house was opened, the corpse of their victim lay alone upon the threshold.

Another brother still, named Hercules Malherbe, was arrested on the 11th of April, 1612, by order of the prefect of Pignerol. But the Vaudois of St. John obtained his release, in virtue of the article of their privileges, according to which no inhabitant of the valleys could be withdrawn from the jurisdiction of his natural judge (in this case the podestat of Lucerna), let the charge be what it might, except for the crime of high treason.

His brother Louis was not so fortunate. Having ventured, notwithstanding advice to the contrary, to go to Busque in the spring of 1626, to receive payment of some money which was due to him, he passed by Verzol, where his wife's family resided. There he had a discussion with a missionary monk, who had been preaching in the church called the church of Les Battus. The monk, who probably had not the advantage in this controversy, assisted by some followers, all ready to use violence in his behalf, caused the old man (for Louis Malherbe had then seen nearly seventy years) to enter into the church, close to where he had his assassin band. They watched the gates; and he sent a messenger in all haste to the inquisitor of Saluces, who, without losing an instant, came to Verzol to bear off the prisoner. No sooner were the Vaudois apprised of this outrage, than they addressed a petition to Charles Emmanuel for the liberation of the prisoner. They grounded their petition on the edicts which authorized them freely to pass through the dominions of his highness, without any one having a right to arrest them, unless in the very act of crime.

Possibly a request enforced by such strong reasons might have engaged the honour of the sovereign to a just compliance with it, for the very maintenance of his own edicts; but the Inquisition, more prompt to slay than the prince to pardon, anticipated the solution of this question by an unexampled catastrophe.

At the very moment when hope began to be entertained of a present happy termination of the old man's captivity, the monks were seen to bear his corpse out of the prisons of the Holy Office, and to cast it contemptuously into a pit digged in the open field, beyond the walls of the city. The dishonour which marked his burial may be held as an attestation of the firmness which he had displayed, to his last breath, in not abandoning his religion; but the cause of his death was not discovered. We know not whether his body was entire or mutilated; whether he had been deprived of life by torture or by poison; nor, in short, whether his death had been violent or natural.

When, about the close of the year 1633, the Vaudois of Praviglelm and Paësane were obliged to quit their abodes for the last time, and to retire into the valleys of Lucerna, the monks of the convent of Paësane set fire to the deserted houses, in order to deprive their fugitive inhabitants of all hope of ever returning to them again. Some of them came back to save from the flames their furniture or linen, which they had not been able to carry with them at first; but as they returned to their new refuge, they were arrested by the soldiers of the garrison of Revel. These imprisonments had no object but spoliation; and by abandoning the relics of their property, which they had with peril rescued from the fire, or by paying a heavy ransom, most of them obtained their liberation.

But in this they were not all successful. Daniel Peillon, a man already advanced in years, was apprehended at Barges, and conveyed from Revel to the prisons of the senate of Turin. There he had to contend against the solicitations of the regular clergy, who promised not only to restore him to liberty, but also to reinstate him in full possession of all his property, if he would abjure Protestantism. "God has given me the grace to know his truth," replied he firmly; "I have been happily enabled to persevere in it to my old age, and I am too near death to sacrifice my soul for the sake of living a few days more." In vain did they attempt to make him say anything else. All who knew him, even Catholics themselves, acknowledged his worth; many efforts were made to obtain his liberation, but in vain; he was condemned to the galleys for ten years. One of his judges, a member of the senate, being solicited in his favour by compassionate persons, who represented how cruel it was to condemn an old man to so long a punishment for no other cause than his doctrines, coldly replied, "Ten years of the galleys! what is that for a heretic?" He was, therefore, compelled to undergo this punishment. He was transported to the pontoons of Villefranche, near Nice, and his fellow-countrymen of the valley of Lucerna sent every year one of their number to convey to him some relief and consolation. Every year, also, these charitable messengers returned to announce to the Vaudois that the evangelical galley-slave remained constant in his piety, enduring his punishment, but without regret for its cause.

Peillon became weak in body, but his soul did not bend; he grew old in the galleys, but renewed his youth for heaven.

The wars which ensued a few years after interrupted the fraternal communications betwixt the mountaineers and the prisoner. When they sought to resume them, and new messengers came to Villefranche to convey to him the accustomed tribute of the pious sympathies of his distant friends, upon their inquiring after the aged galley-slave of the valley of the Po, they learned that he was dead.

Thus the Vaudois left martyrs everywhere—amongst the mountains and in the prisons, on the piles, and on the seas. Such are the great examples left us by that age of heroism, faith, and suffering.

But how many other victims breathed their last with the same faith, and amidst equal agonies, of whom no account has come down to us! Unnoticed soldiers, they contributed to the triumph without having part in the glory. Obscurity attended them throughout their painful pilgrimage, and received them in the tomb; victims forgotten upon earth, but not in heaven, they seem greater still enwrapped in their own self-denial. And what matters it though our names may be unknown to men, if only they be inscribed in the book of life! Martyrdom has no need of circumstances which attract human attention, in order to enjoy the blessing of heaven. To devote one's self to Christ, without regard to glory or display, is the sacrifice which is most pleasing to him; and it may be made in the ordinary life of every day, as well as at the last moment of a world-noticed death. Yea, the Christian may contend for his faith in prosperity as well as in suffering, and die for his God in the bosom of his family, as well as on a burning pile.

PART SECOND.

FROM THE TIME WHEN THE VAUDOIS WERE RESTRICTED WITHIN THE LIMITS OF THEIR VALLEYS, TO THE DATE OF THEIR TOTAL BANISHMENT.

CHAPTER I.

MATTERS PRELIMINARY TO THE SECOND GENERAL PERSECUTION OF THE VAUDOIS OF THE VALLEYS OF PIEDMONT.[1]

(A.D. 1520 TO A.D. 1560.)

Increasing number of attendants at the public worship of the Vaudois—Building of places of worship—Friendly disposition of the Dukes of Savoy in the earlier part of the 16th century—Pope Paul IV.—Commissioners of the Parliament of Turin sent to the valleys in 1556—Fanaticism—Firmness of the Vaudois—Profession of faith—Threatenings of persecution—Charles and Boniface Trouchet, seigneurs of Le Perrier—Their attempt to seize the minister of Rioclaret—Flight of the people of Rioclaret—An aged pastor and another prisoner burned alive at Pignerol—The people of Rioclaret saved by the other Vaudois, who take up arms for their assistance—Remarkable fate of the seigneurs of Le Perrier—Philip of Savoy, Count of Racconis, at Angrogna—Many instances of violence—Poussevin, commandant of Fossano—His argument in favour of the mass—The syndics of the valleys refuse to send away the pastors—An army collected against the Vaudois in 1560—Vain attempts to bring them even to apparent concessions—Friendly interposition of Count Charles of Lucerna.

AFTER having published the Bible, and confirmed their unity in faith with the Reformed Church, the Vaudois entered upon the public preaching of the glad tidings of salvation.

It will be remembered that the houses of their Barbas had hitherto served them for places of meeting. Thus the primitive church, exposed for centuries to assaults from without, long sheltered its testimony in the retirement of private dwellings. But

---

[1] AUTHORITIES.—*Gilles, Perrin, De Thou.*—"*Memorabilis historia persecutionum, bellorumque in populum vulgò Valdensem appellatum, Angrunicam, Luserneam, Sanmartineam, Perusinam, aliasque regionis Pedemontanæ valles*

withal, this unobtrusive ministry was not the less active, and the church all at once manifested an increased strength at the expiry of that first age of concentration. The Vaudois valleys adopted the same method, which must be considered as the method adopted by our Lord. At the date to which our history now refers, all their places of worship were constructed in a single year.[1]

The number of hearers who at that time crowded into the residences of the Barbas became too great to be accommodated there, for they came not only from the valleys, but from the plain of Piedmont; and as the parish of Angrogna was most easily accessible to them, they repaired thither in greatest numbers.

One day the throng, assembled in the square of the village, waited till they should be able to enter the pastor's residence, which was already full of people. It was in the month of August, 1555. The pastor taught within; a schoolmaster preached without. "Yes, the times are come," exclaimed he, "when the gospel must be proclaimed to every nation, when the Lord will pour out his Spirit upon every creature! Come and drink at these living fountains of the grace by which Christ refreshes our souls! Blessed are they who hunger and thirst after righteousness, for they shall be

---

incolentem, ab anno 1555 ad 1561, *religionis ergo gestorum Anno* MDLXII., *Gallicè primum in luce edita; nunc vero a Christophero* Richardo *Biturige, Latine donata*." A small 8vo volume of 151 pages, in italics.—The same work, in French, "*Histoire des persécutions et guerres faites depuis l'an* 1555, *jusques en l'an* 1561, *contre le peuple appelé Vaudois,*" &c., printed in the same year (1562), a small quarto of 173 pages.—The same work in *Crespin,* " *Histoire mémorable des persecutions* . . . ." &c. Folio edition of 1619, from fol. 532 to fol. 547. —" *Hist. mém. de la guérre faite par le Duc de Savoye Emmanuel Philibert, contre ses sujets d'Angrogne, Pérouse* . . . . &c., *traduit de l'Italien.*" Printed in 1561. —The same work, published in Italian, in the same year.—" *Hist. des perséc. contre les Vaudois, de* 1555 *a* 1561," &c. The two preceding works combined into one. Geneva, 1581.—" *Historia ecclesiæ Waldensium,*" &c. 4to. Strasburg, 1668.—" *Histoire des Chrétiens communément nommés Vaudois, pendant les douze premiers siècles;*" printed at Haarlem in 1765. This work had been previously published in Dutch, at Amsterdam, in 1732 ("*Historie der Christenen, die men gemeenlyk Waldensen noemt.*")—" *Chronique des Vaudois, depuis* 1160 *à* 1655," published in German, at Zurich, in 1655; republished at Schaffhausen the same year (by Souter; it was the first work of that celebrated printer); translated into Dutch, and published at Amsterdam in 1656, and in French, the same year, at Geneva. See also the general sources of information indicated at the commencement of Part I.—The manuscript authorities are almost none.—" *Relazione dei successi nelle valli di Luserna e Piemonte, l'anno* 1559-1634 [without date or place of publication).—*Histoire mém. de la guerre faite par le Duc de Savoje, Emmanuel Philibert, contre ses subjects des vallées d'Angrogne, Pérosse* . . . . *et autres circonvoisines, pour compte de la religion. Ensemble les articles et capitulations de l'accord proposé audit seigneur par lesdits subjects, au mois de juing,* 1561. *Nouvellement traduit de l'Italien en Français.* MDLXII. A small 8vo. of thirty pages.

[1] From 1555 to 1556.

filled!" And the people, with increased eagerness, called for the pastor. The pastor was Stephen Noël, whom Gilles, in returning from Calabria, had brought with him from Lausanne. He was obliged to leave his house and preach in the open air. Privacy was no longer possible. A place of worship was constructed upon that spot, and before the end of the year another was built, at the distance of half-a-league. These two places of worship remain to the present day.[1] The pastors read the Bible there, and explained it to the people every day; the people could not be satisfied.

In the other communes the same demand arose for places of worship. Within eighteen months they were all built. What a power there is in evangelical life and activity! "Show me thy faith by thy works," said St. James to the primitive church; and that church pursuing her course of unobtrusive ministration in private dwellings, laboured for centuries to win souls and elevate them heavenwards, as so many temples dedicated to the Lord; and afterwards her places of worship arose everywhere. In the same manner the Vaudois Church, after centuries of hidden life, set open the sanctuary of its teachings, and all the places of worship in its valleys were erected at once. It was not long till they were cemented with the blood of martyrs. Behold the works of our faith! might these worthy inheritors of the primitive Christians have said to the apostle.

But they had been favoured by the kindness of their sovereigns. There is extant a brief of Julius II., of date 8th May, 1506, addressed to the Duke of Savoy, who had interceded for them with the court of Rome;[2] and for twenty years after the great synod of 1532, the Vaudois still lived undisturbed. "The pastors and other leaders of the churches," says Gilles, "had resolved to conduct their religious services with as little display and noise as possible, in order not unnecessarily to irritate those who only desired an occasion to do them harm."

When prudence does not interfere with devotedness, it increases our estimate of its value; and when, at a later period—after having been brought by Providence to enjoy a publicity of ministrations beyond what they had sought—these intrepid propagators of the gospel had notice given them that they must submit to some restrictions, "Why," said they, "should we diminish the work of God and the field of labour which he has assigned us?" "Armed

[1] The first is that of St. Laurent; the second, that of Serres; they have merely been repaired from time to time.
[2] *Nobis humiliter supplicari fecisti ut subditis prædictis ne vexentur.* . . . .— Archives of the Court of Turin, T. 620. *Cat. Valdesi;* No. (of the series) 620.

bands," it was replied, "will come from Turin and annihilate you."[1] "God will defend what he has set up," said they. And they pursued, with the calmness of courage, the work commenced in the calmness of prudence. It is the character of strong minds; it was that of these evangelical mountaineers.

But when seven places of worship were erected at once in the valleys—when, notwithstanding the execution of Laborie, Vernoux, Varailles, and Hector, who suffered martyrdom at that period, it was perceived that the number of Vaudois students in foreign parts, and that of the foreign pastors in Piedmont increased at the same time with the flocks hungering for the pastures of the Bible—the court of Rome took the alarm, and armed itself with its utmost severity.

The Vaudois valleys and the city of Turin belonged at that time to France. The unfortunate Duke of Savoy, Charles III., so justly surnamed *the Good*, had sought the assistance of Charles V., and from his retreat at Verceil he beheld with sorrow his hereditary dominions alternately made the prey of his allies and of his enemies.

Marcel II., a well-meaning and upright pope, who had manifested some dispositions favourable to reformation, and evinced a desire to introduce it into the Church, having been elected on the 9th of April, 1555, died unexpectedly twenty-one days after his exaltation to the papal chair, being struck, it was said, with apoplexy. His successor, Paul IV.,[2] more faithful to the spirit of Catholicism, instead of favouring improvement, endeavoured to put a stop to it. Events, at first, seemed to fall in with his designs. The cardinals of Lorraine and of Tournon, the latter of whom had already proved so dreadful an enemy to the Vaudois of Provence, came to Rome on the 15th of December, 1555, to conclude, in name of the King of France, a league against the Spaniards. At the same time the nuncio wrote from Turin to report the progress made by the Vaudois, and Paul IV. took advantage of the return of the diplomatist cardinals to apply to Henry II., with whom he had just been negotiating an alliance, requiring that he should employ rigorous measures against these heretics.

The French monarch accordingly transmitted orders to the parliament of Turin, and that body named two commissioners, St. Julian and Della Chiesa (in Latin called De Ecclesia), who were appointed to proceed to the spot, to collect information, to prepare a report, to endeavour to bring over the Vaudois to Catholicism, and to take all steps which they might judge necessary for that

[1] This report was current in the valleys in the month of December, 1555.
[2] Elected on the 27th of May, 1555.

purpose. These delegates, escorted by a numerous suite, arrived in the valleys in the month of March, 1556. They commenced by issuing a proclamation, in which, reminding the people of the respect due to the authority of the king and of the church, they threatened with the severest penalties those who should resist. The Vaudois replied that they were, and would continue to be, faithful subjects and Christians.

But the irritation of the Catholics against the reformed was great. A man of St. John, who had got his child baptized by the pastor of Angrogna, was denounced to the commissioners, and cited before them at Pignerol. There he received orders to have his child re-baptized by a priest, with certification that if he did not he would be burned alive. The disconcerted villager stood silent. Being urged to reply, he asked time for reflection. "You shall not leave that spot till you decide." "Permit me, at least, to take counsel." "Of your confessor, perchance?" said the vice-president, with a sarcastic air.[1] "Yes, my lord," gravely replied the Christian. His request was granted. "What is he going to do?" said those who were present, one to another. The countryman retired to the most distant part of the room, and fearlessly kneeling in presence of these great ones, humbly addressed himself to God in prayer.

And was not this, indeed, to go to the best counsellor—the friend to whom all distresses may be confided—the only confessor who is able both to absolve and to direct? "What have you resolved upon?" said the magistrates. "Will you take upon your souls," replied the peasant, "the evil which there may be in doing what you require of me?" The commissioners, disconcerted in their turn, sent him away, without insisting upon his compliance.

But all around them fanaticism was breaking out into deeds of violence, and the basest passions were expressed in the most offensive language. "I will cut off the nose of that cursed pastor of Angrogna, if he continues his audacious preachings," cried a man, named Trombaud, in the public square of Briquèras.

The smallest incidents were significant at that time; they appeared, to the lively and simple imagination of the people, to take place under the guiding hand of God. And why should it not always be so? This same Trombaud, travelling by night towards the mountains of Angrogna, was attacked by a wolf, which sprang at his face, and disfigured it; so that he underwent the same mutilation by the teeth of a ferocious beast, with which his hand

[1] The commissioner, St. Julian, was third president of the parliament of Turin, and Della Chiesa third counsellor.

had threatened the pastor. Common-place as this circumstance may seem to us, it was taken at that time for a providential chastisement, and perhaps retarded the bursting of the storm which gathered over the Vaudois.

The commissioners visited the valley of Perouse; they then went to Lucerna, and afterwards to Angrogna, where they entered both the places of worship, and were present during sermon. When the minister had descended from the pulpit, they commanded a monk to get up into it, requesting the congregation to listen to him also. The monk preached on the unity of the Catholic Church, and asserted that separation from it was a crime. "It is that church herself that has separated from the gospel," said the minister, when the monk had finished his discourse; "and, if the honourable commissioners will permit us, we will prove it from the Bible." "We are not come here to hold discussions," they replied, "but to enforce the observance of the king's orders. Recollect what happened ten years ago to your brethren of Merindol and of Cabrières, for having resisted the laws of the church."[1] The Vaudois, without taking any notice of the confusion which these words made of civil and ecclesiastical laws, or of the threat with which they were accompanied, answered with the utmost simplicity, but firmly, that they were resolved to live according to the word of God, and that if the falsehood of their doctrines could be proved to them from the word of God, they were ready to forsake them. The same answer was given to the commissioners in the other communes of the valleys, which they visited in the same manner.

Hereupon they retired to Lucerna, and caused an edict to be published on the 23d of March, 1556, by which they ordained the Vaudois to abjure, and to receive no more preachers coming from other parts, except such as might be sent to them by the Archbishop of Turin. The third part of the goods of offenders was promised to those who should inform against them.

The Vaudois replied by a profession of faith, founded upon the Bible, in the spirit of which they resolved to persevere, like their forefathers, until it should be proved to them that they were in error. "And as for human traditions," they added, "we willingly receive those which serve to promote order, decency, and the dignity of the holy ministry; but as for those which are recommended in order to the acquiring of merit, and to bind and oblige consciences, contrary to the word of God, we absolutely reject them, and would not accept them even from the hand of an angel."

---

[1] This was an allusion to the frightful massacres which deluged the banks of the Durance with blood in 1545.—*See* chap. v. of Part I.

The commissioners could not hope to prevail more than an angel, and upon this demanded that the pastors and schoolmasters should be delivered up to them. "If they teach the truth," said the Vaudois, "why take them from us? and if they do not teach the truth, let it be proved to us by the word of truth." All the threatenings and solicitations of the parliamentary envoys failed against that impregnable rampart of the Vaudois church—the Bible—the eternal stumbling-block of the Church of Rome. "Very well," said St. Julian, "keep your schoolmasters and your preachers, but you will have to give an account of your keeping them, when they shall be demanded from you again."

After this the commissioners returned to Turin, and made their report to the parliament, which appointed them to proceed to France, to inform Henry II. of what had taken place, and to receive his instructions for the future. It was not until next year that they returned, and revisiting the valleys, said to the Vaudois that the king commanded them immediately to embrace Catholicism. Three days were allowed them for deliberation. But they did not need long time. "Let them prove to us," said they, "that our doctrines are not agreeable to the word of God, and we are ready to abandon them; otherwise, let them not ask us for any abjuration." "We are not here to enter into any discussion," replied the commissioners, "but to know if you are ready to become Catholics; yes or no." "No!" said the Vaudois.

Thereupon, by an edict of the 22d of March, 1557, forty-six of the principal of them were summoned to appear at Turin on the 29th of the same month, under pain of a fine of 500 crowns of gold for each who should disregard the citation. All disregarded it. A month after, new summonses were sent to some of those who had been cited before, and to all the pastors and schoolmasters without exception. This time, also, they refused to attend. The syndics were ordered to apprehend them, but no one durst lay a hand upon them.

About this time Spain and England declared war against France, and the Swiss cantons interposed their influence with Henry II., in favour of the Vaudois. These events suspended the proceedings against them; and they hastened to profit by the intermission, to prepare a code of ecclesiastical discipline, which was formally adopted on the 13th of July, 1558.

In the following year Emmanuel Philibert was restored to the enjoyment of his dominions.[1] On the 9th of July, 1559, he

---

[1] With the exception of Turin, Pignerol, and some other towns, which were given up to him from 1562 to 1574. In 1564, the Bernese restored to him the Pays de Gex, which they had seized in 1536, but retained the Pays de Vaud.

espoused the sister of Henry II., who was favourable to Protestantism; and in the commencement of his reign he showed a friendly disposition towards the inhabitants of the Vaudois valleys, whose valour and loyalty were both well known to him.

But the prelates, the nuncio, the King of Spain, and some of the princes of Italy, at the instigation, as Gilles says, of certain gentlemen of the valleys,[1] so plied the good prince on all hands with their solicitations, that he began by forbidding all who did not belong to the Vaudois valleys from going to hear sermon there.[2] And thereupon commissioners were named, to see that the reformed worship was not celebrated beyond the prescribed limits of these mountains. At their head was no less a personage than Philip of Savoy, the cousin of the reigning duke, who assumed the appellation of Count of Racconis; with him was the Count of La Trinité, whose proper name was George Coste, and the grand inquisitor of Turin, by name Thomas Jacomel. Gilles, who is usually so reserved in his expressions, says of him, that he had the reputation of being an apostate, and a shameless and insatiable plunderer of what belonged to others.

The most really noble of these three personages soon withdrew from the bloody course which they thought fit to open up for the triumph of Catholicism; for it was by their hands that so many stakes were at that time erected, and that the flame of so many piles illustrated the devotedness of our martyr fathers. It was at that time, also, that the valleys of Mathias, Larche, and Méane were so cruelly assailed, of which notice will fall to be taken in the history of Pragela, as well as those of Saluces and Barcelonnette, of which we have already spoken. Amidst such a series of persecutions, it could not fail, ere long, to come to the turn of the Vaudois valleys also. But, forgetful of their own dangers, they were forward in endeavouring to avert those of their brethren. The representations, petitions, and supplications which the Vaudois at that time addressed to the sovereign,[3] in favour of their persecuted brethren, had no effect but to attract attention to their own church, which till then had been spared.

The year 1560 commenced in the valleys with violent earthquakes.[4] At this date, also, the monks of the abbey of Pignerol had

[1] There are letters extant of Count William of Lucerna, showing his participation in this hostility. There are also others of Count Charles, which exhibit him, on the contrary, as the zealous protector of the Vaudois.

[2] Edict dated at Nice, 15th February, 1560.

[3] See on this point the twelfth chapter of Gilles.

[4] The first of these took place on the 8th of February, at four o'clock in the morning, the second on the 13th of April, in the afternoon.

in their pay a troop of plunderers; and, in the words of Crespin, "they sent them out to pillage, beat, and kill the poor people, and to bring prisoners to the abbey, both men and women, of whom some were most cruelly burned alive, and others sent to the galleys, and some few released for a ransom. Those who escaped from their prisons were so sick that they seemed to have been poisoned."[1]

The valley of St. Martin was laid waste by the seigneurs of Le Perrier, named Charles and Boniface Truchet.[2] In the preceding year they had already attempted to seize the minister of Rioclaret (*the valley of the clear stream*). Whilst he was preaching, they had sent to the place of worship traitors, who, under the guise of simple hearers, were to gather around the minister, and lay hold of him. These hireling villains were at their post. Charles Truchet arrived at the gates of the place of worship with his proud and well-armed troop. He sounded the clarion; his secret emissaries rushed upon the pastor, and endeavoured to drag him away. All the people flew to defend him. The troop attempted to carry the church by assault, but was repulsed; its leader, although of great stature, vigorous, and armed with mail, was in danger of losing his life, for one of these robust mountaineers having got into combat with him, and squeezed him up against a tree, could easily have choked him; but because of his rank, says Gilles, and from motives of humanity, he let him go.

Instead of being thankful, his hostility only grew. Thus it is with base natures. On the 2d of April, 1560, before daylight, he returned to Rioclaret with a troop more numerous than the former, broke open the doors, killed the inhabitants, and ravaged the whole hamlet. But the cries of his first victims wakened their neighbours, who fled without clothes, without provisions, and without arms, to the peaks of the mountains, still covered with snow. "The enemy," says Richard,[3] "pursued these poor people far up into the woods, firing many shots at them with their arquebuses: afterwards they came back to the deserted houses, took up their lodgings there, and made themselves comfortable, whilst those to whom the houses and provisions belonged were suffering from hunger and cold: they even asserted loudly that they would not permit them to return, at least until they should promise to go to mass."

Next day an aged pastor, recently come from Calabria, made an

[1] Crespin, fol. 535, second page.
[2] They are designated, in some documents, as seigneurs of Rioclaret, a commune quite close by Le Perrier.
[3] *Hist. persec. ad pop. Vald. ab anno* 1555, *usque ad* 1561.—Translation of MDLXII., pp. 47-52.

attempt to visit and encourage these poor fugitives. The troop of Truchet perceived him at daybreak, pursued him, seized him, and delivered him over to the monks of Pignerol, who caused him to be burned alive, with another prisoner from the valley of St. Martin. It is as needless to say that they might have saved their lives by apostasy, as it was needless to propose it to them.

Three days afterwards, however, the Vaudois of Pragela having learned the unhappy condition of their brethren of Rioclaret, assembled, to the number of 400, and resolved upon going to their rescue. Their pastor, named Martin, marched at the head of this troop. From time to time as they advanced, he flung himself upon his knees, with all his men, and prayed to God to give them the victory. Their prayer was heard. The weather was very gloomy, and it was towards evening when they arrived at Rioclaret. The enemy, being apprised of their approach, had made preparations for defence; but a terrible storm, such that the Alps themselves seemed to be shaken when it burst upon their peaks, poured its fury upon the mountain at the moment when the action commenced. After an obstinate combat, the band of Truchet was driven from its positions, and pursued into the ravines, where the soldiers wandered in the midst of the night, and for the second time the unjust aggressor had difficulty in making his escape.

Hereupon Truchet repaired to Nice, where Philibert then held his court, for the city of Turin had not yet been given up to him. "The Vaudois," he said to him, "are rebels; they bring foreign troops into your dominions," (alluding to that band which came from Pragela, in the kingdom of France,) "and they are constructing places of security on the mountains."

A miserable stronghold, indeed, was that to which they had been obliged to retire amidst the snow, half-naked, and without arms or provisions! But the duke could not know these particulars: he was in bad health, and very irritable; and the Truchets counted on his wrath. Yielding, therefore, to their perfidious suggestions, he authorized them to rebuild the fortifications of Le Perrier, which had been destroyed by the French before the restitution of that place,[1] and to burden the Vaudois with compulsory labour. The Vaudois addressed respectful remonstrances to their sovereign; the seigneurs of Le Perrier returned to Nice to counteract the effect of them; and during a pleasure excursion which they made upon the sea, they were carried off by corsairs, and are no more mentioned in history.[2]

[1] These fortifications were demolished in 1534, or thereabout.
[2] They were believed for a long time to be dead; but they made their appearance again, after having been obliged to pay 400 crowns of gold for their ransom.

Whilst these things were taking place in the valley of St. Martin, the duke's cousin, the Count of Racconis, had proceeded to that of Lucerna. One day, in the month of April, he ascended to Angrogna, and listened in silence to the sermon of the minister. After the conclusion of the service, he expressed a desire to see the proceedings against the Vaudois terminated. To take advantage of these friendly feelings, the Vaudois sent to him a particular exposition of their doctrines, with three petitions, one addressed to the Duchess of Savoy, another to the duke, and the third to his council.

Six weeks after, towards the end of the month of June, the Count of Racconis returned to Angrogna with the Count of La Trinité. The syndics and pastors being assembled, these commissioners demanded of them whether they would make any opposition to the duke's causing mass to be sung in their parish. They said, "No, if we are not obliged to go to it." "If the duke send you ministers who shall preach to you the word of God in purity, will you hear them?" "Yes; if that word itself be not taken from us." "In that case, will you consent to send away your present pastors, under reservation of a right to recal them, if those who shall be given you shall not appear to you to be evangelical?" The Vaudois having asked time to reflect upon this question until the morrow, replied that they could not resolve to send away their present pastors, whom they already knew to be evangelical, in order to receive others who might not be so. This was too reasonable to admit of being answered; accordingly the commissioners, without attempting to answer it, harshly ordered the Vaudois to send away their ministers without further remarks. In vain the syndics mildly set forth that they had always found them of sound doctrine and holy life, and that they could not expel them without a cause. "They are enemies of the prince," replied the Count of La Trinité, "and you will expose yourselves to great dangers in keeping them among you."

The two noble lords then retired without any act of violence; but all the adversaries of the Vaudois redoubled their insolence towards them. The mercenaries of the abbey of Pignerol, in particular, carried on a lawless course of infuriate violence, and it was at this time that they seized the pastor of St. Germain, whose martyrdom has been already related.

"In the month of June," says Crespin, "at the time when the harvest is reaped in Piedmont, a number of the Vaudois people having gone, according to their custom, to work in the plain as reapers for hire, to earn a little, they were all made prisoners at different places and times, without their knowing anything one of another; but by the goodness of God they all escaped from their prisons, as if by miracle. Then came the harvest time in the mountains in the month of July, and the people of Angrogna, being one morning in their *muandas* or summer huts [*chalets*], in the neighbourhood of St. Germain, heard some arquebuse shots in the direction of that place; and a little after they perceived a troop of plunderers, to the number of 120, who were advancing towards them. Hereupon they immediately shouted, to give notice to their brethren, and being all assembled, they formed themselves into two troops of fifty men each, the one of which went higher up, and the other lower down upon the mountain. The latter were the first to rush upon the rascally company, who were all loaded and encumbered with booty, and they put them to flight, and pursued them to the banks of the Clusone, where the half of them were drowned." If the men of Angrogna had chosen then to pursue the fugitives, they might have seized upon the abbey buildings, and delivered all their brethren who were prisoners, for the monks had fled to Pignerol; but they could not venture to do it without consulting their pastors, and thus the opportunity was lost.

A few days after, the commandant of Fossano retired into this abbey, after a polemical conference with the Vaudois pastors; and from thence he sent and seized a number of poor people of Campillon and Fenil, with their families and their cattle. Their brethren, alarmed, took to flight. Upon this one of the seigneurs of Campillon offered them his protection, and assured them that they would be left in quiet, if they would pay him thirty crowns. They gave the money, and remained in their abodes. And who was it that then betrayed them? The same gentleman who had caused them to pay him to be their protector, and who now promoted their apprehension. But being warned in time, they took to flight again, and so escaped from that treachery.[1]

Meanwhile the Duke of Savoy had transmitted to Rome the statement of their doctrines which the Vaudois had sent him. As they offered to abandon their doctrines if they were proved to be erroneous, and as they had never ceased to invoke discussion for this intent, it appeared only fair to commence thereby. But as this involved a question strictly ecclesiastical, it was necessary to consult the head of the church, and the pontifical decision did not arrive at Nice till near the end of June. "I will never permit," said Pius IV., "that points which have been canonically decided should be opened to discussion. The dignity of the church requires

---

[1] All these particulars are taken from Crespin, fol. 536, 537.

that every one submit himself to her constitutions, disputing nothing; and the duty of my office is to proceed with all rigour against those who do not choose to be in subjection thereto." The pope would consent only to send to the valleys a legate, who might absolve from all their past crimes those who should become Catholics, and instruct them in their new duties *without controversy*, that is to say, without their examining for themselves.

Accordingly, the governor of Fossano, by name Poussevin, was commissioned by Emmanuel Philibert, on the 7th of July, 1560, to establish in the Vaudois churches certain of the *Brethren of Christian doctrine*, under whose influence intellectual servility would soon have brought about that precious submission so necessary to the Church of Rome.

Poussevin repaired in the first place to the castle of Cavour, situated upon a solitary eminence, like a verdant pyramid in the midst of the plain, opposite to the valley of Lucerna. The castle belonged at that time to the Count of Racconis, who happened also to be there. The Vaudois were invited to send representatives thither. They named three, and one of them was chosen from Bubiano, a town situated close by the gates of Cavour. This one was the notary Reinier, father-in-law of Bartholomew Coupin, one of the martyrs whose story has been already told. On their arrival at Cavour, the governor acquainted them with his commission, and demanded if they would consent to hear the sermons which he proposed to preach in the valleys. "Yes," they replied, "if you preach the word of God; but if you preach the human traditions, which bring it to nought, No." Poussevin did not seem to be offended at this frankness and energy, and replied that he would preach only the pure gospel.

But during this conference, a Vaudois of St. Germain had complained to the Count of Racconis, that the people of Miradol had carried away his cattle, and had promised to return them to him upon payment of 100 crowns, which he had scraped together with great difficulty. "And have you sent them to them?" "Yes; but they have kept both the cattle and the money." "I commend you to Poussevin, said the count;" "he will give you full and prompt justice." "You are an ill-bred fellow," said Poussevin, in reply to the poor man's request, "and if you had gone to mass, this would never have happened to you. And I can tell you," he added, "that this is only the commencement of what is in store for heretics." Such were the first proofs of justice and of pure evangelical doctrine, given by the representative of the throne and of the church.

This governor, however, had a great reputation for eloquence, and doubtless supposed that his power of oratory, together with the assistance of the secular arm, would procure him the honour of a ready triumph over the consciences of these poor, good-natured Vaudois, who suffered themselves to be so easily duped. Having therefore announced that he would preach at Cavour next day, to set forth in public the object of his mission, he ascended the pulpit of the largest church in the town, and said, in substance, that he was about to convict all the Vaudois pastors of heresy, to expel them, and to re-establish the mass in the valleys. Two days after he went to Bubiano, where he added terrible threats against the obstinate, and splendid promises for those who should abjure—new auxiliary means, of which he began to feel the need. The Protestants of Bubiano, who formed one-half of the population, were not moved; but the Catholics, their neighbours and friends, with whom they had always lived upon good understanding, actuated both by religious zeal and by natural affection, strongly urged them at once to become Catholics, in order to avoid the calamities with which they were threatened.

This, however, was only the prelude to scenes still more remarkable. Poussevin, having come to St. John, invited the leading members of the Vaudois churches to have a conference with him. The conference took place in the Protestant church of Les Stalliats. "Here," he said, "is the commission which has been given to me;" and he caused the ducal letters patent to be read, from which he derived his authority. "Here now," he said, "is the statement of doctrines presented as on your part; do you acknowledge it?" On their replying that they did, he asked them if they adhered to the sentiments which it contained. "We have seen no reason," said they, "to change them." "Well, then," said he, "you are bound by this paper to repudiate your errors so soon as they shall be proved to you." "And we promise it again," said they. "If that be the case," said he, "I will prove to you that the mass is to be found in the Holy Scripture. Does not the word *massah* signify *sent?*" "Not exactly." "Was not the primitive expression, *Ite, missa est*, employed to send away the audience?" "That is true." "You see, then, gentlemen, that the mass is to be found in the Holy Scripture."

Never did a novice of an advocate, thinking to catch his adversary by arguments from which there was no escape, make a more ridiculous conclusion. But, alas! it had been well if such sophistical quirks had not led to frightful massacres!

The Vaudois, however, respectfully replied that he had made a mistake as to the term *massah*, which was not to be found in the Hebrew text with the sense which he had assigned to it ;[1] and that, moreover, if it were, it would not prove the Divine institution of the mass; also that private masses, transubstantiation, the denial of the cup to the laity, and many other things which were in dispute between them, would by no means be justified by such a line of argument. "You are heretics, atheists, and damned," cried Poussevin in a sort of frenzy; "I have not come to hold discussions with you, but to drive you out of the country as you deserve." This contemptible and coarse reply confounded the hearers, who had accompanied the governor because of the renown of his learning and eloquence, and caused the blood to rush into their cheeks. The governor, however, immediately caused notification to be made to the syndics of the several communes of the valley, that they must expel the pastors, and provide for the maintenance of the priests who should be sent to them. The syndics replied that they would not send away their pastors unless they were convicted of errors in behaviour or doctrine, and that they would make no provision for the maintenance of those of whom he spoke as coming, unless they were equally irreproachable in doctrine and morals.

It was upon this that Poussevin retired into the abbey of Pignerol, as has been stated in the commencement of this chapter. There he passed the month of August, and composed a polemical work, which was refuted by the celebrated and learned Scipio Lentulus, then pastor at St. John, and afterwards one of the pillars of the Evangelical Church of the Grisons.

In the beginning of September, 1560, Poussevin quitted Pignerol to go to Emmanuel Philibert, who was always in bad health and irritable; and before him brought the most odious and calumnious accusations against the Vaudois. They, being informed of this, addressed new protestations to the duke, through the intervention of the good Duchess Margaret, the daughter of Francis I., and that of Renée of France, who had just arrived in Piedmont on her way home to her own country. She was the daughter of Louis XII., and had now for a year been the widow of Hercules II., Duke of Ferrara, in which city she had at a former period attended the preaching of Lentulus, who was of Neapolitan origin. He wrote to her to say that he had found in the Vaudois valleys "a people strongly attached to the true religion, faithful to God and to their superiors, and of exemplary life, but cruelly persecuted in these difficult times; wherefore he prayed her to recal to mind the favour which she used to have for him, and to intercede with their

[1] The Hebrew word *massah* signifies a *burden*, appointed or actual.

highnesses of Savoy on behalf of this poor people." But all these efforts remained fruitless.

The beginning of the month of October, 1560, had now come. The nuncio and the prelates strongly insisted upon the duke's complying with the instructions of the holy father. Why consult him if his decision was not to be respected? It was to aggravate the wrong which the church had already endured by the increase of heretics. The argument was correct. Rome is logical: the deference which had been shown was an acknowledgment of her power, and power requires obedience. The Duke of Savoy, therefore, must needs obey.

He levied troops in Piedmont, promised a full pardon to all condemned persons, fugitives from justice, vagabonds and outlaws, who should enrol themselves as combatants against the Vaudois, in whose sight persecuting fanaticism already permitted its triumphant joy to break out. Their friends at a distance repaired to the valleys, to persuade those who were dear to them to leave the scene of danger. The inhabitants of the plain took away the infants which they had sent thither to be nursed. Catholics of kind and humane disposition, who had relatives in the mountains, entreated those whom they loved to abjure rather than suffer themselves to be destroyed. It seemed that all was on the point of being consumed in a total and inevitable destruction. The consternation was general.

Count Charles of Lucerna, at that time governor of Mondovi, repaired in person to Angrogna, and wrote several times to the Vaudois, to whom he was strongly attached, to persuade them to bend to circumstances, and to submit to the commands of their sovereign, were it only for love of him and of their own families. "Worthy Sir," they replied, "we must, above all, do that which the love of God and of truth directs us." However, a deputation was sent to him by the Vaudois, to thank him for the interest which he took in their fate. "If you will consent," said he, "to send away your pastors, at least whilst this storm shall last, I will go and cast myself at the feet of his highness, to try if I can save you." "We are deeply impressed with your great kindness," they replied, "but we are not empowered to make any such engagement in name of our people." "Ah, well!" he said, "go and consult them, and we will try to reconcile your preservation and your faith."

It was agreed that the reply of the people should be conveyed to him by Peter Boulles of Bubiano, the brother of him of whom mention has already been made in the history of the Protestants of that town. But without waiting for the return of that emissary, Count Charles wrote immediately to his mother, that she should do everything in her power to incline the Vaudois to some apparent concessions. The countess, in her turn, wrote to them, and they replied, that having stated to the Duke of Savoy all that their consciences permitted them to do according to the word of God, they were resolved not to change what they had said. "If the circumstances in which we are placed are serious," said they, "our duties are still more serious. The times may change, but the Bible never changes, and our consciences cannot be altered."

The countess transmitted this reply to her son, who left Mondovi, and came himself to Lucerna, on the 22d of October. He immediately caused the principal inhabitants of Angrogna to be called before him — Rivoire, Odin, Frache, Monastier, Malan, Appia, Buffa, Bertin, and some others. He found fault with them, reprimanded them, exhorted, menaced, showed them that an army was already mustered, and quite prepared to proceed to the greatest severities against them; he conjured them not to be obstinate and to incur certain death; to pay some respect to the attachment which he felt for them, to the compassion with which he was filled, to the urgency which he employed; he even entreated them to send away their pastors. "Is your fate inseparable from that of these men?" he added, in conclusion. "No, certainly, we are not slaves to any man, but to the word of God; our pastors are dear to us, but the word of God alone is necessary to us; let them allow us ministers who preach it, and we will send away those who at present teach it to us." "And if the duke cause mass to be celebrated in your parts, what will you do?" "We will not attend it." After urging them, in vain, to obtain some further concession, the count caused these conditions to be written down.

The deputies retired. Some hours after, the report spread rapidly that they had consented to the expulsion of their pastors and the establishment of the mass. The people of Angrogna were furious. "Rather let us die!" they exclaimed; and pressing like a swelling sea around the astonished deputies, they demanded an explanation. It was given, but was not at all in accordance with the minute of conference already mentioned, which, upon examination, was found to be falsified.

It was the secretary's fault, the count said; but his church had accustomed him to *pious frauds*, another invention of Catholicism, like religious wars: the impious combinations of words are characteristic of Catholicism itself as a whole! And the good seigneur had thought he might allow himself to employ one of these pious frauds in order to save the Vaudois.

But they had no thought of saving themselves at such a price. The papers were torn in pieces, and the martyr people declared that they could not make any change in their resolutions.

"Let your pastors at least go and hide themselves for a few days," said the count again; "they will come and celebrate mass at Angrogna; you will not attend it; the duke will be satisfied, and the armies will be withdrawn." "But why this hypocrisy?" rejoined these poor people; "must we do good as men do evil, concealing it? No! may God protect us! we will not be ashamed of his ministers, for then he would be ashamed of us."

The count, Gilles says, manifested much grief at the prospect of the miseries which he foresaw. The Vaudois thanked him with great feeling for all that he had done, and assured him of their attachment and respect, but they retired without yielding anything.

CHAPTER II.

HISTORY OF THE SECOND GENERAL PERSECUTION WHICH TOOK PLACE IN THE VAUDOIS VALLEYS.[1]

(A.D. 1560 TO A.D. 1561.)

The army under the command of the Count De La Trinité marches against the Vaudois—Its excesses even against adherents of the Church of Rome—Remarkable proof of the estimation in which the morality of the Vaudois was held—First skirmishes—Successive defeats of the Count De La Trinité—Attempted negotiation—The Count De La Trinité visits the Pra-du-Tour—His perfidy—Combats—Cruelties—A large sum extorted from the Vaudois to secure the withdrawal of the invading army—Further treachery—The Vaudois send their pastors to Pragela—Outrages and horrible atrocities—Unsuccessful deputation to the Duke of Savoy—The Vaudois swear a covenant in the Val Cluson—They adopt measures for more effective resistance—Partial contests, in which the Vaudois are successful—They take Le Villar—Their *Flying Company*—Further defeats of the assailants—Treacherous attempt to engage the Vaudois in negotiations, and to attack them by surprise—Final defeat of the Count De La Trinité, and terms of peace granted to the Vaudois.

WAR was therefore declared. The Vaudois families made haste to gather together the things most indispensable for subsistence, and to retire with their flocks to the fastnesses of the high mountains. The pastors everywhere redoubled their zeal and fervour. The religious assemblies were never more largely attended. The

[1] AUTHORITIES.—The same as in the chapter preceding.

army approached. It was about the end of October. The Vaudois valleys set apart a time for fasting and prayer. After these solemnities, an extraordinary celebration of the Lord's Supper took place, which united all the persecuted in one act of holy fellowship. Thus, without fear or weakness, but encouraging one another, did "these poor people," as Gilles says, "prepare, with incredible resolution and cheerfulness, to receive from the hand of God all the afflictions to which it might seem good to him to subject them. Nothing was to be heard from vale to mountain but the psalms and hymns of those who transported the sick, the infirm, the aged, the women and children, to the securest retreats of their rocks." "So that for eight days," adds Richard, "you could see nothing but people passing and repassing on these rugged paths, diligently bearing luggage and little articles of furniture; as in the summer time the ants incessantly run and travel hither and thither, storing away provisions against the evil days; and amongst these worthy people none regretted his property, so resolute were they to await patiently all the good pleasure of God." The advice of their pastors had even been not to defend themselves by weapons of war, but merely to retire to a place where they might be safe from attack.

The Count of Racconis, Philip of Savoy, who came at this time to the valleys, wrote to his uncle, Philibert, saying, "These unhappy people persist in their opinions, but they are not willing to take up arms against their sovereign; some of them are going away from the place, others courageously await martyrdom in the midst of their families—a marvellous sight, and very piteous to behold."[1]

Three days after, a proclamation was published and put up in all the villages of Angrogna, to the effect that all would be destroyed by fire and sword if the Vaudois did not return to the Church of Rome. Next day, being the 1st of November, 1560, the army commenced its march, under the orders of George Coste, Count of La Trinité, and encamped at Bubiano. Hastily recruited, and its ranks filled up with adventurers, it wanted discipline; the soldiers gave themselves up to all sorts of excesses, and began to pillage before they had fought. Believing themselves already in the country of the Vaudois, they made Catholics and Protestants indiscriminately the subjects of their outrages. The former, there-

---

[1] This letter is dated 23th October, 1560. The following are its words:—*Persistono nella loro opinione, ma non vogliono pigliar l'armi contra di lui. Alcuni se n'andarono; altri aspettando il martirio con moglia, robba, e gran compassione.* Turin, . . . &c. Archives of State. Correspondence of Em. Philibert. (Communicated by M. Cibrario.)

fore, desiring to secure the maidenly chastity of their daughters from the brutal grossness of that lawless soldiery, did a thing worthy of the most admired times. Knowing the rigid purity of the morals of the Vaudois, the strength of their fastnesses, and the devotedness of those who were to defend them, they saw no refuge for their children more safe than these very retreats, and did not hesitate to confide the honour of their families to the virtuous fidelity of the Vaudois cottages. Accordingly, many of them took their trembling wives and children, and left them amongst these heroic mountaineers.

It was surely wonderful to see these young Catholic women committed with confidence to the care of the Protestants, at the moment when Catholicism was marching in arms against them. But this confidence was not misplaced. The Vaudois defended the sacred charge which had been intrusted to them with as much courage and respect as their own families. Without for a moment entertaining the thought of making precious hostages of these young people who were in their hands, and of taking advantage of the circumstance against their adversaries, they generously exposed themselves in their defence, concealing them instead of exposing them to danger; and after having preserved them from outrage, they restored them to their friends, without dreaming of any recompense. Incredible as this fact may appear, all the historians of the times, Gilles, Richard, De Thou, and Crespin make mention of it; and it affords the most beautiful testimony which their adversaries could have rendered to the virtue and generosity of the Vaudois.

On the 2d of November the whole army crossed the Pélis, and encamped in the meadows of St. John. Thereafter it advanced towards Angrogna, extending its wings over all the hills of the Costières. Many skirmishes took place along this great line. The advantage was nearly equal upon both sides; but the little parties left by the Vaudois for defence, found themselves too far separate from each other to act with vigour. They retired, therefore, still defending themselves, to the more and more confined *plateaux* of the mountain. Many of them had only slings and cross-bows.

But the enemy still ascended. This succession of partial engagements had only retarded them, and made them spend the whole day upon the march. On both sides fatigue began to be felt. Evening was come. The Vaudois were now united on the summit of the Costières, towards Rochemanant. There they halted and ceased to retreat. The enemy coming forward, paused when near them, a little way below, and kindled their bivouac fires, to pass the night there. The mountaineers, on the contrary, fell on their

THE PERSECUTORS REPULSED.

knees, to give thanks to God and to renew their prayers. This act gave occasion to a multitude of railleries and sarcasms in the ranks of their persecutors. Just at this time a Vaudois child, who had got hold of a drum, suddenly began to make a noise with it in a ravine close by. Supposing that a hostile troop had arrived, the Catholic soldiers sprung up in disorder, and seized their arms. The Vaudois, witnessing this movement, imagined that an attack was to be made, and rushed forward to repel it. Hereupon the troops, fatigued and surprised, gave way; they were pursued; they disbanded; and the night preventing them from recognizing one another, or discerning the way, the soldiers took to flight at hazard; the foremost were frightened at the sound of the feet of those who followed them; they flung away their arms, and never halted till they reached the plain, abandoning in one hour all the ground that they had gained by the day's march. But upon their arrival at the base of the mountain, they set fire to a number of houses. In this affair the Vaudois had only three killed and one wounded Having re-ascended to the field of battle, they rendered thanks to the Lord for this deliverance, and bore to Pra-du-Tour the arms of their enemies.

Next day the Count of La Trinité, having rallied his forces, encamped at La Tour, repaired the fortifications which had been demolished, and placed a garrison there; but his troops conducted themselves so outrageously in that town, that there also the Catholics of the place sent their wives and daughters amongst the Vaudois. The little fortresses of Le Villar, in the valley of Lucerna, and of Perouse and Le Perrier, in the valley of St. Martin, were also garrisoned with soldiers.

On Monday, the 4th of November, a detachment issued from La Tour, and having been joined on the way by the garrison of Le Villar, which had just been driven back from the Combe, proceeded to attack Le Taillaret. The Vaudois seeing these troops of the enemy coming upon them, fell upon their knees, according to the custom of their fathers upon all great occasions; and according to the promise of God, that he will not forsake any who wait upon him, they received a spirit of strength and courage which made them victors. Voluntarily allowing themselves to be first attacked by their adversaries, that they might not, even in a single instance, be the aggressors, they firmly awaited them on the rocks, from which a hail-storm of stones and balls soon repelled the assailants. But the latter returned to the charge; the Vaudois resisted them; the combatants became furious; the more disciplined troop regained the advantage; when suddenly there arrived from the heights of La Fontanelle fresh combatants, by whom a portion of that troop had already been repulsed. They joined their brethren, who soon again had the best of the combat; the enemy gave way and disbanded; and the Vaudois pursued the fugitives, who uttered many cries and blasphemies on the subject of their rout; but on the noise of the firing, a reinforcement of fresh troops came up from La Tour, who took the Vaudois in the rear. These brave mountaineers faced to both sides, forming themselves into two bodies, of which the one engaged the new-comers, whilst the other completed the rout of the first assailants; this done, the two bodies reunited, and rushing at once upon their adversaries, passed through the midst of them, without leaving one of their number in their hands. In this combat they had only four killed and two wounded; their enemies, according to Richard, bore away whole cart-loads of their killed and wounded.

On the evening before, however,[1] the Count of La Trinité had sent a young lad to Angrogna, with a letter, in which he pretended that he had learned, with great regret, of the collisions of the preceding day. "My troops," he said, "had no object but to go to Angrogna, in order to ascertain if it were a place favourable for the construction of a fortress for the service of his highness and the defence of the country; but having encountered military posts and armed men, they thought themselves defied, and I am greatly grieved at the conflicts which ensued, as well as at the burning of the houses by my soldiers." The treacherous villain concluded by proposing an arrangement.

"It is matter of great regret to us also," replied the people of Angrogna, "to find ourselves assailed without cause by the troops of our lawful prince, to whom we have always been faithful and obedient. As to an arrangement, if it has for its object to convince us of error, by discussion and not by arms, we willingly agree to it; but if it be meant that we should sacrifice in it the honour of God and the salvation of our souls, it is better for us to die all together rather than consent to it." At the same time that they sent this reply, the Vaudois, readily foreseeing what reception it would meet with, despatched a messenger to their brethren of Pragela, to entreat them to come to their aid.

Their letter, however, having been presented to the Count of La Trinité, he did not seem to take the least offence at it, and demanded that the inhabitants of Angrogna should send deputies to confer with him. He received them very graciously, told them that the Duchess of Savoy was favourable to their brethren, and

[1] Sunday, 3d November, 1560.

that the duke himself had uttered in his hearing the following words: "It is in vain that the pope, the Italian princes, and even my council, urge me to exterminate that people; I have taken counsel with God in my heart, and he urges me still more strongly not to destroy them."

Real or fictitious, these words were to be made good. But it does not appear that this was the intention of the Count of La Trinité; for whilst these negotiations were going on, not only did his troops attack Le Villar and Le Taillaret, but scaling the heights of Champ-la-Rama, they endeavoured to cross the mountain which separates the valley of Lucerna from that of Angrogna, in order to gain the bottom of the latter, and to seize upon the Pra-du-Tour, to which a great part of the Vaudois families had retired. These troops, having set fire to some barns, were observed, and were repulsed, as Gilles says, by a valiant combat. A few days after,[1] their general caused word to be carried to Angrogna, that if the Vaudois would lay down their arms he would go with a few attendants to have a mass celebrated at St. Laurence,[2] and would thereafter employ himself in endeavours to obtain peace for them.

The Vaudois spent a whole night in deliberating whether or not they ought to consent to this. But the desire of showing a pacific disposition—of giving no pretext for the violence of their enemies, and perhaps of not suffering a favourable opportunity to escape for putting an end to this war—induced them to accept the proposal. The Count of La Trinité came, caused mass to be celebrated without compelling anybody to be present, and then expressed a desire to visit that famous place, the Pra-du-Tour. It was difficult to refuse this privilege to the general of an army; but he was requested to leave his soldiers at St. Laurence, to which he consented. Pra-du-Tour is the place where the ancient Vaudois had the school of their Barbas, the secret source of those vivifying missions which they sent to both extremities of Italy. It is not situated on a height, but in a deep recess amongst the mountains. It is the bottom of a valley, savage and austere as the peaks of the Alps, remote from observation, and free from bustle as a nook of the forest. The steep mountain-slopes bring down into this deep dell the head-waters of the torrent of Angrogna, which escapes amongst the rocks. This verdant basin, surrounded with frightful precipices, seems a dark crater yawning at the feet of the traveller

---

[1] On Saturday, 9th November.
[2] The name of the principal village of that valley. At the present day it is commonly known by the simple name of Angrogna; but the Catholic church there is still called by the name of St. Laurence.

who views it from the lofty peaks, and looks like an oasis in the desert when he has descended into it. A difficult path, which winds among and around the rocks, is the only outlet by which visitors can enter or depart from it.

By this path the Count of La Trinité did not hesitate to proceed thither. The more and more savage aspect of the mountains filled him with a sort of dread as he advanced. During the whole journey he showed much kindness, consideration, and affability to the Vaudois, who surrounded him with demonstrations of honour. On arriving at the spot he manifested much emotion.

But during his absence his soldiers plundered the Vaudois cottages. The people became irritated; the general hastily returned by the way by which he had gone. At Serres he encountered a soldier who had just stolen a hen, and caused him to be hanged upon the spot. But at St. Laurence, when he was again in the midst of his troops, he inflicted no punishment on those who had pillaged the houses. He immediately led them back to La Tour, and left his secretary at Angrogna to receive the petition, which he himself had undertaken to present to the sovereign. In this petition the Vaudois assured him of their loyalty, and supplicated him to leave them liberty of conscience, that his own might not be charged with their death, before the judgment-seat of God. Vaudois deputies were sent to Verceil to present it to Emmanuel Philibert, who at that time resided there.

After their departure, the Count of La Trinité summoned the Vaudois of Le Taillaret to lay down their arms, no doubt in order that—their mountains being no longer defended—he might accomplish the design which he had formed of getting past the bulwark of the Pra-du-Tour.

The inhabitants of Le Taillaret met at Les Bonnets to deliberate upon this proposition. Meanwhile the enemy, in too great haste to take advantage of it, seized upon their houses, ravaged, plundered, and burned them, and carried off women and children prisoners. The meeting at Les Bonnets, being apprised of what had taken place, rushed to arms, pursued the ravishers, delivered the captives, and then resumed their deliberations. What singular meetings must those have been which were interrupted by such incidents! Scarcely had this meeting been recommenced in that remote hamlet, when the soldiers surrounded it in silence, approached the place in which it was held, suddenly broke into it, and fell upon the members of the little parliament. But they still had their arms, and defended themselves with great energy; the enemy fell back, the Vaudois gained upon them; the conflict extended into a multitude of partial engagements. An aged man was fleeing away; a soldier ran at him brandishing his sword. The old man, kneeling down, seized the soldier by the legs, flung him down, and then rushing into a ravine, dragged the soldier after him, and flung him over a precipice.

Another patriarch of these mountains, a man of 103 years of age, had retired into a cavern with his grand-daughter. A she-goat, concealed along with them, nourished them with its milk. The young woman was singing a hymn one evening; the soldiers heard her, and, guided by the voice, surprised the cavern, and killed the old man; they would then have seized the girl, but she rushed of her own accord over the rocks, to save her honour at the expense of her life.

All the Vaudois from the lower parts of the valley had retired to the mountains. The troops of the Count of La Trinité plundered and wasted the valley without resistance and without mercy. They soon ascended to Le Villar, where some inhabitants still remained, amongst whom they made a number of prisoners. It was here that a soldier of Mondovi uttered that ferocious saying: "I wish to carry home to my own country some of the flesh of the heretics!" and, rushing like a wild beast upon the first whom he encountered, he bit his face, and tore off a morsel of flesh.

The Vaudois, indignant at such acts of violence, went to complain of them to the Count of La Trinité, to whom, however, they still expressed themselves with much moderation. "Is it not customary," said they, "to suspend hostilities during the time of a capitulation? We have laid down our arms in order to show respect to your word, and to our own deputation, by a calm and reserved attitude; but how is your authority respected by the troops? For we have no doubt that it is entirely contrary to your intentions that such excesses are committed against us." The count excused himself, as usual, by hypocritical protestations. "Ah! if I had been there," said he, "these things would not have happened." And he caused the prisoners to be given up, but he retained the booty.

However, partial vexations still continued everywhere. A band of depredators having commenced to pillage some isolated houses of Rocheplate, seventeen men of that commune successfully repelled them.

A traitor, named Vernon, had promised to seize the pastor of La Tour.[1] He followed him from one place of retreat to another, in order to lay hold of him. One day he got sight of him. "*Here!*

[1] By name Claud Bergo.

here!" he cried to his companions, "*we have caught the chicken!*" But a Vaudois, named Cabriol, who accompanied the pastor, flung so heavy a stone at the breast of Vernon, that the scoundrel was knocked down. He was then killed, and cast over a precipice.

The irritation of the Vaudois still increasing, the Count of La Trinité invited them to meet with him again, that they might examine together the conditions of a solid agreement; and he promised to withdraw his troops, if they would engage to pay a sum of 20,000 crowns. "I will get this sum reduced to 16,000," said the worthy secretary of such a master, "if you will give me now a part of that reduction, in testimony of your gratitude." The amount of this testimony of gratitude was fixed at 100 crowns. The Vaudois, therefore, consented to pay 16,000 crowns (about 50,000 francs).[1] The Duke of Savoy remitted the half of it; there remained 24,000 francs which these poor people must raise. But how was this to be done? Their property wasted, their houses burned, their crops destroyed; unable to borrow, because no one would lend to them; uncertain of what might await them in the future, they were reduced to circumstances of overwhelming trial. They had nothing left but their flocks, which they had succeeded in saving from the plunderers. They resolved to sell them. George Coste insisted that these sales should not take place without his consent; and following the example of his secretary, he sold that consent for a price, to certain rich purchasers, who paid him for the monopoly, and finding themselves masters of the market, bought at a low rate these numerous flocks, the last riches of the unhappy Vaudois. And thus the 8000 crowns were paid.

The army ought to have been withdrawn, but it did not move. A petition was addressed to the general. "You must send me all your arms," replied he. Some arms were sent to him. "Now remove your troops," said the Vaudois. "Give me first," said the count, "a bond for other 8000 crowns; for you agreed to pay 16,000, and you have only paid the half." "But the duke," said they, "has exempted us from the rest." "I do not care for that," he replied; "I know only your agreement." The bond for other 24,000 francs was accordingly signed. "Now send away your troops," they said. "Send away your pastors in the first place," said he, "for that is the essential object of my coming."

The Vaudois, driven to despair, perceiving, but too late, the errors into which they had fallen, fearing lest they might injure the success of their deputation, finding themselves disarmed and enfeebled, and hoping that this privation would be only of brief

---

[1] About £2000 sterling.

continuance, consented at last to send away their pastors, resolving to convey them to Pragela, which then belonged to France.

But the mountains were covered with snow; the road by the plain was infested by vagabonds, assassins, and robbers, especially by the armed recruits of the abbey of Pignerol. They resolved to cross the Col Julian. The enemy, being apprised of this decision, appointed an ambuscade to be placed in the neighbourhood of Bobi, where the pastors were to assemble, in order to seize them all at once. But the soldiers arrived too late; the travellers had set out two hours before. Hereupon they plundered and ravaged everything; entering all the houses of the village, causing their doors, and even those of apartments and closets to be opened to them, under pretext of seeing that the pastors were not hidden within, and seizing upon whatever could be an object either of cupidity or of lust.

The pastors, however, had succeeded in crossing the Col Julian. They stopped at Pral, and descending from thence to Macel, and again ascending the Col du Pis, they arrived safe and sound in Pragela.

Only one of their number did not accompany the rest—Stephen Noël, the pastor of Angrogna. Having been called, a few days before, to a conference with the Count of La Trinité, he had been strongly pressed by him to repair to the court of the duke, to defend the cause of his church. "It is to my parish that I belong," replied the pastor, "and I cannot dispose of myself without its consent." And it was well for him that he did not quit it; for a few days after, the perfidious Coste sent a party of soldiers to make him prisoner. Noël perceived them, and retired to the mountain; but his house was plundered, his books and papers were carried to the general, who committed them to the flames; forty other houses were rummaged, and everything valuable which was found in them was carried away. On the same evening the soldiers, provided with flaming torches, searched about on the mountain, in order to find the fugitive pastor. Not having found him, the count next day ordered the syndics of Angrogna to deliver him up under pain of death. The syndics replied that they knew not where he was.

The Vaudois deputation, nevertheless, having reached Verceil, the Count of La Trinité withdrew his army to the plain which extends from Briquièras to Cavour, but left strong garrisons at La Tour, Le Villar, Le Perrier, and Perouse. The Vaudois were required to provide for the sustenance of the garrisons. "We are," said they, "sheep compelled to nourish the wolves which devour them." However, they resigned themselves to their fate; and the syndics of Angrogna having gone to carry victuals and money to the garrison of La Tour, were maltreated and beaten in the most atrocious manner.

A party of this same garrison having, on the next day but one, taken the road to Angrogna, demanded to be supplied with meat and drink at a hamlet composed of a few isolated houses. The inhabitants of this hamlet clubbed together, and despoiling themselves, brought all the best that they had, and themselves served the soldiers in a close court-yard. This inclosure was bounded on one side by the dwelling-house, and on the opposite side by a shed, whilst on the two other sides were walls, in which the entrance gates opened one over against the other. Having well eaten and drunken, the soldiers closed the gates, seized upon the men, bound them one to another, and prepared to carry them away as prisoners. But the women set fire to the shed, and threatened the authors of all the violence, that they would burn them alive, with their victims, if they refused to let them go. They hesitated; a combat ensued; the gates were opened, and the invaders escaped with their prey, the children pursuing them, and throwing stones at them. Ten of the captives succeeded in making their escape, but four were carried to the castle of La Tour. They were afterwards given up, upon payment of a large ransom; but they had been so cruelly maltreated, that one of them died the day after he was set at liberty; and another, half-killed, only survived the torments to which he had been subjected, to endure an incredible prolongation of martyrdom. The flesh had been torn away from his feet and hands by the torturers; it fell off in pieces; the bones of his fingers and his toes then came away one after another, and he remained a cripple all his life. Their executioner was the captain of that garrison, a man named Bauster, the same who, having attempted to surprise the hamlet of Les Bonnets, bore off John and Udolph Geymet, whom he brought to so cruel a death.

I say nothing of the young girls who were detained in these infernal dens; the reader may imagine for himself to what frightful treatment they must have been subjected. The other garrisons left by George Coste, conducted themselves in the same manner, "*and did no better,*" says Gilles, without adding a word of reproach to that expression, so pungent by its laconic simplicity.

Thus passed the year 1560; a bloody autumn, a fatal winter, misery everywhere, bereavement even in the smallest families; but everywhere, also, the invincible energy of a supreme confidence in the Lord; in every dwelling the reading of the Bible and its consolations; the word of life everywhere rising above these cries of death! Such was the picture which the Vaudois valleys then presented.

The deputation which they had sent to Verceil did not return till the commencement of January, 1561. How many hopes had been founded upon it! and how were they deceived! "Scarcely were we arrived at Verceil," said the afflicted deputies, "when the secretary, Gastaud, who accompanied us, and to whom we had already given 100 crowns for the part which he had taken as to the prayer of our petition, snatched that petition out of our hands, and would have us to sign another. Then, instead of giving us a paternal reception, the duke ordered us to prostrate ourselves before him as suppliants—to ask pardon of him for what he called the rebellion of our people. We were compelled, also, to make a like submission to the legate of the Holy See. After we had done all this, we supposed that we might be permitted to return home; but we were still detained for a month and a half, incessantly tormented every day by swarms of monks and priests, who sought to make us go to mass. Finally it was decided that nothing more should be conceded to us than hitherto, and that we should even be deprived of what still remained to us. For all this priestly tribe, this vermin of abbés, and prelates, and monks, left our sovereign no repose, till he would promise to exterminate us all, without sparing so much as one. Accordingly, they are about to send us a multitude of preachers of idolatry, so that we shall no longer have means of subsistence for them; and, in fact, we have seen such troops of monks, and regiments of priests, and crowds of abbés, that there will very soon be no room but for themselves." Such overloading of society with idle priests, indicates the downfall either of the nations which endure it, or of the institutions which produce it.

How overwhelmed, how desolate, in what a posture of discouragement may we now expect to see the whole Vaudois Church! The very opposite was the case. No longer afraid of bringing any evil upon their deputies, who were now returned amongst them— no longer fearing the loss of goods, of which they had already been plundered, nor that they might cause the failure of negotiations for an impossible peace—no longer occupied by any thought of consenting to proposals whose perfidy had been so often demonstrated to them—the Vaudois, feeling more happy in circumstances more unembarrassed, courageously re-installed in each parish the pastor who had been removed from it, rebuilt their places of worship, unanimously agreed upon defensive measures, and everywhere resumed their hymns, their labours, and the accustomed joys and exercises of their Christian life. At the same time, letters came to them from Switzerland and from Dauphiny, by which their brethren in other countries exhorted them not to give way to despondency, but to persevere in courage and prayer, to put all their confidence in God, and not to found their expectations upon men; the brethren in Dauphiny adducing themselves as an example, for the Reformed Church in France was then violently persecuted by the Duke of Guise and the Cardinal of Lorraine. The feeble Francis II., scarcely sixteen years of age, had placed the former at the head of his armies, the latter at the head of his council; and never had religious fanaticism been so powerful; but toleration and the Bible had also illustrious defenders. The Prince of Condé became the leader of the reformed; the Chancellor De L'Hôpital preserved them from the Inquisition by the institution of the Red Chamber [*chambre ardente*], a tribunal erected in connection with the parliaments, and appointed to take cognizance of the crime of heresy. In spite of this, Protestants multiplied in France; why, then, should they be annihilated in Piedmont?

The hearts of men are drawn together by a common danger. The valley of Pragela, which then belonged to Francis II., was threatened with the same calamities as the valley of Lucerna. Then took place one of those solemn and impressive scenes which sometimes elevate modern times to the level of the ages of antiquity, and which seem to be suited rather to poetry than to history, a scene at once heroic and religious, and, above all, grand in its simplicity. A few lines will suffice to describe it.

Deputies from the Val Pélis went to the Val Cluson,[1] in order to renew before God the covenant which had always subsisted among the primitive churches of the Alps. This covenant was sworn by all the people assembled on a platform of snow, over against the mountains of Sestrières and of the chain of Gunivert; where the Cluson takes its rise from the glaciers. Thereafter, the people of Pragela sent delegates and pastors in their turn to the valley of Lucerna. Not being able to follow the ordinary route, by reason of the troops which would have seized them, they traversed mountains rendered almost impassable by the snow which covered them, climbed that of Le Pis, by which they got to Macel, and thence again ascending to Pral, they crossed the Col Julian, in order to proceed to Bobi.

They arrived there on the 21st of January, 1561. The evening

[1] The valley of the Cluson or of Pragela is separated from that of Lucerna or of the Pélis by that of St. Martin or of the Germanasque.

before, proclamation had been made throughout the whole valley that the inhabitants must, within twenty-four hours, make up their minds to go to mass, or to endure all the penalties reserved for heretics—the stake, the galleys, the rack, the gibbet, and all the other corollaries of Catholicism. The expiry of this fatal term coincided precisely with the arrival of the pastors of Pragela. They had just descended to Le Puy, a hamlet of the commune of Bobi, situated on a verdant hill, covered with gigantic chestnuts, at a little distance from the latter village. Without loss of time, the pastor, the elders, the deacons, and the members of the church in Bobi and in the surrounding hamlets, mounted the hill to Le Puy, in order to make known to their newly arrived friends the sad extremities to which they were reduced; and there, says Gilles, after fervent prayers made to God for his counsel and assistance, considering that none of the Vaudois could think of abjuring, and that they had it not in their power to seek refuge elsewhere, and that the purpose of their enemies was absolutely to destroy them, "a thing to which the meanest worm," adds the chronicler, with inimitable artlessness, "will not submit without resistance," an enthusiastic resolution was adopted that they should defend themselves unto death. From that moment dates the commencement of the most glorious campaign which the heroic persecuted ever maintained against fanatical persecutors.

The delegates of Pragela and of the valley of Lucerna, standing up amidst the crowd, whilst emotion and seriousness at once prevailed, pronounced these solemn words:—

"In the name of the Vaudois churches of the Alps, of Dauphiny, and of Piedmont, which are all here united, and whose representatives we are, we here promise, with our hands upon the Bible and in the presence of God, that all our valleys will courageously stand by one another in what relates to religion, without prejudice to the obedience due to their lawful superiors. We promise to maintain the Bible, entire and without admixture, according to the usage of the true Apostolic Church, steadfastly continuing in this holy religion, although it should be at peril of our lives, in order that we may be able to leave it to our children intact and pure, as we have received it from our fathers. We promise aid and succour to our persecuted brethren, and not to regard individual interests, but the common cause, and not to wait upon men, but upon God."

And 130 years later, these same Vaudois, on their return to their valleys, from which they had been expelled by the united arms of Louis XIV. and Victor Amadeus II., renewed, almost in the same place, on the hill of Sibaoud, the oath of the covenant which we have now recorded.

Scarcely had these words been pronounced, when many of those present exclaimed, "We are required to make an ignominious abjuration of our faith to-morrow: come, then, and let us make a striking protestation to-morrow against the persecuting idolatry which comes upon us with such a demand!" The Vaudois had exhausted all methods of patience and forbearance. It was now the time for them to show some energy. Before dawn of the following day, instead of flocking to the mass, they proceeded in a crowd, but with arms in their hands, to the Protestant church, which the Catholics had already crammed with the trumpery pertaining to their worship. Images, candles, and rosaries were presently flung into the street and trodden under foot. The minister, Humbert Artus, gave out a text from Isaiah xlv. 20: "Assemble yourselves and come; draw near together, ye that are escaped of the nations: they have no knowledge that set up the wood of their graven image, and pray unto a god that cannot save." The resolution of the hearers was wrought up to a higher pitch by his powerful and encouraging discourse. They then set out for Le Villar, in order to purge the place of worship there of the gross fetishes of the Romish idolatry. The Christians of the Alps marched that day, singing that hymn of Theodore Beza—

> Loin de nous desormais
> Tous ces dieux contrefaits, . . . &c.[1]

And this iconoclastic zeal was not at that time a puerile act, but an act of true courage, because it was their response, at peril of their lives, to the capital summons, by which it had been attempted to exact the base abandonment of their religion.

The term allowed by this summons was already past; and the garrison of Le Villar had already marched out to make prisoners. The Vaudois of Bobi met it on the way; it attacked them; they defended themselves, repulsed the garrison, and pursued it even under the walls of Le Villar. The monks, the judges, the seigneurs, and the podestat, who had come thither in order to receive the abjuration of the heretics, had scarcely time to shut themselves up with the fugitive soldiers in the menaced fortress! The Vaudois laid siege to it, placed sentinels and posts of observation and defence, fortified themselves also in their turn, and awaited the progress of events.

The garrison of La Tour, arrived next day to deliver the be-

---

[1] Far from us henceforth be
These gods which are no gods, &c.

sieged; the Vaudois routed it in the plain of Teynau. It returned in greater force on the following day, but they repulsed it again. Three bodies of troops advanced upon the fourth day and underwent the same fate. The siege lasted for ten days. The Vaudois made powder for themselves, also mines, casemates, engines for throwing stones, and loopholes in the neighbouring houses, in order to shoot over the bastions of the citadel.

The army of the Count of La Trinité was put in motion for the deliverance of this place; but the besieged were ignorant of the attempts made to rescue them; and the besiegers pressed on the attack with increased vigour. The garrison was speedily reduced to the last extremities. It was in want of provisions and of ammunition, and was obliged to knead bread with wine, for want of water. At last it surrendered, upon condition that the lives of the soldiers should be saved, and that they should be accompanied by two pastors, thus showing, says Gilles, that they put more confidence in these so much-hated ministers, than in any other parties; and the ministers who were granted to them justified this confidence, for the officers of the garrison thanked them, he adds, for their conducting of them safely, with assurance of all possible courtesy, according to opportunity. The fortifications of Le Villar were immediately demolished by the conquerors.

This advantage of the Vaudois caused the Count of La Trinité to pause, and to resolve upon disuniting them, in order to destroy them. For this purpose he made his army to halt betwixt Lucerna and St. John, and began by giving the people of Angrogna to understand that they had nothing to apprehend from him, if they would not mix themselves up with the affairs of the other valleys. But that people, already so often deceived, allowed this message to remain this time unanswered; or rather, gave their answer to it only by increased activity in their preparations for the common defence.

They got ready entrenchments, posts, and signals; they were everywhere busy in the fabrication of pikes or the casting of balls; the best marksmen were united under the name of the *Flying Company*, in order that they might the more promptly repair to any spot to which the approach of danger should call them. Two pastors were appointed to accompany them, in order to prevent excesses, needless bloodshed, and relaxation in attention to religious duties; and before battle, as well as at the dawn and close of each day, they conducted prayers in the midst of the camp. By their strict equity the Vaudois desired to exhibit the righteousness of their cause.

Their most advanced post was that of *Les Sonnaillettes*. It was attacked on the 4th of February, 1561, and the combat continued until night.

Three days after, the army marched upon Angrogna, in many separate columns, which united on a steep and rocky mountain-slope called Les Costes. But they were driven back in confusion by the Vaudois, who occupied the height above, and rolled down rocks among the ranks of the enemy.

Seven days after, on the 24th of February, took place the terrible attack which had already been threatened. The count brought up all his forces, and availed himself of all the resources of strategy. His endeavour was to surprise the Pra-du-Tour, where all the population of Angrogna were assembled, and where they had constructed mills, ovens, houses, and all that was requisite for subsistence, as in a fort. This citadel of the Alps was defended not only by its rocks, but also by heroic combatants. An attempt was made to enter it by Le Taillaret, but the company of Le Villar maintained that passage. Two bodies of troops then advanced, the one by the valley of St. Martin, the other by that of Pragela. Charles Tronchet put himself at the head of the former, along with Louis de Monteil; George Coste commanded the latter. These two troops were intended to fall upon the Pra-du-Tour—the one by the Col du Laouzoun, the other by the Col de la Vachère. On the day appointed for this purpose, a third corps appeared in the lower part of the valley of Angrogna, burning and ravaging everything, in order to draw away the defenders from the principal post, but the stratagem did not succeed. The troop which came by La Vachère making its appearance first, the Vaudois assailed it and put it to flight. They then perceived that of Le Laouzoun, which was descending the mountain with difficulty. They allowed it to get involved amongst the ravines. The guides who went before it, arriving at an opening from which they had a view of the lower part of the valley, exclaimed, "Come down! come down! all Angrogna is in our power!"

"Say, rather, that you are in our power!" replied the Vaudois immediately, and rushed forward from the covering of the rocks. "And they did their duty marvellously well," says Gilles, in relating this occurrence. Nevertheless the enemy, observing their small numbers, made head against them, and endeavoured to surround them. But just then the Vaudois troop, already victorious at La Vachère, arrived with drums beating, and caused a diversion in this conflict by assailing the enemy on the left flank. The soldiers of Tronchet still resisted. "Courage! courage!" exclaimed the *Flying Company*, coming to the help of their Vaudois brethren, and now making their appearance on the right. Thus assailed upon three sides, the enemy thought proper to fall back. But the ascent of the mountain was more difficult than the descent. Three times they wheeled about and attempted to make a resistance; three times they were repulsed and put to flight. At last they were completely thrown into confusion and defeated. Charles Tronchet was knocked down by a stone, and his head was cut off with his own sword. Louis de Monteil, who had made his way back to the northern shoulder of the mountain, in order to descend again into the valley of St. Martin, was also overtaken and killed among the snow.

All the soldiers would have been put to death but for the pastor of the Flying Company, who rushed to the field of battle in order to defend those who no longer defended themselves. "Kill them! kill them!" cried the Vaudois, still excited with the ardour of victory. "To your knees! to your knees!" exclaimed the pastor.[1] "Let us give thanks to the God of armies for the success which he has just granted us."

And like Moses at Meriba, who, during the whole battle of Israel against Amalek, ceased not to keep his arms raised towards heaven to obtain the triumph of his people, the Vaudois families left behind in the Pra-du-Tour had not ceased, all day long, to lift up their prayers to the Lord for his blessing on the arms of their defenders. Their prayer was answered; and that evening the whole place resounded with the praises of God, and with songs of joy and of triumph; whilst from all sides were brought in the arms and the booty taken from their enemies—arquebuses, morions, cuirasses, pikes, swords, poignards, and halberts. Never had these wild rocks been covered with such magnificent trophies.

To avenge this defeat the Count of La Trinité caused the houses of Rora to be burned, the families of which place did not retire till after a long and vigorous resistance. To attain a place of refuge in the valley of Lucerna, these poor fugitives had to go by the mountain of Brouard, which was at that time covered with snow. Night overtook them. They were opposite to Le Villar, but still at a distance from it, though they saw its lights shining on the other side of the valley. Their cries, however, were heard there, and lights were seen in motion; torches were kindled, and their brethren came to meet them; friendly voices responded to theirs. The cries of distress were soon changed into accents of joy and deliverance; sufferers had met with one another, and the outlawed

[1] The pastor was Gilles of Les Gilles.

had found brethren. Before the day dawned the people of Rora were all lodged in the houses of Le Villar.

And now the Flying Company proceeded to drive from their mountain valley the ravagers who still occupied it. But, presuming that the enemy would not lose much time in attacking Le Villar and Bobi, the Vaudois proceeded immediately to erect barricades in the narrowest parts of the valley. These ramparts, raised especially in order to present an obstacle to cavalry, were hastily formed of trees cut down and laid one upon another, between a double row of stakes, which represented the faces of a wall. Amongst the branches of these trees great stones were heaped together, cemented to one another by snow beaten hard and moistened with lukewarm water, so that, being softened for a moment, it again congealed into a solid mass around the stones and branches, the whole forming a wall of one single solid block.

The Count of La Trinité divided his army into three columns; two bodies of infantry were to ascend by the two sides, and the cavalry by the bottom of the valley. A company of pioneers preceded, to level the barricades.

As soon as this movement commenced, the Vaudois advanced by the left bank of the Pélis till they were opposite Les Chiabriols, and fired upon the cavalry as soon as they made their appearance; then, retreating from tree to tree and from rock to rock, they continued to annoy them until they reached the barricades situated beneath Le Villar. There they halted, and united themselves to the ranks of the Flying Company, which defended that post. The day was spent in perpetual combat, now on one point, now on another, of this barricade, without the enemy being able to make a breach in it anywhere. All this while the bodies of infantry had pursued their way along the heights, and towards nightfall they passed the line so heroically defended.

The Vaudois were then obliged to separate into parties in order to repulse these new assailants. The first who appeared had already crossed the torrent of Respart, and commenced to ascend the vine-covered hills which look down upon Le Villar. The Vaudois, by running along the other slope, gained the summit and partly repulsed the enemy in a hand-to-hand conflict. They were still thus engaged when the infantry on the right side, descending above the barricade, attacked in rear the Flying Company, which still defended it. Some inhabitants of the Val Cluson, who belonged to this company, seeing themselves caught betwixt two fires, judged their destruction inevitable, and retired by the only way of escape which was still open to them—the heights of

Drawn by T.C. Dibdin from a sketch by M. Muston. Engraved by W. Wallis.

TOWN OF LE VILLAR.
IN THE VALLEY OF LUCERNA.

BLACKIE & SON, GLASGOW. EDINBURGH & LONDON.

Les Cassarots, by which they gained the Col Julian and made their way home. But the greater number of the Vaudois kept their ground until evening, and then only fell back upon Le Villar.

The cavalry followed them upon the one side and the infantry upon the other. When they reached the village they were joined by those who had just succeeded in driving the enemy from the upper vineyards, and their combined forces made both horse and foot give way before them. But the enemy, as they retired, burned the houses of Le Villar, and fell back upon La Tour after having suffered considerable loss.

Next week (upon the 18th of February), the count returned to the charge and repeated the same manœuvre, but with an increased number of assailants. He commenced a vigorous demonstration in the direction of Le Taillaret, in order to draw off the Vaudois, and to enfeeble them by that diversion. Having now carried away all that they reckoned most valuable to the most elevated of their mountain villages (if that name may be given to some scattered groups of poor dwellings suspended on the flanks of the precipices like the eyries of the eagle), the Vaudois renounced the defence of the lower part of the valley and confined themselves to the heights. The army of the count was, therefore, by and by concentrated in the verdant basin which extends uninterrupted from Bobi to Le Villar. They first attacked the hamlet of Boudrina, or Les Huchoires, situated upon the ledges of projecting rocks, at the summit of a very steep slope covered with vineyards. The Vaudois repulsed two successive assaults without the loss of a man, whilst their assailants left many dead upon the ground. This success of the Vaudois was not only owing to the valour of the men, and to the protection of God, but to the circumstance, that they were able to fire from above upon the enemy, and to shelter themselves from their bullets behind the numerous parapet-formed walls.

A detachment of 1500 men came to support the assailants, and to bring them back to the charge. But the sound of the firing had brought the Flying Company to the scene of combat, who, from the vineyards of Le Villar, really flew to the succour of their brethren. After all, however, it was only a reinforcement of 100 men, and it may easily be conceived that they could not hold their ground against the efforts of 2000. Abandoning, therefore, that perilous post, they retired higher. The remainder of the army, which was stationed in the plain, seeing these 2000 men take possession of the paltry buildings which had been so long disputed, raised shouts of joy, and made flourishes of trumpets to celebrate their victory.

Here let us allow Gilles to speak for a moment. "The Vaudois," says he, "having retired about a stone's cast, cried with one voice to the Lord, and resolutely united for further combat. Those who had not arquebuses made use of their slings, from which they cast a shower of stones upon the enemy. Three times the enemy rested, and three times returned to the assault. When the enemy took breath the people above prayed to God with loud voice, and when the assault was renewed, all of them, crying to God, did their duty marvellously. The women and children supplied stones to the slingers; those who, by reason of infirmity or old age, could do nothing, kept farther up the hill, crying to the Lord with tears and groans that he would succour them."

The succour was not long in coming, for at the third assault a messenger arrived crying, "Courage! courage! God has sent us the men of Angrogna." And the old men on the hill, and the combatants on the field of battle, eagerly took up the cry, "Courage! help is at hand!"

However, the men of Angrogna were not yet there. They were fighting at Le Taillaret, from which they drove the assailants; but the assailants of Les Huchoires, hearing it announced that assistance was coming to the Vaudois troop, which had already harassed them by six consecutive attacks, now beat a retreat to rejoin the cavalry which remained posted in the basin of Bobi. The Flying Company went in pursuit of them, overthrew the walls of dry stones behind which they had taken shelter, fairly routed them, and annoyed them all the way to the confines of La Tour. There it endured some loss by the unexpected attack of a body of fresh troops which came to the protection of the fugitives.

Notwithstanding this, the alarm was so great in the camp of the persecutors that the Count of La Trinité took flight and retired to Lucerna. Thereafter his army re-appeared no more at Le Villar or Bobi, for in these places, it is said, his loss had been very great.

But Angrogna still remained the central position of the valleys, approachable on all sides but the west, and of this he conceived hopes. Having gathered new troops under his dishonoured banners, he soon found himself at the head of 7000 combatants. On the 17th of March, 1561, being Sabbath, the Vaudois families that were assembled at Pra-du-Tour, with their defenders, had just been addressing their prayers to the Lord, when they saw, as they came out from sermon, three long files of soldiers, who advanced parallel to each other, one by the heights of La Vachère, another by the way of Les Fourests, and the third by that of Serres. The captain of the first battalion was named Sebastian De Virgile. "We shall sweep these heretics off the earth to-day!" he had exclaimed in the morning as he left Lucerna. "Sir," replied his hostess, "if our religion is better than theirs you will have the victory, but if not, you yourselves will be swept away."

The approaches of the Pra-du-Tour, against which the two first attacking columns were directed, were defended by a bastion of earth and stones which the Vaudois had thrown up; but the lower path had not been guarded and barred, although it would have been more easily shut up than any other passage, by reason of the narrow space within which it was inclosed. The natural difficulties of traversing it had been thought sufficient to guard it, and the enemy's column which advanced by it was, in fact, the last to appear in view of the Pra-du-Tour. The Vaudois were already occupied in defending their bastion against the columns which came by the higher paths, when this last battalion unexpectedly penetrated into the lower basin. Immediately they descended to repel it, leaving very few men at the bastion which was attacked; but these men had long pikes, and every enemy who showed himself upon the scarp was quickly hurled down.

After a great succession of exploits, which cost the lives of two of their number, they were on the point of giving way, when the Flying Company, which had just routed their assailants on the lower ground, arrived in a mass upon the higher bastion; whereupon, no longer contented with defending themselves, the Vaudois assumed the offensive. The enemy drew back; it was the signal for pursuit. The Vaudois rushed upon them, broke their ranks, dispersed them, and, by the ardour of their courage, really swept them away. Sebastian De Virgile was carried in a dying state to Lucerna, and the Count of La Trinité wept as he sat upon a rock, and looked upon so many dead. "*God fights for them, and we do them wrong!*" exclaimed the soldiers themselves.

On this decisive day the Vaudois were completely victorious. At the summit of the mountain, where they had another bastion, they had awaited the approach of the Catholics, without moving until they were close at hand, when, by a discharge within a short range, they brought them to a sudden pause. The battalion being taken by surprise, hesitated; the Vaudois, encouraged by this, redoubled their efforts; the enemy yielded; they rushed out upon them, overthrew them, pursued them, decimated, and almost destroyed them. "Never," said their captain afterwards, "did I see soldiers so affrighted, so timid as ours were before these mountaineers." They were half vanquished by the very idea of having to contend with them. Discouragement, therefore, was visible in the hostile army. They began to murmur, and their losses were considerable; whilst in the plains of St. John, of Briquèras, and of La Tour—where, from morning to evening, nothing was to be seen but dead or wounded men carried down from the summits of those dreadful mountains, upon which battalions melted away like snow—a sort of panic seized upon the minds of persons already moved by a war so unjust; and, in speaking of the Vaudois, it began to be said, "Surely God is on their side!"

Many persons at that time were surprised that the inhabitants of these mountains, familiar with every locality, and triumphant on all hands, did not pursue their adversaries to destroy them completely; "but the principal leaders," observes Gilles, "and especially the ministers, would not consent to that pursuit, for they had resolved from the beginning, that *when in the last extremity they were forced to defend themselves by arms, they would keep always within the limits of legitimate defence, both out of respect for their superiors, and in order to spare human blood, and that in every victory granted to them by the God of armies, they would use their victory as moderately as possible.*"[1] It is one of the most remarkable characteristics of greatness, always to combine moderation with courage, and piety also owns the duty of continuing humble and humane in the triumph of strength.

One of the Catholic leaders, by name Gratian De Castrocaro, a Tuscan by birth, and at that time a colonel of the ducal army, was made prisoner upon this occasion. He called himself a gentleman of the Duchess of Savoy, and the Vaudois generously released him; but if an act of kindness excites gratitude in noble minds, it is burdensome to bad hearts, and this Castrocaro showed.

The Catholic leaders ascribed the reiterated defeats of their troops to their being unaccustomed to mountain warfare; whereas, they said they would have beaten the enemy a thousand times on level ground. But a few days after, a combat took place on level ground, and the Vaudois were still victorious. "Thus," says Gilles, "it appears that victory does not depend upon great or small numbers, nor upon fighting in open field, or in narrow glens, nor on the plain, nor amongst the mountains, but only on the compassionate assistance of the Lord, who gives to the supporters of a just cause, the power to will and to do according to his own good pleasure." In this last conflict, however, the Vaudois were so closely engaged with the enemy, that they were actually hand to hand, fighting in this way in the open expanse of the valley, like those Homeric warriors, whose combats have given renown to the plains of Mysia.

[1] Gilles, p. 154.

A BRAVE DEFENCE.

After these numerous combats, in which the Vaudois lost only fourteen men,[1] the Count of La Trinité sent commissioners to enter into an accommodation with them. But amidst their negotiations, he made a new attack upon the Vaudois without notice, marching all his army on the night between the 16th and 17th of April, against the two strongest points in the whole country—the Pra-du-Tour and Le Taillaret.

The last-named place was first assailed at daybreak, by a great number of little attacking parties, who advanced at the same time against all the scattered hamlets that there occupy the different heights.[2] The inhabitants, surprised in their sleep, became in part the victims of that sudden assault—many fled in their shirts, and owed their safety only to their agility amongst the rocks with which they were so familiar. The invaders made a number of prisoners, and laid everything waste; then they descended by Coste Roussine to the mountain-slopes which overlook the Pra-du-Tour, in order to unite with the rest of the army in the projected destruction of the Vaudois there.

But the first act of the latter, at the commencement of every day, was to unite in public prayer. They had terminated this religious exercise before sunrise. The first rays of the morning light were reflected by the gleaming arms and helmets of the ravagers of Le Taillaret, as they descended the mountain upon them. Six determined men immediately went forth to meet them, and posted themselves in a defile, where only two persons could pass abreast. There they held in check that long file of the enemy, who soon accumulated, and were crowded together before this obstacle. Of these six Vaudois, the two foremost had their pieces always charged, and being within easy range, killed each couple of soldiers who presented themselves at the turning of the rock. The two Vaudois placed in the second rank fired over the shoulders of the first—their comrades behind them reloading their pieces.

Thus, for a whole quarter of an hour, the passage was interrupted. The other Vaudois had time to gather. They mounted upon the higher ledges of the defile, in the depths of which the ranks of the enemy's line were inv lved. Suddenly from the higher parts of these steep peaks, rough rocks were loosened, which broke through the line from both sides, destroying the men, making gaps in the ranks, bursting like the thunderbolt, spreading in multiplied frag-

[1] To wit, nine of Angrogna, two of St. John, one of Le Taillaret, one of Le Villar, and one of Fénestrelles.

[2] The name of Taillaret was given at that time to the whole space included within the Chiabriols on the west, Champ-la-Rama on the east, Les Copiers on the south, and Castolus and Coste Roussine on the north.

ments like grape-shot, and rebounding like splinters of bomb-shells, between the contracted walls of that path of death. The rout was soon complete. Unable either to advance or to spread itself out, unable even to fight, this unfortunate troop retreated in disorder, and was torn to pieces ere it retired. The other party, which advanced on the same expedition by La Vachère, to the attack also of the Pra-du-Tour, seeing that those with whom they were to have co-operated were already defeated, retired likewise, of their own accord, renouncing an assault which could now have no object.

A greater number of the Vaudois then proceeded to drive off the first aggressors. It was a horrible situation to have to re-ascend a ravine, into which huge stones were rolling down with fearful noise and power of rapid destruction. But such was the situation of the enemy. And without having been able to touch one of their courageous antagonists, the assailing party withdrew from that narrow and bloody ravine, as a traitor should always withdraw from his own snares—shattered, mangled, defeated, and powerless.

By reason of their number, however, some companies succeeded in still showing front against the Vaudois, who ceased not to pursue them. They re-ascended with difficulty these mountain-slopes, so fatal to treachery, and succeeded in passing again over the Col of Coste Roussine, by which they counted upon regaining La Tour.

The Vaudois, so basely attacked in midst of the armistice which had been offered to them by the commissioners, and which they had accepted, eagerly pursued these fugitive troops; and, in spite of some partial attempts at resistance, by which the enemy sought at intervals to cover their retreat, they annoyed them with balls and stones all the way to the little plain of Champ-la-Rama, situated at a short distance from La Tour. There the Catholics made a stand, hoping to surround the insignificant number of their pursuers; more especially, as the Count of La Trinité had contrived to acquaint them that he would presently send fresh troops. But the Vaudois gave their enemies no time to await this reinforcement, impetuously rushing upon the centre of the troop, whose commander fell.

His name was Cornelio; he was a young man of noble birth, married a short time before. He had a certain military reputation; and the Count of La Trinité had employed the greatest urgency to get him to take a command in his army. His young wife burst into tears when he parted from her. "I swear by the holy Virgin, and I give you my knightly word," said the count to her, "that I will bring him back to you sound and safe." She consented to his going, but she only received back his corpse.

The troops retreated in confusion, and the Vaudois pursued them to the very gates of La Tour; for, after the death of their commander, the soldiers ceased to make any serious resistance; and the Count of La Trinité, seeing them arrive in so great disorder, broke up his camp that very evening and retired to Cavour. It was, he said, to return with cannon. "Let him bring them," replied the mountaineers, "and he shall not take them back." And immediately setting to work they covered the Pra-du-Tour, on the side towards La Vachère, with a bastion so considerable that it could be seen from Lucerna, three leagues off.

At the same time there arrived in the valleys a new legion of defenders. The Vaudois of Provence—who had escaped from the massacres of 1545, prepared for war both by their misfortunes and by the rude life which they had led during their dispersion on the wild slopes of the Leberon—issued from their fastnesses, upon the news that their brethren of the valleys were persecuted; and whether the climate of Provence had inspired them with more violent passions, or the unexampled cruelties of Menier D'Oppède had excited in them a more profound indignation against the Catholics, certain it is that these new combatants were far from imitating the moderation of the Vaudois in respect of the Papists. Their phalanx—animated by a spirit of revenge, which may be accounted for, but not justified, by the frightful wrongs which they had endured—scoured the outskirts of the valleys, ravaging the possessions of the Catholics, returning carnage for carnage, and rapidly spreading on every side that unsurmountable terror which is inspired by those who combat in despair. The inhabitants of the surrounding districts—victims at once of the spoliations of the hostile army, and the devastating incursions of these implacable avengers, who had come from afar to protect the birthplace of their fathers—loudly demanded the termination of this war, so disastrous for all parties.

On the other hand, desertion had commenced in the Popish army; the soldiers would no longer fight against such adversaries; they refused to march in the direction of these dreadful mountains, "where, it was maintained," says Gilles,[1] "that the death of a single Vaudois cost the lives of more than a hundred of their enemies." At last the Count of La Trinité fell sick, whilst the valleys, far from being enfeebled, had defenders more resolute, more powerful, and more numerous than ever.

Serious thoughts then began to be entertained of treating with them. The first overtures consisted merely of offers of peace, upon

[1] P. 172.

condition that the Vaudois should send away their pastors again, and pay the ransom of their prisoners. But these conditions were rejected.

The Count of Racconis wrote to the Vaudois from Cavour, on the 5th of May, asking them to name deputies who should come and treat with him concerning the terms of a definitive arrangement. These deputies went, and after a number of difficulties, the following articles were signed at Cavour, on the 5th of June, 1561:—

1. An amnesty for the past.
2. Liberty of conscience granted to the Vaudois.
3. Permission to the banished and fugitives to return to their native country.
4. Restitution of confiscated property.
5. The Protestants of Bubiano, Fenil, and other towns of Piedmont, to be authorized to attend public worship in the valleys.
6. Those who had abjured to be authorized to return to their own church.
7. A promise that all the ancient privileges of the Vaudois should be confirmed.
8. The prisoners to be given up.

These articles were signed in name of the Duke of Savoy, by his cousin Philip of Savoy, Count of Racconis; and in name of the Vaudois, by Francis Vals, pastor of Le Villar, and Claud Berge, pastor of La Tour, and also by two laymen, George Monastier of Angrogna, and Michel Raymonet of Le Taillaret.

But the Catholic clergy raised a howl of vexation; the nuncio wrote to the Pope; the Pope complained to the consistory; and the Duchess of Savoy said some days after to Stephen Noël, pastor of Angrogna, who had been summoned to her presence, "You could not believe all the evil reports which are brought to us every day against you! But do not concern yourselves—do that which is right—be obedient to God and your prince, and peaceable towards your neighbours, and all that has been promised you shall be faithfully performed." "But in spite of this," says Noël,[1] "the Pope's legate did all that was in his power to have me put in prison." He would have wished all the Vaudois of the valleys to be destroyed, as all their brethren of Calabria had been. He could not conceive how a princess could receive a minister; he was very near raising a disturbance upon that account. Noël was obliged to take his departure next day; but he effected his return to the valleys, resumed his ministry, and long enjoyed the fruits of his labours.

Thus courage and faith prevailed. The articles of the 5th of

[1] *Letter of Stephen Noël*, Gilles, p. 174.

June supplied the Vaudois with a solid basis for the future defence of their liberty of conscience. It was yet to suffer very violent assaults, but it has always triumphed over them; for their protector was always the same. "Call upon me in the day of trouble, I will deliver thee," saith the Lord.

These words may aptly serve as a concluding motto for the present chapter; which is nothing else than an illustration of them, in the whole of its contents.

CHAPTER III.

CASTROCARO, GOVERNOR OF THE VALLEYS.[1]

(A.D. 1561 TO A.D. 1581.)

Distress prevailing in the Valleys—Refugees from Calabria—Castrocaro appointed Governor of the Valleys—His scheme for the gradual destruction of the Vaudois Church—He proceeds to impose new restrictions—His arbitrary proceedings—His duplicity—He misrepresents the Vaudois at court—Kind intentions of the Duchess of Savoy—Gilles Des Gilles, pastor of La Tour, seized and committed to prison—Castrocaro frustrated in some of his attempts—New dangers—A solemn fast—Deliverance from fear—Further arbitrary measures of the Governor—A new covenant sworn by the Vaudois—Charles IX. of France writes to the Duke of Savoy in favour of the persecuted Protestants of the plains of Piedmont—Massacre of St. Bartholomew—Threats of Castrocaro—Consternation of the Vaudois—They are re-assured by the Duke of Savoy—Francis Guérin, pastor of St. Germain, boldly challenges a popish priest to public controversy—Death of the Duchess of Savoy—Controversial discussions—A son of the pastor of La Tour carried off by night—Castrocaro's tyranny and misgovernment become known to the Duke of Savoy—He refuses to appear at Turin, and is carried thither a prisoner—The reward of a traitor and persecutor.

THERE had been so long an interruption of the labours of husbandry, and the Vaudois had been subjected to so much of pillage and conflagration, and so many losses of every kind, that great distress began to be felt in their valleys. The confiscated properties had been spoiled to the utmost before being restored, and some of them were very incompletely restored. The monks of Pignerol continued to

---

[1] AUTHORITIES.—*Gilles*, who is very full in this part, sufficing to make up for deficiencies of documents. His work is the principal source of the information contained in this chapter.—*Rorengo*, "*Memorie istoriche*," ought, lest he mislead, to be compared with Gilles, who was his contemporary. His first work was entitled, "*Breve narratione dell' introduttione degl' heretici nelle valli de Piemonte*," &c., published at Turin in 1632, a small 4to of 114 pages; it has become rare. The "*Memorie istoriche dell' introduttione dell' heresie nelle valli di Lucerna*," &c., were published in 1649, in a 4to of xx and 350 pages.—*Cappel*, "*Vallium Alpinarum*

have a troop of malefactors in their pay, to inflict incessant injury on the inoffensive Protestants of their vicinity. Besides all this, there frequently arrived in the valleys a few unfortunate persons escaped from the massacres of Calabria, naked as those who have suffered shipwreck, issuing from the Apennines, where they had crept along from cavern to cavern, destitute alike of clothing, shelter, food, and the means of procuring it. The impoverished inhabitants of our hospitable Alps, nevertheless, welcomed these brethren and sisters with the warmest sympathy for the misfortunes which they had endured.

Compassion is easily excited in those who are themselves worthy of it. The Vaudois shared with these new-comers the little which remained to them. They were descended from the same ancestors. But the feeble resources of our desolated lands would have been insufficient for necessities so great. Collections were made for them in Switzerland, in Germany, and even in France.

Scarcely had they begun to recover when Castrocaro—the same who had been their prisoner, and whom they had so generously released—expressing, in the presence of the Duchess of Savoy, the best intentions with regard to them, succeeded in getting himself named Governor of the Valleys. His kind disposition towards them was believed, upon account of the gratitude which he owed them. But perfidious both upon the one hand and upon the other, he deceived his benefactress and his benefactors. The Archbishop of Turin had received from him the only promise which he did not fail to keep. He promised to him that he would gradually withdraw from the Vaudois all the liberties which had been conceded to them, and that he would thus labour for the complete destruction of their church.

Instead of seeking to accomplish this object by a sudden stroke, he proceeded by means of successive restrictions, and commenced by demanding, in 1565, a revision of the Treaty of Cavour, concluded in 1561. The Vaudois refused to consent. He then pretended that they had transgressed it. Recourse was had to the duke for the maintenance of its provisions. Castrocaro repaired to Turin, and returned from thence with new articles, which he pre-

trajecta portenta," &c. Sedan, 1621. (He published also "*Doctrine des Vaudois représentée par Claude Seyssel,*" a small 8vo of 111 pages.) See also the general histories concerning the province of Pignerol, and the historical memorials concerning Piedmont and the house of Savoy, by Costa de Beauregard, Chiesa, Cibrario, Muletti, &c.; and with these, the "*Art de verifier les dates,*" for the arrangement of political facts. The manuscript sources of information are not numerous—a few mouldering documents in the Archives of the Court at Turin and in the Royal Library.

sented on behalf of the prince for the signature of the Vaudois. But these papers did not bear the signature of the duke, and the leaders of the Vaudois again met him with a refusal.

He thereupon threatened that he would declare against them a war more cruel than the former. Long negotiations were entered upon; commissioners were named upon both sides; some concessions were wrung from those of the valleys, and the Vaudois people disavowed their deputies. Things then began to get embroiled; which was what Castrocaro wished. He got the command of a body of troops assigned to him to maintain order, and established himself with this garrison in the Castle of La Tour. He then ordered the inhabitants of Bobi to send away their pastor,[1] and those of St. John no longer to admit the Protestants of the plain to their worship.

The Vaudois, by the intervention of the Duchess of Savoy, obtained at first a cessation of these hostilities. But as a suspension of twenty days had been proposed to them by Castrocaro, that they might appeal to the duke against his decisions, he took advantage of the concluding term of that suspension to give his decisions the legal force requisite for their being carried into execution, although the duke might have disallowed them; and on the 10th of September, 1565, he caused proclamation to be made in the valley of Lucerna, that he would put to the sword any who did not conform to them. What anarchy amongst rulers, what arbitrary magistracies, what ignorance of social rights prevailed in these unhappy times!

Castrocaro, writing to the court, represented the resistance of the Vaudois to his orders as a rebellion on their part against the duke's authority, and he obtained from that prince an intimation to the people that they must obey their governor. They, in their turn, sent deputies to court; namely, Domenic Vignaux, pastor of Le Villar,[2] Gilles, the pastor of La Tour, and three laymen. The good Duchess of Savoy procured for them a safe-conduct, and received them at Turin with much kindness; but she could not make up her mind to the recall of the governor whom she had given them, so completely had he succeeded in persuading her of the uprightness of his intentions. On the contrary, she urged the Vaudois to submit to him all their difficulties. "Dear and well-beloved," said she to them in a letter dated 6th of December, 1565, "we shall always commend the good desire which you show towards the service of

---

[1] Humbert Artus, who had made offer to the polemical monks to hold discussions with them in Greek, Latin, or Hebrew, as they might choose.

[2] He had succeeded the old pastor, whose name was Peter Val, two years before.

God, as also of your prince, and we are far from thinking that you speak feignedly; but we have two things to ask of you—the first of which is, that whilst you reserve to yourselves the things which can only belong to the judgment of your own conscience, you would proceed in respect of them with sound discretion as well as with true zeal, for the one without the other is worth very little; the other is, that you would submit your deliberations to those who, being upon the spot, can judge accurately of what is expedient both for the one party and for the other; and if you allow yourselves to be guided by those who understand public affairs, and desire your repose, you will never find yourselves deceived nor have cause of dissatisfaction."

Worthy lady! it was she who was deceived. Noble minds have difficulty in believing evil, whilst the worthless suspect it even where it does not exist. Margaret of France believed in the good intentions of Castrocaro; and, accordingly, she adds in the letter above quoted, that she hopes that time and experience will permit the Vaudois to do him justice. Time only justified their apprehensions. His animosity was redoubled by the complaints made against him; he put to ransom, imprisoned, or persecuted these poor people upon all sorts of pretexts: accusing some of opposing his schemes, and others of finding fault with them; some of not looking upon him with a good eye, others of not showing him enough of deference. He succeeded in this way in expelling from the valleys the learned Scipio Lentulus, on the pretext that he was of foreign birth.[1] He caused the pastor of La Tour, Gilles Des Gilles, to be arrested, on the pretext that he had been at Grenoble and at Geneva with the view of bringing troops from other countries against his sovereign.

This pastor, however, had saved the lives of Castrocaro and of a multitude of Catholics, by many times arresting that terrible legion of sharp-shooters, whom he accompanied in 1561, like an angel of peace, whose mission was only to put an end to carnage. Castrocaro had been one of the prisoners; the laws of war authorized his death. His life was spared; his liberty was given to him; but these natural causes of gratitude tormented him as a thirst for vengeance. He set a troop of soldiers to watch his liberator; and in the beginning of February, 1566, they seized the pastor and cast him into prison, where "he was not less rigidly and rudely treated," his grandson tells us, "than if he had been some noted robber." All the other pastors of the valleys offered to be security

---

[1] He was born at Naples; he was at this time pastor of St. John, and he retired to Chiavenna.

for their colleague, asking that he might be released until the charges brought against him should be submitted to the Duke of Savoy; but the merciless governor refused to allow any mitigation of the hardships of the captive.

When he was transferred to Turin, the family of the duke felt the greatest regard for him; but the clergy eagerly laboured for his destruction by aggravating, as much as possible, the charges under which he lay. One day the advocate-fiscal, Barbèri, said to him, "Your case looks ill; a sentence of death is sure to be pronounced; you cannot escape it but by changing your religion." "Will that change my guilt or my innocence, in respect of the things imputed to me?" said the pastor. "No; but they will cease to be regarded, and you will receive as much favour as you have otherwise to apprehend punishment." "It is not justice, then, that is cared for." "It is your salvation, which is of far more importance. Hold! subscribe you only the things which are contained in this book and your life will be saved." "I would rather save my soul. But, however, let us see this book." "Ah! his highness has required that your case should be proceeded in without delay; you must therefore decide presently." "I cannot sign what I do not know." "Well! I will leave the book with you, and I will come back to hear your answer in three days."

Barbèri having returned at the time fixed, the pastor exclaimed, "It is a tissue of errors and blasphemies; I would rather die than sign such a thing." "What! errors! blasphemies! It is you who blaspheme; and you will be burned alive were it only for these words." "If such be God's will, I am in his hands."

But at that time violent persecutions were carried on against the reformed at once of Saluces, Barcelonnette, and Suza; the Elector Palatine had deputed one of his councillors of state to the Duke of Savoy, in order to get them stopped, and this ambassador did not quit Turin till he had succeeded in having Gilles declared innocent and set at liberty.

Castrocaro then caused proclamation to be made in his government, that all Protestants who were not born within it, must remove from it under pain of death and confiscation of all their goods.[1] But by the intervention of the Duchess of Savoy, the rescinding of this barbarous order was obtained.

On the instigation of the Archbishop of Turin, the perfidious governor made an attempt to have the Vaudois interdicted from assembling in synod. In this he did not succeed. Thereupon he demanded to be present at it, on pretext of securing against plots

[1] Order of April 20, 1566.

which might there be hatched against the safety of the state. "The people protested," says Gilles, "against this innovation, not for fear of his knowing all that was transacted in these assemblies, but out of regard to the future."

In the year following, the religious wars broke out again in France; and the Duke of Clèves, leading a Spanish army into Flanders, had occasion to pass through Piedmont. His first exploits, it was said, would be the extermination of the Vaudois. Fanatics rejoiced, and Christ's followers were depressed; trouble and disquietude again prevailed in the valleys. A solemn fast was observed there in the end of May, to avert the judgments of God in the dreaded future. Was it, then, because of the unanimous supplications of this whole people, humbled in penitence and prayer, that this storm passed by without doing them any harm? Their faith was assured of it; the fact belongs to history. That vast extermination, the danger of which was thought to be so imminent—these prospects of bloodshed, these menaces and fears of death passed away like a cloud, whose presence is only marked upon the earth by the shadow which it casts. And whilst Europe was in combustion, the Vaudois people enjoyed at this time some years of peace.

Castrocaro employed this interval of respite in building, or rather completing, the fort of Mirabouc. The people of Bobi, in particular, saw with displeasure the erection of this fortress, because of the obstacle which it formed on the road to Le Queyras, the free passage of which was of some consequence to their *colayers*,[1] for the exchange or sale of their produce in Upper Dauphiny. Castrocaro, upon his part, vowed a particular enmity against the *Bubiarels*,[2] and in name of the priest of La Tour, he demanded that the place of worship at Bobi, and the grounds attached to the residence of the pastor, should be given up to him. The Vaudois refused; and by a sentence passed upon the 26th of October, 1571, he condemned them to a fine of 100 crowns of gold, payable within twenty-four hours, under penalty of twenty-five crowns of gold of additional fine for every day's delay in the payment of the original sum. All the Vaudois made common cause upon this occasion. They sent deputies to Emmanuel Philibert, and again succeeded in getting a stop put to these proceedings.

But seeing, nevertheless, that those persecuting courses were

[1] The name of *colayers* is given to labourers, or small merchants, whose employment is to traverse the *cols* of the mountains, bearing on their shoulders the merchandise of one valley to another. One of them said one day, to describe the hardships of such a life, "The bread which we eat has seven crusts, and the best of them is burned!"

[2] A Vaudois designation for the inhabitants of the commune of Bobi.

renewed against them, by which their destruction had formerly been attempted, they renewed upon their part by oath, their covenant and bond of mutual responsibility as Christians, the source of their previous triumphs, and subscribed in addition the following articles:—

"When one of our churches shall be assailed in any of its peculiar interests, all shall jointly reply as with one mouth to maintain their common rights. None of us shall act, in any such matter, without consulting his brethren.

"And we all bind ourselves to one another, under an oath, unswervingly to abide in this ancient union, transmitted to us by our fathers, never to forsake our holy religion, and always to remain faithful to our rightful sovereigns."

In these terms was their covenant made and ratified at Bobi on the 11th of November, 1571.

Nevertheless, the system of annoyance was still kept up, especially against the Protestants of Lower Piedmont, and a very curious particular connected with this fact is, that Charles IX. wrote to the Duke of Savoy a very pressing letter in favour of the persecuted. "I have one request to make to you," says he, "which I would make, not in an ordinary way, but with all the earnestness which is possible for me. . . . for during the troubles of war, passion no more permits us to judge aright of what is expedient, than disease permits a patient to judge in his own case . . . . and as you have treated your subjects in an unusual manner upon this account . . . . for my sake also, let it please you now, in kindness to me, upon my prayer and special recommendation, to receive them to your benign favour, to restore them and reinstate them in their possessions, which have been confiscated . . . . This matter is so just in itself, and is so earnestly regarded by me, that I assure myself you will readily comply with my wishes."

This letter is dated from Blois on the 28th of September, 1571. Charles IX. was then twenty-one years of age. "He had received from nature," say the Benedictines,[1] "an excellent disposition and rare abilities; he was brave, intrepid, possessed of extraordinary penetration, of lively imagination, and of sound judgment; he expressed himself with dignity and readiness. But the seductions with which he was surrounded perverted this happy natural character; the queen-mother herself trained him in the art of deceit and dissimulation; the Marshal De Rez taught him to make light of oaths; and the Guises, by their sanguinary counsels, turned the natural impetuosity of his character into cruelty." Placed in other

[1] *Art de verifier les dates.*

circumstances, he would, perhaps, have been one of the most accomplished princes, of whom the records of royalty have preserved the memory. It is impossible to tell what crimes bad example and bad instructions have produced. If Charles IX. had been brought up under the teaching of the Bible, France would have escaped many calamities. But a year after this letter, came the news of the massacres of St. Bartholomew.[1] The most dreadful consternation succeeded in all the Reformed churches, to the hopes which they had conceived with regard to the future.

Castrocaro took advantage of the occasion to terrify the Vaudois valleys with his threats of extermination. "If 60,000 Huguenots have fallen in France," exclaimed he in a transport, "it is not to be supposed that this handful of heretics can expect to survive." And the Papists, the enthusiastic Papists, Gilles says, in his style of grave impartiality, already exulted in the approaching destruction of the Vaudois. And they, alarmed by that distant echo of so great a massacre, and by the infuriate rage which was displayed in their own immediate vicinity, began to convey their children and households to the most inaccessible places among the mountains; the men got ready their weapons, and waiting till they should be compelled to make use of them, they continued to watch and to pray.

But the cry of horror which resounded throughout the whole of civilized Europe, on that vast assassination, startled the Duke of Savoy himself. At the spectacle of such a conflagration, his heart was moved to indignation, and his wisdom dictated caution. He energetically protested against the cruelties of Charles IX., swore that he would never sully his reputation by such crimes, re-assured the Vaudois as to their prospects, and persuaded them to return peaceably to their homes, where they would have nothing to fear.

Some troubles, however, took place at this time in the valley of Perouse, which belonged to France, and the history of which is too intimately connected with that of Pragela to be detached from it. I shall therefore take notice of the events which then agitated the Val Perouse, in relating the history of Pragela, of which the political destinies have been very distinct from those of the other Vaudois valleys.

One fact, however, deserves to be inserted here, because it belongs to the general movement of the countries with which we are now engaged. In the midst of this almost universal fury against the Protestants, the pastor of St. Germain, Francis Guérin, had the courage to undertake, alone and unaided, to combat Catholicism by

[1] From 23d to 26th August, 1572.

arms more terrible and less bloody—those of argument. One day, in 1573, he ascended to Pramol, where Popery reigned in full strength. It was a Sabbath, the people were assembled in the church, the priest celebrated mass. Francis Guérin took his place amongst the hearers, and waited in silence till the services were terminated. No one suspected that in that crowd of obscure persons was a soldier of Christ, who, armed according to the scriptural expressions, with the helmet of salvation and the sword of the Spirit, which is the word of God,[1] was speedily, with all the power of love and courage, to make that word triumphant over the servile forces of superstition.

The priest of Pramol having concluded his service, the pastor rose and inquired if he had finished.[2] "Yes," replied the priest. "What then is it which you have been doing?" "I have been saying mass." "And what is the mass?" The question was put in Latin. The priest knew not what reply to make. Francis Guérin repeated it in Italian, and said to him, "Be so good as to explain to me what the mass is?" The priest was as silent as before. Then the pastor, inflamed with zeal for his God, and with ardent and devout compassion for so many enslaved souls, ascended the pulpit in the midst of an audience dumb with astonishment, and exclaimed, "Poor people! you see by whom you allow yourselves to be guided! By a man who does not know what he does; he says mass every day, and he does not know what the mass is. He feeds you with a thing which neither you nor he know anything about. Oh come! leave behind you your ignorance, and these vain superstitions! Souls are too precious to be thus trifled with. Behold the Bible," he proceeded, laying one down before him, "listen to the word of God and you shall be saved!"

The people, excited and motionless, ventured not to take any

[1] Epistle to the Ephesians, vi. 16, 17.
[2] These details are taken from a manuscript of that period, *Circa la religione, e dominio spirituale. . . . dal Fra Agostino di Castellamonte, Cappucino: e misfatti dei protestanti in queste valli.* Fol., 32 pages.—Archives of the Bishopric of Pignerol.

The following are a few extracts:—" Finita la messa il ministro dice al curato: Monsignor haveto detto messa ?—Rispose il curato: Messer, si.—Replico il Ministro: *Quid est missa ?*—Il curato non seppe rispondere parola.—Il ministro torno ha dire in vulgare, perche forse il povero curato non intendeva il latino !—O monsignor, che cosa e messa ?—Ne meno seppe rispondere. All'hora il ministro monto in pulpito, e comincio da predicare contra la messa e contra il papa, e fra le altre cose, dice :—O povera gente ! vedete che havete qua, un uomo che non sa quelle che si faccia ? Ogni giorno dice messa, e non sa che cosa sia messa, Fa una cosa che ne voi, ne lui intende ! Vedete qua la Bibla, sentite la parola di Dio. . . . E seppe dire tante chiachierie, che perverti tutta quella terra, e al presente non vi è più ne curato ne messa."—Gilles also mentions this occurrence, with fewer particulars, in his 37th chapter.

decided course. "Well," added the pastor, "I do not wish to take anybody by surprise; and to give your priest time to prepare his answers, I will return next Sabbath, to prove to him, both by the Bible and by his own missal, that the mass is full of falsehoods; meanwhile, pray to God that he may enlighten you, and incline you to receive the truth without weakness and without prejudice." Hereupon Guérin left the church and re-descended to St. Germain. In course of the week many of the people of Pramol came to him, opened their hearts to him, and asked his advice; and to each he gave a Bible, saying, "There is your best counsellor, consult it often, and you will have no need of other directions."

Next Sabbath he went up again to Pramol. The concourse of people was considerable; curiosity, surprise, and a multitude of different emotions agitated their hearts. The new apostle made his way into the church; the crowd pressed around him; he seemed to be already their pastor. But the priest did not make his appearance; no one presented himself to celebrate or to defend the mass. "Reverend pastor," said a voice, "speak to us again of the word of God." "Yes, I will speak to you," was the reply, "and I will be your pastor, or rather you shall have only one shepherd, who is Christ! you shall be his sheep; but his sheep must know him." And without delay he proceeded to expound to them the great doctrines of salvation. It may easily be imagined that they triumphed amongst these simple and awakened souls, for whom Popery at first did not think it worth while to contend with the gospel.

This event passed unobserved amidst the great troubles of the times. The Church of Rome was too much intoxicated with the bloody triumphs of St. Bartholomew, to alarm herself about so petty a triumph of faith. But nothing is insignificant which concerns the infinite and immortality; and the salvation of a soul is of more importance in the sight of God than the conquest of a kingdom.

Francis Guérin was decidedly of this judgment; for five years after, he set to work again to win souls in another district of the country. At the head of the Vaudois regiments he made his way into the marquisate of Saluces, for which Savoy and France then contended; and when the armies had retired, the pastor still remained to consolidate the evangelical churches there. The adventurous life of the knights-errant is regarded as full of heroism; but with what heroic emotions, perhaps still more elevated and still more generous, must not apostles, missionaries, and the ancient Vaudois Barbas have been animated, amidst the dangers which they often encountered!

During the various agitations of this period, and especially after the troubles to which the valley of Perouse was subjected, many of the people of that valley had taken refuge in the valley of Lucerna. Castrocaro, on the 28th of July, 1573, ordained all those who were not born within his government, to leave it within five days, under pain of three applications of the strapado and confiscation of goods. A new appeal to the Duchess of Savoy put an end to these proceedings. But this kind protectress was removed on the 19th of October, 1574, and her husband was not long behind her, for he died on the 30th of August, 1580.

During this interval, Lesdiguières wrote to the Vaudois, to request them to allow to the church of Gap, where he then resided, the ministry of Stephen Noël, pastor of Angrogna, who had already, in 1574, been called by the church of Grenoble. His ministry was therefore granted to one or other of these churches.

In February, 1581, polemical conferences were held in the valleys. The occasion was the following:—A Jesuit missionary, named Vanin, frequently made the Vaudois, and especially their pastors, the theme of his preaching. "Let them show their faces," he would say, "these heretics, these false prophets, these instruments of Satan, these workers of iniquity! But they will not come, for I would confound them." "There is nothing rational in abuse," wrote Francis Truchi, the pastor of St. John, in a letter addressed to him, "but if by word or writing you are willing to hold serious discussion with me, according to the usual manner of theologians, you will not find me to shrink from your attacks."

The day fixed for the first conference was a Sabbath. Vanin, presuming that all the Vaudois ministers would assemble to take part in it, and that he would find their churches abandoned at that time, repaired to Le Villar to address the people, instead of going to St. John to hold a discussion with the pastors. But Domenic Vignaux, minister of Le Villar, did not leave the field free to the Jesuit as he expected. "I am astonished," he said, "to meet with you here, at the very hour which you yourself had named for the conference at St. John; but since you are here you can have no objection that I take the place of my colleague Truchi in this duty, and that we proceed forthwith to public discussion. This was precisely what the Jesuit dreaded. He turned a supplicating look towards the governor's lieutenant who accompanied him, and who comprehended his embarrassment. "I forbid all discussion," said that magistrate.

But poor Vanin was not yet at the end of his vexations, for the pastor of St. John, with whom the discussion had been authorized, having learned that his antagonist had gone to Le Villar, had followed pretty closely after him, and soon arrived to call upon him to enter the lists which he had himself demanded. After many difficulties the conference was opened. It may be conceived which side had the advantage.

But Vanin, to avenge himself for his defeat, caused the son of the pastor of La Tour, Gilles Des Gilles, to be carried off by night. This young man was transported to Turin to the Jesuit convent, and thence he was despatched to the Indies, whence no word of him ever came. The grief of his family may be imagined. It endured as long as they lived, says his grand-nephew.

Soon after this, Castrocaro caused it to be reported that a new army was coming to destroy the Vaudois. The Vaudois withdrew their families to the mountains, and the governor wrote to the duke that they were fortifying themselves in order to resist his authority. A commissioner, sent to the spot, acknowledged at once the innocence of the Vaudois, and the hateful annoyances to which they were subjected by their calumniators. "For the cruel Castrocaro cared for nothing," says Gilles, "but to live in luxury in his castle of La Tour, where he became fat and rich, leaving his garrison to commit all sorts of excesses, and sometimes himself causing them to do so. He kept in his palace a troop of dogs, of which some were of prodigious size. His son Andrew was so debauched a fellow that the women of the neighbourhood, who regarded their own honour, durst not go out without being well attended. His three daughters went indiscriminately to mass or to the preaching of the reformed ministers, caring nothing either for the one religion or for the other, but only to be extravagantly and gaudily dressed, whilst his great object was to plunder all that he could."

The Duke of Savoy, being informed of such conduct, resolved to put an end to these excesses. He summoned Castrocaro to present himself at Turin; but, upon various pretexts, the unworthy governor always refused to obey, giving proof of his unfaithfulness by his resistance. The duke then seeing well enough that if there were rebels at La Tour, it was not among the Vaudois, but rather among those who denounced them, ordered the Count of Lucerna, Emmanuel Philibert, to seize Castrocaro and make him prisoner. This was no easy matter upon account of the fortifications, soldiers, and ferocious dogs by which he was surrounded.

Treachery came to the aid of tactics. Traitors are always deceived. A captain, named Simon, upon a private agreement with the Count of Lucerna, sent away, on the 13th of June, 1582, a part of the soldiers of the garrison. The count had posted his troop within a short distance of the castle. He came on impetuously, and surprised it almost without defence; the porter was killed at the moment when he was going to raise the draw-bridge before the assailants; they seized upon all the entrances. Castrocaro and his son were still in bed, and only the huge dogs which watched them attempted to defend them. The governor's three daughters mounted to the belfry of the castle, and sounded the alarm. The people came with all haste from Angrogna and St. John to the assistance of the castle. But the Count of Lucerna exhibited the ducal order upon which he had acted, and it may be supposed that the Vaudois were not very eager to oppose the arrest of their persecutor. He was conducted to Turin, and died in prison. His son expiated his misconduct in the dungeons of the senate. All their goods were confiscated, with reservation of a small allowance which was secured to the daughters and their mother.

Thus ended the disgraceful and mischievous rule of Castrocaro, illustrating the declarations of Scripture, concerning the wicked, whose strength and hope are suddenly destroyed, and who are not permitted to prosper in their iniquities.

CHAPTER IV.
STATE OF THE VAUDOIS DURING THE REIGN OF CHARLES EMMANUEL.
(A.D. 1580 TO A.D. 1630.)
GLI BANDITTI.[1]

Troubles in the valley of Pérouse—The Jesuits in the valley of Lucerna—A solemn fast of four days—Deaths of two aged Vaudois pastors—War between France and Savoy—Sufferings of the Vaudois—Proceedings of the Romish clergy—Apostasy of a Vaudois minister, Andrew Laurent—His consequent miseries—The Jesuits in the valleys—Discussions between them and Vaudois pastors—Ubertin Braida, priest of La Tour—The *Banditti*—The *Digiunati*—Irritation and excesses—A fast—Governor Ponte—Count Charles of Lucerna—Captain Galline attacks Bobi, but is defeated and spared by the Vaudois—Count Charles of Lucerna obtains favourable terms for the Vaudois, and tranquillity is in some measure restored—Deaths of Vaudois pastors—New alarms—A fast—Earthquake—The regiment of the Baron De La Roche in the valley of Lucerna—The Vaudois compelled to pay a large sum of money—Disunion among them—Further injustice and exactions—Destruction of a number of places of worship—Continued vexations—Rorengo, Prior of Lucerna—Resistance to the establishment of monks in the valleys.

EMMANUEL PHILIBERT having died in 1580, his son, Charles Emmanuel, then eighteen years of age, succeeded him. He espoused,

---

[1] AUTHORITIES.—The same as in the preceding chapter.

in 1585, Catharine of Spain, daughter of Philip II., after having been upon the point, two years before, of marrying Catharine of France, sister of Henry IV. But this latter princess being a Protestant, the projected marriage met with so much opposition in Italy, that he could not accomplish it.

In 1583 serious troubles arose in the valley of Pérouse, and led to the interposition of the people of the valley of Lucerna; for the Vaudois had bound themselves by oath never to abandon one another; and the prudence and energy are above all praise which they displayed under the diversity of their circumstances, which was attended with the greater difficulty, that they were the subjects of two different powers. But extricating always from all others the religious question, on which nothing ever could make them yield, they sustained the cause of their church without interfering in the affairs of the state. As the valley of Pérouse is merely a prolongation of that of Pragela, which then formed a part of Dauphiny, it is in the history of the latter valley that these events will naturally find their place.

In 1584 a new Jesuit invasion took place in the valley of Lucerna. The Duke of Savoy having, in the following year, espoused the daughter of Philip II., who was a member of the league against the reformed, it was supposed that Charles Emmanuel would ere long follow his example; "and the monks," says Gilles, "immediately sounded the horn with extravagant vauntings against our people, reckoning them all to be already exterminated. However, they caused them to be exhorted in all quarters, to prevent this misfortune by prompt conversion. The alarm was great, not so much upon account of these monkish lies and boastings, as of the certain accounts received of the league which was formed in France and elsewhere. Accordingly the Vaudois considered, in good earnest, that they had need, by true repentance, and extraordinary waiting upon God, with fasting and prayer, to endeavour to avert the calamities which they dreaded."

Four days were therefore set apart for solemn fasting in the Vaudois valleys, namely, the 15th and 16th, and the 22d and 23d of May, 1585, according to the usage of the primitive church in similar difficulties; and as if the blessing or the might of God always attended the fervent prayers of men, they very soon heard that, throughout the whole of Dauphiny, the reformed were victorious over the soldiers of the league. A third part of the Vaudois valleys then belonged to that province; and the advantage which they derived from these successes, contributed much to confirm and encourage the rest.

A touching but melancholy circumstance occurred in 1588. The two oldest pastors of the valleys, Gilles Des Gilles and Francis Laurens, the last disciples of the ancient Barbas, anterior to the Reformation, and whose whole lives had been spent in the same labours, and in unbroken friendship, expired within a short time of each other, in their ripe but vigorous old age. Gilles died first; and Francis Laurens, being informed of the decease of him who had been the companion of his studies and of his journeys—his colleague for half a century, and his friend throughout the whole of his life—was so strongly affected that he took to bed that same hour, and died a few days after. Such sensibility is rare amongst old men; but the faith which gives immortality does not permit the souls which have obtained it to grow old.

In course of the same year, Charles Emmanuel seized the marquisate of Saluces. There was war betwixt him and France. This war still continued in 1592, for the Duke of Savoy was supported by Spain and Austria. The theatre of hostilities being on the frontiers of Provence and Piedmont, two diversions were attempted by the French forces in the Vaudois valleys. The commandant of Queyras Castle attempted to surprise the fort of Mirabouc, but was repulsed; and Lesdiguières, an abler commander, seized that of Pérouse, and afterwards those of Lucerna and La Tour, from which he re-ascended the valley, and assailing the fort of Mirabouc from the lower side, compelled it to capitulate. He fixed his headquarters at Briquéras, where he caused a fortress to be erected; and from thence he levied contributions upon all the surrounding district. The town of Vigon, having refused to pay, was given up to pillage. The castle of Cavour, defended by Count Emmanuel of Lucerna, made some resistance, but after a siege of twenty days, and 500 volleys of cannon—munitions and provisions being exhausted—it also fell into the hands of the French, on the 8th of December, 1592.

During the time of this siege, a skirmish took place at Garsiliano betwixt the troops of the Duke of Savoy and those of Lesdiguières, in which the latter had the advantage. At this time Lesdiguières had not yet abjured Protestantism, and the Vaudois were not subjected to great hardships under his domination. Finding himself master of the country, he caused the castle of La Tour to be demolished in 1593, as well as that of La Pérouse, which were untenable against cannon. It was proposed to have demolished also those of Lucerna and Mirandol, but the project was not executed. The French general soon found reason to regret this, for the Duke of Savoy seized these two places towards the end of the month of June. The French garrison of the castle of Mirandol allowed themselves to be cut in pieces rather than surrender. The fort of Exiles did not surrender till it had received 3000 cannon shot; and that of Briquéras endured more than 7000 before it yielded.

The Duke of Savoy had with him Neapolitan, Milanese, and Spanish troops. A detachment of these last surprised La Tour one Sabbath morning. The soldiers entered it by the street of Les Bruns, opposite to the town's house, for the principal entry was barricaded. They massacred, without distinction, both Protestants and Catholics whom they met in the streets. Afterwards forcing their way into the houses, they committed cruel acts of violence, "and went the length," says Gilles, " of cutting off the fingers of noble damsels, who were not able themselves quickly enough to pull off the gold rings which these plunderers wanted." But they did not long continue these barbarous spoliations, for the Vaudois having run to arms on all sides, the Spaniards took flight without waiting for them.

However, Lesdiguières having lost all the places which he had taken in Piedmont, except Cavour and Mirabouc, retired before the victorious army of the confederates, and regained Dauphiny.

The Duke of Savoy then re-entered into possession of his dominions; but as, under the French rule, an oath of fidelity to the King of France had been exacted from the Vaudois, the Church of Rome endeavoured to persuade Charles Emmanuel to seize upon this pretext for exterminating them. That prince was too skilful a politician not to wish to avail himself of the repose granted him from foreign wars, in order to other purposes than the ravaging of his own territories; but he consented to make some show of persecution, in order to satisfy the fanatics, who, perhaps, themselves hoped to win from the Vaudois by terror some concessions fatal to their churches.

The army which had taken Briquéras continued to occupy it. The commander-in-chief wrote to the Vaudois to send deputies to him. "My orders are," said he to them, "to enter your valleys, and to exterminate all their inhabitants, in order to chastise them for having taken an oath to the King of France, contrary to the duty which they owed to their sovereign." "Will you massacre also the Catholics," said they, " who took it as well as we?" "That is not your affair," he replied, " but as I am very unwilling to shed so much blood, I would recommend you to go and cast yourselves at the feet of his highness, to ask pardon of him, and submit yourselves absolutely to his will."

A petition was presented to the duke,[1] who allowed himself to be persuaded, and granted its prayer, on condition that Catholicism should be established in all the valleys, and that the Protestant places of worship, which had formerly belonged to the Church of Rome, should be restored to it. This last condition alone was accepted, and with its acceptance the sovereign was satisfied.

In 1595 Charles Emmanuel retook the castle of Cavour, which had still remained in possession of the French, and afterwards, about the end of June, he seized upon their last stronghold, the fort of Mirabouc. On his return from this expedition, he stopped in the public square of Le Villar, and said to the Vaudois who came to congratulate him upon his victory, "Be faithful to me, and I will be a good prince, nay, a father to you. As to your liberty of conscience, and the exercise of your religion, I have no wish to make any innovation contrary to the liberties which you have enjoyed until now, and if any one attempt to trouble you, come to me and I will see to it."

The Catholic clergy were irritated at these kind words, and not being able to obtain the employment of any violence against the Vaudois Church, they attacked them by insidious methods. Their first care was to obtain authority to establish Catholic missions in all the valleys, with right to enter the Protestant places of worship, to which the Protestants should not be entitled to offer any opposition. The Archbishop of Turin came in person to instal the Jesuits in the valley of Lucerna, and the Capuchins in that of St. Martin. Scenes very distressing to the Vaudois occurred at this time.

Their former pastor, Andrew Laurent, who had succeeded Gilles Des Gilles in the parish of La Tour, had been made prisoner during the preceding war, and cast into the dungeons, one after another, of Saluces, of Coni, and of Turin. At first he resisted with great firmness the solicitations to apostasy, which usually followed the torments inflicted by Catholicism upon its victims; but at last, whether it was that his mind was weakened by his sufferings, or whether he had lost the strength of his former convictions, the unhappy Laurent consented to put an end to his tortures by an abjuration. Immediately he was transferred from noisome prisons to a sumptuous palace, whilst his soul was declared to have also passed from darkness to light. A richly-furnished house was prepared for him at Lucerna; the Jesuits, under pretext of boarding with him, never quitted him, watched him continually, and led him

---

[1] The answer to this petition is dated 21st November, 1574.

about as a trophy in the midst of them, in the excursions which they made among the Protestants.

Escorted by these children of darkness, a jealous and suspicious guard, who marked his slightest movements, whilst they professed to do him honour by their attendance, he was dragged about to make polemical addresses in the religious assemblies of the Vaudois, in the very churches where he had preached to them the word of God, in presence of his former colleagues, amidst his former parishioners; and after the sermon he was caused to declare before them that their religion was a heresy, that he himself had taught them nothing but error, and that, being himself converted, he would recommend them to follow his example. What a grief to the Vaudois, and what a humiliation to himself!

His repentant and submissive voice, his air of subjection and distress, made it obvious enough to what tyrannical injunctions he was compelled to render obedience. His appearance and his words excited in his afflicted hearers only a silent pity, more grievous to him than reproaches. Eyes were cast down as he passed, or accusing looks penetrated his soul like heart-rending weapons. O! there is no trifling with remorse! But Laurent died of it, after having been subjected to affronts perhaps more cruel, and humiliations more painful still. The Jesuits took charge of his family; and scarcely had it been confided to them, when his daughter lost her honour. The monk who debauched her fled, as if it were possible for a man to flee from his sin; but the unhappy father remained heart-stricken, afflicted in his soul, and through his dearest affections, till it ended in his losing his life. Distrusted by the one party, and despised by the other, he died, says Gilles, without esteem and without consolation; he died in his apostasy, by a slower and more cruel death than that of which, if he had persevered, his faithfulness would have been in danger. If a man's faults could be expiated by his sufferings, Andrew Laurent would have dearly won his pardon. But it is more pleasant to think that his pardon may have been freely given to him in Christ.

Public conferences betwixt the Jesuits and the pastors succeeded to these fruitless demonstrations. The first conference took place at Les Appias, on the marches of the three communes of Angrogna, La Tour, and St. John; the Count of Lucerna presided. The pastor, after having replied to the Jesuit, begged the president to declare which side had the advantage. "Gentlemen," replied he, "if you were disputing about the qualities of a good horse or a good sword, I could give you my opinion, because I understand something about it, but in your controversies I am not able to meddle." And upon this he dismissed the meeting. Other discussions, however, took place, but without any advantage to the Papists.

Then came sudden injuries and iniquitous acts of violence, unexpected arrests, and executions by sleight of hand (if that term may be used to characterize the secrecy and expedition with which they were conducted), the victims of which were Protestants living by themselves in remote places, whom the monks or their satellites contrived to seize by surprise; in a word, all the ill that wickedness, possessed of power, could inflict upon inoffensive weakness.

In 1597 an attempt was made to rob the inhabitants of Prarusting of the heritages of their fathers, but they resisted by force of arms, and God gave the victory in these conflicts to them and their righteous cause.

In 1598, on the 2d of August, a conference, long announced, took place betwixt the pastor of St. Germain and the Capuchin Berno, who had been specially authorized by the Duke of Savoy to enter into that polemical discussion. Their theses were printed, but the Inquisition prohibited the sale of these books, which would seem to prove that the victory did not remain with Catholicism. After this conference, as after those which had taken place at Les Appias, the monks sought to compensate themselves by deeds of violence for the arguments of their adversaries.

In this way they obtained some venal conversions, not more honourable for the Catholics than for the Protestants; "but the greater part of those who had allowed themselves to be turned aside, afterwards returned to the right way." Such is the testimony of Gilles. "In 1599," he continues, "a priest was sent to La Tour, who strutted about, looking as bold as a lion, and seemed more fit to occasion trouble than to guide the church." His name was Ubertin Braida. His first act was to exact tithes, which the Protestants had never payed. His demand was refused. But "still desiring to work mischief," says our author, "he treated the Vaudois with contempt in a multitude of ways; and, like another Goliath, he even went so far as to challenge them to personal combat with himself, each man in his shirt, in an inclosure marked by four stakes." What a method of promoting the truth! "He always bore about, under his cassock, a coat of mail, and showed himself cowardly whilst he boasted that he was afraid of no man!"

"One evening, after supper, some young men, making themselves merry in the clear moonlight, went to make a racket near the abode of this priest, to try if he were as brave as he appeared. Braida, dreading some act of vengeance, took to flight, without being pursued." The podestat of La Tour, at the instigation of the most respectable parishioners of the fugitive prior, caused the young men to be summoned before him, and condemned them to remain under arrest in the house of a gentleman whom he named. The Vaudois proceeded thither; but ere long they were apprised that a band of constables was to be sent to seize them, in order to convey them to Turin, and cast them into the dungeons of the Inquisition. They fled during the night, were again summoned to appear before the podestat, did not comply with the summons, and found themselves under sentence of banishment from the territories of Savoy, under penalty of the galleys in case of their being apprehended.

These young men retired to places of most difficult access, keeping themselves upon their guard, armed and in one body, but not remaining long in the same place. Their life was very soon that of vagabonds, under the necessity of living upon the voluntary or extorted contributions of others. As they were under sentence of banishment, or, as the Italian term is, *Banditti*, they were called *the troop of Banditti;* and for some years their numbers continually increased. A rigorous prohibition was published, by sound of trumpet, of giving them any relief, shelter, or assistance; but, pressed by hunger, they became only the more formidable.

The podestat of La Tour, who might, by more moderation, have prevented these troubles at the beginning, thought good to march against the outlaws with armed men; but he was defeated, and in danger of losing his life. Hereupon he retired to Lucerna, and did not venture any more to make his appearance at La Tour, even to discharge the duties of his office.

Independent of these acts of resistance and of vigour, there were individual acts of vengeance performed by unknown hands, which were placed, by gratuitous inference, to the account of the outlaws. The outlaws, not being able to settle anywhere, nor to gain their living in a constant and regular manner, were compelled to levy contributions from the surrounding districts, and sometimes made whole townships compound with them. As they had nothing to lose and nothing to hope for, there was no rein to restrain them.

The Vaudois deplored these disorders; they looked for some judgment from heaven, and all the phenomena of nature appeared to them to be its forerunners. "In 1601," says Gilles, "from the month of April to the month of June, although the weather was fine, the sun and moon did not display their ordinary brightness; every morning the sun appeared red and blackish, and in the daytime he looked pale and dull," all which they regarded as the signs of some approaching affliction.

In the beginning of February, 1602, there arrived in the valleys

IRRITATION AND EXCESSES.

the Archbishop of Turin,[1] the governor of Pignerol,[2] and Count Charles of Lucerna, with a great train of Jesuits and Capuchins. They caused much disquietude to the Protestants of Lucerna and of the plain of Piedmont, as we have already seen in the twelfth chapter.

At this period, also, the Protestant churches of the marquisate of Saluces were cruelly persecuted, and the company of the *Digiunati* was there formed, analogous to that of the *Banditti* in the valleys. The Vaudois of Pérouse, and those of the neighbourhood of Pignerol, were alike subjected to prolonged annoyance. From day to day it was expected that the central part of the Vaudois valleys would be the scene of some catastrophe. The troop of the outlaws became greater than ever. The Catholics charged the whole Protestant population with the excesses which they committed, whilst their irritation continually increased; and trusting nobody, and fearing nobody, they made themselves dreaded by all.

The Duke of Savoy was earnestly implored to destroy, once for all, this focus of heresy and nest of robbers. The Vaudois were apprised, from time to time, of the progress of these instigations. They named pastors for the special duty of seeking out, exhorting, reproving, and restraining the outlaws; thereafter a solemn fast was held in the valleys, in the middle of the month of August,[3] to implore the pardon and compassion of Heaven. Affrighted families began already to retire to the mountains, whilst their defenders watched and prayed, knowing that the only good protection is that of the Lord.

Meanwhile, Governor Ponte proceeded to La Tour, where he convoked the syndics of all the Vaudois communes, and required them to deliver up the outlaws. They replied by protesting, in the first place, their loyalty to their sovereign, and then deploring the disorders which had been occasioned by unjust proscriptions:—
"It is our persecutors," said they, "who have thrown all this people into this confusion; for your lordship is not ignorant how fatal are the effects of distrust and despair; and if some of these unhappy men have acted a desperate part, they are not the only guilty parties, and as it would be difficult to punish them all, and calamities enough have been endured already, it seems to us that it would be more expedient to cast water upon the fire, by procuring peace for all." Governor Ponte rejected this method, and commanded them to deliver up to him the outlaws, either dead or alive. There was not time for the execution of this order; for, a few days after, the governor himself was arrested, and deprived of all his dignities, on the presumption of his having been guilty of

---

[1] Broglia.   [2] Ponte.   [3] On the 11th and 12th.

betraying the interests of his sovereign in secret transactions with the French generals.

Count Charles of Lucerna, who enjoyed a great influence at court, then came to the valleys to see about an arrangement. He had previously been at Prague, and afterwards at the court of the Emperor Rudolph, in the capacity of ambassador of Savoy. The Elector of Saxony gave him a splendid reception at Dresden; and the count having asked him how he could show his grateful recollection of it, the elector replied that nothing could be more agreeable to him than to learn that on his return he protected the Vaudois. The count promised it, and kept his word. The Vaudois deputies were now invited to assemble at his palace of Lucerna, on the 19th of November, 1602. Vignaux and Gilles were at that meeting—the one for the valley of Lucerna, the other for that of St. Martin. Everybody desired an agreement; for the troop of outlaws still increased by the addition of a great number of Protestants, expelled from the marquisate of Saluces and from the plain of Piedmont. With this the count at first reproached the Vaudois, treating them as guilty of a crime in having given these banished persons the means of subsistence. They replied that the Catholic townships had done so, much more than they, by paying them tribute. On both sides the excesses which had resulted from the proscription were deplored, and a deputation was sent to Turin, where the count promised to promote their endeavours to obtain a general pardon.

But the Duke of Savoy refused the amnesty requested by the Vaudois; and they in their turn refused the other favours which he was disposed to have granted them. The outlaws still pursued their wandering and warlike course of life, making several expeditions to places in the neighbourhood. After new endeavours to put an end to these disorders, the duke, on the 9th of April, 1603, passed an edict at Coni, by which those of the fugitives who belonged to the valleys were permitted to return to their abodes without being proceeded against. But there remained those banished from Saluces, Fenil, Bubiano, Villefranche, and some other parts of Piedmont. The duke wished to destroy them, and for this purpose he formed a special body of troops, to be maintained at the expense of the valleys, the command of whom was intrusted to Captain Galline; but, under pretext of proceeding against the outlaws, this petty general committed numerous crimes, both against persons and property.

One day in the month of July, having arrived at Bobi with his troop, whilst the people were occupied with their field labours, he fell upon the village sword in hand, killed a young man who came in his way, forcibly entered the dwelling of the pastor, who saved himself in the vineyards of Pausettes—and would have gone further with his ravages, if the villagers, hearing the cries of alarm, which were suddenly echoed from rock to rock, had not run from the higher parts of the mountains, and surrounded him in the heart of the valley. Galline, seeing his case to be desperate, and the superior forces of the Vaudois closing around him in a threatening manner, flung himself all at once into the arms of the most influential of his adversaries, Captain Pellenc, and entreated him to save his life. "It is very evident that it is not the outlaws whom you come to seek," said the irritated Vaudois, "since you kill peaceable people, and fall upon our pastors!" Galline humbly excused himself! He was allowed to escape, being first shown that they had it in their power to exterminate his band or to retain him a prisoner. "But those whom you treat so ill," added the leaders of the Vaudois troop, "know how to render good for evil, and, far from destroying you, we shall escort you to see that no harm happen to you."

The precaution was not unnecessary, for from all sides bold combatants descended before them. The soldiers of Galline thought fit still to brave them; a sergeant, named La Morre, meeting at La Pianta a group of mountaineers, commenced to treat them with contempt, and paid for his insolence with his life. The lesson might have served for his comrades; but as they passed through Le Villar, an indignant and armed crowd could not restrain the expression of their anger; some one replied by stabbing with a pike one of those who spoke; and upon this act of violence, the peasants, losing command of themselves, rushed upon the soldiers, and cut them in pieces. A small number escaped in great disarray. Galline arrived at Lucerna, bareheaded, without arms, and without men. Those who had cried to the Vaudois to spare them had readily obtained their request, and were conducted back to Bobi, to the number of forty, to remain there as hostages, until this affair should be settled.

The duke being apprised of it, sent to Lucerna the provost-general of justice, who disciplined Galline's troop; for, since his misadventure, the captain had formed it anew by many enrolments. It was arranged that it should remain on the right bank of the Pélis, and the Vaudois on the left. The provost then caused the inhabitants of the other communes to be informed that they would have nothing to fear, provided that they would not meddle with the affair of Bobi and Le Villar; but all, without hesitation, made themselves mutually responsible for one another, and refused thenceforth to contribute anything at all for the maintenance of Galline's troop. The provost, therefore, returned, without having concluded anything; but a few days after, Count Charles of Lucerna announced himself to the valleys as a mediator plenipotentiary for the proposed arrangement; and after some negotiations, it was decided that the valleys should pay 1500 ducatoons, and that the banished should be pardoned, a general amnesty covering all past excesses.

The Vaudois were even authorized to retain the properties which they possessed beyond the limits of their valleys,[1] and to make profession of their religion in presence of Catholics when it should be asked of them; for hitherto they were not allowed even to avow it; and they were no longer forbidden to do anything except to defend it by polemical discussions. This was to recognize it as possessing a great power.

These concessions were especially favourable to a large number of the inhabitants of Saluces, who had taken refuge in the valleys, and who were permitted thenceforth to remain there. The liberal collections which came to them from France and Switzerland, now also enabled them to recover a little from the confiscations with which they had been visited.

Vignaux died in 1605, after half-a-century spent in the gospel ministry in the Vaudois valleys. He translated into French certain Italian memoirs concerning the Vaudois, drawn up by one of his predecessors, Jerome Miol, pastor of Angrogna. New documents were added by himself. It was on this work of Vignaux that the first history of the Vaudois was based, which was published by Perrin, in 1618, by order of a synod of Dauphiny.[2] Vignaux was nearly 100 years of age; his son assisted him as suffragan during the latter years of his life. For half-a-century he never revisited the place of his birth,[3] and was a pastor in the Vaudois Church. His first parish was that of Praviglelm, from which he went to Le Villar, and he died pastor of Bobi.

[1] The edict is dated 29th September, 1603.

[2] The Synod of Grenoble, in 1603, had first required M. Chaumier, pastor at Montelimart, to write this history. He devolved it upon M. Crisson, who, in his turn, committed it to Perrin, with consent of the Synod of Dauphiny, in 1605. The work of Perrin was not deemed satisfactory; and the synod held at Pramol on the 15th of September, 1620, charged Peter Gilles, the colleague of Vignaux, to compose a new history of the Vaudois. Gilles was seventy years of age when he commenced it. Notwithstanding his old age, he preached six times a-week. His work was first written in Italian, and he did not shrink from recommencing it in French, at the age of eighty years, when, the plague of 1630 having deprived the valleys of almost all their pastors, the use of the French language was introduced by the foreign pastors.

[3] Panassac, in Gascony.

"Three days before his death, all the ministers of the valley assembled in a company around him," says Gilles, "for he was as noble in heart as in birth and talent: and there," he adds, "this zealous patriarch addressed us in a discourse worthy of himself and suitable to our duties; these were his last advices, for he felt that the hour of his departure was come. I remained with him to the last, more and more comforted by his words replete with piety and wisdom, which he ceased not to speak to us as much as his extreme weakness would permit, and thus he expired without apparent pain." What a grave and calm picture! how pleasant does death seem in that aged Christian! His soul removes in peace and serenity from its dwelling; it parts from it without violence, as a ripe fruit parts from the branch on which it hung.

Two years after died the learned pastor of Angrogna, Augustin Gros, a former Augustine monk, as Luther was; converted to the gospel as the great Reformer was converted; zealous in defending and teaching it as erewhile the famous doctor of Wittemberg defended and taught it. He left three sons and a son-in-law, all four pastors in the valleys. A year before his death, in 1607, he was relieved from the active duties of the ministry—the first instance of emeritation which is connected with any particular name in the annals of our valleys.

The Vaudois having enjoyed at this period some years of tranquillity, their numbers increased daily, and the place of worship at Les Copiers received additions in 1608, which brought it to the size which it still retains.

Intelligence was received, however, that the reformed churches of France were exposed to new persecutions. A regiment was sent into the valley of Barcelonnette, to promote the conversion of the Vaudois of that locality. The Church of Rome is the only church which has set the example of employing such agents in the work of conversion. In Piedmont, also, she exerted herself to obtain the employment of similar means against the Vaudois valleys. A public fast was appointed for Thursday, the 20th of January, 1611. On all great occasions the Vaudois ceased not to have recourse, above all things, to fasting and prayer, penitence and supplications.

On the morning of that day a violent earthquake shook all our mountains. "It was," says Gilles, "one of the most terrible that ever was witnessed." Eight days after the regiment of the Baron of La Roche passed from Barcelonnette into the valley of Lucerna. "They were," says the same annalist, "men well armed, making a fine appearance, and carrying themselves proudly, ravaging and putting to ransom wherever they were able, notwithstanding all that could be done to satisfy their insolence."

Quarters were found for them in the communes of the plain, in order that it might be possible to retire into those of the mountain in case of need. They thought fit to assail these, but were repulsed with loss; and if the wish of the more fiery spirits had been acted upon, they would have been driven out of the valleys; but the pastors, desiring that everything might be marked by the utmost moderation, appeased the people, and exhorted them to confine themselves patiently within the strict limits of legitimate defence.

A gentleman of the valley offered his mediation, to obtain from Charles Emmanuel the peaceable removal of these troops; but the treacherous fellow, on the contrary, urged the Duke of Savoy to keep that regiment of plunderers in the valleys, and to take advantage of its presence to obtain from the Vaudois concessions of servility and apostasy. "Yield nothing," said Captain Farel to the Vaudois, "for at the end of a month these troops must receive another destination, and be sent elsewhere, without any steps taken by you." His expectations were realized; and these troops having thought fit to continue, in their new cantonments, the same excesses which they had committed in the valley of Lucerna, were massacred by the peasants.

In 1613 a great part of the Vaudois were summoned out in arms, and required to leave home for the war of Montferrat. They were commanded by the Counts of Lucerna,[1] and reserved to themselves the privilege of assembling, morning and evening, for their own worship, in every place to which they should be led. They conducted themselves bravely in that campaign, and received the commendations of their sovereign.

The year following, Charles Emmanuel having got into a war with Spain, in consequence of his pretensions to Montferrat, new levies were demanded of the gallant mountaineers of our Alps, who then marched towards Verceil, still accompanied by their pastors. They thus had opportunity of removing many prejudices current concerning them, and of meeting now and then secret friends of

---

[1] Count Charles, the son of him who had so often proved himself the protector of the Vaudois, had the general command of the Vaudois troops. Count Achates was named captain of the companies of Rora, Lucerna, Campillon, Fenil, and Briquéras. The Chevalier Philip of Lucerna led those of La Tour and Angrogna. Captain Joseph Pellenc of Bobi had under his orders those of Bobi and Le Villar. "The other valleys and their neighbourhoods," says Gilles, "had also their captains and officers, taken from amongst the men of their places." The major-general of all these troops was Ulysses Paravicin, of the Valteline, for some time resident in the valley of Lucerna.

their doctrines—minds familiarized with the Bible, whose warm reception of them afforded them the more pleasure, as the darkness of superstition reigned so fearfully over these countries.

Troubles, of which we have already given an account, befell the churches of Saluces, and of the neighbourhood of the Vaudois valleys, in 1620. The people of the valleys having interposed, with the view of bringing them to a termination, their deputies were imprisoned either at Turin or Pignerol. They were compelled to pay the sum of 6000 ducatoons, in order to obtain their deliverance and a termination of the annoyances which the Protestants endured.

It was in 1620, also, that the massacre took place of the Protestants of the Valteline, of which the narrative was published as an appendix to the *Brief Account of the Persecutions of the People of Saluces.*

The valley of Lucerna, which had come forward most prominently and resolutely in the common cause of the Vaudois churches, had paid the 6000 ducatoons which were exacted as the price of their tranquillity; and this sum had been well-nigh trebled by the numerous expenses of law and registration which it had involved. The valley of Lucerna then demanded from two other valleys (Pérouse and St. Martin) to be reimbursed for its advances, by the repayment of a part of the sum furnished for the common interest. This repayment appeared hard; peace had been granted. "It is a business concluded," whispered perfidious counsellors in the ears of the Vaudois of Pérouse; "besides you were no parties to the collisions of Le Villar and Bobi; not having shared in their fault, why should you share in their fine?" Advices favourable to personal interest always appear the best; the Vaudois did not recollect that they ought to distrust those of an enemy.

It was an endeavour to produce disunion amongst them. When peril is over, selfishness resumes its power; selfishness is blind, and peril returns. This was what happened to the two refractory valleys. They refused to pay. "But we became bound for you!" said the people of Lucerna. "What matters it?" resumed the malicious advisers secretly; "disavow the negotiations." They were disavowed accordingly. "Then," said the magistrates, "you cannot take advantage of the edict of pacification, which was founded upon them, nor of the amnesty, which extends to all things past." The Vaudois had nothing to reply. "Let justice take its course," exclaimed their enemies. It would have been well, indeed, that justice should have had its course, if it had been justice. But hatred is unreasoning. The Catholics were in exultation. Their object was attained; they had divided the valleys, and opened up a way for the recommencement of persecution against two of them. And they took advantage of it accordingly.

The wealthiest inhabitants of Pinache, Les Clots, and Pral, were forthwith arrested, on pretext of their having taken part in the preceding troubles; and were obliged to pay more for their deliverance than both the valleys together should have furnished, in order to put themselves under the covert of the protecting edict, which they had so imprudently disavowed. Prosecutions were multiplied; and in order to get a stop put to them, the people of the two valleys, after having already left rich spoil in the hands of their enemies, by the numerous confiscations which had taken place amongst them, agreed to pay to the duke 3000 ducatoons.

It was demanded that they should, moreover, demolish six of their places of worship. They resisted this last condition. Hereupon seven regiments of infantry were sent against them, to treat them as a conquered country. The passes which led to the Val Lucerna were guarded; their brethren could come but slowly to their aid; their churches were demolished, and the villages ravaged, as the reader may see more at length in the history of Pragela and Pérouse, under the year 1623. "This," says Gilles, "has been set down, not so much to recal the faults of the past, as to afford instruction for the future."

Imprisonments and individual instances of annoyance were, however, continued in the valley of Lucerna from 1620 to 1624. But this valley had much better claims to urge for their discontinuance; and accordingly these proceedings had consequences less fatal. Moreover, Lesdiguières interceded for the persecuted, and frequently obtained concessions in their favour. In 1625 this general was called to Piedmont, to support the Duke of Savoy in the war which he had commenced against the republic of Genoa; and his presence in the valleys was of advantage to their inhabitants. But after his departure, the severities of magistrates and the attacks of monks were renewed, and more afflictively than ever.

Theological discussions were instituted with the pastors. The pastors did not fear discussion, but they feared treacherous arrests, and the *bravi* lying in wait in the pay of these *good* monks, who supplemented by daggers the weakness of their arguments. Some circumstances characteristic of this period are related in the last chapter of martyrs.

"About this time," says Gilles, (that is, from 1626 to 1627,) "a certain monk began to be seen making circuits in Piedmont, and particularly in the valley of Lucerna—a man of great reputation among those of his own religion, by name Father Bonaventure.

When he prayed, he was sometimes seen, they said, to be lifted up from the earth by a mysterious power. Some took him for a saint, others for a sorcerer." A number of children, between the ages of ten and twelve years, disappeared as he passed through. It was discovered that they had been borne off and placed in the convent of Pignerol. On the urgent petitions of the Vaudois, an end was put to this carrying off of children.

But on the 9th of June, 1627, a number of Protestant heads of families were arrested at the same hour in the towns of Lucerna, Bubiano, Campillon, and Fenil; they were afterwards carried as prisoners to Cavour, and kept there. We have already seen the sequel of these events in the twelfth chapter of this work.

Shortly afterwards took place the confiscation of the goods of Anna Sobrèra, whose husband had become a Catholic, and had consented that his wife should withdraw to the valley of Lucerna, where she married her three daughters to leading *men of religion*, according to the expression then habitually used. But a son of one of them, in his turn, promised to abjure, seduced by the hope that he would be put into possession of the whole property of his grandmother. She had previously dwelt at Villefalet in Piedmont. The Bishop of Fossano, after many fruitless endeavours to obtain her abjuration, had caused her to be imprisoned. This violence succeeded no better than the fair words previously employed, and her husband, Sobrèra, obtained her liberation on bail. But after the death of the bishop, it so happened that the monks of Pignerol pretended to have found amongst his papers, proofs that his former captive had promised to abjure; hence the pretext brought forward for the confiscation of her goods. She was accused of having relapsed.

It was at this time (in 1628) that the Dutch ambassador to Constantinople, Cornelius Haga, asked from Geneva, and then from the Vaudois valleys, a Protestant minister for the service of his legation. There was sent to him the uncle of the historian John Léger, who was afterwards to shed such a lustre over our afflicted valleys. The uncle's name was Anthony Léger; he was then pastor of the parish of St. John, in which he resumed his functions in 1637, on his return from Constantinople. But the incessant malice of the monks compelled him to flee from it in 1643, and he was then nominated a professor in the academy at Geneva, where he remained till his death. During his sojourn in the East, he had had some communications with the patriarch Cyril Lucar, whose life of trouble is so curious, and so little known.[1]

[1] See Aymar, *Monuments Authentiques de la Religion des Grecs.*—La Haye, 1708.

In 1628, a French army, commanded by the Marquis of Uxel, appeared at the gates of the Alps, in order to go to the assistance of Montferrat against the troops of Charles Emmanuel. The Vaudois were charged to defend the mountains, and acquitted themselves valiantly. The duke himself came twice to visit them upon this occasion,[1] and acknowledged in a becoming manner their patriotism, for they received no pay, but bread only. This, however, was a supply of no small importance, for all the crops had failed in Piedmont in the autumn of 1627; and from the very beginning of 1628 the poor people were under the necessity of selling their cattle, their furniture, and even their clothes, in order to obtain at Queyras the food which they needed.

The presence of Uxel's army on the French frontiers made their condition worse, by interfering with this exchange of commodities; besides that the people of Queyras, alarmed at the great quantity of articles of food which were taken out of their district, prohibited the exportation of them, and went the length of imprisoning the unhappy victims of famine who came to procure them. The monks of Pignerol and their followers took advantage of this state of things to attempt to purchase abjurations amongst the Vaudois, at the price of a morsel of bread—the abjurations of wretches wasted by hunger and at the point of death.

It was at this time that Mark Aurélio Rorengo began to signalize himself. He was the son of a seigneur of La Tour, and was originally intended for the magistracy, but afterwards admitted into orders, and named Prior of Lucerna, upon his promise to do his utmost for the destruction of heresy. He caused his father's house to be purchased by a religious corporation, and it was immediately transformed into a convent of Grey friars,[2] or, according to the expression of Gilles, into a *nest of monkery;* for, adds the historian, "a *brood of monks* multiplied there, to the great detriment of the valleys."

These monastics were settled there on the 23d of June, 1628. Their first care was to distribute provisions amongst the poor of their own communion, holding out brilliant promises to Protestants who should become Catholics. But doubly faithful to the example of the primitive church, the Vaudois from that time forth made all that they had, as it were, common property, and distributed amongst themselves, day by day, daily bread to those who stood in need. The monks, seeing this, directed their attempts at conversion by famine to other communes of the valleys, but with the same want of success.

[1] On the 18th of July and 14th of August, 1628.
[2] *Minimes*—Reformed F   iscans, an order founded by St. Francis de Paule.

At Bobi in particular, notwithstanding the presence of the Count of Lucerna, who made two visits to the spot, the people would not even consent that the Grey friars should celebrate a single mass. The friars at that time took up their abode at Le Villar, in an ancient palace, completely in ruins, which was gradually repaired, and which is now in our days both the Catholic Church and the residence of the parish priest. At Rora they seized upon a deserted house, where two monks made their residence; and at Bobi the governor of Mirabouc lodged two of them likewise in a little chamber which he had hired.

The language of these ecclesiastics was at first full of gentleness and benignity; but "on the 29th of September," says Gilles, "they *discovered the scorpion's tail;*" the Count Bighim then causing an edict to be published, by which "it was forbidden to any one to trouble or *incommode, in any manner,* the very reverend Observantine fathers, in anything whatsoever which they might think it proper to do, under pain of death to the delinquent, and of a fine of 10,000 crowns of gold, to be imposed upon the commune in which the crime might be committed. Every informer, the edict added, shall receive two hundred crowns of gold, and his name shall be kept secret." What fit attendants Popery finds!

The Vaudois, far from murmuring, regarded this measure with a feeling of satisfaction, as it at once disclosed to them the evil designs of their adversaries, and enabled the Christians to take steps from the first to oppose the danger with which they were threatened. The people of Bobi assembled around the house in which the governor of Mirabouc had given the two monks a lodging, and begged them to depart before their presence should occasion troubles of which they might themselves be the first victims. The monks comprehended that this request might become an injunction, and returned to Lucerna. But Count Charles, the protector of the Vaudois in former times, had recently departed from this world, and his successor, Philip, was far from being equally favourable to them. He uttered terrible menaces against the people of Bobi, and against the commune of Angrogna, which would not consent to the establishment of the Observantines, upon any pretext, within its limits.

Count Capris, the governor of Pignerol, then came to the valleys, assembled all the syndics, as well as the pastors, and told them that the pope did not cease to insist with the Duke of Savoy that these monastics should be introduced amongst the mountains— that his highness had the right to command, and that if they would not conform with a good grace to his desires, he would employ force. "To-morrow," added he, "I will come and cause mass to be celebrated in Bobi." He came accordingly, but all the doors and all the windows were closed—not a human face was to be seen. He required the syndic to cause at least a stable to be opened to him, that he might have the cover of its roof. "My authority terminates at the threshold of private houses," replied the syndic. "Well, then," said the governor, "I will open your own house by force." "Let your highness consider well," said the syndic, "before you take such a step." The governor felt that it would be imprudent to insist, and that the defenders of the village were not the less near because they did not show themselves; he contented himself with causing a mass to be sung on the highway, and went away home. Two days after he appeared at Angrogna, on the same errand, and met with a similar reception.

Towards the end of January, 1629, he returned to La Tour, with a French seigneur, named De Serres, convoked anew the Vaudois delegates, and endeavoured to persuade them, by representing to them that in France the Catholic religious orders had it in their power to establish themselves everywhere in the midst of the Protestants. "Yes," replied the Vaudois, "but in France, the Protestants also have it in their power to establish themselves everywhere in midst of the Catholics, whilst here we are restrained within narrow limits, beyond which we cannot pass; let us have permission to extend ourselves over the whole of Piedmont, and if not, let the integrity of our own territory at least be respected."

These endeavours proving unsuccessful, the governor retired, and the Observantines, then settled at Le Villar and Rora, suddenly changed their tactics. With the view of inciting the Vaudois to some acts of violence, which might serve as a pretext for cruel reprisals, they laid aside the mildness and humility which had marked their demeanour hitherto, and became all at once intolerably insolent and provoking. "You will bring some mischief upon yourselves!" said friendly advisers. "So much the better," said they; "let them pursue us, let them strike us, let them kill us, it is just what we desire!"

Then the Vaudois did what they had done at Bobi; they assembled in arms around the abodes of the monks, but the monks refused to go away; and as all men were prohibited from laying hands upon them, the women assailed them; and some of these robust female mountaineers, accustomed to carry heavy burdens, took the poor churchmen upon their shoulders, like loads of wood, and bore them away without resistance. Their furniture, their copes, their relics, and all their baggage, were then carted off, and conveyed beyond the limits of the commune.

The clergy made their complaint at Turin. The Vaudois sent thither deputies to defend their cause; and an edict of the 22d of February, 1629, restored all things to the condition guaranteed in the preceding concessions. Thus were these long vexations [*fâcheries*] terminated, as the most ancient annalist of our valleys expressively but temperately calls them. The troubles which took place at the same time at Praviglelm and at Campillon, have been already related.

Here terminates the long period of Charles Emmanuel's reign. He occupied the throne of Savoy for half-a-century. Crowned on the 2d of September, 1580, he died on the 16th of July, 1630, at the age of sixty-eight years and a half.

The surname of the Great, which he received from his contemporaries, has not been ratified by history. He was a man of benevolence and of ability, but irresolute and changeable. His political course was characterized by restlessness, ambition, and uncertainty, and did not admit of his having faithful allies, for he was not a faithful ally himself. He added to his dominions the marquisate of Saluces, in exchange for Le Bugey and the Pays de Gex; but on his death, France seized upon Savoy and part of Piedmont.

The events briefly sketched in this chapter form two-thirds of the work of Gilles, from which our narrative of them is almost exclusively derived. They are certainly of considerable number; but they did not exercise a sufficient influence over the destinies of the Vaudois to merit so much space in a general work like the present. Nothing of importance has, however, been intentionally omitted.

The period which next follows opens with the calamities of the pestilence, and is closed by unparalleled massacres. To this several chapters will be devoted; but the two principal things which will there be seen continually to increase in importance, as the most active means employed at that time against the Vaudois Church, to wit, the introduction of monks and the cantonment of troops in the valleys, have already been witnessed in their commencement amongst the events just narrated.

But everywhere the protection of God will be seen unceasingly extended to his children; as also the courage of their faith rising to the level of their afflictions.

CHAPTER V.

THE PLAGUE AND THE MONKS.[1]

(A.D. 1629 TO A.D. 1643.)

Famine—The Vaudois prevented from obtaining employment—Extraordinary storms—Convent erected at La Tour—War between France and Savoy—Sufferings of the Vaudois—The plague—Meeting of the pastors at Pramol—Deaths of pastors—Terrible ravages of the disease—Three pastors alone left in the valleys—New pastors obtained from Geneva—Victor Amadeus I.—Rorengo and the pastor Gilles—Government commissioners in the valleys—Polemical works—Public discussions—Anthony Léger.

OUGHT science to reject all notion of a connection subsisting betwixt the extraordinary phenomena of nature and the great events which take place in the world? Such is the opinion prevalent in our day; but the people of other times thought otherwise, and their imagination, attentive to external signs, delighted to bring the testimony of these remarkable facts to the confirmation of their fears or their hopes.

In 1628 there was a famine in Piedmont. Next year the poor inhabitants of the Vaudois valleys—who, having no harvests of their own, were accustomed to go to the rich domains of Piedmont, to offer their services at the rate of so many *emines* of corn for so much work—were deprived of this resource by an express prohibition under which the priests laid their flocks, not to receive a single Protestant labourer. The Vaudois complained, and the duke set aside the prohibition; but in some places, says Gilles, "there were found ecclesiastics who, being as it were infuriated, loudly declared that they would kill with their own hands those *of the religion* who should venture to come to the harvests." *Odium theologicum!* It is a term of the middle ages, when nothing was yet known but Popery.

In 1629, on the 23d of August, about eight o'clock in the morning, a dreadful storm, or rather one of those extraordinary waterspouts, which are like a cataclysm, a local deluge suspended in the atmosphere, broke suddenly upon the peaks of the Col Julian, and produced, in a few hours, a fearful inundation on both sides of the mountain. The village of Pral, in the valley of St. Martin, and that of Bobi, in the valley of Lucerna, were invaded by the waters at the same moment, and with such force, that the inhabitants had

[1] AUTHORITIES.—The same as in Chapter III.

scarcely time to abandon the houses which were most exposed to the danger. The flood filled these two villages with masses of rock which it carried along with it; many houses were swept away; some persons lost their lives; but the scourge disappeared as rapidly as it had come.

This was not to be the case with the pestilence which, in 1630, broke out in all the valleys. It was preceded, in September, 1629, by an extraordinarily cold wind, which, as Gilles says, "marched in company with a very dry haze," and destroyed the last hope of a crop from the magnificent chestnut trees with which our hills are covered; and afterwards unusual rains caused the crop of grapes to perish. There was no expectation but of a famine more severe than the preceding. The Vaudois ministers assembled in synod on the 12th of September, and in that assembly, says the same historian, they had extraordinary religious services in testimony of their fraternal union, not knowing that they were never to meet together again in this world, and that of these fifteen pastors, only two would survive their brethren at the end of a few months.

Towards the close of the year, the convent and church of the Grey friars at La Tour were built, on the site on which the paternal abode of Rorengo had stood. Almost on the same spot, at the present day, stands a house for the education of Protestant girls, and farther off is Trinity College, erected in 1830, precisely two centuries after the erection of this convent, which has long since disappeared.

In 1630 a French army which the Cardinal De Richelieu had placed under the command of three marshals of France, the Marshals De Schomberg, De La Force, and De Créqui, was sent to oppose the Duke of Savoy's projects on the Montferrat. It descended into Piedmont by the valley of Suza, and then drew back towards the Vaudois valleys.

The valley of Pérouse surrendered on being summoned, on the 21st of March, Pignerol on the 23d, and its citadel on the 29th. But the valleys of Lucerna and St. Martin had not yet surrendered. They pressed the duke to send them assistance, and demanded from the generals of the enemy that they should have time to capitulate.

The monk Bonaventure, already mentioned, went to the two parties alternately, saying to the Duke of Savoy, "The Vaudois occupy strong positions in the mountains, and cannot surrender without disloyalty, but the Catholics, dwelling in an open country, cannot resist an armed enemy, and must be excused in the event of their capitulating." To the French, again, he said, "The Catholics will make haste to surrender, but the Vaudois are a rebellious race, who will resist you, and merit all severity."

Meanwhile, the army was allowed to plunder; and conflicts arose between the soldiers and the inhabitants, the former endeavouring to carry off property, and the latter to defend it. The Vaudois hereupon sent deputies to the Marshal De La Force, who commanded a detachment encamped at Briquéras. "Submit to the king," replied he, "and we will protect you; otherwise, we will have you ravaged, killed, burned, and exterminated." The Sardinian troops had already retired beyond the Po; no succour could be expected from them, and the valleys submitted on the 5th of April, upon assurance given them that their privileges would be respected, and that they would never be required to carry arms against their sovereign. "But they were subjected to continual hardships," says Gilles, "by the passage of great bands of armed men going and coming between France and Piedmont; and the roads were covered with a swarm of people, who transported great stores of wheat, which the king (Louis XIII.) had caused to be collected in France for the army of Piedmont."

In the latter part of April, the King of France being at Lyons with all his court, set out for Savoy. The Cardinal De Richelieu went to meet him; and the Vaudois sent to him a deputation, consisting of Joseph Chanforan, John Berton, Joseph Gros, and James Ardoin, who presented to him, at the little village of Montiers, a petition asking the confirmation of their privileges, which was granted to them.

On the 10th of June the troops of the Marshal De La Force took the town of Cavour by assault, and burned it. On the 22d of July the whole army proceeded against Saluces, of which it took possession in the beginning of August. After having remained there for some time, these troops were again put in motion, and on the 26th of October appeared before Casal. This town was at that time defended by the Austrians, and besieged by the Spaniards—allies of the Duke of Savoy. At last, on the 13th of November, the treaty of Ratisbon was signed, which put an end to that war; the valleys of Lucerna and St. Martin were restored to Piedmont, but those of Pérouse and Pragela, as well as Pignerol, remained to France. It was not until September, 1631, that the fortifications of Briquéras were demolished.

But a scourge more terrible than war took away from the Vaudois almost two-thirds of their population in that deplorable year, 1630. The weather was excessively hot; a contagious malady, the plague, which prevailed in France, had augmented the army of Richelieu by a great number of volunteer recruits, who fled from the danger. They brought it with them. With the first days of the month of May, this terrible malady began to appear in the village of Les Portes, situated near Pérouse. It next broke out in St. Germain, whither it was carried, as was said, by a grave-digger; and then also at Pral, to which it was brought with goods that came from Pignerol. And it had very soon spread over all the valleys.

As soon as the pastors were aware of its appearance, they met, according to the usage of their church, to inquire concerning the mind of the Lord, and to seek, by prayer, meditation, and conference, a correct view of the duties which these difficult circumstances required at their hands. They were unanimous in proposing the celebration of an extraordinary fast. "But not seeing," says Gilles, "how it was possible to observe that solemnity in a suitable manner, in the midst of such a bustle of armed men and of people conveying provisions, they agreed that each minister should do all that he could in his own congregation, to produce in the members of the congregation a serious repentance and an effectual conversion. They took counsel, also, to provide themselves with the antidotes proper for the calamity, and to aid the poor by public alms."

This meeting of pastors was held at Pramol. A few days after, the plague made its appearance there, commencing in the quarter of Les Pellencs. Public worship began then to be held in the open fields at Pramol and at St. Germain. This was towards the end of May. A month after, the commune of Angrogna was invaded by the scourge; and on the 10th of July there died, at one time, the pastor of St. John, in the valley of Lucerna, and the pastor of Meane, near Pérouse.

However, the plague had not yet appeared at La Tour. A celebrated physician dwelt there;[1] and there were also there two surgeons[2] and three apothecaries.[3] The presence of these men of skill attracted many persons thither; but they were the first victims of the scourge which then ravaged Pignerol. The persons who were spared made haste to flee from that city. A great number of them retired to La Tour, as well as some of the French generals.[4] Provisions, the rents of apartments, and mercenary

---

[1] Vincent Goss.

[2] Daniel Gilles, son of the historian, and John Bressour, great-grandson of Pantaléon Bressour, one of the former persecutors of the Vaudois, whose family had embraced Protestantism.   [3] Thomas Dassez, Daniel Cupin, and John Cot.

[4] Amongst others, the son of the Marshal De La Force, the Count of Servient, and the Baron of Bonne.

services rose to an excessive price. A mule's load of wine was sold for fourteen or fifteen crowns.

The surgeon Gilles being dead, and his colleague ill, a French surgeon demanded fifty pistoles of gold ere he would let blood for him. Next day he exacted a golden crown, for telling him from the street and in at the window, without entering the house, how he was to place the cupping-glasses. Some persons promised beforehand one of their properties in absolute right, to obtain the assurance that they would be buried; for the dead encumbered the houses, and some were burned with the corpses which they contained.

On the 12th of July the pastor of Pral died,[1] and on the 24th the pastor of Angrogna.[2] Seven other Vaudois pastors died during the following month.[3] Those who survived them, assembled on a mountain which rises by itself in the centre of the three valleys, on the Saumette, near the Vachère, within an easy distance at once of Angrogna, Pramol, and Prarusting. This meeting took place on the 2d of August.[4] After tears and prayers, the six ministers who were still spared divided amongst themselves the necessary care of the churches which had become vacant. Daniel Rozel, the pastor of Bobi, was appointed to conduct the second son of Gilles to Geneva, that he might complete his studies; but they died within a short time of each other, both being cut down before they could accomplish this design.[5]

There now remained in the Vaudois valleys only three pastors engaged in actual duty, and an aged *emeritus* pastor. The latter died soon after. The last three witnesses of the priesthood of the Vaudois Church held a new synodal meeting on the heights of Angrogna, with the deputies of all the parishes of the valleys, to consider the means of providing for the exercise of their religion. They wrote to Constantinople to recal Anthony Léger, also to Geneva requesting the aid of some new ministers, and to Grenoble, entreating those of Dauphiny likewise to come over to console and confirm again this Vaudois Church, thus so severely tried. There remained only one pastor in each of the three valleys; to

[1] James Bernardin, aged forty years.
[2] Bartholemew Appia, forty-five years.
[3] James Gay, at Rocheplate, sixty years; Barnabas, his son, twenty-eight; Brunerol, at Rora, forty-three; Laurence Joli, at Maneille, forty-five; Joseph Chanforan, at St. Germain, fifty-six; John Vignaux (son of Domenic), at Le Villar, fifty-eight; David Javel, at Pinache, fifty. The last-named left by his will all his property to the valleys, for the maintenance of students for the holy ministry.
[4] September ?—Tr.
[5] Rozel died on the 28th of September, and Samuel Gilles on the 23d—the latter being nineteen years of age.

wit, Peter Gilles in that of Lucerna, Valerius Gros in that of St. Martin, and John Barthelemy in that of Pérouse. But the latter having been called to the parish of St. John in 1631, and having gone from thence to La Tour on the 22d of April, to confer with the pastor of that place on the affairs of the church, prolonged that conversation till pretty late in the evening, and then retired to his own home, for he was a native of La Tour, and his father's house was still his home. But he could not say to his soul, "Abide for many years!" for that very night it was required of him. The pestilence seized him at the close of that conference, and he died three days after.

This mysterious and terrible scourge, whose severity had been abated during the winter, became again more violent in the spring of 1631. It then passed through the more elevated districts of Angrogna and Bobi, which it had spared hitherto. More than 12,000 persons died in the valleys;[1] at La Tour alone fifty families were swept entirely away. The harvests rotted on the fields unreaped, the fruits fell ungathered from the trees.

During the great heats of summer, horsemen might be seen to drop from their horses on the middle of the road, and remain dead on the spot. "The great roads," says Gilles, "were strewed with so many bodies of men and beasts, that it was impossible to pass along them without danger. A number of properties were abandoned from want of owners or cultivators. The towns and villages, which recently had abounded with persons of the learned professions, merchants, artisans of every description, and workers of every kind of work, were now without life—the solitude of the desert had come upon them; the grapes hung from the vines, and the corn covered the fields, because labourers were everywhere awanting. The wages of servants increased to four times their ordinary amount. Nurses in particular had become so scarce, that no one could tell where to look in order to find one for the poor babes that were born during these calamities. Their ordinary wages, which had not exceeded twelve or fourteen Piedmontese florins before the plague, soon rose to sixty or eighty, without its being even certain that one could be procured at that rate. Every family lost some of its members, and many families entirely disappeared."

The minister Gilles, whose words we have just quoted, lost the four eldest of his sons; and the aged father himself, alone left of all

[1] The victims, *amongst the Vaudois alone*, were distributed as follows:—In the valley of Lucerna, 6000; in that of St. Martin, 1500; in that of Pérouse, 2200; in the districts of Prarusting and Rocheplate, 550.—Total, 10,250.

the pastors of the valley, found his duties increase along with his sorrows; but God gave him strength to sustain the heavy weight of so many accumulated distresses, and of the service of so many churches. He went into all the parishes, preaching twice every Sabbath, and once at least on every day of the week; visiting the sick and consoling the afflicted, without fear of that death which all his colleagues[1] had met in the fulfilment of the same distressing and dangerous duty. He resolutely prosecuted his ministerial labours; calm and serene in the midst of the dying, he imparted to them his unshaken confidence in him who casts down and who raises up, who wounds and who heals. "I passed," says he, "amidst persons infected with the plague, and through terror-stricken villages, which everywhere presented only spectacles of death and of family affliction;" and, according to the only Latin quotation in which he indulges in his whole work, at a period when it was common to use them very abundantly—"Ubique luctus, ubique pavor, et plurima mortis imago." His indefatigable devotedness seems really more extraordinary than even the danger: and he was preserved to the Vaudois Church throughout all the ravages of that epidemic; and with him the completest monument of the ancient history of the Vaudois, which he has transmitted to us in his chronicles, rich in the details of a period of history but little known.

The pastor Brunet was the first who hastened from Geneva to the help of the valleys: he came in December, 1630, six months before the pestilence ceased. Other ministers of the gospel followed him at later dates; and although the Italian language had until then been used amongst the Vaudois in sermons and teaching, it became necessary at that time to substitute for it the use of the French language, into which Gilles subsequently translated his work, which he had commenced in Italian. From this time, also, date the systematic relations since continued between the Vaudois Church and the Church of Geneva.

The most pressing duties which these new pastors had at first to perform in the valleys, related to the reorganization of their terribly decimated congregations. "It was a marvellous thing," says Gilles, "and such as had never before been seen or heard of in these parts, what a great multitude of marriages took place at that time. . . . . In most places the plague had bereaved families of their children, deprived children of their parents, husbands of their wives, and wives of their husbands; so that desolation extending every-

---

[1] With the exception only of Valerius Gros, the pastor of St. Martin, who was afterwards removed to Le Villar.

where, each one sought to be united with a sister or a brother to build up again their failing or ruined houses." But these marriages were merely the conclusions of funeral solemnities; and were characterized by the invocation of the Divine blessing, instead of the noise of sport and worldly pleasures.

Thus had three disastrous scourges been endured almost simultaneously—famine, pestilence, and war; but the two former having passed away, the latter also was removed at last, during the reign of Victor Amadeus I., who had retired to Queyras in order to avoid the contagion. He signed at that town, on the 6th of April, 1631, a treaty of peace, by which he was restored to possession of all his dominions, and acquired some towns in the Montferrat, in compensation for Pignerol and the valley of Pérouse, which remained to France. Scarcely was he in peaceable possession of his throne, when he set to work to render his reign illustrious by things of lasting benefit to the country, more than by victories. He restored the university of Turin, for which he erected the splendid building which it now occupies, and attracted thither learned strangers, to promote literature and science.

But before going to Turin he made his abode for some time at Montcallier, where the Catholic clergy sought to inspire him with sentiments hostile to the Vaudois. The latter, being apprised of this, sent a deputation[1] to convey to him the dutiful expression of their loyalty, and their prayers for his welfare. The Count of Verrue undertook to communicate their message to the sovereign; but the Vaudois deputies having afterwards obtained an opportunity of an interview with the Duke of Savoy, in the town of Carignan, and having laid before him the object of their mission, he received them graciously, and said to them, as he dismissed them, " Be faithful subjects to me, and I will be to you a good prince."

But the prior of Lucerna (Rorengo), and the superior of the convent of La Tour (Fra Paolo), having been informed of this favourable reception, sought to nip in the bud the hopes which might thence be derived of repose for the valleys, and accused their inhabitants of a multitude of crimes and acts of disobedience. The prefect of the province, named Rezan, proceeded to La Tour to make investigation. A meeting was held for this purpose on the 4th of August, 1630, and the falsehood of the accusations was acknowledged.

What did the worthy prior then do? He sought an interview

---

[1] It was composed of MM. John Geymet for the valley of Lucerna, Francis Laurens for that of St. Martin, and John Meynier for those of Pérouse, Méane, and Pragela.

with the pastor of La Tour, Gilles, whose interesting chronicles have preserved us an account of their conference:—"An excellent thought has occurred to me," he said. The pastor must have thought that it was a thing as fortunate as it was rare. "Why should the Protestants and Catholics persist so obstinately in their respective pretensions?" added the Jesuit. "If we were to yield something on each side all would go on better, and I could reckon confidently on the approbation of the Church of Rome." "I am far from disputing the authority with which you may have been intrusted to that effect," replied the pastor, "but I have much less authority on the part of our churches; and I declare to you beforehand, that I cannot make in their name any engagement which concerns them, without their having been previously consulted. However, let me know what you have to propose." "It is this," replied Rorengo; "If the Vaudois will consent that the monks shall freely dwell among them, I guarantee that we will leave you in peace." "That is to say," answered Gilles, "that in order to your consenting not to do us any harm, you demand that we put you in a condition to do it." It need hardly be said that the prior met with a refusal.

The Vaudois, however, had applied to Victor Amadeus I. for a ratification of their privileges, and at this period they sent deputies to Turin to hasten forward that matter. These deputies were received by the prince on the 8th of September, 1632, and learned from his own mouth that a minister of state would be sent to the valleys, to satisfy himself by exact information as to the acts of disobedience which were laid to their charge, as well as to take cognizance of the grievances which they themselves complained of. Accordingly, a short time after, the collateral Sillan arrived, who, accompanied by Rorengo, went over all the valleys, collecting the remarks of the Vaudois, and the informations which were lodged against them. It is not known what report he made to the sovereign; but next year a new commissioner was sent by him to the same places—a master of requests, named Christopher Fauzon. He arrived at La Tour on the 5th of May, 1633, and convoked a meeting of the Vaudois delegates for the 9th of the same month. When they were assembled, he told them that they were accused of having recently established themselves at Lucerna and Bubiano. The Vaudois proved that they had existed there from time immemorial. Then he pretended that a number of them had promised to abjure, and had not kept their word. "Because the promise had been wrung from them by violence," replied they. "What proof have you of that?" he demanded. "If it had been voluntary," said they, "what hindered them to fulfil it?"

"But you have schoolmasters who teach heresy," said he. "Prove to us," said the Vaudois, "that our religion is a heresy, and we renounce it; but if they only teach our religion, then do you respect the liberty of conscience, which was guaranteed to us by the edict of 1561." "Do not insist upon that," said the commissioner, "for his highness is going to send you better teachers." "And who are they." "Learned and respectable fathers." "What!" exclaimed the deputy of Bobi,[1] "would they make us send our children to school to the monks? I would rather that mine perished on one pile, than give up their souls to perdition."

The referendary Fauzon afterwards disputed the right of the Vaudois of St. John to make use of a bell for assembling the congregation to worship. "The practice is of immemorial antiquity," replied the delegate of St. John, " and the successive confirmations of our liberties have, by implication, sanctioned it."

After this Fauzon set aside the other accusations, of which nothing was found to remain but an echo, which could be traced to no origin and no authority. Then it was that, with one consent, the people broke out in complaints too long suppressed. "What! you leave undisturbed the impostors who work upon the credulity of the public! You leave undisturbed the Jews, who blaspheme the name of the Redeemer, and the vagabonds who infest the highways; but you cease not to prosecute and vex us, peaceful and laborious evangelical Christians, whose only endeavour is to live in the fear of God and in brotherly kindness with all men; you cease not to set at our heels packs of monks bent upon mischief; for these fanatics think nothing more delightful and praiseworthy than to make us the victims of treachery, deceit, imprisonment, and robbery." In support of these complaints, unfortunately too well founded, a multitude of particulars were cited, of which no one could deny the correctness. Hereupon the commissioner assumed a milder tone, and promised to put an end to such abuses; after which he hastily closed the meeting, and left the valleys without coming to any conclusion. But the hidden influences under which he had, in the first instance, acted, were set in operation again to impose upon him.

Accordingly Fauzon returned to La Tour a few days after, in order to oblige the Vaudois to furnish written proofs establishing their legal right to celebrate Protestant worship in each of the parishes in particular. They dreaded some trap set for them

[1] Peter Paravin.

amongst these perpetual delays. However, on the 29th of June, 1633, they furnished the document required. This paper remained unanswered, and the state of things continued unchanged. But the monks only became the more active in their attacks upon Protestantism, and it was at this time that the polemical writings of Rorengo and of Belvedère appeared, in order to refute which Gilles suspended for a time his historic labours. He replied to these writings in a work entitled, *Considerations on the Apostolic Letters of the Sieurs, Marcus Aurelius Rorengo, Prior of Lucerna, and Theodore Belvedère, Prefect of the Monks*,[1] published in 1635. This work, of which a refutation was attempted at Turin, was followed by another, still larger, which the indefatigable pastor of La Tour published in the year following, under the title of *Torre Evangelica*.

These two volumes owed their origin to polemical publications, and called forth others which this is not the place to enumerate. These were succeeded by conferences between the monks and the pastors, in which Anthony Léger, the pastor of St. John, who had returned in 1637 from Constantinople, displayed so much talent, that one of his adversaries, finding himself unable to vanquish him by discussion, resolved to seize him by main force. For this purpose he put himself at the head of a troop of armed men, to whom he said, "I must have the minister dead or alive!" The Vaudois came promptly to the defence of their pastor. They prevented the monk Simond from executing his design; but, in consequence of the continual conflicts and vexations which arose on his account, Anthony Léger quitted the valleys in 1643, and went to Geneva, where he spent the remainder of his days.

At this period, also, close the interesting chronicles of Gilles, which we have so often quoted in this and preceding chapters. As a historian he has the merit of abounding and being exact in facts, and of being calm and grave in his judgments, fluent and simple in his style. His only fault is that of being sometimes diffuse and careless. The fulness and circumstantiality with which he relates events, derive an additional value from the caution and exactness which characterize his narratives. As a controversial writer he has the defects of his time, but he exhibits also its good qualities, and unites with a solid erudition the advantages of a very sound judgment, and of a raillery that is sometimes sufficiently sharp. His mode of conducting an argument appears at first sight lax, in consequence of the length to which he carries out the statement of his views, but his reasoning is close enough in respect of the connection of his views and deductions themselves. Gilles was,

[1] *Considerations sur les lettres*, &c.

moreover, during more than ten years, secretary of the Table, or moderator of the Vaudois churches, and he completed, in 1601, the scheme of ecclesiastical discipline which had been prepared in 1564. These numerous labours, carried on amidst the multiplied duties of his ministry, attest at once his zeal and activity. It is not without regret that we here quit this valued guide, whose memory becomes dear to all students of the history of the Vaudois.

CHAPTER VI.

THE PROPAGANDA.[1]

(A.D. 1637 TO A.D. 1655.)

Charles Emmanuel II. of Savoy—The Duchess Christina of France—Disputes as to the regency—The Propaganda instituted—Rorengo—Placido Corso—Public discussions—Crimes and cruelties—Terrible conflagrations—Civil war—The Vaudois support the Duchess Christina—Protestant worship prohibited at St. John—Other severe edicts—Women in the Propaganda—The Marchioness of Pianesse—Her dying charge to her husband—The residences of the monks burned at various places in the valleys—False charge brought against a Vaudois pastor, of having instigated the assassination of a priest.

VICTOR AMADEUS I., who ascended the throne in 1630, died on the 7th of October, 1637. His eldest son, Francis Hyacinth, aged scarcely five years, survived him only one year; and his second son, then aged only four years and some months, became, on the 4th of October, 1638, the successor to the ducal crown. The title of Charles Emmanuel II. was given to him; and it was under his

---

AUTHORITIES.—The last two chapters of *Gilles*, and chapters v., vi., vii., and x., of the second part of *Léger*.—"*Relatione all' eminentissima Congregatione de Propagandâ fide de i luoghi de alcune valli di Picmonte, all' A. R. di Savoya soggette . . . dal V. F. Teodoro Belvedère.*"—*Torino.* (No date.) A small volume of 323 pages. (The real name of this monk was *Anthony Lazzari*. Gilles refutes his works in his sixty-first chapter. A reply was made to him in a little work, entitled "*Risposta al libro del Sig. Gillio, titolato* Torre Evangelica." This publication was also dedicated to the Propaganda.)—"*Journal of the Conversions which have been made, and of the instances of grace with which God has favoured the Company for the Propagation . . .*," &c. Without date. In 4to, 20 pages.—"*Summary of the Reasons and Grounds upon which his Royal Highness has gone in forbidding the Heretics of the Valley of Lucerna from residing beyond the tolerated bounds.*" Without date, but printed at Turin about the close of 1655, and published both in Italian and Latin.—*Van Breen,* "*Apologetic Memoir concerning the Vaudois, with an Appendix from 1642 to 1655,*" printed in Dutch, at Amsterdam, 1663.— See also the introductory part of most of the works noted at the commencement of the following chapter.

reign that one of the most terrible persecutions took place which ever drenched the Vaudois valleys with blood. But it would be wrong to hold him alone accountable, as until his majority it was his mother who held the reins of government in the capacity of regent. She was Christina of France, daughter of Henry IV. and Mary De Medicis. She inherited the haughty and stern disposition of her grandmother, so that the spirit of the Medicis, rather than that of the princes of Savoy, presided over the carnage of 1655.

From 1637 to 1642, Thomas and Maurice of Savoy, brothers of Charles Emmanuel, disputed with his widow the regency of his dominions. This contest of five years was the cause of most fatal troubles and divisions in Piedmont; then, from 1642 to 1659 (the date when the peace of the Pyrenees was concluded), the war was continued against the Spaniards, who had, in the first place, been brought into the country by the Cardinal Maurice and Prince Thomas, when they were claimants of the regency. These foreigners having seized upon the best places of Piedmont, refused to give them up; so that Christina, in order to reconquer them, was obliged, in her turn, to call into her dominions the troops of France.

In the valleys, where we have seen that the reformed Franciscan monks, or Grey friars, had been introduced by Rorengo, and maintained most pertinaciously by the governors of the country, the regular clergy continued their underground work, destined to burst forth at an after period in prodigious disasters. A powerful coadjutor was at this time also given them by the court of Rome, to wit, the Propaganda. This name was given to a society composed of clergy and laymen, founded at Rome, in 1622, by Gregory XV., under the title of *Congregatio de Propagandâ fide*.

Its institution had, from the first, no other object than to promote the spread of the Catholic doctrines. It was not long of acquiring a predominant influence over the secular clergy, who had imprudently admitted it as an ally; and afterwards it went the length of savagely pursuing—with an incendiary torch in one hand, a sword in the other, and the feet in blood—the extermination of all doctrines which were not its own. Nothing was forgotten in its work except the gospel. And what did it gain? What persecution always gains—the burden of the crimes committed, the responsibility of the blood shed, and the execration of humanity.

It was the prior of Lucerna, Mark Aurelio Rorengo, who introduced into the Vaudois valleys the first seed of this powerful tree, whose branches were very soon to extend over all Piedmont, and to cover it with the bloody fruits of the most odious fanaticism.

A member of the Roman Propaganda, already celebrated by his talent for discussion, was sent from Rome to the valleys, expressly to labour for the conversion of the Vaudois. He was a preaching monk, named Placido Corso. Rorengo, who had already had many fruitless conferences with the pastors, hastened to go and meet this protector champion, whom fame announced to him as a polemical Boanerges.

It was on the 10th of November, 1637, that Placido Corso arrived at La Tour. His first care was to provoke the pastor of the place, Gilles the historian, to a conference. "I have come a very long way," he wrote to him, "to defend the holy Catholic, Apostolic, and Roman Church; and having inquired at several persons of your parish as to the reasons for which the Vaudois had separated from it, they directed me to their pastor, as to one who was better able to instruct me on that point." "What an admirable zeal it is," replied the pastor, "which comes from so great a distance to attack that of which it knows nothing! But, nevertheless, we are very far from recognizing the Church of Rome as being what you designate it; it is for you, therefore, to prove, in the first place, that it is apostolic and holy; and the result of this inquiry will render it much more easy for us to tell you why it is that we have separated from it."

The monk did not shrink from the thesis which he was invited to sustain, and he wrote to the minister all the reasons commonly adduced in favour of the Romish Church. Gilles refuted him. Letters in considerable number were thus exchanged, till in the end Placido Corso left the last unanswered.

Hoping to be more fortunate in a *vivâ voce* conference, where his adversary would not have time to choose and weigh his arguments, he sought to gain, by such means, the ground which he had lost. Anthony Léger, recently arrived from Constantinople, where he had filled the post of chaplain to an embassy, had resumed the humble duties of a village pastor, in his old parish of St. John. It was to him that the propagandist addressed himself; and after various negotiations, it was arranged that a public conference should take place at La Tour, on the 4th of December, 1637, in the court-yard of an elder of the church, named Thomas Marghet. Rorengo demanded that he should preside in this meeting; and it was thought proper to defer to his wish. The youthful Scipio Bastié, on the side of the Protestants, and a Capuchin named Laurent, on the side of the Catholics, were chosen for secretaries. One of the most difficult questions of canonical theology, that of the Apocryphal books, occupied the whole of that meeting.

The second was fixed for the 1st of January, 1638, and took place at St. John, in the court-yard of Daniel Blanc, for no apartment was capacious enough to receive the crowd of hearers; but the sky of Italy sometimes, even in winter, permits meetings to be held in the open air, on ground scarcely hardened by frost, at the base of snow-covered Alps. The monks were very late in making their appearance at this meeting. They excused themselves on the ground of their having been detained by their private devotions; but some of those present smiled, and said to one another in a low voice, that they showed themselves more eager to put an end to the conference than to prolong it. The discussion, however, was not terminated when night came on; but it was the last, for the propagandist would not again enter the lists *"with these wranglers,"* as he said, *"who made a pope of the Bible."* Yes! the Bible was to the Vaudois even more than a pope. But the crouching slave of the Holy See could go no farther in his comparison.

The next to follow and emulate him in the arena of discussion was a Grey friar of La Tour, named Brother Hilarion. He undertook a polemical correspondence with the pastor of Bobi, Francis Guérin, whose last letters he also left unanswered.[1] In the valley of St. Martin, the monks of Le Perrier attempted similar contests, and met with similar checks.

The spirit of hatred, or at least of intolerance, so natural to monks, became exasperation in these. It was no longer by the weapons of logic that they sought to combat the Vaudois; assassinations and abductions were employed. A young man, named Morton, the servant of an Englishman, was assassinated at La Tour. A young girl of Bubiano was carried off by the monks who dwelt there, and placed under the care of a popish woman. The brother of this girl came to claim his sister again, and she eagerly followed him. The guard saw them, and raised the alarm; the Catholics ran and overwhelmed the young man with blows. Then came a priest on horseback, who took the girl behind him, and bore her off to Turin. From that time forth, all attempts made to obtain restitution of her remained ineffective.

But these were not the only wicked proceedings by which the clergy laboured to vex the poor Protestants. At their instigation, an attempt was made to compel the Vaudois settled upon the right bank of the Pélis, in the district of Lucerna, to remove and confine themselves to the left bank only; an attempt was also made to restrict all of them from residing for more than three days conse-

---

[1] Guérin was cited to appear at Turin in 1650, prosecuted in 1651 for not having appeared, condemned for contumacy, and obliged to go into exile.

cutively in any of the other towns of Piedmont, whither business might call them. But through the interposition of persons in high place, these vexatious measures were unsuccessful. At the same time there occurred also certain movements of troops, which the enemies of the Vaudois always sought to turn to their disadvantage.

On the 22d of March, 1639, there arrived at Lucerna, St. John, and La Tour, a great number of people from Bubiano and its neighbourhood, all in disorder and alarm, bringing carts loaded with their furniture, and horses with their stores of linen and their children, whilst they themselves conducted their flocks, as if going into exile. Then came message upon message, rapidly succeeding each other, all to announce that a regiment of Italian cavalry, in search of quarters, was advancing at a quick rate. The regiment arrived that evening at Lucerna, and from thence was sent to Bubiano; next day it attempted to enter the territory of St. John, but the Vaudois had placed strong guards at all the passes, and drove it back into the plain. Upon that occasion the excesses consequent upon the want of military discipline, the trouble and confusion which arise in the proximity of camps, prevailed for some days in Piedmont, without penetrating into the Vaudois valleys. These disastrous agitations expired at the confines of that home of the gospel, where courage maintained peace. And they were well entitled to defend themselves—that people, whose number was so small, and whose rulers were then disputing for the throne of a child.

But terrible conflagrations occurring at this period, contributed also to increase the misfortunes of these districts. On the 6th of March, and on the 21st of November, 1634, fire caught hold of the woods of Briquéras, and despoiled the hills around that place of all their lofty trees. These hills are now covered with vineyards. On the 11th of December, 1639, two fires, also at the openings of the valleys, broke out simultaneously—the one between Briquéras and St. Segont, the other between Lucerna and Lucernette. The north-east wind blew strongly; the first of the fires extended to the heights of Prarusting, devouring everything in its course. That of Lucernette quickly seized upon the woods of Bubiano upon the one side, and upon those of Famolasc and Bagnols upon the other; and its ocean of flame swept over the country as far as the hills of Barges, thus occupying a space of several square leagues. The affrighted inhabitants, not being able to contend against this devouring invasion, took to flight, or endeavoured to isolate their dwellings, by cutting down beforehand the trees by which they were surrounded. Numbers were compelled to defend themselves against the danger, by extinguishing the flames with the wine from their cellars, for want of sufficient water at hand.

This fearful conflagration lasted for several days. The front of the fire might be seen climbing from the plain up the mountains, like a sea of flame, leaving behind its glowing waves the naked and blackened earth, presenting at intervals, over great tracts of country, what looked like immense cauterizations, or frightful blotches of gangrene.

Besides all this, Piedmont was desolated by civil war. Three political parties had formed themselves in the country. Robbery and plunder extended everywhere like another fire. The outlaws, still scattered among the mountains, confidently acted upon their own unhappy pretensions; frequent murders signalized their vengeance. They exhibited, upon a smaller scale, the same conduct which the princes of Savoy then displayed at the head of their armies. One man kills another, and is an assassin; a prince kills a thousand men, and is a hero. When will murderers be weighed in the same balance? When will the nations become weary of shedding their blood like water for dynastic pretensions, which have nothing to do with their welfare? The union of kings is a perpetual conspiracy against liberty; what, then, must their divisions be for the nations of men?

The Marquises of Lucerna and of Angrogna, having embraced the party of the pretenders to the regency, maltreated the Vaudois, who had refused to take part in these intestine divisions, which brought so much suffering upon the kingdom. Another member of the same family, Count Christopher, upon the contrary, espoused the cause of the duchess and her son.

It was dreaded that the usurpers, supported by the Spanish army, might devastate the Vaudois valleys with fire and sword. A general meeting was held at St. John, to consider what was to be done. The count was there. The pastor, Anthony Léger, insisted that the Vaudois should maintain their independence on behalf of the legitimate prince, Charles Emmanuel II., then a minor, and the tutelage of whom his uncles were disputing with his mother. The Vaudois prepared their own militia for service; made provision for the maintenance of the government, already much disorganized; opened the passage of the Alps to the French army, which Turenne and D'Harcourt led to the succour of Christina; and finally restored to that victorious princess one of the best defended provinces of her dominions.

The recollection of all this, which she afterwards showed them that she retained, was far from being that of gratitude; and this princess, when she became powerful, was like the serpent warmed again to life. But at the present time she was in misfortune, and perhaps even afterwards, she was more weak than cruel.

Be this as it may, the enemies of the Vaudois availed themselves of their position around her to irritate her against them; and as Léger had exercised a great influence in the council of his countrymen, they had him condemned to death for contumacy, on the pretext that he had been in the service of foreign powers, without authority from his lawful sovereign. This service had been limited to the discharge of his pastoral functions whilst he was with the ambassador of the United Provinces. But any pretext is good enough for hatred, and hatred was satisfied. Léger was compelled to retire to Geneva, where the academy of that town had long the honour to number him amongst its professors. He was a man of extremely mild character, and of remarkable talent.

Encouraged by this first success, the enemies of the Vaudois went farther in their demands. Agents of the Roman Propaganda had established themselves at Turin, and their influence extended, like an invisible net-work, over the court of Savoy. The father of the duchess, Henry IV., had been a Protestant; fanaticism presented this circumstance to the mistaken eyes, or rather to the servile conscience of Christina, as casting upon her origin a deplorable stain, which the most fervent zeal alone could efface; and we have seen already wherein zeal for Catholicism consists. Everything injurious to the Protestants was fervour in her estimation; the Propaganda encouraged these sentiments, and their triumph was completed through the influence of political views.

This took place in the following manner:—From the vacancy of the ducal throne, and from the moment that Christina's regency was disputed, the clergy gave all their support to her competitor, Maurice, of Savoy, who was a cardinal. Christina, therefore, in order to win back the clergy to her side, thought it necessary to rival her brother-in-law in zeal, that is to say, in concessions, honour, and power, accorded to the clergy; restrictions, rigour, and intolerance, in regard to the Vaudois. One of the first acts of her government was to enjoin the Vaudois settled without their limits to return to them within the space of three days.[1] A month before, she had given instructions to the magistrates in favour of the Capuchin missionaries, ordaining that, upon information lodged, the podestats should act according to their office against those whom

[1] Dated 3d November, 1637.

they denounced.[1] Next year she renewed her orders against the Vaudois extending themselves beyond their own territory.[2]

At this time an accident happened to the castle of Cavour, which was in part destroyed by lightning, but was restored by the French. A year afterwards, at the synod of St. Germain,[3] the younger Léger was ordained to the holy ministry, who at a later period became, by his courage, as well as by his writings, one of the most powerful defenders of the valleys. The congregation which he was then appointed to supply was that of Pral and Rodoret. Some months after, the duchess, still upon solicitation of the Propagandists, gave many injunctions to the prefect of the province, whose name was Rossano, to have the Protestant worship interdicted at St. John, and the church shut up which the Vaudois possessed there.[4] Again she renewed the prohibition against their passing beyond their limits, not only to acquire lands, but even to farm them, and that under pain of death and confiscation of goods.

A special commissioner was sent from Turin to watch over the observance of this edict—a doctor of laws from Montcallier, master of requests to the council of state, and very zealous in the sense in which that term was understood by his sovereign. His name was Gastaldo, and he took up his abode at Lucerna. His first care was to cite all the Vaudois to appear before him who possessed lands or establishments of any kind beyond the limits to which it was thought fit to restrain them—limits which became narrower continually; for, according to a more recent order, even the right bank of the Pélis had been interdicted to them.[5] The persons cited having refused to appear, their properties and establishments were declared to be confiscated and to have fallen to the exchequer.[6]

But it was not enough to oppress the Vaudois; favour must also be shown to their adversaries, and in a very long edict[7] of the Duchess of Savoy, in which she treats at once of duels, of the chase, and of taxes, all the governors of castles in the Vaudois valleys were ordained to accede freely to the requests of the Capuchin missionaries, to attend at the meetings held by the Vaudois, to watch over them and to interdict them if necessary. The Vaudois were at the same time prohibited from assembling without the presence of chaplains, under a penalty of fifty crowns of gold for every

[1] Dated 19th October, 1637.
[2] 9th November, 1638.   [3] 27th September, 1639.
[4] These orders are of date the 4th and 17th of April, 1640. The church of the Vaudois was then situated in the quarter of Les Malanots.
[5] This order was of date 23d December, 1640. Gastaldo's citation was of date 14th January, 1641.   [6] By decree of Gastaldo, 29th January, 1641.
[7] Of 15th and 16th January, 1642.

A PASTOR APOSTATIZES.

one who should contravene the edict; and this singular edict, which contains so many other things, promises, moreover, an immunity from public burdens for five years together, to all Protestants who should consent to become Catholics.

This promise having seduced no one, it was renewed by a special edict still more urgent than the first.[1] A few abjured; but the public contempt, and the affronts which they received from their fellow-countrymen, very soon compelled them to quit the valleys, and to seek a residence elsewhere.[2]

Shortly after succeeded, one after another, measures still more rigorous against the Vaudois. They were prohibited from passing beyond their limits, even for a few hours, except on market-days.[3] The magistrates of the neighbouring towns were enjoined, in case of their so doing, to arrest them without any legal formality.[4] At the same time proceedings were instituted against their pastors[5]— the official celebration of the Catholic worship was appointed to take place in all the Protestant parishes[6]—the Capuchins were encouraged,[7] and new rewards were promised to apostasy.[8]

In 1645, an institution was founded at Lucerna, expressly to receive and provide with marriage portions such young Vaudois girls as might abjure; but this institution could not maintain itself. The same year a Sovereign Council, established in Piedmont by the king of France, adopted still more vexatious measures against the Vaudois of Pérouse and Pragela.[9] The Catholics, and those who had become Catholics, were loaded with the favours of the court.[10] A young minister, named Louis Gaston D'Albret, who was born at Paris, and had studied at Geneva, arrived in the valleys, where he filled the office of pastor for two months, when he was unable to resist the pressing solicitations to apostasy which were addressed to the Vaudois. He abjured on the 26th of July, 1647 —received great honours at Turin—resided with the nuncio, and afterwards disappeared from the country, bearing with him a gratuity of 800 livres which the Duchess of Savoy had sent him,

---

[1] This second edict is of 6th April, 1642. I mark these dates precisely, because these events have been related by no previous historian.
[2] As the family of Durands of Rora, which removed to Bagnol.
[3] 17th February, 1644.   [4] 18th September, 1645.
[5] The judiciary citations relative to Anthony Léger are of date 20th December, 1642, and 10th April, 1643. A petition of the Vaudois, on this subject, bears date 12th June. The order relative to the ministers Guérin and Lépreux, is of 3d April, 1647.   [6] This order is of 13th December, 1646.
[7] Orders of 10th January, 28th April; 8th October, 1646; 22d July, 1648, &c.
[8] 8th May, 1645; 8th March, 1648, &c.   [9] Edict of 17th July, 1645.
[10] For general favours, exemption from burdens, from taxes, &c., 10th September, 1645; 9th and 12th October 1647; 4th November, 1648.

eager perhaps to get him removed from her dominions, as well as withdrawn from Protestantism; for she also was a D'Albret, that name being a patronymic of the progenitors of Henry IV.

The ancient privileges of the Vaudois were, however, ratified at this period more frequently than ever;[1] for the Vaudois thought to make them more secure by confirmations. In this the court granted nothing, and they gained nothing; on the contrary, they robbed themselves; for the fees of sealing, copying, and registration required costly sacrifices at their hand on each new confirmation. But Rome grudged them even this impotent safeguard; and Innocent X. annulled, by a pontifical decree, dated on the 19th of August, 1649, the last favours which these poor people had obtained from their sovereigns. The influence of the Propagandists went on increasing, and ere long all the privileges, guaranteed in such mockery, were arbitrarily suspended by the edict of the 20th of February, 1650.[2] This suspension was to continue until the Vaudois should have demolished the eleven places of worship which they possessed beyond the prescribed limits; dismissed those pastors who were natives of other countries;[3] shut up the numerous schools maintained by them elsewhere than in their own territory; and consented to the universal celebration of the Catholic worship in all the valleys. These severities were all owing to the increasing intrigues of the Capuchins and the Propaganda.

The Vaudois sent up petition after petition, and, by these dilatory means, only succeeded in keeping all their difficulties unresolved. The monks, meanwhile, erected chapels in the valleys, notwithstanding the visible displeasure, and sometimes the formal opposition of the inhabitants: it required an edict of the sovereign to compel the people of Macel to permit the building of the church of La Salsa.[4]

But the claims and representations of the clergy became every day more urgent; and the petitions of the Vaudois having been rejected, instructions were given to Gastaldo, on the 15th of May, 1650, to restrict them within a boundary-line drawn above St. John and La Tour; ordaining all those who were settled in these

[1] An edict of 26th February, 1635, approved on 19th September, confirmed the privileges of 1585; it cost the Vaudois 15,198 livres. Other confirmations were dated 8th May, 1643; 17th July, 1648; 30th June, 1649, &c.

[2] This edict was grounded upon a Report or *Parere* of the Minister of Justice, *Gambarana*, of which the reasoning is curious enough—" *Perchè*," it says, " *detti heretici* . . . . *sono desobedientissimi, e continuamente intravengono alli ordini di V. A. R., e alle loro proprie concessioni* . . ." &c., &c.

[3] The pastor, Daniel Roche, had already been recalled from the valleys to Geneva, where he had entered the academy of that town in the capacity of a professor. The letter recalling him is dated 23d March, 1648.   [4] Edict of 28th January, 1649.

communes, as well as those of Lucernette, Bubiano, Fenil, and St. Segont, to retire from thence within the space of three days, under pain of death, with obligation to sell their possessions within the space of fifteen days, under pain of having them confiscated. The entirely Protestant communes of Bobi, Villar, Angrogna, and Rora, were enjoined to maintain, at their own expense, a station of Capuchin missionaries in each; and, at the same time that all possible means were thus employed to augment the number of Catholics, foreign Protestants were absolutely prohibited from settling in the valleys under pain of death, and of a fine of 1000 crowns of gold, to be imposed on the commune which should admit them.

Charged to put in execution enactments so Draconic, or rather, to designate more perfectly their cruel injustice and savage atrocity, enactments so profoundly Catholic—Gastaldo, however little sympathy he had hitherto shown for the Vaudois, acted with great moderation, it must be said, in the application of this ordinance, which, in his hands, became rather comminatory than repressive. The times fixed by the ordinance had long passed over without the parties, who were so unfortunate as to come under its sweep, having yet complied with it, and Gastaldo kept his eyes closed. He himself supported, by his representations to the sovereign, the petitions which were sent up by the persons interested, against whom, in the meantime, he took no steps; and ere long new confirmations of their ancient privileges were granted to them, on the 12th of January and the 4th of June, 1653. Thus the barbarous ordinance of the 15th of May, 1650, was never carried into effect.

But during this interval the Propaganda had attained unexpected greatness in consequence of the jubilee, which, in 1650, brought to Rome the rich tribute of the superstitions of all Europe. A sort of popular enthusiasm was created for that work, in which it was open to all Catholics, of whatever condition, to take a part. To be engaged in it, was all that was necessary to obtain a plenary indulgence; persons of great note enlisted themselves; princes and artizans took their places together in these ranks; there was no one who did not need indulgences, or, at least, there was no one who had not some need of pardon; this institution of the Propaganda, therefore, rapidly extended, not only in Italy, but also in France. It had special councils in almost all the towns of these countries; and now to its title of "*Congregation for the Propagation of the Faith,*" it added, in Piedmont at least, these supplementary words, "*and for the extirpation of heretics.*"[1] These councils,

[1] Congregatio de propagandâ fide et extirpandis hereticis.

as we have already said, were indifferently, or rather, with perfidious ingenuity, composed of persons *of civil life* and persons *of religious life*, if that name of *religious life* may be given to the gross fanaticism which labours, hand in hand, with corruption and cruelty. Yet this is what Rome calls zeal! If such be not the language of Antichrist, where shall we expect to find it?

As there was a plenary indulgence for the Propagandists, the women also desired to have their share. They formed a special council; and thenceforth the Propaganda was composed of two councils—one of men and another of women. This institution was founded at Turin, under the high favour of a royal ordinance.[1] The archbishop of that city, and the Marquis of St. Thomas, a minister of the crown, were the presidents of the former of these councils. The Marchioness of Pianesse was president of the latter. She had spent her youth in dissipation, and sought to expiate her past faults by the extremeness of her new zeal. Being a woman of strong passions, and easily led away, but perhaps also of a noble and generous disposition, it was no difficult matter for her spiritual directors to impel her into a wrong course, which they could teach her to regard as that of duty. Mankind, in general, are more easily swayed by a command issued in name of truth than by proof of the truth. Here lies the secret of the power of Popery.

All means were set in operation by the Propagandists to attain the object of their association; and as we now enter on the historic chapter of Léger, we shall borrow from that historian some particulars concerning the proceedings of the council, which owned for its president the Marchioness of Pianesse.[2]

"These ladies," says he, "divide the towns into districts, and each visits her district twice a-week, suborning simple girls, female servants, and children, by their cajoleries and fair promises; and causing trouble and annoyance to those who do not choose to listen to them. They have their spies everywhere, who inform them of all Protestant families in which there is any domestic disagreement; and then they profit by the occasion to blow the fire of division as much as possible, to separate the husband from his wife, and the wife from her husband, the child from his father and mother, &c., promising them, and in fact bestowing upon them, great advantages, if they engage to attend mass. Frequently they impel them to institute law-suits against one another, and if once they have a hold of them by this handle, they never let them go until they have either recanted, or are ruined. They know the

---

[1] This ordinance is cited in the edict of 31st May, 1650.
[2] Léger, Part II., chap. vi.

merchant who is unprosperous in business, the gentleman who has gambled away or squandered all that he had, and in general all families which fall into necessitous circumstances. And to seduce them with their *dabo tibi*, these ladies never fail to propose apostasy to these persons when they are almost desperate. They make their way into the very prisons, and accomplish the release of criminals who give themselves up to them. And as they employ great sums of money in keeping all this machinery in motion, and paying those who sell their souls to them for bread, they make regular collections, and do not fail to visit all families in good circumstances, shops, taverns, gambling-houses, &c., demanding alms for the extirpation of heresy. And if any person of condition arrives at an inn, they lose no time in paying their respects to him with an empty purse in their hands. To conclude, they meet in most of the towns twice a-week, to compare accounts of what they have done, and to concert plans for what they are to do. If it so happens that they have need of the secular arm, or of an order of Parliament, it is rarely that they do not succeed in obtaining it. The councils of the lesser towns give in reports to those of the metropolitan towns, the latter to the council of the capital, and those of the capitals to that of Rome, where is the great spider that holds the threads of all this web."[1]

Such was the secret of the power so rapidly and immensely organized and extended by the activity, everywhere multiplied and propagated, of the innumerable agents who served it, and were its devoted instruments. The Marchioness of Pianesse herself, Léger adds, great lady as she was, and unquestionably the first at court, took the pains, as long as she lived, of going in person several times a-week, to make the above-mentioned collections through the town, even in the public-houses.[2] Could we desire greater devotedness or self-denial in a work of Christian charity? Let us do justice to our persecutors! they thought to serve the cause of charity: but let us execrate the detestable Popery which so perverted the idea of charity, and which changed into infernal poisons the most celestial perfumes of the noblest souls!

And these were not the only works of this kind to which these generous-hearted persons were guided by their church of perdition, and to which they might sometimes be seen to flock with a disinterestedness well worthy of a better cause. All the Vaudois children that could be withdrawn from under their paternal roof, and carried off from their parents, were considered as innocent victims saved from heresy, that is to say, snatched from the claws

[1] Léger, Part II., page 74.   [2] Ibid.

of Satan, and rescued from eternal perdition. Zealous Papists did not shrink from making the greatest sacrifices, braving even the terrors of the laws and the vengeance of men, in order to seize upon them. These children were then placed with rich Catholic families, who undertook their maintenance, or in convents, which undertook to make them slowly die to the world, to their native country, to the pure affections of the heart, and to the faith of the Bible. But what anguish and disorder were thus brought into families! And in this way did the abominable power of corruption, deposited in the bosom of Catholicism, transform the natural generosity of the hearts of its adherents into odious deception and barbarous treachery, as it had transformed Christian doctrine into miserable superstitions. The law of Nature was not more respected than the law of Revelation: for indeed both are from the same Divine source, and it is in the nature of Antichrist to oppose everything which comes from God.

It was, however, under the guise, and perhaps in all the sincerity of the greatest benevolence, that the instruments of apostasy were sometimes made to act, whose inflexible and cruel servility was perhaps also nothing else than the Catholic transformation of a genuine devotedness. Thus, by the concurrence of a number of rich persons and diverse legacies, there were opened in all the valleys (at Lucerna, at Pignerol, and at Le Perrier), establishments for lending money upon pledges, which were then called *Lombards*, and are now known as *Monts de Piété*.

The valleys were exhausted by the successive cantoning of different bodies of troops since 1653.[1] The famine augmented the price of wares, and poverty made them scarce. The establishments of which we speak had stores of corn, linen, various kinds of stuffs, and cash, all which resources they placed at the disposal of the Vaudois. When one of them had pawned his last articles of furniture, in order to prolong his life, they offered to restore them to him without any repayment on his part, on condition that he should give his soul in pawn to Popery; or they threatened him with the prison, if he did not reimburse them for the advances which he had received, and afterwards offered to release him from it, to annul his debt, and even to furnish him with fresh assistance, if he would abjure. These means were successful in drawing over numbers of persons, but still they did not accomplish so much as was desired.

[1] Piedmont was then in alliance with France, and opened a passage through its territory to the troops of Louis XIV. to go to the assistance of the Duke of Modena. They were led by Prince Thomas, uncle of the Duke of Savoy.

The death of the Marchioness of Pianesse drew near. Not hoping anything more from this world, she bethought herself of her husband, whom she had not seen for a long time: she sent for him and said to him, "'I believe I have much to expiate, and perhaps in my conduct towards you. My soul is in danger, help me and labour for the conversion of the Vaudois.' The husband promised; he was a brave soldier, and he laboured accordingly in soldierly style, putting all to fire and sword."[1] He had still another motive for obeying, namely, that his wife left him considerable sums, of which he was to have the disposal only upon that condition. The Jesuits presided at this compact of agony and extermination suggested by the Propaganda. From this time forth their only business was to find an occasion, or pretext, or reason for violent measures. The monks became more arrogant than ever, and the Jesuits dispersed agents amongst the Vaudois, whose employment was to provoke and excite the people to some sudden out-breaking.

Léger relates that the wife of Pastor Monget, at Le Villar, took an active part in the burning of the abode of the monks in that place, but the fact is not proved. The habitations of the monks were certainly destroyed by fire, or by the hands of the Vaudois, not only at Le Villar, but at Bobi, Angrogna and Rora; but the punishment of these crimes, in the persons of those who were guilty of them, could not be alleged as a motive for the violent measures of 1655, far less in justification of them; for the last of these acts, the burning of the convent of Le Villar, took place in 1653, and next year, as well as in that same year, the Vaudois again obtained the confirmation of their ancient privileges, after having rebuilt for the monks, the house which had been burned down.[2] This fact,

[1] Extract from M. Michelet's *Course of History*, published in the supplement of the journal *Le Siècle*, of 8th May, 1843.

[2] These confirmations were of date the 12th of January, 1653 (before the fire at Le Villar), and the 4th of June, 1653 (after that event), as well as on the 8th of December, 1654. (This last document relates only to civil privileges). In the greater number of papers relative to the events of 1655, which have come under my eyes, I have nowhere found, amongst the complaints brought against the Vaudois, the fact of that fire, which was then an affair terminated and set right. Monget himself was banished from the country. In the reports addressed to the government on the subject of the Vaudois, about the end of 1654, these two complaints are set forth:—

1. That certain young people of Prarusting, in returning *from a wedding*, had cast down, in sport, a *piloun* already ruined. (This name is given to a kind of isolated pillars which support nothing, but in which is formed a little niche where is placed either a statue or a picture of the Virgin, holding in her arms the infant Jesus. This figure is named the *Madone*).

2. The Vaudois of La Tour are accused of having excited an ass, and then let

to which Léger ascribes too much importance, because of the part which he acted as moderator in connection with it, had nothing whatever to do with the proceedings of 1655. Pretexts more serious, but having as little foundation, were then brought forward. The priest of Fenil had been assassinated. The assassin was seized after another crime. Pardon was promised him upon condition that he should confess plainly that he had killed the priest solely at the instigation of the Vaudois, and in particular of Léger, then pastor at St. John. Berru (such was the assassin's name), not having shrunk from the commission of a crime which entailed upon him capital punishment, could not be expected to shrink from a falsehood which was to save his life.

And it was on the denunciation of this man, guilty of three avowed murders, that the pastor of St. John, unknown to himself, without examination, and without being confronted with his accuser, without any judicial process, and without having even been cited, was condemned to death, as the instigator of one of these assassinations, whilst the assassin was set at liberty. We may easily understand the sentiments of indignation which are expressed in the writings of Léger, and cannot be surprised if the heart of the persecuted man sometimes caused the pen of the historian to tremble.

When hatred was reduced to such accusations as these—when the magistracy could listen to them, there must assuredly have been a world of prejudices on the one side, and a very irreprehensible life upon the other. But the worthlessness of the pretext shows the blindness of the hatred: other machinations show its ingenuity.

Louis XIV. had sent troops to the succour of the Duke of Modena in 1654, and it was resolved to take advantage of their return and their passage through Piedmont, towards the end of that year, to canton them in the Vaudois valleys, and to make them serve for the work in hand. A dreadful success crowned the clerical intrigues in this instance, and there would therefore rest an ineffaceable stigma on the front of Catholicism, like the mark on Cain, the first fratricide, even if bloody pages were not so abundant in the history of that religion.

him loose to cross the ranks of a Catholic procession. Their justification bears that this ass, which had been fastened before a shop, was frightened by the singing, the noise, the appearance, and banners of the procession itself, and that it broke its halter and escaped without anybody having to do with it.

CHAPTER VII.

THE PIEDMONTESE EASTER, OR THE MASSACRES OF 1655.[1]

(SATURDAY, THE 24TH OF APRIL, BEING EASTER EVE.)

Proceedings of the Society *de Propagandâ fide*—Gastaldo, the duke's lieutenant in the valleys—Severe measures—Prolonged and fruitless negotiations—The Marquis of Pianesse—His deceitfulness—He puts himself at the head of troops for the extermination of the Vaudois—Indecision of the Vaudois, who are in part deceived by false pretences—Janavel—The Vaudois resist the Marquis of Pianesse at La Tour, but are defeated—Further combats—Further treachery of Pianesse—Massacre on the day before Easter—Fearful atrocities—M. Du Petitbourg refuses to conduct his troops upon occasion of this massacre—His subsequent exposure of its enormities.

ALL the means hitherto employed to destroy the Vaudois having proved insufficient, others were devised; for the avowed object of the Propaganda, officially established at Turin, and extended over the whole of Piedmont, was *the extirpation of heretics.* Whatever

---

[1] AUTHORITIES.—The works which follow being very numerous, I think it may be advantageous to arrange them in two sections:—
I. *Works written with a design favourable to the Vaudois.*—*Léger.* The most important. His whole work relates to this epoch of the history of the Vaudois. Léger is rich in documents; but being himself a witness of the events which he relates, and a sufferer, he sometimes writes in a style which displays much passionate feeling. His work was reprinted at Lyons in 1699, in one vol., folio, and translated into German, Breslau, 1750, 4to.—Léger embodies in this work the greater part of *Morland's* "*History of the Evangelical Churches of the Valleys of Piedmont,* . . . ." &c. Folio, which was printed at London in 1658, whilst Léger's work was not printed (at Leyden) till 1669. Two vols., folio, ordinarily bound in one.—
"*Rélation véritable de ce qui s'est passé dans les persécutions et massacres faits, cette année, aux Eglises Réformées de Piémont,*" &c. . . . Place of printing not given. M.DC.LV. 4to of 84 pages.—At page 55 commences a second little work, entitled "*Suite de la relation contenant une succincte réfutation de l'invective du Marquis de Pianesse.* . . ." &c. The same work was also printed at Geneva, with this note, *Jouxte la copie imprimée à Turin,* M.DC.LV.—It has been republished, with some modifications, under different titles:—"*Récit véritable de ce qui est arrivé depuis peu, aux vallées de Piémont.*" (No date nor place of printing.) 8vo of 47 pages.—"*Discours sur les calamités des fidèles de Piémont.*" 8vo, 20 pages.—
"*Lettre des fidèles des vallées de Piémont, a MM. les Etats-généraux,*" &c. 8vo, 15 pages. (Dated from Pinache in the Val Perouse, at that period belonging to France, 27th July, 1655.)—"*Lettre des Protestants des vallées de Pérouse à Mylord Protecteur d'Angleterre, avec un cantique sur les actes funestes de leur massacre et de leur paix.*" 8vo. Two little works, each of 8 pages.—"*Rélation véritable de Piedmont, de ce qui s'est passé dans les persécutions et massacres, cette 1655 année, des Eglises reformées,*" &c. Villefranche, MDCLV. 8vo. Not paged. 32 leaves.—"*Histoire d'une ambassade des cantons évangeliques de la Suisse, au Duc de Savoie, en 1655.*" (Revue Suisse, t. iii. p. 260.)—"*Voix de pleurs et de lamentations.*" Printed at Villefranche, MDCLX., small 4to, 402 pages. The second part

might be the reasons to which recourse was had for the institution or justification of the violent proceedings now to be considered, this avowed object was their real cause.

<blockquote>
alone relates to our subject. Its title is "*Examen de la procédure et des cruautés que les massacreurs ont exercé contre les pauvres Chrétiens des vallées de Piedmont, avec les pleurs et lamentations de leurs frères,*" from p. 89 to p. 242. (Not at all historic.) See also most of the works which treat generally of the Vaudois.

II. *Works written in a spirit unfavourable to the Vaudois.*—"*Rélation des événements qui se sont passés entre les Vaudois et le Duc de Savoie, faite par ordre de S. M.* (Ch. Emmanuel II.,) *pour répondre à une autre relation des Vaudois, partiale et inexacte.*" It is to this work that the second part of the "*Rélation Véritable,*" cited in the preceding section, is a reply, derived from the work of Morland.—"*Somma delle ragioni e fondamenti, con quali S. A. R. s' e mossa a prohibiri alli heretici della valle di Luserna, l' habitatione fuori de limiti tolerati, Torino,* 1655." Folio, 10 pages. It is the French translation of this manifesto, which has been cited amongst the authorities for the preceding chapter.—"*Summa rationum quibus Regia Celsitudo Seren. Sabaudiae Ducis adducta est ut prohiberet haereticis Lucernae vallis ne extra limites toleratos domicilium haberent. Augusta Taur.*" Folio, eight pages. The same manifesto in Latin. It commences with an apology for the order of January 25, 1655, and contains some interesting documents.—"*Rélation des succès arrivés en la vallée de Lucerne, l' an.* 1655." Not paged, and with no intimation where it was printed. (Léger has given the whole of this pamphlet in the tenth chapter of his second part, refuting it point by point.)—"*Relatione de successi seguiti nella valle di Luserna, nel anno* 1655." Folio, eight pages, without intimation where printed. (This is the same pamphlet in Italian. Its great object is the justification of the Marquis of Pianesse.)—"*Rélation très véritable, de ce qui s'est passé aux vallées de Luserne, Saint-Martin et Angrogne, cette année de* 1655," &c. 4to, 38 pages. No indication where printed. (This pamphlet is a reply to the "*Rélation Véritable*" of the Vaudois, which is itself a reply to the "*Rélation*" of the Marquis of Pianesse.)—"*Gesta in valle Lucernensi, anno* 1655." 4to, eight pages. (No date nor place of printing.) A translation of it in French. Folio, 10 pages.

To these works relative to the circumstances of this period, and called forth by them, may be added the following:—"*La conversione di quaranta eretici, con due loro principali ministri, d' alla setta di Calvino, alla santa fede catolica; nell' augusta celta di Torino, alla* 18 *di maggio* 1655." (Not paged, and without date or place of printing.)—The pastors here referred to returned afterwards to the evangelical faith, and published "*Saincte palinodie, ou repentance des prisonniers des Eglises Réformées de Piémont, lesquels par infirmité, avaient fait abjuration de la vérité, avec une brièvè reformation des articles de ladite abjuration, dressés par ordonnance de l' archevêque de Turin et du général des Inquisiteurs de ladite cité.*" MDCLVI. 8vo, 87 pages. (No place of printing.) See concerning the facts of this case, *Léger*, part II. p. 65.

To all these may be added the diplomatic papers exchanged between the different Protestant powers of Europe and the Court of Turin, on occasion of these events, which may be found partially embodied in several collections, *Leti, Life of Cromwell; Morland, Léger, Florent, Martinet,* &c. These papers are preserved in the State archives at Turin, where also several manuscripts are to be found: "*Origine de la guerre des Barbets en* 1655 *;*"—"*Relation de ce qui s'est passé à l' arrivée et au départ des ambassadeurs Suisses,*" &c.—"*Mémoire remis par les ambassadeurs Suisses a S. A. R. en faveur des Vaudois;*"—"*Notta delle transgressione attuali che commettono gli eretici,*" &c., all relating to the latter part of the year 1655; and a multitude of other notes, documents of various kinds, and in particular, letters, of which the greater part (but not all) have been published.
</blockquote>

CHARLES EMMANUEL II.

Charles Emmanuel II. was a prince of much clemency and goodness, and with much that was noble in his character. The Vaudois allowed themselves to be drawn into unaccustomed murmurings, and even reprehensible doings, under the excitement of a system of incessant provocations and wrongs to which they were subjected, unknown to their sovereign, by the Jesuits, the Capuchins, and the Propaganda. But again it must be said, that neither the intentions of the duke, nor the doings of the Vaudois, were the cause of the massacres of 1655. The spirit of Popery alone excited that storm. But how was the duke induced to favour it?

It has already been said, that the council *De Propagandâ fide et extirpandis hæreticis* was composed of the highest personages of the court.[1] Its meetings were held in the palace of the Archbishop of Turin. Other councils established in the provinces sent in their reports to it. These reports were invariably hostile to the Vaudois. Their immemorial residence at Saint John, at Briquéras, at Bubiano, and at Campillon, was represented as if they had made new encroachments; their appeals to their ancient privileges as acts of resistance to the recent decrees of Gastaldo, himself a member of this council. Other reports, founded upon these, were presented to the sovereign by ministers who also formed part of this council of extirpation and of death (*de extirpandis hæreticis*).

It is a fact honourable to the Duke of Savoy, that he did not consent at that time to adopt any new measure more severe than preceding ones, but confined himself solely to giving Gastaldo orders that the edict of 15th May, 1650, should be put into execution—an edict which indeed had, since that time, been suspended and legally abrogated by late ratifications of the ancient privileges, but which was still valid as to certain reserved articles, and was far exceeded by the pressing and almost universal demands of the public fanaticism, then clamouring for the complete annihilation of the Vaudois. As to the military operations which followed, the duke had the responsibility of them without directing them, and we shall soon also see by what combinations of insidious and perfidious intrigues both the inhabitants of the valleys and the Duke of Savoy were deceived. The former fell by thousands in a frightful carnage; the latter was rejected by indignant Europe from amongst the number of civilized princes; and the cause of all this

[1] It included the Minister of State, *the Marquis of St. Thomas; Ferrari*, the President of the Senate; *Philippa*, President of the Court of Accounts; the Grand Chancellor; the Archbishop of Turin; the King's Confessor; *the Marquis de Pianesse; the Count Christoforo; the Abbé de la Mena; Gastaldo*, Lieutenant of the Crown, and, from the year 1650, Supreme Governor of the Valleys; as also *Rorengo*, the founder of the Grey Friars of La Tour, Grand Prior of Lucerna, &c.

was Rome—alone remaining barbarous, persecuting, and savage, in the midst of civilization.

Gastaldo, the duke's special lieutenant in the Vaudois valleys, having been ordered to see that the people complied with the requirements of the edict of 15th May, 1650,[1] issued, on the 25th of January, 1655, an edict, bearing that all Protestant heads of families settled in the communes of Lucerna and Lucernette, Fenil and Campillon, Bubiano and Briquéras, St. Segont, St. John, and La Tour, should remove to the communes of Bobi, Villar, Angrogna, and Rora—the only communes of the valley in which his royal highness was disposed to tolerate their religion—and that within the space of three days, under pain of death and confiscation of goods. Moreover, they were bound to sell their lands within the twenty days next following, at least unless they would consent to become Catholics. Finally, it was ordained that the Catholic worship should be celebrated in all the Protestant communes, whilst the Vaudois were prohibited from offering any molestation; and the penalty of death was denounced against any one who should dissuade a Protestant from becoming a Catholic. All these provisions show plainly enough in what spirit and under what influence this edict was conceived.

Gastaldo, however, who was authorized by his instructions to banish all the Vaudois families resident within the prohibited communes, confined himself to demanding, in the first instance, the removal of their heads. The Vaudois obeyed. All the heads of families against whom these requirements were directed retired into the higher parts of the valley. A petition was addressed to the sovereign. He seemed disposed to clemency. The Count Christopher of Lucerna interceded for the oppressed people. "I would willingly allow them to reside at St. John and at La Tour," said the duke, "if they, on their part, would consent to retire from the other localities nearer to the plain, for their adversaries will not leave me in peace without having obtained some satisfaction."

Meanwhile, the Propaganda bestirred itself. In place of the duke's being told that the Vaudois were perfectly ready to obey, he was told that they were in a state of rebellion, and had already assassinated the priest of Fenil. Their deputies arrived at Turin, and were not received. The court remitted them to the council of the Propaganda, saying that they would have to deal with it. This council likewise refused to receive them on account of their

---

[1] These orders were given on the 13th of January, 1655. The ratifications of their privileges, subsequent to 15th May, 1650, were not yet legally *approved*. Of this, advantage was taken to consider them as not granted.

being Protestants, and ordained them to have their petition presented by a Popish procurator. They chose one named Gibelino, who was introduced into the hall of deliberation. The council was sitting, the Archbishop presiding; and the humble procurator of the Vaudois was obliged to present their petition on his knees. The reply of the Council was, that they must send other deputies, authorized to make suitable engagements in name of all the people.

These new representatives arrived at Turin on the 12th of February, but their mandate bore that they should subscribe nothing contrary to the concessions or privileges of their constituents. They were told that this would not suffice, and that they must be furnished with unlimited powers. They returned to the valleys; and the following month was spent in exchanging protocols, and sending memorials and supplications, sometimes to the court, sometimes to the Marquis of Pianesse, who at all events replied very temperately to those which were addressed to him.

Moderation of language sometimes proceeds from hardness of heart. Perverse sentiments permit a man to be more master of himself than generous sentiments do. It will soon appear that these observations are not incorrect in reference to the Marquis of Pianesse, whose conduct has suggested them. He had, moreover, studied in the school of Jesuitism, and its atrocities sanctioned the course which he pursued—perfidious but polished—cruel but devout—shrinking from no means of attaining an object. The fruits of this doctrine are like those of which an old Vaudois poem speaks—

Lical son vernis e lendenas e poelh abimol.[1]

At last, in the beginning of April, 1655, a third Vaudois deputation, composed of two deputies only,[2] repaired to Turin, furnished with a general mandate by which they were authorized to accept all the conditions which it might please his royal highness to impose, provided always that their liberty of conscience was untouched; and, in the event of its being menaced, they were to demand, in name of all their brethren, permission to retire from the dominions of his royal highness.

This was to state the question courageously and unambiguously. It was not to shrink from its difficulties. The answer must needs be decisive.

The Marquis of Pianesse was commissioned to make it. After

[1] Which are outwardly splendid (*vernis*), and of which the interior is abominable dust.—*La Barca*, stanza xvii.

[2] David Bianchi, of St. John, for the valley of Lucerna, and Francis Manchon for that of St. Martin.

some delays he fixed a day for an audience. It was the 17th of April, 1655. The deputies proceeded to the palace; they were told to come back at a later hour. They came back; his excellency was not yet visible. They presented themselves a third time, and were put off for a day or two. "What can be the meaning of this?" said the deputies, full of impatience and anxiety. They were but too soon informed.

On the evening previous to the day which had been assigned to them for an audience, namely, on the 16th of April, at nightfall, the Marquis of Pianesse had quitted Turin to join the armed force which awaited him on the road to the Vaudois valleys; and next day, whilst the commissioners, men of candour and integrity, were confidently waiting to see him at his mansion, Pianesse, in whom Jesuitism had extinguished at once nobility of blood and the honour of the soldier, was already on the verge of their country, at the head of troops intended for the extermination of their people.

These troops were numerous. Besides those which were already quartered in the district, there was the regiment of *Grancey*, commanded by the first captain, *Du Petitbourg*, quartered at Pignerol. There were also the regiment *of the city*, commanded by *Galeazzo;* that of *Chablais*, commanded by the *Prince de Montafon*, and that of *St. Damian*, commanded by an officer of that name. The Marquis of Pianesse had the general command of all the assembled forces.

On the 17th of April, he sent a messenger to La Tour to require the Vaudois to provide lodging and entertainment for 800 infantry, and 300 cavalry, whose cantonment in their commune had been appointed by his royal highness. "How can his royal highness command us to find lodging for his soldiers, in a place where, by his last edict, we ourselves are prohibited from dwelling?" replied the Vaudois. "Then why are you here?" retorted the messenger. "We are here on our business," said they, "but we have removed our residence to within the appointed limits." The messenger therefore returned without having accomplished anything. Towards evening, the Marquis of Pianesse, after having passed, without resistance, the line of Briquéras, Fenil, Campillon, Bubiano, and St. John, from which the Vaudois had retired, arrived under the walls of La Tour with the regiments of the city and of St. Damian.[1]

[1] I shall sometimes desert, in the recital of these events, the narrative of Léger, to which, however, I shall always refer for the facts of which he was an eye-witness, or of which he gives satisfactory proofs. The details following are also from the

It may readily be supposed that this concentration of troops upon the valleys, the avowed designs of the Propaganda, the high position of those who were engaged in its cause, the general excitement of popular fanaticism, the warnings of their friends, and the threats of their adversaries, must have revealed to the Vaudois, clearly enough, the hostile intentions entertained against them. They knew not, however, how far it was necessary for them to be upon their guard, or how far they might trust to the good faith of their sovereign. No official prosecution had been directed against them; they had obeyed the edict of the 25th of January, whilst they protested against it, and had sent deputies for the purpose of obtaining its revocation; and these commissioners were still at Turin. On the one hand the Vaudois could not overlook the violent projects of the Propaganda, but on the other there was room for doubt if the Duke of Savoy would become the instrument or accomplice of that body.

What were they to do? They betook themselves to prayer; they consulted their pastors; they wrote to Geneva; the general voice recommended them to take measures of self-defence; but uncertainty as to the future prevented the concerting of any plan. They perceived that a storm was coming; but could they foresee the extent of the calamities with which they were to be overwhelmed? If they had foreseen them, all hesitation would have disappeared, and the vigour of an unanimous resistance would have

pen of an eye-witness (an officer of the regiment of St. Damian), who appears to have written down, day by day, the things which he saw in that expedition. His notes are unpublished, and are contained in the archives of state at Turin. These archives have also furnished me with a great number of official reports and narratives, written when all was over, to abate the horror of the massacres which had been perpetrated in the valleys. One of these documents declares, for example, that in all the valleys not more than fifty Vaudois perished; another affirms that at most some ten or twelve of them were killed. We learn, on the contrary, from the official reports, that in the commune of Bobi alone, there were (according to a statistical report drawn up on the 11th of May) 160 Vaudois killed, 160 who became Catholics, 32 who fled to France, 10 made prisoners, and 40 who were scattered over Piedmont; in that of Le Villar, on the 10th of May, 150 dead (of whom 36 were buried under an avalanche), 289 who became Catholics (all of whose names are given), 20 dispersed among the mountains, 25 in Piedmont, and 4 retained as hostages. This report gives therefore a total of 310 persons put to death in these two communes alone, and raises to more than 2000 the number who perished in all the valleys together. And we may judge of the horrors enacted by those which are avowed; the officer of the Marquis of St. Damian, in the journal of which we have spoken, says, under date the 9th of July, "Alle ore 20, furono uccisi e scoiati due eretici; e ad uno doppo gavato il cuore fu legato un gatto, per mangiarli linterno."

This officer was far from being favourable to the Vaudois, for with regard to an arrangement which they proposed to the Marquis of Pianesse on the 21st of April, he says, "Their pretensions were so impertinent, that it would have seemed as if they had been in the right and the prince in the wrong."

proved itself equal to the maintenance of their despised rights. But in indecision and ignorance—desirous of obeying the commands of their sovereign, which enjoined them to provide quarters for troops—made anxious, and with good reason, by seeing at the head of these troops, one of the leaders of the Propaganda, who had vowed their destruction—neither daring to comply with confidence nor to resist with vigour, they took only half measures, insufficient on either view of the case. Janavel alone had, in the month of February, raised a small company of resolute defenders, in the anticipation, which events too well justified, that the anterior measures already adopted were only the prelude to a terrible persecution. But he was then regarded by his compatriots as too exclusive and too violent.

It has just been stated that the Marquis of Pianesse had appeared, on the 17th of April, at evening, under the walls of La Tour.[1] It was a Saturday, there was fine moonlight—the whole army of the Duke of Savoy halted in the plain, which extends from Les Appiots to Pra-la-Fèra and Les Eyrals. The commander-in-chief caused the Vaudois to be summoned to provide quarters. They being only some 300 or 400 in the town, replied that it was impossible for them to furnish quarters, that no preparation had been made, and that they requested time to reflect and to consider the matter.

Delay was absolutely refused—they were told that they must immediately receive the troops; and, in case of refusal, the troops would seize by force the posts demanded. Hereupon the Vaudois entrenched themselves behind bastions erected in haste. The entrance of La Tour, opposite to the bridge of Angrogna, was closed with barricades. This barrier arrested the enemy, and was thickly covered with defenders. It was near ten o'clock at night. The Marquis of Pianesse caused the attack to be commenced, the Vaudois made a valiant resistance. After three hours' fighting the assailants had still obtained no advantage. But towards one o'clock in the morning, Count Amadeus of Lucerna, who knew the locality, put himself at the head of the regiment *de villa*, commanded by Galeazzo; and whilst the rest of the troops continued to give employment to the besieged, this regiment turned the town on the side of the Pélis, ascended by the meadows and gardens which extend upon that side, and following the steps of its guide, penetrated to the centre of La Tour, in the street of Les Bruns, and assailed the defenders of the barricade in the rear. The Vaudois now abandoned the barricade, wheeled about, forced their

---

[1] "*Circa le 22 hore*," says the narrative above quoted.

way through the ranks of these new comers, who vainly pursued after them, and retired to the heights.

About two o'clock in the morning, the Catholics being victorious and masters of the place, repaired in a body to the church of the mission, sung the *Te Deum laudamus*,[1] and exclaimed on all hands, "*Viva la santa Chiesa Romana!*[2] *E viva la santa fede*,[3] *e guai agli Barbetti!*"[4] In this affair the Vaudois had only three killed and a few wounded. About 5 o'clock in the morning the Marquis of Pianesse arrived, *con tutta la sua nobilta*,[5] and took his quarters in the mission buildings.

It was then Sunday morning—Palm-Sunday, the beginning of Holy Week. The spirit of Antichrist burned to signalize these Christian festivals by a grand massacre of Christians. On that same Sunday, therefore, immediately after mass, the Catholic soldiers, conducted by Mario, the commandant of Bagnola, set out by way of worldly diversion, or by way of preparation for the approaching Easter, to give chase to the heretics; that is to say, to kill, by shooting with their muskets, all the Vaudois whom they met, hiding themselves in order to take them by surprise, and burning the houses whose owners they had put to flight or killed.[6]

In the evening additional troops still arrived. On Monday, the 19th, the army, according to Léger's account, already consisted of nearly 15,000 men.[7] It was no longer possible to doubt that the old project of the extermination of the Vaudois, so long cherished, matured, and loudly avowed by the more zealous representatives of the Romish Church, was at last to be put in execution. It was thus that Popery prepared to celebrate the Easter of 1655.

The Vaudois, beholding from the heights of Angrogna and Le Taillaret, the devastation and conflagration which were already spread over the plain, took measures of defence. They placed sentinels at the advanced points, and defensive parties at the most

---

[1] "We praise thee, O Lord!" [2] "Hurrah for the holy Roman Church!"
[3] "And hurrah for the holy faith!"
[4] "And woe to the Barbets!" This name of *Barbets*, given in derision to the Vaudois, is probably derived from that of their pastors, anciently called Barbas.
[5] "With all his nobility." An expression of the contemporary writings.
[6] "*Andarono scaramucciando per quelle montagnuole, rentrezzando gli eretici anamazandone molti ed abruciando qui sue case o cassine che possono prendere.*" The writing from which we have taken these particulars cannot be suspected of any partiality for the Vaudois. It is entitled "*Memorie delle irrutione e barbarie fatte dagli eretici Valdesi contro i catholici della Torre, Luserna, San Segondo,*" &c. (Archives of Court at Turin.) To justify this title, the author enlarges much upon the irruptions of Janavel, of which we shall afterwards speak.
[7] Second part, chap. ix. p. 108.

important passes. But they were ill armed and ill organized; besides they could not believe in the perfidies of which they became the victims.

On the morning after Palm-Sunday (Monday, the 19th of April, 1655) the troops of the Marquis of Pianesse attacked these poor mountaineers, at once by the heights of La Tour, Saint John, Angrogna, and Briquéras. The Vaudois contented themselves with defending their positions. They were one against a hundred; but a powerful aid sustained them—their confidence in God. All these attacks were repulsed; the enemy could not drive them from one of their entrenchments. The campaign began, therefore, with a victory on their side. Could they foresee that it was to terminate in such great calamities?

On Tuesday, the 20th of April, only two attacks were made—the one directed against the Vaudois of St. John, entrenched at Castellus, the other against those of Taillaret. Both resulted, a second time, in the success of the Vaudois. The first was repulsed, with great success, by Captain Jayer. The second was not less fatal to the assailants; for the Vaudois lost only two men, in an action in which they killed fifty of their enemies. Léger, who relates these particulars, was himself in that engagement.

The Marquis of Pianesse—seeing the considerable forces at his disposal give way as before a superior force in attacking these advantageous and well-guarded posts—thought it necessary to have recourse to means which but too often proved successful against the Vaudois, because they were ignorant of the way of using them; but which have never been more skilfully employed than in the Church of Rome, and have contributed to it a part of its power. He had recourse to perfidy. On the morning of the following day (Wednesday, the 21st of April), two hours before sunrise, he sent to all the entrenchments of the Vaudois, clarions and heralds, to inform them that he was ready to receive deputies, in order to treat of an accommodation, in name of his royal highness the Duke of Savoy.

The deputies of all the communes of the valley repaired to his presence; he welcomed them graciously, conversed with them till mid-day, gave them an excellent dinner, testified the best disposition towards the Vaudois, and assured them that it had never been his intention to disquiet them in any way. Gastaldo's edict, he added (that of the 25th of January), had reference only to those dwelling in the low country, who must, indeed, be contented to return to the mountains; but as to the communes of the upper valleys they had positively nothing to fear. He seemed much vexed at the excesses which his soldiers had already committed; laid the blame upon the difficulty of causing discipline to be observed by so great a number of troops; expressed his fear of not being able to restrain them, and his desire to send them away; and spoke of the embarrassment which their number caused him, and of the advantage which there would be in scattering them. "You may render a service to your country and to me," he added in conclusion, "by engaging your respective communes, each to receive and to lodge only one of the regiments which have been sent hither. By thus receiving them without resistance, not only will the localities which shall receive them be secure from all violence, but it may be also that the prince, touched with this proof of confidence, will display less rigour in the exclusion pronounced against the towns of the plain."

The deputies promised to exert themselves, as much as they could, in favour of so good a design. Léger and Janavel opposed to it a vain but inflexible resistance. The communes consented to receive the soldiers of the Marquis of Pianesse; and that very evening they took possession of all the passes, installed themselves in all the hamlets; and, in spite of the formal order to conduct themselves with prudence, did not even wait until next day without massacring a few heretics.

It was this which betrayed them. In their eagerness to obtain possession of the strongest positions of our mountains, whilst two regiments pursued the ordinary route of *Villar* and *Bobi*, and a third that of *Angrogna*, a special detachment began to ascend the hills of Champ-la-Rama and of Coste Roussine, in order to arrive sooner at Pra du Tour. This detachment, on its way, set fire to the scattered houses of Le Taillaret; the smoke was seen, and the cries of the fugitives and shouts of the persecutors were heard from the *colette* of Rora, on which a fire was immediately kindled as a signal of distress. It was immediately perceived from all the heights of Angrogna, whither the greater part of the refugees from the plain had retired, who had been compelled to quit Bubiano, Campillon, &c., in consequence of the edict of Gastaldo of 25th February. The people of Angrogna themselves, also, soon saw the rapid march of the invading detachment, which, directing its course towards the Pra du Tour, triumphantly descended by the slope of the mountain. There soon appeared, besides, near the *Gates of Angrogna* and the *Pausa dei Morts*, the regiment of Grancey, which alone had been expected. Then, perceiving the treachery, they kindled in their turn their signal of distress, and the cries—"To Pérouse! to Pérouse! to the Vachère! Every one save himself!

There are the traitors! God help us! Let us fly!"—were raised, and ran along, spreading like an electric flame over the vast flank of these mountains, from which the men, in a condition to carry arms, retired in haste to the heights of the Vachère, and thence by the valley of Pramol, to those of Pérouse and Pragela, which then appertained to France.

On the side of Bobi the alarm was less prompt, for the regiments of Bagnola and Petitbourg (of which the former was to be quartered at Bobi and the latter at Le Villar) arrived peaceably by the ordinary road. Apprehension was excited when the soldiers, instead of remaining at Bobi, were seen to ascend to Sarcena and Ville Neuve; victims had already been slaughtered as they came, but the knowledge of these isolated murders could not spread, and the officers everywhere manifested an intention to maintain a severe discipline amongst their troops.

Even at Angrogna, where they found only some women, old men and children—feeble guardians of their deserted houses—they at first abstained from any excess. De Pianesse contented himself with taking up his position there, and giving rest to his troops, without seeming to think of remaining in the place more than two or three days, according to the terms of his agreement with the deputies. Thus seeking to gain the confidence of the Vaudois women and children, these new comers persuaded them to recal their husbands and brothers who had taken flight, protesting that no harm would be done to them. Some of them came back, to their cost. "*Non servanda fides hœreticis*," said the Council of Constance. "*Ad extirpandos hœreticos!*" cried the Propaganda.

From the head of the valley downwards, in villages and hamlets, on the highways and rocks, the Propaganda, by the help of the bad faith which its church authorizes, had now introduced its soldiers, or posted its assassins. Accordingly the veil was raised. On Saturday, Easter Eve (24th April, 1655), at four o'clock in the morning, the signal for a general massacre of the Vaudois was given to these perfidious troops, from the summit of the castle of La Tour.

The soldiers, apprized beforehand, had risen early; they were fresh and active; they had slept under the roofs of those whose throats they were to cut. Those whom the Vaudois had received, lodged and fed with such confidence, who ought to have protected them, were now at the same moment throughout the whole valley, and with the same fanaticism, transformed into base assassins. Rome carries off the palm for conversions of this kind.

And now, how can we give an idea of the horrors which ensued? It would be necessary to be able, with one glance, to include at once the whole country, to penetrate into all apartments, to be present at all executions, to distinguish in this vast voice of anguish and desolation, each particular cry of a heart or of a living being torn in pieces. Little children, Léger says,[1] were torn from the arms of their mothers, dashed against the rocks, and cast carelessly away. The sick or the aged, both men and women, were either burned in their houses, or hacked in pieces; or mutilated, half-murdered, and flayed alive, they were exposed in a dying state to the heat of the sun, or to flames, or to ferocious beasts; others were tied, in a state of nakedness, into the form of balls, the head between the legs, and in this state were rolled down the precipices. Some of them, torn and bruised by the rocks from which they had rebounded, remained suspended from some projecting rock or the branch of some tree, and still groaned forty-eight hours afterwards. Women and young girls were violated, empaled, set up naked upon pikes at the corners of the roads, buried alive, roasted upon lances, and cut in pieces by these *soldiers of the faith* as by cannibals: then, after the massacre, the children which had survived it, and were found wandering in the woods, were carried away; or children were forcibly taken from what remained of their afflicted family, to be conveyed into the dwellings of these butchers, and into the monasteries, like lambs taken to the slaughter-house; and finally, the massacre and the removal of children were succeeded by conflagration—the monks, the propagandists, and the *zealous Catholics* running from house to house with resinous torches or incendiary projectiles, and ravaging, in the midst of the fires, these villages now filled with corpses.

"Two of the most infuriated of these fire-raisers," says a work of the period,[2] "were a priest and a monk of the order of St. Francis, who marched about, escorted by troops; and if there was any hidden cottage[3] which had not fallen into their hands on the first occasion, they might be seen repassing on the morrow; and to finish their work the priest had only to discharge his carabine, loaded with an artificial fire, which stuck to the walls." Let the reader imagine these mad wretches running about amongst the burning houses, urging on the carnage and destruction, and these mountains resounding with the fall of ruins, of avalanches, of rocks, and of living bodies cast down the precipices!

Such was the frightful, unparalleled, unprecedented scene which

[1] Part II. chap. ix.
[2] "*Récit véritable de ce qui est arrivé, depuis peu, aux vallées de Piémont* (8vo, 47 pages), p. 23.
[3] [*Recoin de couvert.*] *Couvert*, a *cottage*, a *roof*, but implying the support of walls.—A *shed*, a little building.—*Lou câbert*, the phrase is borrowed from the patois of the country.

was then presented in these regions of despair. "And let it not be said," adds the historian Léger, "that I exaggerate things upon account of the persecutions which I myself personally have endured; I have travelled from one neighbourhood to another to collect the authentic testimonies of the survivors, who deponed what things they had seen before two notaries who accompanied me. In some places fathers had seen their children torn through the midst by strength of men's arms, or cut through with swords; in other places mothers had seen their daughters forced or murdered in their presence. Daughters had witnessed the mutilation of the living bodies of their fathers; brothers had seen the mouths of their brothers filled with powder, to which the persecutors set fire, making the head fly in pieces; pregnant women had been ripped up, and the fruit of their womb had been seen taken living from their bowels. What shall I say? O my God! the pen falls from my hands. Dead bodies lay scattered about or were planted upon stakes; portions of children, torn in quarters, had been flung into the middle of the road; brains were plastered against the rocks; trunks of human bodies were to be seen destitute of arms and limbs, or bodies half-flayed, or with the eyes torn out of the head, or the nails torn off the toes; others were fastened to trees with the chest opened, and without heart or lungs; here might be seen bodies of women still more horribly mutilated; there graves scarcely filled up, where the earth still seemed to give forth the groans of the unhappy victims who had been buried alive; everywhere misery, terror, desolation, and death! These are the things which I can tell!"

The universal destruction of the Vaudois houses by fire followed the massacre of their inhabitants. In many hamlets, the witness of the martyrs proceeds, not one single cottage remained standing, so that the beautiful valley of Lucerna then presented only the aspect of a burning furnace, where cries, which became more and more unfrequent, attested that a people had lived!

Léger adds after this a long series of notarial depositions, giving the particulars of martyrdoms of which there had been eye-witnesses, the horrors which were committed in the face of the sun, the names of the victims, and the vauntings of their butchers. I shall not copy the representation of these frightful scenes. Why should we stay to contemplate individual martyrdoms when we see an entire people suffer martyrdom at once?

All these noble and courageous persons, thus put to death, might have saved their lives by abjuring their religion; and the torments inflicted upon many of them were still prolonged in prison without making them yield. Ten years, twenty years afterwards, there were still in the galleys of the sovereign, galley-slaves who were *martyrs*. In the dungeons of Villefranche and of Turin there were forgotten victims whose tortures, firmness, and joyful death, Heaven alone could know.

However, there were also numerous abjurations in the Vaudois valleys. Originating, as they did, under the impression of terror and despair, every one can appreciate their value. A deed obtained by violence is considered as null in law. Will it be so before the Supreme Tribunal? It is not for us to resolve that question, but rather to render homage to those who have persevered with unshaken fidelity in the manifestation of their faith.

Poor Michelin of Bobi (whose son was then pastor at Angrogna), after being treated in a way the most ignominious and painful that can be imagined, having survived these sufferings, was cast into the prisons of Turin. All means possible were employed to make him abjure, but all without success. One day there descended into his dungeon two ministers of his own church, the one named Peter Gros, and the other Francis Aghit. Did they come to encourage him, or to partake his sufferings? But how could they have been permitted to get access to him? They were accompanied by Jesuits. Ah! perhaps they might be brought to be buried in this dungeon with their faithful parishioner. God be praised! they would at least be able to comfort, to confirm one another, and to pray together. No; these pastors were of the number of the feeble souls whose convictions had been given up in exchange for a miserable life; they came, driven on by the hideous hand of Popery, to persuade the prisoner also to follow their example, and to abjure his religion. The surprise which poor Michelin felt was so cruel, the shock so great, and the wound so deep, that it caused his death.[1] These two pastors afterwards returned to the Protestant church, but the old man of Bobi had not made his religion a garment, which he could change according to circumstances—he had made it his life; and beholding those who had instructed him disown their own instructions, it might be said that he died for them.

Other prisoners also died, rather than abjure. James and David Prins of Le Villar, of the hamlet of La Baudèna, were committed to the prisons of Lucerna; and there, says Léger, they having resisted all solicitations to apostasy, with which they were plied by the monks, "their arms were flayed from the shoulder to the elbow, the skin being cut into stripes, which were left attached by the upper end, and which thus rested loosely on the quick flesh; the rest

---

[1] Léger, p. 125, Part II.

of the arm was flayed in the same manner, from the elbow to the hands, and their thighs down to the knee, as also their legs, from where the garter is tied to the ancle; and in this state they were left to die."[1] These stripes of skin, to remain hanging in this way, must have been torn off and raised from the flesh from their lower extremity upwards. What an atrocious refinement of barbarity!

"I cannot refrain from remarking here," adds the historian, "that there were six brothers of these Prinses, and that they had married six sisters, and all of them had numbers of children, and that they lived together without having ever made any division of their property, and without the slightest discord having ever been observed in that family. It was composed of more than forty persons, each of whom had his own department of labour; some in the work of the vineyards and cultivation of the fields—others in the care of the meadows, or in that of the flocks. The eldest of the brothers and his wife, who was also the eldest of the sisters, were like the father and mother of the whole family."[2] Yet these patriarchal scenes, so worthy of respect, so beautiful, so simple, and so Christian, furnished prey to the demon of Popery, trained to cruelty by superstition, and descending beneath the level of the savage!

Sometimes, in these barbarous mutilations, hæmorrhage occurred, which was arrested by fire, in order to prolong the agonies, and multiply the torments of the victim. A man of Freyssinières, a farm-servant at Bobi, after having had the soles of his feet and the palms of his hands pierced with a poignard, was deprived of the sexual organs, and suspended over a burning torch, that the flame might arrest the effusion of blood. After this, his nails were torn away by pincers, to compel him to abandon his religion; but as he continued resolute, he was fastened by the feet to the harness of a mule, and in this way dragged through the streets of Lucerna. Seeing him well nigh dead, his executioners encircled his head with a cord, and drew it so tight, that the eyes and the brain were forced out, after which they threw the corpse into the river.[3]

It had not been so bad if these accumulated horrors had been the result of a transport of vengeance, of a fit of madness, of one of those outbursts of rage, those feverish excitements, those sudden frenzies, those irresistible impulses of blind, imperious, and brutal fury, of which men are sometimes the victims! But no: it was the issue of the great work of Popery, coolly prepared, patiently expected, accomplished with premeditation. All crimes and vices seem then to have combined for the service of Popery: Popery

---

[1] Léger, p. 122.—*Notarial Depositions.* [2] Léger, Part II. p. 122.
[3] Léger, p. 118.—*Notarial Depositions.*

alone, like the monarch of the infernal regions, could have thought of disciplining them, that they might do the more harm.

It was from the steeple of a Catholic church that the signal of St. Bartholomew's Day was given;[1] it was from the minsters of Palermo that the *Sicilian Vespers* sounded; it was from an edifice which bore the name of the Virgin Mary[2] that the signal was given for the *Piedmontese Easter*, the frightful celebration of which filled the Vaudois valleys with tears and blood. O holy mother of Christ! the highly-favoured Mary! if a sword was to pierce thy soul, was it not in the church which pretends to honour thee most, which calls thee queen of angels, and has made thee queen of demons?

In a pious song, printed about this period, we read the following lines:—

> "Seigneur, ici le sang d'Abel
> Crie encore sur les supplices;
> Vois Zacharie encor parmi ces sacrifices,
> Mort entre le temple et l'autel.
> Gloire de l'Eternel, justice des justices,
> As-tu les yeux fermés et ta puissante main
> Endormie en ton sein?"[3]

They are not equal to the sonnet of Milton, but they are an echo of the feeling which was excited throughout all Europe in favour of the Vaudois.

Many persons, even amongst those who had been chosen to serve as the instruments of this work of extermination, reprobated it with horror, and refused to have any part in it. Of this number was the first captain of the regiment of Grancey, M. Du Petitbourg, of whom we have already spoken. When he knew to what employment his troops were destined, he refused to conduct them to that disgraceful massacre, and resigned his command. The court of Savoy having caused a sort of apology to be afterwards written, in which all the odium of these events was cast upon the leaders of the French army, the commandant, Du Petitbourg, published a declaration, by which he disclaimed all participation in the barbarities committed, and at the same time attested the reality of them in a manner which puts it beyond all doubt,[4] and with extracts made without alteration from this document, I shall conclude this chapter.

---

[1] The steeple of Saint Germain l' Auxerrois.
[2] The fort of La Tour was named the fort of Saint Mary.
[3] "O Lord, the blood of Abel still cries here of violent deaths; thou still beholdest Zachariah amongst these sacrifices lying dead betwixt the temple and the altar. Glory of the Lord! Judge of judges! are thine eyes closed, and does thy mighty hand sleep in thy bosom?"
[4] In the *Apology, or Faithful Relation of the War of* 1655, are set down, to excuse the deeds of violence which are acknowledged, many calumnies against the

"I, the seigneur Du Petitbourg, first captain of the regiment of Grancey, in command of the regiment, having been ordered by the Prince Thomas to go to join the Marquis of Pianesse, and to receive orders from him at La Tour, ... *I have been witness* of many deeds of great violence and extreme cruelty, committed by the outlaws of Piedmont [1] and by the soldiers, on persons of every age, sex, and condition, *whom I saw* massacred, dismembered, hanged, burned, and violated; and of many frightful conflagrations. . . . . I *saw* the order that every one must be killed. As for his [the Marquis of Pianesse's] protesting that no one was ever touched except in battle, nor the least outrage committed against persons unable to bear arms, I maintain that this is not the case, and that *I with my own eyes saw* men murdered in cold blood, and women, aged men, and little children miserably put to death.

* * * * * * * *

So that I positively affirm and protest before God that none of the cruelties above-mentioned were executed by my orders; on the contrary, seeing that I could do nothing to prevent them, I was constrained to retire, and to renounce the command of the regiment, that I might not be present at such wicked actions.—Done at Pignerol, this 27th of November, 1655.

"(Signed), "DU PETITBOURG."

This declaration was made and signed before witnesses; the witnesses are M. St. Hilaire, captain of the infantry regiment of Auvergne, and M. Du Favre, captain of the infantry regiment of Sault. Léger gives this document entire, in his second part, at the end of Chapter IX.

I must now proceed to relate how the Vaudois were enabled to recover from such an extermination. Ezekiel saw the dry bones restored to life by the breath of the Lord and becoming a people; and if we see a people die who are animated by the Spirit of God, it can only be to obtain a life more perfect and more happy than this earthly life. But the Vaudois were to recover possession of their country. It is time that we should pass to these glorious events.

Vaudois. I have not thought it necessary to take notice of them. To render infamous, to kill and to calumniate, was the rule followed by the Marquis of Pianesse.

[1] Outlaws and volunteers of every condition had been invited to the standard. The Irish assassins, driven from their native country by Cromwell, and received in Piedmont, distinguished themselves by their savage ferocity in these cruel massacres.

CHAPTER VIII.

JANAVEL AND JAHIER.[1]

(APRIL TO JUNE, 1655.)

The fugitive Vaudois find an asylum in the French dominions—Janavel, with a small band, obtains wonderful victories over the troops of Pianesse—Pianesse has recourse again to the arts of treachery—He ravages Rora, but is attacked and defeated by Janavel as he retires with his booty—Pianesse marches against Rora with almost ten thousand men—Janavel's wife and daughters made prisoners—His constant resolution—The Duchess of Savoy and the French court—Mazarin refuses to take part against the Vaudois as she desires—Cromwell offers them a refuge in Ireland—Intercessions of foreign powers—Collections made for the Vaudois in Protestant countries—The Vaudois continue in arms—Another Vaudois troop takes the field under Jahier—Janavel makes an attempt to seize Lucernette, but fails—Jahier and he effect a junction—They seize St. Segont—Further successes—Janavel is severely wounded—Jahier is killed.

It has been already stated that the Vaudois of Angrogna, and the refugees of the plain of Piedmont, had, in great part, retired into the valley of Pérouse; those of St. Martin, forewarned by a man who, although a Catholic, was compassionate,[2] of the arrival of the troops of Galeazzo, with commission to put all to fire and sword, made haste to gain the valley of Pragela; and such of the inhabitants of Bobi as contrived to escape the massacre sought an asylum in that of Queyras, across frightful snows, precipices, and rocks. All these places of refuge were then within the dominions of the King of France.

With the view of shutting that hospitable country against the Vaudois, the Duchess of Savoy,[3] who appears to have taken a much greater part in these disastrous events than her son, wrote to the court of France.[4] She wished to prevent her subjects from leaving the valleys, and to have them massacred there. Mazarin did not enter into her views; he replied that humanity imposed upon him the duty of opening an asylum to the fugitive Vaudois.

This gave them facilities for rallying, arming, and organizing themselves. They were even able to re-enter their country in

---

[1] AUTHORITIES.—The same as in the preceding chapter.

[2] His name was Emmanuel Bochiardo. He warned the Vaudois "*Che il Signor Marchese Galeazzo a ordine di abbruciare e d'estirpar ogni cosa,*" &c. His letter is of date May 5, 1655.

[3] Called *Madame Royale* in the documents of the time.

[4] Anne of Austria was then regent; Louis XIV., a minor; Mazarin, prime minister.

much greater numbers than they had left it, for a multitude of their brethren from Queyras and Pragela joined them. Meanwhile, a man of energy and ability, Captain Joshua Janavel, who alone had foreseen the treachery, supported, doubtless, by the hand of God (in which no one ever put more absolute confidence than this intrepid warrior), kept in check the enemy's army, and, by slow degrees, drove it from the valleys.

This came to pass as follows:—It will be recollected that the 24th of April was the day fixed for the general massacre of the Vaudois. Troops had been cantoned in the principal place of each commune, except Rora; not, however, that that place was to have been spared. Accordingly, on the morning of that day of extermination, the Marquis of St. Damian had sent a battalion of 500 or 600 soldiers from Le Villar, in order to surprise Rora, under the command of Count Christopher of Lucerna, who was designated the Count of Rora, because his *apanage* had been given him in that *seigneurie*. These soldiers climbed the steep slopes of the mountain of Brouard, which lay between them and Rora. Janavel, whose residence was at the base of a long ridge which that mountain sends out in the direction of Lucerna,[1] saw the soldiers ascending on the way towards the menaced village; and he, ascending also by a different way, gathered together as he went, six determined men like himself, with whom he posted himself in a favourable position on the path by which the troops must pass, who advanced in expectation of taking the village by surprise. There he awaited them with his little party, behind some rocks that left a narrow passage only, through which they must of necessity pass.

So soon as they were engaged in this defile, Janavel and his companions united in one loud cry, and discharged their pieces, of which every one took effect; six soldiers fell, the rest drew back; those who followed, believing the ambuscade to be formed by a much larger body than it really was, wheeled about, and the advanced guard was then separated from the main body of the squadron. The Vaudois, concealed amongst rocks, where the enemy could form no estimate of their numbers, poured in their fire, and cleared the ground of the advanced guard, causing it to disband and take to flight. The rearguard, which had yet scarcely arrived at the summit of the mountain ridge, seeing that the foremost ranks were endeavouring to re-ascend it, made all haste to get down again

---

[1] He resided in a quarter called *The Vineyards of Lucerna*. In the reports and despatches of the time, which make mention of his first exploits, he is designated in this way, "The Captain of the Vineyards of Lucerna." But his name was not long of being sufficiently well known.

by the side on which it was advancing, without having even seen those by whom it had been attacked; the fugitives likewise, turning their backs upon the Vaudois, saw them as little; and thus a whole battalion retired before a corporal's party, or rather before the exaggerated image of a perilous ambuscade. Such incidents are rare, but they can be conceived. It was thus that the entire army of Brennus took to flight before the temple of Delphi, at the noise made by the priests of Apollo, transformed, by the affrighted imagination of the soldiers, into supernatural combatants.

Janavel, returning by Rora, apprised the inhabitants of that village of the danger which they had run. Ignorant of the massacres which had been perpetrated on that same day in the valley of Lucerna, the people of Rora immediately went to complain to the Marquis of Pianesse, of the invasion attempted against them in the morning. "If they meant to attack you, it was not by my orders," he replied; "the troops which I command never made any such wicked attempt. It can only have been a horde of Piedmontese robbers and vagabonds. You would have done me a pleasure if you had cut them in pieces. However," added he, with an air of kindness, "I shall take care that such alarms do not take place again." It was not an alarm, in good sooth, which he intended, but a surprise which should crush them all. Proof of this was soon afforded.

On the following day a new battalion was sent against Rora, by the mountain of Cassulet. This time Janavel had seventeen men with him; the number seems very small, but under his guidance they were worth an army. Of these eighteen men, twelve were armed from head to foot, six had only slings. He disposed them in three bands of six men each, to wit, four musketeers and two slingers. His position was chosen beforehand; it was again a defile, in which ten men had scarcely room to manœuvre: he had almost twice the number, and occupied the most advantageous position.

As soon as the battalion of the Marquis of Pianesse had advanced into the depths of the scene of ambuscade, the Vaudois made their appearance. An officer and ten foot-soldiers fell at their first discharge. Stones flew like hail, whistling amongst the ranks of the enemy, who fell into disorder. "Every man save himself!" cried a coward. The troops began to disband. Janavel and his men rushed upon them from the rocks above, a pistol in one hand, and a sword in the other. Their agility, vigour, and intrepidity multiplied their numbers; it seemed as if jaguars or lynxes flew from crest to crest of the rocks, as lightly as winged insects from flower to flower. The battalion, already surprised, thrown into confusion, and half routed, saw its discharges of musketry wasted amongst empty bushes, or upon impenetrable rocks, and yet men resolute and completely armed, springing up, falling down, and leaping about before their eyes from these bushes and these rocks, and scattering death around their steps. The battalion, or rather the companies which were first surprised and most engaged, recoiled involuntarily before them. The retrograde movement extended, the contagion of terror spread, one was carried along by the example of another—and presently these 600 men, who had been led to a field of battle with which they were not acquainted, fled towards Lucerna, ignorant alike of the number of their adversaries, and of the number of the dead whom they left behind them.

Men who flee do not defend themselves—they do not see the danger, they aggravate it by their flight, giving arms to the enemy by their own weakness, and doubling the energy of his assaults. It was thus with the battalion on the mountain of Cassulet. It had lost only twelve men in the defile, it lost forty in the flight. The following are the words in which Janavel, thirty years after, when banished from his country, recalled in his exile that glorious event: "We were but very few in number; a few fusileers, and six or seven slingers, who were not yet able to use the musket, and we defeated the enemy; if we had not, we would have been all destroyed. When they fought down hill, the stones of the slings and the ten fusileers did more execution than you could have believed."[1]

From these few words it appears that amongst that little handful of combatants who saved Rora, and who ere long became the salvation of the valleys, there were some young men who were not yet able to use the musket. It is impossible not to be all the more struck with the success of this heroic phalanx; we know not which most to admire, their courage, or the Divine protection which gave them the victory. But valour is not to be measured by age, nor the strength of an army by the number of its soldiers. Janavel's troop had already given proof of this, and was to give further proof of it.

The Marquis of Pianesse, a second time frustrated in his projects, sent to Rora, Count Christopher, the seigneur of the place, to restore confidence amongst the Vaudois, and to repudiate, as a mistake, the sending of troops into their valley. "Reports have been made against you," said he, "whose falsehood has been discovered; you have only to keep yourselves quiet, and you shall live in peace." At the same time he caused a battalion, more numerous than the

---

[1] Letter written from Geneva to the valleys by Joshua Janavel, in 1685, to forewarn the Vaudois of the terrible persecution which broke out in 1686. (Archives of the Court at Turin.)

former, to be collected, for the purpose of annihilating them. It seems marvellous that the Vaudois could allow themselves to be caught by such promises; and such impudence of falsehood seems surprising in a man of noble birth; but we must not forget that they considered lying to be a sin, and that he regarded it as a virtue. Has not the highest organ of Catholicism, an ecumenical council, declared that it is lawful to break faith with heretics? And did not the Propaganda, Jesuitism, and all that constituted the life and power of the Romish Church at that period, make it a duty? What a Protestant would reckon disgraceful, is matter of pride to a Papist. To accomplish the shedding of blood by treachery was a legitimate triumph for Rome. Yet we may suppose that confidence was not completely restored to the minds of the Vaudois.

Next day, being the 27th of April, an entire regiment moved into the valley, pressed on towards Rora, took possession of all the paths, occupied all the positions, burned a number of houses which lay in its way, and carried off a load of plunder and the flocks of the inhabitants, who had retired to the heights of Friouland. Janavel, with his men, beheld from a distance the ravaging of the valley, but durst not approach because of the great numbers of the enemy. However, when he saw them encumbered with booty, and embarrassed by the flocks which they took away with them, he encouraged his seventeen men, fell upon his knees, offered a fervent prayer to the God of armies, and with undaunted boldness conducted his little troop to an advantageous position named Damasser. The regiment was arrested in its passage—did not know the number of the enemy—did not choose to abandon the booty—lost its foremost men, and thought it best to turn back and retire upon Le Villar.

But the Vaudois knew their own mountains better than these stranger troops; they took a short path, got before them, posted themselves on their line of passage, and again cut off their retreat. This was near the summit of the mountain which separates Rora from Le Villar, on a little grassy plain, named the *Pian pra*, which means the *smooth meadow*. The army of Pianesse advanced, bearing along with it an immense booty. It marched in disorder and carelessly, for the foes over whom it had been unable to gain any advantage had disappeared from its path, and as no trace of them was to be perceived, it seemed that they had thought it best to make no further demonstration. All at once a destructive fire was opened at a short distance from amongst the trees. The soldiers, instead of defending themselves, hurried forward in their course. They were already on the descent of the mountain. Janavel's party rolled down upon them an avalanche of stones. They dispersed themselves in order to avoid them. Hereupon the Vaudois rushed in amongst these disbanded soldiers. In vain they attempted to rally; the ground did not any longer permit it; many of them lost their footing and were helplessly killed, or fell over the precipices. However, the greater part of the army arrived at Le Villar, but they had left their booty by the way; the Vaudois lost none of their men, and recovered possession of all their property which had been carried off.

Having re-ascended to the *Pian pra*, Janavel caused his men to halt. "Let us give thanks," said he. His men fell on their knees. "O God!" exclaimed their intrepid leader, "we bless thee for having preserved us. Protect our people in these calamities, and increase our faith!" This short prayer was followed by the Lord's Prayer and the Apostles' Creed. Meanwhile the fugitives arrived at Lucerna. The Marquis of Pianesse, furious, humiliated, burning with rage, yet desirous to restrain himself, perceiving that it would be vain to have recourse to new acts of deceit or perfidious protestations, convoked the whole forces under his command, from Bubiano, from Barges, and from Cavour. They were all to assemble at Lucerna in order to march upon Rora; the day and the hour were appointed; but the zealot who conducted the massacre at Bobi, Mario De Bagnol, wished to have the glory all to himself of destroying this miserable handful of adventurers, for so they designated these heroic mountaineers who defended, with so much courage, their unhappy families.

Captain Mario accordingly set out with his musketeers two hours before the other troops. He had three companies of regular troops, one of volunteers, and one of Piedmontese outlaws, a fifth of Irish, expelled from their country by Cromwell, in punishment for the massacres of which they had been guilty of the Protestants of that island. It was a good reason for their being received amongst the slaughterers of the Vaudois. They had even received a promise beforehand, that a free grant would be made to them of the dispeopled lands of the valleys. They fought, therefore, for their own interest. Fanaticism and self-interest! by what more powerful motives for carnage could they have been inspired?

Captain Mario divided his troops into two parties, of which one took the right, and the other the left side of the vale of Rora. They advanced without resistance to the rocks of Rummer, already signalized four days before as the scene of Janavel's first victory. Janavel was again intrenched there, his little troop augmented by a number of new combatants, and thus raised to the number of from thirty to forty men. But the right of the Count of Bagnol, having deployed upon the heights, had got above Rummer, and threatened to attack the Vaudois in the rear, whilst the rest of the assailants would have attacked them in front.

Janavel saw the trap in which he was on the point of being taken; and with the promptitude of decision and energy of action, which mark military genius, he exclaimed, "Forward! to the *broua!*[1] the victory is up there!" and wheeling about, he left the position which he had occupied opposite to the front of Captain Mario, whose movement in pursuit was retarded by the necessity of scaling rocks, and turned against the upper detachment which was already deploying upon the smooth brow of the hill; all the Vaudois had their pieces loaded; Janavel turned them directly upon the right wing of that detachment which was manœuvring in order to surround them. "Fire!" cried he. A terrible discharge was poured in upon the enemy; the bulk of the troops inclined in that direction to resist the Vaudois; but Janavel had flung himself upon his belly on the earth, and the bullets passed over his head: and immediately taking advantage of the clouds of smoke which still covered him, instead of pressing on in his original direction, he made a sudden bend, and proceeded, sword in hand, to cut his way through the left wing, where the enemy was already weakened by the movement of concentration which had taken place to the opposite side. Breaking in this way the line of the invaders, he passed through them, and attained the summit or *broua* which he had pointed out to his soldiers. Here he had the advantage of the ground; and all the Vaudois ranging themselves in order of battle, with their backs against the rocks, with the triple energy which is given by a good cause, trust in God, and success, they faced their foes with an intrepidity that daunted them. In vain did the two divisions of the Count of Bagnol's troops re-unite, in order to assail them; they could make no impression upon the Vaudois.

The enemy formed a circle embracing all the base of the hill, and as the level of the water rises around a promontory, the circle closed as the enemy ascended towards them; but it did not pass a certain limit, for the soldiers who formed it fell dead as they came within the range of the bullets of the Vaudois. As the snow melts on the side of a mountain, this army became gradually less; and here its course of invasion was stayed. "The Vaudois," says Léger, "made so long and courageous a resistance, that at last confusion and a sense of dismay manifestly seized on that great multitude of assailants, and they took flight, leaving sixty-five of

[1] A patois word, signifying the *summit*.

their number dead on the ground, without reckoning the wounded and the corpses which were carried away."

Seeing that the enemy retired by the opening of the valley, the Vaudois would have pursued them. Janavel stayed them. "Better than that!" said he; "they must be utterly destroyed." And passing along the heights till he had got before the fugitives, he ran to post himself again, with his invincible fusileers, at a narrow pass called *Pierro Capello*.

The enemy's troop came up, now beginning to recover breath. At the moment when they least expected it, the Vaudois fired upon them again, hurled down masses of rock, rushed upon them, and redoubled their affright, their disorder, and their loss; there was not a shadow of resistance—a panic, or rather the fear of the God of Jacob seized upon these disbanded soldiers, so that not being able easily to flee, because of the difficulty of the paths, they flung themselves headlong over rocks, and into ravines and torrents, and were drowned or lay dead beneath precipices, if they did not fall by the swords or the bullets of their terrible assailants. Captain Mario himself was with great difficulty drawn out of a hole full of water, in which he must otherwise have been drowned; and was carried back without his accoutrements, and without hat or shoes, to Lucerna, where he died a few days after.

We come now to the record of a fact which one could not venture to introduce into a work of pure imagination, so improbable it would appear. But history must not shrink before prodigies sufficiently authenticated; and it is well known that truth is often that which is least truth-like.

Astonishing as were already the repeated victories of Janavel over enemies fifty times more numerous, it is not without surprise that we observe that the Marquis of Pianesse now called to arms all the disposable troops under his command, and caused nearly 10,000 men to march against the little commune of Rora, so perseveringly defended by a simple company of brave mountaineers. It was in the beginning of May, 1655: 3000 men set out from Bagnol, 3000 from Le Villar, and 4000 from Lucerna, to make a simultaneous assault upon a village of fifty houses.

The division from Le Villar was the first to make its appearance. Janavel repulsed its attack; but whilst he was engaged in battle, the two other divisions entered the lower part of the valley, plundered the village, burned the houses, massacred the inhabitants, committed monstrous outrages, and carried off as prisoners the unfortunates who had not been killed. The position was no longer tenable; Janavel had no longer anything to defend; Rora was destroyed; its inhabitants were slain or taken captive; and he withdrew with his heroic cohort into the valley of Lucerna.

Next day he received from the Marquis of Pianesse a note in these terms:—"To Captain Janavel. Your wife and your daughters are in my hands—they were made prisoners at Rora; I exhort you for the last time to abjure your heresy, which will be the only means to obtain pardon for your rebellion against the authority of his royal highness, and to save the lives of your wife and your daughters, who shall be burned alive if you do not submit. And if you persist in your obstinacy, without putting myself to the trouble of sending troops against you, I will set such a price upon your head, that were you the devil incarnate, you must certainly be brought to me dead or alive; and if you fall into my hands alive, you may lay your account with it that there are no torments so cruel that they shall not be inflicted upon you. This warning is for your guidance—consider how you may turn it to your advantage."

The following is Janavel's reply: "There is no torment so cruel that I do not prefer it to the abjuring of my religion; and your threats, instead of turning me from it, confirm me in it all the more. As for my wife and my daughters, they know if they are dear to me! But God alone is Lord of their lives; and if you destroy their bodies, God will save their souls. May he graciously receive these beloved souls, and likewise mine, if it so happen that I fall into your hands." Such was the answer of the heroic mountaineer. A price was immediately set upon his head.

He had still one son, a young boy, who had been committed to the charge of a relative belonging to Le Villar. Fearing lest he also might be made prisoner, the intrepid and afflicted father took with him this child, bore him across the snows to the other side of the Alps, descended into Dauphiny, and there deposited his son—re-victualled his little escort, and took some days' repose, of which he availed himself to recruit his band—and then, still putting his trust in God, he crossed the Alps once more, re-entered the valleys, and took the field again, more powerful, formidable, and intrepid than ever.

Meanwhile, Léger, the moderator of the Vaudois churches, had proceeded to Paris, where he published a statement, addressed to all the Protestant powers of Europe. Many proofs of the liveliest sympathy and most active interest reached the Vaudois churches from all parts. On the other hand, the court of Savoy, or rather the duchess,[1] urged by the Propaganda and by the pontifical (I dare not say the apostolic) nuncio, pursued with vigour amidst the

---

[1] Most of the papers of which we shall have to speak bear her signature.

applauses of the dignified clergy, the real object of so much agitation, namely, the expulsion or complete extermination of the Israel of the Alps, these evangelical children of the valleys.

After having requested of Mazarin that an asylum should be refused them in France, and having failed to obtain her request, she next requested that he would have them removed from the frontiers of Piedmont, at least three days' journey. The execution of this scheme having been also refused, she requested and obtained a prohibition against French subjects coming to the help of the Vaudois who still remained in the valleys.

She was so active in her proceedings—her designs were so loudly proclaimed, that even in the valleys themselves, many persons doubted if the Vaudois would ever be able to recover their position. Francis Guérin, minister of Roure, in Pragela, confidently prophesied to the refugees that they ought to renounce the hope of returning to their native country, the time being come when the candlestick must be removed out of its place.[1]

The captain of the Duke of Savoy's Swiss guards being from the canton of Glaris, where there were a few Catholic families ill-contented to dwell in a Protestant country, proposed to Charles Emmanuel II. that he should receive these families into the valleys, and send the Vaudois in exchange, into the canton of Glaris.[2]

Cromwell, on his part, made offer to the Vaudois to receive them into Ireland, in place of the natives whom he had expelled from that island. But the reply of the moderator was more in accordance with the interests of his native land; he entreated the Protector to send a plenipotentiary to Turin, to exert himself for the re-establishment of the Vaudois in the valleys, instead of their removal from thence. The plenipotentiary sent was Morland, who rendered such important service in the pacification of that unfortunate country, and who afterwards wrote a remarkable history of the events which had there taken place.

Most of the foreign powers, from the King of Sweden to the Helvetic Cantons, wrote to Charles Emmanuel in favour of the Vaudois. "This business makes a great noise in Switzerland, as well as in France and Germany," wrote the Sardinian ambassador, De La Borde, to the Duchess Christina.[3] "Your highness will give it such consideration as you deem fit at a time when the com-

---

[1] These facts are mentioned in a letter of the Duchess of Savoy to Lesdiguières, Governor of Dauphiny, asking him to adopt measures in conformity with these arrangements. The letter is dated 2d June, 1655, and is in the Archives of State at Turin. Lesdiguières received orders to the same effect from Louis XIV., 4th and 18th June, 1655. (In the same archives.)

[2] Léger, II. 365.   [3] Letter of 18th June, 1655. (Archives of Turin.)

mon arms might be more profitably employed elsewhere." In another letter,[1] the same ambassador expresses himself still more clearly. "This war," he says, "can only have been recommended by the friends of Spain, to turn away the arms of his royal highness from the Milanese."

Thus every one judged of this matter according to his own way of thinking. Diplomatists ascribed it all to political causes, and ecclesiastics to religious causes; but all were unanimous in their condemnations. And let us ask in passing, would the whole of Europe have been so moved, would so many sovereigns have addressed such strong representations to the court of Savoy, on the subject of the massacres perpetrated in the Vaudois valleys in 1655, if these massacres had never taken place? The court of Savoy, however, presently adopted the course of contradicting the news. But the feeling of the sad reality was so deep amongst the sufferers, that twenty-five years afterwards, the year 1655 is still designated in their correspondence by these simple words, *The Year of the Massacres;* and authentic documents do not permit a doubt to remain as to the veritable character of these events, in which the hideous consequences of Popery are exhibited in all their magnitude.

In Switzerland, in England, in Holland, and in almost all Protestant countries, collections were made, and public fasts were held upon account of the Vaudois. Many Catholics also testified the deepest sympathy. I love always to distinguish the principle of Catholicism from the virtues which may be concealed in generous souls beneath the external forms in which it has clothed them. Louis XIV. himself commanded Lesdiguières to receive the Vaudois fugitives kindly, and to assure them of his royal protection.[2] In the valleys of Le Queyras and Pragela, which belonged to France, the people took up arms for the help of the persecuted.[3] The regular troops deserted with the same view.[4] A formal order was placarded at Grenoble prohibiting these desertions.[5] Captain Janavel had already returned to the valleys with his valiant party, augmented by numerous recruits from Le Queyras.

Captain Jahier, a native of Pramol, had retired into the Val Pérouse, in the French territory, with the refugees of Bubiano and the people of Angrogna, who, on the 22d of April, had fled before

[1] Of 25th June. (Archives of Turin.)
[2] These were the terms which he employed in stating the matter to Cromwell. (Léger, II. 226.)
[3] Letter of Christina to Lesdiguières, 2d June.—Letter of Louis XIV. to the same, 18th June. (Turin. Archives of State.)
[4] Letter of Louis XIV. to Lesdiguières, dated 4th June. (Archives as above.)
[5] 14th June. This order is printed as a placard.

the army of Pianesse. He returned a month after at the head of these exiles, supported by their brethren of Pragela, and settled them again in the valleys of Angrogna and Pramol. Then he wrote to Janavel to come and join him.

Janavel had at first taken up his position on a high mountain, called the Alp of the *Pelaya di Geymet*. Thence, descending by the valley of Rora, which he knew so well, he attempted to take possession of Lucernette, a Catholic village situated half a league from Lucerna. But, at the sound of the tocsin, the troops from Lucerna and from Bubiano gathered to the spot in such numbers, that Janavel was compelled to relinquish his project. He was already surrounded by the enemy when he beat a retreat; and this retreat was so skilfully executed that his enemies themselves could not speak of it without admiration. In this affair the gallant captain received a bullet in his leg, which remained lodged in the flesh as long as he lived. But this wound did not prevent him from proceeding in his expeditions. His attempt upon Lucernette, though it had failed as to its object, was not without important consequences, for it gave a new aspect to this war of extermination. The Vaudois now, for the first time, took the aggressive part.

An inexpressible terror began to trouble the towns of Piedmont which lay nearest to the mountains. Each wished fortifications and a garrison. Irish troops were quartered at Bubiano, but they committed such excesses that the inhabitants themselves were very soon obliged to take arms and expel them. Thus the persecutors began to destroy one another.

It was just at this time that Janavel effected his junction with Captain Jahier (on the 27th of May), on the banks of the Angrogna. These two warriors, uniting their forces, became more formidable and more powerful in their expeditions. The first enterprise which they attempted in common was against the little town of Garsiliano, which they endeavoured to seize that very evening. But it happened, as at Lucernette, that, numerous troops coming at the sound of the tocsin from all the neighbouring townships, they were compelled to retire, carrying off with them only some cattle and six pairs of oxen, which they had seized.

Next day, at daybreak, having sought encouragement in prayer, and feeling the necessity of some energetic demonstration to save their country, they assailed the town of St. Segont, and made themselves masters of it. To preserve themselves from the enemy's fire, the Vaudois rolled before them great casks filled with hay; and in this manner they approached the walls of the town, from which a shower of balls fell upon them, but the balls were lost in the casks, without striking the men, who were sheltered behind these rolling screens. Arrived at the bottom of the fortifications, they set fire to bundles of faggots and vine twigs, the smoke of which concealed them from the eyes of the besieged. Having then broken through a gate, they penetrated into the town and loaded themselves with booty. An Irish regiment was surprised in its barrack and cut to pieces. The number slain by the Vaudois amounted to 700 or 800 Irish, and 650 Piedmontese. The unarmed inhabitants were spared,[1] and in part retained prisoners; afterwards the village was destroyed by fire.

It was a terrible execution, and which, perhaps, it might not have been requisite to carry so far, but for the necessity imposed upon the Vaudois of making such a display of their force as should produce an impression amongst the enemy, who had not shrunk from butchering them when defenceless. Moreover, in time of war men do not reason with the coolness of a calm judgment. And the Vaudois valleys had been so cruelly destroyed, the blood which had been shed cried so loudly, the irritation had become so profound, that without attributing such reprisals to the spirit of vengeance alone, we may regard them as a necessary consequence. They had, indeed, the effect of leading the persecutors to see that they must treat this sacrificed people with more consideration. And if it be true that men have no respect for any but those whom they love or those whom they fear, the Vaudois, certain of not being loved, had no alternative but in making themselves feared. They succeeded in a few days.

The capture of St. Segont was already equivalent to a battle won. They had made 1400 of the enemy bite the dust; on their side the loss was only seven men;[2] and these almost incredible facts were well known. The terror inspired by Janavel and Jahier seized all the neighbouring towns. They concerted schemes of mutual defence, and arranged a telegraphic signal, which was to appear on the tops of the steeples, giving notice of the coming of the Vaudois, and indicating their position.

The people, who suffered from the interruption of trade, the cantoning of troops, and the incursions of the Vaudois, began to express a very strong indignation against the cause, or at least against the effects of these troubles; and the public voice became still more urgent as the exploits of Jahier and Janavel, with their intrepid partizans, became more numerous. The Marquis of Pianesse

[1] One girl only, Mademoiselle Alix Marsaille, was killed by a stray shot.
[2] To wit, one of La Tour, two of the Val St. Martin, one of Rocheplate, two of Angrogna, and one of St. John. They had also six wounded.

endeavoured to cut them off by setting a price upon the heads of those amongst them who were of most note;[1] but their troop, instead of being reduced, was augmented every day by new recruits or new refugees, who came to them from Queyras and Pragela. On the 2d of June it consisted of four companies, commanded by the captains with whom we are already acquainted, and by captains Laurens and Benet. In their little council of war they resolved to make an attack upon Briquéras. To execute this design the four companies marched by different directions, so as not only to be able to surprise the town, but also to oppose the approach of the troops, whose assistance it might demand.

In consequence, Janavel kept upon the borders of St. John and La Tayarca, in order to arrest the progress of the troops which might come from La Tour and Lucerna; Captain Laurens took the direction of the last spurs of Rocheplate, ready to intercept those which might be sent from St. Segont; for notwithstanding the recent burning of that village, it had been rendered habitable again by prompt repairs. Jahier descended into the plain of Briquéras, and began to ravage the surrounding fields; but on a signal given, the garrisons of the neighbourhood hastened to the assistance of Briquéras with such rapidity, that no assault could be made upon that place.

Jahier then retraced his steps towards the hills of St. John, where Janavel had kept in check the troops whose progress he had

---

[1] In this way we may learn the names of the most distinguished of these last defenders of their country. They are thus given in the edict of 23d May, 1655. The figures which follow the name indicate the sum promised for the head of each of them:—Joshua Janavel, 300 *ducats;* Bartholemew and James Jahier, 600; Paul Vachère, of Lucerna, 300; Francis Laurent, of Les Chiots (Vale of St. Martin), 200; John Malanot, of the same place, 200; Daniel Grill, of Pral, 200; Abel, John, Anthony, Philip, and Gioanino Peirotti, of Pral (a whole family), 200; Charles Fautrier, 150; Paul Fautrier, 150; Stephen Grass, of Bobi, 150; Lorenzo Buffa, of Angrogna, 150; the brothers John, Peter, and James Tron, called Gianetti (of the Vale of St. Martin), 150; Peter Chanforan and Bartholomew Imbert, of Angrogna, 150 each; Bartholomew Bonous and James Perronel, of Rioclaret (together), 150; and, finally, Daniel Arbareu, of Angrogna; Bartholomew Gianolet, of St. John; William Malanot, of the same place; Gianone de Gianoni, of Angrogna; David Bianchi, of St. John; Joshua Mondon, of Bobi; Daniel Pellenc, of Le Villar; Paul Goante, of La Tour; Paul Bernard, of Rodoret; James, William, and Michael Bastie (without other designation); price set upon their heads, 100 ducats for each. For the brothers John and Francis Meruson, of Traverses, in Pragela, 100 ducats for both.

A price was likewise set by this edict upon the heads of the three Vaudois pastors; to wit, John Léger, the historian, 200 ducats; John Michelin, of Bobi, and Isaac Lépreux, 300 ducats each.

The edict is signed by Charles Emmanuel, and counter-signed Morozza. The names of all the staff of the Vaudois troop are given by Léger, p. 199.

been appointed to arrest. Thus mutually reinforced by one another, the two captains attacked the enemy with such impetuosity, that one hundred and fifty of their number were left dead upon the field of battle. The Vaudois had only one man killed.

A few days after, a convoy of three hundred soldiers was sent from Lucerna to the fort of Mirabouc. Janavel was at Bobi; he was aware of this movement, and awaited the enemy at the defile of Marbec, where he kept them in check for five hours, but was at last obliged to let them pass, after having killed many of them. The valiant captain had on this occasion only eight men with him, and although they retreated, yet it must be granted that they showed great intrepidity in daring to attack three hundred. It is true that they were favoured by the admirable position which their leader had chosen. None of them was killed.

After this, Janavel fell back upon the Alp from which he had made his first expedition against Lucernette, namely, the *Palea di Geymet*, situated opposite to Le Villar. This village was the only one which had not been burned, upon account of the great number of its inhabitants who had become Catholics, and whom it was thought proper to leave at peace in their dwellings. Janavel sent word to them that they must join him, to augment the number of the defenders of the country, in default of which they would be treated as apostates, traitors, and enemies. On this energetic language, the people of Le Villar, whether from fear or from patriotism, joined the standard of the rude warrior who so addressed them.

Janavel then united his efforts once more with those of Jahier, and they formed the project of jointly retaking the Protestant capital of their valleys, the town of La Tour. In this they failed, but they slew more than three hundred soldiers.

The combined troops of these two captains, at this time, amounted to more than six hundred men. They established their headquarters on one of the heights of Angrogna, named Le Verné. But it was necessary to provide for the maintenance of these soldiers; and this could only be done by putting the enemy to ransom.

The inhabitants of Crussol, a village situated in the valley of the Po, having done much harm to the Vaudois at the time of the last massacres, Jahier resolved to lay them under contribution. He set out during the night with one hundred and fifty men; and next morning, at break of day, before the people of Crussol could take any steps for their defence, their village was attacked. The inhabitants retired in consternation to a deep cavern; and the

Vaudois carried off, without resistance, more than four hundred cows or oxen, and six hundred sheep. This booty was conveyed for division to the Alp of Liouza, which, by a very ancient charter, was granted to the abbey of Staffarde.

Whilst this expedition was accomplished on the banks of the Po, the Catholics of St. Segont, and the neighbouring villages, attacked the one hundred and fifty Vaudois who remained at Angrogna. Captains Laurens and Benet, with the brothers Jahier, repulsed these assailants, who, in their retreat, surprised a defenceless man, and satiated their cruelty upon him.[1]

However, Captain Jahier had gone to Pragela to sell, or place in safe custody, a part of the booty which he had made at Crussol. Janavel having in vain expected him for eight days, resolved to attack the town of Lucerna himself. This delay caused the failure of the expedition; for a new regiment, which had arrived in that town on the previous evening, repelled the attack.

Two days after, the Marquis of Pianesse, having called to active service all the troops of the district, supported by the new regiment under the command of M. De Marolles, made an attack in his turn upon Janavel's troop, in the very centre of Angrogna. This was on Friday the 15th of June, 1655. The troops advanced up the valleys, at the same time upon La Tour, St. John, Rocheplate, and Pramol. It was intended to attack them all at once; but this simultaneousness of operations could not be attained, because of the different routes which the army of Pianesse pursued, and the distant points which it occupied. The detachment which came by Rocheplate gave the signal of attack some minutes too soon. Janavel had with him only three hundred men. He went against these first assailants, and repulsed them before the troops from Pramol could come up in their rear. In order to divide them he inclined towards the heights of Rochemanant, when suddenly he found himself opposed to the detachment which had come up by the *côtières* of St. John, and at the same time he saw the detachment advancing which came from La Tour.

In this critical position—assailed on all sides, and lacking half his men, who were still in Pragela—the hero of Rora, with that quick confidence of judgment and energetic promptitude of execution which characterize great captains on the field of battle, fell back ere the battalion of Rocheplate could rally on his flank—dashed into the midst of that which came from Pramol—cut it

---

[1] They passed a cord round his head, and twisted it with a stick till it penetrated into the flesh. The man's name was Peter Reggio; he belonged to Pinache, and died a few days after, in consequence of this treatment.

JANAVEL AGAIN VICTORIOUS.

in two—passed through it—and, as he had formerly done with so much success at Rora, posted himself with his men on the summit of a hill. The hill, thus crowned with this band of heroes, is formed by a bending up again of the mountain-slopes, of gentle inclination on the side which they ascended, but suddenly cut off and broken into precipitous ridges on the opposite side.

The four battalions of the enemy drew together at the base of this slope. Janavel was now shut in betwixt a precipice and an army ten times more numerous than his own. It was nine o'clock in the morning. He resisted in this position till two o'clock in the afternoon; then, judging that his men had been sufficiently exposed in maintaining the conflict, without flinching, for five whole hours, and perceiving already some marks of weariness, impatience, and hesitation amongst the ranks of the enemy, Janavel raised his arms towards heaven and cried, "It is in thy name, O God! support and preserve us!" Then to his men he said, "Forward, my friends!" And, like an avalanche of pikes, swords, and balls, these courageous men rushed to the bottom of the hill with all the impetuosity of a valour too long restrained. Without awaiting their shock, the enemy attempted to spread themselves out in the plain, and recoiled before them. By this manœuvre, in extending, they weakened their line. The Vaudois succeeded in breaking it, and disorder ensued. Confusion readily arises amongst bodies under different commanders. It was habitual with these troops of different origin whenever they were worsted, and followed immediately upon this bold movement of the Vaudois. The 3000 men disbanded. The Vaudois pursued them, killed more than 500, and themselves had only one killed and two wounded.

But all was not ended. Having purged the vale of Angrogna from its invaders, Janavel retired to his entrenchments. At the same moment Captain Jahier arrived from Pragela; their troops were fatigued—the one party by the combat, the other by the march, and those of Janavel had had no food since morning. Whilst they took a hasty refreshment he went to reconnoitre the position of the enemy. He saw them rallying their bodies of dispersed troops in the plain of St. John, and far from thinking of any attack.

This indefatigable warrior called again upon his men; caused them to descend by the borders of the valley, and fell like a thunderbolt unexpectedly upon the army, which was a second time put to the route before him. The Vaudois killed more than 100 men; but the death of Janavel had well-nigh proved at that juncture a greater calamity to his compatriots than a defeat, for that leader, to whom they could not have found a successor, was struck by a bullet which passed quite through his body, entering by the chest and coming out by the back. His mouth filled with blood; he lost consciousness, and was thought to be on the point of expiring. The grief of those around him was extreme. He gave over the command to Jahier, to whom he also gave his instructions, amidst tears, prayers, and liveliest testimonies of affection on the part of his soldiers.

However, Providence was pleased not permanently to deprive the valleys of their intrepid defender, and after six weeks' suffering the cure of Janavel was completed. He had caused himself to be carried to Pinache, in the French territory, to recover or die there. His last advice to Captain Jahier had been, not to attempt anything for that day by reason of the fatigue of their troops; but an emissary having come to apprize Jahier that he might take possession of the town of Ossac, that too impetuous captain, as Léger calls him, whose intrepidity always got the better of his prudence, burning to signalize himself by some grand exploit, took with him 150 soldiers and set out under the guidance of the emissary.

The emissary was a traitor. He led Jahier into an ambuscade, where a squadron of cavalry surrounded and defied him. In this moment of extremity Jahier rose above himself by his extraordinary valour; seeing himself betrayed he killed the traitor, invoked God, caused his soldiers to take to their swords and pikes, rushed upon the cavalry of Savoy with an intrepidity worthy of a better fate; and there, thrusting and striking, disembowelling horses, killing their riders, and breaking through the ranks of his adversaries, he made terrible ravages all around him—killed with his own hand three officers of the enemy, and at last, overcome by the number of his wounds, fell dead upon the spot. His son, who fought by his side, died with him. All his soldiers, with the exception only of one, were cut in pieces. The survivor hid himself in a marsh, and passed the Cluson at night by swimming, to bear this deplorable intelligence to his compatriots.

That 15th of June was a fatal day! The Vaudois were deprived at once of Janavel and Jahier. "The latter," says Léger, "had always shown a great zeal for the service of God and the cause of his country; having the courage of a lion, and, moreover, meek as a lamb, always giving to God alone all the praise of his victories; extremely well versed in the Holy Scriptures; perfectly familiar with controversy and a man of high ability, who might have seemed to possess every estimable quality if only he had been capable of moderating his courage."[1]

[1] Léger, Part II. p. 104.

CHAPTER IX.

END OF THE CONFLICT, NEGOTIATIONS, AND PATENTS OF GRACE.[1]

(JUNE TO SEPTEMBER, 1655.)

Foreigners come to the assistance of the Vaudois—Further successes of their arms—They fail in an attempt, conducted by the French General Descombies, to take the Fort of La Tour—Intervention of Cromwell—His ambassador, Morland, at Turin—Treaty of Pignerol.

THE adversaries of the Vaudois exulted over the death of Jahier and the loss of Janavel, whose wound they regarded as mortal. The hopes which had been formed of an accommodation vanished once more. The army of the persecutors, which had for a moment been held in restraint, assumed the offensive with new vigour. But during this time also, public opinion had declared itself with greater energy in favour of the Vaudois. The fame of the exploits of Jahier and Janavel advanced their cause in a military point of view, as the sufferings of their martyrs had already exalted it in its religious aspect.

Men of arms, from different countries,[2] came to offer their services to this heroic people, whom their enemies had thought to destroy. The French Lieutenant-General Descombies and the Swiss Colonel Andrion were of the number. The latter had already distinguished himself in Sweden, in France, and in Germany. There remained also amongst the Vaudois certain captains of merit; amongst others, Bertin and Podio of Bobi, Albarea of Le Villar, Laurens of Val St. Martin, and Revel and Costabelle, the lieutenants of Janavel and Jahier.

The moderator, Léger, had also returned to the valleys. On the first day after his arrival he thought it proper to pass to Angrogna, where his compatriots were assembled. He repaired thither with Colonel Andrion, who had likewise just arrived. The Vaudois were encamped on the Vachère. During the night they sent soldiers in the direction of La Tour to reconnoitre the positions of the enemy. These soldiers, having come to the hamlet of St. Laurent, there discovered a detachment of Piedmontese troops, who awaited the dawning of the day to ascend higher and attack the Vaudois. These troops were scattered as in a halt; the darkness of night

---

[1] AUTHORITIES.—The same as in Chapter VII.
[2] "There arrived every day a good number of them," says Léger (II. 197).

was still thick; and the two Vaudois soldiers mingled with them and conversed with them in their own language. They thus learned the designs of M. De Marolles, their commander; and, quitting the tents at break of day, hastened to inform their comrades of what they had learned.

Some musket shots were fired after them in vain to arrest their flight; and the enemy, finding themselves discovered, seized their arms and followed on their track. The Vaudois got in advance so far as to forewarn their companions. Léger then took refuge with all haste behind the barricades which had been erected. The enemy divided themselves into four battalions; and from five o'clock in the morning till three o'clock in the afternoon, ceased not to attack the barricades of the Vachère upon three different sides. They were defended only by a few hundred Vaudois.

After this long and unequal combat, the lower barricades, called the *Cases* [*Les Casses*] were carried, and the Vaudois retired to a more elevated spot called the *Keep* [*Le Donjon*]. The Piedmontese army raised a shout of victory, and came forward to the assault, exclaiming, "Come on! come on! ye remains of Jahier!" But from the summit of this keep, down steeper and higher slopes than those of their first fortifications, the Vaudois rolled stones, or rather rocks, which came with thundering rapidity, and made chasms in the ranks of the enemy, dashing them to pieces or crushing them into the earth. The army paused, "Come on! ye remains of St. Segont!" cried the Vaudois then in their turn.

Many of the Piedmontese soldiers had talismans, such as relics and medals dedicated to the Virgin Mary—so many amulets, to which they ascribed the power of turning the balls of the heretics. Those who still survived attributed their preservation to these precious safeguards. They had not seen at what distance from them the balls passed; and danger unseen sometimes seems to have no existence. But in view of these rocks bounding so furiously down, and seeing their companions in the attack falling on their right hand and on their left, the soldiers recoiled for fear of death. They came in contact with each other, jostled upon each other, and impeded each other's movements; disorder got into their ranks, and the Vaudois took advantage of it to rush upon them cutlass in hand. The rout was now complete; the army was defeated and fled, leaving a hundred dead on the field of battle, and bearing off almost as many corpses, with twice that number of wounded.

The syndic of Lucerna seeing these deplorable remains of the army enter the town, it drew from him a saying, whose point cannot easily be perceived except in Italian,[1] "The wolves used to eat the *barbets,* but now it seems that the barbets[2] have devoured the wolves."

A few days after, the garrison of La Tour again revisited the valley of Angrogna, to waste the little that remained of crops in the fields, and to burn the miserable cottages which had escaped the previous burnings; but they were repulsed by Captain Bellin, who pursued them to the very entry of the town. The disorder with which they rushed in caused so great a panic, that the Vaudois captain might have made himself master of the place, if he had known how to make the most of his advantage.

An attempt was made a few days afterwards to accomplish this object; but the opportunity was past, and the attempt was not crowned with success. The enterprise was, however, conducted by an experienced officer, M. Descombies, a native of Languedoc, who had arrived in the valleys on the 17th of July, and had almost immediately been named commander-in-chief of the Vaudois. The Vaudois at the same time equipped a little squadron of cavalry, of which the command was intrusted to another French refugee, named Charles Feautrier. Whilst the adversaries of the Vaudois were gradually weakened, the defenders of the valleys became more and more numerous; they had at this time almost 1800 men in active service. Moreover, Janavel had recovered of his wound and returned to join his brethren.

The whole of these forces being assembled together, advanced by night to the hill of Le Chiabas, distant scarcely ten minutes' walk from La Tour. There the Vaudois halted until the day broke. "Certainly," says Léger,[3] "if, according to the advice of those who belonged to the valleys, the attack had been immediately commenced, it would have been all over both with the town and the fortress; but the fatal prudence of M. Descombies was the cause of the fort not being taken." This general not having yet seen the Vaudois engaged in action, not knowing the localities, and not daring to rely upon what was told him, sent Frenchmen, who had come with him, to reconnoitre the approaches of the Châtelard; for so the fort of St. Mary or citadel of La Tour was called. These emissaries described it to him as impregnable; and Descombies then gave orders for a retreat, that he might not throw away, in this first affair, the lives of the men who had intrusted themselves

---

[1] *Altre volte li lupi mangiavono li barbetti, ma lo tempo è venuto che li barbetti mangiano i lupi.*

[2] A contemptuous epithet given to the Vaudois, derived from the ancient name of their pastors, *Barbas.* [3] Page 197.

to his command. However, the presence of the Vaudois had by this time been telegraphed, and M. De Marolles issued from Lucerna at the head of his regiment. Descombies was going to conduct his troops and his cavalry to the Vachère, when two Vaudois captains, Bellin and Peironnel, exclaimed, "Those who love me, follow me!" The troops hesitated; the officers rushed forward; 100 men followed—the rest fell back. "I will remain here to sound a retreat," exclaimed Janavel, who was still too ill to fight. The half of the Vaudois army then abandoned its commander-in-chief; and even a few Frenchmen joining them, they made an assault upon La Tour. Upon this occasion Captain Fonjuliane performed prodigies of valour. The Vaudois, who knew the weak places in the fortifications of La Tour, made their assault near the convent of the Capuchins. A shower of balls was poured down upon them from the fort and convent. Nevertheless they demolished the wall, penetrated into the interior, seized the cloister, set it on fire, rushed into the town, occupied all the outlets, and made themselves masters of it in a few moments. The slaughter was great; but the conquerors spared all who sought mercy. The Capuchins were of this number, and remained prisoners. The intrepid assailants then mounted to attack the citadel, sheltering themselves, as they had already done at St. Segont, behind casks either empty or stuffed with hay, which they rolled before them, and in which the balls safely spent their strength.

The garrison, seeing the convent lost, the town on fire, and the bastions of the fort scaled on all sides, began to capitulate, and asked only to retire with their lives. But just then the regiment of M. De Marolles arrived from Lucerna. The garrison seeing it approach, persisted in resistance. Presently the cavalry of Savoy surrounded the place, to cut off the escape of the attacking party. If the Vaudois had only had a small body of cavalry on their side to guard the approaches of the town, they would have been able to have completed their conquest; but M. Descombies had led his cavalry back to the Vachère. Janavel, seeing his brave compatriots almost surrounded, sounded a retreat from the top of the hill of Chiabas. He was a man so intrepid and so experienced that they could not but regard his orders with confidence. The Vaudois therefore retired. It was full time: the pursuit was hot; but Janavel had calculated so justly that they were all saved. "What a loss it was," said they to Descombies, "that your troops were not there to support us!" "I regret it more than you do," he replied, "for my honour is compromised. Ah! if I had seen you fight before! I knew very well that the Vaudois were brave soldiers; but I did not think that they were lions, and more than lions." It was his desire then to find an opportunity, as soon as possible, of showing that his bravery was not unworthy of theirs; but again the opportunity once lost never returned.

The report of the Easter massacres spread over indignant Europe. The representations made by European sovereigns to the court of Savoy became stronger and stronger. Cromwell, in particular, manifested extraordinary zeal and activity in favour of the Vaudois; not contented with addressing Charles Emmanuel himself, he solicited the other powers to follow his example. Louis XIV. replied to him as follows:[1]—"Most Serene Protector, . . . To show that I nowise approved their turning aside my troops for this business, although under pretext of quartering them in the valley of Lucerna, I immediately sent several of my officers to the Duke of Savoy to put a stop to the proceedings [against the Vaudois] which were still being carried on under his authority. . . . And I even gave orders to the Duke De Lesdiguières, governor of Dauphiny, to receive them, treat them humanely, and assure them of my protection. And as I am informed by your letters of the 25th ult.,[2] that you are touched with the calamity of this miserable people, I am very happy to have anticipated you in your desire; and I will continue to address myself to that prince for their consolation and re-establishment. I have gone so far as to make myself answerable for their obedience and loyalty, so that I have good hopes that my mediation will not be ineffectual."[3]

The French ambassador in Piedmont, M. De Servient, received orders to act according to the spirit of this letter. Holland and Switzerland also sent to Turin mediators for the Vaudois. Morland, the youthful plenipotentiary of Cromwell, arrived on the 21st of June at Rivoli, where the court was. On the 24th he was admitted to a public audience; and after the customary compliments he added, "The Most Serene Protector himself adjures you to have compassion on your own subjects in the valleys, so cruelly maltreated. Misery has followed the massacres; they wander upon the mountains; they suffer from hunger and from cold; their wives and children drag out their lives in destitution and consuming affliction. And of what barbarities have they been the victims! Their houses burned, their members torn, scattered about, mutilated, sometimes even devoured by the murderers! Heaven and Earth shudder at it with horror! Were all the Neros of past and future times to view these fields of carnage, infamy, and inexpressible atrocities (let it not wound your royal highness), they would conclude that they

[1] 12th June, 1655.   [2] May, 1655.   [3] Léger, Part II. p. 226.

had never seen anything but what was good and humane in comparison with these things! I say it without offence to your majesty. O God! Sovereign ruler of Heaven and Earth, avert from the heads of the guilty the just vengeance which so much bloodshed calls for!" Such was the harangue of Morland.

This speech, characterized by Puritan energy and unction, pronounced with the manly assurance of youth and courage, more like the severe accents of the prophets than the complaisance of diplomacy, produced a profound sensation. Never had prince been so boldly found fault with to his face. Charles Emmanuel made no reply: but the Duchess spoke. The Jesuits had moulded her mind. "I am very sensible," she said, "of the interest which your master testifies in my subjects. Only I am astonished that he should have lent an ear to the inaccurate reports of which your address gives evidence. The distance at which he resides can alone excuse them; for it is impossible to represent as barbarities, chastisements so mild and paternal, inflicted upon rebellious subjects, whose revolt no sovereign could excuse. Nevertheless, I am well contented to pardon them, in order to show to the Most Serene Protector the desire which I feel to please him."

Morland left Turin on the 19th of July, promising to return in order to assist the Vaudois in the negotiations which were to be opened with regard to them. But the government made haste to have them concluded in his absence, in order that they might be more free to grant less. On the 18th of August, 1655, in presence of the Swiss ambassadors[1] who had arrived at Turin after Morland's departure, and under the influence of Servient, the ambassador of France, was concluded at Pignerol the treaty named the *Patents of Grace*, which re-established the Vaudois in part of their privileges, and by its perfidious reservations became the occasion of incessant vexations to them. It cannot be doubted that if the return of Morland had been awaited, this treaty would have been much more advantageous; for about the end of July Cromwell had sent a new ambassador, Mr. Downing, with orders to take with him from Geneva the Chevalier Pelh, his resident ambassador to the Helvetic body. They were then both to join Morland, and all together

---

[1] These ambassadors came in name of the Protestant cantons; but there exists a letter from the deputies of the *Catholic* cantons in the *Diet*, in which they say to the Duke of Savoy, that they had intended to unite delegates of their own communion to that embassy, to intercede likewise in favour of the Vaudois; but that their offer not having been accepted, they expressed their sentiments on this point to him by writing. The letter is dated 21st July, 1655. (Archives of Turin.) The court of Turin wrote on the 3d of August to the Pope's nuncio in Switzerland, to entreat him to remove from these Catholic cantons their too favourable prepossessions respecting the valleys. (Same Archives.)

to repair to Turin, to act in concert with the ambassador of the United Provinces (Holland). But the treaty of Pignerol was unfortunately signed before the arrival of these influential personages, and was thenceforth to afford too evident proofs of their absence. The following were its principal provisions:—

"The Vaudois, having taken up arms against their sovereign, deserved to be punished; however, through clemency they will be pardoned; and the Duke of Savoy wishing to make known to the world with how much tenderness he loves his people,[1] consents to accord to them:—

"I.—The confirmation of their privileges. (Liberty of conscience, of trade, and of transit.)

"II.—An amnesty for the excesses committed during the troubles.

"III.—The annulling of the prosecutions commenced, and of the decrees of outlawry issued against Léger, Janavel, Michelin, Lepreux, and other outlawed persons" (on whose heads a price had been set).

"IV.—The Protestants are prohibited from dwelling henceforth on the right bank of the Pélis, below Lucerna, and at Lucernette, Bubiano, Campillon, Fenil, Garsiliano, Briquéras, and St. Segont." (This clause would assuredly not have been admitted by the representatives of Great Britain and the United Provinces, since it was expressly contrary to the treaty of Cavour, 1561.)

"V.—The possessions of the Vaudois, lying within the districts where they are prohibited from dwelling, shall be sold within three months, in default of which they shall be paid for by the exchequer to their proprietors, according to the price which they cost.

"VI.—The Vaudois may inhabit the commune of St. John, but they are prohibited from practising any public religious service there.

"VII.—They shall be exempted from divers taxes for the space of five years (because," adds the patent, "they are not in a condition to pay them, by reason of the losses which they have suffered).

"VIII.—Mass shall be celebrated in all the valleys; but the Vaudois shall not be required to attend.

---

[1] *Volendo far noto al mondo, con quanta tenerezza d'affetto amiamo i nostri popoli.* . . . These expressions need to be read in their exact form in order to be believed genuine. There is at the end of this preamble an expression which shows that Charles Emmanuel had only acted under the directions of his mother, *Madame Reale, mia Signora e Madre quale habbiamo sempre tanto deferito.* And she had only acted according to the suggestions of the clergy who were under the influence of Jesuitism, the language of which may be recognized at the slightest glance in the very first words which we have cited.

"IX.—Those who, having abjured their religion during the late troubles, shall think that they have been constrained thereto by violence, and wish to return to Protestantism, shall not be punished as relapsed.[1]

"X.—The prisoners on both sides, including women and children, shall be restored as soon as they shall be demanded." (In virtue of this article, the wife and daughters of Janavel were delivered up. But these words, apparently so precise, *The prisoners shall be restored as soon as they shall be demanded*, were the cloak for bitter deceptions; for the greater part of the children carried off during the war had been dispersed in Piedmont, had been passed from hand to hand, from castle to castle, from monastery to monastery, so that their parents knew not whither to go to seek them; and the authorities responded to their complaints, "Tell us where your child is and we will secure your obtaining it." Thus Jesuitism triumphed still by its crooked policy, even under the protective provisions of an official edict.)

Some clauses of a mere temporary interest terminate this treaty, consisting in all of twenty articles.[2]

The plenipotentiaries had, it is true, demanded more solid guarantees for the repose of the Vaudois; amongst others, the demolition of the fort of La Tour, but they were refused or eluded; and, as we shall very soon see, the want of them became the source of new difficulties and misfortunes.

---

[1] But, on the 6th of August, the greater part of those who had become Catholics had been removed from the valleys and conducted to a great distance. The principal stages they were to pass through are marked as follows:—*Paësane, Moretta, Piombes, Leyni, Vische, Borgo d'Alea, Saluzzola*, &c.

[2] The negotiators of this treaty were, in name of the Vaudois, the four ambassadors sent by the evangelical cantons of Switzerland, viz., Solomon Hirzel of Zurich, Charles de Bonstetten of Berne, Benedict Sossin of Basle, and James Stockart of Appenzel. On the part of France, the Ambassador Servient; and on the part of Piedmont, MM. Truchi, Gastaldo, and De Grési.

CHAPTER X.

INFRACTIONS OF THE TREATY OF PIGNEROL—LÉGER'S VICISSITUDES.[1]

(A.D. 1655 TO A.D. 1660.)

Grievances not redressed by the Treaty of Pignerol—The Fort of La Tour—Continued operations of the Propaganda—Gastaldo, governor of the valleys—New vexations—Violations of the treaty—Question of the right to meet for public worship at St. John—Léger, pastor of St. John, the object of the particular hostility of the Romish party—He is condemned to death, and flees from the country—His labours and trials in his exile—Odious conduct of Charles II. of England, with regard to money collected in that country during the time of Cromwell, for the Vaudois.

THE treaty of Pignerol could not all at once diffuse the tranquillity of a regular and peaceful government, over a country so torn by extraordinary troubles. The conditions of the treaty were far from being satisfactory to the parties concerned. Hastily concluded by the plenipotentiaries of France and Piedmont, to escape the influence of the ambassadors of Holland and England,[2] whose arrival was not waited for,[3] they left modifications to be desired, which all subsequent efforts[4] were ineffectual to obtain. On the one hand, however, the Propaganda found the concessions too great; on the other, the Vaudois judged them insufficient, and ere long were forced to complain that they were not carried into effect.

The fort of La Tour, which Charles Emmanuel I. had caused to be demolished in 1603, and whose walls had begun to be rebuilt during the late war, became one of the first subjects of discontentment. A recollection of the base conduct of Castrocaro, Gallina, and other persecutors of the Vaudois, was sufficient to excite distrust in the bosoms of the persecuted. In the conferences preparatory to the treaty of Pignerol, it had been agreed that that citadel should be demolished. The Swiss negotiators even wished that this demolition should be guaranteed by a special article. The Sardinian delegates replied, that the Duke of Savoy could not consent in this way to seem to disarm himself before his own subjects, but that he wanted no other fortress than grateful hearts, and

---

[1] AUTHORITIES.—The same as in Chapter VII. Principally *Léger* and *Morland*.
[2] Letter of M. D'Ommeren to the Swiss cantons, 19th October, 1655. (Léger, p. 238.)
[3] Attestation of the Secretary of the Embassy at Turin, 17th Sept., 1655. (Id. p. 223.)
[4] Acts of an Assembly held at Payerne, on the 13th of Oct., 1655. (Id. p. 223.)

that the fortifications of La Tour would be razed immediately after the signature of the treaty.[1] "What would be the use," they said also, "of introducing into the treaty a clause which would be humiliating to the sovereign, and which would be without an object after the lapse of a few days?"

The patents of Pignerol were therefore silent on this point, and the enemies of the Vaudois congratulated themselves upon it; but Jesuitism aimed at still more, and sought to introduce into this charter provisions altogether opposed to these positive promises. The charter was signed; but in the space between the text and the signatures was inserted a new paragraph, bearing that "His royal highness accorded to the Vaudois the right of addressing petitions to him for the demolition of the citadel of La Tour, or its reconstruction in another place."[2] This implied the right of refusal; it was to bring again into question all that had already been agreed; it was to commit a forgery; and when it was complained of, the reply made was that this interpolation was owing to the negligence of a clerk.[3]

The Vaudois, however, sent up the petitions, the vain right of sending which had, with so deceitful an intention, been thus granted them. The duke replied, with much apparent kindness, that he was happy to have it in his power to give them a new proof of his good-will, and that he would destroy as much of the fort of La Tour as was not necessary for the defence of his dominions. He did, indeed, cause a little useless fort to be demolished which stood in the plain of La Tour, but at the same time he redoubled his activity in the construction of the citadel situated on the height. The works were so vigorously carried on that the building was terminated in the course of the same year, and a garrison was placed in it in the year following. Thus the honeyed duplicity of a cruel political expediency trifled with the good faith of the people, and laboured to oppress them whilst affecting to establish a claim to their gratitude.

However, the French authorities saw with dislike a fortress of such strength constructed so near their frontiers. The governor of Dauphiny[4] and the commandant of Pignerol[5] expressed their dis-

---

[1] Letter of the Swiss ambassadors to those of France and Piedmont, 30th Nov., 1657. (Léger, p. 283, al. 3.)

[2] Some editions of the *Patenti di grazia* do not contain this article (Guichenon, Hist. p. 1017). In others it is preceded by a special declaration on the part of Servient, the ambassador of France. (Raccolta degli Editti, p. 103.) Léger discusses this point at length, Part II. pp. 263, 264, 265.

[3] See Léger, pp. 250, 283, &c.

[4] Lesdiguières.   [5] La Bretonnière.

approbation of it;[1] and Louis XIV. then offered to the Vaudois to become guarantee for the full execution of the treaty of Pignerol concluded under his auspices.[2] A synod was held at La Tour to deliberate upon this offer.[3] The Vaudois thanked the monarch for his protection, which they entreated him to continue,[4] and put into the hands of his envoy a memorial,[5] setting forth all the grievances of which they thought they had cause to complain, since the signing of the *Patents of Grace*. These patents, said they, have not been carried into effect;[6] the release of our prisoners is refused,[7] our children are still carried off,[8] and the soldiers who garrison the fort of La Tour commit with impunity the gravest crimes against our persons and properties.[9]

Thus pillage and assassination, rape and violence, continued the Catholic *work of faith*. The Propaganda had not renounced their design—the extirpation of heresy. Did they not proclaim the lawfulness of all treachery against heretics? Did they not brand all those as heretics who rested on the authority of the Bible? Was it not therefore their duty, at all hazards, to destroy the Vaudois?[10] Thus the report spread far that new conflicts were about to arise in these afflicted valleys.[11] And meanwhile an attempt was made to create division amongst their inhabitants by the vilest insinuations. Some Jesuits, who had introduced themselves by pretending to be Protestant refugees from Languedoc, excited the poor people to distrust of their pastors, propagating, with perfidious ingenuity, reports of malversation against those of them who had been intrusted with the distribution of the considerable sums col-

[1] Guichenon, p. 1077.
[2] Letter of Louis XIV. to Lesdiguières, 22d February, 1656. (Léger, p. 246.) Lesdiguières himself wrote to the Vaudois on the 4th of March, 1656, sending them Louis XIV.'s letter by a lieutenant-colonel named M. *Du Buis*. (Id. p. 247.)
[3] On the 28th and 29th of March, 1656.
[4] See the letters of the Vaudois in Léger, pp. 248 and 249.
[5] This memorial is given by Léger, p. 250, *et seq*. It contains fifteen articles.
[6] See Art. v., vii., viii. and ix., xi. and xii. of the memorial.
[7] Art. x. Léger, p. 251.
[8] Art. xiii. The *Patents of Grace* still authorized this carrying off of children within certain limits, whilst seeming to prohibit it—"*I figluoli non potranno esse tolti a loro parenti, mentre che sono in età minore cive li maschi di dodeci, e le femine di dicci anni*. (Art. xv. of the *Patents*.)
[9] Those of the assassin soldiers who had been apprehended by the peasants, and delivered over to the authorities for justice, promptly obtained their liberty, through the interposition of the Castilian Cordeliers, with whom the valleys were then infested. Their presence also occasioned serious grievances. Léger reports numerous instances of deeds of violence committed by them (pp. 250–266), of which the Swiss ambassadors speak as eye-witnesses.—(Letter of 30th Nov., 1657. Léger, p. 283.)
[10] The designation of the Propaganda assumed it as a duty: "*Congregatio de extirpandis hæreticis*."
[11] Léger, p. 247.

lected in foreign countries.¹ The calumnies most ready to be credited are those which concern the meanest interests; the unfortunate, moreover, are more easily moved to suspicion, and ignorance favours such an attempt. The Vaudois, accordingly, soon presented the melancholy spectacle of intestine divisions and recriminations about pecuniary affairs, whilst yet they had scarcely well escaped from their greatest calamities.²

New trials very soon came upon them to re-unite them again against a common danger. The auditor Gastaldo, who had been made governor of the valleys, without ceasing to be a member of that body so hostile to the Vaudois—the Propaganda, issued, on the 15th of June, 1657, a decree, by which he prohibited them from setting up any kind of worship at St. John, under pain of a fine of 1000 crowns of gold for the minister conducting it, and of 200 for every one of his hearers. At the same time new Popish missions were founded in the valleys; the Jesuits got a footing in them everywhere; exemptions from taxation, and other indulgences, were granted to the Catholics and those who had become Catholics, whilst an extreme rigour was shown in the execution of all measures burdensome to the Protestants. The latter were not left, however, without the comfort of receiving lively proofs of the interest with which they were regarded by others. The synod of Dauphiny gave the Vaudois churches marks of its fraternal sympathy by sending them several pastors, but the Piedmontese government took advantage of their foreign origin to expel them from the country.³

In a letter addressed to the Swiss ambassadors who had negotiated the treaty of Pignerol, the Vaudois complained of the increasing annoyances to which they were subjected; and the ambassadors wrote in their turn to Piedmont to complain of the infractions of the treaty.⁴ After mention of the promises relative

---

[1] Guichenon estimates the collections in England at two millions of livres (p. 1014). Those of Holland amounted, on the 5th of September, 1655, to 640,637 florins. These sums were not entirely remitted to the Vaudois pastors; but a great part remained in the hands of divers committees charged with their management in London and Geneva.

[2] The complaints of this kind, which, in 1656 alone, were addressed by the Vaudois to the pastors of Geneva, are more numerous than could have been credited. (See the Registers of the Venerable Company, vol. K, p. 40, 95, 190, 192, 194, 195, 198, &c.) The probity of Léger was often called in question; but he was honourably acquitted after an investigation subsequently made into this business.

[3] Some of them, however, received permission to reside in it on condition of their taking an oath of allegiance to Charles Emmanuel II., viz., Michael Bourset, of Ussau, in Val Cluson, pastor also of Pragela (which belonged to France), and Armaud, of Vagnes, in the Gapençois. They took the oath on the 9th of November, 1657, in the palace of the counts of Lucerna.

[4] The letter is dated from Zurich, 30th November, 1657. It is signed by the four ambassadors, and is given by Léger, pp. 233-235.

to the demolition of the fort of La Tour, and the excesses of which the soldiers of that fort were then daily guilty, they said concerning the Vaudois, "What liberty of conscience, then, have they obtained, if the pastors of their churches, for the simple reason of their being foreigners by birth, are compelled to leave them—if all religious service is prohibited where only the right of private worship is demanded—if the Protestants are forbidden to make proselytes, and at the same time are exposed to all the proselytizing endeavours of their adversaries? Finally," they add, "whilst the Vaudois are forbidden to acquire, or even to rent, any property without the limits which are fixed for them, the Catholics are forbidden to sell them those which they possess within these same limits. Now all these things," say they, reminding the Piedmontese government of the treaty of Pignerol, "touch our hearts so much the more sensibly, because we took part, in the name of our lords and superiors, in the framing of that treaty, and are parties interested therein."

The President Truchis replied with much ability, to show that the stipulations granted to the Vaudois had not been violated, but that, on the contrary, they themselves had been guilty of not observing them.

The synod of the Vaudois valleys then drew up a statement of the violations of the treaty which they had to complain of, adding evidence in support of them. This memorial was printed at Haarlem in 1662, and reprinted in the same town, with new particulars, in 1663. But the Piedmontese government was deaf to all these complaints, and seemed only, on the contrary, desirous of giving every day new cause for complaints yet louder.

In virtue of the sixth article of the Patents of 18th August, 1655, the people of the valleys were to be exempted from paying the outstanding public burdens of that sad year, in which all the crops and every fortune and every family had suffered so deplorably throughout that afflicted country; yet, in spite of their profound misery, which the product of foreign collections could but very incompletely relieve, these public burdens were rigorously exacted from the Vaudois. Moreover, as if on purpose to render this exaction more flagrantly offensive, an exemption from these very charges was at the same time granted to the Catholics of the valley of St. Martin, "in order," says the decree, "that they may be able to repair the loss which the Protestants have caused them."[1]

It was not, however, with a view of clearing themselves from

[1] *Acciò si possino rimettere dalli danni patiti da Religionarii.*—Edict of 16th December, 1657.

these heavy taxes, that the Vaudois at this time made the most urgent applications to the government. A money wound is not a mortal one, said the popular good sense: that only is deadly of which there is no healing; and the prohibition of religious exercises in the parish of St. John was, in their estimation, that mortal wound, from which, therefore, they wished to secure themselves. By this arbitrary prohibition all their churches were menaced at once. The edict of Cavour (1561) guaranteed the free exercise of their worship in all places in which it was then established; St. John was of the number—the patents of Pignerol had neither restricted nor enlarged these limits. (Art. VII.) If one of their parishes could be attacked, what security could remain for the rest? It is true that public preaching had been forbidden at St. John since the year 1620, in which the church of Les Malanots was shut up; but private meetings, the instruction of catechumens, and the discharge of the other pastoral functions had been always continued there.

A general synod was held in the month of March, 1658, with reference to this grave question. It decided upon making application to the sovereign, and that, in the meantime, the pastor of St. John (Léger the historian) should continue to exercise his function until the question submitted to the judgment of the duke should be decided.

This decision of the synod caused great irritation at the court of Turin. "The first duty of subjects," it was said, "is to obey their prince: in resisting his orders the Vaudois make themselves guilty of rebellion—they must be treated as rebels and guilty of high treason." The Protestant powers,[1] to which the synod had written to obtain their intercession in this matter, having addressed the court of Turin with this view, received only a reply expressing still greater inflexibility. "You do not know the people on whose behalf you interest yourself, they are rebels, unworthy of any regard."

It may readily be supposed that the Propaganda and the Catholic clergy would seek to irritate men's minds rather than to tranquillize them. The particular object of this irritation was Léger, that powerful supporter of the valleys, and courageous pastor, who remained at his post in spite of menaces and dangers. Already twice condemned to death,[2] he braved it still, and his enemies no

---

[1] To wit, the Elector-Palatine, the Elector of Brandenburg, the Landgrave of Hesse, the States-General of the United Provinces (Holland), and the evangelical cantons of Switzerland. Their letters were carried by Colonel Holzhalb, in July, 1662. (Léger, B. ii. pp. 295, 325-357, and 278-281.)

[2] The first condemnation was on the 23d of May, 1655. It was pronounced

doubt hoped that this time would be the last. They sent him a citation to appear at Turin; the citation bore no cause assigned, and Léger paid no attention to it. A second summons was not more effectual. The Count of Saluces, who seemed to take a real interest in the Vaudois,[1] then sought out the minister, and said to him, "You have entered on a wrong course; why do you not obey this summons? This is to make men believe that you are guilty. A legal order has forbidden public worship in your parish; why do you not comply with it until it be revoked?" "I cannot suspend my pastoral functions in expectation of that revocation," replied the pastor. "The way to obtain it soonest," said his adviser, "would be to plead your cause at Turin." But Léger refused to go. "At least," said the count, "suspend the public services of your religion till a new order be issued." Léger still refused. "Will you," added the count, "contend with a high hand against your sovereign, and do you think he will permit you to prevail against him?" "I contend only in the way of right and duty," said Léger. "It is my duty to minister in our congregations; and it is a right which they exercise when they maintain their worship." Thus war was declared; Léger was to be defeated.

On the 3d of May, 1658, he received a third citation, requiring him to appear under pain of banishment and confiscation of goods. The pastor of St. John thought it proper to consult his brethren against twenty-nine inhabitants of the valleys, of whom Léger was one. The edict charged them with having assembled illegally, and with conspiracy in that meeting. (They had only sought, in concert, the means of defending their country.) This condemnation was annulled by the first article of the Patents of Pignerol.

The second condemnation was pronounced against Léger personally, on the information of an assassin, of whom we have already spoken, and who, to obtain his own pardon, declared that Léger had engaged him to execute the murder which he had committed. The assassin was set at liberty, and Léger was cited to appear before the podestat of Lucerna, in July, 1655. It was at the hottest time of the war; the citation never came to his hands, and he was condemned for contumacy. A month after, having come to Pignerol during the negotiations which put an end to the war, he was informed of this condemnation. He immediately demanded to be confronted with his accuser; but it was replied that the accuser had been released, and that it was not known where he was to be found. The Vaudois pastor was, however, hastily freed from the sentence under which he lay, and that with as little formality as had attended the pronouncing of it.

Meanwhile, the Vaudois themselves seized the murderer with whom the accusation had originated, and conducted him to Pignerol; but the authorities still refused to confront him with Leger, saying to the latter that it was enough for him to be relieved from his condemnation. From this example we may judge what sort of protection, or even of equity, the Vaudois had to expect from the pretended justice of their adversaries.

[1] Generous sentiments seem to be hereditary in this noble family, whose present representatives have recently expressed to an author belonging to the Vaudois valleys the liveliest interest in his compatriots.

as to the course which he should pursue. A meeting was held for this purpose in Pinache, a town at that time belonging to France, where it was decided that a petition should be presented to Charles Emmanuel to preserve Léger in his congregation. This should have been done at the first; but it was too late to hope that this petition would be granted now. It was not. Three years were spent in fruitless negotiations; and on the 12th of January, 1661, a decree of the senate of Turin condemned Léger to death, and those who were accused along with him to ten years of the galleys.[1]

No longer able to remain in his native country, Léger withdrew from it to continue his labours in its service; but new trials were reserved for him in foreign lands. In 1659, he had been sent to England to receive the collections made on behalf of the Vaudois. During his absence, the Jesuits, who had made their way into the valleys, under the guise of Protestant refugees, spread the report that the Vaudois pastors in general, and Léger in particular, had appropriated a great part of this money. The synod of the valleys exposed these impostures; but the calumniators, not owning themselves defeated, carried their accusations before the synod of Dauphiny,[2] which named a commission to investigate them. This commission proceeded to the valleys in name of the churches of France, which, having contributed to the collections, were entitled to be informed as to the use made of them. A detailed report was presented next year to the synod of Veynes, and by this report the proceedings of the Vaudois pastors were fully justified.

The complaints were then carried to Geneva, where they were no better received. But the dissatisfaction to which they had given rise in the valleys, amongst the worst-informed persons, having been carefully fomented by the enemies of the Vaudois, some of the latter thought fit to address a petition upon the subject to their sovereign. Thirty-seven persons, drawn from the least enlightened ranks of the population (for more than one-third of them could not write), signed[3] an accusation of peculation, which was thus brought by the Vaudois against their own pastors. They requested that a government officer might be named to inquire into the real amount of the collections, and to take charge of their distribution.

---

[1] These were the deacons and elders of the congregation of St. John, named Bianquis, Bastie, Danna, Magnot, Fervout, and Curts.

[2] Held at Die in 1660. There existed at that time a Protestant Faculty of Theology in that town, which was suppressed in 1672.

[3] Those who could not write signed by making a simple *mark*, generally in the form of a cross ; and the name of the person signing was inscribed by those who prepared the paper opposite the mark which each had made.

The government affected to regard this paper as the expression of the general sentiment of the valleys, and Charles Emmanuel immediately named the Count of Lucerna to attend to the complaint. The senator Perrachino, intendant-general of the court of justice, summoned the Vaudois pastors to give in their accounts to him. It cannot be denied that the distributions were not wholly such as might have been desired;[1] but certainly it was not for the persecuted thus to submit to the control of their persecutors, and the pastors being assembled in synod, replied with dignity that the employment of all the money which had passed through their hands would be found to be justified by exact accounts, and that they were ready to produce regular receipts, when and where they might be required.

Meanwhile Léger, accompanied by two other delegates of the valleys, pursued his labours in England. The period was one of great agitation in Great Britain, where the sceptre had just passed into the feeble and inexperienced hands of Cromwell's son. The Vaudois deputies were witnesses of his fall, and of the return of Charles II., recalled after twelve years of exile, by the voice of a new parliament, the convocation of which was owing to the devoted exertions of the famous General Monk.

It was to this young sovereign that the Vaudois had to address themselves, to obtain the first annual payment from the considerable sums which Cromwell had collected on their behalf, and converted into an annuity on national security.[2] These sums amounted to more than £16,000 sterling; but the new prince refused to account for them, declaring that he would not pay the debts of an usurper. This, however, was not a debt, but a trust; this money had not been furnished by Cromwell, but by the English Church, and Charles II., in seizing these offerings, was guilty of an usurpation less glorious than that with which he reproached his predecessor, but as real. The commissioners of the valleys could, therefore, only recover certain small sums which had been deposited in the hands of private parties.[3]

The bad success of this negotiation was shortly followed, in

[1] Léger died without having completed a statement of accounts as to the sums which he had received.

[2] By an act signed at Whitehall, 18th May, 1658, Cromwell had assigned to the Vaudois churches a perpetual annuity of £614 sterling, the interest accruing from a capital of £16,333, 10s. 3d., the balance which remained of collections amounting to £38,241, 10s. 6d., of which the other portion had already been sent to the valleys.

[3] The generous voice of an illustrious protector of the Vaudois, who owes his power to his talents alone, has recently made a successful appeal to the British Parliament for the restitution of these funds.

Léger's case, by a blow still more severe. Libels were published against him.[1] He was cited to appear at Turin;[2] and on the pretext that he had travelled to foreign countries to foment bad feeling against the Duke of Savoy, he was again condemned to death for the crime of high-treason. Hereupon he retired to Geneva, and thence to Leyden, where he wrote his *General History of the Vaudois Churches*, which is simply a collection of papers relative to the events of the year 1655. The church of Leyden received him as one of its pastors; he lived there for a number of years, contracted a second marriage in 1665, and ended his days there.[3]

CHAPTER XI.

THE WAR OF THE OUTLAWS.[4]

(A.D. 1660 TO A.D. 1664.)

De Bagnol, commandant of the fort of La Tour—*Gli Banditti*—This troop of proscribed and desperate men makes reprisals on the persecutors of the Vaudois—Edict of 25th June, 1663—Treachery and violence—The Vaudois assailed by troops under the Marquis De Fleury—Defeat of the assailants—Edict of 10th August, 1663—The Vaudois, under Janavel, continue the defensive war—An attempt to divide the Vaudois by getting a few of their number to consent to the conditions of the edict of 10th August—Intervention of foreign Protestant powers.

LÉGER and Janavel had been condemned to death.[5] Twenty persons had been sent to the galleys, and others had been prosecuted for resisting the orders of the sovereign in the exercise of Protestant worship at St. John, where it had been interdicted.[6]

The condemned persons had fled; a price had been set upon their

---

[1] They were taken up and refuted in a special *Apology*. See sect. I. § ii. No. 3, of the Bibliography at the end of this work.

[2] On the 7th of December, 1661, although already condemned to death.

[3] I do not know the precise date of his death, but he no longer survived in 1684; for under date 27th August of that year, there occurs a royal edict which makes mention of the confiscated property of *the late* John Léger. (*Records of the Court of Accounts* at Turin. *Regio controrolo, Finanze*, 1684. No. 179, fol. 55.)

[4] AUTHORITIES.—The same as in Chapter VII., and the introductory parts of most of the works cited as authorities for next chapter.

[5] The edict condemning Janavel is dated 25th January, 1661. Fifty persons were condemned to death along with him. A price of 300 ducats was set upon their heads. A fine of 3000 ducats was decreed against the communes which tolerated the outlaws within their bounds.

[6] On the 31st of May, 1661, but the interdict was not published in the valleys till the 10th of August. (Léger says the 12th—p. 272.)

heads, but no one dared to give them up, and force was employed in order to apprehend them; the officer of justice, Perrachino, put himself at the head of a troop of soldiers, who commenced their exploits by ravaging and plundering. They proceeded to raze Léger's house at St. John, and that of Joshua Janavel at the vineyards of Lucerna.[1]

The command of the fort of La Tour was, moreover, intrusted to the Count of Bagnol, one of those who had been concerned in the massacre of 1655, and who continued a zealous servant of the Propaganda. His soldiers committed all sorts of excesses; they arrested travellers and robbed them, plundered the houses of the Vaudois, carried off their daughters, and killed those who resisted their violence. Many of the poor villagers abandoned their dwellings, to seek a safer asylum in the deeper recesses of their mountains. The outlaws who had fled thither descended from their fastnesses to defend their brethren. De Bagnol threatened the severest penalties against all who should receive them. The house of any one who should even give an outlaw anything to eat was to be razed to the ground. Everything possible seemed to be done at that time to irritate the Vaudois.

The commandant of the fort of Mirabouc followed the example of the commandant of La Tour. The governor of Lucerna, Léger tells us,[2] was famous for more than sixty murders, committed before the marriage of the Duke of Savoy, on which occasion he had received pardon;[3] and as to the Sire De Bagnol, who reigned in his fort over all the valley, we may mention by anticipation, that he died upon the scaffold convicted of 120 odious murders. What could the valleys become in such hands? What opinion can we form of the government which set over them such rulers?

Janavel, at the head of his troop of outlaws, was their sole defender. This troop was rapidly augmented by the addition of all the Vaudois who were driven from their dwellings. They were enjoined to return to them under pain of death and confiscation of goods. Then, under pretext of seizing the confiscated goods, the soldiers extended their ravages and pillage on all sides. The troop of outlaws, called, as at a former time, *gli banditti*, opposed these expeditions by force.

It may be imagined what this troop must have become under the conduct of Janavel. Every day was signalized by new exploits,

[1] In March, 1662. [2] Léger, p. 267.
[3] Charles Emmanuel II. had espoused, on the 4th of March, 1663, Frances of Orleans, who died ten months after. He married again, on the 11th of April, 1665, Joan of Savoy, who died on the 15th of March, 1724, forty-nine years after her husband.

and all attempts to apprehend him were fruitless. In vain were the Vaudois ordered to resign their arms into the hands of the magistrates,[1] and the former penalties denounced anew against the outlaws;[2] in vain did the Vaudois, on their part, betake themselves to the intendant of the province[3] and to the sovereign,[4] to obtain the protection of the law against the robberies of the Count of Bagnol. It was difficult for those not on the spot to estimate the justice of their complaints; the authorities could not believe that such crimes were committed, and regarded their complaints as exaggerated. The intendant of the province replied that they must return to their dwellings within the space of three days,[5] and Charles Emmanuel promised an investigation concerning the disorders of which they alleged that they were the victims.[6] Meanwhile, De Bagnol continued his extortions and violence.

The troop *degli banditti* defended the poor mountaineers; but they could not subsist without levying contributions on their part also, which they did most frequently on the Catholic villages. Janavel seized on several of these, laid siege to others,[7] and took ransoms for Catholics of the plain to sustain the persecuted people of the mountains. He sometimes pursued his adversaries to the walls of Lucerna and Briquéras. There was no day, says Léger, on which some action did not take place[8] between these warlike troops and those of the Marquis De Fleury or Captain Pool, who commanded the forces of the province; the latter, notwithstanding their numbers, being always worsted in their conflicts with Janavel.

On the 25th of May, 1663, however, the Vaudois were driven back from the quarter of Les Malanots, which they occupied at St. John, as far as the hills of Angrogna; but there, assuming the offensive in their turn, they charged their pursuers so impetuously, that they drove them back again over all the ground which they had gained, and even into the fort itself. In none of the encounters which took place in 1655, says a letter of that period, did the Vaudois kill a greater number of the enemy than in that affair.

Another skirmish took place on the 17th of June, in the immediate vicinity of La Tour. The combat, says a letter of the 21st, lasted the whole day; and the Vaudois from the upper part of the

---

[1] Order of 19th December, 1660, cited in the *Conferences tenues à Turin en 1664*, p. 24.   [2] 25th January, 1661. (Léger, p. 290.)
[3] 13th and 22d May, 1663.   [4] 26th and 30th May, 1663.
[5] 19th and 24th May, 1663.   [6] 31st May, 1663.
[7] We only know these facts from the preamble of the edict of 25th June, 1663.
[8] Part II. p. 302. Léger, so prolix in other things, is laconic to the utmost as to historic facts. "*I omit,*" he says, "*a multitude of notable encounters,*" &c. (p. 303). "*I shall not spend time in relating the remarkable victories,*" &c. (p. 299).

valley[1] having arrived upon the ground without being aware that a fight was going on, flung themselves into the midst of the enemy, and killed a number of them without sustaining any loss.

But, as the bringing of military forces against the valleys had no other ostensible object than to apprehend men who had been outlawed by a judicial sentence, it was held a crime in the Vaudois to support their defenders, as if they had been guilty of favouring the escape of criminals. More than once the syndics of the communes were obliged to repudiate all connection with the troop *degli banditti*.

On the 25th of June (1663), the Duke of Savoy, wishing to inspire the Vaudois with admiration of his unexpected goodness,[2] issued a long edict, which, under pretext of pacifying the valleys, ordained them all to take up arms and make war upon the outlaws. Two hundred and sixty men, drawn from different communes,[3] were appointed to assemble at Le Chiabas, opposite to La Tour, and to await the orders of the commandant of Briquéras. Each commune was, besides, to give an hostage as security for its loyalty. An investigation was to be commenced at Turin, under the direction of the Count De Bagnol; and to crown all these benefactions, his highness pardoned all the Protestants, on condition of their returning to their dwellings within the space of fifteen days.

By the same edict, the preamble of which expressed so much benignity, Joshua Janavel was condemned to have his flesh torn with red-hot pincers, to be quartered, and to have his head cut off and planted on the top of a pike in an elevated place. The sentence of death against Léger was reiterated; a person named Artus, one named Bastie, one named Rivoire, two named Muston, one named Revel, and a number of others, amounting to thirty-five persons in all, were condemned to death and confiscation of goods. These were the most intrepid leaders of the little Vaudois army. Six persons also were condemned to the galleys for life, and four to be put in irons for ten years. And it was actually proposed that the Vaudois themselves should take the lives of their own leaders and pastors! And this was called a clemency worthy of admiration! We may judge what must have been the severity of those who deemed it so.

The governor of La Tour and the treasurer-general of his highness urged the Vaudois, in the most pressing manner, to accept these

---

[1] From Le Villar and from Bobi.
[2] *Volendo* . . . . *dar occasione agli religionarj di restar ammirativi d'una benignità, tanto da essi inaspettata.* . . . Preamble of the edict of 25th June 1663.
[3] Bobi and Rora were to furnish fifty of them, Le Villar fifty, La Tour sixty, and Angrogna one hundred.

terms. They had eight days to make up their minds. But if ever there was dignity in silence, it was on this occasion. The Vaudois allowed the duke's ultimatum to remain unanswered. The commune of Prarusting alone declined all responsibility for the proceedings of the valley of Lucerna.[1] The seigneurs of the neighbourhood did their utmost to augment this division, to obtain the acceptance of the conditions of the edict by at least a part of the Vaudois. Not being able to obtain this, they particularly insisted that the inhabitants of the valley of Lucerna should give a proof of their peaceful and loyal disposition by escorting a convoy, which it was proposed to send, for the revictualling of the fort of Mirabouc. This fort commands the narrowest part of the valley of Lucerna, and shuts up the pass by which Dauphiny may be reached, whither, it will be remembered, that the Vaudois had oftener than once retired in time of persecution.

It was not without some hesitation that, by conveying warlike stores to this fort, they contributed to close this retreat against themselves in the event of their utmost need of it. But the protestations of the governor of La Tour and the treasurer-general were irresistible. "In return for this act of submission," said they to the Vaudois, "the most complete peace will be granted you. Bring back your families to their dwellings, and entertain no anxiety as to the future."

The Vaudois were already conforming to these advices, when all at once they received information that troops were being secretly sent out from Turin. And they very soon learned that these troops were marching against them. In fact, six regiments of Royal Guards had left the capital on the 29th of June, under the command of the Marquis De Fleury. This army had therefore set out eleven days before the expiration of the time allowed to the Vaudois for returning to their dwellings, and four days before the time when they were to make their reply as to the conditions of the edict. It came to be afterwards known that reinforcements of troops had been secretly directed to Lucerna and La Tour[2] even before this edict was published. It is a vain attempt, therefore, which is made to justify the aggression upon the Vaudois by saying, that the duke meant to punish the inhabitants of the valleys for not having conformed to the edict of the 25th of June, since the assailants were already on the march, not only before the Vaudois could make known their intentions in this respect, but even before they had heard of the edict.

[1] Resolution adopted at the General Council of St. Segont, sitting of 1st July, 1663.
[2] Investigations. *Conferences tenues à l'Hôtel de Ville, à Turin, en* 1664, p. 57.

The Marquis De Fleury marched direct upon Angrogna, taking the road by St. John. The Marquis of Angrogna,[1] commanding the cavalry of St. Segont, bent his course towards the same point by the heights of Rocheplate, whilst the infantry ascended to it by the hills of Briquéras. These bodies of troops united at daybreak on the higher plain to which these different roads conduct. This was on the 6th of July, 1663. Their object was to seize on the Vachère, which rises above the plain, and commands, from its central position, the openings of the three Vaudois valleys.[2] But a corps of observation, placed by the Vaudois, defended this important post.

The bulk of the Vaudois army, commanded by Janavel, occupied a position farther down, on the borders of St. John. It was therefore threatened with the danger of being attacked in the rear by the troops of the Marquis De Fleury. At the same time those of the Count De Bagnol would have assailed it in front, ascending the valley at once on the side of La Tour and on the side of St. John. They accomplished this movement, and effected their junction in Janavel's sight.

The Vaudois patriot recoiled before forces superior to his own. Arriving at the summit of the slope, he found it already occupied by the enemy, who cut off all his communication with his rearguard, which had just been moving in the direction of the Vachère. Never had Janavel been in a situation of greater danger; his destruction might have been deemed inevitable; it appeared as if nothing but a miracle could save him. But Janavel's trust in God was unshaken, and in him the confidence of the Christian was as eminently displayed as the intrepidity of the warrior.

With that perfect knowledge of the locality which he possessed above every other man, and that coolness which never forsook him in presence of danger, he sent sixty men into a defile called the *Gates of Angrogna*, opening upon the little plain then occupied by the Marquis De Fleury. "There," said he, "you may arrest an army, and you will cover at once the Vachère and Rochemanant. Go and pray, and be resolute." Then, continuing to fall back before the lines of the Count De Bagnol, he arrived at those impregnable precipices called Rochemanant, having with him only about 600 men. "Here is our Tabor," said he to his men; "to your knees and take courage!" The bible-reading warrior recollected the victories of Barak and Deborah. His men had got ahead of the

---

[1] Of the family of the Counts of Lucerna.
[2] Those of Angrogna and Lucerna on one side, those of Pramol and Pérouse on another, those of Faët and St. Martin on a third.

enemy; they fell upon their knees. "O God!" exclaimed their leader, "shield us by thy mighty hand!"

But the enemy approached. The Vaudois spread themselves among the rocks; they barred every entrance; and from every aperture issued their death-dealing bullets. De Bagnol paused, and examined the ground. After having given his troops some repose, he attempted to carry the post, but was repulsed. The troops drew breath and returned to the assault; they were repulsed a second time. The count had already lost more than 300 men, and his army could do nothing against a rock. He attempted to scale it, but his soldiers were flung down one above another. Then a superstitious terror seized them. Could it be true that these heretics had made a compact with the devil to be made invulnerable? It was even said that the Vaudois collected in the folds of their shirts all the bullets which pierced their garments, without their bodies being injured. Janavel, indeed, had been pierced through and through in 1655; but that wound, which would have been mortal in any one else, had left him valiant and vigorous. These thoughts, more or less strongly entertained, and more or less general, were indicated by the increasing hesitation of the Catholic troops. The Vaudois perceived it, and made a vigorous sortie. "Let us sweep away these hordes of cowards at once," said Janavel. And his experienced warriors rushed from all the places in which they were intrenched. The enemy gave way and disbanded. The Vaudois, sword in hand, pursued with vigour. The Count of Bagnol in vain sought to oppose the rout, in which he himself was carried along; his soldiers rushed in a disorderly manner to the lateral slopes of the mountain; ten Vaudois put a hundred of their enemies to flight. The latter did not halt till they had reached the plain; many of them perished as they fled; the whole mountain was swept clean of its invaders.

Janavel now rallied his heroic army, mounted to the higher ground, gave thanks to God for the victory which he had just gained; and then all exhausted with fatigue, went to rejoin the sixty men whom he had sent to the *Gates of Angrogna* to protect his rear-guard.

As he had anticipated, these sixty men had sufficed to keep in check, since morning, all the forces of the Marquis De Fleury. They had intrenched themselves behind an earthen bank five feet high; this barrier crossing the defile, sheltered them, and permitted them to make continual discharges against the front of the enemy. But the enemy had also natural bastions which served them for bulwarks; and from rock to rock, they had come almost, it might be said, to surround this little post of the Vaudois. One effort more and the post would be carried, the defile passed, the Vachère occupied, and the valley lost. The Vaudois perceived this, and sent an emissary to Janavel to obtain some reinforcement. But Janavel had already cleared the ground of the Count De Bagnol, and arrived in person with all his troop.

Thenceforth the advantage was no longer doubtful. Whilst Janavel attacked the flank of the enemy's army, the Vaudois, who had so long remained without moving in their defile, now issued from it with great ardour. Nothing so raises the spirits of troops as the certainty of success. With Janavel's help and their confidence in God they had no doubt of the result. The enemy, on the other hand, seeing this redoubted captain arrive with his 600 men, understood that the Count De Bagnol was already vanquished. Nothing deprives men of courage like the contagion of a defeat. The Marquis De Fleury, likewise, now saw his army yield and disband before these new assailants. The intrepidity of the Vaudois increased; victory declared for them; the Catholics everywhere took to flight, and poured their confused legions over all the hills of Angrogna, St. Segont, and Briquéras. They left as many dead upon the field of battle as the Vaudois had of combatants altogether. More than 600 men were killed, more than 400 were wounded, and the greater part of these died of their wounds, whilst the evangelical party lost only five or six men, and had only twelve wounded, of whom none died.

Having pursued his adversaries half-way down the hill, Janavel paused, and his 600 warriors knelt around him, to give united thanks to God for the victory, and for having so completely delivered them.

They were only at a very short distance from the communes of Prarusting and Rocheplate, which a few days before had detached themselves from the common cause of the Vaudois. But seeing the victory gained by their brethren, the people of these communes now went in pursuit of the enemy's troops; so that after prayer, Janavel led his little army into these villages thus brought back to their alliance, in order to fraternize with the auxiliaries who had issued from them.

Less considerable encounters and skirmishes, in which he had almost always the advantage, still signalized his operations on the following days; so that he not only diminished the forces of the enemy, but every day he augmented his own; for besides the Vaudois, who ranged themselves in greater and greater numbers under his command, many French Protestants hastened to the support of their brethren.[1] The reverses of the Marquis De Fleury became numerous in proportion; and, as it seemed to the court of Savoy impossible that, with the considerable forces which had been placed under his command, this general ought not to have succeeded in bringing into subjection a handful of rebels (for so our heroic mountaineers are always called), the command of the troops directed against the Vaudois was taken from him, and the Count of St. Damian was sent in his stead.

The Count of St. Damian augmented his army by some new recruits, and commenced his operations by setting out from Lucerna at the head of 1500 men, to take possession of the little commune of Rora. It was at that time defended only by fifteen Vaudois and eight French, in all twenty-three men! They were posted in an advantageous position, but what could they do against 1500 assailants? They did much: they did more than the victors! They fought for six hours, and were cut in pieces with the exception of only one man, who was taken prisoner.

Inflated with his success, St. Damian, on the following day, made a sortie into the valley of Lucerna. But scarcely had he arrived at the village of St. Margaret, to which his soldiers set fire, when the Vaudois, to the number of 200, descended from the heights of Le Taillaret, so often assailed, and never assailed with success. They came upon his troop by the ravine which descends from Les Copiers, put it to flight, killed many of the incendiaries, and on their own side had neither killed nor wounded.

Charles Emmanuel, seeing that this intestine war was taking a turn so disastrous for him, and beginning to understand that the unskilfulness of his generals was not the only cause, thought that he might succeed better by intimidating these valleys, so devoted to their religion and so valiant in its defence. With this view he published, on the 10th of August, 1663, an edict, in which he began by declaring all the inhabitants of the valleys rebels, and guilty of high-treason, and accordingly condemned them to death, with confiscation of goods. There is nothing very formidable in a sentence of death pronounced upon those whom it has been found impossible to vanquish, and who slay more of their enemies than there are living men of themselves. These declarations, however, were merely a preface to numerous exceptions, by which the duke hoped to disunite this warlike and faithful people in order to bring them to

---

[1] An edict, printed and placarded at Grenoble, 21st July, 1663, by M. De La Berchère, First President of the Parliament of Dauphiny, interdicted all subjects of the King of France from *going to take part with those of the pretended reformed religion in the valley of Angrogna, and from giving them any assistance.*

a readier submission. But the Vaudois did not accept this edict, which kept in force the condemnation of their most valiant compatriots and most devoted defenders.

The war continued. After having weakened his adversaries, Janavel assumed the offensive against them. He pursued the Count of St. Damian to his very head-quarters, and afterwards renewed his incursions into the plain. The town of Lucerna demanded the protection of walls[1] to shield it from this terrible invader. The works were commenced, but a new attack of the mountaineers interrupted them.

We can here only make hasty mention of the principal of those little expeditions which took place during the rest of the year. The Vaudois made an incursion on Bubiano and were repulsed: the enemy made one towards Le Villar and was repulsed. St. Damian prepared an ambuscade in the district of the vineyards of Lucerna; but he allowed himself to be surprised there, and his troops were cut in pieces.

The army of the Propaganda was disheartened, the duke's finances were exhausted, and new overtures were made to the heroic mountaineers. Peace was offered them upon condition that they should lay down their arms, that there should be no question about religion, and that each community of the valleys should, in all time coming, send up its petitions by itself. This would have been, on their part, to cease to be a people, a church, or a body, whose parts are all mutually responsible amongst themselves; it would have been to break up their unity. The Vaudois understood this, and these conditions were still rejected.

However, they wrote from the valleys, "Our poor people are very miserable; our men have been long constrained to live under arms, feeding on bread and water, and worn out by continual fatigue. God have pity upon us! But we will resolutely resist. The very children in the streets may be heard saying that they would rather die in the caverns than abandon their religion."[2] The melancholy facts becoming known in foreign countries, the Protestant powers were moved by them, and collections began to be made for the unfortunate Vaudois.[3]

The Piedmontese rulers, unable to reduce them by arms, at-

[1] This demand is dated 11th September, 1663.
[2] Letter of 2d September, 1663, addressed to Léger, who was then at Leyden.
[3] These collections were stopped by the report (of which this circumstance proves the great prevalence) of the peculations committed at the time of the previous distributions. But these charges referred to 1655: they had then been found false; collections had been again made in 1662; how could these charges arise anew between 1662 and 1663? This is now very difficult to clear up.

tempted to gain their purpose by creating division amongst them. Six Vaudois, five of whom could not sign their own names (but the reality of whose assent is attested by a captain of the guards of his royal highness, a Capuchin missionary, and the prefect of Pignerol), in their ignorant simplicity, and perhaps through the use of undue means, permitted themselves to be drawn into an inconsiderate procedure which favoured these designs. They agreed to a declaration by which, making a full and entire submission to the will of his royal highness, they implored his clemency, disavowed the conduct of their brethren in taking up arms, and accepted the conditions of the edict of the 10th of August.[1]

History would take no notice of incidents in themselves so unworthy to occupy it, if the most insignificant occurrences, and the meanest tricks, had not sometimes been the grand resort of the government in pursuance of that cowardly, cruel, and deceitful papal policy which often prevailed over the natural nobility and goodness of the princes of Savoy.

Some historians tell us, that the persons who signed this paper had no other object than to obtain for themselves a few days' truce, to enable them to gather the grapes, then hanging ripe, without being disquieted at their work.[2] But the ducal council treated the declaration of these five people of Prarusting as a consequence, a ratification, and a development of that resolution to which the whole commune had agreed at St. Segont on the 1st of July, afterwards annulled on the 6th of August, when the troops of Janavel fraternized with the inhabitants of Rocheplate and Prarusting.

The people of these communes protested against such an interpretation; and the five persons themselves who had signed retracted the declaration which they had made, saying that it had been obtained from them by surprise.[3] It might have been thought that the matter would now have been at an end; if so, it would never have been mentioned here.

The notary who drew up the paper, and the witnesses for the adherents who could not sign their names, maintained the validity of that deed,[4] notwithstanding the protestation of the reputed subscribers, who withdrew their names from it.

During the time of those pitiful debates, these abortive attempts at division and dishonourable negotiations, which could be brought to no issue, disorder spread in the valleys; acts of private revenge

---

[1] This declaration bears date 27th September, 1663.
[2] Léger, Part II. p. 301, paragraph 3.
[3] This retractation is dated 3d October, 1663.
[4] This new document is dated 8th October, 1663.

were mingled with those of public defence; the Count De Bagnol and his robber troops conducted themselves at La Tour as if they had been in a conquered country; discontentment extended everywhere; the wretchedness of the people increased rather than diminished; and, to crown their hardships, the severity of winter began to come upon the mountains, aggravating still more the terrible afflictions with which they were visited.

Fortunately, the Protestant powers of Germany, Holland, and Switzerland had already addressed urgent representations to Charles Emmanuel in favour of the Vaudois. The Propaganda, on the other hand, exerted themselves to the utmost to prevent them from being considered otherwise than as rebels and malefactors; but, notwithstanding all their activity in exciting irritation, and assisting to provide for the expense of this war, the Duke of Savoy, whose intelligence was too great, and his disposition too noble, not to regard many things in it with dislike, showed an inclination to receive the ambassadors of the powers that had undertaken the part of mediators; and they arrived at Turin in November, 1663.[1]

A safe-conduct was immediately despatched to the Vaudois, that they might be able to send commissioners to Turin. But the preamble of this document was not of a nature to re-assure them. "Being desirous," said the duke, "that it should be manifest to people of other countries that our subjects are rebels, and that we have all cause for chastising them, we authorize those of them to come to Turin who may be designated by the secretary of legation, attached to the extraordinary embassy of the six Protestant cantons of Switzerland."[2] Such was the substance of this document. For the Vaudois to have taken advantage of it would have been to have owned themselves really rebels; they feared, moreover, that it might have been to expose themselves to some surprise like those of which they had so frequently been the victims. They refused, therefore, to send any commissioner to Turin. "You see,"

---

[1] Léger says, on the 15th of December. Part II. chapter xxiii. p. 304, paragraph 2.) But this date is proved inaccurate by what follows in the next page of the same author; and that which I give rests upon the authority of the safe-conduct granted to the Vaudois, *that they might be able securely to present themselves before the ambassadors already arrived at Turin;* and this safe-conduct is dated the 14th of November. These ambassadors must, therefore, have arrived in the month of November: to wit, those from Switzerland;[*] the ambassador from Holland arrived later; and as Léger was at Leyden, it may be supposed that this circumstance led him into his mistake. Boyer, and almost all subsequent writers, have copied his inaccuracies.

[2] *Raccolta dagl' Editti,* p. 136. 14th November, 1663.

[*] *MM. Gaspard Hirzel,* grand councillor of the canton of Zurich, and former prefect of Thurgau, and *Gabriel Weiss,* grand councillor of Berne, and former colonel of a Swiss regiment in the service of the republic of Venice.

the Piedmontese rulers then said to the ambassadors, "they dare not come, they have nothing to say in their own defence; they are avowed rebels! Is not their refusal to appear before us a proof of their contempt for their sovereign? Is it not an insult to Switzerland itself?"[1] The secretary of legation set out in person for the valleys, re-assured the Vaudois, and returned to the capital accompanied by their eight deputies.[2]

And now the conferences, of which we must proceed to speak, were opened at the town's-house of Turin.

CHAPTER XII.

MEDIATION OF SWITZERLAND; TREACHERY OF ST. DAMIAN; CONFERENCES AT THE TOWN'S-HOUSE OF TURIN; ARBITRATION OF LOUIS XIV.[3]

(A.D. 1664 TO A.D. 1680.)

Conferences between the ambassadors of the Protestant cantons of Switzerland and delegates of the Duke of Savoy—Complaints against the Count De Bagnol—His defence—Charges brought against the Vaudois—The question of public worship at St. John—Treacherous invasion of the valleys during the conferences—Further negotiations—Terms agreed upon—Difficulties still renewed—Death of Charles Emmanuel II.

THE six Protestant cantons of Switzerland having sent MM. Weiss and Hirzel to the Duke of Savoy, to mediate in favour of the

---

[1] These imputations are not set down on presumption; they are a faithful summary of the official speech made by the Baron De Greysi, on the part of his royal highness, to the Swiss ambassadors. This speech is reported in the *Histoire des Conférences de* 1664, p. 217.

[2] These were *David Léger*, pastor at Le Clos (Val St. Martin), the brother of the exiled John Léger; *James Bastie*, pastor at St. John; *Peter Baile*, pastor at St. Germain; *Andrew Michelin*, syndic of La Tour; *David Martinat*, delegate from Bobi; *James Jahier*, of Pramol, and the *Laurents*, father and son, of Les Clots or Chiots, in the parish of Ville Sèche.

[3] AUTHORITIES.—"*Conférences faictes à Turin, dans l'Hostel de Ville, en présence de MM. les Ambassadeurs Suisses, entre les ministres de S. A. R., et les députés des vallées de Luserne, à la fin de l'année*, 1663, *et au commencement de la courante*, 1664. *A Turin*, MDCLXIV." (A small folio of 232 pages.)—"*Récit de ce qu'il y a de plus considérable aux affaires des Eglises réformées des vallées de Piedmont, depuis les massacres de* 1655, ... *jouxte la copiè imprimée à Haerlem*, 1663." (A small 4to of iv. and 60 pages. The title is very long, and contains a complete analysis of the work.)—"*Très-humble remontrance, touchant le pitoyable estat où se trouvent à présent réduittes les pauvres Eglises Evangéliques des vallées de Piémond, a cause de l'altération et violation de leurs concessions, et*

Vaudois, and Charles Emmanuel having authorized[1] conferences between these ambassadors and his own deputies, to examine into the complaints made by the valleys against the governor of La Tour,[2] these conferences took place in the town's-house of Turin.

They were opened on the 17th of December, 1663,[3] in presence of the Swiss ambassadors, eight Vaudois deputies, and the deputies of Charles Emmanuel commissioned to justify the measures adopted by their sovereign. These last commenced by stating, according to their own view of them, the events which led to the war, which, according to them, had no other cause than the repeated rebellions of the Vaudois. The Vaudois deputies replied that the real cause of the conflicts, which they deplored, was to be found in successive aggressions, and in the continual acts of violence of the governor of La Tour. It was necessary, therefore, to enter into the investigation of the complaints brought against the Count De Bagnol.

A great number of documents were produced on both sides. The Vaudois instanced murders,[4] robberies,[5] tortures,[6] and acts of violence of every sort committed by the count.[7] The count replied on these various heads,[8] that the murders of which he was accused had been committed either by accident, or through the private revenge of those under his command; and that if any other persons had been killed, it could only be such as had been outlawed, and whom no one was bound to regard. And in conclusion, he added, that if the murders had not been committed upon the persons of

partic. de la patente de 1655, faite en Novembre, 1661, à Haerlem . . . l'an 1662" (4to, 12 leaves, not paged).—"*Apologie des Eglises évangéliques des vallées de Piémont, faite en défense de Jean Léger.*" This *Apology* was drawn up by the Vaudois Synod, held at Les Malans, in the valley of Angrogna, on the 13th of September, 1661. Léger speaks of it in Part II. chap. xix. It was he who got it printed at Geneva: see p. 371, near the bottom.—A similar pamphlet, which I have not been able to procure, is entitled, "*Les Assemblées sur les affaires des Protestants des vallées de Piedmont.*"—See also, on the same subject, "*Relation d'une ambassade des cantons évangéliques de la Suisse, au Duc de Savoiè, dans le* xvii. *e siècle, au sujet des Vaudois.*" (*Revue Suisse*, t. iii. p. 260.)—The general histories of the Vaudois and contemporaneous works.—The manuscript sources of information are few in number, and are to be found at Turin, in the Archives of the Court.

[1] By edict of 10th August, 1663.   [2] The Count De Bagnol.
[3] They were held on the 17th, 21st, 30th, and 31st of December, 1663, the 5th, 16th, and 20th of January, 1664. The minutes have been printed.
[4] *Hist. des Conférences*, p. 6, No. i.; p. 12, No. xvi.; p. 24, &c.
[5] Id. pp. 10–13, Nos. vi., vii., viii., ix., xvi., xvii., and xx.
[6] Id. p. 12, No. xv. and p. 23, Nos. xviii. and xix.
[7] Against women, *Hist. des Conférences*, p. 30; against property, pp. 8, 10, and 13; against inoffensive persons, abused out of religious hatred, pp. 16 and 17; without known motives, p. 22; by threats, p. 11, No. xii.; p. 12, Nos. xiv., xv., xvi.; by injurious words, p. 9, No. ii.; p. 10, No. iv., &c.
[8] By a memorial in justification, not by speech.

the outlaws themselves, they must have been committed upon some of their friends or near relatives.[1] This singular defence could scarcely have the effect of placing his scrupulosity in such matters above suspicion.

As to the other points, he continued, if there have been houses broken open, and homes violated, as is alleged, these were only domiciliary visits made for the purpose of seeing that none of the outlaws were concealed there.[2] "Moreover," adds his defence, "there arrived other soldiers in the valleys after the 25th of June, so that the accused cannot answer for the outrages which may have been committed there."[3] He positively denied the injurious language and threats[4] which were ascribed to him; but he acknowledged that he had in his service a band of ravagers, intended to oppose those of the valleys.[5] "In short," concluded the memorial which was presented in his name, "the Sieur De Bagnol has laboured *with all mildness,* and with particular care to *keep the valleys in peace,* and to preserve them from intercourse with the outlaws who have rushed into such an inexcusable rebellion." These last words were an insinuation intended to make the position of the Vaudois in the conference more unfavourable; but we may judge of the *very particular* care which he had taken of their repose by the troop of hired ravagers, whom he acknowledged that he had in his pay, for the purpose of plundering and robbing them.

The Vaudois were thereafter formally accused of a multitude of offences; and it is with pain that we see how questions of form and etiquette were put in the balance—in the case of these poor mountaineers, against crimes alleged to have been committed in the most revolting manner—by the very magistrates whose duty it was to have prevented them.

The following is a summary of these accusations:—"You ought to have sought legal redress for the acts of violence of which you complain; not having done so, you have failed in compliance with every rule of law." "We would have sought legal redress," it was replied,[6] "but they refused to attend to our complaints." "You ought to have done so sooner, for then the crimes alleged could not have been longer persevered in." "We informed concerning them previously, but no reply was made to us." "You should have applied to the council of the sovereign." "We did so, begging that it would ascertain for itself, and repress the violence to which we were subjected." "That was not the right way; this does not

---

[1] *Conférences*, pp. 49–52, and p. 54.   [2] See *Conférences*, pp. 49–52, and p. 54.
[3] Id. p. 57.   [4] Id. p. 56.   [5] Id. p. 58.
[6] They had done so on the 26th of May, 1663.

CHARGES AGAINST THE VAUDOIS.

belong to the council; you have failed to comply with all legal forms and rules of procedure." Such was the substance of the discussion on this point.

As to the celebration of public worship at St. John, contrary to the orders of the sovereign, the Vaudois maintained that these orders themselves were contrary to their privileges. They proved by former edicts that they were authorized to celebrate that worship; and this subject brought on a new discussion on the value of these edicts, the extent of these privileges, and the limits of the places in which religious exercises were authorized, according to the usages (*il solito*) which regulated that matter; and all these questions were debated at great length.

It is worth while, however, to observe to what quirks the adversaries of the Vaudois were reduced, to confound, by chicanery, the simple and honest good sense of these poor persecuted people. Certainly, if it had been possible to have reproached them with a crime, with any serious offence or delinquency, the accusation would not have been awanting. A strong effort was made to do so; but their replies, in this respect, were too peremptory to leave any ground for the accusation.

They were reproached, for example, with having formed a camp at the Pra, and attacked the citadel of La Tour; but, after investigation, it was discovered (1) that this pretended camp was only a sheepfold, and (2) that some children having rolled stones down the hill of La Tour, these stones had struck the ramparts of the citadel, and that the attack of which they were accused consisted of nothing more than this! Is it possible that puerilities like these can have been the subject of such grave conferences, and that they can have served as a pretext for such great cruelties? But the great complaint brought against the Vaudois was that of having given assistance to the outlaws. "Can any one be astonished," they replied, "that so great a number of persons condemned to death should have combined together to defend their lives? And, if they obtained some assistance from their families, or found shelter in the houses of their relatives or friends, can the responsibility be made to fall upon the whole body of the valleys?"

Such was the real substance of these long and wearisome conferences. The commissioners of the government, however, concluded by saying, that the Vaudois had had no cause of discontentment; and that if they took up arms, it was "to cause themselves to be molested, that they might complain thereof to foreign powers and have abundant collections sent them."[1] But if such an accusation

[1] *Conférences*, p. 82.

is only ridiculous, it cannot be denied that what it now remains for us to speak of is truly odious.

Whilst the ducal commissioners thus insulted at Turin the good sense and loyalty of the Vaudois during these conferences—which most unquestionably ought to have been accompanied by a complete suspension of hostilities, and whilst our poor mountaineers were hoping for a favourable result—the Propaganda were contriving their destruction, and perfidiously proceeding to a bloody extermination. The second sitting of the Turin conferences had not yet taken place when the plan of this treachery was already entirely arranged.[1]

On the morning of the 21st of December, the Count of St. Damian marched upon Prarusting, by the borders of St. Segont, at the head of 1655 infantry and 50 cavalry. The Marquis of Parelles ascended in the direction of Angrogna, by the Garsinéra, with 1576 infantry and 50 cavalry. Count Genèle, skirting the hills of the *Portes* and St. Germain, advanced upon the same point, by the opposite side, with a battalion of 786 men. Captain Cagnolo occupied the plain of St. John, at the head of 100 cavalry, ready to move in any direction that circumstances might demand; and, moreover, the Count of Bagnol, the governor of La Tour (the same who protested so much solicitude for the repose of the Vaudois, and who perished on the scaffold a few years after), was to make an attack by Les Copiers and St. Margaret, conducting against the Protestants 1118 men.

It was in this quarter that the attack commenced. The Vaudois were successively driven back from St. Margaret to Les Copiers, and from Les Copiers to the heights of Le Taillaret. But there they stood and contrived to keep their ground for some time, intrenched behind the rocks. Supposing that they alone were assailed, they sent to demand assistance from their brethren of Angrogna; they imagined that this attack was only a new villainy of the Count of Bagnol, but they were soon undeceived. They saw,

---

[1] The second sitting was held on the 21st of December, 1663; and there exists an order, dated on the 20th, which is entitled, "*Distribuzione delle trupe per li 4 attachi che si devono fare dimani,* 21 *Decembre, alli ribelli delle valle di Luserna e San Martino.*" (Turin, Archives of State.) That it was not intended only to attack, under the name of rebels, the little troop of outlaws, is proved by the simple consideration, that the forces directed against the valleys at this date amounted to 5135 infantry, and 200 cavalry.—Léger and Boyer say 18,000 men. (Léger, p. 305; Boyer, p. 188. They also place this attack upon the 25th of December. But as the reports which they give coincide with the way in which the troops were disposed, according to the written scheme which I have before my eyes, and this document points out the 21st for the attack, I think this latter date is to be preferred. Léger, moreover, was not upon the spot, and Boyer has merely copied him.)

in the hostile army, a troop more numerous than the governor of La Tour ordinarily had under his command. Their fortifications were already outflanked, and they thought of retiring. They seemed about to perish under the assault of forces ten times stronger than their own, when a voice was heard to cry, "Courage! stand fast! we are here! God for your help!" These last words are a common form of speech in the Vaudois language.[1] Those who now spoke them were the people of Angrogna come to the help of their assailed brethren, whose valour was redoubled by the hope of success.

The enemy, supposing them already vanquished, were astonished at this resistance. The courage of the Vaudois rose on the arrival of these new forces, and their ardour increased as the attack was slackened. The Count of Bagnol, more vigorously pressed, lost courage, and became weaker rather than stronger. Victor but recently, he now only fought, and was soon to yield.

The Vaudois now assumed the offensive in their turn. They rushed out impetuously on the front of the assailing army; and, the detachment from Angrogna arriving, fell upon it in flank. That superstitious terror, which the presence of the Vaudois had so often awakened in the breasts of their adversaries, was now manifested again. The minds of the Catholics were seized with a perturbation which passed along the ranks—they disbanded, the bravery of the mountaineers completed their rout; and, like a torrent breaking its banks, which carries all before it, the triumphant Vaudois pursued their enemies to the very plain of La Tour.

On the side of Angrogna, where Captain Prionel defended at once the Vachère, Rochemanant, and Le Chiabas (three points distant several kilometres[2] from each other), the Marquis of Parelles gained no advantage. On the side of St. Germain, on the contrary, where the Count of Genèle had advanced with only one battalion, the Vaudois were completely beaten. The enemy laid waste their fields, vineyards, and crops, and set fire to the houses which lay along the hills from St. Germain to Rocheplate. In the latter hamlet, a poor impotent woman, almost 100 years of age, was burned alive in her dwelling. At St. Germain, a younger woman had her flesh torn in shreds without being put to death. Many old men were likewise mutilated. Such was the use which Popery made of its victory!

[1] *Dio ajutaci! Diou v' s' agiutou!* (God help you!) These are the words most frequently to be heard to this day amongst the Vaudois mountains, in reference to any one going away, or to any journey, any malady, any project or undertaking whatever—*God help you!* What better wish can there be, or what words more Christian?

[2] [The French kilometre is equal to $1093\frac{2}{3}$ yards, the British mile to 1760 yards.]

But although defeated, the Vaudois yet caused their enemies, on the field of battle, losses much more numerous than their own, having themselves lost only six men, whilst they killed 100 of the enemy, and amongst that number the Count of La Trinité, a lineal descendant of him who had so cruelly persecuted their fathers a century before; also the young Count of St. Frons, a descendant of the ancient persecutors of the Vaudois church of Praviglelm. This young man was the inheritor of a great fortune, and had been married a few days before to a lady to whom he was very strongly attached. But neither wealth nor love protected him in this combat; and with much confidence we may say, that the iniquities of the fathers were visited upon the children. Amongst the combatants killed by the Vaudois were reckoned, likewise, other great personages, such as Captain Biala and M. De Grand-Maison.

No sooner were the Swiss ambassadors at Turin informed of these disastrous events, than they complained bitterly to the ministers of the ducal court of this incessant and outrageous violation of the armistice agreed upon at the opening of the conferences. The reply made to them was, that the troops of his royal highness wanted provisions, and had merely taken some steps for the purpose of obtaining them in the valleys.[1] How, then, were the burnings and massacres to be accounted for? "The Vaudois having opposed the movement of our troops," it was said, "some collisions took place, and a few houses were burned by inadvertency." Many other outrages were then represented which had been perpetrated against the Vaudois; and the count replied, that the fault lay with the Vaudois themselves, who had so oppressed, vexed, and molested their Catholic neighbours, that these latter had seized this opportunity to be in a slight degree revenged. Let us leave the falsehood of this statement unexposed, and attend to the conclusion of the negotiations.

It was agreed that the bases of an arrangement should be presented to the Vaudois under the title of *Patents of Grace;* for the Duke of Savoy could by no means consent, in his exalted sovereign dignity, to treat on equal terms with these miserable heretics. He was resolved to grant them nothing whatsoever, except as of his grace; and this grace granted to the Vaudois, and accepted by them, must of necessity involve an acknowledgment on their part that they had been guilty of rebellion, which, according to the report of the ambassadors, was very far from being the case.[2] The Vaudois

---

[1] The order of 20th December, hitherto unknown, shows what value is to be attached to such professions, and what steps had really been taken by the troops of Charles Emmanuel.   [2] Report of 2d July, 1664.

made some difficulty about accepting such propositions; but their protectors themselves entreated them not to insist upon matters of expression which were of no importance except for vanity; and accordingly the following heads of agreement were concluded at the hôtel of the embassy :—[1]

"A general amnesty shall be granted to the Vaudois, with the exception of those previously condemned." (The latter were the *outlaws* mentioned in the edict of the 25th of June, 1663. At their head were Léger and Janavel. The former was already in safety in Holland, where he occupied himself in writing the history of the Vaudois; the second retired to Geneva, where he afterwards rendered the greatest services to his countrymen, by tracing out for them, in 1689, the course which they should follow to return to their country, from which they had been totally expelled in 1687.)

By the second article of these stipulations Charles Emmanuel ratified the *Patents of Grace*, granted at Pignerol on the 18th of August, 1655; but he reserved the right of demanding from the Vaudois securities for the future, and suitable amends for the present, referring this point to the arbitration of France.

This arbitration, the judgments of which were pronounced in the name of Louis XIV.,[2] became the source of innumerable difficulties. The Most Christian king decided that our unfortunate valleys, already ruined by war, exhausted by the depredations of the Count of Bagnol, devastated by fire, and by robbery and outrage of every sort, to which they had been subjected, should pay to the Duke of Savoy, for the expenses of war, an indemnity of fifty thousand francs, and cede to him their richest lands (the district of the vineyards of Lucerna), in compensation for the losses which had been caused to him by the pretended *rebellion* of the Vaudois. And the Vaudois could not complain, for they had implicitly acknowledged the reality of this rebellion in accepting the amnesty as of grace. Such was the consequence, in artful and greedy hands, of the disinterested counsel which the Swiss ambassadors in their sincerity had given to the Vaudois, causing them to accept these humiliating terms as a simple sacrifice of conventional dignity designed to satisfy courtly pride.

The third part of the *Patents of Grace* of 1664 relates to religious exercises at St. John. Public worship there was interdicted. A pastor of the valley might come twice a-year to visit

---

[1] Concluded on the 3d of February, 1664; ratified on the 13th by the Vaudois deputies; signed on the 14th by the Duke of Savoy; and registered at the Court of Accounts on the 17th. (*Raccolta dagl' Editti*, pp. 137-141.)

[2] On the 18th of January, 1667. They are printed in one vol. folio.

the members of the Protestant Church there, but he was not to reside in that parish, nor even to pass the night there, except in case of absolute necessity. He was to be permitted to visit the sick, but not to hold any religious meeting, nor even to instruct his catechumens within the limits of this commune.—(This article became the source of the most frequent and prolonged disagreements, and of accusations most easily got up, and disproved with the greatest difficulty, even when they were unfounded. The narration of what the Vaudois suffered on this score would occupy a whole volume of itself.)

The last conditions contained in the edict of 14th February, 1664, were—

(Art. VI.) That the pastors of the Vaudois churches should henceforth be natives of the country. (This condition did them no harm; but, on the contrary, confirmed their evangelical individuality, which ran great risk of being lost under the too prolonged guidance of foreign pastors.)

(Art. VII.) The Catholic chapels and churches destroyed in this last war shall be built again at the expense of the Vaudois. (More demands still against the oppressed!)

(Art. VIII.) The prisoners on both sides shall be released.

A convention of disarmament of the respective combatants followed immediately[1] upon the publication of this paper; and the Duke of Savoy wrote to Switzerland by the ambassadors on their return, that he would conform entirely to its provisions.[2]

After so many cruel agitations, the Vaudois valleys began to enjoy a little repose, when, unexpectedly, they received orders to send delegates to Turin, with a mandate authorizing them to treat in name of all the people.[3] Each commune was obliged to send a representative; and all these delegates must be assembled at Turin on the 17th of May, 1664. The object was, to take into consideration the securities and indemnities demanded by Charles Emmanuel in virtue of the second article of the late edict.

The Duke of Savoy wished the Vaudois to pay more than half a million of francs (531,000) for the expenses of the war, and 330,367 francs besides, to indemnify the Catholic villages which had suffered in the recent events. Alas! which had suffered most? Was it the Catholics who had been obliged to forsake their properties and dwellings, to flee to the mountains, and to sacrifice their flocks, in order to maintain in misery a persecuted life? Was

---

[1] It took place on the 18th of February, 1664.
[2] The letter is dated 28th February.
[3] The letter making this demand is dated 18th April, 1664.

it the Catholics whose crops had been wasted, and their houses burned, and who had not been able to save themselves from sword, and fire, and famine? No; but it was thought proper to take from the persecuted the last relics of their fortune, to pay for the barbarities of their persecutors.[1] As to the securities demanded for the future, Charles Emmanuel required the erection at the entry of each valley, and at the expense of the Vaudois, of a fortified post, of which the garrison should be maintained at their expense. He also required that they should no longer be entitled to hold their synod save in presence of one of his officers, that the communes of the valleys should not be connected together any longer in one body, but that each should henceforth treat separately of its own private affairs without consulting the rest. This was to reserve to himself the right of destroying the Vaudois in detail, by depriving them of all corporate life. Other conditions were also demanded, but they were all rejected.

A minute was drawn up of the refusal of the Vaudois; and this document was sent to Louis XIV., as the judge in the last resort. We have already stated his decision; and it must be acknowledged that, when it is compared with the exorbitant pretensions of the Duke of Savoy, he showed great moderation in this business. Many foreign powers wrote to him, moreover, in favour of the Vaudois. His arbitration was not terminated till 1667; and, meanwhile, abundant and numerous collections had been made in the Protestant churches of other countries, to give some relief to their oppressed sister of the Alps of Piedmont. The strictest precautions were taken by the distributors of these collections, to preserve themselves from the slightest suspicion of malversation.

From 1667 to 1672 numerous obstacles still retarded the fulfilment of the conditions fixed by Louis XIV.; for the decision of that monarch bore, not only that the Vaudois should pay 50,000 francs and surrender the vineyards of Lucerna, to be added to the private domains of Charles Emmanuel II., but also that they should make a declaration to him, binding themselves and their successors beforehand, to submit to the loss of all their property and the abolition of all their privileges, if they ever again took up arms against their sovereign. The people of the valleys very reasonably refused to engage for their successors. They said also that it was impossible

---

[1] Besides these enormous sums, there were demanded of the Vaudois 50,000 francs for the walls of Lucerna, 40,000 for the customs, 25,000 for the salt tax; also the sum necessary to repair the fortifications of La Tour and of Mirabouc; the price of the provisions and ammunition consumed by the soldiers during the war; the pay of the troops for the same time, and many other expenses of which an exact account has not been preserved. (See Léger, p. 313.)

for them to know precisely what were the domains designed by that vague expression, the *Vineyards of Lucerna;* and finally they demanded time to pay. These things were not soon settled.

In 1670,[1] the duke enjoined the intendant of the Court of Justice, Louis Beccaria, to compel the Vaudois to fulfil the conditions which had been imposed upon them. The intendant wrote to the valleys accordingly, but with much moderation;[2] and at last the Vaudois submitted with a good grace.[3] The bearing of the court of Savoy towards them became milder, and new favours were granted them.[4] The soldiers of the valleys distinguished themselves at the siege of Genoa, and their sovereign wrote them a flattering letter in testimony of his satisfaction.[5] These sentiments of goodwill and tardy justice towards the Vaudois cannot be suspected of insincerity, for at this period the Duke of Savoy wrote to the apos-

[1] On the 10th of February.

[2] The letter is dated the 15th of February, 1670, and is to be found in Borelli.

[3] The deed by which they bound themselves to pay 50,000 francs in ten years, and never again to take arms against the service of his royal highness, forms a folio volume. The deed by which he entered on possession of the *Vineyards of Lucerna* forms another; and the partial deeds of purchase, discharges, transactions, abatements, procedures, procurations, &c., relative to the different domains situated therein, form a considerable bundle of papers. All these documents are to be found in the Archives of the Court of Turin, and belong to the year 1670. But it does not appear that the payment of 50,000 francs was ever completely effected; for there are only to be found three discharges in deduction from this account—one of 4079 francs, 45 cents, of date 18th December, 1679—a second of 750 francs, dated the 23d of the same month—and a third of 2250 francs, of date 23d November, 1680.—Archives of the Court of Accounts at Turin, *Regio Controrolo, Finanze*, No. 168, fol. 24 and 33, and No. 171, fol. 120, on the back. (Communicated by M. Cibrario.)

[4] Exemptions from charges, 24th May, 1670. Liberty of commerce and industry, 22d May, 1672. Authorization to carry arms, 9th July of same year. New exemptions, 30th November, 1674.

[5] This letter is given in the *Histoire de la dissipation des Eglises Vaudoises, en* 1686, p. 36. It is there given under date 5th November, 1678, and with the signature of Charles Emmanuel; but there must be some error either in the date or in the signature. The words of the letter are these:—

"As we have been much pleased with the zeal and promptitude with which you have provided men, who have served to our entire satisfaction in the contests which we have recently had with the Genoese, we have thought good to testify to you, by these presents, our satisfaction, and to assure you that we shall keep it in very particular recollection, to make you feel, upon every occasion, the effects of our royal protection, as the Count Beccaria will signify to you more particularly, to whom we have given charge, more fully to express to you our sentiments, and also to take note of the officers and soldiers, both dead and remaining prisoners, that he may make a report concerning them to us, so that we may be able to act with regard to them in a suitable manner. However, the present letter will serve for an assured testimony to you of our satisfaction and contentment; and we shall pray God that he may preserve you from evil."

This letter was accompanied with conformable instructions, addressed to Beccaria, intendant of the Court of Justice.

tolic nuncio, "If I only consulted the counsels of sound policy, I ought to desire that the Vaudois should multiply rather than diminish in number; for they are loyal, laborious, well-disposed, useful to the country," &c.[1]

Charles Emmanuel died in 1675;[2] and although he was not surnamed *the Great*, like his predecessor of the same name, he had a noble and lofty spirit. He encouraged arts and sciences; and it was he who constructed the palace which the kings now occupy at Turin. The modern part of that capital was also his work. In opening the magnificent road of Les Echelles, which connects France and Savoy, he accomplished an enterprise which the Romans appear to have attempted in vain; and, moreover, important reforms were introduced by him into most of the departments of public administration.

His son, Victor Amadeus II., succeeded him under the regency of his mother; for he was only nine years of age when the ducal crown was placed upon his head, upon which it was to become a royal crown.

The regent wrote, in 1679,[3] to the Swiss cantons, to assure them of the care which she would take to cause all the privileges of the Vaudois to be respected; who, at that period, gave new proof of their valour and generous loyalty, by defending the cause of the crown in a rebellion which took place in Mondovi. The uncle of the young king, Don Gabriel of Savoy, mentioned this fact in a very honourable way, in an order of the day in 1680, and wrote himself to the Vaudois to thank them.[4] They in their turn asked the ratification of their ancient privileges, and obtained it from Victor Amadeus II., the son of Charles Emmanuel II.[5]

[1] "Copia di littera scritta a Monsignor Nuncio Mosti rimessagli dal conte di Buttigliera d'ordine di S. A. R.," January, 1677. There is reference here to measures adopted for the conversion of the Vaudois; and it is said, "S'havesse risguardo alla sola politica, e all' interesse temporale, non sarrebbero necessarie taute fatiche e spese e tornerebbe a canto a queste Altezze Reale; il lasciare diffundere e multiplicare gli huomini delle Valli che sono fedeli, ben affetti, laboriosi, utili al paese," &c. (Archives of the Court. Turin, No. of Series 437.)

[2] On the 12th of June, in consequence of the shock which he received by seeing his son fall from his horse. Boyer, p. 192, places his death in 1678. I prefer to rest upon the authority of *L'Art de vérifier les dates;* with reference to which, moreover, I have carefully examined all the dates which that learned work gave me the means of verifying whilst engaged with this history.

[3] On 28th January. This letter is given in the *Histoire des negociations de* 1686.

[4] This letter is dated 29th September, 1681, and is given in the *Histoire de la dissipation des Eglises Vaudoises en* 1686, p. 36.

[5] The petition of the Vaudois bears date, 16th October, 1680. It prays for the confirmation of the Patents of 24th November, 1582; of 3d January, 1584; of 26th February, 1635; of 8th May, 1643; and of 11th September, 1663. The

It seemed as if this event should have placed upon a solid foundation, for all time coming, the independence and repose of the Vaudois churches; but God's ways are not our ways, and these poor churches, already so much tried, were then nearer than ever to being destroyed by an extraordinary catastrophe, which in its mysterious counsels heaven reserved for them.

CHAPTER XIII.

EXILE OF JANAVEL, REVOCATION OF THE EDICT OF NANTES, PRELIMINARIES OF A FOURTH PERSECUTION.[1]

(A.D. 1680 TO A.D. 1685.)

Janavel retires to Geneva—Louis XIV.—Revocation of the Edict of Nantes—Janavel becomes apprehensive of danger impending over the Vaudois—The Duke of Savoy in a condition almost of vassalage to France—Demands of the French monarch with regard to the Vaudois—He urges the duke to extreme measures—The Propaganda and the Papal nuncio second his efforts—Janavel's letter to his brethren in the valleys, and directions for their conduct in the approaching struggle.

JANAVEL, having been excepted from the amnesty which terminated the *War of the Outlaws*, was under the necessity of seeking an asylum in a foreign country. He retired to Geneva. There living apart, he ceased not to occupy himself with the affairs of the valleys. The heroic old man, notwithstanding so many adverse occurrences, had retained all the energy of his patriotism and of his faith. In solitary glory, proscribed but not forgotten, he devoted his last days to prayer for the country which he had so valiantly defended; and with the foresight of his great experience, he watched with anxiety the increasing indications of a new storm, which he saw preparing to burst on his beloved native land.

intendant of the Court of Justice, Béraudo, supported this petition by a letter of 28th November, 1681; and Victor Amadeus II. ratified these Patents and privileges on the 4th of December, 1681. This ratification was registered on the 31st of January, 1682; and the whole was published in a little volume of sixteen pages—*Confirmazione de privilegii*, &c.—at Sinibaldo's, Turin, 1682.

[1] AUTHORITIES.—Historians previously cited.—Benoist, "*Hist. de l'Edit de Nantes*," vol. vi.—"*Réponse pour les Eglises des vallées du Piémont.*" . . . Geneva, 1679, a 4to of more than 600 pages.—Diplomatic Archives of France. Despatches exchanged betwixt Louis XIV. and his ambassador at Turin. (Communicated by M. Guizot.)—Archives of State at Turin.—Archives of Berne and Geneva. Archives of the Venerable Company of Pastors of the last-named city.—Private communications, &c.

France was then, of all the states of Europe, that of greatest weight in the balance of their respective destinies; but in proportion to his greatness, Louis XIV. had also great weaknesses. Noble and resolute before earthly powers, he submitted to the yoke of superstition, and bowed with the credulous terror of ignorance before those mysterious powers which his church showed him in the gloomy and dreadful twilight of her spiritual domain. His dissolute life, interrupted by fits of devotion, his proud spirit and selfish disposition, could have been ruled only by the accommodating and ambitious power of Popery. The latter, again, was disposed to take advantage of this influence only to crush liberty; and as the great enemy of superstition is the Bible, whoever appealed to the authority of that Divine book was pursued with all the hatred of Catholicism.

The confessors of Louis XIV., therefore, persuaded that monarch that he might promote at once his fame and his salvation by the extermination of the Protestants; the glory of his reign, by raising up again, in its imperious and majestic unity, the tottering but inflexible frame of the Romish Church; his own salvation, by offering, as a sort of expiation for his personal faults, the conversion of heretics—a holocaust before the appeased altars of that church, in which everything is bought, everything is sold, everything becomes matter of merchandise.

As it was only to procure a sort of ransom for himself, he at first employed money to obtain conversions. This cause of apostasies had only the effect of purging the Protestant Church of all whose souls were venal and their consciences worthless. A current account of expenses and receipts—the former in money, the latter in conversions—was carefully prepared, and regularly submitted to the re-assured conscience of the Most Christian King, for such was the title which, from the days of Louis XI., who deserved it so well—the kings of France had assumed on ascending the throne. Bands of beggars, calling themselves Protestants, might then be seen abjuring in mass in one town, from which, after having been paid, they went on to another to abjure again, to receive more wages, and to pursue this scandalous trade from one end of France to the other.

The resource of venal apostasies was therefore soon abandoned. But the royal consort of Maria Theresa could not so readily abandon also his vices. He committed a new adultery,[1] and thenceforth was always more affected with anxiety for his salvation. This the Protestant Church was soon made painfully to feel.

[1] About 1670, Madame De Montespan; in 1679, Madame De Fontanges.

Twenty-one places of worship were demolished in the Vivarais in 1680. Proscriptions were multiplied; and the Reformed were declared incapable of holding public offices, and even of exercising ordinary professions.[1] The persecutions to which they were subjected went on increasing, along with the criminal pleasures of the monarch.

Then came the *Dragonnades*. Louvois, already odious for the disasters and conflagrations with which the Palatinate had been visited under his command, wrote to Louis XIV. concerning the Vivarais, "It is necessary to make such a desolation in this country that the example shall be always remembered."

Even this was not enough! To strike all Protestantism with one blow, the Edict of Nantes was revoked on the 18th of October, 1685. The effect of this revocation was sudden and terrible. A great number of French Protestants carried their intelligence and their virtues to foreign countries, as well as their fortunes acquired or to be acquired. This one act weakened France more than all the victories of Louis XIV. ever strengthened her.

But, in interdicting the Reformed worship, he had not yet interdicted opinions. To this length also he now went. All Protestants were pronounced dead in law. Consequently all their acts—their very marriages—were declared null; and the children born, or to be born of these unions, were reputed illegitimate. And any one who, having abjured or appeared to abjure Protestantism, refused on his death-bed the sacraments of the Catholic Church, was dragged through the mire, and cast on the dunghill in case of his decease, or condemned to the galleys in case of his recovery; but whether he recovered or died, his goods were escheat to the king.

The king, growing old in pride and lasciviousness, had lost even the dignity of his former glory. Puerile terrors flung him in helpless servility at the feet of his confessor. Letellier at last succeeded in getting him to sign an edict, impregnated throughout with the rancour and dishonesty of Jesuitism. By this monstrous edict all the Protestants were declared converted to Catholicism; and those of them who refused to conform to the rites of that religion were to be treated as *relapsed;* that is to say, to be dragged in the mire after their death, or flung into the galleys whilst alive.

Never had the history of the Dukes of Savoy been stained with such revolting crimes. Victor Amadeus himself expressed disapprobation. All generous hearts were moved with indignation. Many

---

[1] The ordinance of 2d December, 1681, interdicted notaries, physicians, printers, &c., belonging to the Reformed Church, from exercising their professions from that time forth.

distinguished Catholics, as the Cardinal De Noailles, Fléchier, and Fénélon, protested against the wrong thus done to France. Vauban, the celebrated architect, who fortified so many towns for war, drew up a memorial, in which he represented this voluntary exile of 100,000 Frenchmen as a political and social calamity. He exhibited the revocation of the Edict of Nantes and the subsequent measures as entailing the ruin of commerce and industry, bringing disorder into families, strengthening the fleets of hostile nations with 9000 seamen, and foreign armies with 600 officers and 12,000 of the best soldiers.

And what did the king then do? He ordained that every one who left his country should be condemned to death and confiscation of goods. It was in effect to say to his Protestant subjects, "You shall be massacred in my kingdom, and exterminated if you attempt to leave it!" Is it possible that the title of Great shall still be attached to the name of the immoral and cruel despot who, in his factitious dignity as a potentate, manifested so total a disregard for the dignity of human nature!

I have thought it necessary to make brief mention of these tyrannic measures, because they all applied to the valleys of Pérouse and Pragela, which then belonged to France; and also because of the effects which they occasioned to the other Vaudois valleys, for the news of this proceeding so operated in Piedmont, as to bring upon the Israel of the Alps the most terrible storm that ever threatened its existence. Janavel perceived it with a sad but courageous foresight, living as he did in exile, but full of patriotic solicitude. Aware of the relations which subsisted betwixt Louis XIV. and Victor Amadeus, he saw too clearly that the Duke of Savoy could only be the vassal of the King of France.

Accordingly, on the 12th of October, 1685, the King of France wrote to the Marquis D'Arcy, his ambassador at Turin—" I have given orders to the Sieur D'Harleville,[1] to attempt the conversion of the valleys[2] which are within my dominions, by quartering my troops in them;[3] and as these valleys are adjacent to those of Piedmont, which are subject to the Duke of Savoy, and in which his predecessors have always shown how unwillingly they suffered the exercise of the Protestant religion, I desire that you communicate to that prince what I write to you, and exhort him in my

[1] King's Lieutenant at Pignerol.
[2] Pérouse, Pragela, Cazane, Usseaux, Méane, Exiles, Traverses, Salabertrans, and Bardonnèche.
[3] By means of *dragonnades*. Protestants unconverted and obstinate in their heresy were obliged to lodge, feed, and maintain soldiers, whose business it was to torment as much as possible those with whom they were placed.

name to employ the same measures in his dominions, not doubting that they will have the same success."[1]

Fifteen days after, the Marquis D'Arcy replied to his sovereign, "I have discharged the duty which your majesty was pleased to impose upon me, by your despatch of the 12th of this month. I have taken occasion to exhort the Duke of Savoy to profit by the happy opportunity which the neighbourhood of your majesty's troops presents to him, for compelling the conversion of the people of the pretended Reformed religion, and for so bringing back all his people to one and the same faith—an object earnestly desired by his predecessors, without their ever enjoying so favourable an occasion for succeeding in it as the present moment affords. The Duke of Savoy assured me that he receives with all possible sentiments of respect and gratitude, the counsels of your majesty, . . . but that he must examine into the matter more thoroughly; for several of his predecessors have in vain attempted to do it, and have even brought great disorders into this district by such attempts. I replied that his predecessors had never enjoyed the facilities for this object which your majesty offers to him, and that it might be long before he found so favourable an opportunity again. And with this I seemed to leave him to think of it, as of a thing in which his own advantage alone was concerned. The Marquis of St. Thomas and the President Truchi are the persons who most relish the counsels of your majesty; and the latter in particular thinks, that at the present moment it would be as easy as glorious to follow them," . . . &c.[2]

This despatch is dated 27th October, 1685; it was the commencement of a negotiation, which was to have the most serious consequences for the Vaudois and even for the house of Savoy. I shall continue to borrow from this correspondence the very language employed in it, in order to throw light upon the mysterious preludes to the persecution, which took place in 1686. The exact words will reveal, better than any analysis, that imperious influence of Louis XIV., of which so many events in our history bore the impress.

The King of France replied to his ambassador[3] in the terms following :—

"It seems that the Duke of Savoy has not yet adopted a firm resolution to labour efficaciously in this great business, which will

---

[1] This and the following documents, to the 26th of January, 1686, are extracted from the *Diplomatic Archives of France*, and were obligingly communicated to me, in 1844, by M. Guizot, at that time Minister of Foreign Affairs.

[2] The despatch is much longer; but I have made these extracts as faithfully and exactly as possible.

[3] From Versailles, 10th November, 1685.

never be successfully accomplished by slight efforts, such as I clearly see that he proposes;¹ but he must be given to understand that his glory is concerned in bringing back his subjects, *at whatever cost*, to submission to the Church." "And if the Duke of Savoy has not sufficient troops in that quarter" (added Louis XIV., in a despatch of the 16th of November), "you can assure him that he will be assisted by mine, and that I will give him all the help which may be needed for the execution of so pious a design."

In his reply of 24th November, 1685, the Marquis D'Arcy begins by saying, that he had reminded the Duke of Savoy, in a very urgent manner, of the offers of his Most Christian Majesty for the conversion of the Vaudois. "I have particularly called him to consider," says he, "what powerful assistance he would receive from the alarm which would be created amongst them by the approach of your troops. The Duke of Savoy, who is a very reserved prince, confined himself to the reiteration of his expressions of gratitude for the interest which your majesty takes in his affairs. The Marquis of St. Thomas has assured me that his master is inclined to profit by your majesty's example and assistance. He told me that a number of the Calvinistic subjects of Victor Amadeus are in a very hopeful condition; but I replied that the object would never be attained without the employment of force, as has been done by your majesty; and that it would never do for the duke to delay the employment of it until your troops were at a distance from his dominions. The President De Truchi again signified to me that it was difficult to know what were the duke's intentions in this respect, for he is of a very independent and reserved character; and it may be doubted if he will really labour for the conversion of the Vaudois as your majesty advises him, because when his ministers have ventured to speak of it to him, he has scarcely chosen to listen to what they had to say."

The original of this despatch is of much greater length. Abridgement was indispensable; but the sense and the most notable expressions have been exactly preserved. The same remark equally applies to the following reply of Louis XIV.:—²

"I see that your representations to the duke have been fruitless; and although his ministers acknowledge that nothing could be more agreeable to God, or useful for the dominions of Savoy, than

¹ Another despatch of the Marquis D'Arcy, dated 2d November, 1685, had apprised Louis XIV. that the Duke of Savoy, "*not thinking that it is for him*" (such is the expression) "*to do in his dominions what your majesty has not been able to do in yours*, has sent the intendant Marousse into the valleys, *to see what course he ought to adopt.*"

² Dated at Versailles, 7th December, 1685.

the entire banishment of heresy, they think that their prince will refuse to take advantage of the present conjuncture, that he may be under obligation to no one either as to the design or the execution. You must, nevertheless, explain to him that, so long as Huguenots exist on the frontiers of my dominions, his authority will never be sufficient to prevent the desertion of my Calvinist subjects; and as he may well judge that I will not suffer this, and that the insolence of these heretics will be a cause of displeasure to me, it may likely enough come to pass that I will not any longer be able to entertain for him the same sentiments of friendship which I have expressed for him up to this time. I feel assured," he says in conclusion, "that he will reflect very seriously upon this subject."

This language announced, upon the part of Louis XIV., views too decided to yield to the hesitation of the Duke of Savoy; and when he speaks of the *insolence* of the poor victims of persecution, it cannot but be felt that such a designation is more fitly to be applied to his own language, which, by haughty insinuations, signified to Victor Amadeus that he must lay his account with being threatened into compliance with the wishes of his ally.

The Marquis D'Arcy replied, on the 1st of December, 1685, that he had renewed his efforts with the Duke of Savoy and his ministers. "I have represented to them," he says, "how easy it would be to compel the Vaudois to change their religion, by the aid of the troops of France; that it would be an honourable thing for the sovereign, and would much conduce to the tranquillity and profit of his dominions, and that it might even be held so meritorious by the pope as to obtain for him the investiture of the principality of Masseray,[1] which his Holiness has hitherto refused. To these offers, advices, and representations, I receive for answer, Sire, plenty of polite speeches, thanks, and acknowledgments of obligation; but I do not see any symptoms of anything effectual likely to be done." At the end of this despatch he adds, that the ministers always seem disposed to exact the conversion of the Vaudois by all means possible. In his reply, dated 14th December, Louis XIV. said, "There is no time to be lost in order that success may be easy, and I shall be very glad that the Marquis of St. Thomas[2] fix the time when he is to act, and that you let me know as soon as possible."

"Sire," replied the ambassador,[3] "I sought an audience of the Duke of Savoy, the day before yesterday, to know if his ministers

---

[1] Recently purchased by Victor Amadeus for a pension of 87,000 livres.
[2] Prime minister of Victor Amadeus.
[3] Under date 5th January, 1686.

had faithfully communicated to him what I laid before them on the part of your majesty." His account of the interview is rather long; but it appears from it that Victor Amadeus had made a commencement, by promising to revoke the ancient edicts favourable to the Vaudois, and that he hoped to gain over their ministers to the Catholic religion, by offering them the double of what they received as pastors in their own church. "The prince added," says the ambassador, "that if he was rather long in doing it he must be excused, upon account of the desire which he had to know and do things himself, in order that he might become the more capable at a future time to serve his friends and allies."

"I observe with pleasure," replied Louis XIV.,[1] "that the Duke of Savoy is disposed to employ, without further delay, all his authority, and even his forces for the conversion of his Calvinist subjects; but I fear he may content himself with imparting his projects to you without executing them. For this reason you must strongly represent to him, that all gentle treatment of such a set of people will only serve to render them more obstinate. The only course for him is, by one stroke, to take from them all favours and privileges which have been granted to them by his predecessors—to ordain the demolition of their places of worship—to prohibit them from any exercise of their religion—and at the same time to lodge his troops with the most obstinate of them; . . . and by this firmness of conduct he will succeed so much the more easily, that these wretches will hope for no assistance; and that even if they should be able to resist the forces of the duke, they will reflect that he will always be supported by mine in the execution of this design."

On the 25th of January Louis XIV. wrote again to the Marquis D'Arcy to the same purpose;[2] but one part of his wish was already realized, for in a despatch dated on the 26th that ambassador sent him the following statement:—

"I was apprehensive that he wished to save himself by protracting time, and I insisted that he should indicate to me the precise day for carrying this matter into execution. So that a promise was given me, Sire, that on Wednesday next[3] the Duke of Savoy would make public the resolution which he had adopted, not to

---

[1] By a despatch, dated from Versailles 17th January, 1686. During the interval a new despatch had been sent to him from Turin, by the Marquis D'Arcy, dated on the 12th. In it the ambassador said, "*I am not a little surprised and vexed to see him (the Duke of Savoy) always defer the execution of this design, which I continue, however, to urge to the utmost of my power.*"   [2] In reply to his despatch of the 12th.

[3] This must have been the 30th of January. The edict of Victor Amadeus, proscribing the Protestantism of the valleys, was issued on the 31st.

suffer the Huguenots of the valleys of Lucerna any longer in their religion, for it is to these valleys that they have almost all retired. The prince has not yet opened his mind distinctly to any of his ministers, following in this his usual manner of dealing with them; but I continue to proclaim so loudly here your fixed resolution not to suffer such a retreat so near your dominions—that notwithstanding all the bad grace[1] and slackness with which this enterprise is gone about, I cannot think that it will terminate otherwise than to the satisfaction of your majesty."

The Propaganda and the nuncio, on their part also, urged the execution of this design. The Duke of Savoy had, perhaps, hoped to succeed in it by means less cruel—by bribes, which would have left to apostasies the appearance of voluntary acts; and with this view he had multiplied for some years all his means of operating upon the Vaudois,[2] and all his allurements of recompense;[3] but, as his royal *suzerain* took for granted, who was already of long experience in persecution, *the Reformed Church could not be destroyed except by force.*[4] Force, therefore, must needs be employed.

Janavel, in his exile, had foreseen this catastrophe. Before it took place he intimated it to his compatriots, telling them in what way they would be attacked, and in what way they ought to defend themselves. The accuracy of his opinions, which the events justified with so melancholy an exactness, gives a high value to the letter which contains them.[5]

"These few words,"[6] says he to his brethren, "are to salute you

---

[1] This diplomatic correspondence places beyond a doubt the repugnance with which the Duke of Savoy consented to the expulsion of the Vaudois, on the exigencies of a policy whose grandeur we cannot unreservedly admit.

[2] In 1679 was founded at Pignerol, the *Opera del rifugio ed ospizio pè catholisati e catholizandi*—an establishment intended to receive, maintain, and provide with portions, those Protestants who had become, or wished to become, Catholics. Hither it was that—in the first instance, from this time forth—all the children were conveyed who were carried off from the Vaudois valleys. These children were sometimes purchased or given.

A few years before a similar establishment had been founded at Le Perrier, in the valley of St. Martin, under the name of the *Monte Dominicale*, but it continued only for a short time. That of Pignerol, on the contrary, subsists to this day. In 1634, a new Catholic *mission* was established at St. Barthélemy.

[3] Exemption from taxes, and other favours, were granted to those Vaudois who became Catholics, 8th October, 1677; 28th January, 1678; 15th March, 1682, &c.

[4] Louis XIV. to the Marquis D'Arcy. Despatches of 10th November, 1685, and 17th January, 1686.

[5] It is not dated, but evidently belongs to 1685. It is to be found in the Archives of Turin, whither it found its way in consequence of the same incident which brought thither the journal of the return of the Vaudois in 1689. (See *Arnaud*, first edition, p. 175.)

[6] I quote exactly. All that is between inverted commas is in the words of Janavel.

with my whole heart, and to testify to you the love which I bear you. You will not be unwilling to be informed what are my sentiments about a number of things which concern you. *If God should be pleased to put your faith to a trial,* as is said and believed, I pray you to take in good part the contents of this letter. Although I doubt not your prudence and conduct, *the first thing which you have to do is to be well united.* It is necessary that the pastors be required to follow their people day and night, that they may be honoured and respected by them, as the servants of God ought to be. They will not intermeddle with anything but the duties of their office—to console the dying, to provide for the safety of poor families, and to encourage the combatants by their prayers. Those who have sufficient zeal and capacity to enter the council of war may be received into it, provided that they do not dread the effusion of blood. Their first duty" (he adds) "will be to assemble all the people, great and small; and after having exhorted them from the word of God, *to make them, with hand lifted up to heaven, swear to be faithful to their church and country, even unto death.* And so doing you will see that the sword of the Lord will be on your side. In the event of war, the first thing which I have to say to you is, to address very humble supplications to your sovereign; but, in the meantime, already, do not omit to have two men in the level country—one to go, and the other to come, that you be not taken by surprise.

"In case they should proceed to quarter troops in the valleys," he goes on to say, "the syndics of the communes should represent to his royal highness that the people take umbrage at it; and as apprehensive lest anything unpleasant should happen to the soldiers or officers, they should pray that it may be dispensed with, offering, however, to pay their share in money. You are entreated in the name of God to admit none, upon any pretext whatever, nor for any possible show of reason assigned—*otherwise it is your certain destruction.* Remember the massacres of 1655, and all the perfidiousness used even at the present time—all which ought to serve you as sufficient example. If, unfortunately, you are attacked, you must defend yourselves the first day without officers, and after that, you must labour day and night to establish amongst yourselves the military arrangements requisite."

He then gives them instructions at great length on this last point. The companies are not to consist of more than eighteen or twenty men. There are to be no lieutenants, "in order not to copy the fashion of the great ones of the world." They are to have a secret council, composed of one man of each valley, *faithful and fearing God*, with one or two of the most resolute pastors, and a commandant-general over all the people of the valleys. "All these are to be nominated *by the voice of the people, and with good order;* and, if God give you time," he proceeds, "you will take care to purchase a little wheat, and to convey it to a retired place amongst the mountains, that it may serve for the relief of the most distressed, and to maintain the flying companies."

Then follow a number of details concerning the most important positions of the valleys—those which ought to be strengthened as points of defence—those which ought to be fortified as places of refuge—and concerning the intrenchments which ought to be made, and the posts which ought to be destroyed. "For Angrogna," says he, "*Revengier* must be strongly barricaded, because it is a place of great importance, which, if well guarded, secures Rocheplate, St. Germain, and Pramol, as well as Rioclaret and St. Martin." He gives up the idea of defending the commune of Rora, the people of which are recommended to retire to Bobi. "You will all be men of strength and of labour," he continues; "spare neither care nor pains to make barricades wherever you think them proper, cutting up the roads and felling trees, in order to impede the passage of the enemy."

After this he points out to the Vaudois the manner of fighting to the greatest advantage, the arms which they ought to use, and the order in which it is best for them to draw themselves up. He recommends them never to be the first to beat a retreat. "Because," says he, "this makes your own people to lose courage, and increases the courage of your enemies. When you pursue them, do it in two bands—the one by the flank, and the other pressing right on, to preserve you from ambuscades. All the captains must be warned that they do not expose their soldiers, *for in preserving them they provide for the safety of the church of God.* As for ammunition, give yourselves no concern about the want of it; I will tell you something on that subject on the first secure opportunity." It is probable that this great captain had placed some ammunition in reserve in some of the deep caverns which had been wont to serve him for places of refuge, magazines, and strongholds; and this, in anticipation of new calamities which the future might still be to bring upon his afflicted country.

Agreeably to his advice, the Vaudois began by sending a deputation to Turin; but it was not received.[1] The intendant, Marousse, had returned from a visit made to the valleys, in order to study their weak points, their means of resistance, and the dispositions

[1] The Marquis D'Arcy speaks of it in his despatch of 26th January, 1686.

of their inhabitants. His report was entirely in favour of the attempts of proselytism by arms, which were so urgently recommended by Louis XIV., and seconded by the Church. M. De La Roche had then been named governor of the province, and had gone to Lucerna to cause several posts in its neighbourhood to be fortified; amongst others, La Tour and Mirabouc. All the officers of the regiment of guards had also been recalled to their colours. All those of the regiment of the White Cross—who were, without exception, Knights of Malta—had received orders to provide themselves with horses. Both these and the officers of the guards were required to hold themselves in readiness for marching; so that everywhere the precursory signs of a new persecution began to appear.

To realize it, the Propaganda made more exertion than ever. It had councils organized in Turin, Pignerol, Grenoble, and Briançon. These councils combined their efforts; and it must be admitted that the intentions and the zeal of a real charity did, in many instances, animate the persons who composed them. The sacrifices which they made for the conversion of the heretics attest their generosity, but the means employed prove their ignorance.

The first pretext employed for disturbing the repose of the Vaudois was derived from the great number of French refugees who had retired into the valleys after the revocation of the edict of Nantes. Louis XIV., blinded by the pride which gave the ambitious and extravagant flatteries of the Catholic party such a hold over him that he became an instrument in their hands without a will of his own, made use of his power for the service of their low intrigues, and engaged more and more in a political course unworthy of the age to which his name has been given. Wishing at once to oppress the people in his own dominions, and to prevent them from leaving them, he had obtained from Victor Amadeus the barring of his frontiers against French fugitives. In the end of the year 1685, the Duke of Savoy had, therefore, at the urgency of his formidable ally, promulgated an edict by which the Vaudois were forbidden to receive any of their refugee brethren; and the latter were ordained to leave Piedmont, or to abjure within the space of eight days, under pain of incarceration.[1]

In the meantime, the Propagandists proceeded with a perseverance and a fertility of invention as to means, which were worthy of a better cause, in the application of all the old measures of repression applicable to the Protestant religion. These measures affected the valleys of Lucerna and St. Martin, which belonged to

[1] This edict is of date 4th November, 1685. It is to be found in Dubois, II. 239.

Piedmont, whilst the royal council of Pignerol and the Parliament of Grenoble prosecuted the same work in the valleys of the Cluson and the Doire, which belonged to France. Such were the circumstances in which the year 1686 began; and the ambassador of France was able to write to his master on the 26th of January: "The Duke of Savoy has promised me that he will make known, on Wednesday next, the measures which he is about to adopt in order to enter into the views of your majesty."

We are now come to a decisive epoch in the history of the Vaudois; the catastrophe is imminent; the conflict will be terrible; but the most extraordinary wonders in the history of the Israel of the Alps were destined to arise out of the most disastrous calamities.

CHAPTER XIV.

COMMENCEMENT OF THE FOURTH GENERAL PERSECUTION IN THE VALLEYS.[1]

(JANUARY TO THE END OF APRIL, 1686.)

Edict of 31st January, 1686—Consternation in the valleys—Delegates meet at Angrogna—Petition to the duke—Attempted intervention of the Protestant cantons of Switzerland—The valleys invaded by French troops—Organized resistance—Endeavours of the Swiss ambassadors—Proposal that the Vaudois should leave their native country—Division of opinion among them—They finally resolve to abide by and defend their valleys—Celebration of the Lord's Supper at Easter, 1686.

ON Thursday, the 31st of January, 1686, appeared the fatal edict which caused so much woe in the valleys, and was attended by such consequences, that for some years it was supposed that the

---

[1] AUTHORITIES.—"*Hist. de la perséc. des vallées de Piémont; contenant ce qui s'est passé dans la dissipation des Eglises et des habitants de ces vallées, arrivé en l'an 1686.* Rotterdam, MDCLXXXIX." 4to, pp. 36. There exists a German translation of this work, published in 1690—an 18mo volume of 155 pages, with the title, "*History of the Vaudois Persecution in Piedmont.*" (Library of Berne.)—Another work in German, on the same subject, is entitled, "*The Palm-tree of Christian Truth; or, The Persecutions of the Protestants and Vaudois.*" (Nuremberg, 1690.)—"*Hist. de la négociation des ambassadeurs envoyés au duc de Savoie par les cantons évangéliques* (of Switzerland) *l'année*, 1686." Published in 1690. One vol. 32mo, pp 172.— "*Le feu de la reconnaissance et de la joie, pour la glorieuse victoire remportée sur les hérétiques vaudois, dans les vallées de Luserne, par S. A. R. Victor Amé II., duc de Savoye, prince de Piémont, roy de Chypre, donné dans la ville de Rumilly par le comte de Saint-Joyre,* &c. .... *le 14 mai 1686, jour de la naissance de sadite A. R.*" (Chambery, 1686.) Not paged.—"*Rélation de la guerre contre les religionnaires nommés Barbets.*" (Quoted in the first of the works here named, at the fifteenth page.) A little work upon which I have not been able to

Vaudois church had entirely disappeared. This document is so important, that its contents must be fully exhibited.[1]

"The heresy," it is here said, "has found its way from the midst of the valley of Lucerna to the very heart of Piedmont. . . . Our ancestors have often attempted to extirpate it; but in consequence of the aid which the sectaries received from foreign countries, the sacred work of their restoration to the Church of Rome could not be accomplished; and as the principal reason which existed for tolerating them has recently disappeared—through the zeal and piety of the glorious monarch of France, who has brought back to the true faith the heretics bordering upon the Vaudois valleys—we think he would have cause to accuse us of ingratitude for his distinguished favours, which we still enjoy, if we were to allow the opportunity to escape of executing this important design, according to the intention which our glorious predecessors have always entertained." Such is a succinct but faithful abridgment of the preamble of the edict.

These words might be skilfully selected in a political point of view; but when we recal the haughty language which Louis XIV. had addressed to Victor Amadeus, to compel him to destroy his most faithful subjects, we cannot help noting in the latter a great want of dignity, in thus giving the name of *distinguished favours* to the shameful vassalage to which he was subjected by France. The following, however, is the enactive part of the edict which has so strange an introduction.

"For the preceding causes, and *for other urgent reasons*,[2] we

lay my hands; perhaps the title only refers to the following—"*Relation de la guerre de 1686, contre ceux des vallées,*" &c. 4to, pp. 8. No place of publication given. At the end appears, "*Suite de la rélation de la défaite des sujets rebelles de S. A. R.,*" &c. —Amongst recent works there is one which specially relates to this subject—"*The Exiles of Lucerna; or, The Sufferings of the Waldenses during the Persecution of 1686.*" Edinburgh, 1841, 8vo, pp. 195, with wood engravings, of two tints, representing various places in the Vaudois valleys.

The *Archives of the Court of Turin* are very rich in documents connected with this period, as well as the *Archives of the Court of Accounts*. There exist, also, manuscripts and memoirs of individuals, amongst which notice ought to be taken of the "*Memorie di me, Bartolomeo Salvajot, di 1686 al 1688.*"—Also the *Diplomatic Archives of France* contain the correspondence of Louis XIV. with the Marquis D'Arcy, his ambassador at Turin. (Communicated by M. Guizot.) See the documents quoted in the preceding chapter.

[1] The substance of this edict has been published in the "*Hist. de la négociation de 1686*" (32mo, Geneva, 1690). It is to be found entire in the *Archives of the Court of Accounts* of Turin, *Regio controrollo, Finanze da* 1678 in 1687, No. 165, fol. 224, second page. I believe it is awanting in the great collections of Borelli and Duboin.

[2] The duke felt that those which he had just set forth were not sufficient; but how could he base measures so cruel on reasons which he does not state? Such, however, is the fatal dilemma of tyranny, always suspended betwixt the two terms— servility and oppression.

have, of our perfect authority, certain knowledge, good pleasure, and absolute power, decreed as follows:—

"I. The Vaudois shall cease immediately and for ever from all the exercises of their religion.

"II. They are prohibited from holding religious meetings, under pain of death and confiscation of goods.

"III. All their ancient privileges are abolished.[1]

"IV. All their places of worship, places of prayer, and edifices set apart for their worship shall be razed.

"V. All the pastors and schoolmasters of the valleys shall be obliged to embrace Catholicism, or to quit the country within the space of fifteen days, under pain of death and confiscation of goods.

"VI. All the children born, and to be born of Protestant parents, shall be compulsorily educated as Catholics.

"Consequently, the parents to whom a child shall be born are required, within eight days from its birth, to present it to the priest of their parish, under pain, for the mother, of being publicly beaten with rods, and for the father, of five years of the galleys.

"VII. The Vaudois pastors who shall abjure the doctrine which they have hitherto preached, shall receive a pension one-third greater than they have previously enjoyed, with a reversion of one-half of this annuity to their widows.

"VIII. All foreign Protestants settled in Piedmont are ordained to become Catholics, or to leave the country within the space of fifteen days.

"IX. By a special act of his high and paternal clemency, the sovereign will permit them to sell, within that interval, the properties which they have acquired in Piedmont, on condition that the purchasers shall be Catholics only."

We would need to go back to that period, so widely different from our own, not to see in these pretences of clemency the language of insolent pride and cruelty, by which tyranny aggravated the revolting injustice of its acts. "The state! I am the state!" said sovereigns in those days. "The state! we are the state!" say the people now. May the hand of God aid them to the full attainment of their freedom! But the Bible tells us, that it is only if Christ make us free that we are free indeed; and so long as the spirit of Popery, striving against the Bible, shall cause its enervating yoke of superstition to press upon the degraded nations—so long as they consent to its tyranny over conscience and oppression of

---

[1] It ought to be recollected that Victor Amadeus had solemnly ratified these very privileges on the 4th of December, 1681; and Popery called it a *holy piety* to trifle in this way with the rights and the blood of human beings.

the mind, every pretence of liberty on their part will be a mockery. How can a man be free when his mind is enslaved? The Vaudois, who preserved the integrity of their religion at the expense of leaving their country, when it was trodden down by tyranny, carried with them more of independence than belongs to a people exempt from oppression, but destitute of moral energy and true liberty.

It is impossible to paint the profound consternation, the scenes of baseness and carnage, the tears of grief and anguish which filled the Vaudois valleys at this time. All the parishes were requested immediately to name delegates, who should meet at Angrogna, to consult for the defence of their common interests.

"Your first care," Janavel had said to his fellow-countrymen, "must be to address supplications to your sovereign." They recollected this advice. A petition was drawn up; but it remained unanswered. Three times they renewed their petition, which was lost in a silence as of death. With difficulty did they obtain a little delay in the execution of the edict of which they asked the revocation. At the same time, they wrote to Switzerland to solicit the advice, interposition, and sympathy of that generous nation, whose government had always been amongst the most active protectors of their people.

The first letter which the Helvetic government addressed to the court of Turin, in favour of the Vaudois, remained likewise unanswered. All the deputies of the Protestant cantons of that noble country then met in an extraordinary meeting at Baden.[1] They resolved to send commissioners to Piedmont without delay, with instructions actively to employ all means possible to save from complete ruin, the Israel of the Alps so cruelly menaced. These ambassadors extraordinary were Gaspard and Bernard De Murat, both of them councillors of state. They arrived in Turin in the beginning of the month of March, and immediately solicited an audience of Victor Amadeus, which was refused them.

But there was no time to be lost; the urgency of the French ambassador, the nuncio, and the Propaganda, allowed the duke no repose; the longer period which he had granted to the Vaudois was nearly expired. The persecuting zeal, which seemed at that time to have seized upon the public mind like some disease of the brain, had already hurried on some small bodies of Catholic volunteers to commence hostilities against the people of the valleys. The French troops, cantoned at Pignerol, waited with impatience for the signal. "There is nothing spoken of here but exterminating

[1] This meeting took place on the 26th of February, 1686.

and destroying everything, and hanging great and small," wrote a French officer from Pignerol a few days before that date.[1]

In these partial encounters the mountaineers had had the advantage. But there were traitors among them; a French refugee, named Desmoulin, made known daily to the commandant of La Tour[2] the plans and arrangements of those who had sheltered him. "They are very impatient for battle," he wrote on the 4th of March. "The prisoners of Le Villar have been brought, part to Bobi and part to Angrogna.[3] They reckon upon 3000 combatants, and expect many foreigners."

To increase their strength by a powerful military organization, the Vaudois embodied the instructions which Janavel had sent them, in a sort of code of discipline, of which the following were the principal articles[4]:—

Article IV. Every one is prohibited, under severe penalties, from using offensive language to another, from blaspheming the holy name of God, and from insulting the enemy by abusive words or useless cries.

Art. V. Debauchery, robbery, and other similar actions contrary to the law of God are severely prohibited. (The council of war was to judge of the penalties incurred and of their infliction.)

Art. IX. Care shall be taken to keep watch over those who shall behave as cowards in battle, or who do not choose to obey their officers, that they may be punished according to their disobedience.

Art. XIII. No one shall fire a musket unnecessarily, in order to spare the ammunition.

Art. XIV. Soldiers amongst whom any subject of dispute shall arise, must present themselves before their officers and report it for their decision.

Art. XV. Each officer shall be held answerable to the council of war for his soldiers.

Art. XX. The women and girls shall attend at the places of

---

[1] The letter is dated on the 26th of January. (Archives of Berne, compartment D.)

[2] The commandant was Major Vercelli. The letters of the spy are in the Archives of Turin.

[3] The fact that there were prisoners proves that there had already been fighting.

[4] The exact title of this document is the following—"*Regulations to be observed by the watching party, and generally in all the exercises and services of the war waged against the people of the valleys of Piedmont on account of their religion.*" This expression, *the people of the valleys* [ceux des vallées], suggests the supposition that these regulations, which embody all the instructions of Janavel, were prepared out of the valleys, and probably by Janavel himself. The precise date cannot be stated.

battle to bear off the sick and wounded, as well as to roll down stones when there is need.

It is appointed, moreover, that signals shall be established, by which they are to give notice to one another of the approach of an enemy. Slings and scythes are numbered amongst the weapons recommended. All the soldiers are required to assemble an hour before daylight, to be present under arms at morning prayer.

The singular simplicity of these articles brings prominently into view the manly and religious character of this people of the Alps; the courageous fervour of the sentiments which they breathe accords well with that of the hero of Rora, Janavel, who knew how to combine the calm intrepidity of the warrior with the humility and sobriety of the Christian; a strict regard to duty in the first place, and a deep sense of the wants of man appear, especially in these few lines, placed at the head of the regulations :—

"As the war which is commenced against us arises from hatred against our religion, and our sins are its cause, it is necessary that each one amend his ways; and that the officers be careful to cause good books to be read in the watching parties by those who are not actively employed, and to cause prayer to be made evening and morning, as is set down at the end of these articles."

Is it not remarkable to see the reading of good books, prayer, reserve, and moderation, put in the order of the day for an army on the point of battle? The daily prayer appointed to be said morning and evening in the Vaudois camp is also full of a humble and courageous faith, suitable to persons whose surest reliance is on the arm of God. We shall lay it before our readers when the course of events shall have brought us into the heroic camps of the Israel of the Alps.

But, before entering into conflict, the Vaudois were anxious to exhaust all means of conciliation. Already surrounded by the ducal and French troops, they knew not that Switzerland had sent ambassadors to defend their cause. These ambassadors themselves, not having been able to gain an audience of Victor Amadeus, drew up a memorial in strong language, reminding that young prince of the edicts which guaranteed liberty of conscience to the Vaudois, and representing to him that the faithful observance of treaties is the strength of states, and can alone secure their repose— that if the word of kings were no longer to be counted on, Protestant princes might treat their Catholic subjects as he himself treated his Protestant subjects—and that his own glory, humanity, justice, and the prosperity of Piedmont, were interested in his not making himself the destroyer and executioner of his own people, of whom he ought to be the protector, and to whom he had promised that he would be a father.

The Marquis of St. Thomas, one of the ministers of the Duke of Savoy, was charged with the duty of replying to this memorial. "The inhabitants of the valleys," he said to the ambassadors, "are guilty of having taken up arms against their sovereign, and can no longer be protected by the edicts to which you refer." "The Vaudois did not take up arms until they were attacked," replied the ambassadors, "and in this particular it is his highness himself who has been the first to break his engagements." "Other engagements by which we were strongly bound to the King of France have dictated our conduct," the minister went on to say. "Say not, then," replied the ambassadors, "that the Vaudois are guilty; and cease to persecute them." "Things are now too far advanced to leave any possibility of drawing back," said the Marquis of St. Thomas; "however," he added, "if the Vaudois choose to save appearances by conforming outwardly to the provisions of the edict of the 31st of January, things may perhaps be arranged."

These terms were too vague; and in accepting them the Vaudois would have placed themselves in a position as uncertain as their former one, and much less honourable. So thought the ambassadors, and rejected with dignity this proposal of temporizing and false appearances. Moreover, what assurance could have been entertained that this half promise, this hope held out without guarantee, would not have proved deceitful, when solemn edicts had been violated?

The ambassadors resolved to proceed in person to the valleys. A safe-conduct was granted them for this purpose. The Elector of Brandenburg, as well as Holland and England, addressed fresh representations to Victor Amadeus on the subject of the Vaudois. It might have been hoped that these things combined would have exercised a happy influence in their favour.

The Swiss commissioners arrived in the valleys on the 22d of March, and immediately asked the representatives of all the Vaudois communes to do them the favour of meeting with them on the morrow. This meeting took place at Le Chiabas. It was opened with a fervent prayer from the lips of Pastor Arnaud. Messrs. De Morat then stated all that they had done since their arrival at Turin, and inquired of the Vaudois what was their resolution. "Be so good as to give us your own advice," replied they. "Would you consent to quit your country," said the Swiss, "if we should obtain from Victor Amadeus permission for you to dispose of your properties and to leave his dominions with your families?" It is impossible to describe the stupor which seized the meeting upon this proposal. The Vaudois sought assistance, expected a conflict, hoped for victory; and now, before they had fought at all, it was proposed that they should submit to all the consequences of defeat. Even a defeat could be repaired; but exile involved the loss of their country, the ruin of their church, and a complete termination of their existence as a people.

The ambassadors strongly represented the impossibility of their rendering assistance in any way but by negotiations. "Your valleys," said they, "are inclosed by the dominions of your enemies; all the passes are guarded; no nation is in circumstances to make war with France upon your single account; no army could even penetrate hither; and as for yourselves, you have scarcely 3000 combatants; nevertheless you have more than 12,000 mouths, which you must feed; all your doings are watched; the regular troops wait only for the signal of massacre; how can you resist?"

But the love of their native country still struggled in the breasts of the Vaudois against the sad conviction which these words brought to their minds. "It would be cowardly," they exclaimed, "to lose courage in the presence of God, who has so often delivered our fathers, and who saved the people of Israel from so many dangers."—"It would be folly," replied the prudent diplomatists, "to count upon miraculous events now. It is impossible for you to contend against the greater force of your enemies; it is impossible for you to receive any assistance. Consider your situation. One way of escape from it remains for you. Would it not be better to transport to another place the lamp of the gospel, which has been intrusted to you, than to let it remain here to be extinguished in blood?" On these words the meeting was divided in opinion, and replied that it could not conclude any engagement on so grave a subject, without having consulted the whole people.[1]

The ambassadors could not wait for this decision, and returned to Turin. They requested a safe-conduct for Vaudois deputies to bring them the reply of the people, but this was refused. Their secretary therefore went for it to the valleys. He arrived there

[1] Moser (*Geschichte der Waldenser* . . . . § 25) pretends that at this conjuncture, Victor Amadeus sent to the valleys the *Chancellor Vercelli*, and that the Vaudois seized him and kept him as an hostage. Perhaps they would have done very properly. But I have found no proof of this fact anywhere; and I have met with only one bearing the name of Vercelli, the major of the fort of La Tour, and not a chancellor. Moser does not say on what authority he founds. The rest of his history is often incorrect, and always incomplete. I have not, therefore, thought it proper to regard his testimony in this instance.

on the 28th of March. The assembly of the communes was holding constant sittings at Angrogna, where he found a great agitation prevailing. "Your case," said he to them, "grows worse every day. Louis XIV., through his ambassadors, expresses a burning rage at the procrastinations of the Duke of Savoy. The nuncio promises the duke the investiture of Masseran so soon as he shall act in this business; the Propaganda labour amongst the army and the people: make you haste to quit this country whilst you still have it in your power." "Who shall assure us," replied the Vaudois, "that they will not seek to destroy us whilst in separate groups we are passing out of the country? They have not respected the edicts which guaranteed our residence in these valleys; will they show more respect for the engagement by which they permit us to leave them?"

A memorial setting forth all these objections was addressed by the assembly to the ambassadors. The Vaudois added, in a private letter, that they left the matter to their decision. This letter was signed by nine ministers and eight laymen. The ambassadors now reported to the Marquis of St. Thomas, minister of foreign affairs, that they hoped to bring the Vaudois to the decision of quitting their native country, provided that they received a guarantee of perfect safety on their journey of emigration. To this proposal Victor Amadeus replied, through the Count of Marsenas, that the Vaudois having already taken up arms against him, had merited the most rigorous treatment; but that if they chose to send deputies to ask pardon, in name of the whole people, he would see what could be done.

The Messrs. De Morat expressed their surprise, that after having hitherto so obstinately refused to receive the Vaudois at Turin, he should now require their presence in that capital. Was it not intended, by forcing them to come and ask pardon, to bring them to own themselves guilty, in order that they might therefore be treated accordingly? But there was no time for hesitation; and they advised the Vaudois to show deference to their sovereign by conforming to his desires, rather than to irritate him still more by a refusal.

A safe-conduct was thereupon granted for the deputies from the valleys. The secretary of the embassy himself carried it to them. But the assembly of the communes, which still continued its sittings, was not yet prepared to resolve upon such a course. The greater part of the pastors were in favour of submission; the people preferred to defend themselves. The debates were prolonged without any result for a whole day. Next day a part of the Vaudois

CHAP. XIV.]   DIVISION AMONGST THE VAUDOIS.   435

communes resolved to submit[1] and to send deputies to Turin; the rest persisted in their refusal.[2] These, however, also sent a deputy, but with instructions only to thank the Swiss embassy for their kind endeavours, declaring at the same time their resolution to defend themselves to their last breath.

The enemies of the Vaudois triumphed in this division; and to derive from it all possible advantage, they induced Victor Amadeus to sign an edict on the 9th of April, which treated the emigration of the Vaudois as a settled point.[3] It was published in the valleys on the 11th of April, and at first had only the effect of increasing the agitation which already prevailed there.

Three days after, the delegates of the communes assembled at Rocheplate to deliberate upon it, and agreed that the conditions imposed by this edict were such as could not be consented to. Accordingly, they unanimously agreed to resist to the utmost, to commit themselves to the care of Providence, and valiantly to de-

[1] These were the communes of La Pérouse and St. Martin, Prarusting and Rocheplate, Rora, Le Villar and La Tour; the latter not adhering unanimously.

[2] Namely, the communes of Bobi, St. John, and Angrogna, with the dissentients of the commune of La Tour.

[3] Meanwhile, the Swiss ambassadors had sent to the valleys the deputy of Bobi with a letter, in which they exhorted the party who were for resistance to unite in the submission of their brethren, rather than to create a division in what concerned their churches. Each of the three communes, resolved upon maintaining their rights by arms, appointed deputies commissioned to reply in their name.

This reply was drawn up on the 4th of April. It was signed by *John Muston* and *Michael Parise*, deputies of St. John; *Négrin Danne* and *Bertin*, deputies of Bobi; and *John Buffa*, deputy of Angrogna.. They expressed their regret at being compelled to resist the mind of the ambassadors, and declared again their resolution of defending themselves to the utmost. During this time, the Marquis of St. Thomas strongly urged the five deputies from the submitting communes, who had remained at Turin, to make their submission. But they always put it off to wait for the deputy of Bobi. These delays excited the impatience of the court, and especially of the ambassador of France, who urged Victor Amadeus with his own edict in his hand, and almost with threats in his mouth, to proceed to put into execution the measures required by Louis XIV. In these circumstances news came that two Frenchmen had been killed; and this murder was imputed to the Vaudois. The Marquis De Grancy exhibited a violent irritation. It was upon this, that in order to avoid the massacre of the Vaudois, and with humane designs, Victor Amadeus issued the decree of the 9th of April, which laid down regulations for their departure from the country, as if it had been a thing already agreed upon. According to this decree, the people of the valley of Lucerna were to assemble at La Tour on the 21st of April; those of Angrogna, Prarusting, and Rocheplate were to assemble at St. Segont on the 22d, and those of the valley of St. Martin at Mirandol on the 23d, that they might thus remove in three detachments. Ten days were allowed them to sell their properties; they were to lay down their arms immediately, and to demolish their places of worship with their own hands before they went away. This edict, signed on the 9th, was registered on the 10th, and published in the valleys on the 11th. It contains also other provisions. It may be seen in *Duboin*, II. 243, and in the *Histoire des négociations de* 1686, p. 42.

fend their homes and their altars as their fathers had done. And so this measure, which had been adopted in order to disunite them, produced a contrary effect. The pastors, however, did not approve of this decision; and they wrote to the Messrs. De Morat to deplore the infatuation of their people, who were going to engage in a resistance that was desperate; but at the same time to say, that they were resolved not to abandon them.

The ambassadors, afflicted to see all that they had accomplished with such difficulty undone in a moment, made a last effort, and addressed a last appeal to the Israel of the Alps by a letter, in the most urgent terms, which was read from the pulpit in all the Vaudois parishes.

"Undoubtedly," said they, "one's native country has great attractions; but the heavenly inheritance is preferable to those of earth. You still have it in your power to leave your country, which is at once so dear and so fatal to you; you have in your power to carry away your families, to retain your religion, to avoid bloodshed; in the name of Heaven, then, do not obstinately set yourselves upon a useless resistance! Do not close against yourselves the last remaining path of escape from a total destruction!"

We may imagine what sort of effect these words must have produced on an audience partly composed of timid persons, old men, women, and children! All the churches of our valleys were full of weeping and sobs. But presently the grave voice of prayer rose alone above these lamentations. They implored the assistance and direction of God. Their breasts were calmed, their souls were strengthened; and confidence was re-established in their agitated minds.

A solemn assembly of all the delegates of the valleys was held at Rocheplate on the 19th of April. It renewed the declaration of the 14th, by which, on the ground of the righteousness of their cause, the Vaudois bound themselves to defend their country and their religion unto death. The meeting was held on Good Friday. "O Lord Jesus," said the pastor Arnaud, "who hast suffered so much and died for us, grant us grace that we may be able also to suffer and to sacrifice our lives for thee! Those who persevere to the end shall be saved. Let each of us exclaim with the apostle, 'I can do all things through Christ which strengtheneth me!'" It was resolved that the people of the valleys should be universally exhorted to repentance and amendment, so that they might humbly submit to the trials to which they were to be subjected, and that the Divine hand might be pleased to moderate their severity. Moreover, it was appointed that on the following Sabbath, being Easter-day, there should be celebrated in each parish, a solemn communion of all the children of these mountains—heroic disciples of the gospel, resolved to defend themselves against their base oppressors!

In some communes the concourse of people to this solemnity was so great, that the Lord's Supper was celebrated in the open air—an august and affecting ceremony, a sublime and mournful communion! Thus feeding upon their Saviour's sacrifice, the Vaudois bound themselves to brave torture, and to shed their blood in defence of his religion. They united at the footstool of the Lord in the same devotedness, the same love, and the same prayers. Alas! to the most of them it was the sacrament of the dying which they received on that occasion. To all of them it was the last communion at which they were to have it in their power to be present before the terrible catastrophe which we are now to relate, and which brought on the total dispersion of this heroic people, whose existence then seemed entirely at an end. But—like the two witnesses of the Apocalypse, who are called the "candlesticks standing before the God of the earth," and of whom we are told, that after having been overthrown for three days and a half they are re-animated by the spirit of life [1]—the Vaudois, these ancient depositaries of the Old and of the New Testament, these two heavenly witnesses, after three years of exile and apparent death, were to reconquer their native country, to re-appear on their mountains, and to set up again, no more to be removed, the symbolical candlestick of eternal truth on the bloody but blessed theatre of so many atrocious persecutions.

CHAPTER XV.

WAR AND MASSACRE IN THE VALLEYS.[2]

(APRIL TO MAY, 1686.)

The Swiss ambassadors endeavour to secure a place of refuge for the Vaudois in Brandenburg—The valleys invaded by the combined troops of France and Piedmont—Catinat, the French commander-in-chief—His treachery—Successes of the invaders—Cruelties and outrages—Gabriel of Savoy—His treachery towards the Vaudois—Fearful cruelties—Conflicts—Massacres—Prolonged sufferings and martyrdom of Leydet, pastor of Pral.

THE generous ambassadors of Switzerland—grieved to see that their most disinterested mediation could satisfy neither of the two parties,

---

[1] Rev. xi. 3, 4, 7, 9, 11, &c.
[2] AUTHORITIES.—The same as in the preceding chapter.

but was rejected at once by the Vaudois and by the Duke of Savoy, and that there was no hope of any benefit from any new attempt at accommodation—resolved, with hearts full of affliction and sorrow, to depart from Piedmont. But foreseeing the inevitable and approaching destruction of that Vaudois church, which they loved so much, they wrote to the Elector of Brandenburg, Frederic William the Great, to learn from him if there were in his dominions any lands which could be set apart for the reception of a colony of Vaudois in the event of their expatriation. The elector replied with the most generous warmth that nothing could be more agreeable to him than to give them an asylum. All these documents show the universal apprehension which the precarious state of the Israel of the Alps then inspired. These mournful and increasing fears were but too well justified by the result.

The united forces of France and Piedmont already approached in good order to the Vaudois valleys. Victor Amadeus II. reviewed his troops in the plain of St. Segont. His army consisted of 2586 men, drawn from the various regiments[1] of the militia of Mondovi, Barges, and Bagnol, one corps of Piedmontese infantry, and one corps of cavalry. It was followed by fifty mules laden with warlike stores, and eighty-five carrying provisions;[2] besides which there were sixteen mules carrying shovels, and hatchets, and empty sacks, intended to be filled with earth upon the spot, to secure the soldiers from the bullets of the enemy; and others which carried various engines fit to be used in fortifications and intrenchments. These precautions had been dictated by the ancient reputation of bravery of the Vaudois mountaineers. The French troops were composed of a number of regiments of cavalry and dragoons, seven or eight battalions of infantry which had been brought from Dauphiny, and part of the garrisons of Pignerol and Casal. Volunteers and plunderers thronged together for booty, like birds of prey, in the train of the two armies.

A new *Piedmontese Easter* was in preparation. The Vaudois came from the communion, the Catholics gathered for carnage. The signal was to be given on Easter Monday, the 22d of April, by three cannon shots, *fired at the first break of day*,[3] from the summit

---

[1] The regiments of Nice and Montferrat were quartered at Bubiano; those of Savoy and of La Croix Blanche at La Tour; those of Aosta and of Saluces at Lucerna; that of the sea-coast at Fenil; that of the *gendarmerie* at Garsiliano; and the body-guards, the regiment of guards, and the cavalry were at Briquéras.

[2] Seventy mules were laden with wine; fifteen carried 150 *rups* of provisions daily.

[3] These are the terms of the order, written according to a plan agreed upon in a council of war.

of the hill of Briquéras. A general attack on the two valleys was immediately to follow, the Duke of Savoy assailing that of Lucerna, and Catinat, commander-in-chief of the French troops, invading that of St. Martin. This general set out from Pignerol at midnight, between Easter Sunday and Easter Monday, 1686. He marched for two hours by the light of torches and flambeaux, before which the dark and gigantic masses of our mountains seemed to recede. By and by a more pleasant light fell from heaven on their loftiest peaks; the snow of the glaciers blushed in the first ray of the morning. The murderers extinguished their torches; they had now arrived opposite to the village of St. Germain.

Thither Catinat sent a detachment of infantry,[1] commanded by Lieutenant-Colonel Villevieille, who took possession of the village, and drove the Vaudois from their first intrenchments; but they, having retired to higher ground, and finding themselves still pursued, wheeled about, and in turn repulsed their assailants. Catinat then sent a detachment of cavalry and dragoons to support his infantry. Battle was joined along the whole line, and the firing continued for six consecutive hours.

The French infantry began to be exhausted, the cavalry could not manœuvre on the slopes covered with brushwood, where our brave mountaineers made so vigorous a resistance; and they, seeing the fire of the assailing army slacken, suddenly made a rush so impetuous, that the French, surprised and overthrown, were cast into confusion, and driven from the territory of St. Germain, even to the left bank of the Cluson. In this affair more than 500 of the French were killed or wounded, whilst only two of the Vaudois lost their lives.[2] The village of St. Germain was then cleared, except, however, of a small body of troops which, along with the gallant Lieutenant-Colonel Villevieille, had thrown themselves into the Vaudois place of worship, where they maintained their position until evening.[3]

[1] *Relatione del succeduto al primo attaco fatto dai Francesi nella valle di San Martino.* (Turin, *Archives of the Court, Valdesi*, No. of the series, 300.) This paper is written in French, although the inscription on the back is in Italian. It begins thus, "Yesterday morning, the 22d, M. De Catinat detached the regiment *Limosin and Du Plessis.* . . . . . This regiment drove the Barbets a little too far, and came to a stand almost at the base of the fort of these Huguenots. The dragoons of La Lande advanced on the right, and got entangled amongst the rocks, where they lost a number of men. The captain who commanded was wounded in the arm," &c. Farther on we read, "The Major De Provence was mortally wounded; M. De Brienne was wounded in the head, M. De Gontaudau in the arm," &c.

[2] *Dissipation des Eglises Vaudoises en* 1686, p. 15.

[3] The following is the account given of this affair in the bulletin above quoted: "The Chevalier De Villevieille was attacked by a numerous troop, which was concealed in a ravine on his left, and by those in the fort, who at the same time rushed out to charge him. He lost a number of men as he retired, ... and all that

Henry Arnaud, a native of the neighbourhood of Die in Dauphiny, had quitted that province with the Protestant refugees who fled to the valleys of Piedmont, to escape from the iniquitous persecutions of Louis XIV. From being a French pastor he became a Vaudois pastor, and from a pastor he became a captain, by reason of the horrid assaults to which the valleys were now subjected. Learning that Lieutenant-Colonel Villevieille had made a redoubt of the church of St. Germain, he hastened thither with a small detachment of men, determined to make themselves masters of it. But a formidable fire of musketry, directed on all points from the door of the church, along the esplanade which stretched in front of it, swept the approaches to that extemporary fortress, with a power too murderous for those who attacked, and too advantageous for those who defended it. It was necessary to give up the attack on this side. Arnaud commanded his men to come upon the church behind,[1] to scale the walls, to cut the timber of the roof, and to crush the enemy under the weight of the heavy slates with which it was covered, whilst another party of his men digged canals around the walls, to fill the church with water, and to drown Villevieille in it if he refused to surrender. But night came on to interrupt these operations; the governor of Pignerol sent fresh troops, and Villevieille was freed from the dangerous position into which his bravery had brought him.

Without turning back upon St. Germain, Catinat pursued his way towards La Pérouse. There he parted his forces into two divisions; the first, commanded by Mélac, turned the heights of Le Pomaret, penetrating into the valley of Pragela by Salvage; the second, led by Catinat himself, was moved in the direction of Les Clots; and next day, the 23d of April, that general attacked Rioclaret, situated opposite to the position which he had taken up.

The inhabitants of the whole valley of St. Martin had declared their desire, four days before, to avail themselves of the provisions of the edict of the 9th of April, and not to take up arms. But their resolution was not known to Victor Amadeus till the evening before the attack; and he refused to accept it, declaring that it was too late. His troops already occupied the approaches to the valleys; the commissioner sent by that of St. Martin could not get back to it again; the inhabitants of that region were ignorant

he could do was to gain a house, with only thirty men, in which he was attacked for more than four hours by 500 men, who proposed to give him good terms to cause him to surrender, but to whom he only replied by discharges of musketry. . . . . ."

[1] Arnaud, in his *Glorieuse Rentrée*, records this fact in p. 49 of the preface. The bulletins make no mention of it.

of the response of the duke; they trusted to the provisions of the edict, and not counting upon being attacked, they had made no preparation for defence. The army of Catinat, therefore, took them by surprise, and cut them in pieces. They had broken the union sworn by all the Vaudois; and this cowardly baseness cost them more dear than all the most desperate efforts of a generous courage would have done.

The enemy's troops spread themselves without resistance over the valley, plundering, killing, and ravaging to the utmost. Six families, taken prisoners and sent to La Pérouse, were there massacred in cold blood. Two young girls of Ville Sèche were killed for resisting the outrages of the soldiers, who satiated on their corpses the savage brutality of which they had not been able to make them victims whilst they lived. John Ribet, of Macel, had all his members burned one after another, upon the successive refusals with which he met the threats and representations addressed to him during the intervals of his tortures, to bring him to an abjuration. At the hamlet of Les Fontaines, near Rodoret, four women were seized as they fled, carrying along with them their children. These innocents were butchered before the eyes of their mothers, and the mothers were then slaughtered over the bodies of their babes.

The horrors of 1655 were renewed everywhere over this unfortunate country; and as if the sword and the burning pile had not been enough for the martyrdom of the Vaudois, the most cruel punishments were also employed. Some were fastened to their ploughs and buried piecemeal in the earth, which was laid open as if to receive the grain for supply of food. Others were flung down rocks, or torn by horses. The trees on the wayside served as gibbets for other victims, and these new martyrs were subjected to abominable mutilations.

After having thus ravaged the valley of St. Martin, Catinat left a few troops there, and marched upon Pramol, where he was ere long joined by Mélac, who had perpetrated the same atrocities at Le Pomaret. He had even gone farther in barbarity and indecency. Not knowing the paths which he must follow on the mountain, he caused some Vaudois women and girls, whom he had seized, to act for some time as his guides, compelling them by the sword to walk entirely naked at the head of his columns.

The united troops of Mélac and Catinat encamped in the vale of Pramol, at the hamlet of La Rua, situated opposite to that of Poemian. The Vaudois had retired into the latter village to the number of more than 1500. They were joined by their brethren of St. Germain, who had repulsed with so much success the first attack of the enemy; they were therefore still in a condition to resist, and probably might have done it with similar advantage. But their enemies formed a plan to vanquish them by treachery. These inheritors of the primitive church were always vulnerable on this side, for they trusted in the good faith of their enemies.

Catinat caused them to be told that the inhabitants of the valley of Lucerna had laid down their arms, and surrendered to Victor Amadeus, who had pardoned them. He exhorted them to follow this example, that they might enjoy the same benefits. The Vaudois sent two deputies to the French general, to receive from his own mouth the confirmation of this news, and of his promises. In the breast of this warrior soldierly honour did not revolt against the course which he pursued, and he certified the lie, giving his word for its truth. "Lay down your arms," he added, "and all is pardoned." "But, general," said the deputies, "whilst we by no means doubt your word, we dread the excesses of these same soldiers who have just shed so much blood in the valley of St. Martin." Catinat replied with an oath, that all his army should pass through their houses without touching so much as a fowl. Was it possible to suspect, in the hero of so many battles, the low perfidy so familiar to the genius of the Papal system? No: the Vaudois entertained no doubts; and they left one of their deputies with him as an hostage, whilst the others went to get their brethren to lay down their arms, and to re-assemble their dispersed families.

Catinat already triumphed in the success of his artifice. These mountaineers were, in his eyes, only heretics, people devoted to hell and to carnage, the killing of whom, without resistance, spared the blood of his brave and loyal companions in arms, who might have perished in the combat. Such is the genius of Popery; pride and tyranny for itself, disdain and cruelty for others.

On the evening of the same day, Catinat sent a courier to Gabriel of Savoy, the uncle of Victor Amadeus, who had invaded the valley of Lucerna, and was encamped at La Vachère. This courier passed by Poemian, and told the Vaudois that he went to apprise the prince of the proposed peace. Next day he came back, and said that the peace was concluded. The Vaudois, therefore, believed themselves assured of peace for the future. It was their destruction which had been resolved upon.

The French troops entered Poemian. They were received without arms and without distrust. The officer who commanded them[1] renewed to the Vaudois the assurances of his general, caused the

[1] Captain St. Pierre.

heads of families to be brought before him, separated the men from the women, and told the former that he was going to cause them to be conducted to the Duke of Savoy, that they might make their submission to himself.

Having thus deprived these unfortunate families of all their defenders—having none before them but women, children, and aged men—the soldiers of Catinat rushed like savage beasts on that inoffensive multitude, so basely deceived; massacred some, tortured others, stripped them of everything valuable; seized the women and girls, to subject them to the most brutal treatment; satiated upon them the most infamous passions, and subjected them to all the horrors of rape and assassination. There were some of them who resisted with so much courage that their destroyers could not succeed in their vile endeavours till they mutilated them in all their four members, nothing but a bloody torso being thus left for the prey of these demons. Others were only vanquished when they were pinned to the ground by a sword through the chest. There were some who could not be forced, and who were buried alive; others, more fortunate, were killed fleeing into the woods, and brought down like timid deer by the bullets of their persecutors. As for the children, they were carried off and dispersed in Piedmont, either in convents or in various Catholic families. What a Christian education they must have received there! Their fathers, who had been sent to the camp of Victor Amadeus, to make their submission to that monarch, were cast into the prisons of Lucerna, Cavour, and Villefranche, where a number of them died of disease and of sorrow.

But Popery triumphed; treachery had served its cause; a half of the people of the valleys were massacred or captive; carnage had done its work; and what remained of the Israel of the Alps could not subsist long. The Te Deums of St. Bartholomew's Day were again to be heard!

Victor Amadeus had remained encamped on the plain which forms the opening of the valley of Lucerna on the side of La Tour and Rora. It was here that, at a later period, after the marvellous return of the Vaudois to their native land, this very prince, himself vanquished and a fugitive, sought an asylum from these same mountaineers whom he now endeavoured to destroy or to disperse.

His uncle, Gabriel of Savoy, commander-in-chief of the ducal troops, had bent his course towards the heights of Angrogna. His line of operations extended from Briquéras to Saint John. The Vaudois occupied, on the summit of the hills of La Costière, a series of little posts situated in an upper zone, parallel, however, to his front of battle. On the 22d of April, Don Gabriel caused these posts to be attacked upon all points at once. The Vaudois fought all day; and, faithful to the tactics of Janavel, concentrated their forces as they drew up their front of resistance to the higher retreats of the mountain, thus drawing themselves together in a line between points less numerous, and nearer and nearer to each other.

Night having come, bivouac fires were kindled on both sides. This luminous girdle crossed the mountain at about a third of its elevation. Les Serres and Castelluz belonged to the enemy; Rochemanant and the *Gates* of Angrogna were in the hands of the Vaudois. In the Piedmontese camp the preposterous worship of relics was mingled with the gross jokes of the soldiers, and the invocation of the Virgin with indecent tales of the atrocities already perpetrated in the valleys. In the camp of the persecuted evening prayer was offered with fervour and humility, amidst religious quiet, grief, and resignation. It will be recollected that this prayer had been placed on the order of the day for all the Vaudois companies, and that it was set down at the end of their military regulations, which have been preserved to our times. It was as follows:—

"O Lord! our great God, and the Father of mercy, we humble ourselves before thy face, to implore of thee the pardon of all our sins, in the name of Jesus Christ our Saviour, that by his merits thine ire[1] may be appeased against us, who have offended thee so much by our perverse and corrupt life. We render unto thee also our most humble thanksgivings, that it hath pleased thee to preserve us until now from all sorts of dangers and calamities: and we humbly entreat thee to continue to us in future thy holy protection and good safeguard against all our enemies, from whose hand we pray thee also to deliver and preserve us. And seeing that they attack the truth and fight against it, bless thou our arms to maintain and defend it! Be thou thyself our strength and our skill in all our combats, that we may come out of them victorious. And if any of us shall die in this cause, receive him, O Lord, in thy grace, pardoning all his sins, and let his soul find admission into thine eternal paradise! O Lord, hear! O Lord, forgive! for the sake of thy well-beloved Son, Jesus Christ, our Saviour, in whose name we pray unto thee, saying, *Our Father which art in heaven* . . . . . . (to the end of the Lord's Prayer). O Lord, increase our faith, and grant us grace to make with heart and

---

[1] ["*Ton ire.*" Explained by Dr. Muston in a foot note, "*Ta colère.*"]

mouth a sincere confession unto thee, to the end of our lives. *I believe in God* . . . . . . (and so on to the end of the Apostles' Creed.) May the holy peace and blessing of God our Father, the love and grace of our Lord Jesus Christ, the guidance, consolation, and help of the Holy Spirit, be given and multiplied to us, from henceforth and for evermore! So let it be!"

These last words were pronounced in name of all who were present, by the pastor or officer who had presided at this simple service. Such is the prayer, which we have not thought it proper to exclude even from a historic abridgment, and which was offered evening and morning in the camp of the Vaudois.

On the 23d of April, the attack upon them was recommenced. They still fell back towards the higher parts of the mountain, but in good order, and without ceasing to fight throughout the whole day. Towards evening they assembled in a single camp at the foot of the Vachère, and fortified that advantageous position by intrenchments of earth and large stones, promptly raised by their intrepid vigour and hands long accustomed to work.

Next morning, Gabriel of Savoy had information of the surrender of the Vaudois of Pramol, who had trusted their enemies and delivered themselves into their hands, and whose families had been thereafter massacred without resistance. He resolved to employ the same means against his own opponents, and caused them likewise to be told that their brethren of the Val St. Martin having laid down their arms and obtained pardon, he would advise them to follow that example, in order to avoid great calamities; for, if they did not surrender, the French troops, which occupied the valley of St. Martin and the little vale of Pramol, would come upon their rear, and then they would infallibly be destroyed.

The Vaudois of the Val Lucerna, intrenched at the foot of the Vachère, could not believe this news. Janavel, in the advices which he had addressed to them, had given the first prominence to the necessity of all the people of the valleys remaining constantly united; how, then, could one-half of them have treated with the enemy, without having communicated their intention to their brethren? However, they likewise adopted the course of sending commissioners to Gabriel of Savoy, who confirmed this news, and sent them a note, signed with his own hand, in which he said to them, "Do not hesitate to lay down your arms; and be assured that if you cast yourselves upon the clemency of his royal highness, he will pardon you, and that neither your persons nor those of your wives or children shall be touched."

After a promise so express, signed by a royal hand, there could be no hesitation. But that august hand was a Catholic hand, taught to sign the most wicked treacheries without shaking. I would fain, indeed, think that the uncle of the sovereign was sincere in his promises; but he was aware of the perfidy of Catinat; he himself had taken part the day before in faithlessly making the Vaudois of Pramol captives, and yet he could venture to say that pardon would be granted. His bad faith appears evident; and if the judgment of history ought to be severe against all that is degrading to the dignity of human nature, it cannot pronounce too stern a reprobation of actions so base on the part of one so exalted.

Moreover, we may judge of the character of this engagement by the fruits which it so speedily produced. The Vaudois of the Vachère opened their intrenchments to Gabriel of Savoy, and came forth themselves without arms and without distrust before his troops. These mingled with them under the most pacific guise, surrounded them, and then seizing them and binding them like felons, carried them prisoners to Lucerna, where they were cast into the dungeons, already in part filled with their brethren, who had also been betrayed. How forcibly must the advices of Janavel have then presented themselves to their minds! But it was too late. The enemy had possessed themselves, almost without striking a blow, of those formidable valleys, where the Vaudois "*had posts so advantageous*," says a contemporary, "*and intrenchments so strong, that they might have kept their ground in them for ten years.*"[1]

The defenders of this ancient sanctuary of the church were loaded with irons; their children were carried off and scattered through the Catholic districts; their wives and daughters were violated, massacred, or made captives. As for those that still remained, all whom the enemy could seize became a prey devoted to carnage, spoliation, fire, excesses which cannot be told, and outrages which it would be impossible to describe. Joseph David, being wounded, was carried by the soldiers into a neighbouring house, where they burned him alive. The mother of Daniel Fourneron, a woman eighty years of age, was rolled down a precipice because she did not walk quickly enough. Susanna Olviette and Margaret Baline, having endeavoured to defend their honour, lost their lives in the struggle, and yielded only their corpses to the unbridled lust of the soldiery. Mary Romain, who had been betrothed only a few days before, allowed herself to be slaughtered rather than submit to their desire.

Whilst these things were taking place in Angrogna, Victor

[1] Letter written from Pignerol, 26th April, 1686. Archives of Berne, C. II., 2.

Amadeus had continued to advance in the valley of Lucerna. There the Vaudois still occupied two important posts; the one at the hamlet of Les Geymets, and the other at Champ-la-Rama. Thus they covered the entrance to the Pra-du-Tour on the one side, and the road to Le Villar on the other. These two posts, being attacked at once, were firmly held during a whole day. The enemy could not gain an inch of ground, and lost many men, amongst others the commander of the militia of Mondovi. The Vaudois had only six killed, and as many wounded. Towards evening, the assailants, whose ammunition was exhausted, seemed to think of retreating; but in the fear of being pursued, they resolved at all hazards to deceive their adversaries by some illusory promise, and, under the name of a stratagem of war, to make them the victims of some such perfidy as had already proved so successful at the Vachère and at Poemian.

A number of Piedmontese officers, having laid their arms and their hats upon the ground, approached the fortifications which the Vaudois had erected at Champ-la-Rama, waving a white handkerchief on the end of a stick, and saying that they were the bringers of peace. They were allowed to advance. They exhibited a paper, saying that it was a letter of Victor Amadeus, who had granted pardon to all his subjects, and that he ordained his troops to retire, and requested the Vaudois to do the same. The podestat of Lucerna, whose name was Prat, a magistrate well known to the Vaudois, accompanied these officers, and attested the truth of their declaration, assuring the poor mountaineers that they would have life and liberty, on condition of their immediately ceasing from hostilities.

The Vaudois might, by a vigorous sortie, have routed these exhausted troops, or at least have seized their officers. But trusting in their word, they fired no more, allowing the enemy to draw back in peace, and themselves going to seek some repose. Scarcely had they retired, when the Catholic soldiers retraced their steps with new reinforcements, and took possession of the abandoned post. Those who still defended themselves at the hamlet of Les Geymets, less elevated than the Champ-la-Rama, finding their position commanded by the enemy, abandoned it likewise, and retired to Le Villar.

It might seem that so many reiterated acts of perfidy must have exhausted the amount of Catholic dishonesty, and of the too easy confidence of the Vaudois; but such was not the case. The troops of the enemy, after having pursued the mountaineers, who fell back on the *combe* of Le Villar, halted at the hamlet of Les Bonnets, and remained there for two days without venturing to give battle. But during this time they sent to the Vaudois several successive emissaries, to assure them, in the name of all that was sacred, that those who would surrender would obtain pardon, whilst the severest chastisements would await those who stood out. Many surrendered themselves, and were cast into prison. Thus the number of the Vaudois diminished daily. They might still be about 500 or 600 men. This troop would have sufficed Janavel to perform prodigies; but that illustrious outlaw, having been banished for thirty years from his native country, could no longer serve it except by his advice, and his advice had not been followed. The intrepid captain had lost nothing of his courage; but the infirmities of age had deprived him of his strength, without bending his noble spirit.

After some time, the Vaudois of Le Villar, finding themselves decimated by perfidy or by treachery, and weakened by the intrigues of an enemy destitute alike of honesty and of courage, abandoned also the post which they occupied, and fell back upon Bobi, the last important village of the valley.

Thus passed the month of April. On the 4th of May, Gabriel of Savoy marched all his troops against them. This attack was repulsed. The Vaudois, intrenched on the heights of Subiasc, killed some of his officers and many of his soldiers.

On the 12th of May, the French army, having united itself with that of Victor Amadeus, renewed the attack, which was again repulsed by the Vaudois with great success. But next day the Marquis de Parelles, who had ascended the valley of St. Martin with a detachment of Catinat's troops, passed over the Col Julian, and attacked the gallant defenders of Bobi in the rear. Finding themselves thus placed between two fires, the Vaudois abandoned a position which it was impossible to maintain, and dispersed themselves on the lateral mountains of La Sarcena and Garin.

New emissaries were presently sent after them, to promise them liberty if they would surrender themselves to their sovereign. A number did surrender themselves, and, like the former, were cast into prison. The mind revolts at the thought of a continued rascality always successful and always disastrous! The triumph of what is shameful is a dishonour to human nature.

However, the bloodiest horrors did not cease to be enacted everywhere over this desolated land. Two sisters, Anne and Madeleine Vittoria, were burned alive in the straw of the shed where they had been ravished. Daniel Pellenc was flayed alive, and as the soldiers could not succeed in making the skin of his body pass up

Drawn by T.C. Dibdin from a sketch by Dr. Muston.   Engraved by S. Bradshaw.

THE TOWN OF BOBI AND MOUNT BARIOUND.
FROM THE WOOD OF BELSILLE

BLACKIE & SON, GLASGOW. EDINBURGH & LONDON.

over his shoulders, they laid him on the ground, threw a large stone on his mangled but still breathing body, and left him to expire in that condition. Twenty-two persons were flung into the ravines of Le Cruel, from the heights of Bariound and Garneyreugna. A number of them, suspended on ledges of the rocks, with their bones broken and their flesh torn, still remained alive for some days. A young mother, who fled carrying her child in her arms, and who carried another also within her, was overtaken by the murderers. They took her babe from her, seized it by the feet, and dashed its head against the rocks; then falling, sword in hand, upon the fainting mother, they committed two murders more by a single stroke. Another woman was placed naked, with her infant in her arms, amongst the soldiers, and they amused themselves by standing at a distance and throwing their daggers, some at the mother and some at the child. The name of this ill-fated woman was Margaret Salvajot. Another woman had retired into a cavern with her child and a she-goat. The goat, browsing on the herbage amongst the brushwood, nourished the poor mother with its milk, and she gave suck to her child. The soldiers came upon them by surprise. The infant was flung into a hole, as the redundant progeny of beasts are flung upon the dunghill when we want to be quit of them. The mother was conducted into the presence of the Marquis of Bénil, colonel of the regiment of Savoy. They wished to learn from her the hiding-place of her Protestant brethren who had disappeared. She knew nothing of the matter. To make her speak, they crushed her fingers between bars of iron; but it was in vain. Then these defenders, heroes, and pillars of the Catholic faith, broke her legs, and having tied her head to her feet, they rolled her down into the same chasm into which they had cast her child.

"Why relate such atrocities?" more than one voice will exclaim with emotion. To inspire a horror of the odious principles which have produced them. Do you suppose that an account of the blood which was shed will never be called for? Nay; these vile oppressors of mankind, tyrannizing by the sword, tyrannizing by deceit, tyrannizing by cupidity—these heroes of superstition and intolerance, who would have put an end to Christianity a thousand times over, if it could have been destroyed—these authors of so many wounds still bleeding in the world—must endure history to the last; their works are their condemnation.

The Marquis De Parelles himself was moved with indignation on meeting bands of his soldiers bearing on their hats the hideous trophies of the various mutilations to which they had subjected the unfortunate Vaudois.

Daniel Mondon, one of the elders of the parish of Rora, was the agonized and helpless witness of the murder of his two sons, who were beheaded with the sabre, and then of his daughter-in-law, whose body was ripped open the whole length of the belly. The four little children of this ill-fated woman were also butchered before the eyes of their mother. The old man was reserved, that he might be compelled to bear upon his shoulders the heads of his two sons, and the bloody relics of his slaughtered family. In this manner he was obliged to march from Rora to Lucerna. On his arrival in the latter town, he was hanged on a gallows.

"All the valleys are exterminated, the people killed, hanged, or massacred," wrote a French officer, announcing to foreign parts the result of this fratricidal contest, by a letter of date the 26th of May, 1686. On the same day Victor Amadeus issued a decree, by which all the Vaudois, without exception, were declared guilty of the crime of high treason,[1] because they had not laid down their arms on the first summons, and all their property was confiscated, to the increase of the royal domains.[2] The few Vaudois who escaped carnage and the prisons, wandered miserably on the mountains. Those who still remained in their lonely dwellings, received orders not to leave them.[3]

Thus the destruction of these Vaudois churches, so long exposed to trial, appeared now inevitable; their overthrow seemed to be complete. A number of their sons still maintained the struggle even in this extremity, some by their courage, others by their martyrdom. The pastor of Pral, named Leydet, had retired to a cavern to escape the murderers. After the lapse of two days, he supposed that the troops had retired, and rendered thanks to God, by singing in a low voice a song of deliverance. But these pious accents, issuing through the clefts of the rock, betrayed his retreat. The soldiers heard him, rushed into the cavern, seized the pastor, and conducted him to Lucerna, where he was brought before Victor Amadeus as a prisoner of importance. He was promised his liberty and a pension of 2000 livres, if he would consent to change his religion. He refused. He was then imprisoned in a tower, his legs being made fast betwixt two beams united by a screw. Here he remained for a long time, receiving only bread and water, and unable to lie down, because of the stocks in which his legs were painfully held. In

---

[1] [Fr. *Lèse-majesté.*] What *majesty* is there in an unjust power?

[2] Turin, *Archives of the Court of Accounts*. *Ordini*, 1685–1686, No. 103, fol. 33, and 104, fol. 6. It is to be found also in the *Archives of the Court*, portfolio of the Edicts of His Royal Highness from 1686 to 1698.

[3] On the 28th of April. (Dubois, II. 243.)

this afflictive situation he had to sustain long theological discussions every day, with the priests and monks who were sent to convert him.

Like some kind of vermin always engendered around torture, this brood of death is everywhere to be found, from the dungeons of the Spanish Inquisition, to those of the Holy Office of Rome and of Turin. Their *holy office* is well enough known; but what had it ever to do with the gospel?

At last, not being able to convince the prisoner, the priests told him that he must presently die. "The will of God be done!" he tranquilly replied. "You may save your life by becoming a Catholic," said they. "That would not be the will of God," was his answer. New discussions were then again commenced, and as a last argument, they were concluded once more by a new announcement of death. But nothing shook the constancy of the prisoner. Thereupon he was condemned to death, and as a pretext for his condemnation, the sentence bore that he had been taken with arms in his hands.

The day before his execution, and that day itself, the monks assailed him again, to make him abjure; they hoped that the emotion always inseparable from these last moments would have broken his resolution, or discomposed his mind. But he remained calm, serene, firm in his faith, and resigned. As he left the prison to go to execution, he said to the executioners, "This is for me a double deliverance, in which both my soul and my body ought to rejoice." Then having mounted the scaffold, he uttered, without ostentation, only these words, "O my God! I commit my soul into thy hands."

CHAPTER XVI.

TERMINATION OF THE CONTEST; MEMOIRS OF A PRISONER; CAPTIVITY AND DISPERSION OF THE VAUDOIS IN VARIOUS TOWNS.[1]

(A.D. 1686—MAY TO SEPTEMBER.)

The last body of defenders of the valleys—Further treachery practised against them—The valleys, after great massacres and devastations, seem entirely reduced—The invaders depart—New bands of Vaudois appear in arms in the valleys of Lucerna and St. Martin—It is at last stipulated that all the surviving Vaudois shall be permitted to go into exile—Journal of a prisoner—Sufferings of the prisoners.

OF the whole number of their courageous but too credulous defenders, there now remained in the Vaudois valleys only a little troop of combatants, who still continued the contest on the mountain of Vandalin. The last hope of their prostrated country, the last ray of expiring liberty depended on their noble efforts. But a spirit of destruction seemed to have breathed over all these countries. A fatal vertigo threw men of the most undaunted courage into the gross snare of those deceitful promises of which such base use had already been made.

The governor of the province, M. De La Roche, after having caused some unsuccessful attacks to be made upon this small but heroic band, had recourse to treachery, in order to take from their valiant hands that glorious banner of liberty which they still made to float over the valleys. He wrote to them to promise, as a magistrate, as a citizen, and as a man of honour, pardon for their families, and their own liberty, if, according to the terms of the edict of the 28th of May, they would consent to retire to their respective dwellings. The Vaudois had too much forgotten that to the simplicity of the dove they ought to have joined the prudence of the serpent. They believed these perfidious promises, and retired to their dwellings; whereupon the faithful governor immediately took possession of the intrenched post which they had just abandoned, tore from their hands the note which he had written to them, and flung them into the prisons already filled with their brethren.

"In the valley of St. Martin," says Brez,[2] "a few men, having

---

[1] AUTHORITIES.—The same as in Chapter XIV. To which add the introductory part and the preface of the *Glorious Return of the Vaudois*, by HENRY ARNAUD.

[2] The published portion of the *History of the Vaudois*, by Brez (although it does not bear his name), comes down only to the events of 1655. The remainder of this

still rallied, had resolved to defend their natal soil to the last extremity. The persecutors could not be indifferent to these feeble relics, whom it was less easy to subdue by force than by stratagem; and, as there were amongst the prisoners many Vaudois who enjoyed the confidence of their compatriots, the Marquis De Parelles caused them to march at the head of his army, that he might make some progress against their brethren, and then forced them, with a pistol at their breast, to write a number of notes, exhorting their compatriots to lay down their arms, and cast themselves upon the clemency of the sovereign, who had offered pardon, they said, to all who chose to profit by it. On seeing these well-known persons, the Vaudois, wasted by fatigue, hunger, and hardships, almost all surrendered; and, instead of obtaining their pardon, were added to the number of the captives."

Thus, after more than 1000 persons had been massacred, more than 6000 prisoners taken by fraud, and 2000 Protestant children dispersed in all directions—after all the Vaudois who still remained in the valleys had been declared guilty of high treason, and an universal confiscation of their property had been pronounced—it seemed as if there was nothing more to be done with this unfortunate country but to abandon to its own silence the tomb of the Vaudois churches, and to leave solitude and desolation to spread over them for ever.

But, on the contrary—strange as it may seem—it was just then that the Vaudois took fresh courage, and found a new source of energy in the excess of their despair. The spirit of might blows where it will: they had neither places of worship, nor homes, nor country; no vision of clemency could deceive them again; they could have no hope of safety, but in themselves and in God; and now it was that they appeared again, animated with a confidence more invincible than before.

The French troops had retired. The militia of Mondovi had returned to their homes. Thus the principal adversaries of the Vaudois had disappeared—the former being so reckoned on account of their number, the latter on account of their ferocity; for, in 1681, the rebels of Mondovi had been vanquished by the Vaudois militia, and the spirit of revenge was combined in them with the

work is unpublished. My venerable friend, M. Appia, a native of the Vaudois valleys, and pastor at Frankfort-on-the-Maine, had the goodness to procure me a copy. It is from the eighth chapter of this second part of the work of Brez that the sentences are extracted which I here quote, not as an authority, but as a narration; for, in a scientific point of view, this work contains no new fact and no profound research. A few bombastic or incorrect expressions have been modified, even in this quotation.

excitements of fanaticism and of war, to augment, in 1686, the cruelty of the reprisals which they took upon us. The Piedmontese army began also to abandon this impoverished, bloodstained, and depopulated land. Wealthy Savoyards already came to examine the properties which they proposed to purchase in these devastated regions. The Duke of Savoy wished to repeople them, as if to prevent even a desert from preserving there the recollection of a people who had disappeared.

Then, from the depths of the woods, from the recesses of the ravines, from the clefts of the rocks, from the summits of steep peaks, came forth emaciated men, half-naked patriots, outlaws battered by the storm, inured to danger, familiar with fatigue and hunger, who, to escape persecution, had maintained their lives for whole months on the herbs of the mountains and the flesh of the chamois, or even on the savage brood of wolves that wandered about to devour the corpses left unburied. By degrees these rude mountaineers drew together, united, organized themselves, and, having taken an account of their numbers in the valley of Lucerna, on the umbrageous heights of Le Becès, they found themselves in all forty-two men, with a few women and a few children. An almost equal number made their appearance from the valley of St. Martin.

What were their names? Who was their leader? What acts of extraordinary heroism and valour did they thereafter perform to set free, unaided, their oppressed country, to release from prison their compatriots who had been betrayed, to regain all their confiscated properties, and to obtain, for themselves and their people, a glorious retreat with arms and baggage to a foreign country? All this is unknown. No one has written the annals of these, the forlorn hope, but victorious, of the Vaudois mountains. Their expeditions must be judged of by their results. Ah! what might these have been if all the force of such a people had been found, from the first, well united and well directed—if Javanel had been listened to,—if he had been there!

But his spirit, at least, appears to have animated these last defenders of the valleys. Urged on by the hand of God, they fell like a thunderbolt on the persecutors, who supposed them destroyed—defeated in succession the garrisons of Le Villar, La Tour, Lucerna, and St. Segont—intercepted convoys proceeding to revictual Pignerol, and thus refitted their own equipment, and provided themselves with ammunition and provisions. Then retiring again to those unconquered mountains, of which they alone knew the paths, they multiplied their number by their activity, their strength by their valour, their power by the fear which they inspired, and their chances of safety by the repeated losses which they made their enemies to experience. Unexpected in attack, and not to be overtaken in flight, they fell suddenly upon some neglected post, or on soldiers sleeping in their quarters, gave all to fire and sword, and retired as quickly as they came. At other times, in the middle of the night, they surprised some one of the villages of the plain, setting it on fire at both ends, and threatening to burn it entirely if it refused to pay a heavy contribution.

The Marquis De Parelles put himself in motion again on the side of Rocheplate and the Vachère; Gabriel of Savoy ascended again towards Lucerna and Rora; for it was never by the bottom of the valleys, but by the projecting lateral ridges of the interjacent mountains, that these bold freebooters made their incursions. Like pirates of the Alps, treated as enemies by all their neighbours, these desperate mountaineers caused a terror which increased with their victories. The troops which marched against them were twice repulsed. The Marquis De Parelles occupied the heights of St. Germain and Angrogna, which separate the valley of Lucerna from that of St. Martin, in order to prevent the junction of the two small bodies of flying troops which occupied these valleys.

Offers were made to both of safe-conducts, that they might be enabled to retire freely to a foreign country; but they insisted that the same liberty should be granted to all their compatriots who were in prison. There seemed to be a disposition to enter into negotiations with them upon this basis; but they would not capitulate unless hostages were given them. The negotiation went on favourably for themselves; but reservations were made regarding the prisoners. They broke it off sharply, saying that they would all die in the valleys, which they would not leave unless accompanied by their compatriots. At last the retreat of all the surviving Vaudois was granted. The mountaineers stipulated that an officer of the royal guard should accompany each division of the exiles in the capacity of an hostage. They demanded, moreover, and with success, that their journey to the frontiers of the dominions of Savoy should be made at the expense of Victor Amadeus.

They were to set out in two brigades, after which all the other prisoners were to depart in succession in the same manner. Each of them was free to dispose as he pleased of his property. But alas! all had been the prey of pillage or of fire; and from those frightful prisons into which their brethren had been crowded, how many of them never came out! A greater number died at that time within a few days, through the long sufferings of captivity, than had fallen in battle, during three centuries, in all the persecutions.[1] Courage is always attended with less danger than weakness.

A journal, written in Italian by one of these afflicted people, enables us to acquaint the reader with a part of their sufferings. "On the 23d of April," says he,[2] "commenced the desolation of our valleys. On the 26th I retired to the mountains of Rora, for nowhere else could one sleep, and all appeared so ravaged that nothing could be found to eat. Ere long I knew not what way to turn; but I thought that God would not forsake me if I remained faithful to him;[3] and accordingly he sent a man to me on whom I could depend.[4] He resided at Lucernette, and said to me, that if I would go with him I should have nothing to fear. We descended the mountain, and as night approached, we having arrived at the hamlet of Les Bonnets, where my house was, he asked me if there was any wine in it, that we might refresh ourselves. I showed him some of an inferior quality, but told him that I had also some of another quality, which was the best which was produced in the Giovanèra of St. John."[5] On their arrival at Lucernette, Salvajot

---

[1] "There died," says Arnaud, "as many as *eleven thousand*." (*Return*, first edition, fol. 25). We read also in a letter written from Geneva to the Minister of Foreign Affairs at Turin (the Marquis of St. Thomas), "*The Vaudois are arrived in Switzerland to the number of* 2600, *a miserable remnant of the* 15,000 *who existed a year ago*." Dated 19th March, 1687. *Archives of Berne*, compartment C. (Communicated by M. Monastier.)

[2] The following is the title of this manuscript:—"*Memorie di me Bartolomeo Salvajot, nelli anni* 1686, 1687, *e* 1688." The author was one of those Vaudois of whom ERMAN and RECLAM speak (t. vi.), who went to Brandenburg in 1688 and returned in 1690; for in these *Memoirs* we find his itinerary as far as Stendal, and we meet with him again present at the Synod of La Tour, as the lay deputy of Rora, on the 15th of September, 1693.

His manuscript, which has long remained unnoticed, begins with the 23d of April, 1686, and ends with the month of August, 1688. It contains 64 pages. M. Torn, a tutor belonging to the Vaudois valleys, was so kind as to transmit me a copy. Salvajot was an old captain of the Vaudois troops; he was born at Les Bonnets, resided at Rora, and married a woman from La Baudeina, near Bobi, in 1678.

[3] The following are the words of the manuscript:— ... "*Di modo che non sapeva is che divenire; e diceva, con il profeta, che megli mi sarebbe la morte che la vita. Ma Iddio, per la sua grande misericordia, non lascia cadere un solo capello della nostra testa, senza la sua volontà: porchè se li siano veramente fidele, mi salvera miracolosamente.*"

[4] And this man—this friend—was a Catholic. His name was Martina. It is refreshing to see, amidst so many crimes committed in name of religion, one poor man remaining faithful to sacred humanity. The Protestant confided in the Catholic, as at a former time the Catholics had confided in the Protestants, committing their daughters to their charge. The people are always better than their directors.

[5] The reader will pardon the quotation of these particulars. They show life as

gave up his arms to his friend, who hid them, and who then made the fugitive lie down in a loft, that the neighbours might not remark his presence; for it was forbidden, under very severe penalties, to give asylum to any Vaudois. He remained in this garret three days and three nights, after which he asked Martina to go and seek the seigneur of Rora, whose vassal he was, and who dwelt at Campillon, to entreat him to give him some employment.

"I wrote a note to him with my own hand," says he; "but when he saw it he commenced swearing, and tore it, saying that he could do nothing for me. I knew not what to do, and hesitated about returning to the mountains, when Martina went, without saying anything to me, to Lucerna, to speak to the prefect of La Tour, who immediately went to his royal highness, to obtain my pardon. I spent all that day in great uneasiness. My friend did not arrive till 10 o'clock in the evening, and greatly rejoiced my heart, by telling me that I might return home without danger of my life. I gave thanks to God, and next day, the 4th of May, I went to Lucerna in company with the priest of Lucernette and with Martina. They escorted me as far as the convent of Le Pin, where they bade me farewell with much affection (*grande carezze*), thinking that I would change my religion. But I told the monks that, for the present, my mind was occupied with very different matters—that my wife and my little daughter were still in the mountains, and that I entreated them to aid me in getting them out, lest the soldiers should kill them. They immediately went to speak to the President Palavicino, who kindly (*della sua grazzia*) went to his royal highness, and caused me to be informed that as many of our people as chose to surrender themselves to the prince, might have opportunity of doing so."

Salvajot was still ignorant of the fate of those who had already surrendered themselves; for the defenders of Poemian, betrayed by Catinat, were already in prison. He himself was ere long imprisoned also, in the cellars of that very convent, as soon as the impossibility had been discovered of getting him to apostatize. He thus continues his narrative:—

"I therefore sent two children to bring my wife; for I did not choose to write a note, which might make our people think that I had forsaken them. These children were accompanied as far as Le Villar by their own fathers, who carried to the Count De Massel the note of Palavicino, requiring that they should be allowed

---

it is, with its vulgar wants and cares (without which, however, there is no subsisting); and the abstract character of historic events cannot always supply their place. "*E poi*," says Salvajot, "*tiremo fuori un di quei bottali e bevemo bene.*"

to pass and to return with my family. Thereafter, these children went on alone to seek my wife, as far as *La Baudeina*, where they found her making bread. Before descending, she wished to go to seek her daughter, who was in the forest; but the enemy came up, and they were all obliged to conceal themselves for ten days.[1] . . . . At last my wife arrived at Lucerna with our child; they urged her to become a Catholic, but she said that she could do nothing without speaking with her husband. The father president[2] conducted her to my prison, and told me to make her believe that I had already become a Catholic;[3] but that was what I could not. She was going to enter the prison with my daughter, whom she held by the hand, but the father said to them, 'Take care, poor women, for if you go in there you will never come out.' But I was so glad to see them again, and they were so happy to be near me, that we could not make up our minds to part. They came in, and passed that night by my side amongst the other prisoners. They slept upon the ground, without straw, or covering, or supper; for happy was he who could get a stone to lay his head upon—the ministers as well as the rest.[4] Every one snatched for himself as much food as he was able, and some who had been friends became enemies." Such a cruel demon is hunger! "Next day my wife wished to go out, to go to seek something at Lucerna, at the house of our friend Martina; but it was necessary to apply to the major, and to pay two *crosasi* to the captain of the guards, in order to get out. I then directed my wife to a place where I had dropped a large copper vessel into the torrent of Laigha, and told her to carry it to Martina's house; for it had cost me an Italian *doppia*,[5] and it was almost new. She was also to put into his hands a sum of 100 francs, which I had in crowns and small money; as well as twenty pounds of salt and eighteen pounds of bacon, which still remained

---

[1] *Si riscrarono in* Barma d'Hant, *e così scamparono la loro vita. Ma molti altri, che il nemico ricontrava, gli amazzavano, e gli impicavano agli alberi; violovano le donne; saccheggiarono tutto, e brucciavano in molti luoghi, talmente che* . . . . *da tutte le parte, non si sentiva altro che grida, spavento* . . . . *che faceva orrore!* I do not quote these words to increase the horror of the scenes which I have described, but to show that they have not been exaggerated; and if I had chosen to multiply frightful particulars, the documents were not exhausted.

[2] The *superior* of the *mission* established at the convent of Le Pin.

[3] Which proves that they had affirmed to his wife that he had become a Catholic. What can we think of a system which pretends to conduct to the truth, and which employs lying as an instrument?

[4] *E beato era colui che poteva aver una pietra sotto il capo; gli ministri, come gli altri.*

[5] The *doppia* or double ducal livre was worth, before 1755, 41 francs 7 cents; after that time, in accordance with an edict on the subject, the *doppia* was worth only 30 francs 2 cents.

to us. Martina promised to her that he would take good care of all these things, and restore them to me when I came to reclaim them."

These details may seem too minute; but the ordinary cares of life can never cease to force themselves upon attention, even amidst the gravest events. They are not without their value, moreover, as making known the spirit of order, economy, and equity which animated our poor mountaineers. Many other details of the same kind are to be found in the memoir from which these are copied.

"During the first days of my captivity I saw 400 persons arrive from Pral—women, children, and aged men—and all in a state so deplorable and wretched, that the prisoners themselves were afflicted to behold it. These poor people had brought with them a few asses and mules; but the soldiers caught hold of the beasts, and flung down the poor women and children with such violence, that it was really pitiful to see it. Two of them, being pregnant, gave birth to children on the spot, and they took them to another dungeon.

"One day the President Palavicino called me into the garden of the convent, and asked me if I knew the road by the Col Julian and Barma d'Hant; but I told him that I had never been in these quarters. Then the Signor Glaudi Brianza, taking me apart, said to me, 'Now, Salvajot, you must manage so that the rest of the people of the valleys surrender themselves, and thereupon you shall be set at liberty.' 'Ah, Sir!' said I, 'I positively can do nothing of the kind.' 'Take heed,' said he; 'if you are obstinate, you will find cause to repent of it.'

"Two days after, the president came to ask me if I would like to see our ministers. 'Very much,' said I. 'Well!' said he, 'come with me.'—He took me from the convent of the missionaries; we passed before the marquis's palace, where I saw the Duke of Savoy at a window, and presently we arrived at the prison of the ministers. On entering, I saluted them; and seeing their miserable condition, I asked if they had nothing to sleep on, for there was nothing but the paved floor. They replied that they had not. Then the major of Lucerna, who had come in, said to me jeeringly, 'Well, Mr. Captain Salvajot, what think you of this? But we are not at the end, and you shall see, you shall see how we shall do with all these!' He even spoke of hanging me if I would not abjure, and vomited out[1] this sort of stuff for a good while. I wished to return with him, but he told me to remain there till evening, and I was left there for two weeks. Every day new

[1] *Fece grandissima goula.*

bands of prisoners were brought in. Sometimes entire families were brought; but the soldiers tore the little children with such violence from the arms of their mothers, that numbers of these feeble creatures were strangled in the act, and remained dead in their hands. There is no humanity in these folks!" observes Salvajot, with laconic simplicity. "We remained so long without straw," he adds, "that the vermin covered the walls; and no one could go out of the apartment, because a watch was at the door. Nor could we get water to wash with, or even to drink; and we had likewise very little to eat. At last we were conveyed to a new dungeon, under the vaults of a house which anciently belonged to Signor Bastero. But there we were still worse! Fortunately we were not allowed to remain there for more than two or three days.

"One evening the Chevalier Morosa came to see us, and said to the ministers, 'It is you that have caused this rebellion! you would have done better to have obeyed.' 'You know,' they replied, 'that we have done all in our power to prevent it; for it was our desire that our people should take advantage of the orders of his highness, and leave the country; but we could never make them listen to reason.' 'You say that to excuse yourselves,' rejoined he; 'but I know well what took place in your meetings.' However, he did not insist upon this, and as he went away, he said to them, 'Good evening, gentlemen;' and the ministers replied, 'Good evening to your lordship.'

"It was on the 16th of May that the order arrived for our removal. I took my daughter by the hand; my wife went to deposit with various persons the things which we could not carry with us.[1] We were about 160 persons. The men were bound together two and two; there were twenty-seven couples, bound also to one another by a long cord. As we went out of Lucerna, there were a great number of people assembled, and they addressed to us many bad words—'Satanical heretics, your end will soon be seen,' &c. And when we took the road to Turin, they cried, 'Take another look of your mountains, for you will never see them more!' There were some amongst us who wept. Our chained line was flanked by soldiers on the right and left, and in this way we went as far as Briquéras. There we paused for a little under the roof of the market-place, and those who had money purchased some bread. Then we resumed our journey, and that night we slept at Osasco. Those who had their hands tied, and who were besides fastened to one another, were much incommoded, for when it was necessary to

[1] Here I suppress some unnecessary particulars.

cross streams on narrow planks, if one of them made a false step, they were all in danger of falling; and when they were thirsty, they could not drink unless some one gave them water.

"At an early hour next day we arrived in Turin. At the entry of the town we halted, to wait for the carts, which were still behind, laden with the sick, and with women and children. Scarcely had we entered Turin when we found it necessary to keep a sharp watch, lest our children should be taken from us. They had already seized my little daughter, and were bearing her off in haste, when the wife of Bartholomew Ruetto, perceiving it, ran after the ravisher, and brought her back to me. But the crowd was so dense, and the dust so thick, that it was scarcely possible to see. We reached the citadel about ten o'clock in the evening. The prisoners were called over, and the ministers sent into a place by themselves; then those who were bound together were thrust into a chamber so narrow that they could not move about in it, and were choked with the heat. I remained with those of Rora.[1] They put us in a tower where there were mattresses, and we were much better treated than at Lucerna. From time to time we received some alms; soup and linen were given us, and a little wine, which did much good to all, but especially to the sick and those who had no money. There were also persons belonging to the city who showed us great kindness.[2] At intervals we were allowed to go out and walk on the bastions. But this did not take place till after the return of the Royal Guards;[3] for, until then, the citadel was intrusted to the keeping of the citizens of Turin, and we were not so well treated by them as by the soldiers. With the latter we could at least go to seek water to wash our linen, and enjoy some degree of liberty. This state of things continued to the 26th of July, when there arrived an order from his royal highness for our removal to Verceil, for it was necessary that we should make room for others.

"Signor Blaygna, who kept watch over us when the Count Santus was compelled to be absent, appointed Bastie and me to watch over the rest.[4]

"I entreated him to allow me a little private apartment for my

[1] Here again I suppress details. Salvajot gives the names of all his fellow-prisoners, fifteen in number. The prisoners detained in Turin at this time amounted to 222. But there were prisoners also in many other towns; and the multiplied sufferings to which they were subjected, are attested by the enormous mortality among them. Seven-tenths of the Vaudois died in prison.

[2] . . . . *E vi erano ancora molte persone che facevano carità grande.* I dwell with pleasure upon these particulars, omitting no fact which can soften the picture of the cruelties which I am compelled to relate.

[3] A regiment which had been sent against the valleys.

[4] *Il signor Bastia ne aveva 60 da tener conta, ed io 43.*

wife, who was on the point of her confinement. 'Do you not know,' said he, 'that you are to leave this place to-morrow?' And accordingly, next morning, all who were in the tower were brought out of it, except the ministers.[1] Many were sick, and groaned with pain, but it was necessary to have patience, since such was the command of his highness.[2] Scarcely were we out of doors, when M. Blaygna said to me, 'Salvajot, come hither.' And taking me aside, he added, 'Take your wife and your little girl, and go back.' We did so, and he sent back also M. Paul Gonin and his son.[3]

"Then those were placed together who would not change their religion, and those who had abjured. The latter were treated a little better; they were conducted to mass, and the priests came every day to instruct them in their new doctrines. At first they received much more alms than we; but afterwards, whatever was given us was equally divided amongst all. Those who had abjured were offended at this, and alleged that we were the cause of their being still detained in prison, because we would not abjure.

"Eight days after my wife gave birth to a daughter, and the Count Santus came and said to me, 'She must be baptized.' I was very much astonished at this, because I supposed that he had not yet known of her birth. 'The child is healthy,' said I, 'and can be baptized after a while.' 'Any way,' replied he, 'this must be done without loss of time. Here are M. De Rocheneuve and the Baroness of Palavicino, who will act as her godfather and godmother, and who will make your fortune.' Then I durst not say anything more, and they carried the newly-born child into the chapel of the fort, whither I followed in the train with Mademoiselle Jahier of Rocheplate, who had almost fallen down in a swoon when she saw all the ceremonies which they performed.[4] They gave my child the names of Louisa Caroline, which were those of the godfather

---

[1] They were nine in number, each with his family. Four other families were joined to theirs, namely, those of Messrs. Moudon, Malanot, Goante, and Gauthier.

[2] *E vi era gran pianto e lamento: ma bisognò aver pazzienza, perchè cosi era l'ordine di S.A.R.*

[3] The rest set out, and were sent to . . . . (the name is illegible in the manuscript), where they *all* died, with the exception of *one only*, named Daniel Rivoire.

[4] I would not have copied these details, nor many others, if I had had to extract them from a variety of documents placed at the disposal of the historian, to draw from them, on his own responsibility and at his own discretion, the equally assorted materials of a portion of his work; but as we have here to do with an original work, I have thought it right to preserve, as much as possible, its traits and characteristics, even when these were not of general interest, because the particular character of this narrative brings out in strong relief the general features of the whole scene of which it is an episode, and, so to speak, a sample the more valuable the less it is interfered with.

and godmother. Next day there were brought to the mother a shift and two white woollen sheets, which Father Valfrédo, the confessor of his royal highness, had sent, and an offer was made us that we should go to dwell in a separate room; but my wife refused, fearing lest it might be for the purpose of drawing us into apostasy.

"The governor of the fort said to me an hour after, 'Why would you not leave this tower?' I replied that my wife was still too feeble for that. 'You are a genuine rascal!' he exclaimed; 'but you shall pay for it.' And addressing himself to the ministers, he said, 'It is you who are the cause of their not becoming Catholics, but take care of yourselves!'"

The author of the unpublished memoirs which we have quoted, relates further that his wife died after a few days, and that he made use of one of those sheets which had been given them to bury her in. A month after, the infant which she had brought forth in the prison expired likewise. Salvajot was left alone with his little Mary, then aged five years and a half.

Many other pregnant women, who were delivered in the prisons, lost their children, and almost all of them died themselves. "At last," adds the captive, "there was perhaps not one of us who did not suffer from some malady. By the grace of God I was spared amidst these trials; but we were also better treated than the other prisoners. The sick being attended by physicians, the necessary medicines were furnished them, and Father Valfrédo, and also Father Morand, visited them diligently. If there was any of them who had no money, they gave him a little, distributed soups amongst the weakest, and generally furnished us with everything that we required."

It is with satisfaction that I copy these details. In proportion to the indignation caused by bad faith and inhumanity, is the Christian approbation merited by these considerate attentions.

"And what is rather remarkable," adds Salvajot, in speaking of his benefactors, "is that they made no difference between those who had become Catholics and those who remained faithful to their religion. They even seemed to have more regard and respect for the latter."

I would willingly have concluded this chapter with the circumstance just mentioned, in which we see homage paid to the dignity of conviction. But a few words are still necessary to remind the reader that the Vaudois prisoners had not all been transported to Turin, and that they perished in great numbers by the famine, diseases, and distress which they endured in the ditches, prisons, citadels, and dungeons of Queyrasque, Mondovi, Rével, Asti, Carmagnole, Fossan, Villefranche, and Saluces.¹

"At last," says our narrator, "they began to speak of our speedy departure from the country. Already some of our wives had been allowed to pass through the gates of the citadel, and to go into the town to market; then some of the men were also permitted to go out, provided that they were accompanied by two sergeants; afterwards they were allowed to go alone; *and thus*," he observes, *"things made progress towards our liberty;"* that is to say, towards their exile!

CHAPTER XVII.

TOTAL EXPULSION OF THE VAUDOIS, WHO ARE CARRIED AWAY TO VERCEIL, OR CONDUCTED INTO EXILE.²

(SEPTEMBER, 1686, TO SEPTEMBER, 1687.)

Sympathy manifested by Swiss and other Protestants—Vaudois refugees begin to arrive at Geneva—Vaudois children detained as proselytes—Sufferings of Vaudois who, to escape persecution, had apostatized—Sufferings of those who went into exile—Arrival of successive bands of exiles at Geneva—Their kind reception there—Continued detention of most of the Vaudois pastors by the Duke of Savoy.

DURING the course of the events which have just been narrated, a great number of letters had been written to Switzerland, Holland, and Prussia (then Brandenburg), as well as to Wurtemberg, in

---

¹ There were some of them in other prisons also. I have seen a letter written by the pastors Jahier and Malanot, *from the castle of Nice*, on the 1st of May, 1686, and another written by the pastors Giraud, Chauvie, and Jahier (cousin of the former), *from the castle of Miolens* (near Montmellian, in Savoy), on the 20th of June in the same year. Both these letters attest the profound distress of their authors, and have for their object to ask some assistance. The *History of the Persecution of* 1686, published at Rotterdam in 1689, says that the Vaudois prisoners were divided amongst fourteen prisons or fortified residences in Piedmont.

² AUTHORITIES.—The latter part of the authorities given in Chapter XIV.—Also, *Moser*, "*History of the Vaudois, and of their Admission into the Duchy of Wurtemberg, derived from the most authentic documents.*" Zurich, 1798, one vol. small 8vo, pp. 558. (In German.)—*Dieterici*, "*History of the Introduction of the Vaudois into Brandenburg.*" Berlin, 1831, one vol., 8vo, of xx. and 414 pages. (In German.) —Various Memoirs, by Erman and Reclam (vol. vi.), Lamberty, Keller, &c. (all German authors).—"*Extracts from the Registers of the Council of State of Geneva, from February,* 1637, *to December,* 1690, *concerning all which relates to the Vaudois during that period.*" A 4to MS. transmitted by M. Le Fort.—Various extracts from the Ar-

order to awaken an interest in favour of the Vaudois in Protestant powers who might be able to assist them by their intercession, their contributions, or their hospitality. In answer to this appeal the most generous sympathy was expressed. At the commencement of the persecution, the avoyer of Berne had addressed to all the parishes of that canton, and probably also of the other Protestant cantons of Switzerland,[1] a pressing circular, to recommend the celebration of a public fast, accompanied with a general collection on behalf of the Vaudois. This circular commenced in these words: "As in these sad times our brethren of Piedmont, pursued with fire and sword, killed, made prisoners, and banished from their country, are fugitives, and in the most deplorable condition," &c.,[2] . . . from which it appears that at this time a number of the Vaudois had been already *banished from their country*, and were *fugitives*. Even at the beginning of the year, it would seem that the idea of an inevitable and speedy exile had been prevalent in the valleys, since means were already adopted to secure beforehand an asylum for their people in foreign countries.[3]

We have seen how they were decimated by the massacres and the prisons. The heroic resistance of the last defenders of these depopulated mountains was the means of procuring the deliverance of the captives who had surrendered themselves. These combatants did not consent to terminate their warfare, except on condition of their being permitted to retire freely, and along with them their brethren who were prisoners; and they hastened to give intimation of this to the evangelical cantons. Victor Amadeus, without seeming to come to any terms with *his rebellious subjects*, as they were styled, ratified this condition by implication, saying of his prisoners, in a letter to the evangelical cantons of Switzerland, "I hope that the resolution which I shall adopt with regard to them will prove

---

chives of Berne, communicated by M. Monastier.—Extracts from the Archives of Stutgard, Zurich, and Darmstadt.—Also, the journals of the time; Gazettes of France, Leyden, England, &c.—And for what relates to the condition of the Vaudois in Piedmont, the *Archives of State* and *of the Court of Accounts* at Turin.

[1] This would seem to be a fair inference, from the following terms of this circular—"*All the confederate and allied countries are invited,*" &c.

[2] This circular is dated May 14, 1686, and the fast which it recommends was to be held on the 24th of the same month. *Archives of Berne.* Communicated by M. Monastier.

[3] Letters written with this object, in January, 1686, by the Vaudois deputies: 1. To the Elector of Brandenburg, Frederic William the Great. 2. To the Duke of Wurtemberg. 3. To the Elector of the Palatinate. 4. To the Count of Waldeck. Favourable reply of the Elector of Brandenburg, January 31; and a letter by him to the Swiss Cantons, on March 12, to recommend the Vaudois to their care; and on the 3d of June, to request information as to their number, their circumstances, their trades, &c. (Cited by Dieterici.)

agreeable to you."[1] Eight days after the reception of this letter, the Protestant cantons named deputies, who met at Arau,[2] to confer regarding the projected emigation of the Vaudois, and the asylum which could be offered them. Having taken into consideration all the documents bearing on this subject, this meeting nominated two commissioners, to whom it was intrusted to communicate concerning it with the Count Gavon, the Piedmontese representative to the Swiss government. They repaired to Lucerne, where he resided, and their negotiations simply gave an official character to the terms of agreement on which the last combatants of the valleys had laid down their arms.

As to the route by which the Vaudois were to pass out of the dominions of Savoy, Victor Amadeus had at first intended that they should go by way of St. Bernard and the Valais, but as they could not pass through the latter country without the previous consent of the Bishop of Sion, the delegates of the Protestant cantons, who remained beside the Piedmontese ambassador at Lucerne, demanded that the banished Vaudois should be sent into Switzerland by the pass of Mount Cenis. Count Gavon wrote to Turin accordingly, and this route was agreed upon.

Now, likewise, the two detachments of Vaudois began to arrive in Geneva, who had combated with so much courage in the valleys of Lucerna and St. Martin, and whose glorious capitulation had brought about the deliverance of their brethren. They were the first to enjoy the benefit of it, as they had been the last to surrender; and not having passed through the prisons, they had also suffered least, for the diseases of jails are more destructive than the wounds of battle. The magistrates of Geneva had not yet even been made acquainted with their departure from the valleys, when they entered that city with their arms and baggage, on the 25th of November, 1686. They were eighty persons in all, men, women, and children. The council of state decided that their arms should be deposited under the market-sheds, to be restored to them on their departure from the city.[3]

Intelligence was soon received that the Duke of Savoy had set at liberty a party of prisoners.[4] They were those of Turin. Salvajot, known to us by his memoirs, was one of this first party; but the liberation of the prisoners had not yet become general. The

---

[1] Letter to the evangelical cantons, August 17, 1686. (Archives of the Court, Turin.)
[2] In September, 1686. Introduction to the *Return*, by Arnaud.
[3] Registers of the Council of State of Geneva, sitting of November 26, 1686.
[4] Id. Sitting of December 3.

Swiss commissioners again renewed their application, and on the 3d of January, 1687, there appeared at last an edict, by which it was granted to the Vaudois who had not become Catholics, that they should be set at liberty, whatever might have been the ground of their detention, on condition that they should immediately leave the territories of Savoy, without deviating, under pain of death, from the route which should be pointed out to them.

But they did not get away without new sufferings. The Propaganda saw with regret so great a number of heretics escape, even by exile, from their endeavours of conversion. It will be borne in mind how many eminent persons and great families were engaged in their work, with a fervour very unenlightened, no doubt, but perhaps sincere. Their proselytizing had at first proceeded from zeal, afterwards it came to be instigated by ambition. The favour of the court and of the clergy had recompensed the devotion of the first persons who had generously charged themselves with the maintenance and education of a few Vaudois children. It was found to be a way of obtaining such favour; everybody, therefore, wished to have his *convert*. This zeal became quite the fashion in the fashionable world, and a letter written from Turin says, "You will seldom see a coach pass which has not its *barbet*[1] behind it, and sometimes there are two of them, distinguished by the dragoon's cap which they wear."[2] But like everything else which is a mere fashion, this fancy quickly passed away, and these poor children were forgotten, and often sunk into wretchedness, sometimes into degradation. On the departure of their families attempts were still made to seize upon some of them. "The prisoners of my division," writes the conductor of one of them, "have informed me that as they left the citadel of Turin the major took from them a number of children by force."[3]

The Vaudois who had abjured in the valleys, or in the prisons, were also very numerous.[4] It may be imagined what effect an excitement, amounting almost to madness, must have produced upon weak minds, and how very readily such persons might forget themselves amidst the terrors of persecution. Moreover, many of the *converted* had abandoned their church only in the hope of remaining in their native land; but for this they were severely

---

[1] A term of contempt by which the Vaudois were designated, from the name of *Barbas*, which they anciently gave to their pastors.

[2] Letter of the Swiss commissioners to *their lords* of Berne, March 24, 1687. (Archives of Berne, compartment C.)

[3] Letter to M. Panchaud, March 12. (Archives of Berne, C.)

[4] The enumeration of them gives the number 2226. (Archives of State, Turin, various documents.)

punished. To prevent them from joining those who went into Switzerland, they were not allowed to leave the prisons until the departure of the last of their brethren. The fashionable rage for *converts* was then over; the faithful Vaudois had won for themselves respect and admiration, even from their enemies; the apostates continued suspected, even by their new brethren in religion; and, to crown all, instead of being permitted to return to their native Alps, they were sent to the swampy plains of Verceil,[1] and prohibited from leaving them under penalty of ten years of the galleys. Their life there was very miserable, and many of them died of the typhoid fevers which they contracted in these climates, so different from their own.

Their compatriots, who had preferred exile to apostasy, were free to choose an asylum for themselves in a foreign land, whilst, like the descendants of Jacob in Egypt, these unhappy people were detained in slavery in the mephitic rice-grounds of Verceil, to which they had been carried. A penalty of ten years of the galleys was denounced against any inhabitant of any part of the country, out of that province, who should receive into his house one of the catholicized Vaudois. They were not permitted to leave the province, even for the briefest time, without formal leave obtained from the government; being bound, moreover, to produce, on their return, attestations of their regular attendance on the rites of the Church of Rome, signed by the priests of all the parishes in which they had sojourned. May it not well be said, that in place of the dignity of exile they had chosen the degradation of servitude?

Finally, they were prohibited, in the strictest manner, from ever setting foot again in the Vaudois valleys, upon any account whatever,[2] or in virtue of any permission. Any one who should be taken there was to be punished with death; and a reward of 2000 francs[3] was promised to the person who should apprehend any one transgressing this order.

[1] The order for sending them thither arrived on the 3d of March, 1687. A first departure of 650 persons, all from the valley of St. Martin, took place on the 8th. They were embarked on the Po. A second convoy set out on the 15th. According to an enumeration made at Cigliano on the 17th, it consisted of 792 men, 260 women, 501 infirm persons, and 23 children. The small number of children is explained by the consideration of the numbers who had been carried off. The preceding numbers are taken from a paper entitled *Distribuzione delle cattolizati delle valli di Luzerna, nella città e terre della provincia di Vercelli*. (Archives of the Court). Another table, in which the Vaudois people are grouped in families, gives 1973 as the number of families existing in the valleys before 1686, and 424 as the number that became Catholic. (Archives of the Court; *Ristretto degli abitanti delle Valli*, &c.) [2] *Sotto qualsivoglio pretesto imaginabile.*

[3] *E promesso, e sara realmento sborzato* (language of assurance, which was then added to promises, and which shows how little reliance was placed in them, even

It is evident that the unhappy persons thus carried to Verceil, who had hoped for some mitigation of their sufferings by their apostasy, were, on the contrary, less favourably treated than their faithful and proscribed fellow-countrymen. The latter, after having left the dominions of Savoy without degradation, were received with esteem, affection, and universal sympathy in foreign countries, and at last effected a return to their own land, which they quitted no more; whilst the miserable converts to Catholicism, distrusted and despised by all, and having lost their self-respect, and pined in a region remote from their mountains, and, without a prospect of ever returning to them, dragged out the miserable remainder of their days, forgotten, afflicted, and scorned. What important lessons may be learned from their profound degradation!

Before the arrival of this unhappy colony, Verceil had already a number of Vaudois within its walls; but as they were prisoners, and not converts to Catholicism, they were summoned to go out of the country with their faithful brethren, and commenced their journey at the same time with the prisoners of Turin.

This was in the winter of 1686–7. These mountaineers, once so vigorous, were now pallid, feeble, ill-clothed, without shoes, and afflicted with fevers and dysenteries.[1] Death had thinned their ranks during their long confinement;[2] the severity of winter now threatened to put an end to the enfeebled lives which had scarcely escaped from the hardships of the dungeon.[3]

They arrived at Turin; and there still sadder scenes awaited them. On account of the bad weather, of course, orders had been given that no children under twelve years of age should be allowed to go away; but their parents were promised that they would be sent to them on the return of a better season.[4] These poor people, already so often deceived, saw in this only a stratagem intended to deprive them of their children, that they might be kept away from their parents, *made Catholics*, and taken from them for ever. All

---

when most authentic—a characteristic which appears wherever Catholicism has been triumphant); *il premio di doppie cinquanta*, &c. The exact sum is 2053 francs 57 cents [£81, 5s. 8¾d.]

[1] Reports as to the approaching arrival of the first bands of Vaudois outlaws, drawn up by the commissioners who had been sent to meet them. (Registers of the Council of State of Geneva, sittings of the 14th, 15th, 24th, and 31st of January, 1687.)

[2] . . . *Quei di Torino e di Vercelli erano pochi; il motivo è, che erano quasi tutti morti.* (Memoirs of Salvajot.)

[3] A number died on the road. (Letters and Reports of the Commissioners.)

[4] "*Si era ordine di non lasciar andare nessun figliuoli minori di dodeci anni; e dicevano che gli manderebbero nel bel tempo; e che i signori che ne vorebbe ne pigliassen.*" (Memoirs of Salvajot.)

the prisons were filled with cries, tears, and groans;[1] the mothers especially were in the utmost distress; many of them would rather have seen their children dead than given up to their persecutors.[2] On the first attempt to carry off a child in consequence of this order, blood began to flow;[3] the resistance was so energetic that the execution of the order was relinquished.[4] It was one, the execution of which humanity would have approved, if the recollection of former perfidies had not given too good reason for suspecting its design. Not only were the children which these emigrating families retained then left to them, but likewise a number of those who had been previously taken away, learning that their parents were about to leave the country, quitted the great houses in which they had been placed, and fled to join the company of exiles.[5] However, the greater part of these poor children were pursued, seized, and again dragged from the arms of their proscribed families to the palaces which were their prisons. On the way through Savoy, some of those who had actually set out on the journey were still carried off—some by the monks,[6] some by the gentry,[7] and some by the soldiers.[8] It must, however, be added, that the greater part of these children were afterwards restored.[9]

But thus distress of every kind was added to the sufferings of their parents. "These poor people," says Arnaud,[10] "were worn out with infirmity and languor; some were devoured by vermin, and others exhausted by their wounds; covered with sores and rags, they resembled ghosts rather than human beings." Such was the condition in which the first detachments of this expatriated people appeared under the walls of Geneva.

"At last these brave people arrive—these generous confessors of our Lord Jesus Christ!" exclaims an eye-witness of their entry into that city. "We have, as yet, only the first division, composed

---

[1] "*Era un gran pianto in quel giorno, fra i padri e le madre.* (Memoirs of Salvajot.)

[2] *Molte madre erano risolte, se venivano per pigliar i loro fanciuoli, di tirarli un cotello nel ventre.* (Id.)

[3] "*Comminciarono a pigliar una figlia di Davide Gonino di San Giovanni, e la batevano, e gli fece molto sangue. Il padre volendo difenderla lo misse in prigione, per qualche giorni.*" (Id.)

[4] "*Ma, per la volonta di Dio, quel ordine ne durò che quel giorno.*" (Id.)

[5] *Dissipation des Eglises Vaudoises*, p. 29.   [6] At Aiguebelle.

[7] At Suza, at St. Jean de Maurienne, and at Annecy.

[8] At Frangy and at St. Julien.

[9] "All those who were carried off after passing Mount Cenis have been restored, although after much difficulty, except one young girl, whom a gentleman of St. Jean de Maurienne, named M. Galaffre, refused to give up, notwithstanding my applications, and those of the commissioner of his royal highness." (Letter of March 1; Archives of Berne, C. D.)   [10] *Return*, p. 4.

of seventy persons, of every sex and age, who have arrived amidst a cold which has frozen the Rhone to its bottom. They are all that remain of more than a thousand, who were imprisoned in two different places, and they have left twenty of their number on the roads, where they have died of cold, famine, and wretchedness. These their conductors would not permit them to succour. Perhaps it was a father who left his child, a mother who left her daughter, or children who left their parents."[1]

They arrived at different times, and in several divisions, to the number of about 3000 persons.[2] But they were almost all in such a state of destitution, that the greater part of them could not have reached the frontiers of Savoy without frequently receiving assistance. Some, bent down with age and sickness, had nothing with which to clothe themselves; others, pierced with wounds, which had become more serious and malignant in the neglect of the jails, had scarcely linen to dress them; numbers of them had lost the use of their limbs, which had been frostbitten on the way, and could not employ their hands even to receive or to convey to their mouths the food which was offered them; there were some whose stomachs were so disordered that they could not digest the least nourishment without severe pain. Those whose illness was greatest had been flung into carts or set upon beasts; there were some

---

[1] Jurieu, *Lettres pastorales;* Rotterdam, edition of 1688, I. 287.

[2] The following are the data from which this number is calculated:—
There arrived, on the 25th of November, 1686, 80 persons. (On the 10th of December in the same year, the Council of State of Geneva was apprised that there would presently arrive four divisions more, of *one thousand persons* each.) More of the proscribed arrived on the 14th of January, 1687, to the number of 70. On the 24th of the same month, 208; on the 26th, *item*, 340. After this date I find no precise enumeration, till the 31st of August, 1687, when there arrived at Geneva new troops of exiles, to the number of 800 persons, the most of them from the valley of Pragela. All these numbers together amount to 1498. But the bands to which they relate were certainly not the only ones; there must also have been larger and more numerous companies. We learn from the *Memoirs of Salvajot*, that he was one of a company which arrived in Geneva on the 10th of February, 1687, and he adds that they were among the first. From February to the month of August, a number of other caravans of exiles must have come to Geneva after them. A great number of documents prove this. In the Registers of the Council of State of that city, under date the 13th of August (and consequently before the arrival of the greatest division mentioned in this list), we find the following distribution of the Vaudois already expatriated:—In Brandenburg, 700; in Wurtemberg, 700; in the Palatinate, 800; in the cantons of Zurich and Berne, 150; at Geneva (according to a note mentioned in the minutes of the sitting of the 1st of June, 1687), 150: total, 2500; and adding the number of the division of August 31, we have the number 3300. The memoir presented in June, 1687, to the Elector of Brandenburg by the Swiss delegate, David Holzhalb of Zurich, also gives the number of the Vaudois received at that time in the Helvetic Confederation, 1001 men, 891 women, and 764 children under fifteen years; total, 2656 persons.

who staggered from the burden of extreme debility; others were so far gone that they had not strength left to speak; others were so overwhelmed with mental distresses that they would have preferred death. Some breathed their last on the frontier, as if they could not survive the loss of their unnatural country; others died as they arrived at Geneva, between the two gates of the city, finding thus the termination of their woes at the moment when they might have found some solace of them. All these particulars are derived from the relations of the time: there is not one of them which does not depend upon contemporary testimony.

The people of Geneva displayed an admirable devotedness of generosity, and the most delicate and ardent sympathy in relieving these great sufferings. They welcomed the proscribed Vaudois with a sort of enthusiasm. One-half of the population went out to meet them as far as the banks of the Arve, which formed the boundary of their noble country, so small upon the map, but so great in the world. "The Genevese contended with one another," says a contemporary, "as to the reception of the most miserable of these poor Vaudois, which of them should first conduct them to his dwelling. Some there were who bore them in their arms from the frontiers to the city." This eagerness to give them a kind reception was so great, that in order to prevent the roads from being inconveniently crowded, and houses from being over-filled, the council of state of Geneva was under the necessity of passing a decree, by which it was enjoined that each citizen should wait, before receiving any of the newly arrived exiles into his house, the distribution of their billets of lodging.[1]

But what a distress it was for them all when, on seeking for one another in the crowd, the members of the same family could not find one another! The Vaudois who had arrived first, and to whom the generous hospitality of that Christian city had restored some measure of strength, ran in their turn to meet the new divisions, whose arrival was announced, to inquire after relatives and friends whom they missed. "A father sought his son, and a son his father; a husband sought his wife, and a wife her husband."[2] These searches were often followed only by the saddest disappointments. "This produced a spectacle so melancholy and distressful, that all the beholders wept, whilst these poor sufferers, oppressed and overwhelmed with the excess of their woe, had no strength either to weep or to lament."[3]

Janavel was one of the first to go out from Geneva to meet his countrymen. His sad anticipations were realized; his counsels

---

[1] Sitting of 2d February, 1687.　[2] Boyer, p. 281.　[3] *Dissipation*, &c., p. 34.

had failed to prevent this great catastrophe; and he—who having for thirty-two years eaten the bread of exile, would so much the more have sought to save the children of the Vaudois mountains from its bitterness—may sometimes have felt the pleasure of seeing again those from whom it had been so painful to be separated—those families whose recollection he had cherished, and the people whom he had defended—contending against the grief which this new proscription caused to his patriotic heart. But at the distressful spectacle of so many miserable beings, wanderers without a country—as each portion of this great wreck was cast beneath the walls of Geneva, the sad remains of an entire people expatriated—this generous city, as great in charity as Janavel had been in battle, showed itself ready to give new assistance to the exiles.

Moreover, there were still among these exiles courageous bands, who had comparatively escaped, and privileged families, who excited admiration as well as pity. The Vaudois speak of one of their Barbas, ninety years of age, who brought with him a tribe of seventy-two children and grandchildren.[1] These worthy portions of the wreck of the Vaudois Church seemed to revive amongst the people of modern times the imposing images of the patriarchal emigrations, of which the Bible has made the memory familiar to all Protestants.

The exiles arrived in Geneva, singing, with a grave and sad voice, that psalm of fugitive Israel which Theodore Beza had translated into the language of Calvin—

"Faut-il, Grand Dieu, que nous soyons epars!"[2]

and in which, speaking of the enemies of the people of God, the psalmist has introduced particulars which so exactly accord with the excesses committed in the valleys by the persecutors of the *Israel of the Alps*:—

> "They fired have thy sanctuary,
> And have defiled the same,
> By casting down unto the ground
> The place where dwelt thy name.
> Thus said they in their hearts, Let us
> Destroy them out of hand;
> They burnt up all the synagogues
> Of God within the land."

[1] This family formed part of the third band of exiles. There is mention of them in a manuscript of the time, which has been communicated to me by M. Lombard Odier of Geneva. This MS. says that the Vaudois were already *under the leadership of Arnaud, a pastor of their nation.* But these latter words are not sufficient to establish that Arnaud was a Vaudois by birth, especially when opposed to the proofs which exhibit him as a French refugee to the valleys.

[2] The 74th Psalm, from the collection in use in the Reformed Churches. ["O God, why hast thou cast us off?"]

But the miseries of war had been merely the prelude to the longer and more grievous sufferings which the Vaudois had undergone in the prisons. They had entered them in number about 12,000, and there came out only 3500[1] In some of these places of captivity they got only foul water to drink; in others they had nothing to eat but insufficient and bad food. At Queyrasque and Asti they were crowded into the ditches of the town, exposed to all the inclemencies of the seasons; elsewhere, lying on the pavement or on the naked earth; and sometimes so closely packed in a small place, that they had difficulty in moving. The heat of the summer in 1686, say the accounts of the time, engendered such a quantity of lice, that the captives were not able to sleep; there were even great maggots, which bit through the skin;[2] and numbers of these poor people who were sick, were so devoured that their flesh was falling in pieces. As many as seventy-five sick have been numbered in a single chamber, and when they left it in the middle of winter, passing by a sudden transition from their captivity to their journey, without strength, and without clothing,[3] many of them marched only to their death.

At Mondovi, the order to allow the Vaudois to depart was not communicated to them until the day before Christmas, at five o'clock in the evening;[4] and the prisoners were at the same time told, that if they did not profit by it forthwith, they would not have it in their power to go next day. The prisons were immediately empty; all these unfortunate people rushed, notwithstanding the night and the snow, to the middle of the frozen highroads; they went on five leagues without halting; but *one hundred and fifty* of them died on the way. What barbarity on the part of those who had deceived them, and who celebrated, next day, the festival of Christmas without annoyance in their church!

At Fossan they were caused to set out for Mount Cenis in the midst of a violent storm. Eighty-six of these unfortunate outlaws perished in the snows, and many others had their feet or their hands frostbitten.[5]

[1] This number is an approximation, but I think I can give it as exact almost to a few units. It had been said in the sitting of 10th December, 1686, in the council of Geneva, "*There must come first a thousand of them, and then three other bands, each as numerous.*" There was a greater number of bands, but each of them was composed of a smaller number of emigrants.

[2] Probably the larvæ of various insects.

[3] "Most of these poor people of the valleys are very ill-clad or naked." (Registers of the Council of State of Geneva, sitting of 2d January, 1687).

[4] At Lucerna the order was at first posted up in the streets, without being communicated to the prisoners, whom it exclusively concerned.

[5] *Notice of a Great Misfortune which has befallen the Vaudois on Mount Cenis.*

The next division, who passed over Mount Cenis about the end of February,[1] were still able to recognize, lying upon the snow, the corpses of those who had perished in January. But the complaints addressed by the Swiss government to the court of Turin, on the little attention shown to the Vaudois, and the destitution in which they were left, notwithstanding the article of the stipulations by which Victor Amadeus undertook to provide for their wants until they reached the frontiers of Savoy—the indignation which arose on the spectacle of so many woes, and the voice of humanity itself, led the Duke of Savoy to adopt more efficacious measures for the preservation of their lives. He caused fifteen bales of thick black woollen greatcoats to be carried to Novalèze, at the foot of Mount Cenis, intended for the succeeding convoys. That which passed over this mountain a month after the catastrophe which had covered it with mourning, was composed of two bands of prisoners—the one brought from Lucerna, and the other from Turin, but united at St. Ambroise, and amounting to 202 persons. Forty of these woollen cloaks, sent by Victor Amadeus, were distributed to them. The Chevalier De Parelles had accompanied them as far as the bridge of Frèlerive, and his brother, Captain Carrel, conducted them from thence to the frontiers of Geneva. They were greatly satisfied with the care with which they were treated on the journey, and gave an attestation to this effect to the captain, who demanded it of them. This last circumstance shows that the Duke of Savoy had at last begun to be in earnest, and was sincerely desirous that the unhappy outlaws should be cared for.[2]

A note addressed to the Council of State of Geneva, by the Swiss commissioners sent to meet the exiles. It is dated the 3d of February.—A letter of M. Truchet, written from Annecy to Colonel Perdriol at Geneva, and dated on the 14th, gives the particulars of this catastrophe. (Archives of Berne, C and D.)—The Vaudois troop consisted of 320 persons; it was reduced to 230, not only by this accident, but also by a number of children being carried off as they passed through Savoy. Thus, Mary Sarrette of Prarusting, Mary Cardon of Angrogna, John Pasquet, James Pascal, Paul and John Cardon, were carried off at St. Jean de Maurienne. The three daughters of John Pasquet had previously been carried off at Rivoli, &c. If the limits of this work would have permitted it, I could have given, on this point and on many others, far more particulars.

[1] They arrived in Geneva on the 1st of March. (Letter of M. Paschaud, Councillor of State, to their Excellencies of Berne).

[2] In all which took place most afflictive to the Vaudois, it is not so much the intentions of their sovereign that are to be blamed, as the intrigues of their enemies. There are even things which prove that the latter were jealous of the good dispositions of Victor Amadeus in regard to the Vaudois. Salvajot relates in his *Memoirs*, that this prince came often to hold reviews in the citadel of Turin; but that the Vaudois prisoners were then prohibited from leaving the buildings in which they were shut up, and even from showing themselves at the windows; and

They did not yet, however, cease to have great privations to endure. "They are in a pitiable state," wrote one of the Swiss commissioners sent to meet them.[1] "Almost all of them are sick, and without our assistance half of them would have been dead on the road. I have succeeded in recovering the girl who was carried off at Lanslebourg, and a fine boy whom the Master of La Ramassa had detained at Mount Cenis. I wrote to the commissioner of his royal highness to cause the children to be given up who were detained at St. John and Aiguebelles; four of them have been sent, there still remain five, whom it is promised that I shall receive along with the thirteen sick persons who were left on the way." "These people have suffered much. *Yet they are patient and contented, and thank God with tears,* blessing you continually as they behold the care which is taken to succour them." These last words are quoted exactly from the letter of the commissioner.

Let us now look at some of the particulars which Salvajot gives of the march of the convoy to which he belonged.

"After having made many promises to us to get us to embrace Catholicism, they allowed us to depart on the 27th of February, 1687.[2] We set out in good order. The children and persons who could not walk were put in carts. When the road was too bad for vehicles, they gave us mules, asses, and horses. We passed through nearly the whole of Savoy on horseback; and when the Savoyards did not do their duty, the sergeant gave them blows with his stick." It appears that the manners of the time were scarcely more mild in regard to Catholic subjects than in regard to proscribed Protestants. Both the one and the other, in the estimation of the attendants of sovereigns, were clowns, to be taxed and made to work for them at their pleasure.

"Our sergeants were very good," adds Salvajot. "They were careful that no harm should be done to us." (For fear, no doubt, of the corporal chastisements which would have awaited themselves, in consequence of the new feelings towards the proscribed Vaudois, which had been called forth by the accidents arising from the harshness of the first conductors.)

At Geneva, says the relation of 1689, "the Vaudois were received,

that any one who made the least attempt to ask grace from his royal highness was imprisoned *in un crottone*.

[1] Letter of Commissioner Cornillet, dated from Annecy, ... March, 1687. (Archives of Berne, compartment D.) I abridge it by leaving out some expressions.

[2] The following were their stages from Turin to Geneva:—1, St. Ambroise; 2, Bussolino; 3, La Novalèze, where they arrived on the 1st of March; 4, Lanslebourg; 5, Modane; 6, St. Jean de Maurienne; 7, Aiguebelles; 8, Grisy; 9, Favergie; 10, Annecy; 11, Crusiglia; and after marching for twelve days, they arrived on the 10th of March at Geneva, where they remained till the 24th.

not only as brethren, but as persons who brought with them peace, and a blessing to families."[1] Reserved places were prepared for them in the church of St. Peter, behind those of the syndics of the town.[2] The hospital of Plain-Palais had been put in order for them;[3] but almost all of them, even those who were sick, were lodged and provided for by the inhabitants of Geneva.

The other Protestant towns of Switzerland hastened to concur in this generous welcome. That of Berne offered to the magistrates of Geneva, to clothe the Vaudois at its own expense,[4] but this had been already done.[5]

However, all these successive bands of emigrants could not be accumulated in a single town. Frequent couriers passed and repassed among all the Protestant cantons of Switzerland, to accomplish the division amongst them in the most advantageous manner possible, of so great a number of exiles. Part of them were sent on to Wurtemberg and Brandenburg in the course of the year 1687; but the greater part spent the winter in Switzerland, waiting till a station should be definitively assigned them. Some went to Holland, and thence to America; the greater number, however, were totally unwilling to remove far from the Vaudois valleys. The poor exiles hoped to be able to return to them again in a short time, and deferred as much as possible the fixing of an establishment which would have bound them to a foreign land.

Janavel cherished these sentiments of patriotism in their hearts. They had, moreover, left part of their brethren in Piedmont; for independently of those who were at Verceil, all the Vaudois who, during the war of 1686, had been taken with arms in their hands, far from being released with the other prisoners, were condemned to the galleys, and subsequently were employed on the works of fortifications.[6] Moreover, all the Vaudois pastors, with the exception of Arnaud and Montoux, were retained, notwithstanding the frequent and pressing representations of Switzerland, to which it was replied that Victor Amadeus reserved his decision on their fate till his return from a journey which he had just made to Venice.[7]

"Two days before our departure from Turin," Salvajot says, "all

---

[1] *Dissipation* . . . . ., p. 34.

[2] Council of State of Geneva, sitting of February 5, 1687.

[3] Registers of the Council of State, sitting of January 15.

[4] Ibid., sitting of February 2.

[5] For this purpose the supply was drawn from many sources:—1, The government (sitting of the Council of State of February 2); 2, The *Italian Fund* (sitting of February 8); 3, Private persons (sittings of February 19 and of March 12).

[6] Letter of the Count De Gavon to M. De Murat, read to the Council of State of Geneva, sitting of February 7, 1687. (See the Registers of the Council.)

[7] The same Registers.

our ministers, with their families, were put in a separate chamber; guards were placed at the door that no one might go out of it; and thus our poor ministers remained in prison, who thought they should have been the first to have left it.[1] But Victor Amadeus was in no haste to resolve upon their fate; for we read in a work published in 1690 — "The Vaudois pastors are still prisoners; promises and threats have been tried, time about, to make them abjure; and at this very time they still pine, dispersed and confined, in three castles, where they are exposed to much discomfort and misery, without any apparent prospect of their deliverance."[2] They were not set at liberty till June, 1690, when the victorious Vaudois had regained possession of their valleys, and when Victor Amadeus found it his interest to attach them once more to himself, in consequence of the political rupture which had taken place between Piedmont and France.[3]

The secret of the power of kings is in knowing how to make men oppress one another; their armies are formed of the people, and directed against the people. The wars which arise amongst nations are never for the interests of nations; it is the ambition of dynasties which produces them and profits by them. Thus every oppressed people is the accomplice of the tyrant whose oppression it endures; for if he were left alone no tyrant could prevail against an entire people. But God has permitted this severe tutelage of communities of men, in order that they may know the value of emancipation; and, in order to have liberty, it is necessary to be worthy of it. An independent mind is more free, even in oppression, even in martyrdom, than a servile one when its masters are taken away.

Let me conclude with these words of the gospel, "If Christ make you free, you shall be free indeed."

---

[1] Gli fecero mettere tutti con le loro famiglie in una camera. . . . E gli dissero che prima era per il saluto dell' anima sua; e poi che S. A. R. gli darebbe qualche intretorie; ma che per le valle, non pensassero più ad andargli! E i nostri poveri ministri restarono in prigione, e credevano d'essere i primi a partire.

[2] *Hist. de la dissip. des Egl. Vaud.*, p. 35. These pastors were nine in number. —(*Memoir* of David Holzhalb to the great Elector of Brandenburg, on the condition of the Vaudois, June, 1687. Archives of Berlin.) Six others, to wit, MM. Arnaud, Montoux, Bayle (father and son), Dumas, and Javel, had succeeded in getting out of the country. Only one had abjured, J. P. Danne. A pun was made upon his name, by saying that it wanted only an acute accent on the last letter to indicate what he had become. This man, whom it is easier to suppose misled than convinced, wrote some works in favour of the Church of Rome.

[3] *Mercure Historique*, vii. 667.

THE BAPTIST STANDARD BEARER, INC.
A non-profit, tax-exempt corporation
committed to the Publication & Preservation
of The Baptist Heritage.

SAMPLE TITLES FOR PUBLICATIONS AVAILABLE IN OUR VARIOUS SERIES:

THE BAPTIST *COMMENTARY* SERIES
Sample of authors/works in or near republication:
John Gill - *Exposition of the Old & New Testaments (9 & 18 Vol. Sets)*
 (Volumes from the 18 vol. set can be purchased individually)

THE BAPTIST *FAITH* SERIES:
Sample of authors/works in or near republication:
Abraham Booth - *The Reign of Grace*
John Fawcett - *Christ Precious to Those That Believe*
John Gill - *A Complete Body of Doctrinal & Practical Divinity (2 Vols.)*

THE BAPTIST *HISTORY* SERIES:
Sample of authors/works in or near republication:
Thomas Armitage - *A History of the Baptists (2 Vols.)*
Isaac Backus - *History of the New England Baptists (2 Vols.)*
William Cathcart - *The Baptist Encyclopaedia (3 Vols.)*
J. M. Cramp - *Baptist History*

THE BAPTIST *DISTINCTIVES* SERIES:
Sample of authors/works in or near republication:
Abraham Booth - *Paedobaptism Examined (3 Vols.)*
Alexander Carson - *Ecclesiastical Polity of the New Testament Churches*
E. C. Dargan - *Ecclesiology: A Study of the Churches*
J. M. Frost - *Pedobaptism: Is It From Heaven?*
R. B. C. Howell - *The Evils of Infant Baptism*

THE *DISSENT & NONCONFORMITY* SERIES:
Sample of authors/works in or near republication:
Champlin Burrage - *The Early English Dissenters (2 Vols.)*
Albert H. Newman - *History of Anti-Pedobaptism*
Walter Wilson - *The History & Antiquities of the Dissenting Churches (4 Vols.)*

For a complete list of current authors/titles, visit our internet site at
www.standardbearer.com or write us at:

The Baptist Standard Bearer, Inc.
No. 1 Iron Oaks Drive • Paris, Arkansas 72855

Telephone: (501) 963-3831   Fax: (501) 963-8083
E-mail: baptist@arkansas.net
Internet: http://www.standardbearer.com

Specialists in Baptist Reprints and Rare Books

Thou hast given a *standard* to them that fear thee; that it may be displayed because of the truth. -- Psalm 60:4

www.ingramcontent.com/pod-product-compliance
Lightning Source LLC
Chambersburg PA
CBHW032332230426
43664CB00039B/53